Peace and Counterpeace

A Carl Cohirw BOOK

PEACE AND COUNTERPEACE

FROM WILSON TO HITLER

MEMOIRS OF

Hamilton Fish Armstrong

Nations never go out to meet destiny.
It always catches up with them at an
unexpected turn of the road.

—Anne O'Hare McCormick

1817

HARPER & ROW, PUBLISHERS

NEW YORK, EVANSTON, SAN FRANCISCO, LONDON

FIRST EDITION

STANDARD BOOK NUMBER: 06-010121

LIBRARY OF CONGRESS CATALOG CARD NUMBER: 74-138703

For Christa

Contents

vii

PART THREE: ON THE EVE

POSTSCRIPT: General Bliss's Prophecy   560

Illustrations

General Tasker H. Bliss

Edwin F. Gay, portrait by Alexandre Iacovleff

The following are grouped in a separate section after page 400

Archibald Cary Coolidge

Raymond Poincaré

Joseph Caillaux

Count Carlo Sforza

President Thomas G. Masaryk

Sir Horace Plunkett

Greek Republican leaders in jail, Athens, April, 1922

King Constantine of Greece

King Alexander visiting the American Home

Queen Marie of Rumania

Count Michael Károlyi

Secretary General Avenol of the League of Nations and André Géraud

Foreign Ministers of the Little Entente

The Triglav, from Bohinj, Slovenia

The White Fortress, Belgrade

Opening of the Council House, November 28, 1930

Editorial office of *Foreign Affairs*, 45 East 65th Street, 1930

Note

The time between the two Great Wars began with the United States retreating from world responsibility and, in the end, finding itself with a burden of more responsibility than any nation had ever carried before. In these pages, I describe some of the events and characters that made it a time not to be forgotten.

I am indebted to several friends who have read portions of the book, among them Professor William L. Langer of Harvard, Professor Philip E. Mosely of Columbia, Herbert Feis and the late John Gunther. They have no responsibility, of course, for individual observations or possible errors. Carol Kahn has read the manuscript and has offered perceptive comments throughout; she has also made the index. Philip W. Quigg, James Chace, and in particular Grace Darling and Joan Haverly have also been most helpful; so have Janet Rigney and others of the staff of the Council on Foreign Relations Library and the staff of the New York Society Library. My friends Allen W. Dulles and Major General Sherman Miles let me read correspondence and memoranda of theirs which helped me put into perspective events in the remnants of the Hapsburg Empire just after its collapse. I am grateful, too, to the heirs of General Tasker H. Bliss and Dr. Edwin F. Gay for permission to quote from their letters to me, and to the Yale University Press for permitting me to publish letters written to me by Colonel Edward M. House, which, although in my possession, fall in its jurisdiction as general custodian of his papers.

Slavic names always present something of a problem. Croatian and Slovenian proper names, which are written in Roman characters, are given here with their diacritic marks. So also are Czech names. Serbian names, which are written in Cyrillic characters, are transliterated. In this connection Robin Berman's knowledge of the Slavic languages has been most helpful.

H.F.A.

Peace and Counterpeace

Preface in Paris

When I reached Paris in December, 1918, the gray streets, glistening damply under bare branches, were filled with staff cars. The Peace Conference had not begun, but President Wilson and his advisers had arrived and so had the vanguards of other delegations. Knots of the curious gathered all day outside the Crillon, the Astoria, the Majestic and other delegation headquarters, craning their necks impartially at the important and the unimportant. Names were still better known than faces. Of Henry White: "Voilà! Lord George!" "Non, c'est Sir Balfour!" Nobody confused Wilson with Clemenceau; but Colonel House, entering the Crillon mouse-like, passed unnoticed. Flags—familiar, less familiar, and new since yesterday—were everywhere. The black crepe draping "Strasbourg" in the Place de la Concorde was gone. Suddenly the good restaurants had good things to eat; word spread that a chocolate soufflé could be had at Larue. The stunning fact of victory was gradually becoming believable. Exhaustion and relief began to be replaced by exhilaration at the prospect of the drama about to be enacted and speculation over the character and behavior of the celebrated participants.

The atmosphere, however, was taut, for the controversies which were to rend the conference were already boiling to the surface, and newsmen, subventioned or not, were accelerating them with outrageous rumors to fill the void of fact. Some of the most disturbing rumors were of course true. But was it really conceivable that the waves of cheering which had borne President Wilson along the Champs-Élysées would not carry him

1

on victorious to every goal? Among the Americans only a few doubted it, and he was not one of them.

The few were right. Wilson had proclaimed justice as the essential foundation for any lasting peace; but already the French and others had decided that security must come first—security with justice, of course, so far as possible, but security regardless. From a difference in what at first seemed method but was in fact purpose arose many disputes, chief among them how Germany should be made to pay for her past crimes and what sanctions, territorial and military, would protect her neighbors from a repetition of them. France had laid the bodies of more than a million and a quarter *poilus* on the altar of war, and to Clemenceau, Foch and Poincaré it seemed logical and supremely moral to cripple an enemy who had exacted such a fearful sacrifice. Others argued that, moral or not, the proposed restraints would not work. (Twenty years later it was plain they had not worked.)

How to deal with Germany was only one of the impending controversies. Wilson's determination to right the wrongs of European nationalities long under alien domination collided with the ambitions of Italy in the Balkans and raised problems elsewhere on the continent which could not be solved according to one rule of justice without violating others. Inside delegations as well as among them a controversy raged as to how deeply to intervene in the dimly understood struggles within the vast obscurity of Russia. And there were claims and counterclaims to be reconciled somehow in Asia Minor, the Middle East, Africa, the Far East and even the South Seas. For the first time in history the issues confronting statesmen were literally worldwide.

Could the array of problems be unraveled not simply one by one, each a complex task in itself, but in their interrelationships as well? Could they be taken up more or less simultaneously, passed in orderly review and conducted at last to a reasonably acceptable settlement? The statesmen who would give judgment probably possessed in the aggregate more intellectual and political resources than any such group gathered for a similar purpose for a century, if ever. But the world they must take in hand had become incredibly complex. Had the point perhaps been reached where it could not be comprehended in the round by individual minds, even assuming that all these were (which they were not) equally disinterested and wise? The answer of the next twenty years would be yes, the world had reached and passed that point. But in Paris on the eve of the conference the mood was excitement and expectancy.

I was a very junior army officer, serving briefly in the office of the military attaché in Paris on my way to a post in Belgrade and in touch with only the fringes of the diplomatic preparations. I shared the prevailing sense of exhilaration and do not remember that it was tinged with apprehension. Like everyone else, I of course realized that there would be collisions of purpose and will, national and personal. But then would come the reassuring thought that, although the scope for disagreement and error was indeed worldwide, a worldwide organization would be there to set things right. The League of Nations would unravel problems left unsettled by the conference; the League of Nations would snuff out minor clashes by collective action; the League of Nations would gradually develop techniques and acquire authority to deal even with major threats of war.

Does the expectation sound extravagant? Now that we know it was, it does. But at the New Year of 1919 there were countless millions all over the earth who turned compulsively from the nightmares of the past to dreams of a wholly new future and whose determination to make them come true seemed invincible. I was one of those millions, inspired since my days at Princeton by the idealistic purposes of Woodrow Wilson. At that age everything seems possible—a change in human behavior at the least, perhaps even a change in human character.

II

By spring the Allies had still not agreed on the final text of the treaty with Germany and were not sure that when they did agree they could find German plenipotentiaries willing to sign it. Territorial questions in many parts of Europe and elsewhere were still under study, and while the delegates wrangled the rival contestants on the spot were attempting to foreclose by force whatever decisions might be reached far away in Paris. For the first seven months of 1919 I was stationed in Belgrade and observed some of these operations at close range. From there the picture of what Paris was doing or not doing was obscure, and roundabout communications assured that any facts we gleaned from meager diplomatic dispatches were out of date.

In May the Allied leaders realized that further delay in finishing at least the treaty with Germany would involve immense risks. New revolutionary forces were threatening to seize control there and resume fighting; and in the vacuum of power in Eastern Europe Bolshevism was taking over the starving masses. The Allied peoples themselves were restless. President Wilson was being warned from Washington that his strategy in linking the League to the German treaty did not ensure that it would be accepted by the Senate and was being advised to come home quickly to deal with his opponents. The American public were no longer much interested in the merits of the issues for which their representatives in Paris were fighting, only in seeing everything disposed of rapidly one way or another so that the country could settle back to business as usual. It would be twenty-five years before Americans realized that victory did not signify a release but a beginning of responsibility.

As the Peace Conference approached its climax, the American and British experts who had been in close collaboration for several months made ready to scatter to their homes and resume their peacetime occupations. They knew the innards of everything the Big Three had done or were leaving undone, and were less than happy. Nor were they elated over their own accomplishments. They had worked hard and had tried to be impartial in their recommendations, but often they had seen compromises made which ran counter to what they believed right and necessary. Closer to details of each negotiation than the harassed delegates could be, they were acutely aware of the accumulating discontents—hopes disappointed, cupidity thwarted, revenge postponed. They did not fully realize the speed with which "the acceleration of history," as Daniel Halévy has called it, would proceed in response to the coming burst of scientific and technological progress. But they foresaw that as time passed tremendous pressures would be generated to overthrow the decisions of the conference by force; and they realized that judgments which had been right would be challenged as well as those which might have been wrong. They asked themselves whether something could not be done to strengthen the resources of their governments to deal rationally with these eventual pressures and threats.

The Americans felt this as a particular challenge. Most of them had started work in a preparatory group organized by Colonel House known as the "Inquiry." They had arrived in Paris (as Colonel Frederick Palmer wrote in his biography of one of the American plenipotentiaries, General Tasker H. Bliss) knowing their subjects "as war college students know war before they face real war." Now they were veterans of a grueling campaign. They had added to the knowledge of how diplomacy is practiced in theory the knowledge of how it is carried on in fact, and they wanted to put their experience and hard-won wisdom to use. They wanted on their return home to continue their development individually and perhaps accomplish something collectively in broadening the field of instruction in American universities. Above all they wanted to persuade the American people not to slip back into illusions of self-sufficiency, and thus to give the government support in dealing with foreign affairs without extravagant swings either of isolationism and xenophobia or of too emotional involvement. They hoped to encourage them to widen their horizons, to take more interest in foreign policy than they had done in the past, to study its problems, to understand their complexity, to be less impatient with other nations, to accept more responsibility, above all to recognize the intimate relationship which exists between the national interest and the interest of society as a whole.

The British experts had had longer preparation than the Americans for the diplomatic melee at Paris. Some of them felt that their preparatory work had conformed too closely to the traditional lines by British diplomacy, and of course they felt disadvantaged by their government's prior commitments in various secret treaties. One of them, Harold Nicolson, wrote in his diary one evening that he was "exhausted, hopeless and unhappy" and that he saw "nothing but blackness in the future." Not all, of course, went so far. But there was general agreement among a number of both British and American experts that a way should be found to capitalize on their common discontents.

On May 30—Memorial Day—they met together to consider possibilities for action. Among those on the American side were General Tasker H. Bliss, who had been the American member of the Supreme War Council before becoming a delegate at the Peace Conference; three historians, Archibald Cary Coolidge, of Harvard, James T. Shotwell, of Columbia, and George Louis Beer; Dr. James Brown Scott, authority on international law; Stanley K. Hornbeck, a Far Eastern specialist; and Thomas W. Lamont, President Wilson's financial adviser. Among the British were Lord Robert Cecil, Professor Harold Temperley, Sir Valentine Chirol and Lord Eustace Percy. At Cecil's suggestion, General Bliss presided. The tone of the meeting was set by Cecil's opening statement that the value of their action would be determined by the extent of their dissatisfaction.

It was sufficient. Plans were laid for an organization of two separate but associated bodies, one American, one British, with joint secretaries— Whitney H. Shepardson, an aide to Colonel House, and Lionel Curtis, founder of the *Round Table,* who had been one of Milner's "Kindergarten" in South Africa. After the American members of the group reached home they merged with the Council on Foreign Relations, an organization that had been formed in New York during the war but was by now languishing. Besides taking the Council's name, they gained the financial backing of its public-spirited membership. They also acquired a locus, something vital if they were to continue functioning collectively and not as individuals dispersed in academic and other centers.

Meanwhile, the British group, which had begun as the Institute of International Affairs, was given a charter, added the word Royal to its title, and established its headquarters in Chatham House, London. Almost at once it was realized on both sides of the Atlantic that although the scholarly aims of the two groups were identical the foreign policies of their countries would not always coincide. The relationship was therefore severed, although the two organizations continued in friendly cooperation.

On its side, the Council on Foreign Relations decided to respond to the advice of Isaiah Bowman, one of its directors. "Publish or perish!" That injunction came later on to have a sinister sound in the ears of harried college professors, but at the moment it had the happy result of encouraging the Council to start its new career with a specific undertaking which would give it identity and be an earnest of its future broader purposes. It was thus that the Council established a quarterly review, *Foreign Affairs,* persuaded Professor Coolidge to become the editor and appointed the present writer (no persuasion needed) as his assistant.

But this is leaping far ahead. How did it come about that someone who had been far off in Belgrade while the Olympians were making history in Paris was brought into the picture?

PART ONE

The Chain of Coincidences

We fall asleep to the sound of kingdoms
crashing in the night, and every morning
they are swept up before our doors.

—CHATEAUBRIAND

1

Princeton, September, 1912

Soft hazy days, with few signs that summer was ending: a bowl of yellow apples on the hall table at the Peacock Inn, a suggestion of color on the most susceptible dogwoods and maples. It was a deceptive prelude to the disorderly first weeks of freshman year. I had a "condition" to work off, but after a couple of weeks of cramming felt I had passed the exam and could loaf for a day or two. I found a canoe and floated down Stony Brook, placid under the willows, but a comedown after the rapid little Massawippi of summers in Quebec. The world was at peace; I did not dream it could be otherwise. Did anyone? I felt free, on my own, ready for anything.

The tranquillity of the almost deserted campus ended abruptly; it was a new life. We put on our black skullcaps and black jerseys, linked arms for our first rush, turned our coats inside out, posed for the first class picture on the steps of Clio Hall while sophomores pelted us with flour, and became accustomed to jog-trotting off when the call sounded, "Get going, freshmen!" Hazing had been abolished, but milder forms of humiliation remained. When the command was "Go climb a tree!" you looked around for one you could shinny up fast enough to escape a whack on the behind. Once up, you'd be directed, "Sing like a bird!"—which produced music Keats never heard. If you were wearing forbidden garments you were directed to throw them down piece by piece and eventually sent running home in, appropriately, your running drawers. (We got our own back the next September; but the year following, horsing—except in much milder forms—followed hazing into Princeton's more heroic past.)

9

I had a room at 31 University Place, since demolished. It had a bad reputation with the college authorities as a center of disorder. Inmates were assumed to be in the wrong even though the near-riots were always (almost) started by sophomore intruders. After years of coping with freshmen and their foes, the landlady, Mrs. Kirk, was quite unstrung; she would emerge at the foot of the stairs shouting orders, entreaties, threats. Dean McClenahan had us up before him after a band of sophomores broke down the door of a timid freshman, scaring him out of his wits and literally out of his second-floor window. He broke his leg, which was unlucky for him; what was unlucky for Princeton (and worse in the eyes of the Dean) was that his father, who was very rich, withdrew him from college and with him the chance that he might become one of Princeton's benefactors. After that, the inmates of 31 Univ. were more suspect than ever. Mrs. Kirk exploited this for more than it was worth. One evening when there was a certain amount of movement on the top floor she called wrathfully up, and by bad luck I looked down over the banisters. The next morning she informed the Dean that I had dropped a marble tabletop on her head. I explained that this was unlikely: the marble tabletop was still there and intact, Mrs. Kirk was still there and intact, which would hardly be the case if they had collided. Dean Mac listened wearily with bowed head. Gradually his bald pate, the barometer of his feelings, became redder and redder, but was it with anger or amusement? When he looked up I saw he was grinning.

We began at 31 Univ. eleven strong; the withdrawal of the timid freshmen reduced the number to ten; after midyear exams it became six. One of the casualties was a likable fellow from Brooklyn who simply wanted to be able to say, "I went to Princeton."

He had asked me in October, "Do you think they ever flunk anyone out before February?"

I said I thought not. His mind at rest, he never spent forty-eight hours consecutively in Princeton from then until the inevitable axe fell at midyears. He departed, content with his college career.

It was election year. Woodrow Wilson had left the presidency of the college to become Governor of New Jersey; now he was Democratic candidate for President of the United States. He still was living in Princeton, and this would have made it a center of political excitement even if he had not been a controversial figure there already. Year after year Princeton students had voted him the most popular professor. Even among them, however, his popularity had lessened after he set out to reform the club system; and this and his feud with Dean West over the site of the new Graduate College had also turned many of the faculty against him (though not the younger preceptors) and left him with few friends among the trustees. The town, though not yet in commuting range for New York businessmen, was basically Republican. Thus Wilson was not in any sense Princeton's favorite son, and the local odds favored William Howard Taft. Another factor in campus debates was the Bull Moose Club, organized by admirers of Teddy Roosevelt, ardently led by a popular history preceptor, William Starr Myers, whose Southern accent was anything but a drawl. But Wilson's supporters were the most active; they knew they had to be, for the nationwide consensus was that even with Roosevelt splitting the Republican vote Taft would be reelected. I worked hard for Wilson to make up for the fact that I was too young to vote.

I had come to Princeton a Republican but was attracted by Wilson's "New Freedom." My father, though a Republican in the main, had voted for Cleveland and this year voted for Wilson (he always regretted that his first vote had not been for Lincoln and Hamlin but for Bell and Everett, the latter a family friend). I continued to consider myself more or less an independent—less and less, as time went on, until finally Republican isolationism settled me in the opposite camp.

I was named after my mother's favorite uncle, an eminent Republican, and it caused misunderstandings all my life. Years later, as I came into FDR's office at the White House, he greeted me with: "Ham, I like everything about you except your name. The two men in politics I can't abide are Hamilton Dies and Martin Fish."

He was scrambling the names of the Republican Congressman from his own district in Dutchess County, a grandson of my namesake, and a Democratic Congressman from Texas who was being troublesome as chairman of the Committee on Un-American Activities.

I replied mildly that he should be pleased that there was a Democrat with my name, just as I was pleased that there was a Democrat, for a change, named Roosevelt.

He tossed back his head with that sideways motion of his and roared with laughter.

I don't remember ever agreeing on any matter whatsoever with my cousin the Congressman. Even as far back as when he had attained (as some consider) the apex of his career as captain of the Harvard football team, I had collegiate reasons for wishing his defeat; and during his years in Congress when he was an isolationist and eventually a favorite of the Bundists I continued to hope for the failure of his every cause.

The nearest I ever came to becoming involved in politics myself was just after graduation. That summer a group of Republicans in my Congressional district in New York were looking around for an alternative candidate to Fiorello La Guardia, who had run for Congress in 1914 and had been defeated. They imagined I was safely conservative and were further misled by my Republican name. My refusal of their suggestion that I try for the nomination was certainly *pro bono publico,* for La Guardia became a spectacularly successful Congressman and later the best mayor the city of New York had had in years, or was to have again. I have read in a biography of La Guardia that he was under the impression that Ham Fish wanted the nomination. Could there have been a confusion of names then too?

Once it was my last name that caused me chagrin. I was motoring with my wife to Chartres across the lovely level plain of the Beauce; at one point you suddenly become conscious of the appearance on the rim of the horizon, above the undulating fields of wheat, of a tiny model of the cathedral, which will gradually assume its majestic proportions as you approach kilometer by kilometer. At about that point there is a little restaurant, and as it is well known to travelers I had asked the concierge at the hotel in Paris to telephone ahead to reserve a table. When I arrived and gave my name the proprietor's face fell and a murmur of disappointment came from a little crowd gathered around the door.

"Mais il n'est pas noir!" I heard one girl say.

It was sad to disappoint their expectation of glimpsing the most famous trumpeter since the fall of Jericho.

To return to Princeton: college and town were smaller then and more intimately connected. People who had fine places on the outskirts—the Pynes, Marquands, Russells and others—were most hospitable and made a point of inviting incoming freshmen to their houses. One of them, Moses Taylor Pyne, a charming oligarch, had a kind, gentle and absent-minded wife. At lunch one Sunday I sat on one side of Mrs. Pyne and my roommate Walter White sat on the other.

"Hamilton," said Mrs. Pyne sweetly, beginning a routine she had been through so often that she found difficulty in keeping her mind on it, "whom do you room with?"

"With Walter, here," I replied.

Turning to Walter, she asked, "And whom do you room with, Walter?"

With immense presence of mind, Walter replied, "With Sam Shoemaker."

Sam, the absent party in this benevolent deception, was one of the most admired and best-liked members of the class. Later he was involved in the Buchmanite movement, became one of its leaders in Princeton and as such a center of controversy, for the house parties where members publicly confessed their sins aroused considerable criticism. Sometimes it came from those who had passed through the ordeal and regretted having impetuously disclosed infidelities or (maybe more) having merely owned up to hankering to commit them. It was said that the revivalist meetings led to such exaltation, such enthusiasm for a changed life, that an average person often found himself or herself unable to maintain the promised ideal; then might come a nervous breakdown.

Princeton had survived Billy Sunday; a year after his advent the only reminder of his gospel meetings came on spring evenings when, with all the dormitory windows open, someone began a mocking chant, "Brighten the corner where you are." Soon, mixed with cries of "Cows on the campus!" (always untrue), it would be taken up window by window and so in diminishing progression would gradually be lost to the ear. The Buchmanite movement was different; there was no "hitting the sawdust trail." Dr. Buchman aimed particularly to win permanent followers among the well-to-do, educated and prominent. Any undergraduate, however, was worth a try, and later on when Dr. Buchman often visited Princeton he would stop anyone he met crossing the campus and ask him what he was doing to save a soul. Trustees and parents began to object, and about 1924, I think it was, President Hibben barred the campus to Dr. Buchman. Sam went on to become an admirable Episcopal clergyman.

Attendance at chapel was compulsory on at least half the Sundays in a term. You signed a card to prove you'd been there, and to sign an absent friend's name might lead to your being dropped; it was particularly risky if you lived at 31 Univ. Place, as the custodian at the door was Mr. Kirk —"Saint Peter"—who shared his wife's vendetta against their lodgers. The rule about chapel had one pleasant result, possible religious benefits aside, in that more undergraduates spent their weekends in Princeton than seems to be the case today. You walked out into the country or canoed on Stony Brook; in winter, you skated on Lake Carnegie, played records on your "talking machine" and, of course, spent endless hours in bicker sessions. When you had done your chapel quota you might go up to New York for a weekend, if you could afford it, to see a show. If you went for a dance, you chose among those available that evening the one where Conrad's orchestra was going to play. Conrad was a more decisive factor in the success of a party than who was giving it or where. It was in my freshman year, I think, that he invented the idea of breaking the season's most popular tune, "Come On Over Here," back and forth between one-step and waltz time, provoking pleasant confusion.

A recent Broadway hit had been *The Quaker Girl*. Everyone hummed "Tony from America" and "Thee Loves Me." But the real reason it was a hit was Ina Claire. It must have been her first show and, viewed from the respectful distance of the peanut gallery of the Park Theatre, she was my first stage dream. Clifton Crawford was Tony and Percival Knight was the ogre who stood between. When I went up from Princeton with a friend to see Ina Claire in her new play at the Winter Garden we were drawn irresistibly around afterward to the stage door for a glimpse of her at closer range. There was Vincent Astor, waiting in a Stutz Bearcat, and he carried her off to supper without visible protests. It was very disillusioning. I remembered Vincent at children's parties as a rather gawky boy. I realized poignantly that I didn't have and never would have what it takes to persuade a lovely star to go with me to Shanley's.

It never crossed our minds that one day there would be female undergraduates at Princeton. In any case, girls were a less prominent part of college life than they became later, but I don't think that meant they were less important. You didn't appropriate a girl and consider her your personal property; when you invited one to a prom you didn't defend your rights against all comers all evening, but filled out her card with the names of some of your friends as well as your own. In our senior year, about one-fifth of the class reported—with pride or regret—that they had never kissed a girl. Four-fifths reported, presumably with pride, that they had. But it would not have been a clinch under an arc light on a street corner. Panties were worn, not talked about, and panty raids had not yet become the subject of newspaper reports, as they were for a time, until changes in custom rendered such indirect amenities between the sexes unnecessary. *Newsweek* commented not long ago that although Dink Stover and Anthony Blaine may not have had so much real sex as the modern student, they certainly seemed to have had more real fun. At any rate, the girl friend didn't move into the boy friend's flat to talk about Zen, the *I Ching* and how to adjust to a dynamically changing environment.

Friends of mine at Princeton, the daughters of Professor "Bill Geology" Scott, were friends of Woodrow Wilson's daughters, and I was lucky enough to be taken by them one Sunday evening to supper at the Wilson house on Cleveland Lane. Two or three other boys were there and Sylvia Beach, the daughter of the minister at the Presbyterian Church and future founder of Shakespeare and Co. in Paris, first publisher of James Joyce. I can't say that I remember the conversation at the long table, except that it was strictly not about politics. I kept a strong impression of Wilson as a highly civilized person, elegant in a spare, angular way, lively and talkative, really a charmer. He wore glasses, but they didn't cut off contact as sometimes happens. I remember being surprised that there was nothing pedagogic about the former president of the university. After supper we sang such things as "Swanee River" and "In the Good Old Summer Time." Wilson had a good voice and seemed to love it. It was simply an evening in the home of (one would like to think) a typically intelligent and cultivated American professor, perhaps more than typically unaffected and easy of manner. Seven years and a war later I could find no clue in that Princeton recollection to what we were told about the disabled, isolated, bitter and defamed man in the White House.

It was the only time I had direct contact with Wilson, but I saw him often. On election day a group of us cheered him as he came out from voting at the firehouse on Mercer Street, and that evening as favorable returns started coming in we got a band and red fire ready. As soon as the result was sure, the bell in Nassau Hall began ringing wildly. Instantly a "P-rade" of several hundred formed and marched to Prospect, where President Hibben lived. We brought him out onto the front steps and yelled for a holiday. Though Hibben had supported Taft, and had been Wilson's adversary in the controversy over the new Graduate College, he couldn't refuse to honor the first Princeton man elected to the highest office in the land since James Madison. This settled, we snake-danced off with the band to Cleveland Lane and swarmed onto Wilson's front lawn.

Wilson left for the inauguration on March third. Several hundred students filled the special train to which his car was attached. A dense crowd also gathered around the rear platform, and as the train pulled slowly out of the station he joined in "Old Nassau," waving his silk hat in unison. The trip to Washington was wild, and so was the evening there. The Princeton band went with us, and played with tireless vigor as we marched round and round the streets near the Hotel Willard, where the Wilson party was staying. I don't remember where I slept, if I did sleep. The next morning we gathered near the steps of the Capitol to hear the inaugural address and then marched with our band up Pennsylvania Avenue in the inaugural parade. My recollection of how I got back to Princeton is hazy.

The New Freedom was a time of excitement and expectancy. People

forget that if there had been no war Wilson would have been remembered
as a great President for his domestic reforms—the Federal Reserve System and the Federal Trade Commission, the needed stiffening of the
Sherman Antitrust Act, women's suffrage, an eight-hour day for railway
employees and lowering the tariff. His speeches were literate, eloquent,
composed of his own thoughts, based on his own beliefs, put in his own
words (a feat apparently beyond his successors) and often written out
on his own typewriter. I was reminded what the New Freedom had meant
to my generation when Roosevelt led the country out of crisis and de-
spondency with the New Deal and Kennedy rekindled a short-lived glow
with the New Frontier.

II

A routine incident, insignificant at the moment, followed by a chain
of sheer coincidences, can steer your life into quite unexpected channels.
At least so it was with me. A very early ambition to be a fireman, authorized to slide down the pole in the Tenth Street firehouse when you
wanted, changed after a first trip to Europe to a longing to be an archaeologist or if that was impossible a travel agent or anything else
which provided chances to see the world. Since then I don't remember
ever having planned a course of action to reach a certain goal.

Even if there had been a definite plan in my mind when I reached
Princeton, I would not have suspected that everything was being decisively altered one December evening in my freshman year when I received
an assignment to cover a certain lecture for the *Daily Princetonian*. The
competition among forty or fifty heelers for a place on the board had been
furious from the start in late September. Now, toward the end, the contestants had been weeded down to about half a dozen. We were exhausted,
suspicious, eating little, sleeping little, barely hanging onto passing grades
in our academic work, bleary-eyed, pimply, scavenging for bits of news to
supplement the stories assigned to us, fighting in every way possible, fair
or foul, to add to our linage in the paper; for the winner at the end would
be the candidate with the largest total of printed words. I knew I was
ahead, but not by a safe margin.

My assignment this particular evening, along with two other heelers,
was to report a speech in one of the college halls by a certain Madame
Slavko Grouich, the American wife of a Serbian diplomat, just arrived
from Macedonia, where fighting among the Balkan states was causing
heavy losses and wide devastation. It had no name as yet, but history
would know it as the First Balkan War. Mme. Grouich, a West Virginian,

had been studying archaeology in Athens when she met Dr. Grouich, married him and became a devoted proponent of her adopted country. The fact that she was extremely good-looking did not diminish the persuasiveness of her pleas for support of her good works. After the lecture she told me that besides raising funds for relief she was preparing to organize a small team of college boys to go out to Macedonia with Ford trucks, as soon as the fighting was over, to distribute clothing, seeds, agricultural implements and medical supplies. This story was a scoop, and I managed to stretch it out for a week or so by arranging to get bulletins of her progress at other colleges. Soon I began planning to join the expedition myself and even got a promise from a generous lady in New York, Miss Annie Jennings, to finance my particular truck. The war did end in the spring, but an appendix operation intervened and the three boys recruited by Mme. Grouich from other colleges went without me. All this would not be worth describing (though it helped get me my place on the *Prince*) if, as will appear eventually, it had not given me quite a new direction in life.

All through Princeton I skimped academic work in favor of other interests. Yet I couldn't help absorbing some formal education from the wide mixture of courses then required in the first two years of the Princeton curriculum. In English Lit. I sat under "Doc" Spaeth, who doubled as crew coach and was equally full-throated whether barking at his charges on Lake Carnegie or reading (without the megaphone) from the romantic poets. Dean West, chubby and bald, exuding a comradeship instantly identified as spurious, did us the favor of reading from Horace. For Professor Morey I compiled illustrated notebooks on medieval art and for Professor Gerould wrote in learned language but quite superficially about the Venerable Bede and *Beowulf*. Calculus came so near being my undoing that later on from a vantage point on the *Prince* I waged a vindictive and successful war to get it removed from the list of required subjects. Greek grammar was also painful, but Homer became all the greater reward. Professor Philip Marshall Brown, tall, handsome, with beetling brows, a trifle overdignified after diplomatic service in several capitals, labored to give body and reality to international law, handicapped by the fact that the war in Europe was steadily making it more and more abstract; for the cases he cited mainly concerned contraband, continuous voyage, visit and search on the high seas, and other subjects on which Washington was writing stern but ineffectual notes to Britain about freedom of commerce and then still sterner and equally ineffectual notes to Germany about submarine sinkings. Allen Dulles, who sat next to me in Professor Brown's course, was intelligent enough to disassociate the legal concepts involved from the unpunished violations which distracted me, and so derived more profit than I did. "Buzzer" Hall, whose trademarks were his hearing apparatus, his stout stick and his slobbering bulldog Eli, was (as the seniors sang on the steps of Nassau Hall on spring evenings), one of "those preceptor guys,"

> Fifty stiffs to make us wise.
> Easy jobs and lots of pay,
> They work the students night and day.

He gave us history from a very personal point of view, usually not at all a bad one. George B. McClellan, who had left politics after suffering in repute (unfairly, it was said) as a Tammany mayor of New York, lectured about political economy to overflowing classes. The benevolent habits which he brought to his new constituency led him to give every student a passing mark, and eventually he succeeded Wilson as "the most popular professor." Another safe course was "traveling gut," thus named because no written papers were required and nobody failed unless he cut the field trips to the Trenton prison, the court in Newark, the Vineland Home for the Feeble Minded and other state institutions. There was a rumor that a lingering student was locked in at Vineland overnight and that Professor Fetter rewarded him with an A for zeal.

All this liberal instruction could not fail to deposit a thin layer of remembered knowledge, even though as the years passed the facts and figures faded, leaving only opinions—held, needless to say, as resolutely as ever.

III

At that time Princeton was still a college more than a university. It had not been enveloped and gradually absorbed, as I once watched a largish fish absorbed in the Naples aquarium, by what William James called "the Ph.D. octopus." It remained one of the places described by Jacques Barzun where undergraduates "enjoyed four years of maturing in the old atmosphere of useless study."

The incidental benefits were tremendous. Few if any of my classmates suffered nervous breakdowns; no university psychiatrists were in attendance (now there are three); nobody dreamed or suspected that something like modern analysis might either have beneficial results or add to your "status." There were some eccentrics, but the words "fairy" and "pansy" still had only innocent meaning, and a "fag" was a cigarette. As undergraduates were forbidden to marry, none were being supported by their wives or wheeled baby carriages down Nassau Street on weekends. Most had not yet decided their life's work, so there was no urge to specialize except for those in science and engineering, and even these had to spend an allotted time in "useless study" of the humanities. As graduation approached, nobody prepared his list of job requirements as to promotion, fringe benefits and retirement pay in readiness to hand to talent scouts from General Electric, General Motors or General Anything. Dean Barzun suggests that present-day colleges provide little opportunity for "contemplation and the cultivation of sensibility and judgment." The Princeton of my day did offer that opportunity; whether we made the best use of it is another matter.

Surprisingly, my best-remembered course was with Alfred Noyes—surprising because his manner was stolid and his taste in poetry was even for that day unrelentingly conservative. Later on, after his conversion to Roman Catholicism, he became still more opposed to experiment and change and spoke with contempt, hatred almost, of poetic innovators who "cut the English literary tradition at its roots." But often he could read superbly, with a surge of emotion that contradicted the rather fishy expression of the eyes behind those thick glasses. Margot Asquith wrote in her autobiography that Tennyson's reading of his own poetry had "the lilt, the tenderness and rhythm that makes music in the soul." When Noyes read his own poems he gave them lilt and rhythm but not tenderness; he made music in the ear, not the soul. But when he read from the great poets he was overcome with emotion, and suddenly even the most irreverent students in the bare lecture hall found themselves carried, to their astonishment, into a moment of aesthetic emotion. I never knew anyone who could impart such a sense of excitement to poetry, unless perhaps the Irish poet AE, who on evenings in the twenties would settle down in my library in New York, wedge his body back into a big armchair, stretch out his legs, fold his hands across his great chest and for the pure sensual joy of it declaim till all hours.

Once a week I had an evening session with Noyes in his room at the Princeton Inn. Sometimes he read aloud for an hour or so, sometimes set me a stint of writing to be done then and there (a barbarous denial of any hope of finding real inspiration), sometimes went over verses done betweentimes on a given subject. Of the contemporaries that Noyes used to read I liked Masefield and Flecker best, and then of course Rupert Brooke, just coming into our ken and exercising tremendous influence. By now Noyes's own poetry has quite gone out of fashion, but then everyone knew at least the refrains from "The Barrel-Organ" and "Sherwood." It surprised me that among the American poets the one he quoted most often was Emerson. Once, he compared Emerson's intellectual rapture with what he considered the pseudo-profundity of Tagore, a recent winner of the Nobel Prize and all the rage. I questioned whether Tagore's poems, purporting to hide deep verities in simplicity of metaphor, were as facile as Noyes asserted.

"Give me three minutes by your watch," he said, "and I'll write you one."

Before I could call "time" he began reading in a squeaky, high-pitched voice:

> I remember the temple, my beloved, where you
>   brought me flowers in a basket,
> At break of day, then went away weeping.
> I set the basket afloat on the dark Ganges,
> It floated away I know not whither.
> Perhaps it was to the sea, the distant and salt sea,
> But I know not.
> The stars look down and perhaps they see it,
> Floating away into the darkness,
> My beautiful basket of flowers;
> But the stars tell me nothing when I ask them,
> And in my ignorance, I, too, weep.

"Why that mimsy voice?" I asked.

It seems that Lady Gregory had invited him to come to a Tagore reading in London. When he entered the dimly lit room he thought at first that the "wailing" was Lady Gregory's. Then he saw that the figure wriggled into the recesses of an immense armchair was Tagore.

"This isn't intended as a parody of Tagore," Noyes said, handing me the paper (which I still have), "just an experiment to show you how easy that sort of thing is. You could write three volumes of it in a week." And he went on: "Of course if you took six minutes, say, instead of three, it would be better. For instance, when I read it over to you I saw that instead of 'flowers in a basket' I ought to have put 'baskets of lotus bloom.' It's all so easy. We give a high-jump prize now to anyone who can clear a one-foot hurdle."

Though it ran counter to his standards, Noyes encouraged me to think of sometime publishing a book of poetry, and I went so far as to choose a title, *Skylight*. Fortunately, I realized in time that what I had written or might write didn't and wouldn't measure up to an even less aspiring designation, and I turned to something less ambitious.

From the age of ten I had roamed all over New York on roller skates, and knew it and loved it, from Washington Square, near where I was born, to the waterfront, with the banana boats in from the Caribbean, the barges of brick and sand passing in slow lines from Haverstraw and Roseton upriver, and the ocean greyhounds in dock after record crossings of the Atlantic. I knew the Lower East Side of Jacob Riis as well as brown-fronted lower Fifth Avenue, Washington Market as well as still-fashionable Madison Square. I wanted somehow to celebrate it, and the idea I hit on was to collect poems about New York, old and new, and make an anthology. The authors were of every sort and time, from Philip Freneau of Revolutionary days to Bryant and Whitman and on to Vachel Lindsay, F.P.A. and Ezra Pound. On weekends in New York I dug in old files of magazines at the Public Library and the Society Library, and discovered fugitive verse that might be worth recalling; and on evenings between times I typed, cut and arranged what I had copied out in pencil. Finally I ventured to take a sample section to old Major George Haven Putnam, peppery on the surface, softhearted underneath. He offered to publish the book when it was finished, but not under my title, *The New York Poetry Book*.

"Never give anything a highfalutin name it can't live up to," he said. "Most of this isn't poetry; it's verse. The title will be *The Book of New York Verse*."

After graduation, when I was doing odd jobs on *The New Republic*, I found time to keep on with my research, first widening the choice to about 400 poems, then weeding them down to about 250. I had just gotten the manuscript into final shape, and finished the seemingly endless task of securing permissions (authors delighted to give them, publishers unpredictable, sometimes generous, sometimes tight-fisted), when I went into the army. My sister Margaret took the whole thing in hand, chose sixty old woodcuts and other illustrations with more knowledge and taste than I could ever have done, and followed the proofs through the press. On the title page I put four lines by H. C. Bunner, whose stories of New York are as authentic as O. Henry's:

> Why do I love New York, my dear?
> I know not. Were my father here—
> And his—and *his*—the three and I
> Might, perhaps, make you some reply.

Other poets besides Noyes were heard at Princeton, the most sensational of them Vachel Lindsay, who had just published "The Congo" to a conflicting uproar of acclaim and hostility. Not long ago a reviewer in the London *Times Literary Supplement* wrote, with a note of envy, that "it must have been a grand experience to hear Lindsay chant and rant." It was. The big McCosh classroom became a camp meeting, where the unfriendly acoustics failed to muffle the decibels of the final crescendo— "Boomlay, *Boomlay,* BOOM!" Your feet were still twitching in ragtime even after Lindsay, crouching almost on his knees, let his voice trail off in a last whispered warning of "hoo-day, hoo-day, you, you."

Max Beerbohm was a favorite with my generation; we loved Zuleika Dobson. I forget which American character it was that I thought he should make the subject of his irreverent pencil, or why I presumed to write and tell him so. His answer put me gently in my place. I had been given a Christmas present of rather flossy writing paper with deckle edges and my initials at the top in square black letters. Max's art of caricature was the art of exaggeration, and it was so in this case. His explanation of why the subject was not for him was written on a large square piece of wrapping paper, with rough torn edges and headed by the letters B.M., two inches high, in black ink. My letter had been from Princeton University, Princeton, New Jersey, and his reply was dated from Oxford University, Oxford, Oxfordshire. I was pleased with the attention and mildly ashamed of having revealed how ingenuous I was.

A minor literary renaissance was stirring in Princeton in those days. Noyes did not exactly inspire it and has been given no credit for it, but he did provide it with a focus in a book of verse by Princeton undergraduates which he edited. I helped him arrange it and saw it through the press. The only contributors whose names were to become known were Edmund Wilson, John Peale Bishop and Struthers Burt. "Bunny" Wilson had come from Hill School with a group of classmates who were accustomed to his defensive-aggressive manner and knew the unusual intellectual qualities it concealed. At Princeton, he edited the *Nassau Literary Magazine* and wrote the book for the Triangle Club show *The Evil Eye,* for which Scott Fitzgerald wrote the lyrics; both of them also contributed to the *Lit.* and so did I. As advertising manager for *The Evil Eye,* considered a desirable post because it entitled you to travel with the show to half a dozen cities during the Christmas holidays, I searched the shops of New York optometrists for a picture of a sufficiently Svengalian optic to be used on a poster. Scott was annoyed when I decided not to go on the road with the show at Christmas; he was looking forward to innumerable parties in the cities to be visited and was downcast that anyone should consider New York festivities superior.

Our bicker sessions lasted late when Bunny Wilson was there to argue the negative. At that time, however, he was not in the least interested in anything political and clammed up if the talk turned to the distant war in Europe. He lumped together as unworthy of support, sacrifice or discussion the causes which most of us were excited about. Enthusiasm tired and annoyed him. In spite of this Bunny became a close friend of Scott's, whose enthusiasm was one of his special attractions.

Their temperaments were plainly contrary, even in that distant day when all of us were young and unformed and long before these two came to be analyzed and written about. Scott was open and gay but self-deprecatory; Bunny was shy but dogmatic. Scott was in major key—full of nature, overcharged, mobile, sentimental, ungrudging, curious, appealing, very young. Bunny was in minor key; he neither was nor wanted to be appealing; his heavy-lidded brown eyes were watchful, defensive; his walk, with shoulders hunched forward, arms hardly swinging, suggested withdrawal, defiance. Scott took to lively checks, stripes and plaids; Bunny wore dark reddish brown that went well with his red hair. Bunny had fewer likes than dislikes, but his liking and concern for Scott were real and were to be lasting. The record of their friendship, in Andrew Turnbull's admirable biography and in Scott's letters, shows, I think, that he gave Scott everything he was capable of intellectually, and it was valuable; but he seems not to have been able to give the affection which Scott usually evoked even when he was being annoying, and which most of his friends feel across the years to this day.

Both Bunny and Scott wrote poetry, and Bunny especially took it seriously. His poems were among the best in the Noyes book, but looking down on Noyes as he did he wouldn't admit how pleased he was that Noyes praised them and put them in. The war, in which he volunteered as a medical corpsman, left him depressed and uncertain. The poetry he wrote overseas was nostalgic, and when we met in Paris in late 1918 in a little hotel on the rue Cambon where he was staying he talked about Princeton with an affection hitherto concealed from his friends. He wondered what sort of niche he could fit himself into at home, doubting his talents as nobody who knew him would have dreamed of doing. Several of his things and Scott's, as well as mine, were in *The Princeton Book of Verse, II,* edited by Henry van Dyke with far less discrimination and taste than Noyes had shown in preparing the first volume.

I remember Bunny's discovery of Baudelaire and the sensual impact on him of *Fleurs du Mal.* He was self-conscious about sex, and the only times he became flustered were when allusions were made to it, whether in the form of a crude and boring collegiate joke or during a ponderous midnight discussion. Soon after the war we had dinner together one evening at Barney Gallant's, south of Washington Square. Bunny brought a girl's rather frayed round garter out of his pocket, evidence that he had managed a conquest. It lay on the table between us without my bringing myself either to make the expected inquiries or offer congratulations, and after a bit he peevishly put it back into his pocket. *Hecate County* years later was another round garter.

My clearest recollections of Scott are as he came out of the West that first fall of his at Princeton, walking lightly, sure that the fabulous East of his imagination really existed and eager to explore its every dimension. Freud says that neurosis is the price paid for being civilized. Scott did not arrive at Princeton "civilized" to any dangerous extent. He already had a liking for the rich, but whatever it may have become later, at this time it was inquisitive not sycophantic. He imagined that the lives they were living must be exciting, and anything that was new and exciting he was determined to find out about. He even believed the glamorous things he read about them in the society pages. When he told me that he simply had to see what a dance at Sherry's was like, I took him up to a coming-out party there. Our little house in Tenth Street was too full of family for me to put him up, and I left him about three in the morning at the Hotel Martinique, a Princeton rendezvous. He was buoyant with success. He felt he had convinced every girl he danced with that she had made a conquest and that it was one well worth making. Of course he was right. He had not yet spent his good looks. He parted his wavy, pal-ish, almost blond hair in the middle (as many of us did; we would have thought a crew cut something out of a penitentiary and hippie locks those of a castaway on a Pacific isle). He effervesced with good spirits, he danced well, he talked more and took the trouble to talk better than most men at a New York dance. Girls also liked his almost feminine sensitivity. He was not, however, drawn to what was effeminate. Early in his freshman year, we went together to see an instructor in English who lived in the bank building above Jack Honoré's barbershop. This in-structor used to invite in sympathetic spirits on late autumn afternoons to sit around his fireplace, drink tea with rum and talk preciously of Art, Love and Life in the adolescent terms indicated by the capital letters. Walking afterward down University Place to Scott's roominghouse, we agreed to skip future gatherings of these self-conscious aesthetes.

One of the last times I saw Scott he was coming out of the Ritz into Madison Avenue with Zelda and Ludlow Fowler, all of them rather high after a good lunch. They hustled me into a limousine and said they were

taking me to the races at Belmont. Before we got to the bridge I escaped.
I ran into him again in Penn Station, and he asked why I didn't stop off
for a night at his house in Wilmington the next time I went to Washington. I'm sorry I let that and other chances slip; though it wouldn't have
worked, I wish I'd made an effort not to lose him entirely.

IV

In my junior year I sat night after night in the *Daily Princetonian* office reading incoming dispatches that recorded the dead piling up at
Verdun and strewn across frozen marshes in the wake of Mackensen's
drive into Poland. In a daring departure, the *Prince* had subscribed to a
condensed AP wire service and we were printing daily summaries of news
from the fronts. It was appalling to think that as millions were being
rushed to their death in Europe we were going our usual ways, ignorant
except superficially and emotionally of the war's why and whither, unable when we read of colossal battles even to pronounce the names
Przemyśl or Lodz.

Encouraged by Professor Brown, a group of us had planned early in
1914 to organize a discussion club on international affairs, and the outbreak of war that summer brought it into active life. The speakers we
invited to Princeton ran from former President Taft through a variety
of Allied spokesmen to (on the "hear-all-sides" argument) Dr. Bernhard
Dernburg, former German Minister for Colonies, hurriedly dispatched
to the United States when the war began as head of the "German Red
Delegation," actually as Germany's chief propagandist. I was relieved
when the Dernburg meeting ended without a riot. The next day I was
called to the telephone and with horror heard Dernburg's accented voice
suggest that he return for a second meeting to give "fuller explanations"
of the German case. I replied evasively, but at once hurried on my bike
to the telegraph office and sent off a firm refusal. I came back to find a
classmate exulting over his successful hoax: he had telephoned me from
next door in just the correct German accent, neither too heavy nor too
light, and had completely taken me in. He was horrified when I told him
how I had already reacted. Dernburg replied politely to my letter of
apology, saying I wasn't the first to have been taken in by a practical
joke. He added—his only barb—that he would gladly visit Princeton
again when Germany had won the war. After the sinking of the *Lusitania* in May, 1915, he became persona non grata and quickly departed,
not to return.

At the start of the war the American people had been divided by President Wilson's appeal, "We must be impartial in thought as well as in action." Some said angrily that this was both immoral and impossible; others, concentrating on Wilson's sentence "My thought is of America," praised the demand for undisturbed judgment and dispassionate action. The British Orders in Council widening the list of contraband to the disadvantage of American business and finance strengthened the sentiment for neutrality, and wishful thinking made it seem a practicable policy. It was in this mood that in a letter written me on January 13, 1915, President Nicholas Murray Butler, of Columbia University, ventured this judgment: "Let me add that I regard war between the United States and Germany, or between the United States and Japan, as just about as imminent as a war between Jupiter and Saturn."

German-Americans pressed the neutrality theme vigorously. Soon it became difficult to tell where neutralism and pacifism ended and pro-Germanism began. Princeton was less evenly divided than the country as a whole. Professor McClellan was one of the definite minority opposed to condemning German actions. He had taken the lead in urging us to invite Dernburg to speak in Princeton and had given him a large dinner at his home on Battle Road. (When we entered the war, however, he was one of the first faculty members commissioned.) On the other hand, President Hibben could not have been more openly for the Allies. So were most of the faculty and almost the entire student body, including the editors of the *Daily Princetonian*.

In the first months, however, the war seemed unreal, a distant conflict in which the concern of the United States was humanitarian rather than explicitly political and certainly not military. Wilson announced that he aimed to act eventually as mediator between the European contestants, and the hope that he might be able to do so did not seem unreasonable until the results of Germany's declaration of unrestricted warfare and especially the sinking of the *Lusitania* on May 7, 1915, brought death to American citizens on the high seas.

President Hibben had been a militant opponent of Wilson's neutrality policy from the start, and he determined that Princeton should contribute to preparedness for the war which he thought inevitable by introducing military training in the form of a course which would count as credit toward a degree. The proposal met with considerable opposition in the college. A group of which I was one argued against it on various grounds. One, that the need for the preparedness movement was exaggerated, was naïve even at the time and was seen to be more so in light of later events. An argument which had some merit was that college education was at too low a level as it was without diluting the curriculum by the addition of an optional course for which students would receive credit but which would accomplish little of practical value in itself and contribute nothing to their intellectual equipment. If national preparedness must be strengthened, the government should take really effective steps, such as establishing more military and naval academies for the serious training of officers.

The statement which we issued in late February caused a stir, though nothing, of course, like the excitement and violence which possessed colleges in the sixties as a result of student distrust and apprehension about government policy in Vietnam. One difference was that in our time there was no "confidence gap" between generations as such. We were often dubious of the quality and capacities of the Establishment as it then existed, though of course the term had not been coined, and took issue with it freely. But we were not possessed by the certainty of later generations that our answers to problems were infallible and that contrary answers by our elders were conceived in hypocrisy. Our group's stand on military training in the colleges caused President Hibben real pain. He thought it unmanly and unpatriotic; but although he remonstrated with us he respected our motives and honorably did not try to restrain, censor or even (if I remember correctly) publicly take issue with us. The protest failed; a Reserve Officers' Training Corps became part of the curriculum, and close-order drill—something already anachronistic in terms of the war in Europe—began on the Princeton baseball field.

In two years the country was at war and soon most of us were in uniform.

Fifty-odd years later a wave of protest based on similar objections (with others that were more provocative added by the Students for a Democratic Society) was to arise in colleges all across the country. But the times were different and so were the results. The Princeton faculty, in March, 1969, like the faculties at Yale, Harvard and other universities, voted to deprive the ROTC course of academic status.

The *Daily Princetonian*'s entry into the votes-for-women controversy was, of course, of a different order of importance. But the now-forgotten bitterness with which that campaign was fought made our first editorial advocating women's rights a news item all across the country. In my freshman year a student mob had gone out along the Plainsboro road to meet and jeer at Rosalie Jones leading a suffragette march from New York to Washington. The recollection of her rain-soaked but undaunted band trudging down muddy Nassau Street, dogged by hilarious students, gave me the not very original theme of that editorial: educated men must begin to give the issue intelligent thought instead of jeers and sneers. The *Alumni Weekly* remarked that many graduates would "raise their eyebrows and emit a whistle" when they heard of this fresh sign of Princeton decadence. But here President Hibben and most of the faculty were with us. We conducted a postcard poll on the pending amendment to the New Jersey constitution which would extend the vote to women, and announced with satisfaction that the majority intended to vote for it; specifically, members of the Departments of Philosophy and Psychology were unanimously favorable while only the Physics and Chemistry departments were unanimously opposed.

The *Prince* board was divided in an agony of indecision when we learned on unimpeachable local authority in October, 1915, that President Wilson was engaged to be remarried. The story would be a tremendous scoop. Should we print it? A day and a night passed while we debated. Late the next evening the White House issued a confirmatory communiqué. We then of course printed the story, regretting (at least I did) that we had not had the nerve to be the first to break it.

Several members of the *Daily Princetonian* board in my time had notable careers later, among them James Forrestal, Ferdinand Eberstadt and Robert McLean (who from that introduction to journalism went on to be president of the Associated Press). Forrestal heeled for the paper in the same competition I did. He had transferred from Dartmouth to Princeton at the beginning of his sophomore year, saying frankly that he hoped to find more useful contacts there. He still used his middle initial V., for Vincent, and at college some friends called him "Vince," though usually he was known as "Runt." Another nickname he brought from Dartmouth, "Swampy," fortunately disappeared. He abandoned the name Vincent later on when he entered political life; he had severed his connection with the Catholic Church and may have thought it inappropriate to continue using a name usually associated with Catholics. He was active in club and class politicking, and in his senior year his classmates voted him "most likely to succeed"; they also put him fourth on the list of "biggest bluffer." I never felt he was a bluffer; he was perfectly open about his need to make his own way. Just before graduation he abruptly resigned from college. A biography by A. A. Rogow attributes this in part to the fact that he found himself in a financial crisis when "his paying editorship of the *Daily Princetonian*" ended. Actually, there was no salary attached to being an editor; the year's profits were divided among members of the retiring board at the end of their junior year

according to the positions they had held, the business manager receiving
the most because he had brought in the most.

Forrestal may have gotten his start in business through friends made at
Princeton, but his immensely successful career in Wall Street was of
course due to his own drive and brilliance. At college, he did not spend
much time acquiring a formal education. His aim was to "get on." Yet
when he did so, in a most spectacular way, he found financial success by
itself empty and unsatisfactory. I think he then began regretting the
wasted opportunities at Princeton, and turned inward. He started reading voraciously—the standard classics which he had skipped, poetry,
novelists from Conrad and Howells to Steinbeck, economists and historians like Bagehot and Toynbee. Professor Rogow's biography contains much speculation in psychological terms as to the reasons for some
of Forrestal's opinions and policies while Secretary of the Navy and
Secretary of Defense and for his breakdown and suicide. He speaks of
the psychic deprivation in his small-town childhood and traces a close
relationship between his "personality needs and policy recommendations." He suggests, for example, that Forrestal's militant attitude toward
Stalin was a product of "early home life." A reviewer in *The New York
Review of Books* calls this "jargon-jello laced with unshredded cliché."

I didn't find Runt particularly congenial at college, but I appreciated
his energy and single-mindedness; and despite his tight mouth, stubby
jaw, steely eye, grim smile and aggressive stance I found him fair and
friendly in competition. I admired him in public life for similar qualities—complete devotion to his job and a willingness to stick his neck out
and say unpopular things about the conduct of the war, which often
proved to be true. In his post as Secretary of Defense, which he was the
first to hold and which he himself said was "too big for any one man,"
he worked and worried himself into such a state of physical and mental
exhaustion that death seemed to him the only solution. There was, of
course, more to it than that, but probably less than Professor Rogow
imagines in his psycho-social study.

Rummaging about one day in the storage cellar under the *Daily Princetonian* office I came across a bundle of back issues from the winter of
1878–79 when the paper had been a weekly and "Tommy" Woodrow
Wilson had been editor. These issues had belonged to President James
McCosh and many of them bore his signature at the top. I amused myself trying to spot editorials which by substance and style seemed most
likely to have been written by Editor Wilson; then I had the set bound
and sent it to President Wilson with the compliments of our editorial

board. I don't remember all the signposts I followed in making the selection, but one was Wilson's liking for coupling two adverbs, as in his well-known "Cordially and sincerely yours" salutation at the end of letters. He wrote back that he was delighted to have the volume, which he would value "as a token of thoughtful friendship," the more so because some of the numbers "belonged to my beloved President, Doctor McCosh." He said he was afraid he wasn't a sufficient expert in his own style to be sure which editorials he had written, but he thought I was right about the little farewell editorial in the last number, the third in No. 16 and the sixth in No. 17. These may properly be included, then, among the earliest known items in the published works of Woodrow Wilson.

I suppose it was as secretary of the International Polity Club (as the discussion group formed with Professor Brown's encouragement was named) that late in November, 1915, I received a telegram signed Louis P. Lochner, secretary to Henry Ford, inviting me to be Mr. Ford's guest on what became the notorious "Peace Ship." Thirty "most carefully selected" college students were to sail with "two hundred of the most prominent Americans" on a chartered steamer for Stockholm "to bring about a conference of neutral powers to end the European slaughter." The invitation was marked "confidential" but the newspapers soon heard about it, and "Hennery's" motto, "Get the boys out of the trenches before Christmas," became a popular catchword, hopeful for some, derisive for most. The group sailed December 4, so the time in which to achieve the goal was short. I was strong-minded enough to forgo a free trip to Europe, and I hope the decision had nothing to do with the prospect of a stormy December crossing of the North Atlantic.

One of the club's memorable meetings was when we entertained ex-President Taft in something less than Presidential style in the beer cellar of the old Nassau Tavern. A dozen of the long wooden tables, scarred with the initials of convivial souls long departed, were placed end to end, and at the head I put a stout drawing board across two chairs to accommodate Mr. Taft's ample proportions. (A family friend, Sir Horace Plunkett, told me that during his ranching days in the West he had heard a Nebraska farmer describe Taft as "a man of great personal magnitude.") I became enthusiastic about Taft's project for a League to Enforce Peace, which later turned out to be a prototype for the League of Nations. In May, 1916, its sponsors (who included President Lowell of Harvard and Senator Henry Cabot Lodge, not yet warped into isolationism by hatred of Wilson) held a two-day conference in Washington to which I was invited. Meetings were held all day in the Shubert Theatre, and on the second evening two thousand persons crowded into the Hotel Willard banquet room to hear the speech by President Wilson which made him the first chief of state to give official sanction to a proposal for a world organization for peace. He also announced for the first time the principle of self-determination which later was a dominant theme in his Fourteen Points.

That year, the eating club to which I belonged asked me to find a speaker for our annual dinner and by good luck I snared Frank Crownin-shield, the editor of *Vanity Fair;* his spoofing of college life (he himself hadn't been to college) couldn't have been better, witty without being sarcastic, urbane without being top-lofty. As I walked down Prospect Street with him afterward on the way to the station he suggested that after graduation I might like to become one of his assistants on *Vanity Fair.* The idea was very tempting. "Crownie," as most people called him whether or not they knew him well, was a master impresario of sophisticated entertainment of every sort—literary, artistic, theatrical—and had made the magazine a reflection in text and picture of his own taste, which essentially was very good, and his own personality, which was generous, worldly and versatile.

As *arbiter elegantarium,* Frank told everyone through the pages of *Vanity Fair* what was brightest and best and above all what was newest in the domain of the arts, very spaciously and inclusively conceived. Though he loved gaiety, he refused to open its pages to the doings of either what still undauntedly called itself Society or the gathering horde soon to take over, with the help of the new breed of publicity touts, as Café Society. But he got great pleasure out of helping young professional artists; and many new painters, poets, actors, musicians and dancers got their first leg up the career ladder from him. He had a true eye for the best but a weakness for the ephemeral and fashionable. The combination was not permanently successful, so that after a couple of decades the publisher, Condé Nast, recognizing that fashion was the more profitable element, merged *Vanity Fair* into *Vogue,* a "bra magazine," in which editorial and advertising content are indistinguishable and debutantes are models.

Frank's father and mine, I should explain, both artists, had been close friends in Rome in their younger days; indeed, Frank was my father's godson. Predisposed in my favor for this reason, he had accepted an article of mine while he was still on the old *Century Magazine;* then when he began editing *Vanity Fair* he showed me how to touch up one or two bits of *vers de société* in order to make them printable there; and finally came a formal offer to employ me as an assistant. But when the time came I doubted that I ought to begin with something that would be so much fun. My first job, therefore, was with *The New Republic,* doing odds and ends, more in the advertising than in the editorial department. Meanwhile, I applied that spring to join the Commission for Relief in Belgium, but without success. A letter from the director, Captain Lucey, to one of my sponsors, President Hibben, said that Herbert Hoover had just returned from Belgium with word that no further "junior delegates" were needed in Europe.

The next year most of my class were at one stage or another of going overseas, on business even more sober than war relief. Some of the best did not return. As I read their names in the long lists from many wars inscribed in Nassau Hall—among them, my friends on the *Prince,* Ben Bullock and Al Talley—their faces come before me, smiling, not dimmed by time, "young as when they died."

> They shall not grow old, as we that are left grow old:
> Age shall not weary them, nor the years condemn. . . .

2

The Serbian War Mission

It was August, 1914, ten days after the start of what soon we would be calling the World War. I was at North Hatley, the little Quebec village where my family spent the summers, when suddenly a cable came from Mme. Grouich. Since her visit to Princeton I had heard only that she was running a hospital at Nish, in southern Serbia, for orphans of the Balkan Wars. Her cable said that the Austrians were bombarding Belgrade and that the invasion of Serbia was imminent. She asked help for the Serbian Red Cross to cope with the horrors ahead.

North Hatley was an English settlement, surrounded by French *habitant* country which refused to be concerned with the struggle beginning in Europe. The village itself, by contrast, overflowed with patriotism. Every few hours war bulletins went up on strips of brown paper in the window of Jean Le Baron's general store: the Belgian countryside was in flames, the French were turned back in Lorraine, the British Expeditionary Force was landing at Le Havre. Already two boys from the village had volunteered and left. On Sunday—and for how many Sundays thereafter—the little church was crowded and the stuttering rector's prayers for the R-r-royal Family and, in courtesy to the "summer visitors," for the P-p-president of the United States, took on new significance and brought earnest Amens.

It was far from being an opulent community, but my friends and I decided that something must be done to answer Mme. Grouich's appeal. The only kind of benefit practicable on the spur of the moment was a mammoth card party in the Town Hall. We put up posters in the store window alongside the war bulletins and hawked tickets for a dollar apiece. There were tables for bridge and for the more placid game of euchre, in which my mother and her contemporaries indulged. We cajoled those who didn't buy into donating prizes. In a week I was able to telegraph $200 to New York for Colonel Edward F. Ryan, who was just being hurried off to the Balkans by the American Red Cross to see what kinds of relief would be most needed (he died of typhus later in Persia). Colonel Ryan got gold pieces, put them in a little cotton bag, and within two weeks delivered them to Mme. Grouich in Nish—the first tiny drops actually to reach Europe, I like to think, of the flood of American dollars sent there in the following years. The next spring, when Mme. Grouich came again to America and, of course, to Princeton for another profitable meeting, she brought me a Serbian decoration.

The Serbs at this time were immensely popular. They had done the impossible: they had driven the invading armies of Austria-Hungary back across the Danube, out of the country, and held them there. By the autumn of 1915, however, a new enemy revealed itself alongside the old one. Seven German divisions which had been pounding the Russians in Galicia were brought to the aid of the Austrians, and the combined forces were put under the command of Field Marshal von Mackensen. The Serbs, overwhelmed but refusing to surrender, retreated south. Now still another enemy appeared. Bulgaria, sensing a cheap victory, declared war and attacked from the rear. Britain and France had promised to send help via Saloniki, but it was late and ineffective. The British military critic Colonel Repington said the Germans could be in Constantinople in a week. The Serbs were squeezed westward, across historic Kosovo Plain, into the mountains of Albania. In the snow-clogged passes most of the horses and all the oxen perished; the fieldpieces, to each of which twenty oxen had been hitched, were one by one abandoned. The soldiers struggled on, in blinding blizzards and howling winds, with temperatures below zero, half-starved, weak from dysentery, followed by a train of tattered refugees. As they approached the Adriatic even their supposed allies, the Italians, impeded them as much as possible, for Italy was planning to annex Albania herself. About 140,000 survived to reach the coast.

With these remnants of the Serbian Army went members of the government and the diplomatic corps, among them Mme. Grouich, who had returned to Serbia the previous summer; she survived the ordeal but lost an expected baby. One poignant photograph of the march became famous —a thread of Serbian troops winding from the distance through a gorge deep in snow, with the ailing Voivode Putnik in a litter at the head. Throughout the retreat the young Prince Regent Alexander stayed with the rear guard of his troops despite an agony of incipient appendicitis. On the Greek island of Corfu he set up a government-in-exile; and within three months, to the amazement of everyone except the Serbs themselves, a new Serbian Army was forming on the Saloniki front.

In April, 1917, when the United States entered the war, even those of us who were of military age worried that we might not be able to get into the army. Word went round that only the most perfect physical specimens stood a chance of being accepted at the start; and the war was sure to be over by autumn. Little did we know. Actually, my first effort to get accepted at officers' training camp did almost fail. While I was waiting for the crucial physical examination I had gone with some friends for a preliminary workout at the summer camp at Princeton. (I financed it by acting as correspondent there for two New York papers, the *World* and the *Times*.) Even under the inspiration of Major Stuart Heintzelman (later Major General and Chief of Staff of the Second Army in Europe), the close-order drill and topographic hikes would not have been of much use as preparation for trench warfare; but they had the merit of toughening us up, and this I needed after a winter of office work at *The New Republic*. The Jersey sun sweated away a few necessary pounds, however, and by the time I came to take the tests for officers' training camp I was underweight—too far under, said the medical examiner, for him to dare waive the discrepancy.

"But come back tomorrow," he whispered, "and see if you can't make it. With just a little increase I might let you by."

Stuffed with bananas and with water up to my tonsils, I weighed in again the next morning—and passed. The inconveniences were tremendous but temporary.

By way of insurance, I also took examinations at Sandy Hook for appointment as provisional second lieutenant in the Regular Army. Before anything came of that, my orders arrived to report at the officers' training camp at Fort Myer; and thence I was transferred to Fortress Monroe, for army logic dictated that since I was weak in mathematics I should be set to figuring out the intricate factors of drift, barometric pressures, temperature and so on which condition the proper sighting of heavy artillery. Luckily, before there was time for mathematical disaster to overtake me, I was notified that my commission in the Regular Army had been granted. What was more, I was assigned to the 22nd Infantry on Governors Island. Obviously it must be on the point of embarkation for Europe. In top spirits I hurried north.

The reality was shattering. The 22nd Infantry was at, but not on, the point of embarkation. Our commanding officer was Colonel John C. F. Tillson, upright, stocky, grizzled, high-tempered, a veteran of the Indian Wars (a reminder of how close we still were to frontier days). In 1900 he had taken part in the capture of Peking and later served in the Philippines. Despite his experience he was anathema to General Pershing.

"I never want to see any of these men in Europe," General Pershing told Secretary of War Newton Baker, handing him a list of a dozen high officers, including General Goethals and General Leonard Wood.

Colonel Tillson's name led all the rest.

Pershing and Tillson had fallen out in the Philippines over the vital matter of where the regimental colors should be trooped after evening parade. Were they to be borne to the quarters of Colonel Tillson, the Post Commander, or to the quarters of the newly arrived Commander of the Department of Mindanao, Brigadier General Pershing? the color sergeant had inquired, and the Colonel had sent word with some asperity to follow Army Regulations. Through some mistake, the colors had nevertheless been carried to the General's quarters. Now Pershing had been jumped from Captain to Brigadier General over the heads of 862 fellow West Pointers—as a result, some considered, of political influence. Colonel Tillson was one of them, and he interpreted the mistake with the colors as a deliberate affront.

In a fury he called up Pershing: "Who in hell do you think you are?"

Never one to miss a fight, "Black Jack" Pershing answered: "Why in hell don't you learn to run your Post?"

Thus it was that the 22nd was doomed to watch from Governors Island as the camouflaged transports slid out to sea. For the Colonel forbade any of his officers to put in for transfer.

"If I can take it after forty years in the army," he said, "you can."

It was our frustrating routine to guard munition plants, drill for the sort of war we knew was obsolete, prepare to deal with any disorders that might occur in New York, and supply contingents for Liberty Loan parades. Once a week we held evening parade (the colors were trooped to the Colonel's quarters). I was even sent to preach a patriotic sermon at a church in Harlem. On a painful occasion Washington ordered us to supply the honor guard at the funeral of John Purroy Mitchel, former Mayor of New York. He had been serving as a major in the Air Force when killed in a crash, therefore rated a battalion as escort. At dawn, we began transporting the men to the Battery. As I was battalion adjutant I was mounted, and my orderly also. The troops were drawn up in front of City Hall, the coffin was carried out and placed on the gun carriage, the order was given to start the slow march up to St. Patrick's Cathedral and the regimental band struck up the Chopin funeral march. At the first blast, my orderly's horse started to take cover in the nearest subway kiosk. Mine reared and followed. More by luck than good horsemanship we narrowly avoided taking an underground route uptown.

I came into New York seldom, for the city was not a cheerful place. Houses were cold from lack of fuel and my family, like most, was on short rations. It was said that in some cases privations went to extremes. Miss Wetmore, made aware of the shortage of gasoline, resorted (for the first time) to a bus. In those days the conductor came to collect fares with a little machine into which you slipped your dime. "No thank you," said Miss Wetmore when he approached her, "I have my own private charities." Miss Gerry decided that it would be ostentatious and damaging to public morale if she drove around town with the usual footman beside the chauffeur, so she had him follow in a second car to be on hand to open the door when she wished to alight. Stories of such vicissitudes put humdrum sacrifices into their proper place.

A break in the routine came for me late in 1917 when a Serbian War Mission arrived in the United States to secure equipment for the new Serbian Army established on the Saloniki front and to recruit volunteers among Jugoslav immigrants from Austria-Hungary who had not yet become American citizens. Colonel Tillson received orders to assign an officer to accompany the mission. The notation about my Serbian decoration on my qualification card gave him an idea. (Another link was about to be added to the chain of coincidences.)

"You're detailed as an aide to General Rashich," he said, then added with a sour grin, "Don't catch anything from him." He thought the whole thing ridiculous.

The General whose name had such an unfortunate sequence of syllables was a veteran of the Balkan Wars, a dignified and most amiable officer. The head of the mission, Milenko Vesnich, Serbian Minister in Paris, was adroit and cosmopolitan. I traveled with them for several weeks, first to Washington, then to Pittsburgh, Buffalo, St. Louis and other centers of Jugoslav immigration. Mayors gave banquets and local organizations arranged recruiting rallies, usually at night in some dim and smoky social hall. The walls would be hung with lithographs of Washington, Lincoln and Jugoslav heroes—Marko Kraljevich on his white steed, Sharats, Ban Jelačić, defender of Croatia against the Hugarians, and Kara George, founder of Serbian independence. Following nostalgic songs from the old country came exhortatory speeches. "Zhivio! Zhivio!" roared the sweaty miners and factory workers as Vesnich and Rashich assured them the Hapsburg Empire was doomed and promised the union of the Jugoslav peoples.

In Washington we stayed at the old Shoreham Hotel. The weather was bitterly cold and the steam heat rattled all night in the effort to keep from freezing. A young secretary of the mission, Martinats, coming down to breakfast pale and with deep circles under his eyes, fainted before he could get his first cup of coffee; he had not known how to turn off the steam heat, had been too afraid of "the night air" to open a window, and had alternately sweated and taken cold baths every half hour till morning.

General Rashich had talks with Secretary of War Baker and General Bliss, Chief of Staff, and Vesnich with Secretary of State Lansing. Lansing and Baker accompanied our party to a ceremony at Mount Vernon, and President Wilson had the heads of the mission to dinner at the White House. Secretary Baker gave an informal dinner the following evening, at which he and his wife were as considerate to a young lieutenant as to their important guests.

The uniforms of General Rashich's aides, Colonel Nenadovich, who had lost an arm in the Balkan Wars, and his high-spirited colleague Captain Jovichich, who was half English, excited curiosity everywhere and their names caused much merriment. They were delighted to find that the sleeping car in which we were touring was called "Tehachapi" and made me photograph them standing beside it. After that when anyone made fun of their names they took the picture out and handed it around.

I I

The date January 8, 1918, entered into history, not because on that day Vesnich addressed the Senate and House of Representatives but because they remained in joint session afterward to hear President Wilson deliver his "Fourteen Points" speech. The mission was invited to stay, seated in the front row. From the moment the President began to speak it was plain that this was a momentous occasion. I was within a few feet of him. His manner was austere; he did not gesticulate for emphasis or smile at the applause, which at the start was notably reserved, for nobody knew what might be coming.

The President dealt sharply with the demands being made on Russia by Germany and Turkey at Brest-Litovsk; summarized the general prin-

ciples of American war aims; and denounced "secret understandings."
Then, speaking deliberately, he came to the substance of his speech—
the Fourteen Points of an acceptable peace settlement, to be based on
justice to all peoples and nationalities, strong or weak. Each point was
applauded, though the proposal to remove economic barriers less than
the others. When he reached Points Nine, Ten and Eleven the members
of the Serbian War Mission learned for the first time the extent to which
Wilson favored their plan to create a unified Jugoslav state and how far
his ideas might be an obstacle. They were relieved by the statement in
Point Nine that Italy's frontiers should be adjusted after the war "along
clearly recognizable lines of nationality." This sounds irreproachable,
but it came as a blow to Italian ambitions and put British and French
statesmen in a predicament, for it ruled out many of the territorial rewards which they had promised Italy in the secret Treaty of London to
tempt her to enter the war in 1915. Wilson repudiated all such secret
treaties and understandings. The Serbs also were pleased by the demand
in Point Eleven that Serbia be given "free and secure access to the sea."
Taken with Point Nine, they assumed this meant that Wilson favored
giving them the eastern coast of the Adriatic, where the population was
predominantly Jugoslav.

These two points, Nine and Eleven, were the starting point of the
"Adriatic Question," which became a cause of such acute controversy
at the Paris Conference and which was not to be settled in its last ves-
tiges until the Italo-Jugoslav agreement over Trieste in 1954.

Two of Wilson's concepts disturbed the Serbs in particular. It seemed
to them wildly optimistic to propose in Point Eleven that "the relations
of the several Balkan states [should be] determined by friendly counsel
along historically established lines of allegiance and nationality." What
lines, at what moment in history? Frontiers had fluctuated with victories
and defeats of rival Balkan nations like patterns in a kaleidoscope. Bulgaria had entered the present war with an attack on the Serbian rear, and
the fighting with her was continuing at the very moment.

However, it was Wilson's proposal, in Point Ten, that the subject peoples of the Austro-Hungarian Empire "should be accorded the freest
opportunity of autonomous development" that caused consternation in
the mission. If this was all that Wilson meant by self-determination, it
spelt the end of the hopes of Croats and Slovenes to unite with the Serbs
in an independent state. Vesnich felt particularly hard hit, as it showed
that the strong arguments for the complete independence of the subject
peoples which he had put to Colonel House four days earlier had utterly

failed. I knew that he had been invited to meet House but not that it was to discuss specific positions to be taken by the President in a speech on war aims; indeed, there had been no public announcement that the President was going to make a speech, and even the few cabinet members who had heard of it had no inkling that it was to be of historic importance. Wilson had asked House to sound Vesnich out about the provisions on the Balkans in Point Eleven. House was reluctant. "I have had so much experience," he wrote in his diary, "with foreigners and others who are obsessed with an idea that I felt it would be hopeless to expect a reasonable viewpoint." But the President insisted.

Vesnich gave House his reasons for thinking Wilson's proposed approach to a future Balkan settlement wholly unrealistic. And then, although this had not been either Wilson's or House's intention, he broadened the discussion to cover also the future of the Hapsburg Empire. To cut short an interview which had become even more displeasing than expected, House asked him to write down then and there a brief summary of his views. Vesnich without hesitation placed the problem of Austria-Hungary first. So long as the Empire continued to exist, he wrote, there would be no lasting peace in Europe. The question was not simply whether the Croats and Slovenes would consent to remain quietly under Austrian and Magyar domination; the Czechs, Slovaks and Rumanians would refuse it also. House was vexed by this plain talk. His *Intimate Papers,* edited by Charles Seymour, disclose that it left him "rather depressed," that he advised the President not to change the text of his speech in the slightest and that this was the case.

Seymour expresses surprise that the President and House paid no attention to Vesnich's warning. But Wilson was in a dilemma. To promise the subject nationalities complete liberation would force Vienna into entire dependence on Berlin; and it would mean splitting up an economically interdependent region. On the other hand, to offer them mere autonomy, though it had the advantage of keeping open the possibility of detaching Vienna from Berlin and negotiating a separate peace, would dishearten soldiers of Slav blood in the Austro-Hungarian forces, thousands of whom were ready to mutiny; and thus an opportunity to weaken a major opponent would be lost.

Vesnich was in a dilemma too. He realized how foolish it would be to appeal in his speech to Congress for the breakup of Austria-Hungary if President Wilson were going to take the same rostrum a few minutes later and reject it. Yet, if he failed to do so, the Croats and Slovenes would accuse the Serbian Government of being less interested in their fate than in its own territorial ambitions. They might abandon the whole Jugoslav program and decide to "fight it out" with Vienna alone. These days in the mission were very tense. I supposed that Vesnich was worried about the prospect of speaking before Congress; he was, but it was because on the vital question of the Empire he did not know what to say. He had talked several times with Secretary of State Lansing, who in this matter as in many others disagreed with the President, and felt he had made more of an impression on him than on House; but he knew Lansing had negligible influence compared to House. Vesnich's enforced failure to demand the breakup of the Empire did in fact create difficulties for the Serbian Government. On the other hand, for him to have taken the opposite course would have antagonized Wilson, perhaps to the point where his support would have been lost on issues which were to prove just as vital to the Croats and Slovenes as to the Serbs.

I didn't, of course, attend meetings of the mission, but members blurted out their worries. Their sense of helplessness was overwhelming. Problems which were vital to them were remote from American knowledge and experience; yet when the time came to settle those problems it would be the American President and his advisers on whom they would have to rely almost entirely for understanding and support.

A better chance for Vesnich to argue his views came when the President received him for farewell talks at the White House on January 23 and 24. His warnings seemed to make more of an impression then than when relayed by House. At any rate, Wilson gave a surprisingly favorable reply in March to a cable from H. Percival Dodge, American representative with the Serbian Government in exile at Corfu, who reported that the Serbian Prime Minister, Pashich, was under extreme pressure from his Croat colleagues and asked permission to assure them that the Fourteen Points were only a summary of war aims, not a complete program. Specifically, Pashich wanted to tell them that Serbo-Croat national aspirations would be met so far as possible. Wilson authorized Pashich to make such a statement.[1]

It is to Vesnich's credit that he saw things in proportion. He realized that what was all-important was Wilson's commitment to self-determination, and that though he must be urged and encouraged to hold to that principle he must not be rushed by demands to know precisely how he would seek to apply it in every case. If he did hold to it, he would come

---

1. Professor Victor S. Mamatey has noted in *The U.S. and East Central Europe* that this was the first step toward a modification of the Fourteen Points program in favor of Jugoslav union.

in time to see that it had precedence over strategic and economic factors. This is what occurred, although actually in the end it was not a question of choice for Wilson or the other Allied leaders. As Count Czernin, the Hapsburg Foreign Minister, said later: "Austria-Hungary's watch had run down." The old Empire fell apart, and contrary to what many later observers have maintained (including as serious a student as George Kennan), nothing that could have been said or done in Washington or Paris would have saved it. To hold back the subject peoples from uniting with their kinsmen beyond the frontiers would have required the use of military force on a tremendous scale. Certainly the American public, intent on getting home their sons and husbands as rapidly as possible, would have rejected utterly a proposal to send them off to garrison Central Europe and maintain the old frontiers.

III

Back on Governors Island, I found the 22nd Infantry in a mood of desperation. Not the draftees; as soon as they were half trained they were shipped off to units bound overseas and replaced by a new batch. But the officers remained. Most of the provisional second lieutenants had been trained at Fort Leavenworth by Captain Dwight D. Eisenhower. The captains were West Pointers. One of them, who knew his rights, put in a written application for transfer. Army Regulations required Colonel Tillson to forward it through channels. He glanced at it, tore it up and threw the pieces into the scrapbasket. In World War II this officer was to become a lieutenant general, but no foreshadowing of that future eminence helped him now. The Colonel sent him off with a small detail to guard gasoline tanks in Perth Amboy. It was a sobering incident for all of us.

I decided to try a more underhanded course. Using a one-day leave, I went down to Washington and pleaded with a friend in the War Department, Fred Keppel, for a transfer. In two or three weeks the order actually came through. The morning I placed it on top of the pile of papers on the Colonel's desk I sat down at my place in the anteroom to await the worst. It came.

"Lieutenant Armstrong! Come here! Shut the door! Shut the window!"

The reasons for these precautions became clear as door and window reverberated under the force of the Colonel's explosion. The back of my neck prickled, but I held my nerve sufficiently to keep from saying "Yes, sir" to the demand that I refuse the transfer. When he had said everything possible, without effect, he took up the order and wrote at the bottom: "Forwarded, strongly recommending disapproval in the interest of discipline."

"Send an orderly over with it to Department Headquarters," he said with a little smirk, "and get back to work!"

There had not been any particular friction between the Colonel and the Departmental Commander, General J. Franklin Bell; the regimental colors had always been trooped peaceably to the proper place. But the General, holder of the Congressional Medal of Honor, sad but philosophic instead of resentful that he himself was ending a distinguished army career on Governors Island, sympathized with the young officers immobilized there. Beneath the Colonel's negative endorsement he simply wrote, "Forwarded, recommending approval."

After a training course in the Military Intelligence Division in Washington I was assigned to an infantry regiment at Anniston, Alabama. At this moment the war ended. That delirious first night of the Armistice, as I was milling around in the Washington streets with the singing and shouting crowds, a shade of disappointment intruded. Stupid, but a fact.

A day or so later I happened to see three lines in a newspaper to the effect that General Rashich had been appointed Minister of War in the Serbian Government which was about to return to Belgrade from exile in Corfu. I hastened with a brilliant idea to the chief of the Military Intelligence Division, General Marlborough Churchill. I knew General Rashich, I said, better than any other American. Hadn't I helped write his speeches, buckled and unbuckled his galoshes, supplied the aspirin when American steam heat was too much for him? Why not send me to Belgrade? The most obvious reason why not was that a first lieutenant didn't have enough rank to be a military attaché. But after one or two men of higher rank refused the post the need to have some officer in Belgrade at once, any officer, even one as lowly as myself, prevailed, and I was appointed acting military attaché. Temporarily I was assigned to the American Embassy in Paris for a briefing en route regarding the operations of the Peace Conference, then just assembling. Of more than incidental importance was the fact that this would give me an opportunity to get married, for my fiancée had been in France for the past year and a half working with the American Red Cross—a strong reason, it must at last be confessed, for my impatience to get to Europe.

The wedding took place the last day of 1918 in the Church of St. Roch, or rather in the sacristy, since being a Protestant I was a heretic. The aisle is the longest in Paris, and even to the sacristy was a rather long walk. We were married by Father Hemmick, a talented and *mondain* priest who had been an assistant to Monseigneur Fay, Scott Fitzgerald's mentor at the Newman School (Scott admired Hemmick's silver-buckled pumps), and now was the principal Roman Catholic chaplain with the American forces in Europe. The Cardinal Archbishop of Paris had refused to sanction the marriage of a Catholic with a non-Catholic in his jurisdiction, even if it took place in a sacristy. Father Hemmick, not to be deterred, argued successfully that as the lady involved was an American abroad she could be presumed (quite erroneously) to have such a limited choice—"angustia locae," or something of the sort, was the church phrase—that she must not be deprived of the chance to accept an American, any American, even a heretic.

During the ceremony, two priests in the background discussed whether part of the wedding fee ought not to be returned. The wedding had been paid for at the *grande luxe* rate, which called for a red carpet down the Church steps and across the sidewalk; but as it was raining, the sacristan had rolled it only down the steps. How much, if any, was to be refunded? The discussion became so vigorous—one priest insisting that all should be kept, nobody would notice, the other demanding that a rebate be given—that Father Hemmick finally turned and "shushed" them. After the mass, the same stately *huissiers* carrying gold-knobbed staves who had ushered us in saw us out as majestically as though no doubt had arisen whether the affair was *grande luxe* or merely *luxe*. At the wedding breakfast at the Ritz, Vesnich and I exchanged toasts, full of hope and feeling. A few days later we started for, or rather toward, Belgrade.

3

Belgrade in Ruins

I had left Washington with the sketchiest of briefings.

"You are going out there," I was told, "to find the answers to just the questions you are asking us."

In any case I was in a hurry to get off before someone with more suitable rank asked for the assignment. I supplemented the sparse information in the files of the Military Intelligence Division with several of the excellent little green British Foreign Office handbooks and an old Baedeker of Austria-Hungary containing a section on travel in Serbia, something which the reader was informed must not be entered upon lightly. In Paris I was warned that most population maps of Central Europe and the Balkans were colored to suit a propaganda cause, most census statistics had been juggled when taken and juggled a second time in preparation for arguments at the Peace Conference, and most of the history on which various territorial claims were being based was erroneous. My best acquisitions there were a book by Seton-Watson, *German, Slav and Magyar,* containing chapters on the genesis of the Jugoslav movement—useful even if one-sided—and Harold Temperley's *History of Serbia,* gifts from one of the British experts (I'm ashamed to have forgotten his name), who told me he could get replacements by courier from London.

Europe was living under only an armistice. In the broad swath of ruin cut across the continent from the North Sea and the Baltic to the Adriatic and the Aegean the fighting in several areas had never in fact ended or was being renewed by guerrillas. One such local war was in progress in the disputed borderlands between Austria and the new Serbo-Croat-

Slovene state—already commonly called Jugoslavia—and others threatened where Jugoslav claims clashed with Italian claims along the Adriatic and with Magyar claims in Hungary. In view of this, General Marlborough Churchill, chief of M.I.D., thought that before I set out for Belgrade I ought to be briefed by General Tasker H. Bliss, and he arranged for me to call on him at the Hotel Crillon.

General Bliss, American member of the Supreme War Council and now a delegate to the Peace Conference, wore the four stars of a full general—the first time I had seen that impressive sight. He told me no secrets but dosed me with useful realism. His chief fear was that Germany might make some convulsive and fatal move. The demand "Bring the boys home!" was mounting. Soon the Allied armies would be melting away, leaving no forces available to deal with a Communist revolution in Germany or with fresh outbreaks in the many territories whose ownership might not be decided for months. Delays in getting the conference under way made the danger worse. Reports were coming in constantly that all along the Adriatic coast the Italians were interfering with shipments of American food to starving Jugoslav towns. The French, and to some extent the British, were becoming involved there for purposes of their own, and Bliss feared we might be induced to do so too; this would be an error, he thought, unless we planned to maintain enough military strength in Europe to make our wishes prevail, something he didn't suppose Congress and the public were in a mood to approve.

As I left, he said without smiling, but in a way that I learned to know later was good-humored: "Write what you see, and Christ! write it before you read too much tripe!"

Thus encouraged, but nevertheless pretty much an innocent, I started off. My equipment was mainly friendliness for the Serbs, based on my experiences with the war mission, and enthusiasm for the adventure of going as the first American officer to a newborn country. I knew three words of the language, taught me by Vesnich when he came to our wedding reception.

"When you see a pretty girl in the street," he said, "you say 'lepa.' When you see a very pretty girl, you say 'l-e-pa.' When you see a very, *very* pretty girl, you say 'l-e-e-pa!' "

As this seemed insufficient, I also found in Paris a small French-Serb dictionary which proved to contain the most astounding mistranslations.

For the next seven months my wife and I were to watch from the limited angle of a small Balkan capital as history unrolled a new strip of patchwork. But though the angle was narrow the view had interest and even importance. The country coming unsteadily into existence was composed of three peoples never in modern times joined in a single state and faced on every hand by hostile or at any rate rival neighbors. Almost all its frontiers were in dispute. The form of union had been debated during the last phases of the war to the point of despair; but in the end the prestige of the Karageorgevich dynasty, the prowess of the Serbian Army and the fact that Serbia was a member of the winning alliance had been decisive. On December 1, 1918, Prince Regent Alexander of Serbia, acting for his infirm father, King Peter, had proclaimed the united Kingdom of Serbs, Croats and Slovenes, and the first all-Jugoslav government was constituted in Belgrade on January 8, 1919, only a few days before our arrival. The United States did not recognize the new nation until February 7; but H. Percival Dodge, who had been special agent in Corfu while the Serbian Government was in exile there, had accompanied it to Belgrade and opened our Legation as chargé d'affaires.

This first government, a coalition of politicians from the old Serbian regime and revolutionary leaders from the former Hapsburg realm, faced the task of reconciling the traditions, habits and interests of the three related but not identical peoples and fusing them into at least the prototype of a modern state. It was a task that would not be fully accomplished even in the two decades between the Great Wars, nor in fact to this day. The Croats and Slovenes were oriented to the West, the Serbs to the East. The Serbs and Croats spoke the same language with variations in pronunciation, the Slovenes a different though similar language; but the Croats and Slovenes wrote in the Roman alphabet and were mainly Roman Catholic while the Serbs wrote in the Cyrillic alphabet and were mainly Orthodox, plus a considerable Moslem element. The first test of the new government's cohesion would come at the Peace Conference. The Croat and Slovene leaders were suspicious that the dominant Serbian element in the delegation at Paris, headed by former Premier Pashich, would be more vigorous in defending Serbian interests than in fighting for theirs. And even if the delegation united to do its level best, would Serbia's prestige as an ally of the West compensate, when the final awards were made, for Croatia and Slovenia having been part of an enemy country and their soldiers having fought, even if often unwillingly, in an enemy army?

The Peace Conference would have to reach agreement on the Jugoslav boundaries in Macedonia, where the Serbian armies had played a decisive part in September in the spectacular defeat of the Germans and

Bulgarians, and in southern Hungary, where they had occupied part of the old province named the Banat of Temesvár, populated by a mixture of Hungarians, Serbs, Rumanians and other nationalities. But it was on the Adriatic that the Peace Conference would have to deal with the problems most vital to the Jugoslavs; and here they confronted not a defeated enemy but one of the major allies.

The rewards on the east coast of the Adriatic promised Italy by the secret Treaty of London of 1915 were almost entirely in conflict not only with Wilson's Fourteen Points but also with the Pact of Rome of April, 1918, in which an Italian parliamentary committee agreed with Croat and Slovene representatives that territorial questions should be settled "on the basis of the principle of nationalities." That, however, had been just after Caporetto, when Italy saw the necessity of reassuring Slav elements in the Austro-Hungarian Army that an Italian victory would not merely hand them over to a new master. With victory won, Italy felt different. The "Adriatic Question" became the most bitterly fought issue before the Peace Conference.

The Jugoslav delegation, often split on questions of strategy, was at the far end of an interminably roundabout line of communications, so that even when the government in Belgrade could agree on instructions these often reached Paris days after they had been sent, sometimes after contrary action had been taken. The obstacle constantly before the Jugoslavs was that one of the Big Four—one of the judges—was their antagonist. Under intense Italian pressure, Britain and France held to their promises in the Treaty of London, though they did suggest to Italy that she moderate her claims and urged her not to demand Fiume (not included in the treaty). Wilson was left alone to battle for his principle of self-determination. Ultimately, as Vesnich had foreseen in Washington, it took precedence in his mind over economic and strategic considerations (though not to the exclusion of these) and thus made him a proponent of Jugoslav unification. The story of this historic fight has often been told and will not be repeated here.

While it waged the long-distance battle for the frontiers, the Jugoslav Government was trying to organize itself at home to cope with the ruin left from five years of war and enemy occupation. The economic life of each of the separate areas now joined in unfamiliar union was at a standstill and nothing like a national economy could as yet even be adumbrated. Communications, by road, rail or wire, were nonexistent or uncertain. Starvation and epidemics were prevalent; food and medicines were in short supply and transportation to bring succor to districts where conditions were the most desperate was lacking. Soldiers were being demobilized and prisoners of war were straggling back, often to find only rubble where their homes had been.

The government's efforts to function with anything like efficiency were handicapped by the deplorable condition of the capital. Belgrade had been a rather primitive Balkan town even before the successive Austrian and German bombardments, the four years of occupation and the final plundering. There was no electricity, no telephone, no means of getting about except on foot for any but the highest officials (even the Prince Regent usually walked), no light in the streets at night to help one from tumbling into shell holes, scanty fuel brought in over snow-clogged roads on the backs of peasants or on creaking oxcarts, and water only intermittently. Fewer houses had roofs than were without them, shops had been ransacked or gutted, markets were almost empty. All this we would shortly discover.

I I

As far as Venice we traveled by a mock Orient Express, nothing like the *train bleu* which novelists of the twenties were to people with adventurers and adventuresses. Even on that celebrated train, the many dozens of journeys which I later made were never brightened by romance nor did I ever witness a crime of passion; the men leaning out the windows were always unshaved Rumanians in crumpled pajamas, the ladies on the *strapontins* in those swaying corridors were always elderly English governesses on the way to or from some Balkan capital. Our train in January, 1919, was a string of decrepit carriages, in one of which we were lucky enough to have secured *couchettes*. As companion in our compartment we had an amiable and distinguished-looking French colonel who had recently passed through Belgrade; he did his best to paint it for us in attractive colors, but failed.

Our plan was to secure a car at the American Army headquarters in Verona and drive to Belgrade. Whether this would really be feasible could not be determined in Paris, for regardless of other difficulties the roads might be impassably deep in snow. Any such idea was quashed in Verona. General Churchill had arranged with quartermaster headquarters in France that Verona would supply a staff car for the military attaché's office in Belgrade. Paris imagined that it had jurisdiction over all the American forces in Europe. The general in Verona thought differently. When I presented the order to him he looked at it sarcastically, wrote something at the bottom, sent for a quartermaster major, handed it to him and acknowledged my salute with a nod of dismissal. When we got outside, the major, grinning, showed me the endorsement: "Supply as requested, if convenient."

"That," he said, "means no."

Might an explanatory telegram from Paris help? I asked. This was something of an emergency, and maybe the general could be brought to change his mind. The major replied that if the general had intended to recognize any order from Paris he'd have put a different endorsement on this one.

"It's just not convenient," he said, eying me as a quartermaster officer likes to eye a junior in another branch when he has him where he wants him. "It's too bad, but it's just not convenient."

I remembered the rejoicing in the German press early in 1916 over the announcement that since every enemy between Berlin and Constantinople had now been swept aside, the road was clear for the "Balkan Express" to start running, bringing the Kaiser's "Berlin to Baghdad" dream a step nearer consummation. Nothing remained, of course, of that chimerical German route. But at the concierge's desk in the Hotel Danieli in Venice I found a yellowed timetable indicating that the Paris express continued on to Trieste, thence via Laibach (now to be known as Ljubljana) and Agram (now Zagreb) to Belgrade, and then on to Constantinople (not yet Istanbul). This also was a dream train. Travel by rail even as far as Trieste was impossible. The surge of fighting back and forth along the northern Adriatic coast (there were twelve distinct "Battles of the Isonzo") had wrecked the bridges and the series of bridges which successively had replaced them. We therefore asked the harbor master of Venice for passes to travel by ship to Trieste. He supplied them reluctantly, grieving that we were going to sojourn among "those pigs of Slavs."

At dawn we piled our luggage into a snow-sprinkled gondola alongside the broad steps of the Riva dei Schiavoni and were taken out to the *Prinz Hohenlohe,* a captured Austrian Lloyd vessel now serving as Italy's chief link with Trieste. It moved out slowly from its anchorage, past the Palladian façade of San Giorgio into the still waters beyond, in which were reflected the campaniles of Venice and behind them the pink-tipped Alps. It was a brief interlude. Soon the *bora,* swooping down from the north, tossed the ship like a cork across the tops of the whitecaps, and by the time we came within sight of Trieste was snatching up chunks of water bodily and flinging them high overhead. We waited numbly as the hawsers parted twice with loud reports before the ship could be made fast at the quay, and at last stumbled ashore wondering why anyone wanted any part of such a sea. Above the hotel entrance new white letters gleamed—"Hotel Savoia"—replacing what the letter paper in our room was to tell us had been "Excelsior-Palast." The grandness was faded, the appliances didn't work, the bells brought nobody, the waiters spoke no Italian and were afraid to speak German; but it was a delight to be there.

The streets of Trieste were half empty, for the Slav and German-speaking parts of the population were still unreconciled to seeing so many Italian soldiers about. There also were a few Americans in uniform, detailed from the battalion at Fiume to guard the American Food Administration supplies en route to Vienna. The head of the food mission told us that changes in hotel names were occurring so rapidly they couldn't be kept up with. Thus the former Hungarian hotel in Fiume, re-named "Hotel Wilson" in a burst of enthusiasm after the Armistice, had now been changed again by order of the Italian garrison commander to "Hotel Savoia." He reported that food conditions were serious in the Italian-occupied towns down the coast and worse in the hinterland; but in Trieste nothing was rationed.

In the morning there appeared a young Italian marine to whom I had given my meal ticket on the boat, nothing being further from my desire just then than eating. He brought an "Address to the Noble and Democratic American People," among whom we were described as the noblest and most democratic, written in a beautiful script that must have occupied him most of the night. He also had a double armful of long loaves of Italian bread, piled up to his chin, obtained at the commissary where he worked. We accepted the present with thanks, though not realizing how grateful we would be for it later.

That afternoon as the train for Ljubljana snaked slowly up the Karst mountainside an orange-red sun slid into the Adriatic, now a calm sheet of gold, on the edge of which was outlined, to the right and far below, a toy Miramar perched on its tiny peninsula. After pausing to pant at the top, the engine drew its string of nearly empty carriages across a boulder-strewn plain of scrub pines and occasional stone huts, huddled in gulleys. Italian troops from armored trains on sidings stood about in the snow, waving joylessly at us. About midnight the train pulled reluctantly into Longatico—that is, the near half of the station was Longatico, the other half, separated at the center of the platform by the frontier, had the Slovene name Lojč. Here we disembarked. Italy would not trust its engine and cars to the Jugoslavs, and the Jugoslavs would not be able to find any equipment to carry us forward till morning. The Italian station commander kindly offered to let us share his office, so we drew up around his stove, divided his cheese and one of our long breads, and waited. Just before dawn the Jugoslav train shuffled in backward at the far end of the platform. The Italians refused to carry luggage across the line to a Jugoslav train and the Austrians manning the Jugoslav train at first wouldn't come over to get it, but plentiful Austrian kronen (still circulating on both sides) finally bridged the gap. With much shouting and waving of lanterns we started sliding down the long grade onto the Ljubljana plain.

On the platform at Ljubljana we received a first intimation that Jugoslav unity was not yet complete. The major in charge wore an Austrian uniform but with a new red-white-blue "S.H.S." insignia sewed onto his cap—the initials of the three Jugoslav peoples, *Srbi, Hrvati, Slovenaci*. He reluctantly admitted to speaking a little French, so I told him my unfamiliar uniform was American, mentioned General Rashich as a reference and asked if he could help us get on to Zagreb and Belgrade. The name of the Minister of War made him look at me sourly; the idea of having a Serbian superior seemed to disgust him.

"Pfui!" he said.

"At least tell me," I pressed him, "is there a train tomorrow to Zagreb or isn't there? Oui ou non?"

As he turned on his heel, what sounded like "potato" but I took to be "peut-être" came over his shoulder.

At the Hotel Slon ("Elephant" in Slovene, the gilded figure over the door informed us) we spent the night on the floor under our coats; the German-speaking chambermaid explained the condition of the bed-clothes by the fact that there had been a soap famine for months. Coming down to the café early in the morning, we found what seemed to be the same dejected figures sitting over the ersatz coffee that had sat there the evening before.

Fortunately there was a Serbian military mission in the city. The general said a train was about to leave for Zagreb and offered us the compartment reserved for the military. Pacing down the station platform, we passed car after car in which every window was boarded up; then we came to a compartment where the glass had survived—and that was ours. Perhaps, I thought vaguely, the guards at the two ends of the car were there to convoy us safely. In Zagreb, where we changed trains, they disappeared; their duty had been to protect the window and see that it got back to Ljubljana intact.

In the Zagreb station I courageously decided to put the little French-Serbian dictionary to use. Lowering the invaluable window, I stuck out my head and called for a porter.

"Pismonosha! Pismonosha!" I shouted.

People gazed at me curiously. It was not so much, I discovered later, that no such thing as a porter existed; it was because the dictionary had omitted to state that *pismonosha* was not an ordinary porter but a *porteur des lettres*. No one had known how to respond to the call for a postman.

After another night on a hotel floor we were up at five-thirty to start what was to be the last lap of our journey. Arrival in Belgrade was promised for that evening, but soon snow began to fall heavily and our progress became slower and slower. Finally the engine stopped exhausted in a featureless white expanse, and after a time went off in search of more fuel. Meanwhile I had run forward and gotten the engineer to spurt steam into two cups, where it quickly became hot water; we hoped the flavor it added to the Oxo we had for supper was hygienic. The next day's journey proved more successful. The track led downward across a gently sloping plain, and at nightfall by simple force of gravity we reached the end of the line, the former Austrian frontier town of Semlin (now Zemun). Belgrade lay on the opposite side of the River Sava. No lights showed, but we were assured it really was there. The bridge had been destroyed in 1914 and the afternoon ferry had long since gone, so we settled down for another night in a stationmaster's office.

III

The ferry nudged its way through floating ice and came clumsily alongside the strip of frozen mud that served as a dock. Above, commanding the strategic meeting place of the Danube and Sava, stood the fortress from which Belgrade took its name, the "White City." Built first by the Celts in the third century B.C., it had been destroyed and rebuilt by Romans, Huns, Goths, Franks, Bulgars, Greeks, Turks and Austrians. The tower was pockmarked but still stood. The slopes up to it were covered with debris and rusted wire. Patches of snow outlined the crumbled walls of the former Turkish quarter along the river front. In the gray morning light the city appeared deserted.

My prewar Baedeker listed the Hotel Moscow as the best in Belgrade—"very fair," it said, "rooms with bath," high recommendations for any Balkan establishment. Baedeker put the Grand Hotel second, with a glass-enclosed palm court, and in last place the Hotel Balkan, a primi-

tive half-Turkish ˙ɪn which had been the rendezvous for the conspirators
of the Sarajevo assassination. I had written ahead to Mr. Dodge, just
arrived with the Serbian Government from Corfu, mentioning the hope
that it might be possible to find us a room at the Moscow.

As we drew near we saw that several people (but no vehicles) were
waiting on the landing place. Among them was Mr. Dodge's messenger
with a note saying that after immense effort beds had been found for us
at the Sanatorium Vracha. The Moscow had not operated since 1914;
the roof had been blown off and if bathrooms remained they were without water since most of Belgrade was waterless most of the time. Door-
less and windowless, the Moscow stared at us from vacant eyes all the
time we were in Belgrade. As for the Grand, the ground floor was all
that was left of it; everything above had caved in. Under the mounds of
debris, however, functioned what was then the best of the Belgrade
restaurants, roofed by tarpaulins and sacking instead of the former glass
dome. Mr. Dodge didn't go into these explanatory details, which we
learnt later, just told us to be happy that we could put up in a hospital
and invited us to lunch. So we piled our trunks onto the backs of two
nosachi, public porters who could carry the most immense loads, and
followed our guide for a couple of miles through the snow to the sanatorium.

Mr. Dodge was glad to see us arrive, I found, for he and Mrs. Dodge
were alone in the Legation, with no secretary even, so that he himself
had to peck away at the typewriter and do the coding; any sort of help,
particularly with the coding, was most welcome. But he said at once that
he was disappointed I had so little rank; the British attaché was a general and the place was swarming with high French officers; it was too
bad, I could hardly hold my own with them, let alone help him hold his
own with the British Minister, Sir Charles des Graz, and the French
Minister, the Vicomte de Fontenay. Later, as we became friends with
these and the others, he softened, but was not really happy until in the
spring Major Francis Colby arrived as military attaché, and I became
assistant.

First of all we had to find a house, even though the sanatorium was,
for Belgrade, luxurious. People always asked whether it was true that
one could have a boiled egg there for breakfast. At this point Mme.
Grouich's friendship proved most valuable. She was not in Belgrade,
but she had notified relatives of our coming and asked them if possible
to get her house into condition to rent to us. It was on what at that time
was the edge of town and was much too large, but it had a roof and

plumbing, an exceptional combination, and soon we gratefully moved in. The living room, good-sized, with tall windows, looked out onto Shumadijska Ulitsa, the road from the south. Peasants came trudging by in the mornings regardless of snow or rain, usually with back-breaking loads of wood or sacks of turnips, rarely a pair of chickens slung around the neck (prizes to be spotted, run after and purchased).

From a second-floor terrace you had a view down the valley to the hills of Topchider, and beyond you saw in the distance just the tip of Avala, the mountain of old Serbian song and fable. In the foreground were a small back yard (in the spring we planted flowers and vegetables there) and a little wine garden, where on warm evenings a *guslar* would play his plaintive one-string instrument and recite endless mournful ballads in a meandering minor key. He sang of the defeat of Lazar, the last of the independent Serbian princes, on Kosovo, the Field of the Blackbirds, June 28, 1389, and of the death of the victor, Sultan Murad; of how the Hapsburg heir died in Sarajevo on Kosovo Day in 1914; of Prince Marko on his piebald steed; of the first Karageorge, the liberator; of the retreat in winter to the Adriatic and the return, just yesterday, to Belgrade. He was a wrinkled old man who never left off his black sheepskin hat and long sheepskin coat no matter how hot the weather. On Sunday afternoons, dancers of the *kolo* took over the café courtyard, shuffling in a circle around a *tsigane* fiddler. Sometimes they sang "Tamo daleko"—"There far away"—and other songs of the Serbian soldiers in exile, but they were never obstreperous, and it was cheerful having them there. Fifty years later, I now and then hear echoes at night of the *guslar's* lament for the unforgotten lost battle of over five centuries ago.

The house had been used by the Austrians as a hospital for wounded officers, and the straw on which they had been bedded down was still six or eight inches deep in all the rooms. In the living room, in unsuitable juxtaposition, stood a grand piano and an operating table, and in the hall were several cases which had held detonating fuses. That was the extent of the "furniture." The Austrians probably abandoned the battered operating table gladly, but why the piano remained was a mystery, for in the last weeks they were said to have evacuated over six hundred pianos along with other loot across the Danube. Fortunately, various pieces of Grouich furniture had been hidden away during the occupation in attics and outhouses around the city, and some of it, including twelve lovely Italian dining-room chairs, was loaned to us. General Rashich also authorized us to go down to the Danube and pick out additional furniture from the barges which the Austrians had stuffed with plunder but then lacked time to ferry across the river. What we took was listed, of course, so that we could surrender it to the owners if ever they appeared, but there were no claimants up to the end of our stay.

Now and then stolen articles did turn up. Once when I was walking with a Serbian officer in Panchevo, a town on what had been the Austrian side of the Danube, he stopped short and peered through the lace curtains of a parlor window with an exclamation of delight. Without ado, he knocked, bowed to the lady who opened the door, thanked her for taking such good care of his clock, took it off the table in the window, put it under his arm and walked with it back to the Belgrade ferry.

"It was my grandmother's," he said, "a present to her from my grandfather at their wedding. He got it in Paris, as you see from the name on the face. Now it becomes my sole family inheritance."

Our Legation was installed in the building of the former Turkish Legation. The Turks had gone to war with the Allies at the end of 1914, and their personnel of course fled when the Serbs recaptured Belgrade four years later. The United States had never declared war on the Turks, but we were assigned their building to use until Jugoslavia made peace with them—which promised to be some time off. Mr. Dodge gave me temporarily a ground-floor office containing a large flat-topped tile stove, which would have been delightful if enough wood or coal had been available; a desk with drawers that had no bottoms; and four massive safes which would have been most useful if we could have opened them, but as they belonged to our non-enemies, the Turks, Mr. Dodge did not allow me to have the locks picked or even to ask the Serbs to do it for me. Until I found a small building for my office nearer our house I walked the couple of miles back and forth three times a day, there being no means of transportation in the city.

Meanwhile we were trying to collect a household, and here again we were indebted to Mme. Grouich, for one day a former cook of hers appeared from a village in the Shumadija, twenty-two miles to the south, where she had received word of our need from Mme. Grouich's nephew. She had walked the whole way to Belgrade in one day, and when we engaged her walked home again the next day, and in another day was back, carrying all her belongings and those of her little daughter, who trudged alongside. That was a great occasion, doubly so because it saw the arrival of a kitchen stove which had been dug up in the ruins of one of the Grouich family houses. Till then, when the Grand at the other end of town seemed too far, or when my wife was ill, we had cooked our meals in the tile stove in the corner of the bedroom. Anyone who has tried cooking a chicken inside an Austrian *Kachelofen,* through a small opening in the front, with a door that snaps back on a spring and is too hot to hold open, over green wood, will understand that Valeria was welcome. Valeria, who spoke German, was supplemented by Vinko, who came from the littoral and spoke Italian; his only possessions were an Austrian tunic and trousers and hobnailed boots.

Later we changed Vinko for Valentino, who had been in the employ of Prince Livio Borghese, the Italian Minister. It was a mistake. The story was that when one day Valentino took the Minister's dog out for a walk he had given him a bath in the river, whereupon the dog took cold and died and Valentino lost his job. Prince Borghese was disliked in Belgrade. He had arrived with letters of credence to King Peter as King of Serbia not as King of the Serbs, Croats and Slovenes, a deliberate insult underscoring the fact that Italy was fighting at Paris against the recognition of the new state. The government did not accept these credentials, and Borghese moved in March to Budapest, where he played the Rumanians and Hungarians against each other and both against the Jugoslavs. I came to suspect that in preparation for his departure he had "planted" Valentino on us. He could learn nothing of significance in our house, but it was uncomfortable to have him about and I decided to get rid of him. It happened that on the same day I gave him notice the police appeared, arrested him for having failed to register as an alien but in the end released him in custody of the Italian consul. He held Valeria responsible for his troubles and began haunting the house, shouting insults at her over the garden wall and making faces at her through the kitchen window. After several warnings, I fired a pistol over his head; he ran like a rabbit and we saw him no more. It was my sole use of firearms in my wartime experience.

Before the house was ready for housekeeping we usually went for dinner at the Grand, on foot of course. At every corner of the black streets, full of bomb craters and often icy besides, a soldier would challenge us, since only authorized persons were allowed out after nightfall. The subterranean restaurant at the Grand was gloomy, furnished with derelict red-plush sofas and chairs and attended mainly by tattered little boys. The proprietor, who had once been head bouncer at Terrace Gardens, a tough New York joint somewhere north of Central Park, joined us frequently at our table to show off his English. The menu listed as many as fifteen different kinds of meat, but usually there was so little of each that all but the earliest arrivals were told *nema nishta* as they named their first half-dozen choices. There was a good "black" wine from Dalmatia and a soft white one from the Frushka Gora across the Danube.

When we at last began eating our meals at home our equipment was limited. Everything transportable in Belgrade had been looted, so that although we had the dozen fine dining-room chairs we for some time were able to buy only two knives, forks and spoons to go with them. One day when I had been hunting fruitlessly from one small shop to another a shopkeeper surprised me by pointing disbelievingly to the "U.S." on my collar. If I was truly American, he indicated, why did I speak English and not Spanish? He was a Spanish Jew, descended from the Jews expelled from Spain by Torquemada, the Great Inquisitor, many of whom had fled first to the Low Countries and then drifted down the Danube to Vienna and beyond to the Balkans and the Levant. He thought all Americans were Spanish, but in the end was so pleased to have an American acquaintance, even an English-speaking one, that he produced eight knives, forks and spoons from a private cache, leaving us only two short to match our chairs.

4

Communist Takeover in Hungary

Two years earlier when I had said goodbye to General Rashich in New York he had kissed me, Slav fashion, on both cheeks. Now when I went to see him in his office at the War Ministry he did so again. Not long afterward he retired for age, but whenever we met in Belgrade, which was often, he was sure to speak of some incident of his trip to America. Niagara Falls! The White House! Mount Vernon! The Mississippi! The Woolworth Building! Or perhaps the Broadway show I took them all to, with the girl who sang,

> Won't you wait, wait, wait,
> By the old red gate,
> Won't you wait till the cows come home!

I had had trouble translating it into French for him, but he still remembered it, more vividly perhaps than his military exploits, for those were many and New York had been unique.

The principal military personage in Belgrade now was Voivode Mishich, the chief of staff. Mr. Dodge took me almost at once to call on him and on Colonel Kalafatovich, chief of the Bureau of Operations, also a soldier of high professional reputation.

Mishich is one of the forgotten great commanders of the war. His title "Voivode," Slav for "Leader," corresponding to Field Marshal in Western armies today, was bestowed in medieval times on a general who had won a battle. Mishich had won more than a battle; he had helped win two campaigns, the latter a direct contribution to the final Allied victory.

In 1914, after the Serbian defeat at the Kolubara River, Mishich had

59

led the First Army when it turned on the invading Austro-Hungarian armies and threw them back across the Danube. The world was astounded by the news in the terse Serbian communiqué: "On the territory of the Kingdom of Serbia remains not one free enemy soldier."

Four years later, it was Mishich who recommended to General Franchet d'Espèrey, commanding the Allied forces in Macedonia, that the great assault being prepared against the German and Bulgarian armies be directed at precisely the sector of the front where the terrain was most formidable—so formidable, he argued, that the enemy must rule it out of danger. There on September 15, 1918, six Serbian and two French divisions under Mishich attacked "a gigantic wall of rock that seemed impenetrable," opening a general French-British-Serbian-Greek-Italian offensive along a mountain chain with crests as much as eight thousand feet high. The attack was immediately successful, and the victory grew and grew; within two weeks Bulgaria had surrendered and Germany was cut off from contact with Turkey. As Ludendorff admitted in his memoirs, this "sealed the fate" of Germany. The Serbs pursued Mackensen's troops without pause up the Morava Valley and on November 1 captured Belgrade.

But though military historians like Cyril Falls and Liddell Hart attach the word "genius" to Mishich's name, few persons in the West ever heard it. Partly this was because the fighting in Macedonia was always assumed to be only a side issue, and this opinion persisted even after the victory there had proved to be of decisive importance. Partly it was because all eyes had been on Ludendorff's desperate offensive on the Western front, which had just failed, and all hopes were pinned on the British, French and American victories on the Marne and the Somme, at St. Mihiel and in the Argonne. Partly it was because Mishich was serving under a French general who was never a popular hero. D'Espèrey was brusque and imperious, lived very much to himself, disliked and avoided journalists, had fewer friends than enemies among his colleagues. His theatre of operations was also unpopular. Clemenceau wanted to limit operations in the Balkans so that troops engaged there could be transferred to the West, and Foch grudged any undertaking which diverted attention from the Western front. But Mishich was the architect of the strategy that gave Serbia back to the Serbians, and in the new cycle of Serbian ballads that we heard sung in village wine gardens he and Prince Regent Alexander were the new heroes.

Mishich was in his early sixties, a man of middle size, chunky, with a big nose à la J. P. Morgan set in a ruddy, weatherbeaten face. His manner was charming, so gentle that one had difficulty thinking of him as a tough field commander. English and French officers who had served with him told me he was not only that, as well as a superior strategist, but that his moral prestige had been a powerful factor in holding the Serbian forces together through the conspiracies and counterconspiracies involving the Black Hand in the period when the army was being reformed on the Saloniki front. He was the son of a peasant, and his brother still ploughed the fields; but he had wanted an education, and he got, as he put it, "justement assez," meaning to say, "just enough."

The General Staff Headquarters, like many buildings in Belgrade, was of putty-colored stucco, squat and square, and since it stood on a bank sloping away from the street was dark, dank and fusty. You reached the Voivode's room by a windowless corridor, paved unevenly with bricks, from which black wooden doors opened into cubicles where members of the General Staff had their offices and where their orderlies made their tea and slept at night. Mishich kept the temperature of his tiny office at eighty degrees, regardless of the weather, and as he was never without a cigarette the atmosphere was that of a smoke oven. The doctor had ordered him not to smoke, which meant that he invariably began by offering you a cigarette, and then, remarking that he used them *très, très rarement,* took your visit as an excuse to light another himself. To make him happy I had to begin smoking too. After a few minutes of conversation in that tropical haze your eyes began to water and the lines he was pointing out on his staff maps began to wobble. The unvarnished wooden table at which he sat almost filled the room; it was piled high with papers written in longhand, for the Serbian Army did excellently without typewriters, requisition blanks in quadruplicate and pages of "endorsements through channels." On this first visit he told me that whenever I had questions I must come direct to him or to Colonel Kalafatovich, a brisk man with a crew haircut who inhabited an adjoining cubicle and of course had exact knowledge about the stationing of Jugoslav troops and also the latest intelligence procurable about other forces in the area.

The strength and disposition of all military forces, ex-enemy as well as Allied, were matters of intense interest in Washington and to our delegation in Paris. The Jugoslav Army now being organized fell into both Allied and enemy categories. Croats and Slovenes from the former Austro-Hungarian forces were being amalgamated with veteran Serbian troops. When the Empire had fallen apart, Croat and Slovene officers had set up military headquarters of their own in Zagreb and Ljubljana. At first they paid little heed to what was said or done either in Paris or in the capital of their newly united country. Gradually, however, they recognized the authority of the military missions which arrived from Belgrade, and in January their loyalty to the central regime was well enough established for a number of them to be brought into the headquarters of the old Serbian General Staff. Soldiers and noncoms from the Austro-Hungarian Army were encouraged to volunteer and officers of lower grades were accepted rather freely, but in the higher ranks selection was discriminating. The best-known officer of Slav blood who had served the Hapsburgs was General Boreović von Bojna, who had forced the Russians to lift the siege of Przemyśl in 1915 and faced Cadorna successfully in the frightful battles of the Isonzo. He applied for a commission and was refused.

The attitude toward high officers of the former Austro-Hungarian Navy, many of them Dalmatians, was different, for Serbia had been an inland state and urgently needed their services. Among those accepted was Admiral Metod Koch, who on October 30, 1918, had seized the Austro-Hungarian warships in Pola (now Pula) in the name of the local Jugoslav National Committee. He sent a wireless message to President Wilson asking his protection; and the next day the Emperor Karl transferred the whole Adriatic fleet to the Jugoslav National Council. But the Allies refused to recognize the transaction, took over the vessels in their joint name and sent an Italian naval force to carry out the order.

"When I saw an Italian fleet steaming into Pola on November 5," Admiral Koch told me, "I got ready to welcome them as friends. I found pretty quickly how wrong I was. During the war, the Italian Navy had never been able to take Pola by force. Now they took it by a trick. They said they represented all the Allies, and in fact a few British and French officers did arrive too. But they left. The Italians never left."

Afterward I found an entry about Admiral Koch and his sailors in David Hunter Miller's privately printed diary at the Peace Conference, where he was an American legal adviser. Count Macchi di Cellere, the Italian Ambassador in Washington, who had transferred his activities to Paris, assured Miller that the crews were nothing but "Austrian Bolsheviks." The Admiral, who was half English, was far from that, and so were the crews, who simply were in revolt against the old Empire. Koch had particular affection for America, acquired in the nineties when the sailing ship on which he was a midshipman put into New York in the course of a training cruise. He remembered nostalgically an evening at Coney Island and was always willing to sing, with appropriate gestures of despair, a song learnt there which ended, "But Daddy wouldn't buy me a bow-wow-wow."[1]

Both Washington and Paris were interested to know how much the transfusions of Austrian and Hungarian manpower would dilute and perhaps weaken the Serbian Army, which was trained to be extraordinarily tough. Colonel Nenadovich, for example, told me that when his men made a forced march they had to cover ten kilometers of it before they got breakfast. The Croats were esteemed as fighters, but discipline had been poor in the Austro-Hungarian forces, especially where Slav draftees were officered by Austrians and Magyars. Voivode Mishich said that he had never doubted the bravery of the former Austro-Hungarian soldiers; his worry was about how long it would take to assimilate them into a single military machine. By early February he was able to say that the amalgamation could be considered complete. Did that mean, I asked, that the new army was now ready to act as a unified instrument of the central government in case of an open breach with Italy, for instance, or as part of general Allied operations against a Bolshevik takeover in Central Europe? He said that by spring it would be in shape for any necessary operations and already could handle local emergencies.

This estimate had to be accepted with caution because of the considerable separatist sentiment existing in Croatia. The petty Croatian aristocracy cherished their old ties with court circles in Budapest and Vienna and sniffed at the Karageorgevich dynasty as "descended from a swineherd." Zagreb businessmen did not think much of opportunities for trade in backward Serbia compared to those they were in danger of losing in Austria and Hungary. The great Croatian landlords, ecclesiastic foundations and rich peasants feared the attractions of the Serbian freehold peasant system; and their hostility to union was confirmed when one of Prince Regent Alexander's first acts was to proclaim, on Christmas Eve, 1918, a general land reform, the abolition of serfdom and the division of land among the poorer peasants. Paradoxically, opposition existed also at the other end of the social spectrum. An erratic demagogue named Stjepan Radić, head of the Croat Peasant party, strongly advocated Croatian autonomy in a federated republic; and the Croatian peasants

1. Admiral Koch later wrote his memoirs, and asked my help in getting them published in America. If I succeeded (I didn't), he wanted to contribute any royalties to some fund providing for widows or orphans of American soldiers, "in order to give one tiny indication that Europe doesn't always want American money, but, in the measure that it can, pays back its debt to American idealism."

received joyfully his promise that in his republic no peasant would pay taxes.

I had not been long in Belgrade before I realized that delay in recognizing the new state by all the Allies was having unfortunate results. Although Wilson had given recognition in February, neither Britain nor France had followed suit; and of course Italy was urging them not to do so. This diminished the prestige and authority of the central government; increased its difficulty in holding together the various new elements in the state and resisting their more extreme territorial claims; and above all (in a province where I had more excuse to offer an opinion) prevented demobilization and thus delayed economic reconstruction. Several times in February and March I urged that Washington press the other Allies to grant recognition quickly. Britain finally acted on June 2 and France on June 6. Italy, by the fact of signing the Treaty of Versailles on June 28, was forced to give indirect recognition, much to her disgust, to her co-signer, the Kingdom of Serbs, Croats and Slovenes.

Throughout the spring, Italian agents were exploiting the restlessness in Croatia for all it was worth. Italy also used her stranglehold on Trieste and Fiume (today Rijeka) to interrupt American and other food shipments in the hope of creating disorders that might excuse an Italian move into the country. This blockade extended to Austria and caused distress there. Professor Archibald Cary Coolidge, the head of a special mission sent to Vienna by the American delegation in Paris, reported on March 20 that Italy was demanding works of art from the galleries in Vienna in return for letting food come through. In a letter to Allen W. Dulles, his liaison officer in Paris (who let me see his files), Coolidge suggested that in imitating Napoleon as an art collector the Italian Government might have in mind "to provoke incidents and create a situation which would give them a pretext for occupying the city."

Along the Adriatic coast Italian Army and Navy commanders were very aggressive. A member of the Coolidge mission, Colonel Sherman Miles (who also lent me his files) reported from Spalato (now Split) on March 21 what an "awful time" our Admiral Niblack and the British and French admirals were having "keeping the Italians from stirring up trouble here and then landing to suppress it, much as they did in Fiume."

After the Bolsheviks seized power in Hungary in March it looked as though Communism might spread through the region. It seems strange to hint that Italy went so far as to encourage this movement in Croatia as a means of disrupting Jugoslav unity, but there were plenty of indications of this at the time, some of them reported by as responsible an observer as Harold Temperley, then a major in the British Army, when he came from Zagreb on a visit to Belgrade. If so, the results must have disappointed Rome. Radić advertised a great demonstration by discontented Croatian elements to be held on May Day, but it fizzled out. In Belgrade another May Day demonstration, organized with undercover Communist support, was also a failure; shops were boarded up, mounted patrols moved through the streets and we were all urged to stay home, but nobody paid any attention to the warnings and there were no incidents.

By degrees it became evident that for the time being neither separatism nor Communism threatened the solidarity of the state seriously. Nor did anti-Serb sentiment in Croatia prevent the gradual unification of the national army under the Serbian General Staff. The prestige of the Serbian military was very high, and whatever discontent there was with the new setup seemed to come from ex-enemy officers who had not been accepted.

II

Communications between Belgrade and distant parts of the country were very haphazard that winter, and sometimes we heard of even critical events long after they had occurred. The government itself was often in the dark. When it did receive reports of some particularly high-handed Italian action in Dalmatia it at once informed the Legation and made another urgent plea that President Wilson take steps in Paris to prevent Italian *faits accomplis* which would prejudice the final decisions of the Peace Conference. Mr. Dodge could only pass the information along to Washington, where it supplemented the masses of similar British and French reports accumulating there and in Paris. The British gave us what information they received, but it was spotty. I remember Sir Charles des Graz showing me photographs of posters stuck up in Fiume, one of Wilson in a German helmet, another of Christopher Columbus weeping, with an Italian legend, the equivalent of "Oh, if only I hadn't discovered America!"

Mr. Dodge's contacts with Serbians of all parties and with Jugoslav leaders from Austria-Hungary dated from Corfu days and were excellent; he could report fully on their opinions, agreements and disagreements. It was less satisfactory to have to rely on them for knowledge of developments outside the capital. He was quite right, certainly, not to attempt to cover too much territory with what he referred to as "the limited legation staff"—meaning me. I argued, however, that the smallness of "the staff" indicated that it should be used intensively in areas where Washington and Paris had no satisfactory means of securing information. It seemed, for instance, that a useful intelligence job might be done in the Banat of Temesvár, in southern Hungary, within easy reach from Belgrade, where the thoroughly scrambled population and competing Serbian and Rumanian claims were sure to make trouble. There was no question, obviously, of our trying to cover more distant conflicts on Jugoslavia's borders. One of them, the dispute with Italy over the Adriatic coast, was being threshed out in the very highest quarters in Paris. Another, the situation in the Austrian province of Carinthia, where Austrian and Slovene irregulars were fighting for possession of the ethnically mixed territory north of the ceasefire line, was under observation by two American officers attached to the Coolidge mission in Vienna, Colonel Sherman Miles and Lieutenant Le Roy King.

Miles, who had been an observer in the Balkan Wars with both the Serbian and Bulgarian armies, had been sent with King to Carinthia to report on whether the province wanted to keep its old political and economic ties with Vienna or throw in its lot with Jugoslavia. It was not an easy assignment. The provincial capital, Klagenfurt, a town of lovely sixteenth-century architecture, was typically Austrian; the surrounding countryside was fairly solidly Slovene. After a painstaking survey, Miles and King became convinced, to their surprise, that the majority of the population, Austrian and Slovene together, wanted to stay in Austria, and they so reported.

Meanwhile, to end the local fighting, they persuaded both sides to accept a temporary demarcation line. Professor Coolidge wrote Miles that this accomplishment, "however right in itself," raised "possible complications," for the United States had no authority to act on its own; and indeed, when the American Commission was informed it did rebuke both Coolidge and Miles, though it added, not untypically, that it "neither ratifies nor disavows" the result. Approved or not, the temporary line was being observed when King (a cousin of mine) came to visit us in Belgrade for a few days in February; and in fact it saved lives for another two months thereafter.

At about this time Miles was summoned to Paris, and at Colonel House's direction submitted a strong memorandum to President Wilson recommending a plebiscite in the whole Klagenfurt area. His memorandum (so far as I know never published) was very influential. Eventually the Treaty of St. Germain with Austria provided that a plebiscite be held in two stages, the vote in the southern zone, where the Slovene element was strongest, to be held first. When the vote there (October 10, 1920) recorded a majority for Austria, that settled the destinies of the whole area—by the method recommended by Miles and with the result which he and King had predicted.

Years later I learnt from Miles (by then a major general) that at one point he had suggested to Professor Coolidge that I be called to Vienna to fill in details of the picture in Carinthia as seen from Belgrade. I wonder what the result would have been if my first meeting with Professor Coolidge had been at that time. Very likely he would have decided three years later that I was too young and brash to want me as his assistant on *Foreign Affairs*.

III

As the winter wore on, a situation closer at hand caused anxiety in Belgrade. The republican regime which Count Károlyi had set up in Budapest after the collapse of the Empire was being pushed to the wall by the Communists. One reason for their growing strength was that the city was hungry and full of demobilized soldiers and returning prisoners of war. Another was that the Allies paid no heed to Károlyi's appeals to halt the advance of Rumanian troops from the east. Károlyi, an aristocratic radical, strong in theories, confused in action, had promised the Hungarian people that they would get more considerate treatment from the Allies under his leadership than under one of the old reactionary oligarchy. But as the Rumanians edged deeper and deeper into Transylvania it became plain either that the Allies were in disagreement as to whether or not to stop them or were too weak to do so. In an effort to outbid his rivals and avoid being sucked down into the Communist vortex, Károlyi resorted to more and more radical measures, but this only put him increasingly at the mercy of the Communists without winning over the masses, who saw that he was helpless to prevent the country's further dismemberment.

The threat of a Bolshevik takeover in Hungary alarmed neighboring countries, where empty stomachs made populations ready to try any change, however desperate. Most awkwardly, the very pressures which enabled the Bolsheviks to bring Károlyi down came chiefly from Rumania, and the Rumanian Prime Minister, Ion Brătianu, was intent not on diminishing but on increasing them. He felt that his chance to get the immense territories which had been promised Rumania in the secret Treaty of Bucharest in 1916 was to seize them now by force in Hungary's time of weakness and in the absence of any clear policy in Paris. Britain and

France, who had offered to reward Rumania so generously in order to get her into the war, now were proving reluctant to carry out their side of the bargain, taking as excuse the fact that she had violated her undertaking not to make a separate peace. To Brătianu it was immaterial whether Károlyi survived or was ousted by the Communists; in either case he intended to take Budapest, and the road there through Transylvania did not seem too difficult.

In the Banat of Temesvár, one of the richest of the territories promised to Rumania by the treaty, the problem was more difficult, for here Rumania faced French and Serbian occupying troops. To avoid a possible clash, General de Lobit, commanding the Armée Française d'Hongrie, demanded that the Serbs withdraw, leaving French troops in occupation alone. Voivode Mishich sent for me and warned that it would be most difficult for him to order his troops to retire from territory which was largely Serbian and which they had just taken over from the enemy, merely in order (as he put it) to reward a country which that enemy had beaten and made its vassal. For he was convinced that if he drew his troops out, the French would not—perhaps could not—prevent the Rumanians from moving in. He considered that the big stake which French oil and financial interests had in Rumania hardly made France an unbiased arbitrator.

I longed to have a first hand look at what was going on in the Banat, but Mr. Dodge felt that an American's visit might be taken as interference. Indeed, I was tied down pretty tightly in Belgrade until after Major Francis Colby arrived as military attaché in the spring and I became assistant, at about which time, also, Mr. Dodge mercifully acquired a clerk and secretary.

The immediate focus of danger shifted to Transylvania, however, when the Rumanians staged another advance there. The Peace Conference decided to create a neutral zone by requiring the Hungarians to retire two hundred kilometers and permitting the Rumanians to advance one hundred. The Hungarians interpreted this as a preliminary to handing Transylvania over to Rumania, perhaps to letting her occupy Budapest. A paroxysm of nationalist fury swept the country, the Károlyi republic collapsed and on March 22, 1919, the "proletariat" took over in the person of Béla Kun, a protégé of Lenin's. Béla Kun set up a Soviet-style government and made a treaty with Moscow.

Admiral Ernest Troubridge, the British commander of the little Danube flotilla, who had a representative in Budapest, Commander Wilkins-Freeman, heard from him on March 29 that Béla Kun had begun organizing Red Guards. This was ominous; Admiral Troubridge thought that we should all get ready for "a summer campaign." The report had been brought by a Colonel Baker, ostensibly an economist with the British mission in Hungary but evidently equipped to deal with other matters. The evening of his arrival he gave us our first authentic picture of Béla Kun, whose name had hardly been heard outside Budapest a week before and who now was in supreme power. Colonel Baker's portrait, as I noted it down, was not reassuring:

"Of the clan his name denotes. Once a shopkeeper in Belgrade. Later an 'aspirant' in the Austro-Hungarian Army. Deserted. Became one of Lenin's private secretaries in Russia. Sent back to Budapest as chief Communist propagandist. A thick-set, bestial-looking man. Thick neck with rolls of fat in the back. Cropped hair and not much of it. Rather flat large nose, black eyes, round shoulders. An aggressive manner."[2]

For a moment after this figure seized control the Supreme Council played with the idea of sending General Mangin, a French officer of renown, to subdue him and occupy Budapest with the help of the Rumanians. President Wilson did not at all favor this project. Supposing a Rumanian success, wouldn't a new war for Hungarian independence become inevitable and wouldn't Moscow find a way to help? Second thoughts suggested an attempt at conciliation, and an opportunity for this came with the arrival of a memorandum from Béla Kun recognizing the terms of the Armistice and stating that the Russian alliance did not imply a break with the West. On April 1, therefore, a small mission headed by General Smuts and including Harold Nicolson left Paris to try to persuade Béla Kun to withdraw from the proposed neutral zone facing the Rumanians. Coolidge told me later that Clemenceau had wanted to send a soldier and Wilson had wanted to send a statesman, so Lloyd George had offered Smuts, a combination of both.

News of the Smuts mission caused great excitement in Belgrade—when, that is, it became known there (which turned out to be after it was all over). On April 4, a comedy of misunderstanding began with General de Lobit passing on to me a rumor that Smuts was being sent to Budapest, indeed might have gotten as far as Vienna (the real fact was that he was already in Budapest). French headquarters still had received no con-

2. The biographical facts are open to doubt. For example, Kun's widow has written that he did not desert but was captured, and the statement that he lived at one time in Belgrade is not found in other accounts of his life. But the physical description is corroborated by others who met him, for instance, by Colonel Stephen Bonsal, an American correspondent, who saw him in Budapest in early April; he adds that "undoubtedly his outstanding physical feature was his great pointed ears."

firmation of the rumor the next day (by then, Smuts had been in Budapest and had left). At this point the prevailing opinion was that if Smuts
did in fact visit Budapest he might turn up in Belgrade afterward; for
General Franchet d'Espèrey sent word unexpectedly that he was arriving.
Surely it must be to meet Smuts. My own idea was that Smuts would visit
Prague rather than Belgrade, for the Czech attitude toward Hungary had
become almost as threatening as the Rumanian. "The Bolsheviki," I
wrote in my notes, "talk as much about the Czech 'bourgeoisie' as about
the Rumanian 'boyars.' " On his way back to Paris, Smuts did in fact stop
over in Prague to see Masaryk, but not by order of the Supreme Council.
On the contrary, they had been dispatching telegrams to him all along
the line instructing him to visit French and Rumanian military headquarters in Hungary; none reached him on his swift passage, which outdistanced anything Paris imagined possible.

Smuts received Béla Kun in his train in the Budapest station and told
him that the Hungarian troops must be drawn back. Béla Kun agreed,
provided the Rumanians withdrew also. This was not in Smuts's instructions. Harold Nicolson has described the scene in his book *Peacemaking,
1919*. Without argument, Smuts ushered Béla Kun politely onto the station platform and, as Béla Kun watched open-mouthed, the train
steamed slowly off into the night.

Four days later, on April 7 (incidentally my twenty-sixth birthday),
General Franchet d'Espèrey arrived in Belgrade in a state of high emotion. He came from Bucharest, where it had been his intention to organize
a French-Rumanian-Serbian expedition to overthrow Béla Kun, but to
his indignation Paris had vetoed it. He also was furious about the Smuts
mission. What was a South African general doing in Hungary where the
French Army had major responsibilities? Why had Smuts not come to
Belgrade to see him first? When *was* he coming? (By then, of course,
Smuts was already back in Paris.)

Admiral Troubridge, General E. A. Plunkett, the British military attaché, Major Colby (who had recently reached Belgrade) and I went
down to the dock with all the French to meet d'Espèrey. He came down
the little gangplank with short quick steps, leaning forward as though
straining at a leash, followed more sedately by General Bridges, his British number two. He was a stocky man with a thick neck, high coloring
and black eyes that kept darting about suspiciously. Since his voice could
not carry to Paris he made the best of the situation by expressing his
feelings to General de Lobit in a vibrant staccato. To the rest of us he
spoke two words apiece, about-faced on his heel, and in a total of three

minutes was in a car being driven up past the walls of the old fortress and on into the town.

When Major Colby and I called on him the next morning he was "still pretty excited," I noted, and "old de Lobit was in a twitter." Since he could not blame us for Smuts's bad manners, he devoted our fifteen minutes with him to complaining about the behavior of certain American officers and civilian food administrators in Budapest during the revolution. He alleged (and I had no way of knowing until after how mistaken he was) that they had "bought their way out to safety" on a special train in return for a promise to ship food back to Budapest. Why, he demanded, hadn't they stuck by the French mission as the British had done? The Red Guards had arrested the French officers and for a time threatened to shoot them. Our replies could not be to the point, as we knew nothing of what had happened, but the exchange was not amiable.

Early in the morning, two days later, Franchet d'Espèrey departed for Constantinople by way of Bucharest, still in a huff, declaring he would wait for Smuts no longer. Not a moment too soon. That afternoon word reached Belgrade that Smuts had left Budapest (actually, he had been back in Paris for two days). If the General had discovered that it was Smuts who had snubbed him rather than vice versa he would have exploded. My reaction was to wonder whether, if great men were ordering things in this childish way, our dispatches to Washington, "copies to Amembassy Paris," were not, as I jotted down in my notes, letters to Santa Claus.

Such is a usual reaction of men at "the end of a wire" to what seems the indifference of the home authorities. When there is not even a wire, frustration becomes indignation. Everyone in Belgrade—French, British and American alike—was in that state of mind, and such rumor and report as percolated through from Paris intensified it. General Plunkett had us to dinner a couple of days later with a delightful Colonel Swift, an Irishman, on his way back from Paris to Poland. Serbia, by comparison with Poland, was, he said, a Garden of Eden. His report from Paris was that nobody at his level in British headquarters in the Hotel Majestic could be bothered to listen to his account of the appalling conditions in Poland because they were totally preoccupied with discussing whether the ballroom should be used for theatricals to the exclusion of dancing on Tuesdays and Thursdays or just on Tuesdays. It must have been an Irish embellishment of the truth, but we loved to hear it.

The reports brought to us from southern Serbia by Major Edward Stuart, S.C., U.S. Army, did not make it sound like a Garden of Eden; no theatricals there and no dances. In the Morava Valley tens of thousands of Bulgarian, German and Austrian prisoners of war were living and dying in unspeakable conditions, half-naked in filthy rags, herded into rough sheds without heat, with the scantiest rations, no facilities to rid themselves of lice and no medicines to cope with the inevitable typhus.

Stuart was trying to persuade the Serbian Government that it should repatriate the prisoners of war at once; the idea that they could perform productive labor in reparation for war damage was illusory, and they menaced the whole country with epidemics. Colby and I strongly supported his report in private recommendations to friends in the army. But the near-starvation and misery among the whole population in southern Serbia were so terrible, according to Mary Heaton Vorse, Sylvia Beach and other American relief workers there, that the sufferings of prisoners seemed less horrifying than they should have. Also, memories of enemy atrocities were still vivid, renewed by photographs exhibited in many shop windows—rows of Serbian hostages lined up before firing squads and peasants dangling from poles in village streets. It was some time before repatriation began, and that summer there were still gangs of forlorn Bulgarian prisoners straggling around Belgrade, cleaning up rubble and piling it on ox carts.

On the heels of what Belgrade called "the Smuts fiasco" a French courier arrived with news that the Rumanians had begun a fresh advance on April 16 and that Hungarians of all classes and political beliefs were in a fever of fury and defiance. I wrote: "It solidifies Bolshevism in Hungary and enables the Soviet Government in Budapest to pose as the defender of Hungarian nationalism. It ruins the plans, vigorously propagated by the French, for a counterrevolution. There had been good hopes it might succeed. Both General de Lobit and Mr. Dodge have had talks with emissaries of the anti-Bolshevists, some of them with headquarters in Szegedin. The movement was strong even among the best Hungarian troops facing the Rumanians. Rumania's attack, staged for her own ends, has turned everything around. Now the Bolsheviks will be the patriots, the Allies and the anti-Bolsheviks the allies of the enemy. Of course, Rumania is only following Italy's example, seizing what she wants and trusting to the unwillingness of the Allies to prevent it—and to their military impotence to prevent it even if they want to."

There must have been differences inside the French Government as to how to deal with the Rumanians. My suspicion at the time, in view of Franchet d'Espèrey's mood when he left Belgrade, was that when he stopped in Bucharest on his way back to Constantinople, smarting from

Smuts's behavior and furious at having been denied the chance to lead an expedition against Béla Kun himself, he had encouraged the Rumanian military to act on their own. We had no indication of this from either French or Serbian sources in Belgrade. But the same suspicion that a *coup de main* was being organized by d'Espèrey existed in Paris, as Harold Nicolson noted in his diary on April 16. And later I was told in New York by Frank Polk, who was a delegate at Paris in the second phase of the Peace Conference, that in his opinion "the French—not the French Government, but Foreign Minister Pichon and Louis Barthou—had privately advised the Rumanians to go ahead." If so, they would have found a ready intermediary in Franchet d'Espèrey.

Whatever the origins of the Rumanian decision, it had the foreseen results. News trickling through from Budapest in the next few days reported that the Communists were shouting what a fatal mistake it had been to trust the Allies, who obviously were using the Rumanians to destroy Hungary utterly. Red bands were multiplying and roaming the countryside. The last week in April, Admiral Troubridge managed to arrange for Wilkins-Freeman to send out his first code message since the Communist takeover. It reported that there had been two thousand arrests in the last four days and twenty executions. The Rumanian liaison officer with the French, little Major Dimitru, tightly corseted and high-heeled, told me exultingly: "Now we will take Budapest and occupy the Banat." An alternative prospect was suggested by Commander Perrier, the French officer in charge of Serbian aviation, who often lent us horses and with whom we happened to ride out to Topchider on May 4. My mount this time was "the jiggly, nervous sort that will never walk for wanting to trot, and never trot for wanting to gallop." Between gallops, Perrier said General de Lobit was about to be replaced by General Humbert, "a fighting general," and that the planes of the Armée Française d'Hongrie were to be made ready to go into action within ten days.

As a diversion, a couple of days later, came the great Serbian festival, the "Slava" of St. George. On that day people in every city and village put on their gayest clothes, stream out into the country to pick spring flowers and stick sprigs of green in windows and on gates. This year the fete in Belgrade was dedicated to President Wilson. From a flower-decked stand in the Terazije, the central square, speakers extolled the American President who was working heroically at Paris to assure their freedom and unity. The cheers went up in waves: "Zhivio Wilson!"—"Zhivio Amerikanats!"—"Zhivio Srpska Rijeka [Fiume]!"—"Dole Italia!" Afterward a parade formed, first to the palace, where the Prince Regent waved from a window, and then to the American Legation. Those still were days when crowds gathered outside an American Legation to cheer.

On May 7 a familiar voice said over the telephone, "Hello, Ham." It was Professor Philip Marshall Brown, my Princeton friend, arrived unheralded from Budapest. He had been there as Professor Coolidge's observer since the end of March, but this was the first I had known of his being practically next door. He was in Belgrade to get light on the same questions we were asking. If the Allies were seriously considering military action in Hungary, would they send the Armée Française d'Hongrie to take Budapest and keep the Rumanians out, or were they going to give the Rumanians a green light and wash their hands of the consequences?

"If they don't make up their minds quickly," Brown said, "we'll see the whole thing go smash before our eyes. God forbid they decide to use the Rumanians! The red terror is already beginning. That would turn it into a massacre."

We improvised a bed for Brown and talked late into the night. He had discovered from General de Lobit and his chief of staff, Colonel Dosse, that they had been suspicious at first that he might turn out to be a Communist emissary. His views of the Hungarian situation were appraised by Nicolson, who met him there while on the Smuts mission, as impractical and idealistic. They did not strike me as that and certainly not as soft toward the Communists. He had come to believe soon after reaching Budapest that most Hungarians, even the workers, were lukewarm to Bolshevism, feared the Red Guards and were against renewing the war; they knew perfectly well that many of the lost territories were not predominantly Magyar and that it would be futile to try to save them by force. Brown's plan had been to influence Béla Kun not to give way to the fanatical wing of the Communists and to persuade the Allies not to leave him with no other alternative. He urged Béla Kun to accept a peaceful Allied occupation as the only way to hold off the Rumanians and get the food blockade lifted. As a last resort, he had suggested that Béla Kun be invited to Switzerland to meet Allied representatives and work out a compromise along the lines that Smuts had not been authorized to offer, namely that both Hungarian and Rumanian forces withdraw to form a neutral zone.

Now the fresh Rumanian advance had made it impossible for Béla Kun to negotiate with the Allies about a peaceful occupation or anything else. Brown wanted to make sure that if an Allied military expedition entered Budapest there would be a minimum of killing on both sides, and to this end he thought the Allies should announce in advance that, although crimes of violence would be punished harshly, revenge would not be taken for political offenses. He found, however, that Colonel Dosse wanted "a punitive expedition." If the French Army arrived in that spirit, there would be an indiscriminate massacre of foreigners and hostages, including the bourgeois leaders who might prove useful later in a moderate government. Since Brown himself would be among those liquidated, I thought he had a good point, aside from the political reasons for considering a violent outcome undesirable.

When Brown left the next morning in a French staff car, I wrote: "I hated to see him go back. After his visit here, I don't know what they may not do to him in Budapest if the Rumanians or the French start to advance. But he set out in good spirits." Actually, he did not remain in Budapest much longer. He had played the situation along as best he could in order to give Paris time to reach decisions; but the period when verbal arguments could hold things together had passed. Coolidge agreed. He wrote to Dulles on May 12 that Brown "has done splendid work" but "could not continue indefinitely as the moderator, counsellor and in a way friend of a government which we wish to see overthrown, if need be by foreign intervention."

The Allies never made up their collective mind to occupy Budapest or indeed to take positive action of any sort in Hungary. Yet the worst results predicted by Brown did not occur. For this Béla Kun's own blunders were responsible. Pressed by the fanatical wing of his government, he launched an invasion of Slovakia in the hope of opening up direct access to Russia. Many former Austro-Hungarian officers joined in, taking employment under the red flag "to save Hungary." It is not known whether Moscow promised that Russian comrades would meet Béla Kun's expedition halfway, for his communications with Lenin were by wireless and no record of them exists. Robert Conquest writes in *The Great Terror* that the Russian Divisional Commander Dmitri Schmidt had actually prepared an attempt to break through Poland and Rumania and bring Béla Kun aid. But the attempt was not made and the invasion of Slovakia petered out.

About this time, Paris announced the details of the new Hungarian frontiers. *In extremis,* Béla Kun turned against the Rumanians, was decisively beaten and fled to Vienna. Rumanian forces entered Budapest against only apathetic opposition, and although some reprisals and tremendous looting followed, there was no general massacre. Béla Kun's two disastrous gambles had destroyed not only his prestige but all illusion

that Communism could bring salvation. The counterrevolutionary elements which had been organizing hopefully at Szegedin under Admiral
Horthy moved shortly to Budapest and received a considerable welcome.
Not until the following November could the Rumanians be dislodged,
carrying everything movable with them.

When the Peace Conference got around to dividing the Banat, it
awarded the eastern two-thirds, including the Serbian-held town of
Temesvár, to Rumania, and the western third to Jugoslavia. On the
whole, the division seemed a fair one.

5

The Only Jugoslav

With Major Colby's arrival in Belgrade, Mr. Dodge acquired enough of an entourage to feel warranted in presenting it formally to Prince Regent Alexander. The Prince Regent seldom went out to dinner, and when he did I had had almost no chance to see what he was really like, for as soon as we rose from the table he would disappear with the best bridge players into another room. He was living in a modest house on Kralj Milanova Ulitsa, opposite what was left standing of the ornate and very ugly palace built during the Obrenovich reign. There, just across the street, a group of Serbian officers in 1903 had broken in, killed King Alexander Obreno-vich and flung his wife Queen Draga out of the window. The King's mar-riage to Draga Masin, a childless widow of shady reputation, ten years his senior, had outraged the country; and when she announced that she was to bear a child, something the doctors said was physically impossible, a group of officers decided to forestall the indignity of having to accept a false heir. In the empty and ruined palace I was shown the closet where they found the King hiding and ran him through with their swords, and the bedroom balcony whence they so barbarously did away with Draga.

Now an Alexander of the Karageorgevich line was ruling the country and temporarily occupying a house which, if I am not mistaken, had once belonged to Alexander Obrenovich's mother, Queen Nathalie. It was a squat house in the old Belgrade style, directly on the street, with a gloomy reception room shrouded in heavy lace curtains to keep out the gaze of passers-by. Afterward I came to know Alexander as King so well that it is difficult for me to remember him as Prince Regent. I recall that he came into the room with a quick step, that he had a slim body encased in a tight plain uniform with a standing collar and heavy gold epaulettes, no decorations, that his dark eyes examined us steadily but pleasantly through a pince-nez. He did not appear robust, but his face showed no signs of his past ordeals—the long campaigns, the flight in winter, exile in Corfu, the intrigues and plots at Saloniki which almost cost him his life. Our call was formal, the conversation mostly platitudes; for him it was simply something to be gotten through.

Later on, between the First and Second World Wars, I came back to Jugoslavia at least once every year. At the start, the Balkans were still a rather exotic region, imagined from afar as part Graustarkian, part Merry Widowish, not ventured into much by casual travelers. Usually whichever Balkan country a newcomer chanced to visit first became something of a passion with him. I began with Jugoslavia, a country neither dour nor frivolous, and I was irresistibly drawn back to watch its development. Eventually King Alexander's greeting became "So you're here for your annual report." Year by year the report was of the growing difficulties of a country deeply divided at home and with eager enemies on all sides. The King held it together; he was the only Jugoslav.

At the time of which I now write, Alexander was a young man of thirty, a little shy, with unpretentious manners that seemed out of character with his reputation as a military hero. He gave no evidence of having the capacity to meet demands for decisive political action such as were to be made on him in his fifteen years of lonely rule before the ghastly end at Marseilles.

II

Major Colby devoted most of his attention at first to organizing the office. His military experience was considerable, but it had been in more developed and "civilized" surroundings than he found in Belgrade. The frequent appearance of the word *sutra*—tomorrow—in the Serbian vocabulary especially irked his impatient nature. He did his best in a very charming manner to show his Serbian colleagues that he appreciated and liked them, as indeed he did, but somehow they never quite believed it. He had volunteered in 1915 in the Belgian Army, rose to the rank of commandant and when we entered the war transferred to the United States Army. Understandably, he felt that service in the field with an Allied army entitled him to at least equivalent rank in the still largely neophyte American forces; anything less, he maintained, would be an insult to Belgium. He won the argument, but at the expense of some disagreement within the military hierarchy in Washington that left a residue of bad feeling. In consequence, when he asked after the Armistice to be sent as military attaché at Brussels, where he had many friends, the request was denied. Somewhat reluctantly he accepted Belgrade as a substitute. Now, however, he was prepared to make the best of it and set out to organize the post along the lines of a proper headquarters.

There was not much scope for what Major Colby had in mind. In addition to the two of us, the staff consisted of a sergeant and a nice, rather gawky Serbian ex-soldier who acted as messenger. Nevertheless, considerable discussion was needed to settle a number of points. What would be the most efficient system of bells to install between our three rooms? When the duplicating device for which we put in a requisition to Washington arrived, where should we place it? Where should the messenger be situated in order that he could spring quickly into action when summoned by the Major via Sergeant Weinstein? The talk had to remain largely in the realm of theory, for no bells were to be procured in Belgrade and no wire to connect them with Major Colby's pushbuttons if there had been pushbuttons. We sent in requisitions for these and for other office supplies, but when the courier arrived on alternate weeks he regularly disappointed our expectations; and when I left Belgrade in midsummer the effort to achieve the proper degree of American efficiency in our operations was still unattained.

Major Colby's annoyance at the absence of IN and OUT baskets came back to me several years later as I was walking with President Masaryk through the woods of his country place at Lany, outside Prague. The talk happened to turn on whether there are such things as national characteristics. Masaryk thought there are merely national habits. I suggested that German behavior might indicate something deeper. Masaryk had had a lifetime of experience with the Germans, had fought them and suffered from them, but his view was more optimistic. There certainly can be a national state of mind, he said, but it can be changed. I asked him what he would say, after long observation of American ways, was the greatest American weakness. Masaryk always gave any question conscientious consideration in order to produce the most accurate possible answer. He sat down on a log, poked among the dead beech leaves for a few moments, turned his serious eyes on me and said: "The clear-desk system."

III

Entertaining in Belgrade involved difficulties. Everything had to be washed up quickly enough after each course to be brought back to the dinner table in time for the next one. It was always a gamble, too, which guests would actually turn up. Most Serbian wives, especially the older ones, declined all invitations to dinner. This was partly an inheritance from Turkish times; not much more than fifty years earlier the Turkish flag had flown over the Belgrade fortress and Serbs raised in the old ways had not accustomed themselves to those of the West. Also, of course, ladies were reluctant to accept hospitality they could not return. Sometimes we would be surprised by receiving a wife's acceptance, but usually it was sent because she wanted to be polite and not because she meant to come; she had shown her good will, and that was enough. The severest test of the household was when a wife who had refused turned up after all. Once when we gave a dinner for old Voivode Mishich we received the expected regrets from Mme. Mishich, but at the last minute, as a particular compliment, the Voivode decided to bring her along, with the result that my wife and I in turn quietly declined dishes because there weren't enough knives and forks for both of us to eat the same course.

There were no such handicaps at Admiral Troubridge's headquarters in the old Austro-Hungarian Legation and dinner there was sure to be agreeable and interesting. The Admiral's presence in Belgrade seemed anachronistic. He had started the war in command of a British squadron of four armored cruisers in the Mediterranean; now, at its end, he found himself in command of a few small monitors and regulating river traffic on the Danube. How had this degradation come about?

In the first days of the war, British and French naval forces in the Mediterranean had been uncertain of the position and intentions of two German naval craft known to be lurking somewhere on those blue summer waters—the powerful battle cruiser *Goeben* (23,000 tons, 11-inch guns, 27.8 knots), and its companion light cruiser, the *Breslau*. There ensued a complicated hide-and-seek, described admirably by Barbara Tuchman in *The Guns of August*. Admiral Troubridge, in command of four armored cruisers (14,000 tons, 9.2-inch guns), apparently received instructions from his commander, Admiral Milne, to search for and intercept the two German ships but to avoid entering into action "against superior forces." At one moment—at night, near the mouth of the Adriatic—his squadron did almost intercept the German ships. He lay in wait to engage them in the first light of dawn when the shorter range of his guns would not be a fatal handicap; but this did not prove feasible, and when full daylight came he desisted from the chase in the knowledge that the *Goeben* could stand outside the range of his cruisers, and sink them one by one. The escape of the German ships considerably affected the course of the war. They safely reached Constantinople, where the Turkish Government, which still claimed to be neutral, was so impressed by the exploit that it allowed them to assume Turkish names, hoist the Turkish flag and as a final gesture of friendship put the crews into fezzes. In October it permitted the two ships to sally forth from Constantinople to shell Odessa and other Russian ports. Russia replied by declaring war on Turkey, and Britain and France followed. A new and strategically important belligerent had been added to the enemy ranks.

Troubridge's behavior came under such strong criticism, by reason of the catastrophic political sequel, that he demanded a court of inquiry. He was found "justified in regarding the enemy's force as superior to his own in daylight," and was acquitted of the charge of having failed to chase "an enemy then flying"; but he was denied sea duty and assigned to serve with the Serbian forces holding Belgrade against the Austrians.

In that capacity, in the autumn of 1915, when the Austrians began regrouping across the Danube, reinforced by Mackensen's seven divisions, Troubridge got together a flotilla of launches and other small river craft and fitted them out with torpedo tubes. His eight naval guns he installed on the walls of the old Kalemegdan fortress, where, served by a handful of English marines, they helped defend the city until the fortifications were destroyed and most of his launches had been sunk. Troubridge made the retreat with the Serbs through Albania, finally reaching San Giovanni di Medua. There as port commander he struggled to cope with the horrors of famine and plague among the ragged Serbian soldiers, who were down to one-third of their normal rations; the Austrian prisoners of war, who were near starvation with even less; and the hordes of refugees who were dying in the streets. Now when we reached Belgrade three years later he was back on the Danube.

Such was the climax of what at the start had seemed would be an exceptionally brilliant sea career. Commander J. M. Kenworthy, who served as a junior under Troubridge, described him in his memoirs as an officer of unusual parts. "Peace to his ashes," he wrote. "He was the handsomest officer in the Navy in his younger days, and will make a fine angel."[1] He was still very good-looking in a ruddy, white-haired naval way, not at all a Gilbert and Sullivan admiral, but still not the rugged old sea dog that the dashing young officer Kenworthy knew had seemed destined to become. He never spoke about the ruination of his career, and was good-humored and hospitable, but something inside was broken.

---

1. J. M. Kenworthy, *Sailors, Statesmen and Others*. London: Rich and Cowan, 1933.

Troubridge claimed that Serbian peasants were the most honest people on earth and to prove it told how two old servants of his had just appeared after walking from Monastir in the south, six weeks' journey on foot, bringing back every scrap of his belongings that they had been able to salvage after his escape from Belgrade in 1915, together with seventeen chickens, part of the progeny of his seventeen chickens of that day. Unfortunately, the same standards did not apply in Serbian business or government circles. Turkish oppression and exploitation had taught the Serbs to draw together in self-preservation and to make family or friendship the basis of every transaction. The Admiral was finding that the habit of unabashed favoritism had not died with the end of Turkish rule, even when it operated clearly against the public interest. Thus his ban on private commerce on the Danube was being protested by Serbian shipowners in spite of the dire necessity of utilizing every possible ship to transport food from upstream to regions of actual starvation. The government sidestepped the issue and left him to cope with it. He mentioned that he had recently received a letter from my friend General Rashich, a model of personal honesty, introducing a Mr. Jovanovich and recommending that his five boats be turned back to him.

"It took me an hour to compose my refusal," said Admiral Troubridge, "explaining why it was absolutely impossible for me to break up an organization which, as everyone knows, must keep alive thousands of people till the next harvest."

He had seen General Rashich the next day and started to give him a further explanation.

"Oh," interrupted the General, "I expected you to refuse, and quite right too. But Jovanovich is a relative of mine and it was impossible for *me* to."

The former Austro-Hungarian Legation was one of the rare buildings in Belgrade that remained intact, not even looted. The Austrians must have feared that sometime it might have to withstand a siege, for it was equipped with its own water supply and a brick roof, two layers thick, strong enough to support machine guns. The grand pink-and-gold salon was shabby but otherwise much the same as it had been when it was the *Kaisersaal* of the last Austro-Hungarian Minister, Baron von Giesl. In the adjoining study, Hartwig, the Russian Minister, a notorious Pan-Slavist intriguer, had come on July 11, 1914, to call on Baron von Giesl; after drinking a cup of coffee with him he had fallen down dead. That was just two weeks after the assassination of the Archduke Franz Ferdinand at Sarajevo, and the sensational rumor spread in Belgrade that Giesl had installed an electric chair in his study and had shocked his visitor to death. More conservative gossips accepted the story that Hartwig's coffee had been poisoned. No evidence of the charge was forthcoming (then or later), but it added to the tension prevailing in the capital.

Two weeks later came the rapid events that led to the declaration of war. On the evening of July 23, Baron von Giesl set out from the Legation to deliver at the Foreign Office the ultimatum which Vienna had prepared with the obvious intention of facing Serbia with terms so unacceptable that she must refuse at least some part of them and thus lay herself open to humiliating chastisement. And here, just before the expiration of the time limit of forty-eight hours, Prime Minister Pashich arrived with the Serbian reply, conciliatory but not a surrender on all points. Acting on advance instructions, Giesl rejected it and left for Vienna. The war had in fact begun.

I V

When spring came we were able to get to Trieste, where we had arranged to buy a veteran Ford no longer needed by the American Red Cross. It had the usual ailments of a car which had passed through innumerable unloving hands, plus the idiosyncrasy that it sometimes could not be coaxed up a steep hill except backward. Having succeeded in getting it safe though not sound to Belgrade, we decided not to test it at once on any long expedition, and when a chance was offered us by Admiral Troubridge, we embarked on an old paddle-wheeler named the *Radetzky,* which once a week went down the Danube as far as Turnu-Severin, the first river town beyond the Rumanian border.

From the high stern deck of the *Radetzky* we looked down onto a flat-bottomed scow which was being towed behind, crammed with soldiers, repatriated prisoners of war and peasant families straggling back to their homes after perhaps years of absence. Stacked around the deck were the remainders of peasant household gear—bales of frayed comforters, iron pots and tin kettles, an antiquated sewing machine, a churn, bits of harness, strings of dried onions. There were several pigs, tied to something by the legs, a goat that wandered about scavenging, many chickens mostly but not all in coops, and everywhere babies. An old man with walrus mustaches had secured his rooster inside a stove, through the small pipe hole of which it popped its head, crowed, and was answered antiphonally from a dozen directions. A group of chocolate-skinned gypsies kept to themselves; the women, who were in calico and barefoot, shivered till the sun was really up.

The peasants wore conical sheepskin hats, trousers of brown home-spun, immensely baggy in the seats, ornamented with black braid and patched till hardly any of the original material showed, and, around their shoulders, sheepskin vests, woolly side inside, embroidered in red, green and tarnished gold thread, occasionally decorated also with spangles. The women had embroidered aprons tied across their striped and pleated skirts; these, several layers deep and each two or three yards around, were further distended by heavy linen petticoats, also in several layers. On their feet, men and women alike had contraptions of plaited leather strips, half shoe, half sandal, with long turned-up toes, held by a strap which was woven in among the many strips of leather forming the sole, then coiled around the ankle and fastened with a hook. The feet of the returning prisoners were done up in burlap. When the sun grew warm, the soldiers, about half of whom were in the olive drab of the Serbian Army, the others in secondhand French blue, washed their woolen shirts and long drawers over the edge of the scow and spread them to dry wherever the animals couldn't get at them.

We stopped often to exchange, amid tremendous confusion and excitement, some of this horde for others similarly clad and encumbered. At Smederevo, medieval crenelated walls rose straight from the water's edge. At Bazias, the terminus of the railway from Temesvár was marked by a roofless station, strings of overturned rolling stock, a fallen trestle and stranded steel scows along the river bank. At Gradishte, an ancient strongpoint, about a hundred Serbian fieldpieces stood near the dock in businesslike array. By afternoon we were in the great Defile of Kazan, where cliffs hem in the rush of waters to little more than 150 yards. Holes in the rock show where Trajan's legionnaires fitted beams to carry a road-way high above the water and a timeworn tablet commemorates the building of the road and the success of the Dacian campaign. At this point the sun was blotted out unexpectedly behind the Kazan Mountains and a very pale full moon moved into view between the purple masses of the Iron Gates. Boiling currents took us in charge. It seemed sheer good luck that we were not impaled on any of the half-submerged boulders strewn about. The helpless barge was snapped this way and that, but not even a chicken seemed to go overboard.

The Rumanian border guards at Turnu-Severin forbade us to land, but when we proceeded to do so, and marched off to the hotel, they shrugged and went back to their cards. On the return voyage the next morning the barge was left behind—fortunately, for halfway through the rapids one of the paddles struck a rock and shattered. In a jiffy the *Radetzky* whirled around two or three times, then careened sideways down the river. A little steamer upstream which had been struggling vainly to get through the rapids heard our wild toots for help, raced down, caught a line and steered us out of the main current and into a cove where makeshift repairs could be made. Lashed together, the two craft were able to reach the town of Orsova. Beyond we passed into a stretch of evening calm. A thin line of mist lay along the shore. Inlets and coves reflected splashes of apple-green and soft gray. A faint smell of spring earth and blossoms drifted out to us. The moon came up and silvered the *Radetzky*'s wake.

Now that good weather had come, we often rode out in the late afternoon, along roads lined with acacias in bloom and between fields red and yellow with poppies and wild mustard. The horses were of course borrowed, usually from the French, but the one I remember most vividly was a black gelding lent me by General Rashich, at least sixteen hands high and with a back so broad and flat that it seemed made as a platform for a circus rider. He had belonged to an Austrian Archduke, probably for use on ceremonial occasions. "Il est très gentil," Rashich told me. He was, indeed, good-tempered and beautifully schooled, but as he was seldom exercised except when I rode him he would start off at a canter which though not agitated was inexorable.

On a Sunday we might drive out along the Shumadija road with General Plunkett, Roland Bryce of the British Legation or another friend to picnic on Avala, the little mountain which epitomizes Serbian history from earliest mist-shrouded times. The ruined castle at the top was built in the fifteenth century by George Brankovich, one of Serbia's last quasi-independent rulers, on a spot which had been a favorite with still earlier chieftains and was celebrated in folklore as a gathering place for the spirits of old heroes, real and mythological. When Brankovich was defeated by Sultan Murad he fled across the Danube to Hungary, joined forces with Hunyadi János, succeeded in expelling the Turks and died in a brawl in Belgrade at the age of ninety. But the Turks returned and the castle passed to Turkish governors, one of whom was so fond of the bread baked at Smederevo, twenty miles away on the river, that to make sure of receiving it fresh each morning he stationed servants in relays along the path to the mountain top; if it arrived stale the runners lost their heads.

The road to Avala was so pitted with the shellfire of Austrian invaders and Serbian defenders in the fighting of October, 1915, and so rutted by oxcarts and camions, that wherever possible you turned off into detours across the fields. The bare hills on either side were crisscrossed with water-filled trenches and rusted wire. Here and there a crumble of masonry showed where a cottage or roadside *gostionitsa* had been. From beside the keep of the old castle at the top, under the shade of a hedge of hawthorn, you looked out across rolling country to the hills beyond the Sava. From this height the traces of war disappeared and the brown ribbon of road unwound toward the south clean of gashes and potholes. It was just down there, at the foot of Avala, that twenty-five years later the Partisans would join forces with the Russians coming up the Danube from the east and drive the Nazis out of Belgrade.

6

Wilson Day at Panchevo

We were so accustomed to everything happening in Belgrade without warning that we were not surprised when suddenly in early June there appeared a most engaging acquaintance of mine from New York, Michael Idvorsky Pupin. Son of a peasant, born sixty years before in the Banat, in the village of Idvor, he now was Professor of Electromechanics at Columbia University and a famous inventor. His massive frame was somewhat ungainly and his head was shaped (I noted later) like Molotov's, that is, on the model of a Chinese lantern. But the German proverb, "Grosse Stirn, wenig Gehirn"—"Big forehead, small brain"—certainly did not fit him. His eyes looked out benignly but sharply through thick spectacles as he waited to poke fun at whatever seemed to him pretentious.

Pupin's scientific career, described in his memoirs *From Immigrant to Inventor,* started on the plains around Idvor, "a village too small to be on any map," where he and other boys kept watch over the cattle during long starry nights. To communicate with each other they would stick their knives into the hard earth and by alternately tapping the wooden handles and pressing their ears to the ground were able to send signals back and forth and even estimate the direction and distance of each one from the others. Pupin also noticed that these sounds did not reveal their whereabouts to the Rumanian cattle thieves lurking in the cornfields nearby. He did not know then that the reason for this was that the earth there was too soft to serve as a conductor; but these were the phenomena that guided him to the physcial principle which became the basis for one of his most profitable discoveries twenty-five years later, the Pupin coil, to which we owe it that long-distance telephony is easy and cheap.

Pupin was acquainted with Wilson and had stopped in Paris to give him a description of what sort of people lived in the Banat, at any rate his part of it. But though he was as emotional about his native land as about his adopted one, which is saying a great deal, his attitude toward Jugoslav territorial claims was reasonable. He had tried to persuade Pashich and the other Jugoslav delegates in Paris to be moderate, but had realized he must take care not to press his views too hard.

"I wear Western clothes and tortoise-shell glasses," he said, "and that makes me suspect to begin with."

Pupin reported that fortunately the Italians and Rumanians were being so imperious and so importunate that disagreements among the Jugoslav delegates had not been fatal.

"Sonnino has done more to hurt Italy's case and Brătianu has done more to hurt Rumania's case," he said, "than all our statistics, maps and historical memoranda put together."

The year before, Pupin like many others had believed strongly that Wilson should not go to Paris for fear he would dissipate his influence in negotiation and compromise. "He should stay on Olympus," he said then in New York. I had argued that only the President himself could handle the statesmen in Europe, who would concentrate on satisfying the nationalistic aims and strategic needs of their countries even at the cost of establishing the proper basis for a world organization. Now I said that, watching from a distance how things were going at Paris, I had rather changed my mind; maybe Wilson would have had more influence issuing orders and admonitions from afar than himself negotiating on the spot. I asked Pupin how he felt.

"I have changed too," he said, "so we're still on opposite sides. What I have seen in Paris has convinced me that it was absolutely necessary for Wilson to come to Europe to preach the new order between nations, just as Christ had to come to earth to preach the new order between human beings. Someday the Golden Rule must prevail in politics or the world is done for. Some prophet had to begin preaching it, no matter how much he is opposed and reviled and even if he is a failure."

Most historians believe today that in the light of Wilson's breakdown, which began at Paris and was followed by the repudiation by the Senate of his actions there, he was wrong to have undertaken to negotiate the details of the territorial settlements and do hand-to-hand combat for the

League of Nations. But perhaps Pupin saw it more correctly than the historians. Martyrdom can make a crusader's cause everlasting.

Pupin was on a sentimental voyage to Panchevo, a town across the Danube from Belgrade, not far from Idvor, where he had first read and been inspired by the patriotic verse of Vladika Peter Njegosh, the Prince-Bishop of Montenegro; he had taken there his first elementary lessons in physics and heard for the first time about Benjamin Franklin and his kite. Now the Panchevo Town Council had invited him to "come home" and speak at a Wilson Day celebration. Mr. Dodge appointed me to attend as his representative, so we joined Pupin one morning on the early ferry across the Danube.

The dock at Panchevo was lined with a crowd, some of it town folk in holiday black, the rest peasant women wearing brightly colored blouses, the usual voluminous skirts and embroidered aprons, and men in long sheepskin coats and conical sheepskin hats. Everyone carried little Serbian flags, with a sprinkling of homemade American flags, which were waved so frantically that we didn't notice at first that some had vertical stripes and various numbers of stars. As we drew alongside there was a roar of "Zhivio Wilson!" repeated over and over, and then, solemnly, the Serbian national hymn. It was the first time Pupin had seen the Serbian tricolor on his native soil and tears rolled down from behind his thick glasses. Speeches of welcome followed the presentation of bouquets of flowers and much flinging of rose petals, and afterward boyhood friends crowded around Pupin and kissed him and wept. We then set off in procession, preceded by a barefoot boy driving a flock of geese, an impromptu reminder of the usual concerns of market towns. After him, more formally, limped an aged man with an American flag, the final surviving veteran, we were told, of the last affray with the Turks before they quit Serbian soil for good in 1867.

The afternoon ceremonies began with a chorus of children singing "Long, Long Ago" and ended with "The Star-Spangled Banner," evidently considered of equal rank as American patriotic songs. The words had been transliterated into Serbian for the children, who of course had no idea what the sounds meant but brought them out enthusiastically in sharply clipped syllables. After an hour-long oration by a Slovene professor, Pupin was called on to respond. He had been exasperated by the professor's closing remarks on the theme that Wilson was "an oasis in an endless desert of materialism." His experience as a young immigrant in America, Pupin replied, indeed his whole life there, had taught him that

Americans are generous and idealistic and usually not nearly so money-mad as the Europeans who say they are.

"If America had been a desert of materialism," he asked rhetorically, "how could Wilson's idealism have flourished there and why would two million American soldiers have come willing to fight in Europe for a victory from which they expected and wanted no territories, no mandates, no compensation of any sort?"

Panchevo with its well-stocked shops was an interesting contrast to Belgrade. Like other towns in the Banat it had been stripped of valuables early in the war, and later Mackensen had evacuated the Serbian population to Vienna and other Austrian cities. Then the policy was changed in order to lessen the discontent of Serbian and other Slav conscripts in the Austro-Hungarian Army; the inhabitants were brought back and rationing of local produce became less strict. When the war ended, the towns and villages of the Banat realized how fortunate they had been and sent enormous gifts of foodstuffs and livestock to the starving population of devastated regions to the south. In November and December, 1918, twenty-one thousand pigs alone were sent to Bosnia and Dalmatia, where the famine was perhaps worst; and more than sixteen thousand children were brought from there for a year of "fattening up"—living with Serbian families, going to school, doing farm chores. In appearance the town was Austrian, and one noticed that there was a certain sentimental feeling for the Hapsburgs dating from the time when they had been the protector of the Slavs of the monarchy from the "real" enemy, the Magyars. Yet everyone seemed exuberantly for union with Serbia, in contrast with the anti-Serb sentiment expressed sometimes in Croatia.

We were guests for the night of a prosperous leading citizen. Our bed, situated in an alcove off the parlor and separated from it by an openwork lace curtain, was enormous; it was furnished with a bolster as unyielding as a Japanese wooden headrest and a *Federbett* just long enough to leave either your feet or your chest uncovered. Across the room, in a similar alcove with the same sort of transparent curtain, our host and his wife along with their two daughters shared for the night a bed like ours.

While we were getting ready for the banquet to be held that evening in the town hall, we heard singing and music in the street and a wedding party burst in. They had started festivities at nine that morning and now were calling to pick up the brother of our host, who was the groom's *kum*, or witness; he was to be escorted, according to custom, to the bride's house, where everyone, bride and groom included, would eat, drink, sing and dance till morning. The bride's witness was a German farmer who also owned some land in Serbia and hence, we were assured, was "as good as a Serb"—anyway, he wasn't a Magyar. There was repeated kissing, weeping alternating with laughing, and incessant drinking of toasts in slivovitz. Then as suddenly as they had arrived they trooped off, preceded by their three fiddlers. The next morning when we went down to catch the six-o'clock boat the whole party was on the dock, fiddlers and all, still going strong, seeing the bride and groom off on their honeymoon. We hoped the happy but pallid couple would be alone at last; but at Belgrade a fresh group of wide-awake well-wishers greeted them and carried them off, presumably to another day and night of festivities.

That night as I ran over in my mind the events of the day—the little girls singing their incomprehensible "Long, Long Ago" with such painstaking diction, the flowers showered on the Americans, the handmade flags, the perspiring faces of the crowd turned up in rapt attention as Pupin praised American idealism—I thought that perhaps President Wilson would have been more moved by this country town's deep and ardent feeling than by the adulation of all Paris as he drove down the Champs-Elysées in President Poincaré's state barouche. Only a few weeks after that triumphal progress Paris had changed its mind about him, and the French press had begun telling him to take his foolish ideas and go home; indeed, within a few days of this visit of ours to Panchevo that was just what he would do, and in Washington also would meet the same sort of contempt for his idealism in some of the highest quarters. Panchevo was more consistent. A year later I received in New York a letter from the Mayor enclosing a salutation and memorial. The people of Panchevo, he wrote, had not forgotten Wilson and Wilson Day, and never would.

A dinner which we gave for Pupin a few days afterward was the one to which Voivode Mishich unexpectedly brought Mme. Mishich. His glow of triumph as he ushered her in dissipated any worry about there being thirteen at table or what to do for knives and forks. The arrival of a shipment of American uniforms which we had been expecting for months had put him in high spirits.

"Now we can stop sewing patches on patches on patches," he said.

Mme. Mishich, whose only foreign language was German, told a story which would have been incredible if the Voivode hadn't nodded and said, "That's just what happened." It seems that their son, a major, had been put in charge of a camp of Austrian prisoners of war. They were in a state of nerves because in order to dissuade them from surrendering their officers had told them hair-raising stories about barbarous Serbian customs. One evening a group of prisoners came shivering to his door begging to be spared. Alongside their hut a sheep was being roasted in a cook shed, and as one of the horror tales was that Serbs were cannibals they had convinced themselves that the sheep on the spit was a man and that one of them would be next.

One evening the Dodges were entertaining a high official of the American Red Cross, Colonel Henry W. Anderson, a Virginian, who was on his way home from a mission in Rumania. A young Serbian officer sitting beside me at the end of the table was curious about a decoration which gleamed with unusual brilliance on the Colonel's Red Cross uniform and inquired what the order might be. I evaded answering by saying I hadn't examined it closely, for no possible fib could explain in military terms that large diamond "M" which the Colonel had told us before dinner was the gift of Queen Marie of Rumania. Before the conversation went further, I froze at a remark which I overheard being addressed to a Serbian lady by one of Colonel Anderson's aides, a young Red Cross major.

"The Serbs," he was telling her, "are a cruel people. I looked at the faces in Kalemegdan Park this afternoon, and cruelty was written on every one of them." The ensuing silence made certain that if Vice-President Korošec, sitting beside Mrs. Dodge, hadn't heard this statement he wouldn't miss the next one:

"Anyway, Belgrade is quite different from Bucharest. There you'd never think you were in the Balkans."

II

Early in the following month we were informed that the Armée Française d'Hongrie had decided to make the *quatorze juillet* the occasion for a great victory celebration at its headquarters in Veliki Kikinda, a largish town about seventy-five miles north of Belgrade. The Allies had already announced their decision about the Banat, but although the division had not yet been carried into effect the French were making ready to be relieved from what for some of them had been over four years of service abroad. They made their preparations for the fete, then, with enthusiasm. It was a special occasion for us, too, as we would be leaving Belgrade within a few days.

The invitation to Veliki Kikinda included the loan of a French staff car, a necessary item, for one of our recent trips had been too much for the Ford; it expired on the outskirts of Sarajevo and I sold it to an old Mohammedan for a satchelful of paper dinars. We had gone on from Sarajevo by the narrow-gauge railway to Mostar and Ragusa, not yet accustomed to being called Dubrovnik and not yet cluttered with tourists; and from there we had gone by rowboat, up the Ombla to where it bursts from the side of a mountain, to have tea in Count Gozzi's garden, near the famous ancient plane trees. My recollection of the night on the train is waking up to see my wife, candle in hand, singeing bedbugs as they came over the edge of the seat where she was trying to sleep.

In the spring we had already been north across the Slavonian plain as far as the largest of the renowned Orthodox monasteries near Karlovci, on the fertile slopes of the Frushka Gora—the Frankish Hills. These splendid monasteries had acquired special importance during the Turkish invasions of Serbia, when by order of the Austrian Emperor large numbers of fugitive Serbian priests were given asylum there. The Emperor even granted them religious freedom and thus enabled them to perpetuate a branch of the Serbian Orthodox Church. The beds of bare boards given us on that visit were an answer to allegations of priestly sloth. The dinner, however, which reminded me of a scene in a medieval tale, was not frugal. The travelers were seated in positions of honor, I beside the Patriarch at the head of the immensely long and massive board, my wife at the other end beside the Bishop, with lines of black-robed priests stretching on either side between, indistinguishable from each other except in the length or color of their beards. As everyone familiar with such tales knows, the main dish was carp, and there was plenty of wine from the famous Frushka Gora vineyards. Only a few besides the Patriarch and Bishop spoke anything but Serbo-Croat, and those few only German, but all were anxious to profit from the occasion to glean bits of information about the United States. The conversation remained especially disjointed at my end of the table as I wandered in uncertain German from one fragment of a subject to another. Everyone was impressed, however, by my attempt to indicate the glories of American mass production. "Jede Minute," I managed to say, "eine Ford kommt," indicating by supplementary gestures the constant succession of cars rolling off the assembly line into the hands of the fortunate American purchasers.

This time we skirted Karlovci and followed the road up the Danube Valley to Petrovaradin. The fortress standing there on a height above the river is famous for two events. Here Peter the Hermit assembled his host for the First Crusade, bequeathing thereby his name to the town. And here Prince Eugene inflicted a great defeat on the Turks, killed the Grand Vizier and captured an immense booty. Thence he pressed on toward Belgrade, only to find his troops outnumbered five to one by fresh forces brought up from Adrianople. He nevertheless attacked, drove off the enemy, and two days later Belgrade surrendered. Thus was created the hero of the song beginning "Prinz Eugenius, der edle Ritter," sung thereafter by generations of Austrian soldiers going into battle. From Petrovaradin we turned directly north along the dusty banks of the River Theiss, shrunk at this season to a shallow stream, and on across pancake-flat plains of shimmering wheat, breast high and rippling in the breeze like a vast inland sea.

The climax of the day's celebration was the review of the Spahis and other mounted troops. Led by General Gondrecourt, erect and motionless on a wildly curvetting white mare, they swept across the field in dust-shrouded waves.

At the ball that evening there appeared a group of Hungarian dancers in dresses which the French found vaguely familiar. The dancers were the descendants of French peasants brought to this neighborhood in the time of Maria Theresa; she and her husband the Duke of Lorraine imported so many colonists of various nationalities to farm the Danubian plain that it became an ethnic checkerboard, with entirely German villages next to ones entirely French or Magyar or Slovak or Rumanian. The descendants of the French settlers, who still prided themselves on their French blood, had requested a chance to appear before the French officers on their national day. On a gala occasion like this they wore the dress of their ancestors and still performed remembered French dances entirely different from those of their neighbors. Yet they spoke no French, only German; they had refused to learn Magyar, which would represent a step in the Magyarization process which the Hungarian Government tried to impose on them, but they had been willing to learn German because that also was a minority language. They brought red, white and blue bouquets, which they presented with a salutation in German to General de Lobit after their dance. His reply in French was applauded on both sides and they were rewarded with immense amounts of champagne. He also proposed to us a flowery farewell toast.

On our last Sunday in Belgrade we went out the familiar road to Avala. Now the edges of the path to the top were thick with wild strawberries, and we ate our way up and on into the grassy forecourt of the castle. In the center of the court there stood, at that time, a small wooden cross with an inscription which awakened the liveliest feelings. It was the grave of a Serbian scout, shot here on Avala in one of the early engagements of the war when the Austrians had crossed the Danube for the first time. On the cross an enemy hand had scrawled the words: *Ein un-*

bekannter serbischer Soldat. Here on the top of Serbia's legendary mountain lay the war's first and authentic Unknown Soldier, chosen not by
lot but by Clio herself. King Alexander later caused to be erected nearby
a magnificent monument designed by Meštrović. Four imperturbable
peasant women in the dress of the four chief regions of Jugoslavia bear
stoically the weight of the black marble cenotaph. But the wooden cross,
unplanned, evoked deeper emotions.

7

Why Wilson Broke with Colonel House

Our journey west from Belgrade took two days instead of the ten taken by the journey east only seven months before. The world we were returning to was—*must* be—a new one, wholly unlike the old. Enemies had been beaten, dynasties toppled, peoples freed, visible results of victory won at frightful cost. Surely the nations had suffered enough and learnt enough to be ready to try living by a code of rational behavior. It was exhilarating to realize that the experiment was to be made in my lifetime, and I was determined to have some part in it. Perhaps I was moved more by a feeling of adventure than by high-mindedness; but at twenty-six I was painfully high-minded too. In my history books there had been no Mephistopheles to warn, "I am the Spirit that evermore denies."

The work of translating the purposes of the League Covenant as written in Paris into a functioning organization was already under way in London. Colonel House was there, at President Wilson's request, concerned mainly with the mandates provisions of the League Covenant, but of course involved in all the other planning also. In a burst of unwarranted optimism I determined we should go by way of London and see whether I couldn't persuade him to find some place or other for me in the Secretariat.

But first I must stop in Paris, for General Bliss had told me to give him a report after my tour of duty in Belgrade. I found him in the same room at the Hotel Crillon as in January, but in shirt sleeves instead of the tunic with the four stars. There were piles of papers on the desk and drifts of them on the floor. A wooden packing case stood alongside and as he talked he picked up documents and dropped them into it one by one.

Bliss was about to return to America after winning immense respect on the Supreme War Council and then in the less influential role of plenipotentiary at the Peace Conference. It was less influential because, apart from Colonel House, only President Wilson counted when it came to making the great decisions. Nevertheless, he had been one of the few Americans able to communicate directly with the President—though not often enough—and also willing to give him advice which Bliss knew would be distasteful. A famous example was his strongly expressed but futile protest against according rights in Shantung to Japan. He gave no signs of being distressed or cynical about this and other concessions made by Wilson to secure acceptance of the League of Nations, but he did not hide his pleasure at the prospect of becoming free from attempts to wind up political problems which seemed insoluble—and so proved— and of dealing with opposing proposals to use American troops in postwar situations where he felt they would not serve direct American interests. He queried me about the numbers and misery of the Bulgarian prisoners of war in Jugoslavia, the disposition and proficiency of the new Jugoslav Army, and other matters in the ken of a first lieutenant.

I also called on Bliss's colleague, Henry White, and it was fortunate I did so, for when I told him of my ambition to get a place on the League Secretariat he at once wrote me out a line of introduction to Colonel House.

It was characteristic of House, innately kind and courteous, that he seemed not to grudge the time to see me. He held out no great hopes of getting me into the League Secretariat, but promised to try. Although the Secretariat was not being formed on the basis of national quotas there certainly would be a number of American members. Sir Eric Drummond, of the British Foreign Office, had been named Secretary-General, and the two Under-Secretaries were to be French and American, Jean Monnet and Raymond B. Fosdick. They were already installed in Sunderland House, the garish mansion formerly the home of the Duke of Marlborough on Curzon Street, working under the driving belief that the United States would ratify the Treaty almost at once and that they must get ready for first meetings of the Assembly and Council in the autumn. House sent me to see Fosdick there, and his recommendation worked; Fosdick took me on tentatively as one of his assistants, to begin as soon as his own status was settled officially. For the Secretariat was still only provisional, and what was more—and how much more it proved!—our participation in the League was not yet certain. House, however, felt confident that the Senate would ratify the Covenant in the end, rejecting reservations but perhaps with "interpretations" which would be innocuous. He told me that on that basis he expected sixty-five Senators to vote for ratification.

From a Europe in shambles, counting eight million soldiers dead, the possibility that the United States would hold back from an effort to prevent the repetition of such immense horrors seemed incredible. Only after I reached home did I grasp the fatal significance of the antagonism to the League among a band of isolationist Senators, led by Henry Cabot Lodge, whose feeling for Wilson was unconcealed malice. Suddenly it dawned on me that the incredible might happen.

The story of how it did happen has been told from many different points of view and need be mentioned here in only the briefest way. However told, it is a record of personal and public tragedy.

II

On July 19, 1919, President Wilson laid before the Senate the Treaty of Versailles, in which had been incorporated, at his insistence, the League of Nations Covenant. It was referred to the Foreign Relations Committee, of which Lodge was chairman. He brought it back to the Senate with fifty amendments and four reservations. The President saw that their adoption would make it necessary to reopen negotiations with the other signatories; that each of those would add reservations of its own; that then the Senate would have to act again on the Treaty in light of these reservations; and that, in the unlikely case the Treaty still survived, it would then have to be resubmitted to Germany for signature. To Wilson, Lodge's strategy seemed clear—to kill the Treaty by degrees. He also believed that certain of the proposed reservations would fatally emasculate the League and that if he accepted them he would be betraying his pledge that American soldiers had died for something more glorious even than victory.

He determined to "carry the League to the people," and on September 3 started a journey across the continent. At Omaha he made a memorable prophecy: "If this guarantee is not lived up to, I want to say that in another generation or two we must have another and far more disastrous war." The trip encompassed eight thousand miles, twenty-two days and forty speeches. It became a nightmare. The crowds were immense and enthusiastic; they lined the tracks and called for his appearance at even the smallest stops. But the heat was insufferable and an intense pain in the head kept him from sleeping at night. There came a final ghastly appearance at Pueblo, Colorado, where tears ran down his cheeks and the audience, too, wept. The left side of his face and body were paralyzed. From the moment he returned to the White House, he was largely incapacitated, protected alike from the attacks of his enemies and to a large extent from the counsel of his friends by implacable guardians—Mrs. Wilson; Joseph Tumulty, his secretary; and Admiral Grayson, his doctor.

It can be fairly said that during the ensuing struggle in the Senate Wilson did in fact stand in the way of *a* settlement, for he rejected amendments to the Covenant that even many of his supporters considered would probably be accepted by the other signatories. But he firmly and obstinately maintained his requirement for the settlement which in his deepest being he believed was right. One combination of Senators turned down the treaty with the Lodge amendments attached; another turned it down without them.

The death of the treaty also extinguished any hope of ratifying the Pact which was to bind the United States and Britain to give France military support in case of a new attack by Germany, as had been promised by Wilson in return for Clemenceau's concession not to insist on a French occupation of the Rhine. The blow to Europe was double. The political organization which was counted on to arbitrate disputes and restrain aggressors was crippled by the American refusal to participate. In the same moment, the United States withdrew from the plan to concert military force to provide security against a resurgent German militarism. It was the first step toward the world of Hitler.

The election the following autumn sealed the decision that America was to go it alone down the isolationist road. Senator Harding, who had favored strong amendments to the League Covenant, and his running mate, Calvin Coolidge, defeated James M. Cox and Franklin D. Roosevelt by the astounding count of 404 electoral votes to 137. Democratic supporters of the League, which had been the chief issue of the campaign, were stunned. Early that summer, R. W. Seton-Watson had invited me to write an article on the coming election for his magazine in London, *The New Europe*. In it I explained how the two parties had interchanged their international outlooks; how Wilson had led the majority of Democrats to accept the need for American leadership in the postwar world; and how Lodge, Hiram Johnson, William Borah and other "irreconcilables," as they were called, seizing control from men like Taft and Root, were turning the Republican party away from its enlightened traditions, back into the provincialism of the old-time Democrats. I warned English readers what sort of foreign policy they might expect if Harding was

elected; but I did not warn them that this might happen; in fact I prophesied the opposite, which shows how blind you can become to realities
when you are obsessed by a great cause.

Wilson had appealed for "a solemn referendum." The election was far
from that. Originally the American people had been strongly in favor of
the League, but the struggle for their understanding and support was
one-sided from the moment the President was stricken. They became
more and more confused as the opposition cluttered the debate with
technicalities and wild accusations: the League was a Wall Street plot,
a Socialist plot, a Roman Catholic plot, a British plot against the Irish, a
plot against the Monroe Doctrine, any and every sort of plot that could
be conjured up to create fear and prejudice. Leaderless, the public gradually came to acquiesce in what seemed the safest—and easiest—course.
Even many eminent pro-League Republicans were misled, maintaining
to the last that despite Harding's record and his weasel words in the
campaign he would end by taking the United States into the League.
That illusion faded when two days after the election, speaking from his
front porch in Marion, Ohio, President-elect Harding announced that
Wilson's League was "now deceased."

Raymond Fosdick had remained in London till October, 1919, working
and waiting, hoping for the best, coming gradually to fear the worst. On
his return I went to see him at the State Department and he confirmed
his invitation for me to join his staff whenever he assumed his duties at
Geneva. But after the first adverse vote in the Senate on November 19 he
began to feel that his position as an officer of an organization which the
United States refused to join was anomalous. Nevertheless, he hesitated
to withdraw from the preparatory work for the League without the President's permission. The difficulty was that it was impossible to learn the
President's wishes except at second hand, and when word finally came
from the White House that he should follow his own judgment, this
sounded so unlike the President that he doubted the President had actually been consulted. In January Fosdick decided that it might handicap
the fight for the League, about to enter the final stage, if its enemies could
point out that he, Wilson's choice as Under-Secretary, was so presumptu-
ous as to assume that the United States was going to join, and he therefore cabled his resignation to Drummond.

This decision of course ended the idea of my going to Geneva as one
of Fosdick's assistants, though I clung for a bit longer to the hope of finding some spot in the Secretariat once the League had begun functioning.
Fosdick wrote me on February 6, 1920: "I expect to go overseas in about

two weeks to finish up a few loose ends, although I have no anticipation of resuming my place on the Secretariat. Keep in touch with me so that our plans can be matched." They were matched to the extent that neither of us ended up at Geneva.

III

An unaccustomed feeling of futility and helplessness must have overcome Colonel House as he watched the League's great enemy play on the weaknesses of the League's great champion and, in the end, defeat him. House had been Wilson's confidant and adviser since 1912, constantly at his side or within easy reach. He had helped plan the League Covenant and had been the President's emissary abroad in discussing every aspect of it with the Allied statesmen (and not only that, of course: every important aspect of the conduct of the war and the coming peace). But when he returned from London in September, 1919, ill and for some time kept in bed, he found himself barred from all contact with the President, unable even to get a reply to his letters. Mrs. Wilson was holding her invalid all but incommunicado, and in particular, it seemed, from House. She had come to resent his influence with the President after seeing in Paris what prestige he enjoyed among European statesmen and reading in English newspapers that he was considered the wisest member of the American delegation. However, her dislike came not only from jealousy but from a genuine mistrust. Above all, she was determined to protect her husband from being disturbed by advice which she knew would be contrary to the dictates of his conscience.

At Paris, House had found himself in an unaccustomed role. His appointment as one of the five American Commissioners made him for the first time a public official. Before this he had operated behind the scenes, inaccessible, free from direct responsibility. Now, recognized as a more authoritative spokesman for the United States than anyone except the President himself, he could not avoid talking with the newsmen who besieged him in droves. For the first time he was in a position in which reports that he was overstepping his prerogatives might gain credence. His actions now were official actions, subject to the criticism of the hostile and jealous and to the dangerous overpraise of admirers. Mrs. Wilson heard both. Gossip, conveyed to her by Dr. Grayson, suggested that some of the praise showered on House and even slighting remarks about her husband originated with House's son-in-law, Gordon Auchincloss. This was the beginning of her suspicion as to the Colonel's loyalty.

But more vital factors than gossip and perhaps unfairly hostile womanly intuitions had begun to separate Wilson from his chief adviser. A central difference in their characters became critical when the time arrived for theories and plans to be implemented in often painful negotiation with friends as well as enemies. What compromises were necessary—and right—in order to get the treaty written? What compromises were necessary—and right—in order that it should be acceptable at home? Wilson put his trust in fighting, to win all; House put his trust in compromise, as much as necessary to win as much as possible. When the conference dragged along from one crisis to another, House came to believe that nothing was so important as to get a treaty signed. In March and April a major deadlock occurred on whether or not to meet Italy's demand for Dalmatia, as promised under the secret Treaty of London, plus Fiume, which had not been promised. To break the deadlock, House was prepared to yield on what seemed to him a secondary matter, the future regime in Fiume. However, to Wilson the choice was between integrity and expediency. He already had compromised his principles in giving Italy a frontier on the Brenner, and in agreeing to let Japan keep German economic privileges in Shantung seized in 1919; he regretted these errors and did not intend to make another.

Entries in House's diary even before the President's return to Paris on March 13, 1919, following a short visit to Washington, show that he realized Wilson had been cooling toward him. The disintegration of their confidential relationship continued, and by May 30 he was writing that "for the moment" Wilson is "practically out from under my influence." By the time the Treaty of Versailles was at last ready for signature on June 28 House knew that the relationship could never be the same again. In a talk that day with the President, who was leaving Paris in the evening for Washington, House urged him to meet the Senate in a conciliatory spirit. "House," said Wilson, "I have found one can never get anything in this life that is worth while without fighting for it." Their farewell at the station was the last time they ever met.

Had Wilson's trust in House been eroded by degrees, with the dispute over the Italian claims only one in a succession of causes? Or had it been ended by one decisive event? A final judgment is not possible, but I feel that, regardless of what had happened before, the break did become irreparable on a certain date. This opinion is based on a conversation which took place at my house in New York one evening in 1925 between General Bliss and Dr. Isaiah Bowman. Both had played important roles at Paris, the General as one of our plenipotentiaries, Dr. Bowman as executive officer of the Inquiry and the American delegation's chief territorial specialist. By the time of which I am writing, both were members of the Editorial Advisory Board of *Foreign Affairs*. Dr. Bowman was director of the American Geographical Society; General Bliss, now retired, often stayed with me when he was in New York.

After dinner that evening General Bliss and Dr. Bowman got to reminiscing about Paris. They agreed that there had been many contributing causes for the Wilson-House break, probably dating as far back as when House advised Wilson against going to Paris in person, as he had set his mind on doing, and very definitely including House's repeated advice that Wilson try to conciliate opponents of the League, something Wilson rejected as wrong morally and an error strategically. It had been evident, they said, that when Wilson came back to Paris, after his short and unhappy visit in March to Washington, he was discontented with the way House had handled things in his absence.

The same thing has been emphasized by both Ray Stannard Baker and Mrs. Wilson. Mrs. Wilson records[1] that after the President had talked with House, who came to meet them at Brest, he said bitterly: "House has given away everything I had won before we left Paris. He has compromised on every side." Yet she also writes that a week later he rejected the idea that House was back of newspaper stories which made unflattering comparisons between Wilson's judgment and abilities and his own, saying, "I would as soon doubt your loyalty as his." Mrs. Wilson's book had not yet been published at the time of the discussion between Bliss and Bowman which I am describing; but the above quotations from it would confirm their impression that the President at that stage of the negotiations mistrusted House's judgment but did not question his devotion.

How, then, did it happen that lack of confidence in House's judgment developed into lack of confidence in him personally? Bliss and Bowman believed it occurred as a result of a discovery made by the President the night of April 17.

It was a critical moment in the negotiations with Italy. The American delegation was split: To compromise? Or to risk a showdown that could lead to Italy's quitting the conference? One faction consisted of House's brother-in-law, Dr. Sidney Mezes, director of the Inquiry; House's son-in-law and confidential secretary, Gordon Auchincloss; David Hunter Miller, legal adviser to the delegation, Auchincloss' law partner in New York; and George Louis Beer, expert on colonial questions. Their aim

1. Edith Bolling Wilson, *My Memoir*. Indianapolis: Bobbs-Merrill, 1939.

was to reach an agreement with Italy first, then press the Jugoslavs to accept it; and they proposed to win Italy's agreement by giving her Fiume under some formula or other. Against them were ranged Bowman and the chiefs of the territorial divisions—Clive Day, Douglas W. Johnson, W. E. Lunt and Charles Seymour—plus Allyn A. Young, the economist. They recommended awarding Fiume and Dalmatia to Jugoslavia outright. The two groups had already clashed when Mezes on March 16 sent House recommendations which were totally at variance with those of the territorial chiefs, and which the latter had argued against in a strong letter addressed directly to the President on April 4. Now there was to be a decision.

Bowman recalled how late in the afternoon of April 17, as he was looking for some paper in the filing room, he came across a carbon copy of a memorandum signed by Mezes and addressed to House. He was surprised, because it had not been shown to him. His surprise became indignation when he saw that the memorandum recommended a compromise on Fiume as favored by House and that it began with some such words as "Having consulted the experts"—implying that they had altered their position against any compromise. Bowman described how he, the territorial chiefs and Allyn A. Young at once prepared a letter appealing to the President not to accept the Mezes-House compromise. They recalled his statement to them on the *George Washington* en route to France the previous December: "Tell me what's right and I'll fight for it," and they begged him to stick by that promise. They did not, however, have direct access to the President, and it was a question how to get their appeal to him in time. They agreed that General Bliss would be their most effective intermediary, and Bowman went off to see him at the Hotel Crillon. By then it was late in the evening. Bowman and Bliss laughed as they recalled that Bowman had found the General with his tunic off, lying on his bed, reading a pocket-sized Thucydides. (Such was his habit. When he stayed at my house he regularly produced from one hip pocket a Loeb Library Latin or Greek classic and from the other a flask, which he stood on his bedside table. He read Greek, Newton Baker said, "as easily as I read English.")

When Bliss had read the Mezes memorandum and the protest of the "real experts" he got up, dressed, ordered a car and went off to the Place des Etats-Unis where President Wilson was living. The President received him in his bedroom. Bliss explained his mission without arguing the merits of either case, merely stating that the matter seemed to him important enough to bring it to the President's attention in advance of the meeting which was to be held the next morning. Wilson listened to him grimly and thanked him for coming.[2]

Thus when House put forward the Mezes recommendation the next day as representing the judgment of "the experts," Wilson knew from their letter brought to him by Bliss that this was simply not so: either House was trying to mislead him or House had been misled by Mezes. Bowman himself didn't think the former. He had a high opinion of House's sagacity ("the wisest counselor," he wrote to Seymour, "that ever a President had") and he remained on good terms with him until House's death in 1938. But this need not mean that the President entirely exonerated House. Even if he did not conclude that House was deliberately trying to deceive him, he may well have retained some suspicion that this had been the case. House of course knew from the letter which the experts had sent the President on April 4 that they were bitterly opposed to compromise, and Wilson might have wondered why House did not ask how they had come to change their minds. At a minimum, Wilson would have decided that House was not a counselor whose facts and opinions he could trust. This was how Bowman and Bliss pinpointed a moment when Wilson's feeling toward House would seem to have undergone a decisive change.

I report my recollection of their story because any sidelight on the course of a friendship which was so influential in our country's history is of value. Their interpretation conflicts with statements by House himself and by Charles Seymour, the editor of House's *Intimate Papers*.[3] Seymour stated at the end of the fourth volume of that series that the friendship between Wilson and House "lapsed." "It was not broken." And he quotes a letter by House to him in 1928 as saying that the separation "was and is to me a tragic mystery." And, regarding the April 17 letter of the six experts, Seymour (who was one of them) wrote in *American Heritage* for August, 1963: "There is no evidence that the letter in question affected the relations of Wilson and House."

In that issue of *American Heritage* Seymour printed a memorandum made by him following a talk with House on January 5, 1938, two and

2. Professor René Albrecht-Carrié (*Italy at the Peace Conference*. New York: Columbia University Press, 1938) and Ray Stannard Baker (*Woodrow Wilson and World Settlement*. New York: Doubleday, 1923) have printed the text of the experts' letter; Baker has also printed the President's reply expressing agreement with it; and Paul Birdsall (*Versailles: Twenty Years After*. New York: Reynal and Hitchcock, 1941) has stated that one of the experts who signed the letter told him in June, 1940, that the reply was on Bowman's desk by ten o'clock the next morning.

3. *The Intimate Papers of Colonel House*. Boston: Houghton, Mifflin, 1928.

a half months before the Colonel's death. (House asked him not to publish it for twenty-five years.) He quotes House as saying: "It has been
said many times that the Fiume crisis led to a personal break. This is
quite untrue. . . . He [Wilson] never mentioned the letter of the experts
on Fiume, and I do not remember that he knew of it. It has been said
that Dr. Mezes caused a break. I cannot see how. Wilson never mentioned
Mezes except in friendly terms." In the same interview, writes Seymour,
House also mentioned "Shotwell's curious error in placing the responsibility for the break with Wilson on the shoulders of Mezes." The reference was to Professor James T. Shotwell, chief of the historical division
of the Inquiry, whose reminiscences of the Peace Conference describe
Mezes' role in producing the rift. Shotwell's opinion was that, "whatever
other factors" entered into the incident, "the estrangement dated from
that time."

In September, 1963, I asked Shotwell, then in his ninetieth year, and
so far as I know the only member of the group of experts then surviving,
if he wished to change his estimate. He said not. He had disagreed with
Bowman, he said, over the Adriatic question and Fiume, on the basis
"that a geographer's standards were not the right ones by which to arrive
at political judgments." David Hunter Miller had urged the necessity of
compromise with the Italians, he said, "and I agreed." He added that he
had never had confidence in Mezes, who had been head of an undergraduate college, and had, in his opinion, no real scholarly knowledge
and "no idea of how to deal with scholars." Shotwell added: "He gradually drifted out of the picture at Paris. He spent a lot of time there,
toward the end, reading dime novels in bed."

However, Mezes was very much in the picture that April 17, even
though House later had no recollection of the details. The conversation
which Seymour recorded was near the end of House's life and his memory
may very well have failed. If he had in fact accepted at face value Mezes'
indication that the experts had come around to his view, that, he must
have realized, made him seem gullible; and this was something he seldom
was and would have hated to admit. In any case, he would naturally
have tended to avoid confirming an incident which did not redound to
his brother-in-law's credit, and the fact that he wanted to forget it may
have helped him do so. On the other hand, the almost complete omission
of any reference to Mezes in the *Intimate Papers* would seem deliberate.
All in all, we are indeed left, as House professed to be, with a mystery.[4]

4. I wish that, as was often my habit, I had made a memorandum of the Bliss-Bowman
conversation at the time. However, it was of such interest that it remained clear in
my memory, and the accuracy of the central points is corroborated by Professor

Although I came to know House well, he was reluctant to talk about the cause of his separation from Wilson, even after Wilson's death; and no word that he ever uttered to me about Wilson personally was anything but considerate and indeed affectionate. This did not preclude criticizing his policies. Once, for example, he told me that he thought it a great mistake on Wilson's part not to have taken ex-President Taft and ex-Secretary of State Root with him to the Peace Conference; House felt that if he had not been abroad at the time he might have persuaded Wilson to do so. Root would have been consulted on broad questions of international law. Taft would have sat on the commission drawing up the League Covenant and would have favored the same things Wilson favored. The Covenant, as a result, would have been "just the same, if not better." Henry White, the Republican that Wilson did take, was a very nice man, an experienced diplomat, not influential, however, with the leaders of his party. In contrast, the participation of two such eminent Republicans as Taft and Root would have meant that the League could not be dubbed a Democratic concoction but that it was plainly the handiwork of leaders in both parties.

The newspapers always spoke of House as "the silent Colonel," but I found the opposite when he was in a small group of people interested in the same things that interested him. One evening in October, 1921, he came to dinner with me to meet Professor Alfred Zimmern, author of *The Greek Commonwealth* and one of the *Round Table* group in London. Henry Canby had told me Zimmern wanted very much to meet House and I asked him to bring him to dinner for that purpose. Among other things, House talked about Wilson's diplomatic appointments, which on the whole he thought good, especially as the long gap since the Democratic party had been in power meant that there were practically no Democrats of experience in sight and he had to make his choices from private life. House gave him credit, too, for promoting deserving Republicans and for putting the Consular Service under Civil Service. He said that at the end of Wilson's first term he had urged him to make some changes, weeding out "weak sisters." But this Wilson stubbornly refused to do. It wasn't that he wanted to keep inefficient appointees in place out of feelings of loyalty, but because he disliked reopening matters settled well enough even if not settled as well as possible. He had a horror of the spoils system, and he knew that if he dismissed an ambassador or minister he would have a tussle with Bryan, who according to House genuinely believed in the spoils system and thought it unjust to the

Philip E. Mosely, of Columbia University, who discussed the Paris incident with Bowman in 1941 and again in 1943.

Democratic party not to change every federal employee down to letter carriers at every opportunity.

After dinner Zimmern engaged House in an interesting discussion of mistakes made at the Peace Conference. They were in agreement on the serious results of the delay in assembling the conference, during which time the power of France increased and that of the United States waned; on the "wickedness" (both used the word) of the campaign waged by Lloyd George in that period on the platform "Hang the Kaiser, make Germany pay, and a country fit for heroes to live in"; and on the mistake of not making a preliminary treaty rapidly, taking the Fourteen Points as a basic "skeleton."

"Wilson's foot slipped," House said, "when he failed to remind the Allies in every controversial case that Germany had made peace on conditions and that he was determined to abide by them scrupulously. He should, if necessary, have carried the questions at issue home to Congress, saying 'Germany agreed to surrender on such and such terms; Britain now wants to modify the terms in this way, France in this way, Italy in this way. Now help me decide whether these changes are morally justified.' If he had done that, and been defeated, as he probably would have been, how much better it would have been for the world!" Zimmern emphatically agreed. I hazarded the caveat that this course would not have ended the conference as speedily as all considered so desirable. The whole reasoning seemed to me fallacious.

House also stressed Wilson's error in issuing his appeal to the voters for the election of a Democratic Congress midway in his first term.

"It was legitimate, but politically unwise," House said. "If he had refrained, he would have had the Senate and probably the House of Representatives."

I asked House his idea as to how well Wilson thought he had made out at Paris with the Fourteen Points.

"He is sincerely convinced, and will remain convinced, that the Peace Treaty is in agreement with them in all essentials," he replied.

"And how does he reconcile the Shantung compromise with them, for instance?"

"God knows," said House, very slowly and sadly.

It is fair to comment that at Paris House himself had not opposed the transfer to Japan of German economic rights and holdings in Shantung, feeling that the threatened departure of the Japanese delegates following that of the Italians would all but destroy the conference.

8

The "Evening Post": Denizens and Visitors

If what we fought for seems not worth the fighting,
  And if to win seems in the end to fail,
Know that the vision lives beyond all blighting
  And every struggle rends another veil.

The tired hack, the cynic politician,
  Can dim but cannot make us lose the goal;
Time moves with measured step upon her mission,
  Knowing the slow mutations of the soul.

—H.F.A., *The New York Evening Post*, March 2, 1920

These "Lines for the Hour" reflected both the bitter disappointments and the somehow still surviving hopes of the year 1920, surely one of the most dismal periods in the political life of the United States.

By February of that year I had abandoned the idea of joining the League Secretariat and had begun looking for a job with a newspaper. By luck I found one with the *New York Evening Post,* a paper of distinguished lineage, founded in 1801 by Alexander Hamilton, which exercised an influence throughout the country out of all proportion to its modest circulation. William Cullen Bryant had been editor for almost half a century, and among his successors, after the paper had been purchased by Henry Villard, a German-born newspaperman who became a railway president and capitalist, were such men as Carl Schurz, E. L. Godkin and Rollo Ogden. Godkin, a foe of corruption and jingoism, had been a friend of my father's; he lived near us on Tenth Street, and as a boy I admired his stately air and was flattered by his courteous silk-hatted nod as I went by on roller skates.

The *Evening Post* had been bought in 1919 by Thomas W. Lamont, a partner in the Morgan firm, and put in the charge of Edwin F. Gay, a leading economic historian of his time, the first dean and organizing genius of the Harvard Business School. Gay was heavy-set and dark. His black eyes beneath heavy black eyebrows looked at you humorously but piercingly. He was courageous and determined, perhaps too idealistic and enthusiastic for his own good. Nothing was alien to him: he had what his biographer Herbert Heaton summed up as "a sense of the alto-getherness of everything."[1] He seemed so competent that he had no need to be bossy; others followed.

Gay was freshly back from struggles and fights in wartime Washington, where more than any other man he had forced the adoption, against the protests of powerful shipping and business interests, of measures neces-sary to procure more commercial ships vital for the transport of men and military supplies to Europe. (Gay's assistant, Franz Schneider, answered a protest of a different sort from Herbert Hoover: "If we don't get the men to France there will be no Belgian relief problem.") His fights in the Shipping Board, the Central Bureau of Planning and Statistics and the War Industries Board made him many enemies; he didn't mind, for he won them. Maybe it is as a result of this fact that his name is not mentioned in many of the autobiographies of his wartime contemporar-ies. It ought to be, for, as his biographer demonstrates, he was one of the men who contributed most from the Washington end to winning the war.

Though rejuvenated and expanded under Gay's new management, the *Evening Post* still looked, and was, a sober paper. It took several visits to Gay before my eagerness won me a place as jack-of-all-trades on the editorial staff.

The paper had suffered in reputation and circulation under the direc-tion of Oswald Garrison Villard, a sincere but cranky crusader. Lamont, who was determined to restore it as a voice of liberal conservatism, gave Gay free choice in picking editors and engaging special writers on labor, business and economic problems. The result was a staff of unusual bril-liance, but expensive to maintain. Henry Canby remarked that it was "as rich in eccentrics as a university." As editor, Gay appointed Simeon Strunsky to succeed Rollo Ogden. Strunsky had been born, I think, in Russia and had a slight accent, but by every instinct was unequivocally

1. Herbert Heaton, *A Scholar in Action: Edwin F. Gay.* Cambridge: Harvard Uni-versity Press, 1952.

American. He wrote with style, particularly in his meditative weekly column, "Post-Impressions," whimsical without being maudlin, satiric without being cynical. His satire never degenerated into the heavy sarcasm that risks being read literally, with bewildering results.

Several of Strunsky's assistants afterward made names for themselves. Allan Nevins, later the author of a prodigious number of biographies and histories, was the most single-minded typist I have ever known; the machine over which he bent seemed to become a structural extension of his body, and no commotion in the office slowed the stream of words tumbling out under his staccato two fingers (four, counting both hands).

Ernest Boyd was an Irishman with red hair, a red beard, red-brown suits and a voice that came from the depths. His cynicism was sufficient to make up for any lack of it in all the rest of the staff. Our lunch together the first day he came into the office was the start of a long friendship. He was a city man, who took no exercise, "apart," as he said, "from reading and writing." Sometimes he came out to visit me in the country, but took the last train home in the evening "to get some sleep": the meaningless twittering of the birds woke him up at dawn, unlike the purposeful noises of the elevated trains in the city, which soothed him because they were going somewhere. Mountain climbing had once been a passion, but he had given it up when he left Europe. He knew all the literary Irish of his generation and wrote an outstanding history of Irish literature, dedicated to my wife (who knew Ireland) and to me (who had never been there). Reading and writing aside, I asked him, what did he enjoy? "Conversation, with certain kinds of people." It sounds extravagant to compare Boyd to his countryman George Bernard Shaw. In fact, however, the similarities between them were many, but though his wit was as mordant as Shaw's his talent was critical rather than creative. He had the by-products of genius but not its essence.

Under Henry Seidel Canby the literary supplement became a prominent feature on Saturdays. Later he gave it a life of its own as the *Saturday Review of Literature;* later still it became the *Saturday Review,* with science, medicine, education, music and other special departments added to the literary element. Others with reputations in the making were William Rose Benét, the poet, and Christopher Morley, who called his column on the editorial page "The Bowling Green." Morley, first of the line of authors never photographed without a pipe, was an easy writer of prose and verse, unlimited in range of taste from the highest to the meretricious, at his best when he was not being too jovial or too whimsical or using too big words. *Kitty Foyle,* depicting a life far removed from his own Quaker background, was his most serious and, I thought, his most straightforward and successful novel. Sometimes he filled all of "The Bowling Green" with a charming little essay of his own, but usually it was made up of musings and jottings, gentle witticisms and verse, some by himself, some contributed by friends like Steve Benét, Malcolm Cowley and Edmund Lester Pearson. It was more decorous and less spontaneous than "The Sun Dial," the column which Don Marquis wrote for the *Sun* and later the *Tribune,* recording his doings and those of his immortal creations archy the vers-libre cockroach and mehitabel the cat. Morley was alive to all the minutiae of city life. He jotted down for his column the titles of the books he saw being read in the Brooklyn subway and recorded, with embellishments, the gossip at the Three Hours for Lunch Club, of which he and Frank Shay (always referred to as the blue-eyed bookseller) were the pillars. Boyd ridiculed folksiness and detested conviviality, especially in the blend which he imagined particularly prevalent among pipe smokers, and a quiet feud developed between him and Morley.

Because of Lamont's standing in Wall Street, the financial department was an important feature of the *Evening Post.* At first the financial editor was Alexander Dana Noyes, gaunt, precise, "no foolishness." When he went to the *New York Times* he was succeeded by Franz Schneider, who had been one of Gay's right-hand men on the War Industries Board and other boards in Washington. The managing editor was Charles McD. Puckette, a not-in-the-least-typical Southerner, a graduate of Suwannee, shy, short-spoken, hardheaded and, like all managing editors of great city papers, harassed. Mark Sullivan and Harold Phelps Stokes were in charge of the Washington Bureau. Gay was less happy in his choices—or sometimes in the choices made for him—of business advisers; and even his own acumen and tremendous energy were to prove insufficient to increase circulation and income rapidly enough to meet the heavy financial overhead to which he became committed.

II

The *Evening Post* building on Vesey Street was ornamented with heroic-sized statues ranged across the façade just below the tenth-floor editorial offices. I noted from the street that the window by which I was given a desk was just above the massive figure of a scribe in the garb of a monk, not, I hoped, a sign that I was withdrawing from the world. The offices were old-fashioned and, with the influx of new staff, crowded. Yet the only adverse comments that I recall being made were by Mary Stevens, the harassed secretary of managing editor Puckette, who did not like seeing a mouse on the rim of the water cooler, and by Strunsky, who said his coat closet was too small to hold all the pairs of forgotten rubbers that piled up month by month. There was an admirable library, accumulated under the direction of editors of taste and learning. My window overlooked the churchyard of St. Paul's Chapel, where on sunny afternoons stenographers sat on the flat tombstones to eat their lunch.

At first it was hard to turn out even the short editorials assigned me at the morning conference. On the *Daily Princetonian* I could editorialize as I liked on subjects I knew and cared about. The fact that the fillers I was now writing were short did not make them easier. There were plenty of things of interest happening. President Carranza was fleeing from Mexican rebels, D'Annunzio was on the rampage, ex-Premier Caillaux was being tried for treason, the German reparations problem was becoming acute, the number of vehicles now using the city streets had reached 350,000, and the debate had begun as to who should be and would be nominated at the Democratic and Republican conventions in July; on the sports page were stories about *Shamrock IV* being conditioned for the coming America's Cup races, and even the sedate *Evening Post* could not refrain from giving headlines on the front page to the vicissitudes of Nicky Arnstein and Fanny Brice.

No editorial themes of moment were entrusted to me. Gradually, however, I learned that practice, while it does not make perfect, does lessen the anxiety and toil of producing something at least passable; and as I acquired fluency I began to be allowed to write on European and other foreign topics. After a time I also was allotted a small preserve in the lower right-hand corner of the editorial page, headed "At Random," which I filled with poetry, aphorisms political or literary, in fact anything that struck my fancy over a wide range of sources from the *Arkansas State Journal* to Max Beerbohm. Often, too, I wrote pieces for the Saturday magazine—too often, for I took on assignments even when I had to bone up on the topic in the library—and contributed reviews and verse to Canby's book section.[2] I also was publishing poetry in those days in the monthly magazines (then more numerous than now) —*Scribner's, Harper's,* the *Century* and the *North American Review.*

The summer of 1920 was like most summers before Presidential elec-

2. As a footnote to the state of journalism in that era, I might record that from June, 1920, to July, 1921, I contributed ninety-nine special articles to the editorial page, the Saturday magazine and the Literary Supplement, and was paid $524.10, a bit more than $5.00 apiece.

tions, only more so. The wrangle between Harding and Cox over the League of Nations became particularly rancorous; League opponents implied that those who continued to favor entry were close to treasonable while pro-Leaguers were frustrated and embittered because Harding's evasiveness and ambiguity left them without a line of direct attack. For those who wanted to think the best of him, doubt that he was really against the League continued even after his political mentors, notably Senator Lodge, forced him to state categorically, "I favor staying out." Many pro-League Republicans refused to take this as conclusive, and thirty-one of them, including Taft, Root, Hoover and Hughes, announced their continuing conviction that Harding if elected would eventually take the United States into the League. They had a feeling that if they supported Harding they could influence him in that direction. One of them, Paul D. Cravath, put it to me this way: "I believe in being on the bandwagon." The strategy seemed to me bound to be ineffective, and I helped assemble signatures to a manifesto in reply, in which other Republicans stated their belief that Harding was indeed speaking the truth, and on that basis urged the election of Cox. They were not so eminent as the thirty-one, but the event proved them less credulous.

My chores at the *Evening Post* included devising occasional news features. One was to be an estimate of Woodrow Wilson's place in history, to mark the moment of his leaving the White House. I persuaded General Smuts, then Premier of the Union of South Africa, to write this article. He stipulated that it not be copyrighted but released freely to all other publications; and he refused payment, saying that it was "a labor of love" on behalf of Wilson "at a time when most have fallen away from him." The *Evening Post* published it on March 2, 1921, two days before Wilson, partially paralyzed, rode to the Capitol alongside the affable, noble-looking nonentity who was becoming his successor.

Smuts was critical of Wilson but charitable and not despairing of the survival of his ideals. Describing Wilson's position at the close of the war, he wrote that it was "terrible in its greatness," since "probably to no human being in all history did the hopes, the prayers, the aspirations of so many millions of his fellows turn with such poignant intensity as to him." He had arrived in Paris in an "atmosphere of extravagant, almost frenzied expectation," and he emerged six months later with a Peace Treaty that "was not a Wilson peace" but "a Punic peace." His prime mistake, Smuts thought, lay in giving the impression that the peace was in accord with his Fourteen Points when this was not so. Wilson had plunged into

the pit of human passions like a second Heracles, he wrote, "to bring back
the fair Alcestis of the world's desire." But in fact it was not Alcestis, "it
was a haggard unlovely woman with features distorted with hatred, greed
and selfishness, and the little Child that the woman carried was scarcely
noticed. Yet it was for the saving of the Child that Wilson had labored
until he was a physical wreck." Wilson, "the apparent failure," wrote
Smuts, had "the undying honor, which will grow with the growing centuries, of having saved 'the little Child that shall lead them yet.' No other
statesman but Wilson could have done it. . . . It was not Wilson who
failed there, but humanity itself."

Although Smuts's article dealt so harshly with the concessions made
by Wilson at Paris in order to get the Covenant adopted, Wilson apparently liked it. At any rate, when I sent him a copy he wrote me on March
9 from his new address at 2430 S Street that Smuts "has certainly been
most generous to me"; and he wrote to Smuts, "I know of no one I have
met whose good opinion I value more than I value yours."

It is sad to have to add for the record that one of the worst disfigure-
ments inflicted on the fair Alcestis was the inclusion of war pensions in
Germany's reparations bill, and that this unwise and unjust action, which
had such disastrous effects, was supported vigorously by Smuts.

III

Gay sometimes brought in lively visitors to change the pace of the editorial dinners, usually devoted to somber subjects like the plight of the
railroads, inter-Allied debts, reparations payments and the collapse of
the German mark. One such was a young romantic named Sir Paul Dukes,
who had gone through amazing adventures in what in the spring of 1921
was the almost unknown land of the Soviets.

Bourgeois newspapermen were still barred from Russia at this time (it
was not till August that Floyd Gibbons was permitted to go to Moscow,
followed by Walter Duranty and a few others), and any flashes of understanding about what really was happening there were eagerly sought.
Dukes had lived in Russia for eleven years, first as a student at the Petro-
grad Conservatoire, then after the Revolution as an agent of British Intelligence, changing his disguises and his fabricated identity papers almost as often as his abode. Astoundingly, he had been able for a long
period to pose as an official of the bloodthirsty Extraordinary Commission ("If you live among wolves, howl like a wolf") and had even served
as a draftee in the Red Army. The Russian terror, he reported, though
abating somewhat, continued; city and country alike were in economic

chaos; and famine was taking an appalling toll. He called the basic weakness in the Bolshevik regime the determination to suppress private enterprise, initiative and all ambition based on hope of gain. The Reds had been saved so far by the fact that the Whites had not understood the lesson of the Revolution; they did not see that three things were finished—autocracy, the big landlords, the military caste. Because of the obtuseness of the Whites the peasants had turned against them, but this did not mean they had become Reds. They were waiting for some outside event to end the Red regime (which even the Bolsheviks were amazed to find lasting so long), fearing that if they revolted they would simply put the feudalistic Whites back onto their necks.

What, we asked, could be that "outside event" to catalyze the new revolution? Before he answered, another guest, Boris Bakhmetev, the Kerensky regime's Ambassador in Washington, intervened to say that he hoped Dukes wasn't going to suggest military action against the Bolsheviks, which, he was sure, would solidify Russian national feeling and perpetuate the Bolsheviks in power. Not at all, said Dukes; instead of attacking Russia we should encourage every sort of intercourse with her. Western restrictions on trade and travel were playing into Lenin's hands by enabling him to keep the world in the dark about real conditions in Russia and the Russian people in the dark about the fallacy of his claim that Communism was spreading rapidly throughout the world. The prevailing veil of mystery was leading us to a whole series of miscalculations. A dialogue at close quarters between the Communist ideology and ours would be the surest way of proving our superiority.

Nearly a half century later this was no longer unpatriotic doctrine; indeed, it had become part of official American policy. But the idea that America could only gain from the widest possible comparison between the results of dictatorship and those of free enterprise continued to be rejected through the Harding, Coolidge and Hoover administrations and was viewed with hostility by Congressional committees and conservative public opinion even after the Roosevelt administration recognized the Soviet Union in November, 1933.

It is interesting retrospectively to note that both Bakhmetev and Dukes prophesied that the Bolshevik system in Russia would fail, though they did not agree as to what would come next. Bakhmetev foresaw the atomization of Russia, followed by the establishment of a federalized republic based on land-owning peasantry. Dukes said he would not be surprised if the Soviet system, at that time suppressed, would be restored, and this, he thought, would be the first step in reform. Russia would evolve, not into capitalism, not into socialism, but into a cooperative society. The ultimate form would be determined by education. "The evolution will not be hastened nor will the result be made better by ostracism by the rest of the world."

Someone who dropped in often at the *Evening Post* with a manuscript in his pocket was Konrad Bercovici, a Rumanian gypsy, in appearance a brigand but in fact mild and easygoing; he spoke a muffled English but wrote it excellently. Many in his native Dobrudja were of Tartar descent, but Bercovici was pure gypsy, with swarthy skin, wavy black hair and heavy brows. He smoked only Gauloises and therefore was not eligible for the Three Hours for Lunch Club; so when he appeared at the office Boyd and I usually took him out to a little Greek restaurant near the Battery. He had been in the country for about ten years, but intended going back to the Dobrudja, there to rejoin his boyhood companions, who had not been so foolish as to change the freedom of their bogs and swamps for the constraints of city life. So long as they kept quietly to themselves on their spongy islets, reached only by flat-bottomed scows poled through a labyrinth of water lanes hidden among overhanging reeds, the Rumanian Government sent nobody to collect taxes or enroll them for military service; and in exchange they were delighted to do without roads or post. He never did return to Rumania, I believe, which was well, for when the Fascist Iron Guard seized power they began liquidating the gypsies, and when the Nazis arrived they pursued them even into the bogs of the Dobrudja and exterminated them as methodically as they did the Jews in the cities.

Bercovici complained that although Rumanian literature was very extensive it was practically unknown abroad, and it was true that when he recited the names of novelists and poets I had never heard of any of them; and even Boyd, who was so widely read, knew only two or three authors who had been translated into French or German. The only Rumanian writer famous abroad, Bercovici said, was Carmen Sylva, "a Rumanian Queen but not a Rumanian, who wrote in Rumanian, but badly." Later he might have listed several additional Rumanian writers who had acquired a European reputation, including the celebrated Comtesse de Noailles and Princess Marthe Bibesco, author of *Catherine-Paris;* but though Rumanians, both lived in Paris and wrote in French.

About this time I came to know Mme. de Noailles's cousin, Prince Antoine Bibesco, who had just come to Washington as Rumanian Minister, a man of considerable cultivation who had been a close friend of Proust's. George D. Painter describes him in his marvelous biography of

Proust as follows: "In 1900 Antoine Bibesco was a virilely handsome young man of twenty-three, with stern, chiseled features, implacable eyes, and a slightly cruel twist to his thin lips." Twenty-some years later, I'd have called his frequently sarcastic tone more bantering than cruel. Proust said, "There's only one person who understands me, and that's Antoine Bibesco"; but in the end Proust found him cruel too, for after pursuing him with unsatisfactory results he decided that Bibesco didn't understand him after all.

In Washington, Antoine Bibesco could hardly have escaped a reputation for frivolity, living as he did in the social maelstrom created by his irrepressible wife, Elizabeth Asquith. "Elizabeth is the brains of the family, and the Queen," he told me. "I am only the Prince Consort." But there was more pride than humility in his tone. Elizabeth, who wore black silk to set off her chalk-white face, was witty and *méchante,* but strained too obviously to prove herself a worthy daughter of scintillating Margot. When she and Alice Longworth competed at a dinner table it was a hardy conversationalist who interposed views of his own. Antoine's background actually was at least as cosmopolitan as Elizabeth's; his mother's salon in Paris was frequented by every celebrity of the time, from Liszt to Renan, to Debussy, and it was there that Mme. de Noailles brought Proust and introduced him to Parisian society.

Once in Bucharest when Antoine came to the station to see me off to Paris on the Orient Express he casually pressed a small package into my hands. I saw it was directed to his bankers in Paris and handed it right back. Balkan diplomats habitually carried banknotes back and forth in quantity, but Antoine was momentarily out of office (for entirely reputable reasons) and needed a courier. He took my refusal good-humoredly. At the frontier my baggage was searched with most unusual care; perhaps a kind friend who knew of Antoine's project had alerted the border guards.

In Paris, the Bibescos had a flat in that unique house that seems to form the prow (really it is the stern) of the Ile St. Louis, where downstream currents of the Seine circle back through a narrow branch along the Quai de l'Hôtel de Ville. Reflections from the ripples of the divided river, filtering through the branches of trees on the embankment, dappled the white walls of the drawing room from three sides and were re-reflected down onto the pale old Spanish rugs on the floor. People spoke of Bibesco as "le Prince des Boulevards." This was unfair; he was much more than a *flâneur.* He was a man of taste, amused by the vagaries of the crowd, and with a serious concern for the erratic policy of his country and often out of sympathy with its practitioners.

IV

Another visitor from the Balkans, very different from Bercovici or Bibesco (or indeed anyone else), was Bishop Nicholai, of the Orthodox See of Ochrida in Serbian Macedonia, one of the most remarkable human beings I have ever known. Rebecca West agreed. He was, she wrote in *Black Lamb and Grey Falcon,* the supreme magician, who had "full knowledge of what comfort men set in magic, and how they long to learn that defeat is not defeat and that love is serviceable." He was still only in his middle forties, with a dark face set with luminous dark eyes, a black beard, a calm very deep voice, not impressive in height, indeed with no pretense at majesty. Yet he had the innate dignity of one of his twelfth-century predecessors depicted in the glorious frescoes in the Cathedral of Svetia Sophia on the shore of Lake Ochrida. It is a remote land, bordering Macedonia and Albania, made for hardy saints.

Unlike a medieval seer, however, Bishop Nicholai did not practice only magic or let his visions fade off into idle contemplation. He had come to America, he said, not to ask for money or relief. He knew that America was generous and humanitarian, cheerful and optimistic, but at a crisis in human history qualities like those were not enough. "Nations die," he said, "from either too much prosperity or too much poverty." He thought America might die of prosperity. "If she does not add introspection and self-examination to giving and acting, prosperity can be her undoing. With prosperity, however, and with a soul to animate it, she can do everything." Were there, he wanted to know, reserves of moral strength in America on which the three old continents could draw?

This was how he described the continents: Africa, emotion, heart; Asia, thought, mind; Europe, will, action. Who would synthesize the three in a trinity of heart, mind and action? Only America could undertake that mission. But he found that instead of making ready for it we were busy with incidentals. We were looking back a hundred years to establish a basis for policy in some negative doctrine devised by a President simply for American self-protection. Or we were finding compensation for having fought a great war by getting possession of an island in the Pacific called Yap. (The papers were full of our dispute with Japan over this island which nobody could find on a map.) In his travels through the country he had seen no signs that America was preparing to come forward with the necessary dual plan: to restore the world's economy and to give it moral and spiritual vitality.

Nicholai's ideas were in such contrast to the isolationism of the day that I asked him to give them a political setting in an article for the *Evening Post*. This I then expanded on the basis of long talks with him, printed as a small pamphlet and of this distributed about a thousand copies. Europe, he wrote, was waiting in anxiety to see what substitute the new Harding Administration would offer the world for the League of Nations, which it had rejected. In his words: "There remains at present only one organized system, living and working by day and night for its ends, and that is Communism. At the moment the chief propaganda argument of the Communists is that they are the only peacemakers, the only idealists, the only real workers, the only ones who are willing to go to all lengths in order not to see the world drift back to its old standards and habits." He asked: "What to do in this situation? If the League of Nations is not acceptable, what is acceptable?"

After fifty years his proposal sounds very modern:

Why not found a World Construction Committee, in the formation of which America shall take a leading part, but which two or three of the other most rich and powerful nations should also be asked to support, each setting aside for that purpose a certain fraction of its present war budgets? . . . Let this committee send out (as America has herself sent out, though on an inadequate scale in view of the immense undertaking), engineers and doctors and financiers and builders to bring water to lands where no water is, to bring health to lands ravaged by disease, to bring financial order to lands disorganized and impoverished, to build up where all has been torn down, or where nothing worth building has ever been built. There is hardly a part of the world but has been exploited and crippled and is now reaching a stage of desperation and chronic dissatisfaction—Poland, Albania, Calabria, Armenia, China, Russia, Austria, Persia, Ireland, Senegal, Palestine and the Congo, to mention just the first that come to mind. Turn the best thought of the world to the task of curing these festering sore spots, turn its best energies for once to something positive and constructive and practical.

Americans did give on a stupendous scale after the First World War to fight famine and disease, in Belgium, in Central Europe and in Russia. The undertaking was independently American, suiting the political aloofness of the Harding Administration. Only after the Second War would the United States see the political and humanitarian reasons for planning reconstruction and development more broadly, first with the proposal for a continentwide Marshall Plan, which Western Europe seized on to restore its economy and save itself from Communism, later with the worldwide Foreign Aid Program and, in Latin America, the Alliance for Progress. Other nations set up aid programs in underdeveloped countries, and the U.N. Special Fund and the Colombo Plan represented modest cooperative beginnings. But an integrated international development program, jointly planned, financed and directed, still remains to be attempted on the scale proposed by the Bishop from remote Ochrida in 1921.

Before sailing for home on the *Adriatic*, Bishop Nicholai attended a ceremony in the Cathedral of St. John the Divine at which Dr. William T. Manning was consecrated Bishop of the Protestant Episcopal diocese of New York. A discussion ensued in the press as to whether Nicholai had participated in the ceremony of the laying on of hands. The implication would have been that the Orthodox Church recognized the validity of Anglican orders, "thereby ending," as the New York *World* wrote optimistically, "a centuries-old problem." A day or so later I witnessed a curious scene which seemed to settle the matter. I had gone to say good-bye to Bishop Nicholai at the Hotel Majestic, where he was staying, and found with him Bishop Manning and Charles C. Burlingham, a leading lawyer and churchman.

Bishop Manning asked Nicholai directly: "Did you actually take part in the laying on of hands?"

"No," Nicholai answered, "I did not."

Later, when Manning was leaving, Nicholai accompanied him out into the corridor. Burlingham had gone ahead. As I came through the doorway, I saw Bishop Manning kneel down quickly, high hat in one hand, on the carpet of the corridor. Bishop Nicholai then placed his hand on Manning's bare head and blessed him.

We kept in touch through passing years. A letter of mine reaching him one February in his "wilderness" had come, he said, "like a spring bird." You ask me, he wrote, about "our ragged continent." "There are new situations—not new situations of man to God but of man to man. It is like throngs of people in the gallery of a theatre: nobody is satisfied with his place, everybody is pushing and pulling to make his own seat more comfortable. Meanwhile the play on the stage is over—death comes, and the fools tumble down from their seats without having seen the play of life at all."

V

I can't resist mentioning one more of the *Evening Post* dinners, even though the discussion there was of events now remote. It was on June 7,

1921, and Thomas W. Lamont, just back from Europe, told us of the negotiations which had been going on between Lloyd George and Briand on German reparations and the threat that if there was default France would move deeper into the Rhineland. At this distance, the reparations story is boring. Yet then the question whether Germany would pay, and what the Allies should do if she did not, was a burning one; and eventually, of course, the French occupation of the Ruhr as a sanction for German nonfulfillment figured prominently in the story which Hitler used to stimulate German demands for revenge, and thus affected the lives of us all.

Lamont was hopeful that an immediate crisis had been staved off by a compromise according to which Germany was to pay 132 billion gold marks, the first billion to be raised by German borrowing in London. He was pleased to think that he had exerted a moderating influence on both sides; Americans, he remarked, understood the French better than the British did, and the British better than did the French. He told us that Dwight Morrow, one of his partners, had written him to urge Briand to make up with Lloyd George. "As a starter," he wrote, "tell him, the next time they meet, to kiss Lloyd George on both cheeks in true Gallic fashion." When Lamont passed along this advice, Briand replied: "I've always wanted Lloyd George to kiss *me* on both cheeks"; and his accompanying gesture, Lamont said, "indicated the exact anatomical cheeks he had in mind."

One day in July, 1921, Boyd said that if I wanted to see what an authentic Irish rebel was like I should come to lunch with him and Osmond Grattan Esmonde, whose experiences as Sinn Fein "chargé d'affaires" in Washington had been noted copiously in the newspapers and whose subsequent adventures in Australia and Canada had not been neglected either. Boyd watched with amusement my badly concealed surprise when he introduced Esmonde, who wore a monocle, carried a stick, spoke like an Englishman and dressed like one. These had been sufficient reasons to make him totally unacceptable to Irish-American Sinn Feiners, despite the fact that he was a rabid Republican and had been repudiated by his father, a well-known Irish Unionist M.P. From Washington he had been dispatched to Australia, where he found that the authorities, like all colonial authorities, were more vigorous than those at home in prosecuting sedition. For three months they held him on a ship in Sydney harbor. On Sundays, however, he was allowed on shore to attend Mass, after which he would be surrounded and cheered by the Irish-Australian population and then entertained at lunch at the mansion of one or another Irish sympathizer. He described it as a most rewarding experience. Weekdays he spent in reading history and biography, and in the evening he watched the water fetes arranged by partisans to keep him from being bored.

After three months Esmonde was allowed to start back via Canada for England, where he expected to have no trouble being admitted in view of the truce just negotiated between Lloyd George and Eamon de Valera. But at Vancouver he was mobbed by rival bands of friends and foes, put in jail by the mayor, bailed out, showered with presents and brickbats and allowed to proceed to Montreal. There the mayor, a French Canadian, gave a public reception in his honor. He applied at the U.S. Consulate for a visa to go to New York to take ship, but was refused. He had come anyway, slipping across the border without difficulty, and was in the city without the knowledge of the authorities. He nevertheless didn't seem worried about appearing in public, made no attempt at disguise and was very evidently, not to say spectacularly, himself. He expected to sail in a day or so, before anyone was the wiser; and did.

Sometimes Canby handed me a book which it was a delight to review, either because it could be praised sincerely or "given the works." I soon saw which it would be in the case of a new edition of *The Balkans, Laboratory of History,* just brought out by an eminent historian, Professor William Milligan Sloane, Seth Low Professor of History at Columbia University. I remembered the original edition, published just before the war, and turned back to it now to find the place where he dismissed contemptuously the Serbian hope of becoming the Piedmont of a unified Jugoslav state. "This is the land," he had written, "which by reason of its name and language aspires to leadership and control in the creation of Greater Servia. The passion for this ideal among all Serbo-Croats is a species of imperial insanity. The Servians of little Servia expound it in their newspapers, set it forth in their schoolbooks, nourishing their young on wind; it is the stock in trade of the demagogue, the theme of the rhymer, the subject of baby talk and cradle song."

Professor Sloane had not been fortunate in his timing, for hardly had his book been published in the spring of 1914 than the Serbs had the occasion to prove whether their national aspirations were something to die for or just to sing about. Five years later, when the Serbian cavalry rode back into Belgrade it was plain which had shown "imperial insanity"—little Serbia or the ancient House of Hapsburg.

I looked into the new edition of Professor Sloane's book to see how he had adjusted to this unforeseen situation. He had done so by ignoring it. The whole face of the Balkans had been transformed; most conspicuously, the Serbs and the Croats had formed a national state. But, though history had overruled him, Professor Sloane refused to admit it. The sentences quoted above remained unchanged. He did admit that there had been a war; for example, although he did not alter the body of his text, he had substituted certain new terms for certain old ones—"Jugo-Slavia" for "Austria-Hungary," "the Italian people" for "the Dual Monarchy" and "the settlement made at Versailles" for "the settlement made at Bucharest." It was a fascinating example of how to keep up with history without too much trouble and with almost no expense, for as the substituted words were carefully chosen to be the same length as the originals, the publisher did not have to pay for resetting more than a single line of type—never mind that the result made nonsense. The cruelest thing I could think of was to print excerpts from the two editions in parallel columns.

9

"Traitors" Caillaux and Malvy

The excitement of working for a daily paper had not palled, but I was delighted when Dr. Gay assigned me to cover the Institute of Politics, which President Garfield of Williams College had organized to meet in Williamstown the last week in July. This 1921 session was the first of what became, for several years, an annual assemblage of foreign and American statesmen and scholars to discuss international problems in lectures and small groups. The *Evening Post,* always ready to support countermoves to the prevalent isolationist tide, decided to give the Institute wider coverage than the wire agencies would provide.

A day or two before starting I was called up by Roland Bryce, who had been in the British Legation in Belgrade while I was there. He had arrived with his uncle, Lord Bryce, to attend the Institute, and I at once offered to drive him up to Williamstown. It was the renewal of a friendship and the beginning of a friendship with his uncle, or perhaps discipleship would better describe the feeling I had at my age for a man of eighty-three who, in the words of the *Encyclopaedia Britannica,* "had been everywhere, known everybody and read everything." This was particularly true of his relationship to the United States. He had first landed on American soil fifty-one years earlier; for six years he had been British Ambassador at Washington, by common consent the best ever; and he was the author of the classic *The American Commonwealth.* His interests, however, were not limited to politics, law and diplomacy but were as boundless as his energy in pursuing them was inexhaustible. As I drove him and Lady Bryce about the roads near Williamstown, he knew the name of every wildflower, and when he didn't recognize one from the car he asked me to stop and hopped out to examine it. He was amazed to find a rose pink on the edge of a meadow; it was not supposed to occur as far north as Massachusetts.

Whiskers and beard spread so profusely across Lord Bryce's face that little remained to be seen except the nose and the meditative but quickly alerted eyes, peering out under shaggy eyebrows. The impression was of a benign but observant schnauzer. As to "having been every-where," I asked him once when he was talking about the Far East whether he had missed any country there. Yes, he said quickly, Sumatra; "and I'm particularly sorry, as the horned roofs of the Batak houses are said to be most beautiful." Nor had he been to Tibet or Mongolia. In Iceland he had spent most of a winter when he and his traveling companion, the bursar of Brasenose College, had missed the last ship. They used the long nights to learn Icelandic—"very useful," he commented firmly.

Lord Bryce's public addresses attracted large audiences and were re-ported in papers throughout the country, but not usually at the length allowed me by the *Evening Post*. In the first he criticized the Paris Peace Conference severely. Metternich and Talleyrand might have had bad principles and employed despotic methods, but at least they knew what they were doing and their peace lasted more than thirty years. By com-parison, "there is not one of the treaties of 1919–1920 which is not already admitted to need amendment, while some are seen to lead straight to future wars." He agreed that the statesmen at Paris faced tasks of un-precedented difficulty, but thought they had often revealed their in-adequacy and inability to rise above domestic political considerations. "There is no saying more false," he remarked sadly, "than that 'the hour brings the man.' "

Bryce acknowledged that the Peace Conference had avoided some pitfalls, for example giving the Rhineland to France, an error which would have matched Germany's annexation of Alsace-Lorraine in 1871. Most of his specific criticisms centered on the treaties with Austria, Hungary and Bulgaria, with which he coupled an attack on "the extra-ordinarily lenient" treatment accorded the Turks. In his opinion, the Peace Conference should have ordered plebiscites in disputed territories rather than attempting to make awards on the basis of historical, ethnic, strategic and economic factors. Members of the Institute who had been at Paris, most of them from various university faculties, were of the unanimous opinion that to have postponed decisions would have brought chaos, new wars and Communism in Central Europe.

Among these was Archibald Cary Coolidge, professor of history at Harvard. One afternoon when I drove him to Bennington he went over Bryce's arguments pro and con. He felt that Wilson had been entirely right on Dalmatia and Fiume, but that he had not realized how much his acceptance of the Brenner line in the Tyrol violated the principle of nationality. In that matter he had been misled by a "commentary" prepared by Colonel House's Inquiry on how the Fourteen Points should be interpreted in action, and might also have been influenced by the thought that if he had to give way to the Italians on some point it was better to do so in the Tyrol than on the Adriatic. Having been chief of the American mission in Vienna, Coolidge had followed the discussion of the Austrian and Hungarian treaties closely. There was some ground for Bryce's criticism of the Austrian settlement, he thought, but his attack on the terms imposed on Hungary was less valid. In any case it was an error to suppose that the Peace Conference could have avoided liberating the ethnic minorities; the Empire had gone to pieces from its own intrinsic weakness; Austria and Hungary themselves had split apart. The Allies had faced a situation over which as a whole they could exert little control. They simply tried to put the new frontiers in the "least wrong" places—least wrong, because there was no absolute right in weighing the conflicting factors involved. "The ideal state does not and cannot exist in Central Europe."

Coolidge talked interestingly about the strange impression made on him by General Smuts at the time of his famous journey to meet Béla Kun in Budapest. Coolidge had traveled with him from Paris as far as Vienna, and during all this time Smuts either concealed or did not himself know precisely what he was after, and he avoided asking questions which might reveal he was in need of information. I asked whether it was true, as we had heard rumored in Belgrade, that the Allies thought of allowing Béla Kun to send representatives to Switzerland to discuss a compromise. Coolidge said the proposal was quite specific, though the discussion was to have taken place in Paris itself. The first Coolidge heard of the plan was from Alizé, the French representative in Vienna, who showed him and Cunningham, the British representative, orders to communicate directly with Béla Kun and propose a meeting. Both Coolidge and Cunningham were thunderstruck, for they were convinced Béla Kun was tottering. They persuaded Alizé to delay a day while they communicated with Paris. Meanwhile Cunningham's assistant would go to Budapest and, unless he received counterorders, give Béla Kun the invitation. Cunningham, who knew Balfour personally, got busy, and so did

Coolidge, and the order not to approach Béla Kun reached Budapest just two hours before the time limit expired. The face of Central Europe would have been very different if the Allies had saved Béla Kun and gone on to recognize his Communist government.

At breakfast one morning Coolidge to my surprise asked me to come to his round table that afternoon and talk about Jugoslavia, especially the provisions of the new constitution and the roles of the various parties. So many of the group knew Central European problems at first hand that I felt very much on the spot, especially as I was to cover the subject in half an hour and had no time to make real preparation. I would have been more jittery if I had known that (as was shortly to appear) my performance was to have lifelong consequences.

In self-protection Lord Bryce had made a rule against giving interviews, but found himself in trouble after mentioning in a lecture that he considered President Masaryk one of the three really great men to come forward during the war. Everyone immediately began speculating as to the other two. Baron Sergius Korff, one of the lecturers, remarked that he hated Lenin with all his heart, but was there anyone greater in the world today? Other answers ran from Wilson to Keynes and from Foch to Eugene Debs. Then Lord Bryce ended the debate as far as he was concerned: Venizelos was one, Smuts the other. It was noticed that no Englishman, Frenchman or American had deserved his accolade. Apparently the direct and chiefest protagonists in the greatest conflict in history had been too busy waging war and making peace to find time to develop the moral quality required for true greatness; for Bryce made clear that this was his standard of judgment.

You never knew what direction talk with Lord Bryce might take. On our drives around the Berkshires it naturally turned often to Ireland, about which he was terribly concerned. He had watched with abhorrence the burnings and murders by the Irish Republican Army and the savage reprisals by the Black and Tans. He had no use at all for Lloyd George, and viewed his negotiations with de Valera with suspicion. Perhaps, I suggested, Lloyd George was thinking of coming to the Washington Naval Conference in the fall and pulling off some coup to restore his diminished prestige; if so, he must realize the necessity of moving first to end the fighting in Ireland or he would be hounded and perhaps assassinated by Irish-American fanatics. To Bryce this explanation was unnecessarily complex. "He acts by what he thinks is expedient. England has been slowly waking up to the true situation in Ireland, and public pressure for a settlement has been growing stronger and stronger. The urge to make a popular move has convinced him to do what logic and morals could not make him do."

After the Institute was over I happened to see Lord Bryce at Northeast Harbor in Maine, where he was staying with his long-time friend ex-President Eliot of Harvard. He resumed the same line of thought about Ireland when I showed him an interesting letter which I had received from Sir Horace Plunkett, a close friend of my father-in-law, James Byrne. Plunkett was optimistic about the Lloyd George–de Valera negotiations "because neither could afford to shoulder the onus of resuming out-and-out war." Lloyd George, he said, had fled before the wrath of the Irish people. Bryce agreed as to the flight but not as to the cause. "He did not flee before the wrath of the Irish, but because he felt the ground swell of an awakened English public conscience. It was the warning of a great storm, which would have swept away the Coalition Government."

While he was in America, Lord Bryce was on the lookout for facts and opinions that might help him with a revision of his latest book, *Modern Democracies*. It was his belief that the judiciary in the United States, apart from the Federal bench, was inferior, and that this was because in many states judges were chosen by popular election instead of executive appointment. The result was the election of second raters who had toadied to the public. He considered this an innate weakness in the democratic system. I mentioned that I thought Mr. Byrne, who was president of the New York Bar Association, would disagree, and when he said how much he would like to talk out this "surprising point of view" I asked them both to my house in New York, along with Gay and Strunsky. Mr. Byrne admitted that the public could be wrongly influenced in choosing state and municipal judges, but he considered the political deals which often dominate a governor's or mayor's appointments more insidious and likely to lead to more serious abuses. He compared the judges in New York State, who were elected, with those in Massachusetts, for example, where they were appointed. "I'd greatly prefer to argue a case with political or partisan overtones before the Supreme or Appelate Court in New York than similar courts in Massachusetts," he said. "I'd feel safer that they would not be swayed from giving judgment solely on the law and the evidence." How much this discussion affected Bryce's opinion I don't know, though at the time it seemed to; for the revision of *Modern Democracies* was never made.

He and Lady Bryce were planning a trip to Rome in the spring to do more research on a long-planned life of Justinian. Lady Bryce said when

I urged that he write his memoirs: "That must come later. He is too busy now." But he was an octogenarian, and even in the three months which he spent in America he became visibly older. He tried to keep up his optimism in spite of the world's refusal to learn the lessons of the war. His hope for the future centered on a close Anglo-American accord, without which war would come again and civilization in so far as it derived from Europe would slowly fall apart. He sailed for home in October, spoke in the House of Lords in favor of the Irish treaty in December and died in January.

II

That autumn of 1921 I had to tell Gay that I must break off my work at the *Evening Post* and take my wife for a rest in Europe, preferably, the doctors said, somewhere with a soft and relaxing climate—and the fewer diversions the better. Pau, in the foothills of the Pyrenees, turned out to fit these requirements only too well. To lessen my pangs, Gay commissioned me to write foreign correspondence for the paper whenever opportunities occurred, and I at once went down to Washington to get visas and letters of introduction, especially for use in France and in Eastern Europe, where we hoped that by spring we would be able to travel.

Washington was charged with excitement over the largest international conference ever to assemble there, summoned by President Harding in an effort to head off an incipient naval arms race between the victor powers in the war.

The head of the British delegation, Arthur J. Balfour, had consented, though most reluctantly, to something which I believe no top British statesman had ever submitted to before, namely to cross-questioning by the assembled correspondents. Fifty or more of them crowded into the dining room of the old British Embassy to interview him, and thanks to Mark Sullivan I was among them. From one wall King George, rather idealized as to figure and bearing, looked down in flowing coronation robes from his throne; over the mantel was a small picture of Victoria as a girl. Balfour came in warily, hands clasped behind his back, peering about in a rather aloof manner, preceded by Geddes, the Ambassador, and followed by a tall, spare, lantern-jawed gentleman, Lord Riddell, owner of the mass-circulation *News of the World* and one of the directors of British publicity. Balfour sat down as directed at the far side of the dining table, drawn to the end of the big room, but soon moved around in front, murmuring something disarming about age and deafness.

At once it became evident what an advantage Balfour's gentlemanliness and distinguished bearing gave him over his questioners, who found it hard to press anyone so courteous but remote. To this advantage Balfour added every benefit that could be exacted from hardness of hearing; whenever the question was indiscreet his deafness at once became several degrees more acute, and in the respite while the questioner was repeating his query you could sense his brain whizzing around, devising a diplomatic answer, while his face maintained a politely mystified look.

David Lawrence, for instance, asked in a smooth voice whether England was prepared to abandon the Anglo-Japanese alliance if pressed by the United States. Nothing could have been more provocative, for although the Four Power Pacific Treaty signed at the end of the conference did in fact accomplish this, the alliance (which caused much hard feeling in the United States, as well, of course, as with the Chinese) was currently the subject of intensive bargaining. Mr. Balfour—Lawrence called him Lord Balfour, either by intuitive foresight or out of respect for his dignified appearance—was at once struck by an attack of deafness which could not be relieved for some time. Eventually, however, after cupping his ear to a repetition of the question, he replied meaninglessly that he was in general in favor of any agreement broad enough to be acceptable to everyone.

Someone then asked about the Chinese demand for the removal of special privileges for foreigners in China. Balfour replied that on many Chinese requests he could, of course, look with favor, as for instance the Open Door, "a traditional British policy." Thereupon a small Japanese popped up and asked what the Open Door meant, and amidst laughter Balfour admitted, without changing his serious expression, that for years statesmen had been trying to define it—which led nowhere, as Balfour of course intended.

The correspondent of the London *Daily News,* an opposition paper, asked about reduction of land forces, on which the sea-minded British disagreed with the land-minded French, and elicited the reply that neither the United States nor Britain was likely to take the initiative on this question—though he personally thought it vital for Europe's future— since the arms of each were already at a minimum. "Of course you must remember," he added, "that the British Empire is a very big place. I don't know how many troops it has, but I can assure you it is a minimum, which is very few for an Empire of—let me see—I seem to have forgotten how many inhabitants we do have." "About 400 million," prompted Geddes. "About 400 million," echoed Balfour, bringing down the house.

At the end, Lord Riddell jumped up and said how good it was of Mr. Balfour to meet the press on this unusual occasion, but his figurative "Three cheers for the British" didn't warm the atmosphere; Mr. Balfour had won each round but lost the match.

The French press nevertheless attributed the pressure which France was under throughout the conference to British guile. Thus the *Journal des Débats* asserted that American statesmen, reporters and society in general had been taken into camp by the polished manners, easy conversation and good dress of the British delegation. (It failed to mention the language barrier which walled off the French delegates, not one of whom spoke English.)

By the three measurements of the French newspapers Aristide Briand, the French Premier, did not indeed score high points. He was on the *Paris* when my wife and I crossed to Le Havre ten days later, and whether walking the deck during the voyage, or as I often watched him later in the Chambre des Députés, his figure was slouched, his leonine head thrust forward between bent shoulders, his clothes rumpled, his neck sunk in a standing collar, his face, flushed a dark red, draped with a scraggly mustache, and with a cigarette dangling from his lower lip. On shipboard, a little visored yachting cap did not add to the dignity of his appearance. But (as the world came to know) Briand was a highly impressive orator, and his single-minded pursuit of peace by any and every means, realistic or visionary, made him a dominant figure at Geneva.

As the *Paris* came into Havre, Briand gave me my first opportunity to send home a dispatch as a foreign correspondent. He promised that France would do as much in reducing land forces as the primarily naval nations would do in limiting sea forces; rebuked Lord Curzon, the British Foreign Secretary, for alleging that French policy was militaristic; and said that France would not permit the German Government to evade reparations payments simply by pretending that it could not control the German people or by the expedient of devaluing the mark. My story was not properly skeletonized and was received most unkindly at the *Evening Post*. In the process of computing how much could have been saved if it had been written in careful "cablese," the city room delayed it, cut it and finally printed it on an inside page. Puckette, the managing editor, happened to be away from the office, and the next day wrote me the humiliating details. An experienced hand, he said, could have saved about $25, not an inconsiderable sum for a paper in straitened circumstances (the announcement of its sale by Lamont to a syndicate came, in fact, within a month). But he added, "As a matter of fact, I think the message was frightfully mishandled in the office. It was an important dispatch and should have been played up for all it was worth as a message to the American people through the *Evening Post.*" It was a mortifying experience.

Anglo-French amity was in those days at a low ebb; the common denominator of press comments in the two countries seemed to be mutual mistrust and recrimination. François Goguel put the reasons succinctly in his book on the political parties in the Third Republic: Germany had announced that she could not continue paying reparations because of the continuing fall of the mark; France thought Germany was depressing the mark deliberately in order to have an excuse not to pay; Britain thought that reparations were an economic mistake and were responsible not only for Germany's financial difficulties but for the whole European economic crisis. French anger on economic grounds was multiplied by resentment at the British and American pressure for a schedule of naval disarmament felt to be discriminatory against France. *Avenir* was moved to write a sentence which might have been uttered years later by General de Gaulle: "We are not willing to have our security depend on any other nation, whether friend or ally."

It was to cope with these mounting discontents that Briand had hurried home. He did not cope successfully. In January, Lloyd George linked reparations to the problem of French security by offering Briand a British guarantee in return for an agreement to discuss how to end the economic crisis in Europe. The French public did not consider continued German payments and security against future German attack as alternatives. The mere idea that Briand might be led into discussing Lloyd George's proposition gave French intransigents, led by President Millerand, an opportunity to overthrow him. Poincaré came to power as Premier with the avowed intention, "Make Germany Pay."

Two months later, on a visit to Paris, I found Briand in a much more relaxed frame of mind than he had been on the *Paris.* He said it would be out of place for him, now out of office, to give an interview, then added a "but" which proved to cover quite a lot of territory. He was delighted that the United States had just ratified the Four Power Pact negotiated at Washington and was sure France would now do the same, and without grave reservations. What was important for France was that her signature was now on a treaty alongside the signatures of other great powers guaranteeing peace in one part of the world. He advocated, he said, a similar treaty among the European nations. In an early version of what has become known as Atlantic Union, he thought the two groups might then unite in a pact to promote world peace.

III

To give us an idea of the countryside around Pau, Ernest Boyd had sent us a book by Francis Jammes, *Le Curé d'Ozeron*. Jammes had lived at Orthez, some twenty-five miles away, and drew his scenes of everyday provincial life from the valley of the Gave de Pau. Boyd also recommended that in Paris we get the *Propos d'Anatole France*, edited by Paul Gsell, a record of the period before the war when Anatole France opened his house to visitors every Sunday morning. "It will remind you what good talk can be," he wrote me, "and act as an antidote to your orgy of oratory at Williamstown."

Pau had been the residence of the Kings of Navarre, but the castle where Henry IX was born is too heavily restored to have much character. The country round about is pleasant and the climate what Baedeker describes as salubrious even in winter. A coterie of retired English and Americans provided a mild social life; the fact that the weekly hunt meet was the chief feature shows the style. On Christmas Eve we went to midnight mass with French friends, who afterward invited us to a magnificent supper of roast goose accompanied by something I never saw before or since—truffles, a *spécialité* of the region, cooked whole in brown sauce and served as a vegetable. We motored in all directions—to Cauterets and Luchon in the Pyrenees, where hotels were closed but surprised innkeepers were able to provide a bed and *truites au bleu,* caught for us promptly in the swift cold streams; across the fertile plains of Bigorre to Tarbes, and beyond to the village of St. Gaudens, where I liked to imagine that the family of my father's friend Augustus St. Gaudens had originated before migrating to Ireland and then America; and to the ancient cathedral of St.-Bertrand-de-Comminges, on a great rock rising abruptly from the plain, certainly one of the most splendid spots in France.

To vary this uneventful existence I went two or three times in pursuit of news stories to Paris and once to Toulouse, the seat of the famous and powerful *Dépêche de Toulouse,* edited by the Sarraut brothers, to one of whom I had a letter. They were said to control the votes of forty deputies. Maurice Sarraut's talk, and that of his editors, was antimilitarist, anticlerical, antiroyalist.

With the Spanish border so near, I also decided to try to see one of the most controversial figures in French politics, Louis-Jean Malvy, Minister of the Interior during the first three years of the war, now living in exile on the Basque Coast—in summer at Passajes, in winter at San Sebastián. He had been forced from office by Clemenceau, who attacked him for laxity in dealing with defeatist agitators; then was accused of treason by Léon Daudet, venomous reactionary and royalist; and finally was tried for treason by the Senate, sitting as a High Court. Though acquitted on that charge he was found guilty of culpable lenience toward subversive trade-union elements and sentenced to exile from the country for five years. His name was often bracketed with that of Joseph Caillaux, a more important and spectacular figure, former Prime Minister and Minister of Finance, charged in 1918 with negotiating with the enemy and later sentenced by the High Court to loss of civil rights for ten years and to five years' banishment from the capital. I determined to interview both Malvy and Caillaux.

Malvy welcomed the diversion of receiving a visitor. His furnished rooms at San Sebastián did not exhibit signs of the wealth which Léon Daudet and other enemies accused him of having amassed in office. On the walls of his little parlor, papered in a faded Japanesque design, hung gilt-framed pictures of dead fish and sliced melons; here and there on tables stood the painted shells mounted on plush familiar in seaside lodgings the world over. Desk and tables were heaped with correspondence, papers and books, among them Caillaux's *Mes Prisons,* a companion to Malvy's own *Mon Crime.* He came in carrying *Humanité, L'Oeuvre* and other Paris newspapers just arrived by the Sud Express. In appearance he was younger than I had expected, slight and wiry, with heavy prominent eyes, a dark mustache and a high forehead sloping back to wavy dark hair. He made rather too much effort to be agreeable.

It became plain at once that Malvy expected to stage a political comeback as soon as his exile was over. "I was accused," he said, "of the most terrible crime—selling my country. I will dispose of that accusation and show it was simply the product of party politics. Clemenceau made it seem I stood in the way of winning the war, when all I stood in the way of was his political progress. Today the psychology of France is very different from what it was at the height of the war fever. Facts count more, oratory and sentiment less." It sounded overconfident, but I recalled that Anatole France had said: "The *affaire Malvy* was a judicial monstrosity; it would be impious to doubt that someday we shall right it." In his favor was the strange fact that exile did not in his case carry the usual loss of civil rights. Technically he could have been reelected to the Chamber of Deputies even while in exile.

At the time of my visit, however, the Left had just suffered the setback which ousted Briand and brought in Poincaré as Premier. Malvy criticized Briand for never being willing to settle down as chief of one party, for being obsessed with ideas of deals, devices and coalitions.

"Caillaux and I are different," said Malvy. "We are openly party men. We will fight for our party program."

I asked how Caillaux (who unlike Malvy had lost his civil rights) could resume political life before the end of his ten-year term of political ostracism. Because, he replied, changes in French psychology would soon require that Caillaux's conviction be wiped off the slate. "France is headed toward liberalism and democracy. Poincaré's ministry is merely an interlude."

How would the new leftist majority deal with France's two principal foreign problems—relations with England and Germany? Malvy considered an understanding with England essential, although not a special alliance.

"With Germany too?" I asked.

"Why not?" Malvy replied sharply, showing his first defensiveness. "Our place on the globe is alongside Germany, as it was yesterday and will be tomorrow. Mutual concessions would have avoided wars in the past. A policy of good will can avoid them in the future."

Malvy was right about the formation of a wide grouping of the Left. The success of the Cartel des Gauches in 1924 forced Millerand to abandon his attempt to assert the President's right to dissolve the Chamber and led to his resignation. He was wrong, but only partly so, about Briand. Briand became Foreign Minister in the spring of 1925, and after his success in negotiating the Locarno agreements became Premier that autumn. But after reconstructing his ministry twice, the second time with Caillaux as Minister of Finance, he found the continuing financial crisis too formidable for him to master. He again became Minister of Foreign Affairs under Poincaré in the summer of 1926 and from that position continued to direct French foreign policy for the next five years, preeminent at Geneva, joint author of the Kellogg-Briand Pact for the renunciation of war, winner of the Nobel Prize for peace.

Malvy himself was reelected to the Chamber in the same crucial elections of 1924, and two years later Briand appointed him to his old post as Minister of the Interior; but outcries arose and he resigned in order to save Briand embarrassment. He remained in the Chamber for many years, however, almost but not quite clear of the wartime shadows on his character. I remember him as a small man.

I V

Joseph Caillaux, in contrast, was a figure of undoubted stature. Finance Minister for the first time at the age of thirty-six, and several times afterward, Premier at forty-eight, he was at one period perhaps the most powerful political personage in France, at another one of the most execrated. He was Premier during the Agadir crisis in 1911 and handled it with skill; but to avoid risking war and to secure France's position in Morocco he ceded a strip of the French Congo to Germany. From that time on he was known as a "negotiator," which his nationalist enemies translated into "appeaser." Early in the war he let it be known that he doubted an Allied victory and favored a negotiated peace. He was arrested January 14, 1918, accused of dealings with enemy agents, found guilty of something less than treason, namely "damage to the security of the state," and sentenced to exile from the capital. Hatred against him rose so high that for several years he was unable to move about the country without being hissed, run out of restaurants and sometimes, with his wife, physically attacked. Everything he did was sensational, often theatrical. His fiscal intelligence and independence ran counter both to the shibboleths of his own leftist supporters and to what the bankers and industrialists presumed, wrongly, were their special interests.

His marriages were spectacular. His second wife, deciding to revenge the scurrilous attacks being made on him by Gaston Calmette, editor of *Le Figaro,* and to prevent the publication of her love letters written to Caillaux before their marriage, which wife number one had stolen, went to Calmette's office and shot and killed him. The trial was a worldwide sensation. All the great of French political life were involved, one way or another, some as witnesses, and the scenes leading up to Mme. Caillaux's acquittal were wild.

The date, July 28, 1914, made it significant in a more sober sense. On that day Austria declared war on Serbia, four days later France was mobilizing and two days after that Germany declared war. The trial intensified the divisions that afflicted France throughout the conflict (or at least until Clemenceau established iron order in November, 1917). Caillaux had resigned at the time of the assassination and was not in a position to influence events in the crucial days while peace hung in the balance; he was outside the "Union sacrée" proclaimed by Poincaré; and he continued an outsider, rebellious, a known dissenter, labeled a defeatist, even believed to be meditating a *coup d'état* at a time when French military fortunes were at their lowest.

As Malvy predicted, the Chamber of Deputies abrogated Caillaux's sentence as of January, 1925. Until then he lived at Mamers, the market town in the Sarthe from which he had been elected deputy as early as 1898. I went there to see him about three months after visiting Malvy at San Sebastián.

An instructive prelude to this visit was a scene of wild disorder in the Chamber of Deputies at which I happened to be present. By chance Caillaux's name came into the debate. At once there was an uproar. Léon Daudet sprang to his feet in a paroxysm of rage, denouncing democratic and pacifist traitors, then switching to a eulogy of the royalists who would be governing France were it not for the illegal powers seized by the republican *vaches* now squandering the Bourbon heritage and sacrificing the nation on the altar of their animal ambition. The Communist deputies snarled back, banged the covers of their desks like spoiled children with a new governess and shouted obscene epithets. The glass dome quivered; M. Peret, the presiding officer, shot out his hands ineffectually this way and that in a pleading gesture; the monitory bell was rung, and rung again, without effect; and just when the opposing deputies were picking up inkwells and taking aim, M. Peret in despair seized his silk hat and made in pantomime as though to put it on. At once the catcalls sank to mutters and all resumed their seats; for if that hat had actually landed on M. Peret's head the session would have been over and everybody would have had to stop talking and go home, at which prospect quiet was restored.

With this mad scene in mind, I took an express to Le Mans, the capital of the Department of the Sarthe, there changed to a little train which, like one described by Proust on the way to Balbec, meandered in a leisurely manner among well-cultivated fields between stops at every wayside village.

Mamers did not look like a center of conspiratorial or indeed any sort of activity; one understood at once why direct connections with the capital were considered unnecessary. In former times it had been an important place, the winter headquarters of the provincial aristocracy, and some grand houses remained. But while most of them had been changed into shops and bistros, Caillaux had maintained his family house and made it a charming place, the high-ceilinged rooms filled with fine old furniture, and behind it a garden now in May in full bloom. His study in the front part of the house had once been used as a dining room, and Caillaux told me that in the adjoining small alcove someone used to sit during meals and read aloud to the family. This niche was now filled with a great gilt lectern in the shape of an eagle with spread wings.

"It is ancient," he said, "and very valuable, from a church in a neighboring village."

Imprudently, I laughed and asked if it was one of the churches which as an anticlerical he had had a hand in disestablishing. He was annoyed, and after explaining that it was the gift of an old and dear friend, an abbé, he took me to the foot of the stairs to show me a statue of Saint Joseph, which, he assured me, he carried with him wherever he happened to be living. "He is my patron saint," he repeated several times. (A few months later, in a letter discussing an article of mine which indicated that his attitude to the Church had not always been benevolent, he added a postscript: "Why the devil do you present me as a persecutor of religion?" He even had broken for a time with his party, he said, by voting against unnecessarily harsh measures to restrict the religious congregations.)

Caillaux's features and his habitual monocle, spats and stick were as familiar to the French at that time as Teddy Roosevelt's spectacles and grinning teeth had been to Americans. The most prominent thing about him was his shining bald head, which when he became excited flushed a bright red. Eagle eyes flanked his beaklike nose; his black mustache did not hide the impression of nervous force given by his mobile mouth.

Returning to the study, Caillaux motioned me to an easy chair, sat in another and curled one foot under him. Would he profit, I asked, from the shift taking place (as Malvy had predicted) in French political sentiment? Certainly, he answered. The recent elections for the Conseils-Généraux proved that the conservative "Whites" were losing to the liberal and republican "Blues." It was true that the Bloc National had faced extremely difficult problems, but what the public notice is not that problems are hard but that they are not dealt with successfully.

"Events shape men, not men events," he continued platitudinously. "Therefore I cannot predict in detail what policy we republicans will follow when we come to power. Our general aim will be to improve the spirit of good will throughout Europe and forget as much of the past as possible."

It was a period of intense French dissatisfaction with both Germany and England over reparations and war debts. The Genoa Conference had just ended in disagreement and the reparations commission was discussing, over French objections, a temporary moratorium on German payments. I therefore asked Caillaux to be more specific about French policy toward Germany. Could the French really forget the past when the present was so unpleasant?

Caillaux began with a categorical statement: "I think Prussia has spoilt Germany." He wished for peaceful relations with Germany, even friendship, but a prerequisite was for Germany to exclude all Pan-Germans from power. "Until then," he said, "even people like myself who always were well-disposed to Germany and tried to avoid war must consider a rapprochement impossible." Genuine peace could be established "only after Germany becomes really and thoroughly republican." This did not mean that Germany must become a federation, but that the Prussian spirit must cease to dominate; this might happen if more influence were given to the states of West Germany, "where German-French relations are understood as Goethe and Schiller understood them."

For a change, he took me out for a stroll along the grass paths of the garden. I saw a lady retreating from one corner to another. Caillaux apologized, saying that his wife had just washed her hair and wanted to avoid meeting a stranger while it was drying. I was sorry to miss a close glimpse of someone who had caused such an immense furor.

As we walked, he told me he had been occupied in his "forced tranquillity" in writing two books, one already published, *Mes Prisons,* the other, *Où va la France? Où va l'Europe?* which he had just finished. Could he get this published in America? I said I would try to find a publisher as soon as he sent me a copy. In the end, my wife undertook the translation and the book was published by Knopf the year following. At my suggestion, he wrote a special preface for this edition, in which he spoke especially of the unintelligence of "captains of industry cowering behind their customs lines" and of the unlikelihood that developments fostered by science would be enough by themselves to save Western civilization; and he quoted Rabelais, "Science without conscience is the death of the soul."

I remember how he went out of his way to castigate the French press. He said that all the leading French journalists—or rather, almost all— were being subventioned by some domestic group or by some foreign government or by both.

How could he be sure about something both sides must keep secret, I asked?

"Because I have been on the paying side myself," he replied. "I have paid every one of them on one occasion or another." And he named three honorable exceptions—August Gauvain of the *Journal des Débats;* André Géraud, the "Pertinax" of the *Echo de Paris;* and another whose name I have forgotten. Interestingly, all three were conservatives.

I was reminded of this indictment of the French press several years later when I read a book by Kosta Todorov, a Bulgarian diplomat who was trying to get attention for his views in the great French daily, *Le Temps.* The business manager of that respected paper told him that Paris real estate was sold by the square meter, but that space in his paper was sold by the square centimeter.

When we were back in his study Caillaux became more personal. "One can dispute indefinitely about responsibility for the war," he said. "I do not claim that every scrap of responsibility rested with the Germans. But I do claim that without the Pan-German spirit the war could have been avoided. People say that I was for a Franco-German rapprochement. This is not quite true. As an economist, I knew what a war would do to Europe. In order to avoid it I did not seek a Franco-German alliance, but only, like my predecessors, to maintain a fair attitude and pursue a steady policy of conciliation. Obviously that was easier in the period when I was in office than it is today, but it still must be done."

Here was an indication of why a man with Caillaux's record could dream—his sentence for near-treason not yet run—of vindication and a new lease of power. He was careful not to announce that he sought an alliance with Germany at the expense of Britain, but he nevertheless profited with the public by that implication. Each time Lloyd George and liberal English economists attacked France, more Frenchmen wondered whether Caillaux's old policy of conciliation toward Germany might not have been right and might not serve now. Thinking of the German fleet sunk and Britain safe on the seas, of the pressure on France to forgo submarines, of the German colonies taken over by Britain, of their own devastated regions only partly repaired, of their sky-high debts to Britain and the United States and of the endeavors of these latter to reduce Germany's payments to France—thinking of these and other grievances, they became discontented and bitter. It was this restlessness which Caillaux and his allies, even while still in disgrace, were trying to increase, and from which they soon would profit.

Caillaux might have been, as he assured me, favorable to the Franco-British entente and more prepared to cooperate in quashing fresh intrigues across the Rhine than to foster them. But his attitude toward Germany was on the record, reminding Frenchmen, even those who still mistrusted and criticized him, that his genius for negotiation might in a crisis present an alternative to Poincaré's hard policy of fulfillment. After coming away from Mamers I wrote: "If that idea gains sufficient ground in the next twelve months the unthinkable will happen—Caillaux, cried down as a traitor, will again become Premier."

He was not to become Premier, but three years later, in April, 1925, only three months after his sentence had been finally abrogated, he once again was named Minister of Finance, the last hope of the Cartel des Gauches to save the franc.

Malvy and Caillaux had been figures in the political life of the French Republic in one of its most debased periods. Malvy, the small man, a trafficker in the customary favors, infidelities, briberies, concessions and betrayals of the day, had been unable to adjust his moral concepts and behavior to the requirements of wartime when the nation's existence was at stake. He escaped the sentence of death meted out to Bolo Pasha and the *Bonnet Rouge* crowd and Lenoir of *Le Journal*, who took money from the enemy, because unlike them he was not a traitor although, like Caillaux, he did have intercourse with them. He was nothing much worse, probably, than a practitioner of shady arts which could not be tolerated in a national crisis.

Caillaux was a man of far greater talents than his minor colleague. Yet he lived in the same political milieu, and in spite of his superior powers of intellect, and indeed higher moral concepts, could not satisfy his ambition, his sense of superiority and his love of the theatrical without carrying over the accustomed intrigues of domestic political life into the infinitely dangerous field of a nation's foreign relations in wartime. He was too meddlesome to let the constituted government from which he was excluded handle those relations, too disdainful not to feel sure that he had a better goal for France than outright victory and too arrogant not to imagine that he was entitled to try to reach it by his own personal transactions. He was dominated by conceit, and it was the ruin of his talents.

10

Greek Tragedy

The chain of coincidences was now about to add a final link—final, because I have never wanted to add another, whatever the direction in which it might lead.

At Princeton in 1912, Mme. Grouich fired me with enthusiasm for the Serbs; and she brought me, in recognition of my small help, a Serbian decoration.

This gave Colonel Tillson the idea of assigning me to the Serbian War Mission as aide to General Rashich.

When the war ended, General Rashich became Minister of War, and because I knew him I was appointed acting military attaché in Belgrade.

The *Evening Post* sent me to report the Institute of Politics at Williamstown, where Professor Coolidge asked me to talk on Jugoslavia.

Now in the spring of 1922 word reached me in Europe from Gay that the Council on Foreign Relations was being reorganized, that it planned to start a quarterly review, that Professor Coolidge had been invited to become editor and that he seemed likely to accept if "someone like A" would become his assistant. He told me that "A" meant me. Coolidge had remembered me from Williamstown.

The ten-year chain of coincidences was complete.

II

This was how it happened.

In a letter dated March 22, 1922, Gay wrote me: "Let me prepare your mind for a possible cablegram which we may be sending you within the next month. The Council on Foreign Relations, on the basis of a report made by a sub-committee (of which I was appointed chairman), has voted to establish a quarterly journal of foreign affairs and it has undertaken in a general way to provide ample funds for this journal. The fund is contingent upon our obtaining a first-rate editorial staff. The Council on Foreign Relations has a possibility of ample means and also the possibility of a work of great usefulness in the United States. The publication of a journal of absolutely first-rate quality, with an editorial staff in New York ultimately forming a kind of center for information and conference, is the ideal which we have in mind." He had gotten in touch, he went on, with Professor Archibald Cary Coolidge, who had arrived home from Russia the week before, and found that "he would probably be willing to undertake the task of editing such a journal provided he could get you to act as assistant editor in the headquarters in New York."

Coolidge was reluctant to give up entirely either his teaching at Harvard, which he had been doing for nearly thirty years, or his management of the Widener Library. He had hoped, therefore, that the main editorial office might be in Cambridge; but the Council officers looked on the review as only the first step toward creating a center of intellectual activity in New York and could not agree to having the editorial headquarters anywhere else. He now wrote Gay that if the proposal could be modified to allow him to continue his work at Cambridge he might feel able to accept. Harold Jefferson Coolidge tells how when his brother had asked for his opinion he had warned him against adding an entirely different job to the burdens already on his shoulders; and he had also commented (reinforcing Professor Coolidge's own feeling) that the undertaking was so important that "it would be best handled by its really responsible head making decisions in the atmosphere most favorable to his own intellectual processes," which in Coolidge's case meant in the comparative seclusion of the Widener Library, surrounded by its great collection of books.[1] His brother commented later: "I knew then as well as I do now that he had probably made his decision before consulting anyone." It turned out that this was the case: the temptation to take the lead in a notable venture became too strong to be resisted.

Coolidge's counterproposal was that "the current work of administration should be done by a younger man who should be enough of a person in himself not only to do mere routine work but to take part in all the activities connected with the magazine. This man should be as interested in the success of the magazine as anyone else, including myself; indeed

1. *Archibald Cary Coolidge: Life and Letters*, by Harold Jefferson Coolidge and Robert Howard Lord. Boston: Houghton Mifflin Co., 1932.

he should think of aspiring to be at the head of the concern if he makes good. I think I should want a man of about thirty, old enough to have already some knowledge of the world as well as intelligence, and to be able to meet important people on a reasonable footing of equality, but young enough to be willing to do active work of almost any kind and not to feel that he was entitled to run the show. The difference between my age and his would offer a certain security that he would not have to wait too many years before stepping into my shoes." He continued: "Let me suppose the right man can be found; let us call him A (for purposes of discussion). He would then do almost all the regular work as editor. The office and the work of administration would be in New York and I should go down from time to time when it was necessary: on other occasions A should come up here to talk matters over with me."

He realized, he went on, that this involved a considerable overhead "for pretty uncertain results." And he added: "I also doubt whether the Council on Foreign Relations appreciates sufficiently that I am totally without experience in editorial work, that I see no reason for thinking that I have any peculiar capacity for it, that I am quite without knowledge of the cost of many of the things I should wish to do and should need not only expert guidance but control."

This was being vastly overmodest, as the event showed. In his own field Coolidge was self-reliant and positive. He had strong convictions about historical accuracy; and if now his view was to be turned not so much backward as forward and outward, he was determined to apply, and to be free to apply, the same scrupulous standards in the wider field as he had always shown in the past in his own historical work and had exacted from his students. In finally accepting the Council's invitation he therefore made plain that he expected to continue as editor only as long as the Council was satisfied with his performance; but he insisted as a corollary that while he was editor he must have full and complete editorial freedom. The officers and directors of the Council lived up to the bargain scrupulously. Over the years, neither he nor I was subjected by them to a scintilla of pressure to act otherwise than as our independent judgment directed. In the world of journalism and politics that may be a record.

Gay's letter reached me in Paris, where we were making ready to set out via Rome for the Balkans and Eastern Europe. I had been sending cables and mail stories to the *Evening Post* whenever French politics provided material, but the intention had been that I should act for a time as the paper's correspondent in Eastern Europe, and I looked forward to visiting countries where the prospect was as promising journalistically as

it was, in some cases at least, discouraging politically. I cabled Gay that
the project he described was most appealing, that we were leaving on our
trip, but that I could curtail it and return to New York in June or, if
necessary, sooner.

The scene toward which we were headed was tumultuous. Fascists and
Communists were rioting in Italy, pushing impotent moderate governments further and further to the wall. Greece was caught in a losing war
with Turkey in Asia Minor and torn internally between the royalist adherents of King Constantine and the republican followers of Venizelos.
In the musty Yildiz Palace in Constantinople, the Sultan, apprehending
correctly that he was destined to be the last of the seven-centuries-old
House of Osman, was quaking on his cushioned throne; while in Ankara,
Mustafa Kemal and the new generation of Turkish nationalists were preparing to take over such remnants of the old Ottoman Empire as were
not already in their control. In Hungary, Count Bethlen, the Prime Minister, was endeavoring to restrain the partisans of the Hapsburgs, curb the
"Awakening Magyars," limit anti-Semitism and prevent these and other
nationalist excesses from embroiling the country with its neighbors. In
Jugoslavia, King Alexander was struggling to maintain internal unity
while opposing aggression by Italian Fascists in Fiume and Albania.
Czechoslovakia, despite differences between Czechs and Slovaks, was relatively stable under President Masaryk and Foreign Minister Beneš. To
counter the threats of Hungarian revisionists and armed attempts at a
Hapsburg restoration, Jugoslavia, Czechoslovakia and Rumania had come
together in an alliance known as the Little Entente.

Realizing that our time might be limited, we decided not to stop in
Italy and took ship from Brindisi to Piraeus, with only a passing glimpse
of lovely Corfu, where the Serbian Government had taken refuge in the
war.

III

A first sight of the Parthenon is a sensation one thinks cannot be repeated; but for me it can be, and has been, over and over again, year by
year and whatever the season. Even seen from Piraeus, distant and tiny,
it has a unique beauty for the inner eye, colored by history and romance;
and with each glimpse as you follow the ugly road up toward the city it
rises a bit higher, grows a bit larger, glows more golden, takes on a more
distinct outline against Lycabettus and the mountains beyond. Always
when I am in Athens I make sure to go up to the Acropolis each afternoon toward sunset, preferably on foot by the steep cobbled path on the

north side, past the Tower of the Winds and the miniature Byzantine church. It is never the same, whether in spring, with wildflowers filling every cranny in the rocks, or when summer has dried everything to burnt sienna or yellow ochre, or in winter, when the paths turn to streams and the wind carries gobbets of water at almost right angles from all the eaves and cornices. Each evening the shadows creep up Hymettus and Aegaleos in a way you do not remember having ever seen before, changing them, minute by minute and slope by slope, from color to color and from one depth of opalescence to another, at first clean and translucent, then vaporous and murky; even the higher peaks turn gray at last and lights come on along the raw city streets pushing out into the foothills.

In 1922 the old Grande Bretagne Hotel had not yet been westernized. At the main entrance on Constitution Square, darkened by heavy felt curtains, boys with feather dusters stood ready to flick the dust from your shoes. The high-ceilinged rooms, shuttered against the sun, were sufficiently cool by any but later air-conditioned standards. The inevitable clusters of little flies circled silently just outside the radius of the fans in the ceiling. All night through, you heard above the whining of the fans the chatter of Greeks at tables around the edge of the square, sufficiently fortified in loquacity by a single tiny cup of coffee.

As always, there was plenty to talk about, and in any café group you saw from the gesticulations that there were more talkers than listeners. Venizelos, despite dazzling diplomatic triumphs at Paris which had doubled the size of Greece, had lost his popularity. To his amazement, a wave of emotion had carried the royalists to victory in the November, 1920, elections which he most unwisely ordered to be held in his absence. All sorts of factors had combined to undermine him—his long absence in Paris, the corruption of his lieutenants at home (which led him to remark once, "I am not a Venizelist"), his acceptance of too-open and often maladroit Allied support, the eight-year-long mobilization, the disheartening sequel to the great military successes which at first had followed the landing at Smyrna the year before. The Greeks dislike the dominance of even a benefactor and take malicious pleasure in decapitating the tallest poppies in the field. They had decapitated Venizelos, and he now quit the country for what he said was forever.

This political turnabout was only one in the long series of Greek vacillations between love and hatred of the monarchy, devotion to and repudiation of the republic; always the split in personality has been and is there, deep and seemingly incurable.

The surprising election of 1920 was followed by a plebiscite in which

King Constantine, expelled by the Allies in June, 1917, was restored to the throne. But now, in the spring of 1922, he was threatened with losing it again. The plebiscite, like the election, had been indisputably free and the result had been almost unanimously in the King's favor. But the Allies had given advance warning that if he was restored to power they would withhold further support, and when this happened they refused to recognize him. They did not like his being the brother-in-law of the Kaiser and they remembered that his pretended neutralism in the war had been the thinnest sort of disguise for pro-German sympathies. There was also a not unnatural feeling in Allied countries (mitigated by traditional philhellenism in England) that a people so fickle as the Greeks were not dependable; they could be left to pay for their own mistakes.

The Allies, however, had differences among themselves. Lloyd George had been upset by Greece's repudiation of Venizelos, but he did not withdraw his espousal of the Greek cause. France and Italy suspected that this signaled Britain's determination to maintain Greece as an ally in securing domination of Constantinople. France made overtures to Mustafa Kemal and in the autumn of 1921 signed a treaty recognizing his government and relinquishing Cilicia to him in exchange for the promise of future commercial concessions. Italy, for her part, knew that the reason the Supreme Council in Paris had authorized Venizelos to land at Smyrna was to forestall an Italian occupation. As far back as 1919, Count Sforza, then Italian High Commissioner at Constantinople, had foreseen that Kemal was the man of the future and had made friends with him. Now as Italian Foreign Minister he favored allowing the Kemalists to drive the Greeks back to Europe; if they got all they asked for, he said, they would die of indigestion.

All this complicated maneuvering was evidence that the end of the Ottoman Empire was far from being the end of the Turkish Question, over which European statesmen had wrangled for generations. The Sultan had paid for becoming entangled with Imperial Germany and sharing its defeat by losing half of his prewar subjects and a third of his territories. Even in Anatolia itself Turkish rule was curtailed by the Greek administration of Smyrna and the advance of Greek armies halfway to the new Turkish capital at Angora.

But the discord among the Western nations prevented them from dealing with the new phase of the Turkish Question in a firm and orderly manner. Gradually the position of Greece had become extremely hazardous. Everyone except King Constantine had foreseen it. An editorial of mine in the *Evening Post* on July 27, 1921, had noted that even if Greek victories continued they might not break the Turkish nationalist resistance and that "the Greek leaders will be forced to drag out the campaign until finally the Constantine Government becomes about as unpopular as the Venizelist Government was before it." By avoiding large-scale engagement with the Greek armies, Kemal prevented King Constantine from winning a decisive victory and ending his people's long-drawn-out physical and psychological strain.

When we reached Athens in April, 1922, it was plain that a crisis was at hand in the military operations and in Constantine's relations with his people. The King's problem was how to get out of the war without losing the empire, too large for Greece's own good, which Venizelos had won on paper. For the Greek people, the question was whether to stick by the King in adversity or turn back once more to Venizelos in the hope that he might somehow save what was on the way to being lost.

Late each afternoon, the elegant Minister of War, Mr. Theotokis, a red carnation always in his buttonhole, would stroll in a leisurely way into the Grande Bretagne bar. Both he and Mr. Baltazzis, the Foreign Minister, were "playing it cool." They professed not to fear a military debacle in Asia Minor, but did discuss the possibility of a Greek withdrawal—this only on the assumption, however, that it might be forced by the Allies, who in that case must see that it was properly handled. Their conditions were that the political rights of the Greek population in Anatolia must be protected; that the safety of Christian churches and schools must be guaranteed; and the Greek population must have the right to free economic development. These guarantees must be counter-signed by the Allies and the execution of them must be overseen by an inter-Allied commission or by the League of Nations. Had not the Allies recognized in the Treaty of Sèvres that the populations involved were Greek? If now they changed their mind and wanted Greece to give them up, the least they could do was assume some responsibility for their future safety and prosperity.

"Foreign observers must not arrive," Theotokis told me, "only in time to count the Greek graves."

He maintained that the public were not in favor of withdrawal; but he left no doubt that the government was prepared to yield to the Allies with the guarantees mentioned. He minimized the risk that the Greek forces would reject such a settlement and join the million Greek inhabitants of Asia Minor in forming an independent state and continuing the war on their own. However (as I reported to the *Evening Post*) , this eventuality was not to be excluded, and it would pose serious questions for the Allies, already at loggerheads.

Foreign Minister Baltazzis could not deny with a straight face that he was apprehensive, but he tried to draw encouragement from the news from the Genoa Conference that Germany and Soviet Russia had signed a treaty of alliance at Rapallo. Turkey and Russia had done so earlier. He hoped that the Allies would now "wake up" and realize that once Greek troops left Asia Minor, the Kemalists would be free, with the blessing of Russia, now fortified with assurances of German friendship, to turn their attention to getting rid of the French and British from Syria and Mesopotamia.

"The Allies changed their Near Eastern policy half a dozen times during the war," he said, "and have changed it once since. Why not hope they will change it again, this time back to support of Greece?"

But events were taking over from diplomatic moves and countermoves. It was entirely visionary at this point to suppose that even if the Allies agreed among themselves on an effort to save Gréece, they had the ability to dictate terms to Kemal and guarantee the execution of the conditions put forward by Baltazzis and Theotokis as the price for a Greek withdrawal.

I V

Venizelos was in exile and his house on University Street was mostly in ruins. Next door was the villa which had belonged to Heinrich Schliemann, the great and erratic archaeologist, the discoverer of Troy (as he believed) and of the immense treasure by the Lion Gate at Mycene. He was said to have chosen his second wife while still a young girl because of her knowledge of Homer and to have led her a hard life while making his expeditions in pursuit of Homer's topographical hints (in which he placed great confidence) and conducting his controversies with more orthodox classical scholars (not silenced even when he turned up the Treasure of Priam) . I had a letter to Mme. Schliemann from Mme. Grouich, who had known her in her very young days when she was a student at the American School for Classical Studies in Athens. Mme. Schliemann spoke of Mme. Grouich's beauty and her affection for "everything true and aspiring." She herself was very spirited, an ardent admirer of Venizelos. Her son Agamemnon was not. To show me the depth of their political differences, she led me outside and pointed to a ragged row of holes traced by machine-gun bullets across the front of the villa.

"He took soldiers with a machine gun over there," she said, pointing to an opposite corner, "to fire at the Venizelos house, and couldn't resist writing his signature on my house too."

Later she invited me to a family wedding, held in the same house which he had autographed with a machine gun. Political differences remained but were in abeyance for the occasion.

Years later, I was talking about Greece with Lady Dixon, wife of the British Permanent Representative to the United Nations, who had been born there. I mentioned that I had known Athens as far back as 1922, and when she expressed disbelief I mentioned various people I had met there at that time, among them two members of a famous family of patriots, John Koundouriotis, whom I had known as Greek Minister in Belgrade, and his brother Admiral Koundouriotis, both Venizelists. The Koundouriotis family had taken a prominent part in Greek history since the War for Independence; one was President of Greece at that time, and his grandson, the Admiral, was President of the Greek Republic and twice, in emergencies, Regent. Mme. Schliemann was credited with a biting story in connection with the Admiral. A royalist lady asked scornfully at some function, "Who is this President of the Republic?" Mme. Schliemann answered: "He is the man whose grandfather was selling his property and putting it into the War for Independence when your grandfather was minding someone else's goats in his village."

As an added detail, I mentioned to Lady Dixon that I had even been to a wedding at Mme. Schliemann's house.

"Really?" she said. "What was it like?"

I said I didn't remember the Greek Orthodox ceremony in detail except that the bridal couple wore gold fillets in their hair and the priest went through a ritual with salt and oil.

"And do you remember what the bride looked like?" she asked.

I confessed I did not.

"I was that bride," she said.

What a missed opportunity! I should have remembered that all brides are beautiful, and said so. Ismene Dixon's looks forty years later would have confirmed the judgment. (She had separated from Schliemann and married Pierson Dixon in 1928.)

Mme. Schliemann offered to introduce me to Professor William Dörpfeld, her husband's collaborator (and usually though not invariably his friend) despite the fact that he belonged in the royalist camp. Although Dörpfeld had carried on important work at a number of sites for over forty-five years, with Schliemann as well as after his death, he is perhaps best known for his ingenious theory that the Ithaca described in the *Odyssey* does not fit the modern island of that name so well as it does Levkas, just to the north; for he was as apt as Schliemann himself in identifying Homeric with modern geography.

For the time being, however, Dörpfeld's interest had turned back to the excavation he had done at Corfu before the war by order of the German Kaiser. Wilhelm II owned the Villa Achilleion on Corfu, a vast, low, Pompeian-like structure, built originally for tragic Elizabeth of Austria. He fancied himself as an archaeologist and spent long periods on the island, working at an immense desk in front of which was a saddle, with stirrups, mounted as a chair. Sforza, who had been the Italian representative to the Serbian Government in exile at Corfu and who told me about the contraption, said it summed up the Kaiser's character. He had lately been preparing to publish a book on the island's classical antiquities. Dörpfeld had done the digging and the research and, so far as I could make out, had written the book too (though he disclaimed having done more than "help") . The Kaiser's name would nevertheless appear as author on the title page, and Dörpfeld seemed pleased that His Majesty said he would deign to mention him by name, an honor which he evidently considered full compensation for his services.[2] Dörpfeld had just arrived in Athens from Doorn, on his way to Corfu to make the photographs for the book.

Among the antiquities discovered at Corfu by Dörpfeld was the famous pediment of an archaic Doric temple, called either the Temple of Artemis or the Temple of Gorgon. At first it was accepted that the central snake-girdled female figure was Artemis, especially as two lions crouched beside her. But Dörpfeld evolved the theory (to be expounded in the Kaiser's book) that the figure was a pre-Hellenic goddess whom Greek invaders found and adopted as Artemis. It was his idea that the first settlements at Corfu, as at Mycene, were not Cretan (Minoan) in origin, but Phoenician, and that the Phoenicians came from the East. To support these unorthodox ideas, Dörpfeld pointed out that the only part of the ancient world where the Sun was represented as a female was in southern Arabia. I could, of course, only listen. No amateur would dare intrude into the still-continuing disputes among rival classical scholars as to the origins of Greek art and culture.

An amiable gentleman, Balanos by name, whose visiting card carried the modest legend "Architect of the Parthenon," invited me to see the

2. When it was published, Professor Dörpfeld's name was in fact mentioned—in a footnote on the first page.

ambitious restorations which he was carrying out on the Acropolis under the direction of a series of transient ministers of education. The northern colonnade of the Parthenon had been blown out by an explosion of a Turkish powder magazine in the seventeenth century, and most of the great Doric columns lay scattered where they had crashed, deep in grass and flowers, in wild but picturesque confusion. I recalled my father's description of how lovely the Roman Forum had been when he first saw it in the eighteen-fifties, with ivy climbing the columns and arches, flowers in every cranny and sheep grazing on the grass which covered the accumulated soil of ages. The inevitable excavations and restorations that came later added immensely to its historical interest but not to its beauty.

Balanos was proposing to neaten everything up, beginning by restoring the columns to their proper places. To get a general view of the interior, he first took me up by inside steps, which may or may not still exist, to the top of the portico at the west end. He pointed out several of the well-known devices of the architects—the original architects, that is—to add to the majesty of the building, for instance, how the columns diminished slightly in size toward the top so as to add to the impression of height when seen from the ground. We then examined the preparations to raise the fallen columns on the north side of the temple, quite an undertaking, given the weight of the enormous marble drums. Some columns toward the western end which had survived the blast and remained upright had been patched with bits of modern marble or with cement colored to match the original marble as closely as possible—but never closely enough. The blotches were as prominent as cement fillings in a front tooth.

As Balanos was describing the magnitude of the work and how he would like to find generous donors to help it along, I had a mischievous thought, inspired by a recollection of eight granite pillars originally placed in the choir of the Cathedral of St. John the Divine, in New York, each of which bore on its base the name of a donor, "John Jacob Astor," "George Gordon King" and so on. If the Parthenon columns were to be erected by subscription, I suggested jokingly, Mr. Balanos might offer the inducement that they would bear the names of the benefactors, "John D. Rockefeller, Jr." and the like. He thought this would be going too far.

I have often seen the Parthenon since the broken columns were hoisted back into place and patched out where necessary, and though as satisfactory as could be expected, I wonder whether even skillful restoration is not sometimes carried to extremes. Indefatigable Sir G. G. Scott (architect of the Albert Memorial in London) laid heavy hands on innumerable churches throughout England, saving them structurally but often leaving them bereft of charm; and even Viollet-le-Duc, the most renowned restorer of all, left the towers and ramparts of Carcassonne too perfect.

While I was at *The New Republic,* I had had some correspondence with Sir Charles Waldstein (later changed to Walston), director of the American Archaeological School in Athens in the eighteen-eighties. He sent me a letter of introduction to A. J. B. Wace, at this time head of the British School. One evening Wace took me to the Club Athénien and there, seated at a long table in a room overlooking a panorama of Athens, told me an anecdote which had been told him in turn by Sir Charles. Many years before, when Lord Curzon was young but already full of the pomposity of a future Viceroy of India, he had passed through Athens in the course of one of his travels in the Middle East and Asia; and one evening he had been taken to the club by Waldstein. There at dinner, an elderly retired British diplomat, of whom everyone was fond in spite of his being rather a bore, was in his accustomed place at the head of the table. He had come back to live in his beloved Athens and spent every evening at the club. At the far end of the table sat Lord Curzon.

Soon after sitting down to dinner the old diplomat told a meandering story, not very interesting, in excruciatingly long detail. Then at dessert he forgetfully took ten minutes to tell it all over again.

"That," said young Curzon icily from the other end of the table, "reminds me of a most interesting story also." And without changing expression he told the same story word for word for a third time, omitting no detail and if anything drawing out the agony.

The old man realized suddenly for the first time what a bore he must be, left silently as soon as dinner was over and never came to the club again.

V

Western diplomats called Dr. George Streit, King Constantine's schoolmate and still his closest friend, "the German devil at the Greek court." His grandfather had come to Greece with King Otto as part of the numerous Bavarian administration brought along by the new monarch in 1833. He himself had been Greek Foreign Minister at the time of the Austrian attack on Serbia, and like King Constantine had been delighted by Prime Minister Venizelos' refusal to consider the attack as a *casus foederis* requiring Greece to go to Serbia's aid. But there the similarity between the policy of Venizelos and the King and his Foreign Minister stopped. Venizelos, who believed in the victory of the Allies, was determined to bend Greek neutrality in their favor, whereas Constantine and Streit, counting on a German victory, wished to follow a pro-German policy. Within a month after the war had begun Venizelos required Streit to resign.

With his short-cropped hair and bristly mustache Streit was more the picture of a Teutonic professor than of a politician. He talked to me quietly in French about the King's difficulties with Venizelos.

"Venizelos is very impetuous," he said. "He calls me a traitor. I don't say that of him. He is a patriot, but his political ways are not the King's ways. He brought Cretan habits into Greek politics, and that has been unhealthy, for the Cretans are contentious and irreconcilable, and what Greece needs is compromise and unity. He wants the Allies as protectors of Greece. The King wants Greece to be independent. When the King refused to accept his advice he became a revolutionary."

When I remarked that it looked as though Greece would need the help of the Allies to extricate her army from Asia Minor without a debacle, he did not argue, merely looked sad. He readily agreed to arrange for me to see King Constantine, and said that I would hear about an appointment from Count Mercati, the marshal of the court.

This would be something of an achievement, as I had been told that the King had not talked at length with an American newspaperman since the end of the war. The American Ambassador, like the other Allied ambassadors, was under instructions to have nothing to do with him. When I called at the Embassy residence, then on University Street, not far from Mme. Schliemann's, I found that the Ambassador had little conversation about the political situation except that it was inconvenient in entertaining as it divided Athenian society into two groups not on speaking terms. He urgently desired a transfer, especially since the city water pressure was so low that it left the only bathroom, located on the second floor, dry. He laid the fact to royalist mismanagement or possibly deliberate discrimination.

Before seeing the King, I wanted to find out more about what the opposition was thinking. The cafés were said to be buzzing with reports of discontent among the troops in Asia Minor and even of plans for a military coup against the royalist generals. Perhaps some of the younger Venizelist leaders to whom I had letters could tell me how far things might go. I never seemed to be able to find them, however. Telephones didn't answer and messages left at doors brought no response. I read over the names to the concierge at the Grande Bretagne.

"Where," I asked, "can I find Alexander Papanastasiou, the former Minister of Communications?"

"In jail," he said laconically.

"And Alexander Karapanos, former Minister of Foreign Affairs?"

"In jail."

"Petmezar, Professor of International Law?"

"In jail."

"George Vilaras, who used to be Consul General in Philadelphia?"

"In jail."

"Former deputy Theodoropoulos?"

"In jail."

"Deputy Constantine Melas?"

"In jail."

"Is everyone in jail?" I ended in desperation.

"The best ones," he said without a smile.

However, he volunteered to get word to them that I was inquiring about them. A day or so later he handed me in the front hall of the hotel, quite openly, a group photograph of the six of them looking out through prison bars, autographed by each.

King Constantine, tall, dome-headed, courteous, did not impress me as very bright when he professed to be no more perturbed than his ministers about the unrest at home or the precarious military situation which was causing it. He was hopeful, he said, that before a final showdown the French would realize that it was not in their interest to see Greece eliminated as a counterbalance to Turkey in the Levant and would join the British in extricating her from her difficulties. He had to admit that there were few signs of this; instead, France was encouraging the Turks to take back towns "which all the world knows are Greek." He predicted that if the Turks were not curbed, Moslems and Christians would eventually be drawn into the conflict all through the Near and Middle East.

"Why have Americans lost interest in protecting the Christians against the Turks?" he demanded. "They used to talk a lot about it. Turks still hate Christians of whatever race and want to kill them. Why isn't there an outcry in the American press at the idea of leaving them to be massacred?"

At each question he increased the pace at which we were walking in his garden. Suddenly he stopped, turned, took hold of my lapel and made two prophecies, one of which was fulfilled, the other not.

"It would be very difficult to persuade the Greek troops to withdraw from Asia Minor even if I order it," he said. This was the unfulfilled prophesy; the Turks wiped out the difficulties.

"If we ever did withdraw," he continued, "there would be massacre of the most fearful sort." That prophesy was fulfilled. Smyrna was burnt, and the Greeks who had not escaped earlier were burnt with it or bayoneted and their corpses thrown into the sea.

In answer to a polite hint that perhaps his regime was a factor in the way the Allies were treating Greece, he rejected the idea that either the monarchy or his person was in any way involved. Since he knew even better than I did that this was simply not so, I asked abruptly whether this meant that there was nothing to the rumors that he thought of abdicating in favor of Crown Prince George, or even of bowing to Allied pressure and making way for a republic.

"Why should I?" he asked. "The Allies are being completely illogical. Either my government is an outlaw government, imposed on the Greek people against their will, or it is in power because it has a popular mandate. Since it does have a mandate given all but unanimously by the people, it is a legitimate government, and I, its head, am the legal and proper King of Greece.

"The Allies do not adopt either one line or the other. I appointed Gounaris as Premier and sent him to the Genoa Conference with credentials signed by me. Without those credentials he is nobody. The Allies accept him as representing Greece but refuse to recognize me, from whom he draws his power."

I felt like asking why he did not mention the United States, for to my mind American policy was being conducted with as little consistency as Britain and France had shown during the war when they shifted about among Serbia, Bulgaria and Rumania, and as they were showing now in their divided dealings with Greece and Turkey. Congress had forced the United States to withdraw from the Near and Middle East where Wilson had said it would share responsibility for Constantinople and Armenia. Our current policy of nonrecognition did not seem to me to be based on principle.[3] Were we withholding recognition because Constantine was a king? We managed to be on good terms with the King of England, the King of Italy and others. Was it because his wife was a German? We had made our separate peace with Germany and sent Ambassador Houghton

3. A year and a half later, Secretary of State Hughes gave a résumé of the reasons in a speech before the Council on Foreign Relations, January 23, 1924. (Published as a supplement to *Foreign Affairs*, Vol. II, No. 2.)

there to restore friendship with the Germans after the recent "misunderstanding" (Houghton's term). But the King needed no prompting.

"It seems particularly strange that the United States refuses to recognize me," he went on. "Your country joined the war only a month before I went to Switzerland and therefore you were not involved in my disputes with the Allies in my effort to spare Greece another war.

"I have undertaken formally, in writing, to recognize the validity of all undertakings made in my absence by the government of my second son, Alexander. I cannot say that Alexander properly assumed the prerogatives of King, because it was neither constitutional nor legal, but I can and do acknowledge of my own free will the obligations he assumed toward foreign countries.

"In the year and a half since the Greek people gave me a mandate there has been no evidence that the plebiscite was conducted by force or fraud. If that is not the sort of democracy which appeals to Americans, I give up."

The phrase was prophetic, but he tried playing one more card first. In July he took the decision to force a showdown with the Allies. He did not dare delay, as the Kemalists were now securing munitions from the Russians to supplement those they had received from the French when they evacuated Cilicia, and from the Italians. He shifted two divisions from Smyrna to a point near Constantinople and prepared to seize the city. In this he might have succeeded, but the Allies warned that they would use force if necessary to prevent it. This was a fatal loss to him in prestige and spirit and a corresponding gain in both to Kemal. On August 18, the Turks launched a great offensive, scattered the Greek Army and put the Greek quarter of Smyrna to the torch. A military insurrection led by General Plastiras followed. King Constantine abdicated in favor of his son George and left Athens for the last time.

It was the decisive moment of classical Greek tragedy. Prime Minister Gounaris, Foreign Minister Baltazzis, Minister of War Theotokis, two other ministers and the general who had commanded in Asia Minor were shot. Years later, a son of Baltazzis pointed out to me in the distance, but visible from his apartment terrace, the spot at Goudi where the execution took place. Echoes of the shots reverberate sullenly in Greek politics to this day.

11

Capitals and Statesmen

To my consternation, a cable from Dr. Gay caught up with me in Athens, forwarded by mail from Paris, suggesting that pending a final decision as to publishing the review we ought to go from Paris to Genoa, where European statesmen were attempting to reach a settlement with Russia. His idea was that I might make some useful contacts there. Instead, here I was on the other side of Europe, which then signified a formidable gap in time; even an unbroken journey between Paris and Athens took six or seven days, and Greeks still spoke of "going to Europe." Gay meanwhile discovered my whereabouts and a second cable read: "Publication settled. Will you accept assistant editorship beginning salary $3,500. Return Paris for Coolidge letter, then London, home." I at once cabled acceptance, but pointed out that the trip we were just starting would enlarge my usefulness and suggested that by shortening it to three weeks we could be home the first week in June. Gay agreed, and added that Coolidge had accepted the editorship, modest office space was being reserved and specifications were being obtained from a printer.

It was a relief to get a chatty letter from Professor Coolidge, "an Easter Sunday scribble," written before formalities had been completed but assuming we were to work together in running a quarterly review "which we mean to make the first authority in the United States on foreign affairs." For the first time, I realized how exciting it would be working under him. Already his mind was busy with editorial plans. He said that I would find a letter in Paris introducing me to André Tardieu, Clemenceau's closest confidant, in the hope that he could be persuaded to write for our first issue. He also mentioned the possibility of inviting an article from Eduard Beneš, the Czechoslovak Prime Minister, and this decided me to substitute Prague for Constantinople on our itinerary. It was a hard choice, for the war in Asia Minor was approaching a crisis and I was keen to check on the conflicting reports about it circulating in Athens; but with only three weeks to go something had to be left out.

The idea of a French author among our first contributors came naturally to Coolidge. His memory of his first sight of Paris in 1871, at the age of five, when the Germans had not been long gone, could not have remained very distinct, but since his college days hardly a year had passed that he had not been there, going or coming on one of his indefatigable yearly travels. In 1906, he had been a great success as an exchange professor at the Sorbonne, an achievement because his predecessors, Barrett Wendell and George Santayana, had set very high standards.

French policy was under heavy attack by American and British liberals, who blamed Clemenceau, Poincaré and Foch indiscriminately for much of the evil they saw in the Treaty of Versailles, ignoring the subsequent strategic and psychological difficulties created for France by the refusal of the U.S. Senate to ratify the tripartite treaty which would have guaranteed her against German aggression and forgetting that it was this promised protection which had persuaded Clemenceau not to seize territorial guarantees on the Rhine. In addition, Washington was insisting that France pay her war debts to the United States while maintaining that Germany could not meet her reparations payments to France. As if this were not enough, Congress was preparing to raise duties on imports to the highest level in American history. Americans were calling France chauvinistic and ungrateful; Frenchmen were calling America callous and forgetful. The basic causes for this mutual disenchantment could be the subject for an influential article, and Tardieu, who had been foreign editor of *Le Temps,* seemed the right man to write it.

"In general," wrote Coolidge, "hint gently to possible contributors that the American people are tired of eloquence, generalities and compliments. What we seek are facts and reasons." The advice was good then, and still is (though the danger of compliments for Americans has dwindled) . Occasionally, when a Prime Minister or other eminent foreign statesman sends us not the article we invited but a piece of outright propaganda or sententious platitudes in praise of the good and the beautiful, lifted from an afterdinner speech or ghostwritten by a public-relations officer, we have to return the manuscript. It is accompanied by our honorarium and, of course, a letter of profuse apologies and regrets. We thoroughly understand, we say, how heavily burdened he is and how grateful we are that he nevertheless endeavored to fulfill his promise. We may add that we trust he will be able to snatch time from affairs of state to give further thought to the article, and we recall the interesting points we mentioned originally, and which he has ignored. But, whatever we say, the end is usually, on his part, injured silence.

Coolidge also provided some details about the venture on which I was embarking, so far quite nebulous. There was to be an Editorial Advisory Board, three members of which would be "the fathers of the whole scheme," Gay, Isaiah Bowman and Stephen Duggan. For additional members, Coolidge wrote, "I guess we can have about whom we want." A plan was afoot to take over the *Journal of International Relations,* a quarterly with limited circulation published at Clark University, and adopt the title. By agreement, that periodical was in fact discontinued, and its editor, Professor George H. Blakeslee, an expert on the Far East, became a member of our Editorial Advisory Board and its associate editors, Professor Harry Elmer Barnes and Denys P. Myers, became respectively bibliographic editor and editor of our source-material section. The idea of adopting the title did not appeal to me at all. "It sounds to me unnecessarily dull," I wrote Gay, with the result that the decision was held over till after I got home.

Such was the status of the projected periodical, not yet even named, little more than three months before manuscripts for the first issue were supposed to be in hand and only four months before it was to appear in September, go out through the mails and fight for a place on the newsstands. The public had not as yet been informed that it was to come into existence, and of course nobody had been asked to subscribe. No subscription rate had been suggested. Funds were promised for the first year, but (as I found on my return) not beyond that. Printers had been approached, in Gay's phrase, "for specifications." But a printer's specifications had to be based on *our* specifications, and no decisions had been made as to format, paper stock, typography, cover stock and design, size of edition, whether to carry advertisements, and other elementary physical factors. Without them, no printer could make an estimate of costs worth examining and without that any budget of ours was purely speculative.

No wonder Coolidge wanted me home as soon as possible. He wrote that while he saw the value of the "general enlightenment" I was receiving and the contacts I might make, "There is a lot to do, I am perfectly green at the business, and above all I am keen to consult with you from the start and have you feel that you are taking an important part in making plans, forming policies and everything else." Perhaps he had heard from Gay that in my innocence I had written how much I hoped I could continue doing part-time editorial work for the *Evening Post* on the side, and that Gay, equally optimistic, had said he hoped and thought so.

Coolidge confessed himself green. Obviously I was just as green, the difference being that I didn't know it. Otherwise I would have quailed at the prospect of settling questions of format, making a printing contract, finding a business manager, securing lists of possible subscribers and writing promotion letters and leaflets, all in the three months between my return to New York and the date we would go to press, to say nothing of securing and editing and proofreading the dozen articles which were to introduce our magazine to the public and set the standard for future issues. What I did not know was that I also would take over running the Council on Foreign Relations, which meant seeing to its financing, membership and meetings. Simultaneously, of course, we also would have to be looking and planning ahead. As Coolidge wisely remarked, the second issue would in a way be even more important than the first, for people would look at it to see whether the first had been a flash in the pan or an earnest of what we could sustain.

Nevertheless, I proceeded with my trip, I won't say serenely, but undaunted, first to Belgrade, Budapest and Prague, then to Paris, then home, writing along the way cables and mail correspondence for the *Evening Post,* but above all "with eyes, ears and mind open" (Coolidge's admonition, really not needed) for possible topics for the review and talking with people of all sorts, in and out of public life, who might sooner or later deal with them.

II

Twice a week the Orient Express started north from Athens amid all the flutter of an Atlantic liner sailing from New York, with bunches of flowers for departing ladies and much handkerchief waving and weeping. From the moment it creaked out of the station its progress was strictly Balkan. It crawled up the steep grades in the moonlit gorges of Thessaly (or was it Xanadu?), waited everywhere and nowhere, was snarled in red tape at the Jugoslav border, stopped for all-clear signals before venturing onto temporary bridges across the Vardar and the Morava replacing those destroyed in the war, and reached Belgrade at last on the third day.

We had been told that Belgrade would be unrecognizable to us after three years, and in fact the change was remarkable. It was not yet a modern city, but it had water and electricity, some streets had been paved and streetcars were running on them, the Hotel Moscow still stood empty but a small new hotel had been built in which none of the appliances worked but which permitted the Sanatorium Vracha, our refuge on our first arrival in 1919, to return to its proper function. Kalemegdan Park, where people walked to watch the sunset and exchange small-town greetings, had been cleared of debris and planted; new shops had last year's styles from Vienna in the windows; scaffoldings and lines of oxcarts bringing sand and bricks showed where government buildings were going up.

Everything was being pushed to make the city ready for King Alexander's wedding the next month to Princess Marie of Rumania, plump, shy and indolent, outshone and overwhelmed by her imperious mother, Queen Marie, renowned for her beauty, a granddaughter who would not have amused Queen Victoria. She had visited Belgrade a couple of months earlier to inspect the Konak, the gray stone and stucco palace on Kralj Milanova Ulitsa which was being made habitable again after the Austrian bombardments and three years of ill use as a barracks. The main section, across the courtyard from where King Alexander Obrenovich and Queen Draga had been murdered, was being done over for the new married couple. Queen Marie had been outraged to find that her daughter's rooms were to be in the opposite wing from those allotted the King. It was not the right idea of married life, she said, royal or not, and new arrangements were ordered at once. The feature that struck me most was the enormous bathroom. The architect must have been instructed to dispose of the rumor that bathrooms were rare in the Balkans and that such as existed were cubbyholes or alcoves. At any rate, he provided a royal bathroom thirty feet square at least. The King was away, but a year later, from the balcony of his study, he pointed across the roofs of the city to where the Sava curves around the Topschider hills. He said he hoped someday to build a country house there in the woods. Eventually he did so, and it is now used by Tito for state receptions.

Adjoining the large kitchen in the basement was a storeroom where chests of newly purchased gold and silver plate, kept under guard, indicated that King Alexander would not be able to follow in future the rather austere regime to which he had become accustomed during years in the field. The boxes of silver, enough for a dinner of a hundred, were marked "Demi-gala," and those with gold plate, enough for one hundred twenty, were marked "Gala." The pattern was not ornate. In fact, apart from too much gilt paint on the double staircase and in the ballroom, most of what the interior decorator from Paris had done was in good taste. It was the ballroom which the people of Belgrade loved to hear about, for whether they had been exiled during the war or lived under the Austrian occupation they yearned now for some gaiety, some display. I wondered how it all was to be paid for, with dinars worth about a cent and a half, but nobody else seemed to. The wedding had taken on symbolism as the dividing line between the hardships of war and the new era of better times. For the moment, it outdid the perpetual parliamentary crisis as a theme of discussion. Everyone was pleased that there seemed to be money to spend, even if it was for gilt coffee spoons.

The wedding would also mark the end of a year of mourning for old King Peter, who had died the summer before, leaving a memory of patriotism, bravery and simplicity. He had been exiled by the rival Obrenovich family, had served as a volunteer in the French Army in the 1870 war with Germany and had fought under an assumed name in the Bosnian rising against the Turks in 1876. While in exile he translated Mill's *On Liberty* from French into Serbian, and when he was brought back to the throne following the murder of the Obrenovich King and Queen (in which he was in no way implicated), he showed a liberal spirit unusual in Balkan rulers. During the war, though old, ill and crippled, he constantly visited the troops in the field and stayed with them in the retreat over the Albanian mountains. His behavior, dynastic and personal, had given the Karageorgevichs a popularity and prestige which were of great help now to his son.

In the nearly three years since we had left Belgrade no stable government had been formed. The first national assembly was representative of most elements in the country, and the best make-do possible, but it was not regularly elected. The two most important blocs were almost evenly divided. One centered around the old Serbian Radical party, led by Nikola Pashich, who had been Prime Minister of Serbia for the first time in 1891 and again three times afterward, the last extending through the two Balkan Wars and the World War. The Democrats formed a group of about the same size, headed by Ljubomir Davidovich, a Serb, and Svetozar Pribichevich, the strong-willed and combative leader of the Serbs of Croatia, sometimes joined by the Slovenes under Father Korošec. Stjepan Radić was offered three seats for the Croat Peasant party, the same number it had held in the prewar Croatian Sabor, but refused them and stayed away.

The natural choice to form the first cabinet would have seemed to be Nikola Pashich. But many Serbian politicians had rebelled at his authoritarian rule in the years of exile, when his thought was always and only on how to survive, how to win, regardless of normal parliamentary requirements. Croat and Slovene leaders also had been dissatisfied, for although Pashich agreed in the 1917 Pact of Corfu to the formation of a single Serb, Croat and Slovene state under the Karageorgevich dynasty, he had put off discussing the future legal structure and sometimes seemed to them to be thinking more in terms of a Greater Serbia than a true federation. Pashich feared that too loose a federation could not stand up to the three-sided pressure of hostile Italians, Magyars and Bulgars, and he undoubtedly had more confidence in the endurance and fixed purpose of his primitive Serbs than in those of the westernized Croats and Slovenes, whose political experience had been limited to parliamentary maneuvering in opposition to the rule of Vienna and Budapest. Yet he was much more than a Serbian nationalist. Count Sforza, who as Italy's representative at Corfu had opportunity to study his character, wrote: "The theory that Pashich was a prototype of the Pan-Serbian and the antithesis of the Jugoslav ideal is egregiously false."

Justified or not, the opposition to Pashich could not be ignored by the Prince Regent, who was striving in every way to strengthen national unity. He therefore sent him to Paris as head of the delegation to the Peace Conference and gave the mandate to form the nation's first cabinet to another Radical leader, Stojan Protich. Party forces in the provisional assembly were so evenly divided that Protich was rumored to have mustered the two necessary votes to secure confirmation by having the name "Popovich" called three times too often, and his inability to procure a quorum prevented him from passing a single measure.

Looking about for a leader able to rise above party lines, Prince Regent Alexander sent for the Minister to France, Milenko Vesnich, who in short order was able to put together the most widely representative government the country had yet had. It succeeded at last in promulgating an electoral law and passing a bill which set a date for elections to the Constituent Assembly. Vesnich was particularly experienced, of course, in the international field. This proved invaluable when D'Annunzio seized Fiume and installed himself as "Commandant." Vesnich disregarded cries for reprisals (which might have led to war) and appealed to the Council of Ambassadors at Paris. Then, while most politicians were off electioneering, he and Foreign Minister Ante Trumbić entered into negotiations with the Italian Foreign Minister, Count Sforza.

The result was the Treaty of Rapallo, by which Italy at last gave up her claims to Dalmatia, though retaining a small enclave around the city of Zara (now Zadar) and two islands. To secure this Italian concession, the Jugoslavs agreed to a frontier which left several hundred thousand of their co-nationals under Italian rule in Istria and Gorizia, though with promises of freedom of language and culture. Neither won Fiume; it was to be a free city. Public opinion felt that Vesnich's concessions had been disastrous; but the Prince Regent approved, and the fact that one of the negotiators had been Trumbić, himself a Dalmatian and a veteran Croat nationalist, quieted opposition and the government was able to stay in office until after the elections. D'Annunzio declaimed vociferously against the treaty, but surrendered to an Italian expedition sent to oust him.

Once the elections were over, Vesnich resigned, and Pashich, back from the Peace Conference, formed a government equally divided between Radicals and Democrats. A portentous element was missing. The Croat Peasant party had emerged from the elections with fifty seats, but this surprising victory only made Radić more intransigent; he refused to recognize the central government or come to Belgrade to join in the great constitutional debate. This confirmed Pashich in his conviction that only a strong central government could hold the country together, and the Prince Regent also came around to the same view. In the end, the Constituent Assembly voted by a large majority for a centralized form of government and the constitution was adopted on Vidovdan, anniversary of the proclamation of the national union, June 28, 1921. This failed, however, to assure domestic peace. Croats like Trumbić who favored regional self-government were gravely dissatisfied. When, within a month, a Communist shot the Minister of the Interior, the Communist party was banned and henceforth revolutionaries received severe treatment from the police. One of them, a young returned prisoner-of-war from Russia, Josip Broz Tito, did not forget it.

From time to time, correspondents would telegraph that Pashich's resignation was "only a matter of hours," but he was still Prime Minister when we arrived in Belgrade in May, 1922. A recent automobile accident would have been serious even for a man who was now almost eighty, but he hobbled downstairs from his bedroom to see me. A servant girl in peasant dress came in at once with Turkish coffee. Mme. Pashich appeared long enough to take the two little copper pots, tap them the proper three times to settle the grounds, pour the frothy coffee into two tiny cups and set them on an ebony stand between Pashich and me. The stand was covered by a small black and red rug, easily distinguishable as coming from the Pirot region where Pashich was born. In accordance with the Turkish custom, the maid also set down two saucers of sweet-meats and two glasses of water, in each of which stood a spoon.

It was warm, and the air around the locust trees outside was heavy and sweet, but the windows were shut, the heavy lace curtains drawn, and Pashich wore a winter overcoat with the collar turned up and a cap pulled down to shade his eyes. The eyes, very blue, were his chief charac-teristic, apart from the patriarchal white beard, which had made him conspicuous at the Paris Peace Conference. They were eyes that looked many years away from eighty, as sharp and direct as his speech in French was muffled and hesitant. It was said that he spoke even Serbian badly, supposedly because he came from a district near the Bulgarian border where nationalities were mixed. Slobodan Jovanovich, rector of Bel-grade University, told me there even was a dash of Armenian in his Bulgar blood. Whatever the reason, after every few words he would fill a pause with a thick "comme ça" as if to keep one guessing how his line of thought was going to come out.

As it did come out, the thought seemed clear enough. His principal concern was Italy's delay in executing the Treaty of Rapallo. Close now to the end of his life, he still had as his two goals to create a strong cen-tral government and to give the country settled frontiers. The first, he felt, had been accomplished. The second was incomplete because two disputes remained over the application of the treaty. The most important concerned Fiume, to which the treaty had given independent status. Both sides claimed a small basin there, Port Baroš, adjoining the agreed frontier. Baroš would be most valuable to the Jugoslavs as a trade outlet on the Adriatic. Just for that reason Italy wanted to control it, through the control she fully intended to exercise over the Free City, and make the Jugoslavs use the Italian port of Trieste. Pashich said he could easily reach agreement directly with the authorities of the Free City, who real-ized their precarious situation, but Italy insisted on being arbiter.

"We have made our last concessions," Pashich said. "We have a treaty. Both of us have recognized the city's independence. From now on, where the Free City is concerned we deal only with the Free City."

Pashich held one card. At Rapallo, Sforza had refused to let Jugoslavia have Baroš but he had secretly given the Jugoslav delegation a letter recognizing that it lay outside the historical limits of Fiume proper, thus leaving the way open for a later adjustment. His excuse afterward for this double play was that he planned to link Italy and Jugoslavia in a trade consortium, thus saving Fiume from being killed in favor of Trieste:

Port Baroš, he claimed, must be kept as part of Fiume in order to force the Jugoslavs to participate. When the plan was revealed, Sforza resigned as Foreign Minister.

The other obstacle to something like normal relations with Italy was the unhappy condition of the little city of Zara on the Dalmatian coast, Venetian in history and architecture, which the treaty had allotted as an enclave to Italy. The inhabitants were surprised to find that this meant that the Jugoslav villagers in the surrounding countryside no longer brought in their vegetables and milk as before. They complained loudly to the Italian Government, which demanded in turn that since the villagers were so unfriendly they and their farms must be annexed to Italy.

"I pointed out to Signor Sonnino at Paris that this was bound to happen," said Pashich. "If Zara—or rather if Italy, speaking for Zara, which is not at all the same thing—wants to be separate from its neighbors, those neighbors are going to respect the fact, but they can't be expected to like it. Now, having annexed Zara contrary to the town's real interests, the Italian Government demands revision of the treaty by which it acquired title to it, on the grounds of the very difficulty which I predicted all along. To make us pay for the blunder, Italy now asks for twenty square kilometers of territory inhabited entirely by Jugoslavs. These are determined not to be annexed by Italy and we are determined not to allow them to make such a sacrifice."

For Pashich, this was quite a flight of eloquence. The son of a peasant, he was wary and reserved, usually making his points by calm statements isolated between imperturbable and disturbing silences. Sforza remembered him from Corfu as having "a certain grandeur." The few times I saw him, then and later, it did not seem to me that he made any conscious pretensions in that direction. His "grandeur" was simplicity and his weapon was stubbornness.

Having dealt with the Italians, he turned to other neighbors. The Bulgars, he said, could not work with the Magyars to find ways to overturn the peace treaties and still expect reconciliation with Jugoslavia. Greece he hoped to make a friend and ally again, but he must work for that slowly. He wanted to avoid a dispute with Greece over its failure to join the Serbs when they were attacked by Bulgaria in 1915, and for that reason he had not taken up officially the treaty of alliance which was about to expire. If he began to discuss it with Athens, there would be newspaper attacks on Greece which would make eventual agreement impossible. He did not indulge in recriminations for Bulgaria's stab in the back or for Greece's failure to come to Serbia's help, but looked ahead.

"We have much to do at home," he said, "and want only, comme ça, to smooth out things with our neighbors—those that accept the facts of the war and the peace, some of which are very disagreeable to them because of, comme ça, the mistakes they made."

He struggled to get up to say goodbye, but I dissuaded him and left him sitting by the curtained window, compact and composed.

All over the Balkans, at that time, Russian refugees in forlorn uniforms, weather-stained, patched, crumpled from sleeping in odd corners, wandered around city streets and trudged along country roads. They did not beg. In Athens, we had seen them selling newspapers or little cornucopias of dusty candies. Just below the Acropolis, one couple of strapping Cossacks had a collection of Tsarist decorations and paste jewelry which they were polishing on their sleeves and offering awkwardly to passers-by. I turned back and dropped a small coin in the tray. This was not allowed. One of them came jumping down the steps and made me take in return a tin stickpin set with a large glass ruby.

Of all the capitals of the region, Constantinople excepted, Belgrade had the largest collection of Russian exiles. When Baron Wrangel was forced out of the Crimea in November, 1920, he took about 120,000 soldiers with him; they were transported in Allied ships, mostly from Odessa to Constantinople, and thence the greater part of them made their way across Bulgaria, which they found inhospitable, to Serbia. Through history, Serbs had looked to Mother Russia with veneration; Russians were brothers and at the Serbian frontier none were turned back. The inrush left Serbia gasping. With her own war orphans, war widows and war *mutilés* to be tended, the burden of these visitors became almost unbearable. Prince Alexander had spent eight years, from ten to eighteen, at the Ecole des Pages in St. Petersburg, indeed had seen Belgrade for the first time when his father was called from exile to take the throne. It was said, too, that in St. Petersburg he had fallen in love with one of the Tsar's daughters and had been given permission to pay court to her. War came and she was murdered. Every instinct told him to receive the refugees from the Tsarist armies compassionately.

At the beginning the Jugoslav Government gave each Russian soldier a small pension equivalent to about five dollars a month. Alexander contributed to the fund as well. It was a painful drain on the treasury and on his personal fortune. As the refugee tide continued to swell, the subvention could be continued only for the wounded and ill. Wrangel established a bureau, first in Belgrade, then at Petrovaradin sixty miles to the north, to help his men get settled and find work. The Jugoslav Government also permitted B. N. Strandmann, the former Tsarist chargé d'affaires, and General Artamanov, the former military attaché, to continue occupying the old Russian Legation. I visited them there, and found them living in austere conditions. That they were able to exist at all, I gathered, was due to the Prince Regent's help.

These facts were exploited in the European press, usually under datelines from Budapest or Rome, to suggest that the Jugoslav Government was permitting, or even subsidizing, efforts by Wrangel and Artamanov to organize an expedition against Bolshevik Russia. Friends of mine in the government, as well as Wrangel and Artamanov themselves, all categorically denied it, and so far as I could tell, the denials were accurate. I found that Wrangel's lists of his former soldiers were so incomplete, their exact whereabouts so uncertain, that nothing like even a skeleton military organization could be said to exist. If such a forlorn enterprise had been plotted, Alexander and his government would not have been so foolish as to permit it to be organized on Jugoslav territory. They cared for the Russian émigrés out of feelings of pity and kinship.

Baroness Wrangel confirmed this when I crossed the Atlantic with her from New York in 1925. She had managed to get to Belgrade from Constantinople in the spring of 1922 and said that the only time she had seen King Alexander was on the day of her arrival. When her husband reached Saloniki on a French destroyer, Alexander sent his own railway car to meet him at the Greek frontier and his motor to meet him at the Belgrade station. "They had one interview," Baroness Wrangel said, "and have never met since." Once when Princess Nicholas of Greece came to stay at the palace, the Wrangels were asked to use a side door when they went to visit her. Each year, the General toured the towns where groups of his former troops were living, but always when Parliament was not in session, "so as not to cause questions to be asked." Baroness Wrangel lived with her husband at Petrovaradin, except for occasional visits to America and England to raise money to support her fifty-bed sanatorium in Belgrade and another in Sofia. Once a week, she said, she came to Belgrade to look after the sanatorium, but saw no government officials except in that connection. "No politics ever!"

Leaving Belgrade that spring, I wrote Coolidge and Gay that I was in two minds about the country's future, optimistic for the long run, but with some forebodings about the next few years. Pashich had said he was confident that, if the government exercised a firm hand, the regional controversies would not be disastrous and within ten years would give way to a sense of independence. Then the reins could be loosened safely. But those ten years would be a period of great hazard. The old politicians who would still be in charge would find it hard to learn new ways: the Serbs to forget their feeling of superior virtue due to the sufferings they had undergone, the victory they had won; the Croats to stop emphasizing how much more cultivated and wise in the ways of the world they were than their backward Serbian brothers and to take a constructive part in building a new state. On both sides a time lag had to be made up.

There undoubtedly existed such a thing as a Jugoslav national spirit, but it had come into being among the different South Slav peoples at different periods and with different motivations. Before and during the war, when Serbs, Croats, Bosnians, Macedonians or Slovenes had used the slogan "independence and union" they had meant different things. To some extent they still did. Until the country had time to produce new young leaders who thought of it as a single inheritance from the struggles of the past, there would be jealousy and contests for regional preference and differences as to the role of the central government.

The next decade did indeed prove to be one of discord. It did not produce the hoped-for fresh, young leadership; and the obstinacy of the old leaders led the King eventually to act without them and against them in order to save the country's unity in spite of itself.

III

Arriving in Budapest was like coming back to yesterday from tomorrow. In Belgrade, every shop window had a picture of King Alexander and his bride-to-be. In Budapest, it was everywhere the same picture of the Emperor Karl who had twice attempted to regain the Hungarian throne and on the second try had been shot at by the soldiers of the Regent, Admiral Horthy, who was supposed at the time to be holding the throne for him, the legitimate Hapsburg monarch. Now Karl was dead, having died in exile on the island of Madeira only a month earlier, and his photographs were draped forlornly with wisps of black crepe. In Belgrade, people talked of the city they would have one day, when the streets would have been changed from Turkish cobblestones to asphalt, and discussed a supposedly pending American loan (never in fact forthcoming) with which Serbia would build a railway of her own to the Adriatic, an opening to the West that would free her commerce from Italian interference as well as make it less dependent on the Croatian middleman. Now Hungary was surrounded by peoples who had learnt to hate her, and her former foreign markets were for the time being shut; business was at a standstill. In compensation, people spoke of how lively night life used to be before the war, of the hussar officers who had thronged the sidewalks in their brilliant braided uniforms, fur-edged dolmans slung around the shoulders, of the gay crowds that used to be attracted to the May races at the Jockey Club.

The old city of Buda rises, as does Belgrade, on a height above the Danube. There the similarity ceases; neither the Royal Palace, the Coronation Church or the other imposing edifices on Castle Hill, nor the broad boulevards, splendid hotels and vast factories of Pest, the more modern half of the capital spreading over the plain across the river, have anything in common with the small Balkan city. Belgrade was bustling, making do with oxcarts and primitive equipment of every sort; the people walking out in the crowded evening *corso* greeted each other animatedly; the sidewalk cafés were filled; business was being done even in the doorways of tumbledown shops not yet rebuilt owing to the shortage of materials. The boulevards of Budapest were unkempt, scraps of paper eddied about and were caught at the bases of the heroic-sized statues, the sidewalks were half-empty, many stores boarded up. The *tziganes* played at teatime in the gilded hall of the Hotel Hungaria for a drably dressed group as apathetically as it is possible for *tziganes* to play, very unlike their tireless brother fiddlers in earth-floored Belgrade night clubs. Pasted onto the revolving doors of the Hungaria, tram windows, post boxes and other convenient places were stickers with the legend "Nem, nem, soha!" —a defiant "No, no, never!" to the Treaty of Trianon and the loss of Hungary's non-Magyar lands. After the war and defeat, the Károlyi revolution, the Béla Kun revolution, the Rumanian occupation and the Horthy counterrevolution, Hungary looked backward to the old days, resentful and unreconciled.

It was the universal mood. From the Regent and Prime Minister Bethlen down, everybody thought, even if they did not speak, of the time when the treaty which "put the blacks above the whites" would be reversed, when the "occupied territories" would be returned.

One who did speak of it was the dignified Count Apponyi, who had been such an imposing figure at the Peace Conference, chosen to represent his country for his name, one of the greatest in Hungary, his Western manners and his magisterial bearing. If Bishop Nicholai seemed a medieval saint and Pashich a venerable patriarch, Apponyi was an Old Testament prophet. It was remarked at Paris that a man of his appearance must be a man of peace and justice. But like Old Testament prophets he was given to self-righteous anger, and did not conceal from me his expectations of a day of reckoning with Hungary's despoilers. He had been a supporter of Emperor Karl and was standing as a monarchist in the forthcoming general elections. The legitimists had posters everywhere carrying pictures of little Archduke Otto and slogans demanding his immediate coronation with the thousand-year-old crown of St. Stephen. Socialist posters showed pictures of starving mothers and children side by side with those of quarreling politicians. Government posters pictured Apponyi and other legitimists as punctured balloons. (The elections produced a landslide for Horthy and Count Bethlen; Count Apponyi was one of the very few surviving opponents.)

Count Apponyi, not sounding like a punctured balloon, spoke with scorn about Hungary's enemies. At Paris, he had argued Hungary's case against the Serbs, Croats, Slovenes, Czechs, Slovaks and Rumanians in vain, but he remained certain that a way would be found to reverse the Allied decisions. How soon might that be, I asked?

"I am an old man," he replied, "and I may not live long enough to see Hungary restored. But the day is coming, and my son certainly will see it."

"How much of your former territory do you think you will get back?" I asked.

"All," he said. "The Slovaks already have come to hate the Czechs more than we do. The northern territories will come back to us first, but the south will follow soon. The civilized Croats will not tolerate being run by the oriental Serbs, their inferiors in every way. They will turn back to us as surely as morning follows night." He waved his hand as though ushering in the accomplished fact.

When I left Count Apponyi's cream-colored baroque house in old Buda I walked through silent side streets and across an empty square for a brief audience with Admiral Horthy at the Royal Palace, where the royal flag was flying for him as Regent. Ruddy-faced, clean-shaven, monocled, in naval uniform with decorations, he received me without rising from behind his desk. Apponyi had hinted that Horthy did not really mind the monarchist propaganda and only objected to its being pushed so early, the implication being that later he might himself be able to assume the royal title as well as the royal power. To questions he replied that he was a convinced monarchist and legitimist, but he decried the present discussion as to who should be the Emperor Karl's successor. It was too early to settle the matter. To place the young Archduke Otto on the throne would be an "encumbrance" on the peaceful evolution of the state and an excuse for hostile neighbors to attack. If he was being Machiavellian, he hid it successfully under matter-of-fact and thoroughly insensitive behavior.

Count Bethlen, Hungary's most adroit diplomat, received me in a huge room in the half-deserted Parliament House, a pseudo-Gothic edifice covering more than four acres. He thought Count Apponyi was doing harm to Hungary by his impatience and injudicious talk.

"We must work and keep quiet," he said. "Time is on our side. We must not postpone the day of treaty revision by frightening our neighbors with extreme talk."

He went on to express strong regret that those neighbors "refuse to trust us," but before an hour was up he was rapping the corner of his desk to emphasize that though he wished to conciliate them they were in fact of inferior stock and inadequate culture and had no moral right to individual nationhood. I waited for the fatal word, and it came in the statement that though his government wished to live in peace with everyone the Treaty of Trianon could "never" be accepted as fair and lasting.

"Never" is a long time, and Hungarians who used the word with confidence in 1922 did not take into account that the nationalist revolution which had destroyed their ancient realm was still proceeding. As the Succession States which now surrounded them consolidated their position, Hungarian plans for revision became more and more unrealistic. Hungary was too angry to understand. Instead of cooperating with the Succession States in stabilizing Danubian peace and learning to sell by persuasion and merit instead of monopoly and privilege, she remained unreconciled and alone, succumbed eventually first to Hitler and then to Stalin and found an unpremeditated adjustment of her relations with her neighbors inside the Soviet orbit.

IV

The authenticity of Prague was refreshing after the made-to-order grandeur of Budapest, magnificent in its ensemble but disappointing in detail. Even where the grandiose structures of the Hungarian capital rest on ancient foundations or incorporate parts of original buildings, they have been reconstructed by nineteenth-century architects after wars and fires. By contrast, the antiquities of Prague are real and more lovely the more closely you examine them. In Budapest, the Hapsburg palace staring across the Danube from the countless windows of its quarter-mile-long façade must have overwhelmed visitors from the provinces with a crushing sense of Magyar wealth and power. Very different were one's sensations climbing the long cobbled stairways to the top of Hradčany hill and passing through the successive arches that lead into the vast inner courtyard of the castle built by the kings of Bohemia bit by bit during five centuries.

The medieval and baroque palaces, squares and monuments, refined and elegant, scattered throughout Prague; the Gothic cathedral of St. Vitus in the castle courtyard, the burial place of Bohemian monarchs and archbishops; the statue-lined Charles Bridge across the Moldau, linking the busy commercial districts with the tangle of quiet streets on the Malá Strana, described by Karel Čapek and other habitués—all are so much in the tradition of European civilization that even in later years when the menacing visage of Stalin stared out incongruously from shop windows you reassured yourself with the thought that surely a physiognomy so unlike that of Masaryk the philosopher, the father of Czechoslovak independence, could not misrepresent the country's soul and destiny forever.

Like Jugoslavia, Czechoslovakia was facing internal as well as foreign problems. The Czechs, primarily Western, industrialized and highly educated, with many free thinkers and Hussites among the Roman Catholic majority, had to be merged with the much less developed, primarily agricultural and mostly Roman Catholic Slovaks living to the east, as well as, further eastward still, in the Carpathians, with the Greek Catholic Ruthenes, desperately backward as a result of long neglect by their former Hungarian rulers. In the Sudetenland, the German section of the population was dissatisfied with their rights in the new state. Even at that time, 1922, I was told by a member of the cabinet that despite Prague's conciliatory policy the Sudetenlanders were hoping for a new war that would put them back in Germany.[1] The task of organizing all these and other discordant elements into a sound society and viable state fell to two leaders of different but brilliant talents who fortunately worked in harmony.

Thomas Garrigue Masaryk's intellectual and spiritual power, his tenacity and fearlessness, gave him a decisive influence during the war on the thinking of the Allied statesmen, especially President Wilson; and afterward as President of the Republic he had unrivaled prestige at home and was easily the outstanding figure among the leaders of the new states. His protégé and colleague, Eduard Beneš, was for a short time Prime

1. After Munich, of course, they got their wish both for war and for reannexation (temporarily) to Germany.

Minister and then remained as Foreign Minister for seventeen years.

When we reached Prague I found that Beneš was still at the Genoa Conference, and I feared that this would defeat one of the principal objects of my visit, to induce him to write an article for the first issue of *Foreign Affairs;* but a letter of invitation which I left for him was so persuasively backed up by a young friend in the Foreign Office, Josef Hanč, that when I got back to New York a couple of weeks later word came of Beneš' acceptance, followed soon afterward by his manuscript. Hanč did everything for us. He persuaded Masaryk and others in the government to see me, showed us the beauties of Prague, even took us to where it was planned to lay out the city's first golf course. The site was enclosed in a narrow valley, and I said I wondered whether it would not be too small. "Oh, but Czechoslovakia is a very small country," Hanč explained.

When I wrote Professor Coolidge from Athens that I intended trying to get an article from Beneš I naïvely remarked that I supposed he was really more interesting for that purpose than Masaryk. Without making invidious comparisons now between two remarkable men, one whose course was determined by deep moral convictions and a philosophic sense of history, the other whose activity was pragmatic and primarily political and who was to carry his responsibilities through a time of searing tragedy for his country and himself, I can say that the impression I had had of Masaryk sight unseen was changed drastically after spending a day at his country place at Lany, some miles outside Prague.

It was an unpretentious château, set in wide lawns and surrounded by beech woods. I found the President dressed in an unpresidential manner, something halfway between a hunting outfit and what might have been worn by a small country proprietor—belted loden-green jacket, breeches and leather leggings. Incongruously, his throat was constricted in a standing wing collar. The space between the wings was filled by a neat Vandyke beard, down to which the ends of a bushy mustache swooped rather untidily. He spoke deliberately, with many pauses, looking at you the while intently, almost severely, through pince-nez. After lunch with his daughter, Dr. Alice Masaryk, Richard Crane and one or two others, he took me off for a stroll through the woods, moving stiffly and holding himself very erect. Before setting out he covered his domed and nearly bald head with a militarylike cap with a hard visor.

This brief description does not, I see, present a very alluring picture. It is accurate in externals but misleading in every respect that matters. At Williamstown Lord Bryce had named Masaryk, Venizelos and Smuts as the three greatest men produced by the war. I had asked him to go further, to name the three who in his long life had seemed to him most endowed with the attributes of greatness. "Kossuth and Mazzini," he replied, "but, most of all, Masaryk." So far I had put only Wilson in that category (Bryce did not) ; now Masaryk took a place in my mind beside him. Writing a letter of thanks afterward, I said I would never forget the day at Lany. Unlike most polite platitudes, it proved literally true.

Before lunch Masaryk showed me a memorandum which he had prepared for Herbert Hoover relating Russia's need for aid to Bolshevik psychology, doctrine and policy, and gave me a copy.[2] Even a glance through it was enough to show that it could be the basis for a most valuable article, and Masaryk agreed to write it. But a few weeks later he was forced to go to Capri for a rest, and meanwhile Beneš prepared a piece for our first issue describing the purpose and role of the Little Entente, of which he was the principal author. Masaryk's article as eventually printed in *Foreign Affairs* in July, 1925, turned out to be very different from the memorandum; instead it was a meditation on the theme of national character and psychology as they determine political action. He used as a principal example the way in which the German people had gradually separated themselves from the cultural body of Europe and taken more and more to militarism in a violent flight from morbid subjectivity and what he described as a suicidal mania.

To remind me of my talks with Masaryk all that I find are some headings, never filled in, scribbled on the back of an envelope—"Czarist govt. weaknesses, neglect"; "ignorance esp. of officers"; "legionnaires," and so on. In speaking of his despair over the lack of intellectuality in Russia he emphasized the disastrous results of the ignorance of army officers who understood nothing about the nationalities problem in Austria-Hungary, supposed that the Czechs and Slovaks they took prisoners were Austrians and treated them as enemies. Reports of this ill-treatment discouraged Slav soldiers in the Austro-Hungarian armies from surrendering and handicapped Masaryk's efforts to make the Allies understand that the disaffection of the subject peoples constituted an enemy weakness that should be exploited. From the start the Russians mistrusted the two divisions of Czech Legionnaires whom Masaryk organized to fight on the Allied side; and when the Bolshevik regime came to power and made a separate peace with Germany it actually ordered them disbanded,

2. I have made inquiries about this memorandum, dated February 10, 1922, both at the Hoover Institution on War, Revolution and Peace, Stanford University, and at the Library of Congress, and have consulted leading Slavic scholars and persons who were closely connected with Masaryk. No knowledge of it exists.

forcing them to fight their way out by way of Vladivostok and circle the globe to reach home.

Masaryk was well-disposed toward me because I was an American. His liking for America came not only from knowing it at first hand but from having read everything American worth reading from Tom Paine to Thomas Jefferson to Walt Whitman to Edith Wharton to Edgar Lee Masters. He married an American, Charlotte Garrigue, of New York, whom he met at Leipzig while he was studying philosophy and she was studying music, and added her name to his. He admired Wilson in the same way that he admired American civilization, not ignoring its shortcomings but believing deeply in its essential character and purposes. It was from Washington that on October 18, 1918, he proclaimed Czechoslovak independence and it was from his house there that there flew for the first time the colors which now floated over his country place at Lany.

In Paris, Coolidge's letter of introduction brought a prompt invitation from André Tardieu to come to see him at the Chambre des Députés, and I was able to persuade him that he should try to put a new face on American misunderstandings about the course of French policy, which was being described in America as merciless toward France's vanquished enemies and grasping in her demands on her allies. Tardieu singled out Lloyd George and Keynes as chief culprits, the one for accusing France of militarism and intransigence toward Russia, the other for accusing her of forcing Germany into bankruptcy. I assured him he would be free to answer American criticism as sharply as any other—as in fact he did, point by point and, though courteously, with unsparing directness.

I didn't think it was a bad bag with which I was returning to New York—articles from Beneš and Tardieu for our first issue, a promise from Masaryk for the future, another from Caillaux (balancing rightist Tardieu) —and with a headful of ideas, some good, some less so, about other things that must be written about as soon as possible.

PART TWO

Against the Tide

History is a scenario without an end.
—WINSTON CHURCHILL

12

The Making of "Foreign Affairs"

"Our office will be in New York," Coolidge had written in one of his first letters, "and there you will sit and do things." One room in the two-room office at 25 West Forty-third Street was for me, the other for the as yet nonexistent business manager, with a cubbyhole for the secretary who would take care of both of us at the start. On my desk I found a dummy of what a printer thought the magazine might look like. It was about nine by six inches in size, bound in what felt and looked like blotting paper, except that I had never seen blotting paper of exactly that bilious greenish-brown. The title, *The Journal of International Relations,* was in smallish caps, with space underneath for the names of the editors and the Editorial Advisory Board and the titles of a few selected articles. Inside, a sample text was set in 10 point, in two columns, with skimpy margins, on a smooth but lackluster paper. The attractiveness of this sample was not enhanced by the fact that the printer had chosen at random from some medical journal a passage describing intestinal functions.

Someone experienced in publishing might have found this an inauspicious start toward getting out the first issue of a magazine within the next three months. I did not know enough to be daunted. The first task was to find a business manager, and with the help of friends at the *Evening Post* our search resulted most fortunately in the selection of Frank D. Caruthers, Jr., who became an efficient colleague and remained such for nearly forty years. After some argument, my suggestion of the title *Foreign Affairs* was accepted, and, that settled, I was given more or less a free hand to design the format and make a printing contract, subject of course to consulting Coolidge at every point and securing his approval, and within the limits of the operating fund established for the first year. Caruthers knew the printing business inside out, and although his main experience had been in publishing a two-thousand-page mail-order catalogue, he proved equally adept at getting printing bids for a two-hundred-page quarterly and identifying their pros and cons with an eye to more than dollars and cents.

The Council on Foreign Relations was by this time a new body with an old name. As I have mentioned in the preface, it represented the amalgamation of the American Institute of International Affairs, started at Paris in 1919 by members of the American delegation at the Peace Conference, and a group organized in 1918 by leading lawyers, bankers and other men of affairs in New York to discuss wartime problems and entertain foreign visitors. That original Council on Foreign Relations had been active from June, 1918, to the summer of 1920, holding meetings mainly on topics of concern to the New York business, professional and banking communities. With the end of the war, interest in it lagged. In April, 1919, a fund raiser was engaged, but he met with no success. A year later the Council had become, as one member put it, "old and waning," without a definite focus for its activities and without funds to carry them on.

The American Institute was also adrift. Its members had scattered after Paris to their usual academic and other occupations, leaving it a paper organization with high purposes but no locus or definite program and no finances except the $10 annual dues of its twenty-one members. In the fall of 1920 several of them became conscience-stricken that they were doing nothing to combat the relapse of the American public into the easy belief that they could ignore the war's lessons and slip back into the nineteenth-century concept that the United States need not engage its influence in critical international discussions. Probably all the members, Republicans and Democrats alike, had favored American membership in the League of Nations, though differing about desirable or necessary reservations. They had no intention of using the Institute to propagandize for the League, but they were perturbed over the irresponsible character of the isolationist attack on it and what this portended for the future course of American foreign policy.

They were also startled by the discovery that, while the American Institute languished, the British Institute, which had been organized as a sister body at the meetings in Paris, had suddenly sprung into independent life with an impressive inaugural in London, at which the speakers were Viscount Grey and A. J. Balfour, both of them former Prime Ministers, the one a Conservative, the other a Liberal, and Lord Robert Cecil and J. R. Clynes, leader of the Labour party. Was the comparable organization in the United States, where education in foreign affairs was so much more urgently needed, to lag behind, perhaps fade out of existence?

As the elections of November, 1920, approached it became evident that the isolationists were in command of the Republican party, that they controlled its candidate, Warren G. Harding, and that his election was inevitable. It was in this depressing atmosphere that Whitney H. Shepardson, the secretary of the Institute, called a meeting in New York on October 18 and presented a proposal from the Council on Foreign Relations that the Institute join it, take charge of the new organization and shape a new program. A committee was appointed, with Shepardson as secretary, to explore ways and means. Also, eleven new members were elected, several of whom were thereafter to be very active in devising those ways and means.[1]

In a memorandum to Institute members describing the terms of the proposed merger, Shepardson asked three critical questions. The fee for Council membership was $100, but since Institute members belonged mainly to the academic rather than the business world the Council was suggesting that their dues be lower. Would this difference prevent members from associating on equal terms? The Institute had been created as "an organization wherein all shades of political and economic thought might have a hearing, and where the sole criterion of membership should be the candidate's scholarly and continuous interest in the foreign affairs of the United States." Could this standard be maintained in the proposed merger? The Institute had determined to avoid the ordinary social amenities of many international societies and devote itself to a scholarly study of international questions. Would the many members of the Council who were occupied with other matters find it possible, "however earnestly they might desire it," to devote sufficient time to Institute matters?

With the answers to these questions in hand—some of them cautious, several negative—Shepardson asked a few members of the Institute, myself among them, to meet at dinner January 10, 1921, to decide, as he

1. A list of members of the American Institute of International Affairs, including those elected October 18, 1920, is printed in Appendix I. For further details, see *Early History of the Council on Foreign Relations,* by Whitney H. Shepardson, printed privately for the Council at the Overbrook Press, Stamford, Connecticut, March, 1960, 20 pp.

sternly put it, either to join the Council "or simply disband." We gave
an emphatic "No" to the second alternative and agreed that the problems
raised in his memorandum were no bar to the proposed merger. This
decided, the way was open for a Committee on Policy appointed by the
Council to take over, under the chairmanship of George W. Wickersham,
former Attorney General. Members of the Institute preferred that the
new body take the name of the Council in order to indicate that it was
entirely distinct from the British Institute. When the committee had
settled organizational details, one of its members, Frank L. Polk, former
Under Secretary of State, was instructed to draw up by-laws and file
articles of incorporation. The committee then turned over its responsibility to a Board of Directors, who chose the following officers: Elihu
Root, honorary president; John W. Davis, president; Paul D. Cravath,
vice-president; Edwin F. Gay, secretary and treasurer. The Council on
Foreign Relations, Inc., was officially in being.

What would be its future? An unfavorable augury might have been
found in the comment made by William Allen White about the American experts of the American delegation as they set off for the Paris Peace
Conference. They were, he wrote derisively, "a desperate crew of college
professors in horn-rimmed glasses, carrying textbooks, encyclopedias,
maps, charts, graphs, statistics and all sorts of literary crowbars with
which to pry up the boundaries of Europe and move them around in the
interests of justice, as seen through the Fourteen Points." It was precisely
these academics who had formed the American Institute and now were
to join forces with a group of presumably hard-headed men of the world.
Would time show that the amalgam was either too soft or too hard? Or
might the mix perhaps prove valuable, and endure?

A group of members, drawn from both components, were determined
that the experiment should succeed. None was more determined than
Gay, who in spite of his labors and anxieties at the *Evening Post* found
time to engage in organizing the Council and planning its future activities. He insisted, as has already been told, that the first step toward giving members of the Council a sense of responsibility and making the
organization an influence in American life was for it to establish a
periodical of unquestioned authority in its field.

The board agreed to Gay's proposals with alacrity and soon thereafter set about raising the necessary underwriting fund for a quarterly
review—$25,000 for the first year and, hopefully, the same amount an-
nually for a five-year term. Success for the first year was assured when
Otto H. Kahn underwrote whatever portion of the sum could not be

found. There proved to be no need to take up his generous offer. The final total was composed of contributions ranging from $50 to $2,500. (The budget did not include overhead, since the Council was to pay for the office separately.) I have already told how Coolidge was finally tempted into acceptance as editor (on a half-time basis), and how I became his assistant. His salary was to be $4,000 (equal to the half of the Harvard salary which he was relinquishing), mine was to be $2,000 as managing editor, plus $2,000 as general manager of the Council (in succession to William R. Grace, who had managed the Council on a part-time basis in the past). The budget also provided for an office manager, but as no provision was made for a business manager of *Foreign Affairs* I was allowed to shift the item and engage Caruthers.

Now on June 7, the very afternoon of my arrival on the *Homeric,* I was sitting for the first time in the Council office, under instructions from Coolidge to "do things."

II

"Doing things" was a commodious term, covering not only editorial and mechanical preparations for getting *Foreign Affairs* started but organizing as well the Council in its new form; I was to find ways to invigorate the parent as well as bring its offspring into the world. The magazine obviously must come first. And the first step must be to hurry up to Boston to see Coolidge and settle innumerable things, small and large. It was our first meeting since Williamstown. I stayed with him in the big house on Beacon Street which had been his father's and discovered at once how considerate and hospitable he could be. Later he bought the house and described why in a letter to me: "I have concluded to follow the line of least immediate resistance and to do the thing which is most expensive and some would say ridiculous. I mean to remain just where I am. That is, I look forward to residing alone henceforth in a large corner city house which will cost much even to keep dusted, and where I shall rattle about like a small pea in a large pod. On the other hand, it is the place I love." It was a most comfortable pod, as I found whenever I visited there.

The visits were to be less frequent, actually, than Coolidge had expected or had warned me to expect, for he found trips to New York exhilarating and frequently made excuses, connected with *Foreign Affairs* or otherwise, to come down, and, usually, spend a couple of nights with my wife and me. Our small house on East Thirty-sixth Street was a contrast to the spacious old-fashioned house in Boston, where Coolidge was tended in a curious combination of luxury and spartan bachelorhood by a sedate all-Irish team of cook, waitress and parlormaid (I suppose to do the dusting). For the first time I encountered "picked up codfish" for breakfast and a cream clam chowder for at least one other meal.

I see I have said nothing about Coolidge's looks. He was of medium height, square shouldered, broad chested. In college he had been a boxer and featherweight wrestler, and his appearance showed it, though by now his sturdiness was more to the eye than in fact. He walked with a nervously rapid step. His countenance was frank and tranquil. His blue-blue eyes looked at you steadily, whether benevolently or in exaspera-tion. He parted his rather sparse hair in the middle, and as he wore it cut short it gave an old-fashioned effect of a fringe across his broad and high forehead. He spoke with a slight lisp, which of course aroused the amusement of his students in History I; nevertheless it was the most pop-ular course in the curriculum. A book about Harvard once published a caricature of him as Napoleon, with hands clasped behind his back, partly because his figure did in a way resemble Napoleon's, partly be-cause of the severity with which he judged the scholarly attainments of his students; witness to this was a cartoon which appeared in the Harvard *Lampoon* showing him dressed as an Indian chief hacking to pieces scores of freshmen with one of his principal instruments of torture, a copy of Putzger's *Historical Atlas.* Years later, one of his students, Bruce Hopper, retained a mental picture of Coolidge in a seminar, a map lying flat on the table before him, his hands hovering eloquently over spots relatively inconsequential in 1925, and saying: "Watch the Gulf of Aqaba, a potential cause of war in the Middle East; it was safer when it was controlled by the Turks."

Before going to Boston I had thrown the printer's unhealthy-looking dummy into the wastebasket. It had been settled from the start that we were not to use illustrations or pictures on the cover. This meant that if *Foreign Affairs* was to be attractive-looking it would have to rely on elegance of format and readability of type. Caruthers and I decided, after much sampling, to use Caslon 12-point type on a slightly off-white laid paper, with the "Exeter" water mark and deckle edges. The paper was 50 percent rag, so that the contents would be preserved for (we com-placently told ourselves) appreciative future generations. Later, when microfilming was invented, this precaution was less necessary. We also specified that issues should be stitched rather than stapled, so that they would open conveniently and lie flat. Later, to economize, we adopted stapling for a time, but the protests of subscribers when they found their copies snapping together like a trap showed us our error, and we adopted a new form of binding having many of the advantages of stitching.

Coolidge felt, as I did, that the cover was highly important, and we spent a morning looking at all the periodicals in the Widener Library at Harvard, trying to find a guide to a design that would be dignified but not stodgy and attractive without being arty. About that time, American monthlies had begun changing their covers with each issue. We felt that they sacrificed some of their identity by this, and that at any rate for a serious periodical the sense of continuity given by a familiar cover was more of an asset than the novelty of continually new ones. Our hope was to secure a design which might prove acceptable indefinitely.

With Coolidge's approval, I appealed for ideas to my sister Margaret, who had designed hundreds of book covers for leading publishers. Almost by return mail I received two little sketches, and a day or so later several more. These were partly her work, partly that of my sister Helen; they often collaborated, Margaret being particularly good at lettering, Helen at figures. Helen hated lettering; it bored her so that she hurried ahead, only to find after she had finished a long inscription on one of her stained-glass windows that she had left out a letter somewhere and had to do it all over. She had a similar aversion to letter writing, so my

The Foreign Affairs Colophon

Suggested Alternative Designs

correspondence was, naturally, with Margaret. She advised that the cover be as uncluttered as possible, omitting names of editors and selected articles, that the lettering be simple but distinctive and that a colophon be the only ornamentation. One of her suggestions was that the colophon show the Pillars of Hercules, the gateway between the eastern and western hemispheres, and using the old form of the motto, "Plus Oultre," as being more picturesque than the modern "Plus Ultra." She remembered that my father, an artist, had had this out once with the Geographical Society and they had let him use "Oultre" in a window he was making for them. Another sketch was based on the device of Emanuel of Portugal, showing the earth and the sea, but with a motto from Galileo, "E puor il muove"—"And yet it moves"—the idea being that it might be taken emblematically to indicate the (hopeful) progress of the world. Another was of a globe with the inscription "Veritas: Lux." Another, showing a horseman, with the motto "Ubique," was the one we eventually agreed upon. One detail troubled Coolidge: he didn't like the two "Rs" in the title having tails of different lengths, but was persuaded that the slightly off-balance effect was deliberate and, anyway, showed it was hand lettering and not from a commercial font. For cover stock we adopted a crisp gray-blue Fabriano paper. Thus designed, the cover has remained unchanged ever since, an almost unique phenomenon in the magazine world.

It seemed advisable to establish a business relationship with our authors, if only to be able to pay for an article which we had invited without feeling bound to use it if unsatisfactory. As our budget was limited, we began with an honorarium of $100, modest even for those days (since increased). We knew that in any case we could not tempt a leading statesman by the size of the monetary offer but by the fact that *Foreign Affairs* was nonpartisan and noncommercial, that he would be free to say what he wanted (short only of being libelous) and would have elbow room to say it as he wanted. As for members of the academic world, Coolidge said they would at least think our check better than the twenty-five reprints offered as payment by most of the professional reviews. We always named our honorarium in advance, to save argument or disappointment.

A good slice of my time in the first weeks was devoted to trying to secure an impressive leading article for our first issue. Our quarry was Elihu Root, former Senator from New York, former Secretary of State and Secretary of War, at seventy-seven the most eminent and weighty elder statesman of his day. As I knew he had high regard for my father-in-law, James Byrne, my first approach was through him. The Senator hesitated whether or not to accept, which seemed a good sign, but when time passed and he still hesitated I first enlisted the help of his son, then of John W. Davis, then of George W. Wickersham, finally threatened to go up to his place at Clinton, New York, to see him. Meanwhile he returned to town, and Elihu, Jr., reported that he had actually prepared his letter of refusal but had held it up as he was loath to refuse a favor to Mr. Byrne. I asked Mr. Wickersham to see him and tell him something much more important was involved than doing a favor for Mr. Byrne. By now I was in despair; more than a month had passed and still I could not get a yes or even a no. Suddenly on July 13 I was able to send Coolidge the good news: I heard Root was going to accept. Then three days later I had to inform him "a thunderbolt has fallen"; a letter from Root himself had arrived, explaining that while he would do an article for us it would be "something very brief, rather to indicate my interest in your venture than anything else." After the weeks of effort and waiting, this was exasperating. ("These old men," I blew out to Coolidge, "are really intolerable.") Should we tell him to delay until he had time to do us a real article, or wait to see what he sent in? I recommended the latter. "I suppose," I wrote sourly, "we could at least use it in advertising."

We had been racking our brains what to do if Root failed us. To fill the gap, Gay suggested Charles W. Eliot, for forty years President of Harvard and a national figure. My recollection from meeting him while Bryce was visiting him in Maine was one of awe. Coolidge was of two minds; he shared Gay's admiration and affection, he said, "but there is no telling what the old gentleman will say," since he was liable to go off at a tangent and make remarks that provoked sharp criticism "and sometimes make the judicious grieve." Nevertheless he was persuaded, and sent Eliot a masterly letter. The reply was a simple "I will see what I can do about the article for the new review," plus these sentences of advice: "I hope it will prove to be more than a forum for 'writers with widely differing views.' What this country is suffering from in many fields is lack of leadership. It seems to me that *Foreign Affairs* ought to set out to be a leader or guide for a cause warmly embraced." Coolidge realized, of course, that Eliot spoke as a strongly partisan Democrat (he had been asked by Wilson to be Ambassador in London, but declined because of age), and wrote back that he did hope that the magazine's articles would help guide public opinion but that he thought its express avoidance of an editorial stand in favor of any one party "ought to increase rather than diminish its influence." Despite this firm reply, I think the feelings entertained toward Eliot by even as stout-hearted a Bostonian as Coolidge were slightly tinged with the same awe that Eliot inspired in me. When the manuscript came it proved to need some minor editing, and I wisely left Coolidge to persuade him to agree. Regarding one larger change Coolidge wrote me: "I am more puffed at having got Mr. Eliot to strike out a sentence he had written than by any success I have had in years."

In July I met Coolidge at Williamstown and drove him over to Squam Lake, in New Hampshire, where he and his brothers had bought an old farmhouse and considerable land, including a wooded island. We went by the beautiful pass over Peru Mountain, which he said he had always wanted to see. The road was steep for cars of those days, but the views were superb. Coolidge was building a stone house on a high spot overlooking Squam Lake and we used it each day as a base for walks, with stops now and then to sit on some stone wall for talks on editorial problems. Coolidge was getting great fun out of building his house, and even the long delays while local materials were being selected and assembled were more pleasurable than frustrating. The exterior was of smooth-faced stone quarried from nearby mountain ledges and the paneling inside was of wood from his own forest. In the center of the courtyard was a wide-spreading sugar maple. (The house was finished only the summer before his death, and he actually lived in it only a few weeks.)

One of those summers while the house was building, Coolidge lent a camp on a small wooded island in the lake, named Hoag Island but locally called Hogg, to Bruce Hopper, one of his graduate students, later assistant professor of history at Harvard and one of my closest and most admirable friends. He assured Bruce's wife, Effie, that no animal more dangerous than a porcupine was on the island; the main inhabitants were fifteen sheep that he had put there to give the Hoppers company and help keep down the birches springing up everywhere. Between reading and writing, Bruce employed himself chopping and scything a path around the edge of the island. One morning he came upon a pile of leaves and twigs underneath which he discovered the carcass of one of the sheep. He supposed it had been killed by a dog but sent word to the game warden, who on arrival pronounced it the work of a bear. No bear had been seen near the lake for forty years. Nevertheless, the next day the warden assembled several farmers who slowly traversed the island beating tin pans. Suddenly, sure enough, a small bear started swimming for the shore. An assistant warden and a farmer stationed there shot him. Bruce said neighboring farmers feasted for several days on roast bear steak. The skin was cured and hung up in the stone house. The bear was dead—one bear was, anyway—but Effie did not find the island as restful afterward as it had been.

But I must wind up the story of the first issue. Toward the end of July word came unexpectedly that the invitation to Beneš was bearing fruit and the manuscript was actually on its way. Just then, too, I saw in the shipping news that an old friend of Coolidge's from Vienna, the historian Dr. Joseph Redlich, of whom he had often spoken, was arriving in New York. I met him at the pier and took him to his hotel, then to lunch at the Century, secured a visitor's card for him there, and the next morning blarneyed him into sitting down and doing us a piece on the new Danubian relationships emerging from the debris of the Hapsburg Empire (in which, by the way, he had been the last Minister of Finance). Coolidge warned that he was "effusive and elusive," but the article materialized as promised and was a good companion piece to that by Beneš on the Little Entente. Tardieu cabled, too, that his article was finished. Besides these three articles, Eliot's and the snippet expected from Root, we also had in view several others, including one by a young lawyer whose brilliance had impressed Coolidge and many others at Paris, John Foster Dulles, who agreed to tackle the thorny problem of the inter-Allied debts. No one (except Dulles himself) had any idea that he would be Secretary of State thirty years later, nor did we foresee that he would often contribute articles to *Foreign Affairs* over the years, including two while he held that office.

Coolidge enjoyed all the editorial ups and downs tremendously. At one point he confessed, "This is an exciting game." As the date when the manuscripts must go to press drew nearer and nearer I became too time-conscious to get proper pleasure out of the excitement.

III

There was an important last-minute addition to the roster for the first issue. Masaryk, we had hoped, would deal with Russia, but he had defected. Who were the leading American authorities on Slavic affairs? Undoubtedly one of them was Coolidge himself. Very tentatively he indicated the possibility that he might "take his coat off" and write the missing article, and I snapped eagerly at the idea.

If there was a country that interested Coolidge more than France it was Russia. He had studied at both the University of Berlin and the Sorbonne (and later—uniquely, I think—had been exchange professor at both) and had taken his doctorate at Freiburg, but it was Russia which became his chief concern. It began when he served for the winter of 1890–91 as secretary at the American Legation in St. Petersburg, which gave him a chance to perfect his Russian. Afterward he traveled through southern Russia and the Caucasus and into Asia as far as Meshed, in Persia; in 1895 he visited Russia for the second time, spending some time in Siberia; three years later he again traveled in the Caucasus; and in 1902 he went by the newly-opened Trans-Siberian Railway to Vladivostok. These first-hand experiences, probably unequaled among Americans at that time, led the State Department to send him in the summer of 1918 to report on Russian conditions from Archangel, where he found the fateful inter-Allied intervention already breaking down in chaotic disagreement and futility. He was again turned to in 1921, this time by Herbert Hoover, who enlisted him as a member of the American Relief Administration in Russia; during his five months there he had dealings with Chicherin, Radek, Litvinov, Kamenev and other high Bolshevik personages.

This chronological summary gives no indication of Coolidge's constant preoccupation with Slavic studies, till then largely neglected in the United States but, as he saw, of tremendous future significance. He showed the way in remedying that defect by his energy (and success) in pushing the novel idea that they become a part of the Harvard curriculum and, as head of the Widener Library at Harvard, by developing the Slavic collection to the point where, in large part by his own donations, it became one of the richest such collections anywhere outside of Russia.

"We must have plenty in *Foreign Affairs* about Russia first and last," Coolidge had written me. His own article was the first; just how much "plenty" meant he may not have foreseen. In the next forty-five years *Foreign Affairs* printed 248 articles dealing directly with Russia, more, I believe, than any other Western periodical not specializing in the field. And in that period it commented on more than 2,000 books on Slavic topics in its quarterly bibliography. In agreeing to set to work and write an article under forced draft Coolidge made two stipulations. One was that he should write anonymously (the letter "K" was the pseudonym he chose), so as not to involve our editorial policy in whatever controversial opinions he might express; "an article by me, if cussed out, might hurt the whole Review." The other condition was that his piece should be placed last in the issue, not out of false modesty but because he thought an unsigned article in that position would attract attention and indicate that readers ought to persevere with their reading of an issue to the bitter end.

Coolidge took his stint hard and worked over it, I won't say tirelessly, it did tire him, but indefatigably. "By sitting up to two o'clock for the last couple of evenings I have managed to get theoretically to the end of my Russian article," he wrote, adding in a resigned vein, "At the present moment I have very little idea what it is about." What it proved to be about was, in essence, the problems of the new Russian state just entering actively into world politics, enumerated without bias and with amazing foresight.

Among those whose attention the article at once attracted was Lenin himself. Word of this came from Coolidge's former student, friend and A.R.A. colleague in Russia, Professor F. A. Golder, who had returned to Moscow from Riga in the autumn of 1922. He wrote Coolidge that he found "our friends of the red calico"—Trotsky, Lenin, Bukharin, Radek "and the other Olympians" (mentioned, strikingly, in that order) — very much occupied with the Fourth International Congress, but not too much occupied to be interested in the first issue of *Foreign Affairs,* a copy of which had already reached Moscow. Golder wrote to Coolidge on November 22, 1922, that he had had an interesting talk with Karl Radek, chief Soviet propagandist and member of the Central Committee of the Communist party, who told him he had just seen that first issue and had read it from cover to cover. He spoke of the anonymous article in the highest terms and gave a guess that Coolidge was the author. "I hope he is right," Golder commented. Radek said he had given his copy to Lenin, "who is now reading it."

Golder remarked that he was astonished at Radek's grasp of the world situation (I was similarly impressed when I met Radek at Geneva several years later) and his information about American politics. The Soviets certainly had an excellent intelligence system, Golder said, and not many things were happening in the State and Commerce Departments that they didn't know about—and this not only as regards facts but motives also.

The sequel was told by Golder in a second letter, recounting how Radek had just been to dinner with him, bringing his copy of *Foreign Affairs,* in which he had marked in the bibliography a number of books which he would like to get. "He offered to copy," Golder continued, "but I proposed that he leave his copy and I give him mine. He agreed. When I looked into it I found that he and Lenin had marked up a number of passages in the Russian article as well as some of the other articles. You would give a good deal to see that, wouldn't you?"

Coolidge did see it, for when Golder returned home he first lent and then gave it to him, and it is now in my possession, a generous gift from Coolidge's nephew, Harold Jefferson Coolidge, Jr. The markings in it are mostly underscorings and heavy marginal lines, made by two hands with different pencils. The article by Root is not marked and the pages by Tardieu and Beneš remain uncut, contradicting Radek's remark that he had read it from cover to cover. Among the other articles, one by Professor Blakeslee entitled "The Mandates of the Pacific" was marked at a number of places, all of them dealing with strategic considerations, including the reasons for the American claim to Yap. The article by John Foster Dulles was heavily underscored throughout, and folded into it Golder found a two-page memo in which Radek had analyzed Dulles' figures. It is identifiable as Radek's because the writing is the same as that on the envelope in which he later sent an article to *Foreign Affairs* and also because it contains words in Polish, his native language. Some of the most heavily underscored passages are those where Dulles expresses the opinion that Europe would not be able to reverse her unfavorable trade balance in the next ten years to the extent that she could extinguish the principal of her debts to the United States or even to pay interest on them. Singled out for four black strokes in the margin was Dulles' statement that "while Great Britain may make some payment, the Allied debts as a whole will never be repaid."

The Coolidge article is marked at many points. A section of a paragraph underscored and circled begins, "The Russia of today declares she has renounced imperialistic ambitions but that this does not mean she is indifferent to legitimate national interests even if she is not now in a position to assert them effectively," and ends, "She will therefore not accept as valid any international arrangements concerning them made without her participation." Another of Coolidge's passages singled out in the same manner reads as follows: "Shall we refuse to sell sorely needed farm instruments to the Russian peasants because we dislike the Moscow Soviet? To recognize the government of a country does not imply that we admire it, it is merely to take note of an existing fact. If the crimes of Sultan Abdul Hamid were not deemed a bar to American commerce and to the necessary official relations with Turkey, why should trading with Russia make us responsible for the practices of Lenin and Trotsky?" Both statements must have raised hopes in the minds of the readers in Moscow; and the suggestion about the proper basis for recognition, a subject bitterly debated in the United States until Roosevelt finally recognized the Soviet Union in 1933 (trading on short-term credits, however, had been carried on from 1925), still provokes controversy both in principle and as applied to, for instance, Red China. Lenin could hardly have smiled at a reference by Coolidge to his possible disappearance from the scene, "an event which in view of the state of his health may occur at any time, if it has not occurred already." He had been seriously ill for a year, had suffered a stroke in May and was to be disabled by another only the week after Golder wrote his second letter to Coolidge.

Besides checking the approximately two dozen books listed in the bibliography which interested him, Radek also wrote in the margin that he wanted recent books on Wilson by Tumulty and Backer (Baker?) as well as "alle Bände" of the Temperley history of the Paris Peace Conference. Assuming that most of the markings in the bibliography are by Radek, and that those in the same pencil and style elsewhere are also his (including, of course, those in the Dulles article), the others can be taken to be Lenin's. When A. A. Sobolev was the Soviet representative at the United Nations he heard of the existence of this annotated copy, and, wishing to learn what might have been interesting to Lenin in his last active days, asked to borrow it; I of course agreed. If Sobolev read Coolidge's article with attention he would have found that the problems facing Soviet diplomacy in those days of Soviet weakness before and after the crucial conferences at Genoa and The Hague were, strangely enough, less complex, if anything, than those of thirty-five and forty years later, when the Soviet Union had become one of the world's two colossi.

September 13 was the great day when I was able to send Coolidge a copy of the first issue. I said simply: "I hope you will like the looks and feel of it as much as I do. We already know about its contents." Then I went on to talk about plans, already well along, for the issue to follow. Copies were in the mail that day also to those who had had enough faith (or curiosity) to subscribe in advance. We had hoped there would be about five hundred; actually, the number of paid subscribers on publication date was about twice that. The list grew steadily, and in two and a half months reached twenty-seven hundred, plus the sales through booksellers and newsstands. A second printing of one thousand became necessary in order to satisfy subscribers who wished to begin with the first issue. Ivy Lee, an important member of the new tribe of public-relations advisers, had warned some of his clients who thought of contributing to the underwriting fund that if they did so they must be prepared either to continue their support indefinitely or let the magazine close down, because, in his belief, a sober review such as we planned could never secure more than twenty-five hundred subscribers. By spring we had something over five thousand.

The good reception given our first issue was helpful in raising the full five-year underwriting fund, which would allow enough time to show whether or not *Foreign Affairs* could make a place for itself. I had written Gay from Belgrade in the spring that I was less concerned about the review's being financially guaranteed for a long time than about Coolidge's being "free and unhampered." When an undertaking is owned by an organization or group, I wrote, there might be many people who thought they had a say in it. "I suppose it is understood," I said, "that Coolidge is boss." One way to have complete editorial freedom was for the editors not to be involved in raising money. Coolidge made this an explicit condition in accepting the editorship.

When I reached New York in June and found that the underwriting fund had been completed for only the first year I made no move to enlist subscribers to it myself but did press that someone be found to give the task full time. Gay as usual supplied the solution by proposing to lend us Cass Canfield, a member of the business staff of the *Evening Post*. When we think of the enormous sums given by the great foundations today for all manner of educational purposes, and the large gifts of public-spirited individuals, it is hard to imagine the difficulty Cass experienced in obtaining pledges for such a modest sum as $25,000 a year for five years. He turned to the job with immense energy and determination, and when in spite of his best efforts things lagged, he put the problem up to the directors without mincing words. Polite letters of introduction were not enough. Would they solicit subscriptions directly themselves or give up the enterprise? They responded nobly to this goading, and by the end of the winter the fund was complete. My sneaking hope was that when Cass had put *Foreign Affairs* on a firm financial basis, he might take over as general manager of the Council. Instead he joined the old established firm of Harper & Brothers and in time gave it an even more eminent position than it had had in the past among the great American publishing houses.

There was some debate on whether or not *Foreign Affairs* should accept advertising. Coolidge tended to oppose it, but I thought it necessary if we hoped to become self-supporting, also because it would help make plain that the review was more than a house organ. My promotion methods, though the most innocuous possible, also came under discussion. For example, I asked my sister Helen to design a card to be used by subscribers who wanted to give Christmas gift subscriptions to friends. Charles W. Eliot, with whom it was not difficult to have differences of opinion, was critical of any attempt to secure subscribers other than by a simple announcement that the review existed and that it cost such and such a sum. He criticized the fact that I "asked" people to use *Foreign Affairs* as a Christmas gift. I wrote Coolidge that I agreed that we must not descend to cheap promotion but that "a polite mention of our name in the Somerset Club Library or the office of the Third Assistant Secretary of State was not going to be enough to give us a circulation that will allow us to continue or a broad enough influence to be really useful." (The Christmas-card device was adopted by many other periodicals. We still use it.)

Contributing to the success of the first issue was the fact that we had not let disgruntlement with Root's proposal to give us only a testimonial to our good intentions rather than a full-fledged article develop to the point of asking him to postpone his contribution. In sending his manuscript to Coolidge, Root wrote: "I yielded to Mr. Armstrong's polite insistence." Did this conceal a gentle rebuke? At any rate, I was thankful he had not guessed the depth of my exasperation—or maybe he did. His article turned out to be a magnificent statement of the criteria for the successful conduct of foreign policy in a democracy. We gratefully gave it the leading place in the issue; and it has been referred to and quoted from innumerable times ever since. The reason this has been so can be indicated by the following passage:

When foreign affairs were ruled by autocracies or oligarchies the danger of war was in sinister purpose. When foreign affairs are ruled by democracies the danger of war will be in mistaken beliefs. The world will be the gainer by the change, for, while there is no human way to prevent a king from having a bad heart, there is a human way to prevent a people from having an erroneous opinion. That way is to furnish the whole people, as a part of their ordinary education, with correct information about their relations to other peoples, about the limitations upon their own rights, about their duties to respect the rights of others, about what has happened and is happening in international affairs, and about the effects upon national life of the things that are done or refused as between nations; so that the people themselves will have the means to test misinformation and appeals to prejudice and passion based upon error.

Thus succinctly, and in magisterial language, Root summed up the whole reason why *Foreign Affairs* was coming into existence.

13

"The Tiger" Revisits America

Practically paralyzing all work on *Foreign Affairs* was the arrival in New York in November, 1922, of Georges Clemenceau, the world's most conspicuous and controversial figure. Although the Council on Foreign Relations had not originally invited him to America it had agreed to sponsor his appearance in New York.

Today New York has become completely blasé about political celebrities. Crowds may still turn out for an astronaut, but the United Nations attracts prime ministers and foreign ministers in such endless succession that hardly anybody notices their comings and goings; even when the Mayor gives one of them a key to the city the papers mention it only perfunctorily. It is hard to imagine, then, the intensity of excitement caused by the arrival of the eighty-one-year-old "Tiger," the man who more than any other was taken as the wartime embodiment of indomitable France and of Victory itself. The Council had been drawn almost unawares into the maelstrom of competing well-wishers and would-be exploiters as well as xenophobes who were ready to hiss any foreigner venturing to sully American soil by setting an alien foot on it. The original invitation had been pressed on Clemenceau by Colonel House and others, several of whom happened to be Council members; then, when they realized what competition there was going to be between persons and organizations for the glory of entertaining him, and the risk of his welcome being marred by isolationists, pacifists, pro-Germans and other mutually hostile but temporarily united elements, they persuaded the officers of the Council, still pretty loosely organized, to take the whole thing over. A committee of four was put in charge, consisting of Frank L. Polk, George W. Wickersham, Otto H. Kahn and myself, and since I was young and incautious I enthusiastically assumed responsibility for settling the details. The principal problem seemed solved when Kahn arranged for the Council to have the use of the Metropolitan Opera House for the evening of Tuesday, November 21, without charge. Actually problems were only beginning.

The excitement over Clemenceau's visit was due mainly, of course, to enthusiasm and veneration for him as *Père la Victoire,* but curiosity about him had been brought to a high point by the unbridled attacks being directed against him from all directions and for contrary reasons. In France, superpatriots reviled him for not having insisted on harsher terms against Germany. One of these was Foch, whom Clemenceau had made Marshal of France in the black days after the Chemin-des-Dames. Foch had urged the Peace Conference to let France annex the Rhineland or control it indefinitely and had been thwarted mainly by Clemenceau, who thought this would rupture the alliance with the United States and Britain, neither of whom would condone it, and would plant the seeds of a new war. Foch announced: "Wilhelm lost the war, Clemenceau lost the peace." At the leftist end of the political spectrum, leaders like Caillaux opposed his going to America on the grounds that he intended to start an anti-German campaign.

Simultaneously, pro-German groups in New York and Chicago issued statements attacking him; Irish-Americans had a grudge against him because of a mistaken assumption that he was in league with Lloyd George; pacifists said he was a militarist and imperialist; and isolationist Hiram Johnson, Senator from California, demanded to know why he should not be barred from spreading "alien propaganda" in the country. Johnson was vociferously supported by Mayor William Hale Thompson of Chicago, the same who later achieved fame by announcing his desire to give King George of England "a poke in the snout."

The French Government, fearing that Clemenceau might provoke anti-French demonstrations but even more that he might annoy the Harding Administration by telling Americans undiplomatic truths, had refrained cautiously from giving the trip official sanction. Foch predicted sarcastically in an interview with the New York *Tribune:* "He will cry and be sentimental like all old people." The *New York Times* thought this insulting. It replied sharply, "M. Clemenceau doesn't cry, he laughs."

He was welcome, it said, as "a great part of living history," as "a marvellous old man with a wonderfully youthful spirit" and with "the volcanic power and fire of the demi-gods of the French revolution."

It was in an overcharged atmosphere, then, that a group went down the Bay on November 18 to meet the *Paris* bearing this illustrious personage on his first visit since he had left America in June, 1869. He had quit France four years before that, after his attacks on Napoleon III had landed him for two months in jail. For a time he lived in Greenwich Village, on Seventh Street near Sixth Avenue, writing for *Le Temps,* then taught French and riding at a girls' school in Stamford, Connecticut. He fell in love with one of his pupils, married her in New York three years later and took her back with him to France.

Then he was twenty-eight; now, after a lifetime of tumult, he was arriving on the *Paris,* aged eighty-one. The group to greet him included French Ambassador Jules Jusserand, Assistant Secretary of State Robert Woods Bliss (representing, it was rumored, a rather reluctant President Harding), Colonel House, Bernard M. Baruch, the Acting Mayor, Colonel Stephen Bonsal and the four members of the Council on Foreign Relations committee. Ambassador Jusserand was said to be risking his government's censure by welcoming Clemenceau; but he told me he had not hesitated. We boarded the Mayor's boat, the *Macom,* very early, for the *Paris* was due at Quarantine at seven. When we approached the starboard side of the great ship it was seen that she had a slight list to port, and after the *Macom* had maneuvered unsuccessfully for a time under the doorway which had been opened some twenty feet up in the black wall we passed around to the other side. A thousand heads peered down and cheers drowned out our little municipal band as well as the distant ship's band playing on the upper deck. Even on the port side it was necessary to bring in a police boat to serve as a sort of bridge. Clemenceau, who had been watching these maneuvers impatiently, descended to the police boat with great agility and before frantic assistants could reach him had clambered around the narrow ledge of the pilothouse and down the second gangplank onto the *Macom.* There his valet helped Colonel House button the fur collar of his greatcoat up around his neck. The weather-beaten gray felt hat pulled down to his eyes was a change from the deer-stalker cap made familiar by the photographs of him visiting the trenches.

By the time our band had played the "Marseillaise" and "The Star-Spangled Banner" the newsmen and photographers had caught up and now began shouting directions and questions to which Clemenceau paid not the slightest attention, conversing with House as though they were alone on the windswept deck. During the national anthems he had held his hat against his heart and you saw the contour of his massive head: a rather flat forehead running up to a dome covered with only sparse hair. In compensation, his eyebrows and mustache were phenomenal. The bushy eyebrows, widely separated, stuck out so straight that they would have outdistanced any mustache but this one, which drooped at the sides but bristled forward in the center in a white hedge. The mobile wrinkles on his forehead gave his face a quizzical look, made somewhat menacing by the violent motions which he was able to give his eyebrows and mustache, adding emphasis to his successive expressions of surprise, annoyance, skepticism, arrogance. One reporter noted that although the face was very much alive the tightly-drawn rather yellowish skin gave it, paradoxically, a curiously withdrawn Oriental appearance. He was hardly "the gorilla of yellow ivory" described by Harold Nicolson, but the whole bearing of his chunky, rather hunched figure was somehow defiant, almost insolent. He inquired sarcastically of one photographer who stuck his camera into his face whether he was trying to measure the length of his nose and remarked loudly to the whole horde that he would gladly see them all killed. One pressed him twice with the inane question whether he had been invigorated by the voyage. "I do not want to be invigorated," he said. "I want to be left alone." Was his health better? "It is always better." What were his plans? "I will confide them to you privately at the Metropolitan Opera House on Tuesday." And so on.

The Statue of Liberty soon came into sight, a new landmark since he had last seen the harbor. He said laconically to Jusserand: "It is good." On the trip to the Battery, where the *Macom* landed, he was handed a message from his colleague and (sometimes) antagonist at the Paris Peace Conference, Woodrow Wilson, now an invalid in Washington, sending him "an affectionate welcome to America, where you will find none but friends." He angrily winked tears from his eyes. After a ceremony at City Hall, he was escorted uptown to the house of Charles Dana Gibson on Seventy-ninth Street, chosen by Mr. Polk partly because it was comfortable but unostentatious, partly because he knew that Mrs. Gibson, like himself a Southerner, would treat Clemenceau with warm hospitality. She paid the penalty of losing her cook, who rebelled at getting up in time to give Clemenceau the onion soup which he required every morning at five o'clock.

There was some worry that at Clemenceau's age his voice might not carry to all parts of the Metropolitan Opera House, and at my suggestion

Kahn arranged for him to go down there the next day at the end of the Saturday matinee and try out his voice and if necessary one of the new-fangled amplifying appliances.

"I don't want to scream," he agreed. "Perhaps I'll sing."

He arrived at the stage door sooner than expected, toward four o'clock, and I took him and House to Box 48, which Kahn had arranged to keep empty for him. The opera was Boito's *Mefistofele,* with Alda, Gigli and Chaliapin. Drawing aside the curtain at the back of the box, he peered in. It was the scene in Hades, the stage filled with crawling toads and snakes, bats flitting ponderously above. Clemenceau stood glowering for a moment, then turned and went out, pulling the curtain behind him.

"Trop Italien!" he said curtly.

For the rest of the opera he sat in the little anteroom of the box. He was annoyed when at the end the orchestra played the "Marseillaise" and "The Star-Spangled Banner," and said several times in refusing to recognize the thunderous applause that it was not for him but for the singers. As he obviously would have no chance to try out his voice, we put off the test till the afternoon of the speech. To his relief, we found then that he could probably be heard sufficiently well without any mechanical aid.

To head off a scramble for seats I distributed those in the front rows of the orchestra to Council members and assigned the boxes to Council directors and distinguished persons who had been associated with Clemenceau during the war, such as General Pershing (who preferred, however, a seat on the stage), General Bliss, Colonel House and Paderewski, until recently Prime Minister of Poland, now just resuming his career as pianist, also to Miss Anne Morgan and others who had been identified with wartime aid to France. The rest of the seats, put on sale for the benefit of the American Field Service, the charity chosen by Clemenceau, were snapped up at once even in the peanut gallery. It was fortunate that all was done quickly, for there at once arose a great clamor from any number of persons who felt they deserved consideration. One day I came back to our little office to hear our harried telephone operator, Miss Coleman, an efficient eighteen-year-old protected by calm indifference, a sense of humor and an Irish accent, saying:

"Mrs. Vanderbilt, it doesn't matter *who* you know." Then, pausing between each word for emphasis: *"There—is—not—any—box!"*

As Clemenceau walked softly onto the stage to meet the ordeal he had come to dislike particularly, a public speech, the first person he saw was General Pershing. Flinging himself into Pershing's arms, he began talking animatedly to him, oblivious of the four thousand people watching. "God bless you, my dear Pershing!" was all I could hear before the cheers drowned everything out. That afternoon he had rejected the dais prepared by the opera management ("I don't want to look like Queen Victoria"), and took his place on a small cane-bottomed chair like those on which Elihu Root, John W. Davis and other officers of the Council were seated beside and behind him. He had been up at three to work on his speech; had had his onion soup at five; breakfast at seven of four hard-boiled eggs, Gruyère cheese and cold tea; lunch of soup again, oysters, chicken and the invariable Gruyère cheese, and now after a nap seemed very alert and brisk.

He began speaking quietly, with a simplicity which at once put him in rapport with the audience. The blood of France and America had, he said, been commingled. Could that romance between them really have died? It looked as though it had. He had come to see. He spoke of self-determination, gesturing up toward Paderewski's box. He turned to Pershing, near him on the stage, and flinging out a white-gloved hand swept aside their past disagreements over the early entrance of green American troops into battle. Both of them had been right, he said. When he mentioned Wilson and the Fourteen Points a great cheer went up. Touching on a controversial subject, he said that if he had known that there were to be no real German reparations he probably would have insisted that Foch and Pershing go through to Berlin without pausing for an armistice. He put much of the responsibility for the delay in executing the Peace Treaty on England. He warned that stores of arms were being assembled in Germany and that they might be used by militarists led by Hindenburg. Would not America relent and say a word of sympathy and support which would help bring Britain and France together again against the new danger?

During the speech I left the stage and hurried from one part of the opera house to another, from the peanut gallery to the line of standees in back of the orchestra. The decision not to resort to an amplifier had been right. Clemenceau's voice carried everywhere. When the speech was over I took him to sit for a few moments in the office of the Metropolitan's director, Gatti-Casazza.

"Mr. President," I said breathlessly, "I went all over the house. Everywhere every word you said was heard perfectly."

He looked at me a long moment, then said: "Ah! Mes pauvres jambes!"

Fortunately the Council had no responsibility for Clemenceau's trip outside New York, so I did not have to argue with Mayor Curley and

Mayor Thompson whether they would receive him courteously (or at all) in Boston and Chicago. As a precaution, General Pershing went to Chicago to ride in uniform with him through the streets in order to deter pro-German elements from making hostile demonstrations. In Springfield, Illinois, Clemenceau's dislike of photographers was confirmed. He had insisted that Springfield be included in his journey so that he might lay a wreath at the grave of Lincoln, whom he particularly revered. He asked to be allowed to go into the tomb alone. But two photographers had concealed themselves inside, in advance, and as the old man came into the darkness they set off their flashes. He stumbled out dazed and furious, still carrying the wreath. He sailed for home December 12, having proved to detractors on both sides of the Atlantic that he was, as one newspaper said, "a greater soldier than any soldier."

II

Clemenceau's feud with Marshal Foch, which was still so relentless in 1922, had first become conspicuous during the Peace Conference, but in fact went back to the controversies of the last spring of the war over how to meet the tremendous new assault which Ludendorff was then preparing. It proved to be Germany's final effort, but before it failed it had brought the Allies nearer defeat than probably at any other moment in the four years of struggle. To face it, Clemenceau insisted that American units, arriving in France at a rate soon to approximate 300,000 men a month, must be integrated into the depleted British and French armies, and he told Foch to "order" General Pershing to do this without waiting to form a separate American Army. Foch, knowing that his authority did not go so far, refused; as commander in chief of the French Armies he was subject to Clemenceau, who was Minister of War as well as Premier, but as chief of the Allied Armies he was not.

The longer Foch and Clemenceau lived with the memory of these disputes the more furious they became, and eventually each sought to justify his role before history. Foch told his side of the story to Raymond Recouly.[1] The ensuing controversy saddened General Bliss, who of course had known Foch well. He wrote me from Washington:

Poor Foch! I don't think some of his friends are doing any good to his memory by some of the things they are writing about him. They are attributing to him in the last moment of his life (at least that is the impression they must leave on the mind of the average reader) ideas which he had in the days when

1. Raymond Recouly, *Foch: My Conversations with the Marshal.* New York: Appleton, 1929.

everyone was "hot in the collar" about this or that in the Treaty, and which I am sure he modified long before he died. At the end of the war he lived in mortal dread of a revived military Germany. He had seen two invasions and he had a horror of them. He could think of nothing but taking the Rhine as the new eastern frontier. Clemenceau and most of the French political men were wiser than he. The question to him was a purely military one. Political psychology meant nothing to him. He did not see, as the others did, that to annex the Rhineland would result in a far worse problem for France than Alsace-Lorraine had been for Germany.

Clemenceau's caustic and contemptuous rejoinder to Foch was *Grandeur and Misery of Victory,* published in 1930 in several languages. It created a sensation, for it brought up for fresh review the whole question of the Allied preparation, and lack of preparation, for meeting Ludendorff's assault, termed by Colonel Frederick Palmer "the most powerful and fully prepared military offensive in all history." I hoped to get General Bliss to analyze the rival interpretations of those events in *Foreign Affairs.*

We often speak of "the scholar in politics." General Bliss was the rarer phenomenon, the scholar in uniform. He knew the broad sweep of history as thoroughly as the military art in which he had been trained and was as familiar with Acton and Trevelyan as with Herodotus and Tacitus. His stern judgments of individuals were tempered by compassion for the human race.

His reply to my invitation was sorrowful. He could not describe, he said, how deeply Clemenceau's book had affected him; someone else must be found to review it, someone who did not feel as he did. He hoped that Recouly had put into Foch's mouth words which he had never uttered. In any case, Foch "was lying dead at the time they were published and could neither correct nor deny them." Of the Clemenceau polemic he wrote:

It is the utterance of an old, old man, completely disillusioned as every old man becomes, with the senseless rage of an old man-child at what he does not like. They were the two men in France that I most liked—even loved—in spite of the little weaknesses that anyone who knew them at all could and did notice. But they were, after all, the two biggest men and history will always link their names together. And now the picture that is left in my mind—well, it is as if Homer had left Achilles and old Nestor, after all the glorious memories of their association in the War of Troy, in the hero-haunted Asphodel Meadow of the Elysian plain, forever snarling at each other in childish, unreasoning hate.

Bliss afterward told me more about the wartime relations of Clemenceau and Foch. Though he had seen them together countless times, he never had noticed signs of irritation and rivalry between them beyond the disagreements on details which he put down as bound to occur when forceful persons work together; nor had he noticed friction between either of them and Pershing. He felt that Clemenceau simply had never really understood the relationship between the various Allied commanders and Foch as supreme commander; this in turn was due, Bliss felt, to the confused way in which the unified command had come about. He gave some details of what had actually occurred.

From January 30, 1918, to February 2 the Supreme War Council met at Versailles. Present were Haig and Robertson; Foch, Pétain and Clemenceau; Pershing and Bliss. The discussion was about manpower and how to meet the great German attack due in the spring. Foch proposed that a General Reserve be constituted at once; Bliss supported him, but the best that could be secured was the appointment of a committee to prepare plans and request contingents.

Bliss said the discussion of manpower tended to come back to the question whether the American forces should be put into the lines piecemeal or held back until they could be used as a unit. After comments by Robertson and Haig, Pétain and Foch, in that order, Bliss decided that it was absolutely necessary for the American view to be put forward. He, therefore, stated that "nobody in his senses could imagine that the American intention was not going to continue to be what it had already been described as being, namely to create as rapidly as possible an American Army working in cooperation with the other Allied Armies." This was the unanimous desire of the American people, of the American command in France and of President Wilson, and even if the President or the War Department wished to follow another course, they would find it very difficult to do so. He felt certain, he told the Allied leaders, that if their governments pressed for a categorical answer from Washington, President Wilson, either on his own initiative or after consultation with General Pershing and himself, would give a categorical No to a proposal to distribute the American troops along the Allied front in small units under the command of other Allied officers. At that point Clemenceau remarked that this closed the discussion—as in fact it did. The meeting came to an end with the Allied commanders agreeing on the steps which they might take among themselves for meeting the German attack, but counting on the use of important American forces only by midsummer.

General Bliss considered that the General Reserve was not only an essential step in preparation for meeting the impending German attack but that it might also lead toward what he had constantly been urging, the creation of a unified command. Neither had been achieved when Ludendorff's offensive broke on March 21 against the Allied front north and south of the Somme. The makeshift collaboration between General Haig and General Pétain collapsed and the British-French front was ruptured at the point of juncture. The roads to the Channel and to Paris seemed about to open to the Germans, and the gap in the front threatened to widen fatally if Haig drew his forces to the northwest to block the way to the Channel while Pétain fell back to the southwest to cover Paris. Under the shadow of defeat, a council of war assembled at Doullens on March 26 (the Americans were not invited). Haig had suddenly seen the light: it was necessary that Foch should control Pétain. The meeting decided that Foch should "coordinate" the action of the Allied Armies; but he still was not given power to issue orders. Bliss's impression was that, even in this extremity, "Haig held back as far as possible."[2]

At last, eight days later, it was decided at Beauvais (this time with Pershing and Bliss present) that there could be no further delay. Foch was not given the formal title of Allied Commander in Chief, but he received all powers necessary for coordinating the action of all the Allied Armies on the Western front. The national commanders kept tactical control of their armies and retained the right to appeal to their governments if they felt that Foch's instructions placed them in jeopardy. In fact, however, if not in name, Foch from then on exercised the functions of inter-Allied Commander in Chief which should have been accorded to him, in Bliss's opinion, at Versailles two months earlier.[3]

Pershing opposed the policy of amalgamating U.S. troops into the British and French armies; but he recounts in his memoirs that on March 28 he told Foch "that the Americans are ready and anxious to do their part in this crisis and that I was willing to send him any troops we had." The distinction is important. In his book, Clemenceau spoke of Pershing's fine gesture at the Beauvais conference in offering to put the American troops under the supreme command of Foch. Bliss claimed that this was an exaggeration. The Beauvais meeting had to be considered

2. Haig's own papers covering the period from the Versailles conference to March 25 seem to confirm the impression; but Liddell Hart in the *Encyclopaedia Britannica* expresses a contrary view.

3. See "The Unified Command," by General Tasker H. Bliss, *Foreign Affairs*, December 15, 1922. Bliss notes that as early as December 17, 1917, he reported to President Wilson that a pre-condition of the American military effort should be the establishment of "absolute unity of military control," "even going if necessary (as I believe it is) to the limit of unified command." See also Frederick Palmer, *Bliss, Peacemaker*. New York: Dodd, Mead, 1934.

in the light of the Doullens meeting—i.e., what was done at Beauvais was the outcome and consequence of the desire for a strategical high command. Nobody dreamed that Pershing's action implied that Foch was to have power to break up the American or the British Army and move the component parts about, merely that he was to be able to take strategical decisions without having to get in his motorcar and run around the country consulting Haig and then Pétain.

As for Clemenceau's belief that "he could command Foch to command the Allied commanders," this, said Bliss, "was quite erroneous." Foch, he said, remembered the way in which the supreme command had evolved; "Clemenceau, at any rate by the time he came to write his book, had forgotten."

The story must be read as history only, the history of certain days when the future of nations, ours among them, hung in the balance. It provides no lessons for nations burdened with the irrevocable weapons of the atomic age. Generals will not be scrambling, if a supreme crisis ever comes between great powers, to concert strategic actions that should have been planned in advance. There will be a single decision, an instant response, then oblivion.

Woodrow Wilson and Colonel Edward M. House (U.S. War Department, from the
National Archives)

Gavrilo Princip being arrested after his assassination of Archduke Franz Ferdinand, Sarajevo, June 28, 1914

Georges Clemenceau arriving in New York, November, 1922. Front, left to right: George W. Wickersham, Robert Woods Bliss, Secret Service agent, Clemenceau, Frank L. Polk. Rear, left to right: Hamilton Fish Armstrong, Colonel Stephen Bonsal. (Museum of the City of New York)

H.F.A. with members of Serbian War Mission, Washington, D.C., 1917. Left to right: Martinats, Major Jovichich, Colonel Nenadovich.

Serbian War Mission at Mt. Vernon. Milenko Vesnich, Serbian Minister to France (speaking), and (right) Secretary of State Robert Lansing.

King Alexander of Jugoslavia

Voivode Mishich

Prime Minister
Nikola Pashich

Stjepan Radić

Ivan Mestrović

Bishop Nicholai
of Ochrida

Mme. Slavko Grouich

H.F.A. by Mestrović

Woodrow Wilson
Foundation Medal
by Mestrović

General Tasker H. Bliss

Edwin F. Gay,
portrait by
Alexandre Iacovleff

14

Three French Leaders

Of the three leading French statesmen that I came to know in the twenties—Caillaux, Herriot and Poincaré—it was with Poincaré, curiously enough, that I developed the most sympathetic relations. Curiously, because of the three he seemed the most impersonal, less warm in manner than Caillaux, less warm at heart than Herriot.

Poincaré's voice when he spoke on ceremonial occasions or in the Chambre des Députés was hard and tight as though passing with difficulty through too small a larynx. His argument was as cold as the delivery, but because of its relentless logic it was persuasive even with those who did not wish to be convinced. Nor were his looks appealing. It was not true that he was cross-eyed or dumpy, as hostile caricaturists suggested, but his precision in speaking, his sedentary habits and formal dress added to the general impression of stiffness. He disliked signing typewritten letters and instead wrote in his own hand about even trivial matters such as fixing an appointment. Thanks to his meticulous promptness and the speedy French mails, you could arrive in Paris one morning, write asking whether he could receive you, and get back his handwritten reply the morning following, usually fixing a rendezvous for that same afternoon. He was surprised when I thanked him for answering so quickly; he didn't have time, he said dryly, to put things off. Of course he signed typed or printed official documents; but even the manuscripts of the two long articles which he contributed to *Foreign Affairs* were in actual fact "written" from start to finish, without erasures and almost without interlinings, down to the signature, "R. Poincaré" period.

Professor Louis Eisenmann, of the Sorbonne, explained this phenomenon. "C'est une machine," he said, shrugging, "très bien montée."

Yet when you saw him, either at his house on the rue Marbeau or in
his office, you felt that he was much more than a machine, that he was
really and not just formally glad to see you. This was in part, I admit, for
a special reason.

Perhaps to compliment me, but more likely to put me on notice, he
explained once that he did not receive newspapermen often. "It is a waste
of time," he said. "They do not give me as much as I give them. An exception is M. Jammes [Edwin James of the *New York Times*]. I see him
because he tells me more things that are useful to me than I tell him that
are useful to him."

Compared to Poincaré, Edouard Herriot was impulsive, exuberant,
almost boyish, at least when I first knew him in the early years of his
career. "Early years" is in a sense misleading, for although when I met
him in New York in the fall of 1923 his career as a national leader was
just beginning, he had already been Mayor of the great industrial city
of Lyons for eighteen years. He had come to America on an uncharacter-
istically French impulse; he felt it grotesque that even following the war
few French statesmen bothered to cross the Atlantic (Clemenceau was an
exception; Poincaré never did) and decided to know something at first
hand about a country with which he felt sure Europe's fate was inevitably linked. He saw Coney Island and Harvard, Ellis Island and
West Point, Chicago and Cleveland, was impressed by America's commercial and engineering greatness and hoped that "someday her spirit
will grow up to her body."

While Herriot was in New York I arranged for him to have dinner
one evening with some members of the Council on Foreign Relations. I
had just read in a London paper that he was unlikely to have a great
future in politics: "He has no bite," the English journalist wrote. That
evening he had plenty. He chewed up "those royalist nuisances, Daudet,
Léon, and Maurras, Charles," whose doctrines would now be called
Fascist (in fact they did influence the development of an intellectual
climate favorable to Fascism in Italy) ; Briand—"not a socialist of whom
M. Morgan need be afraid"; Malvy—"poor Malvy, a minister *très insuf-
fisant,* not clever, but not a traitor"; Tardieu—"There sits Tardieu, surrounded by his party—Tardieu!"

By contrast, he spoke of his political antagonist Poincaré with respect:
"A real republican, a patriot, trying to govern with a rightist government on a program which he has little sympathy with." Poincaré had

asked him to join his cabinet, he said, but he could not in conscience do it. He had voted against the French occupation of the Ruhr, considering it an ineffective means of pressuring Germany to pay reparations as well as sure to strengthen the German elements already preaching revenge. He objected to it also because he believed that Franco-British cooperation was the foundation of peace in Europe and that neither country should act separately. But from his tone I gathered that although he maintained the purity of his democratic doctrine he was not sorry in his heart that the action had been taken—less sorry, certainly, than the official attitude of his Cartel des Gauches indicated. At any rate, he had voted for the credits necessary to carry on the occupation once it was a *fait accompli*. He spoke bitterly about the German industrialists and predicted that within fifteen years they would try to restore Germany to her former position by force, even if it meant another war. He said Foch had made a tremendous mistake in not going to Berlin and taking a hundred thousand hostages to ensure the fulfillment of just reparations— he emphasized "just" by adding "I don't mean indemnities and I don't mean payments for pensions"—and also to show the German militarists and industrialists that they really were beaten.

"That was war," he said; "this is peace; which is why I was in favor of going to Berlin then and was against the occupation of the Ruhr now."

Was it too late to win Germany for peace, somebody asked? Not too late to try, but probably too late to succeed.

At that time Herriot stood midway in the new Left which was forming in France. He had some fear, he admitted, that the revulsion from the politics of the Bloc National might swing too far. His aim was to secure a leftist majority, but one which was "democratic, republican, not anti-Catholic, not Communist." When I asked about Caillaux's place in such a scheme of things he shrugged and said, "Caillaux est à la campagne"— meaning in the wilderness. He did add a word or so about Caillaux's financial ability, but said he was "restless" and "tired," that though his ambitions were endless his career was behind him. Briand he condemned as "lazy" and he felt that he, too, was "through." His remarks about their characters were more correct than his estimate of their future roles.

By the time I saw Herriot in Paris in the spring of 1924 the Cartel des Gauches had swept Poincaré out of power and there was no doubt that when the Assembly met on June 1 Herriot would be named Premier. He was staying at his usual unpretentious hotel near the Gare de Lyon and was to go later that morning for a precedent-breaking conference with Poincaré, whom he was turning out of office. It was early, and he looked rather frowsy with unbuttoned vest and hair rumpled as usual. Actually he had been working since six. In the cramped little room, strewn with newspapers and books, his bulky body seemed always to be knocking against something. Sweeping a chair clear for me, he sat down on the bed. The rather pathetic impression he gave of being entirely at home in a drab hotel was correct; he had spent five days a week in this room or another like it during his many years of commuting between Lyons and Paris. The bed sagged uncomfortably and almost at once he got up, dumped things off two other chairs, sat down on one, put his arms on the back of the other and rocked his big body back and forth, gradually edging in my direction. The chair creaked complaints but held up.

He was more troubled by the victory which was bringing him to power than Poincaré probably was by his defeat. One of his hopes had been that a leftist French government might be able to ameliorate relations with Germany, but yesterday the Berlin *Vorwärts* had published what it termed a "colossally important" interview with him (he called it "colossally untrue"), accusing him of intervening in domestic German politics by the statement that he would never cooperate with the German Socialists, Nationalists or Communists. The fabrication would be particularly damaging because *Vorwärts* pretended to favor a Franco-German reconciliation. He was prepared, he said angrily, to cooperate with any German government which showed good faith. This did probably exclude, he admitted, the Nationalists; and the exception in fact seemed necessary, for I had just read predictions by as pro-German a commentator as Robert Dell that the Nationalist program aimed at "the restoration of the monarchy, the revival of conscription, the repudiation of the Treaty of Versailles and an eventual war of revenge against France." Herriot said he was eager to give the Germans every chance for rehabilitation by peaceful means, but thought it a bad omen that they assumed that because Poincaré had been intransigent the man elected to succeed him would be weak and could be taken advantage of.

"I do not have a cut-and-dried program which Germany must take or leave as a whole," he said. "I want to negotiate a reparations settlement because I want to restore Europe. I want to be able to reduce French military expenses. I want to revive enthusiasm for democracy all over the Continent. I want to encourage it in Germany. I will not sacrifice the French right to security and reparations, but I will not claim what is not possible and practicable."

That evening, again in the same little hotel room, I saw a less anxious Herriot. His discussions with Poincaré had been successful; they had agreed on a friendly transition from the old to the new government and he was off in an hour to catch the night train to Lyons to see old friends, collect his thoughts and sort out the items on his program. He would be particularly glad, he said, to be rid of the reporters, who "come at me by fifties, each with the same vapid questions."

"I mumble over and over, 'Yes, I believe in the League of Nations. Yes, I believe in the Dawes report on reparations. Yes, I believe in democracy.' " He laughed and clapped me on the back. "But you won't be satisfied with that." Going to a bureau drawer he pulled out a copy of his privately printed *Impressions d'Amérique,* tore off the band and handed it to me.

As I opened it my eye caught the words "la Société des Nations." I asked how he was going to set about giving more strength to League decisions, warnings and advice.

He rolled up the band he had taken off the book into a little ball and gravely placed it on my head.

"I hand you back your question. What is America going to do about the League? She made it. Only she has the prestige to develop it, make it the instrumentality for opening a new era for Europe and the world. The world has been changed by the war, and is ready for still greater changes. What it lacks is a directing hand. If America would lead with her spirit and soul—which is even more important at this moment than to lead with her physical power—none would dare refuse to follow, not Germany, someday not Russia. In the long run, the danger for America in not taking the lead will be infinitely greater than the danger American politicians imagine they see in taking it."

He mentioned without enthusiasm a proposal just made by Colonel House in *Foreign Affairs,* that the United States might begin by accepting some form of associate membership in the League, then commented: "But perhaps a half loaf would be better than no bread."

What did he think, I asked, of Moscow's ultimatum as published that morning in *Humanité,* in which the Soviet Government let fly a string of threats against what it termed contemptuously the new "bourgeois" French Government?

"If those people," he replied (emphasizing with contempt the words *"ces gens-là"*) , "think I am going to trade epithets with them and deal in ultimatums, they are mistaken. I am ready to talk sincerely and quietly with any nation, but the first requisite is politeness. Abuse and threats are not a substitute for sensible argument. The longer it takes the Communists to learn this, the worse for all of us, and by all of us I mean them as much as any."

He had been collecting his papers as he shot these comments over his shoulder and now headed for the door, waving his round black felt hat at me in place of saying au revoir. By the time I had got on my coat and shut the door behind me his ungainly figure had disappeared down the corridor.

The next morning, all the French conservative papers which had predicted that Herriot could not be elected referred in contemptuous terms to this national leader who felt at home only in his own provincial town and fled there to escape the responsibilities of the capital. Just as before the election, they were forgetting that there was another France outside Paris, and that this France of Bordeaux, Lyons, Toulouse and Le Mans was the strength of the Cartel des Gauches. Unfortunately for Herriot, that strength did not last. For a year he fought to hold the franc and limit inflation, but his financial projects were rejected in turn either by the financial community or by the left wing of his coalition.

Herriot was thwarted in foreign affairs also, specifically in his hope of bringing to success France's six years of effort to supplement the security provisions of the League Covenant and make them more effective. He seemed to have scored a spectacular success when he and Ramsay Mac-Donald went to Geneva in September, 1924, and secured the unanimous adoption of the Geneva Protocol, which would have bound signatories to submit for peaceful settlement every dispute which might lead to armed hostilities, unconditionally, and engaged them to participate in sanctions against an aggressor if these proved necessary. But MacDonald's government fell shortly, and his successor, Stanley Baldwin, decided not to go ahead with the agreement. This reversal of British policy was a body blow to Herriot; and as time went on there could be no doubt that the defeat of the Protocol was a fateful blow to the League itself.

In the end the Herriot government was brought down on another issue —the discovery that in its financial agony it had been borrowing illegal amounts from the Bank of France. Herriot proposed a capital levy; a panic on the bourse followed; and the cabinet fell in April, 1925, to be succeeded by a government formed by Herriot's colleague Painlevé, with Briand in charge of foreign affairs and Caillaux of finances.

II

Poincaré, meanwhile, had been living out of the public eye. Since his defeat by Herriot in the spring of 1924 he had served in the Senate but had seldom intervened in debates. It seemed a good moment to urge him to write for *Foreign Affairs,* and the obvious subject for him would be how the war had come in 1914 and how the responsibility should be apportioned.

In a long talk at his house on March 12, 1925, Poincaré discussed the aspects of the war-guilt question which he felt Americans were most apt to misunderstand. He did not doubt the sincerity of the American historians who were beginning to write on the subject, but he felt that they were under serious handicaps. Historians who had been far from the scene and had not known the participants were forced to base their conclusions on the written record. They made microscopic examinations of what the records told them had happened, day by day, hour by hour, even minute by minute. Did they never stop to remember that the telephone existed and was known to have been used, for instance, in critical moments between Berlin and Vienna? Telephone conversations might have reversed or modified the telegrams found in the archives: indeed, certain telegrams might have been sent cynically just "for the record."

In any case, Poincaré went on, reports of important conversations are not conclusive evidence of what was really said. It had been his experience that even the most capable diplomat can fail to understand the significance of some cautiously phrased suggestion, some *ballon d'essai,* some intimation of disagreement, some warning of the need for restraint. Or he may forget to report it to his Foreign Office. Or, worst of all, he may twist his report in order to support his personal policy or interest.

The last risk was the one that had given him the most anxiety during the war. The French Intelligence was able rather quickly to break the codes used by all the Allied or neutral embassies and legations in Paris —with a single exception. The exception, however, was the one which for Poincaré was by far the most important. Despite all efforts of the French cryptographic experts, the Russian code remained intact. Thus he was prevented from reading the dispatches exchanged between the Russian Foreign Minister, Sazonov, and his Ambassador in Paris, Izvolsky. Since it was well known that Izvolsky disliked Sazonov, who had replaced him as Foreign Minister, the French suspected that he would take every opportunity to mislead, embarrass and defeat him. Poincaré described Izvolsky as "a malevolent intrigant" who had done immense harm to his own country and to France. He was bellicose and rash, Poincaré said, in contrast to the Russian Government itself, which in his opinion had been extremely cautious, especially to the extent that it was influenced by the timid and pacific Tsar. Poincaré suspected that Izvolsky was deliberately reporting incorrectly what he told him about French wishes and French intentions; but since he was not able to read Izvolsky's dispatches, he had no opportunity to correct misrepresentations through the French Ambassador in St. Petersburg. This could well have been of fatal importance in connection with Izvolsky's dispatches on the critical days of July 29 and 30, 1914.

Poincaré emphasized the great handicaps on students who try to disentangle the likely and credible from the unlikely and incredible if they are ignorant of the character of the individuals involved and their personal relationships with each other. He had just noted, for instance, the statement of an American professor that one of his colleagues, Léon Bourgeois, had deliberately undercut his policy. No French writer, whether hostile or friendly, would have fallen into that error; Bourgeois was one of his closest friends, "created by me," and nobody who knew anything about French politics would have imagined Bourgeois capable of deceiving him or crossing him in the slightest particular.

"Naïveté is sometimes more dangerous than bias," he said. "Bias can often be detected, while the man who is simply naïve is credited with being honest, matter-of-fact and therefore right."

Another difficulty for Americans was to appreciate fully the difference in the roles of an American and a French President; they knew that the French President's functions and powers were strictly limited, but they forgot it. Thus some asserted that what they termed his harsh and intransigent views had made French policy harsh and intransigent. Regardless of the fact that he had not had any such tendency, it was Prime Minister Viviani, a Socialist, who headed the government in the critical days of July, 1914, and it was he, not Poincaré, who was responsible for decisions.

Viviani and he had gone to Russia that July on a long-planned state visit. He was convinced that the presentation of the Austrian ultimatum in Belgrade had been deliberately delayed until after he and Viviani were safely isolated at sea on their way home. They had news of it in fact only when they reached Stockholm. His first impression was that the ultimatum was not of fatal significance; he sent advice to the Serbian Government to be conciliatory to the utmost, and proceeded to Copenhagen. But there word reached him and Viviani that the situation was most critical and they turned back to Paris.

Ever since the Bosnian crisis of 1908, Poincaré said, he had realized that the question of whether or not there would be a war rested in the hands of the Hapsburg monarchy. "There would be war whenever Vienna wished it. If the Archduke Franz Ferdinand had not been murdered in Sarajevo in 1914, he would have been killed on some similar occasion.

Sooner or later, Vienna would have had the choice whether or not to go to war."

Up to the last hour, Poincaré was convinced, general war might have been avoided. Viviani, on his advice and with his support, had endeavored to avoid war by two methods: by indicating to Germany that the Entente powers would stand together against attack, and by themselves refraining from any menacing action. He gave as an instance his advice to Russia that any mobilization (which in any event would take from eight days to two weeks longer than German or Austrian mobilization) should be begun only by degrees and without fanfare or threats.

Publication of Poincaré's article in *Foreign Affairs* in October, 1925, set off heated discussions. Some historians criticized it, some approved, but none could ignore it, for it formed part of the historical record. In Germany it caused considerable commotion. We gave the former German Chancellor, Wilhelm Marx, the opening pages in the following issue to present the opposite thesis.

Later on, I sent Poincaré the two-volume histories of the origins of the war by Sidney Fay and Bernadotte Schmitt. They confirmed his feeling that the overpreoccupation of American scholars with meticulous studies, their lack of knowledge of human factors and their distrust of "the known stream of history" tended to make events seem more complicated than they were. Of the final plunge into the abyss he said: "The one act which is irretrievable is when an army crosses a frontier. Until then there can be negotiations. At that point it is war."

Such a neat thesis, tenable in 1914, is no longer sufficient. The threat now does not point to a march across frontiers but is immanent in a capacity to destroy from afar, which at a given moment may be taken as a reason or excuse for preclusive action.

III

I happened to be in Paris during the crisis that brought Caillaux back to office. Although he expected to become the *deus ex machina* of a situation which no one else seemed able to control, he nevertheless clung to the idea that he could write an article about the very financial problems he was going to be struggling with. He had no house in Paris, so asked me to visit him at a friend's brand-new and obviously most expensive residence at Neuilly. While I waited I fixed in my mind the full horror of the room into which I was shown. The walls were of imitation marble, mottled in several shades of bilious green. Imbedded in them were bas-reliefs made of brick-red terra cotta set in imitation marble plaques. One showed a head of Ceres, surrounded by the fruits of harvest; below were a soup tureen flanked by oil and vinegar cruets and bunches of asparagus framed by trailing squash and cucumber vines. The bas-relief opposite depicted Neptune with lobsters caught in seaweed, as well as a hunter holding dead rabbits and birds. Against one of the other walls a naked terra-cotta lady, life-sized, joylessly raised a brick-red goblet toward a hedge, under windows opposite, composed of alternating glazed rubber plants and paper palms set in verdant artificial moss. The temperature was about ninety and the smell of fresh paint made it seem more. I was dispirited long before Caillaux came in gaily, flinging open a pair of shiny yellow double doors and admitting strong odors of cooking that outdid the smell of paint. A week in these surroundings seemed not to have depressed him at all. He looked as virile as he had seemed in exile at Mamers two years before, but the impression he had made then of being a caged animal had given way to one of cockiness.

I reminded him of his parting words: "Au revoir—next time in Paris."

"Well," he said briskly, "here we are."

There he was indeed, and everyone, including his partners in the Cartel des Gauches, was wondering what magic he could possibly work in the national emergency which was bringing him back to power from dishonor and political exile. Two years before I had been laughed at for making the tedious journey to Mamers to interview him—"a goner," as one newspaperman told me, "who hasn't a friend left in France." But it was just because I had heard him so abused in the Chambre des Députés that I had felt I must see him; nobody would waste so much attention on a dead dog. Now he was suddenly France's new hope. It was only three months since the Chambre had abrogated his sentence, and he was about to be put in charge of a situation which was threatening the stability of the regime itself. He wrote later in his memoirs that the offer of the Ministry of Finance had come "either too soon or too late." Either way the situation was desperate. His proper course would be to raise taxes and direct that they be collected ruthlessly, but he had been advising publicly against just that (to court popularity, his enemies said). Shaking his shining bald head decisively, as though that might be a substitute for saying something specific, he repeated several times that the watchword of his new regime would be "order."

Order was the last thing in evidence after his installation at the Ministry of Finance. The corridors and anteroom were crowded with visitors shoving to catch one of his secretaries or even get a word with one of the *huissiers* who were shuffling hurriedly around, jangling their silver badges of office. After half an hour, I was summoned into the office where Caillaux sat at a cluttered desk. The room blazed with lights, three or four people in a corner hissed in angry whispers, a telephone jangled unheeded, stopped, and jangled again. Secretaries hurried in with documents which Caillaux waved away without looking at or signed without reading. In snatches he told me, what seemed obvious, that he was too busy just then to write an article, but he assured me that once he had put French finances in order he would do so gladly. His confidence was obvious but wrong. The franc continued to plummet.

The next time I entered that office was in July, 1926. The corridors were empty. In the anteroom a single *huissier* sat sleepily by the door. He took my card and immediately signaled me to enter. The Minister of Finance sat at the great bare desk, a single lamp making a circle of light on the two or three papers that lay before him. The rest of the room was dark. No telephone rang. We were alone and remained uninterrupted during the next half hour. I might have been talking with the Minister of, say, Transport, during the August lull when everyone is on holiday and not even railway workers think of demanding a pay increase. Since Caillaux had left office three ministries had followed each other like quicksilver. By the spring of 1926, French bonds had been selling below par, the treasury was nearly empty, the franc, normally worth about five to the dollar, had fallen to forty-eight to the dollar.

Now, in July, the situation was transformed. The man who sat tranquilly in the chair where Caillaux had fidgeted was Raymond Poincaré. He had no need to simulate confidence or talk grandly about order. He had taken the drastic and very painful steps necessary to increase revenue and reduce expenditures. The public had reacted with hardly a murmur. The confidence which they had withheld from Caillaux they gave him enthusiastically. By December of that year he had cut the exchange rate of the franc almost in half and stabilized it at 25.19 to the dollar.

15

❧ ═══ ✦ ═══ ❧

Difficulties of Being Open-Minded

Publishing can eat up fortunes and shatter hopes and reputations. It showed how brash I was that my first worry when I was asked to become Coolidge's assistant was not whether I was competent to organize and run a publishing venture, or whether the money would hold out long enough for it to prove itself, but whether we were going to have real editorial independence. Would Coolidge be free from interference even from the organization which would be meeting the bills? My enthusiastic letter of acceptance to Gay raised the question whether in such a group undertaking a number of people might not get the idea that they could share in policy-making, and I added a delicate warning, half from worry, half in hope, "I suppose it is understood all around that Coolidge is boss." This concern vanished when I got home and found that Coolidge had undertaken to do the job as long as the Council directors liked his way of doing it, and no longer; it was evidence of their disinterestedness that they had a similar concept of the relationship between publisher and editor. When eventually I succeeded Coolidge it was on the same basis; neither of us ever had a contract.

I have already mentioned the understanding that, while the editors went their chosen way, the Council had the exclusive privilege of raising the necessary money. This not only relieved us of a chore for which neither of us was suited but also fortified our editorial independence; we never asked a financial favor and so never had to repay one. Another accepted policy was that *Foreign Affairs,* like the Council itself, would not ask or

take aid of any sort from the government. This principle, firmly established from the very first, was never breached over the years. The Council
usually remained on excellent terms with the State Department, whatever
its current political complexion, but never felt, or was, under any obligation to treat its views with more than polite respect. The magazine rose
and fell in the estimation of whatever administration was in office, depending on whether we happened to print articles in which the authors
praised government policy or criticized it.

Security from pressures was essential at the start when our nonpartisan
policy, though firmly professed in words, was not yet proved in practice;
and the more so because in the early twenties the American public was
sharply divided on foreign policy and ready to call in question the motives of anyone expressing an opinion on either side. Colonel George
Harvey, whom President Harding sent as Ambassador to London, was reported as saying that the foreign policy of the United States was to have
no foreign policy, and though he complained that he had been misquoted
it was a view widely held even if not usually so frankly expressed. Battles
were being fought over all the problems created by the war and not just
the key question of the League of Nations. Who had been responsible
for the war? How and why had the United States become involved? What
reparations should and could Germany pay? How settle the war debts
owing from our allies? Should Germany be punished or revived so that
we could do business with her?

Editing *Foreign Affairs* in these conditions was something like war
gaming. We were bound to be attacked, and our hope only could be that
in the course of time we could balance the number who criticized us for
being pro-French by those who criticized us for being pro-German. It
wasn't until we achieved the feat of printing articles by Foreign Minister
Stresemann of Germany and former Premier Herriot of France in the
same issue in the spring of 1924 that we felt we were in an impregnable
position. There were bound to be other criticisms, too, from readers who
considered us conservative and those who thought us dangerously radical.
And there were a few who, in the temper of those days, considered that
the mere fact of our printing articles by foreigners at all proved we were
unpatriotic. More than Coolidge, who enjoyed immunity because of his
scholarly distinction and the fact he was in Cambridge and not New York,
I heard the criticism and received the advice as to how we might reform
and do better.

My reply was to refer to the editorial statement signed with Coolidge's
initials which opened the first issue:

In pursuance of its ideals *Foreign Affairs* will not devote itself to the support of any one cause, however worthy. Like the Council on Foreign Relations from which it has sprung it will tolerate wide differences of opinion. Its articles will not present any consensus of beliefs. What is demanded of them is that they shall be competent and well informed, representing honest opinions seriously held and convincingly expressed. We do not expect that readers of the review will sympathize with all the sentiments they find there, for some of our writers will flatly disagree with others; but we hold that while keeping clear of mere vagaries *Foreign Affairs* can do more to guide American public opinion by a broad hospitality to divergent ideas than it can by identifying itself with one school. It does not accept responsibility for the views expressed in any article, signed or unsigned, which appears in its pages. What it does accept is the responsibility for giving them a chance to appear there.

A shortened version of this statement has appeared in all issues of *Foreign Affairs* ever since.

II

As we settled down into our jobs, Coolidge in Cambridge, I in New York, we found ourselves writing each other practically daily letters, more often two pages than one and sometimes three or four. This sounds as though we spent more time in talking about what we ought to do than in actually doing it. Certainly it was a most unusual way to edit a magazine. At first the letter at the end of a long day seemed a chore, but very quickly I found that it was forcing me to develop opinions and make judgments which I could support with arguments that Coolidge would respect. I wasn't inhibited from making far-out suggestions so long as there was an arguable case for them; in fact I felt encouraged to do so, knowing that he would examine them with a cool but unprejudiced eye.

The style of his letters was usually dignified and polite, but nothing interfered with his saying exactly what he meant. He abhorred pomposity and his estimates of a statesman or scholar whose reputation he thought inflated could be caustic. "Nansen I look on as a bit of a windbag," he'd write; or of Georg Brandes, "a well-known star, but not giving much light on this occasion." His comment when I suggested Bertrand Russell showed that an opinion of that famous philosopher's political judgment which later became widely shared was already fixed in Coolidge's mind: the idea was tempting, he wrote, but Russell was "an ardent not to say unbalanced person, and I hate to think what he might give us." The eminent historian Ferrero, he remarked, "would give us nothing but hot air and I think we are past the stage where we need that from anyone short of an ex-President or deposed sovereign." His rejections could be touched with compassion: "I return Count Apponyi's article. I can't imagine our wanting it under any circumstances, but it certainly is a bit pathetic. I am sorry for the old man and for his kind." Sometimes the nice things he said carried a barb, as when I sent him an effusively complimentary letter about a recent issue from Henry White, who had been one of the less effective American plenipotentiaries at the Paris Peace Conference. "Henry White is an old dear," Coolidge commented. "I must try never to speak disrespectfully of him again."

Those who thought the review was destined to be stuffy were surprised to find John Dewey and Harold J. Laski among early contributors. A most interesting offbeat article by Karl Kautsky, however, did not please the editors of *The New Republic* and *The Nation* any more than it did more conservative commentators. Kautsky had been a friend of Karl Marx and after Engels' death was looked upon as the most authoritative interpreter of Marxian philosophy; if he had not opposed the Russian Revolution his face would now look down on May Day throngs in the Red Square from one of the enormous banners strung up opposite the Kremlin. But he was a pacifist, organized an independent socialist party in Germany in opposition to the German Communist party and entered into a long series of polemics with Lenin and Trotsky. His article on German foreign policy was a strong criticism of prewar Germany as well as of the Allied policy in holding the German people responsible for the misdeeds of the Hohenzollern regime after they had repudiated it. One reader wrote in to say that he was disgusted to find a renegade from Socialism like "Earl Kautsky" admitted to our pages—ennobling him, apparently, in order to strengthen the indictment.

An article on the hotly debated German reparations question in the autumn of 1923 started a controversy which kept up for months on both sides of the Atlantic. The author was George P. Auld, accountant-general of the Reparation Commission, who because of his official position used the pen name "Alpha." His article—twenty-eight pages of analysis and argument, supported by a tipped-in three-fold table of statistics—analyzed the value in gold francs of the French claim for damage in the devastated area; replied to the charge made by John Maynard Keynes, in his much-praised book *A Revision of the Treaty,* that this claim was a "faithless and extravagantly unveracious exaggeration"; and in answer to Keynes's statement that the French people were tax shirkers as well as Shylocks showed that in 1922 they paid taxes equal to 18.3 percent of their prewar income compared to 20 percent paid by British taxpayers and 6 percent paid by German taxpayers. The ensuing argument was too technical, complicated and prolonged to bear summarizing here.[1]

Keynes was a formidable antagonist. His first fame had come through his brilliant and devastating sketches, or caricatures, of Wilson and Clemenceau at Paris. His monetary views were accepted with acclaim by many economists. Auld's accusation that he had been incompetent in handling figures and intemperate in stating conclusions infuriated him and his rejoinders abounded in vituperative adjectives. Auld, a cool Vermonter, was stung into replying in kind, with new batteries of facts and figures. The doubt thrown on Keynes's accuracy angered economists who had accepted his figures and found themselves labeled innocents, as well as organs like *The New Republic* and *The Nation* which considered the Versailles Treaty pernicious (as in respect to the inclusion of pensions in the reparations bill it in fact was) and objected heatedly to being deprived of some of their favorite complaints. *The New Republic* took three pages to blast Auld's argument as a "nauseating concoction of half-truths, fiction, sophism and fallacy."

In my first letter to Gay I had said it was my idea that we should not have too many contributors from the famous. A busy man would be tempted to send us something dictated while he was shaving. This ran counter to A. E. Housman's experience that his best poetical thoughts came to him at that time; however, we were not in the poetry market. Alongside the statesmen we should aim to print younger or at least less well-known writers with unorthodox ideas in order to stir things up. I also felt strongly that a principal reason for the existence of *Foreign Affairs* was to deal with subjects not likely to find a place in other magazines. This often meant turning to specialists and technicians, and in fact, over the years, many of our writers were making an appearance in a nonspecialist journal for the first time. Such, for instance, were the authors of a long series of articles on commodities important in international trade relations, such as coal, oil, cotton, fertilizers, rubber, iron and steel, wheat and gold. Gay gave invaluable help in securing writers in this series. Since specialists rarely were experienced in writing for a general public, they did not realize the importance of form if their views were to be read and have influence. "Officialese" of government servants

---

1. It was pursued by Auld and Keynes in letters in the London *Times* (two), the *Economic Review* of London (three), the *New Republic* (three) and the *Evening Post* (one). See also George P. Auld, *The Dawes Plan and the New Economics*. Garden City: Doubleday, 1927.

often had to be decoded, too. As a result we had to spend an unusual amount of time working over manuscripts. Occasionally it happened that when an author saw the proofs of an article which Coolidge or I or both of us together had toiled to get into printable form he would write back, happily unconscious of all that effort: "I had not realized that my article read so well."

Coolidge never boggled at suggestions of unpopular subjects or unfamiliar writers. He was amused and pleased when some Boston friend or a former pupil by now high in the State Department expressed surprise that he allowed unorthodox ideas to creep into our pages. Rather early in the game I sent him for approval an article which I very much liked from an American Negro leader, W. E. B. Du Bois, a wandering, speculative, prophetic piece of writing defining the problem of the twentieth century as the Problem of the Color Line, with somber warnings as to the coming effects of British and French colonial rule as he had observed it on recent journeys in Africa. Coolidge was delighted with it. "It will provide some criticism," he observed, "but many who object to it will do so because the thoughts it suggests make them feel uncomfortable, as in my own case." Thirty years later Du Bois, frustrated and resentful, had become the fellow-traveling idol of the most radical black circles in America. I am especially glad that we printed that first article of his (and four more subsequently). It was like Coolidge to want to do so, even though, or perhaps because, as he said: "I squirm under the conclusions."

Coolidge's knowledge was encyclopedic, yet sometimes a name cropped up which he didn't place, as happened when I mentioned Mr. Byrne's recommendation of F. E. Smith in case we wanted a smashing article on the effects of the war on international law. Coolidge identified him as an F. E. Smith in *Who's Who in America,* a newspaper correspondent. He confessed to more enthusiasm for the idea on discovering that Mr. Byrne's F. E. Smith was Lord Birkenhead, former Lord Chancellor. He was just as ready to accept an article on Irish agriculture by George Russell, as suggested to me by Sir Horace Plunkett, before being told that Russell was the famous poet AE, as he was afterward. For all his erudition, he was not in the least pretentious and was merely amused to find gaps in it. He often had his innings too, as when I suggested the Marquis di San Giuliano, Italian Foreign Minister at the beginning of the war, to write on prewar diplomacy. He would be extraordinarily good, Coolidge replied, if he had not died nine years ago.

The one thing for which Coolidge was a stickler was absolute historical accuracy. Here there was no compromise. In order to verify or correct an author's facts he would plunge into whatever amount of research he thought necessary to confirm his own quite fabulous memory. He would firmly set a distinguished geographer right on the detail in a map illustrating the Tacna-Arica dispute between Chile and Peru, or the ethnography of the Vilna region, or the route of the Chinese Eastern Railway.

The letters which Coolidge and I exchanged day by day constituted in effect an intensive correspondence course for me in history and politics. His letters showed, what members of the history department at Harvard recorded in a memorial after his death, that "when he hesitated it was not from vacillation." He hesitated until he was clear what *was* the truth.

Often he ended his letters, "Yours as usual." To some this may sound cool, but in light of the relationship which developed between us, trust on his side, affection and admiration on mine, it was, to my ears, comfortable and reassuring.

III

We didn't always find it easy to live up to our principles, but not for lack of trying. For one thing, it was difficult to keep a balance between Democratic and Republican points of view. The problem was to find representative Republican spokesmen. We did not espouse specific policies, but we did assume that the United States had interests and responsibilities which were worldwide. This was contrary to current Republican party doctrine. Republican isolationists said haughtily that their defeat of Wilson's policies had closed the debate not only about future relations with the League of Nations, but about the general relationship of the United States to Europe. Those Republicans who had favored the League and argued for a Senate compromise, and then had voted for Harding in the hope that eventually he would propose some form of participation in the League, felt rebuffed and betrayed. Some of these were disinclined to pursue a lost cause; others who fought on were not representative enough of current Republican thinking to provide the needed balance to the many Democratic spokesmen ready to be heard.

We had been fortunate to lead off our first issue with the article by Elihu Root, the most respected elder statesman of the Republican party (even though his counsel was often disregarded). That coup, however, would not serve as a passport of respectability in Republican circles forever. The situation was not helped when we obtained contributions from Colonel House and Oscar W. Underwood, the Democratic leader in the Senate. True, in the issue with House we carried an article by a Republican Senator, Arthur Capper, of Kansas, describing the interests of the

American farmer in foreign policy; but it was cautious, provincial and rather ineffective. Senator Underwood's attack on artificial trade barriers and his argument for a reasonable degree of reciprocity would later be accepted, but at the time it was very unpalatable to the Republican administration.

When I suggested the House article Coolidge demurred, partly, perhaps, because of his recollection of what he thought had been House's subterranean methods of operation at the Peace Conference, but the reasons he gave were less subjective. "In the first place," he wrote, "the gentleman, though pretty frank in conversation, is more cautious in anything like a public statement and I am afraid we should get only some pleasant commonplaces from him." I too realized the risk, but secured Coolidge's permission to sound House out in a preliminary way. He was surprised to hear that by now *Foreign Affairs* had a respectable circulation and seemed impressed that the papers and wire agencies were quoting regularly from its articles. Gradually he warmed up to the idea that in principle there ought to be an article on the future of the League and began talking about points which it could make. One was that, if the League had been functioning with the support of the United States, France would not have felt the need of invading the Ruhr in pursuit of security, indeed might very well have been prevented from doing so—an argument that he thought might lessen German-American hostility to the League. Similarly, the opposition of Irish-Americans might be modified by pointing out how useful a really effective League might be to an Ireland that was self-governing.

House had been careful not to intervene actively and openly in the Senate wrangle over the League. His counsels in favor of compromise would, if expressed directly, have led him into conflict with President Wilson, something he was determined to avoid; they would also have upset whatever remnant of common purpose still existed in the Democratic party and put the League cause in further jeopardy. I felt sure he wasn't simply sulking because of hurt feelings at being shut off from the President. He simply recognized that any intervention of his except directly with the President would be ineffective; and the President himself he was unable to see or even reach with certainty by letter; if his letters were seen by the President, which was doubtful, they remained unanswered. After Harding's election had foreclosed American membership in the League for at least four years, he settled down to trying to make sure, through personal contacts with friends in both parties, that the League would not be forgotten.

Nevertheless, as the election year of 1924 opened, he opposed the desire of devotedly pro-League Democrats to make the League the central campaign issue. In his talks with Democratic hopefuls (he was making a point of seeing as many of them as possible) he was urging them to commit themselves definitely to the League, but on grounds of principle rather than party, and certainly not to plan the campaign around it, since in that case a Democratic defeat would mean "the end of the League forever." After we had discussed the idea of his writing the article pro (on my side) and con (on his) several times, he suddenly called me up to say, "I wrote that article yesterday." My desire to get him to write now turned into worry about what he had written. What if after so much urging the screed turned out to be as thin as Coolidge had warned it might be? I went up the next morning to his apartment to read the draft, trembling because of the speed of composition and his news that the manuscript was only about half a dozen pages long.

It was my impression that since our last talk he had looked at his copies of *Foreign Affairs* closely for the first time. He had been impressed, he told me, not only by the contents but by the cover, the paper and the type. "It's the best magazine I ever saw," he said, and to prove it was going to have it bound regularly for his library. The main thing, however, was that he had written an article, his first magazine article, as he said, of any real substance. When he said that for this reason he wanted to make it very important and would like to have all possible help in strengthening and expanding it, my apprehensions were eased. On the spur of the moment I made a few suggestions and promised more. When I informed Coolidge what was afoot he gracefully threw responsibility on me: "I have great faith in your diplomatic skill and tact in bringing up the child in the way it should go." When he saw the draft he was enthusiastic and became more so as it grew with each repeated revision. I was seeing House every few days and each time, I told Coolidge, "I got a new paragraph out of him." To this the natural response was: "See him as often as possible."

As an exception, I suggested that House cut out a story which might be turned against Wilson, something he wished to avoid. House had written of Wilson's only half-concealed intellectual contempt for Senators, and how this made them itch to discipline him whenever they could. As an example, House recalled that soon after the President's return from Paris he was asked whether he expected trouble with the Senate over the Shantung clause in the treaty.

"Oh, yes," he replied, "when they find out where Shantung is. At the moment they think it is a county in Ireland."

I remembered this anecdote several years later when one evening at dinner an innocent remark by Mrs. House put the shoe on the other foot. Who, she whispered to me, was Dr. Bowman, sitting across the table? I reminded her that he had been in Paris with the Peace Commission and that he was the leading American geographer.

I cannot reproduce her lovely Southern drawl, but the words were something like this: "Ah, geography is very important. One night at the White House, the pore dear President and Mr. House were down on the flo' around a gre't big map and neither of them *could* find Bucharest."

Mrs. House must have been very beautiful as a girl, and her lovely complexion, white hair and sweet smile made her charming still. Memory was not one of her strong points, nor was she immune to Mrs. Malaprop's weakness. I remember another dinner at which she sat next to me, shortly after a trip to Europe in the course of which she and the Colonel had visited Holland.

"The pore dear Kaiser," she remarked, "is shut up almost like in prison, and guards *parole* him night and day."

In her kindness of heart she referred to anyone dead or in trouble as "pore dear."

House himself slurred his consonants. Thus "Lloyd" George came out indistinguishable from "Lord" George, unfairly confirming suspicions that he paid less attention to things in print than to what came in by the ear.

The title finally agreed on for the House article, "The Running Sands," appealed to Coolidge as poetical. House had always been a man of mystery, and Coolidge expected people looking at the title page to say, "What the dickens are the running sands?" and buy the number to find out. At any rate, the newspapers were intrigued, but House's hope that they would not take the article as partisan was not fulfilled. The Republican papers construed it as a slam at Wilson and gave it particularly generous space.[2] They found the basis for this in House's description of the "irreconcilable conflict between the legislative and executive branches" which had brought about the rejection of the League, and his statement that the cause was as follows: "The President was determined to have his way, and the Senate was equally determined to have theirs. Unfortunately, the Senate had the power to compel the President to yield or lose confirmation of the Treaty, and equally unfortunately, he refused to give

2. The Rochester *Herald* headline said, ungrammatically but unequivocally: "Colonel House Thinks Wilson Fought Wrong." More accurate was the Buffalo *Evening News:* "House Nearly Blames Wilson in Article."

way. As far as his approach to the Senate was concerned, in my judgment, the President's purpose was impeccable but his manner unfortunate." Recalling that the President shared the treaty-making power with the Senate, he wrote: "It is unfortunate, on the one hand, that he did not realize this more completely; on the other it is unfortunate that the opposition party did not take a broader and more patriotic view of the situation."

This on-the-one-hand, on-the-other-hand, interpretation of the reasons for the Senate's failure to approve the League was objectionable to many of Wilson's adherents, and of course did not suit the Republicans either.

For some time our search for a matching Republican stalwart was fruitless. We approached without success Senator Hiram Johnson of California, who in today's slang would be called "Mr. Isolationist," and Senator William E. Borah, of Idaho, also ardently opposed to "foreign entanglements" and free of all taint of Wall Street and the Europe-oriented East.[3]

Our problem was not solved until Coolidge persuaded his friend Senator Henry Cabot Lodge to enter the lists. Senator Lodge's article, which led the summer issue of 1924, began briskly by charging that Democratic allegations that the Republican party had no policy were only a political device to draw attention from its many achievements. Because we were not in the League and not "entangled in European affairs" did not mean, he wrote, that we were incapacitated from taking any part in international questions. "The United States has never been isolated," he went on, "and has no desire to be isolated." It can best serve the world by preserving its own strength and the fabric of its own civilization. "America and Europe are entirely different." Many Americans had come here to be free of the "long war-habit of Europe." Let us not entangle ourselves in age-old quarrels which Europe understands but we do not. "Let the League, which was made in Europe and belongs to Europe, go on there and prosper." But let us refrain from permanent alliances, as Washington warned, and try disinterestedly and without taint of foreign influences to help Europe in every possible way—"the way to be determined by us."

Lodge's powerful defense of Republican foreign policy was followed by a second contribution from House, "America in World Affairs." The fact that he let us attach the subtitle, "A Democratic View," indicates how far the passage of a year and the approach of the Democratic Na-

3. We later got Senator Borah to come to New York to address the Council on Foreign Relations and printed his speech as a special supplement to *Foreign Affairs,* January, 1934.

tional Convention had lessened his reluctance to engage in party discussions. But there was also a reason of a personal nature why his former
scruples had disappeared.

IV

On Sunday, February 3, 1924, Woodrow Wilson died. We heard the
news dramatically. As our taxi put my wife and me down at Colonel
House's apartment house on East Seventy-fourth Street, where we were
to lunch, there on the sidewalk was a newsboy with his extras, as though
sent by fate to that particular door, crying the news. It had been inevitable for several days, but House was very much shaken and I think wanted
to give the party up, as would have been well; but I heard Mrs. House
say *sotto voce*, "But lunch has been cooked." It was dismal and awkward.
The Colonel was repeatedly called to the telephone by newspapers or by
friends in Washington. No subject of conversation seemed possible. We
left as soon as possible with the others who were there—Belle Roosevelt
and Eugene McAdoo and his sister. House said he would go to Washington for the funeral, but I wondered whether in view of Mrs. Wilson's
implacable hostility he would be asked. The foreboding was correct. He
was informed that no arrangements were being made for him to attend
the funeral and he listened to the service by radio.

It was only a few weeks after Wilson's death that I discovered what a
direct hand House had begun to take in party politics now that he no
longer risked finding himself at cross-purposes with his former friend and
patron. One day in March he telephoned to ask me to drop in at his
apartment; he had been looking around for Presidential timber with an
eye to the Democratic Convention, now only three months off, and was
inviting several New York Democrats and a few others to "have a look
at" Governor William E. Sweet of Colorado. House's first choice ("by a
long shot," he told me later) had been William G. McAdoo, Wilson's
son-in-law and Secretary of the Treasury. But McAdoo, by bad luck and
worse judgment, had become involved in the uproar which had broken
out following the discovery of Secretary of the Interior Fall's secret lease
of public oil lands in the Teapot Dome Reserve to Harry F. Sinclair and
in the Elk Hills Reserve to E. L. Doheny. This scandal was now being in-
vestigated to the accompaniment of immense publicity and public indignation. The day following Wilson's funeral, it was revealed that McAdoo
was serving as legal counsel for Doheny at a retainer of $150,000. House
feared that this had put him out of the running as a Presidential candidate (in fact, it didn't, for he received the support of a near majority of

the delegates at the convention in Madison Square Garden that fall and only lost out to John W. Davis on the 103rd ballot) .

In his search for alternative candidates, House had invited Governor Sweet to visit New York. The Governor was a stocky, rotund, well-spoken man, who despite the fact that Colorado was normally Republican, and in the face of the united opposition of the local newspapers, had carried the state to a Democratic victory by favoring everything that farmers and labor were supposed to want. What was important to Colonel House, he believed in the League of Nations (as he said repeatedly that afternoon) "up to the hilt." I wondered whether he had the qualities that go to make a national leader.

Evidence of how deeply House was engaging in politics was a cue for me to go back to him for another article. We were planning a pair of articles on the foreign policies of the two parties. Would he speak for the Democrats? He told me to come up and read the speech which Governor Sweet was to make the next week before the Foreign Policy Association. The speech was sincere, right and supremely obvious. When I said it didn't have the makings of a *Foreign Affairs* article House was not surprised; he said he had already realized that Sweet wouldn't do as his candidate. I saw he was tempted by the thought of writing the article himself.

A week later House's "perhaps" had become "yes," dependent only on his getting the approval of enough party leaders to give the pronouncement real significance. He bemoaned the habit of picking candidates mainly for their geographical availability and personal innocuousness. Yet he could not claim very much, apart from those very qualifications, for those he named as currently available: Senator Ralston of Indiana, a nice, conventional old "Harding"; Senator Carter Glass of Virginia, who had succeeded McAdoo in Wilson's cabinet; and several other Senators, including Underwood of Alabama, Homer Cummings of Connecticut, Copeland of New York and Thomas J. Walsh of Montana, who had become famous by conducting the Teapot Dome investigation. Unfortunately, he remarked, John W. Davis' connection with Wall Street as counsel for the Morgan firm almost ruled him out. McAdoo was "always in the running," he said. He was caught in the oil mess only "technically, you might say," and there was a chance his connection with Doheny might be disregarded. If McAdoo wasn't nominated, it would be his own fault, since House had earlier lined up 620 delegates pledged absolutely to vote for him on the third ballot, insuring his nomination and giving every prospect of his election. "We would have been in the League," he said, "before 1925 was over."

It was not surprising that although House said nothing directly critical of John W. Davis he did not include him among his preferred candidates. Davis had been Solicitor General while Lansing was Secretary of State and they had remained on intimate terms. Although Lansing had formally favored entry into the League he did not in his heart believe in it, but considered it, as Raymond Fosdick wrote to Huntington Gilchrist while the Senate fight was on, "a jumble of legislative, judicial and executive work." And of course House knew that from the time he set up the Inquiry before going to Paris he had been looked on in the State Department as a menace to its authority and a rival influence with the President. Many State Department people welcomed House's fall with enthusiasm, and those who by nature were conservative and Republican carried their dislike of him to the point of discreetly opposing "House's League." Thus Lansing and his friend Davis were not among House's favorites.

We had first thought of Davis as the logical author of the Democratic article, since it would give him a chance to make a policy statement on the eve of the convention where he would figure among the leading candidates. The proposal both attracted him and alarmed him. If he ventured to write at such a crucial moment in his career, he would have to produce a masterpiece of one part courage and several parts caution. That in itself didn't appeal to him, and besides would take a lot of doing. "It isn't the labor of putting down ideas on paper that I dread," he said, "but of giving birth first to the ideas." He suggested various substitutes but meanwhile I hooked House.

House's first plan was to present his article in the form of numbered paragraphs which could serve as planks in the Democratic platform. He would get them approved by Senators Glass, Cummings and Walsh, besides, of course, McAdoo and one or two other key men "who will then fight for them in the convention." What became of this ambitious project, I don't know; there were no numbered points in the first draft that we saw. House began by appealing for a platform of "something more than a mere grouping together of familiar platitudes to be used as convenient stepping stones to public office." He advocated making the government more responsive to popular will by giving the House as well as the Senate the right to act on treaties, with approval for both to be by simple majority vote (a reform never adopted). Coolidge asked why House fought shy of the World Court, in view of the resolution for United States adhesion then pending in the Senate. House's reply was that without membership in the League, membership in the Court was a mere gesture, and he inserted a statement to that effect in the text.

Coolidge also brought up the Japanese question. Was it so "unpleasant and ticklish," in view of the discriminatory provisions against the Japanese in the proposed Immigration Act, that House did not want to talk about it? Although House decided he must avoid the topic for political reasons, his own feelings came out forcefully a few weeks later when I went to lunch with him to meet Sir Campbell Stuart of the London *Times*. Just the day before, the Senate had adopted the clause in the immigration bill aimed at totally excluding Japanese immigrants, thus abrogating the "Gentlemen's Agreement" of 1908. House's harsh comment included words like dangerous, unnecessary, bumptious and silly. The bill, signed by President Coolidge on May 26, was strongly protested by the Japanese Government and caused lasting resentment among the Japanese people. Like House, many foresaw that there would be tragic consequences.

Needless to say, House's picture of American responsibilities in the world was the exact opposite of that painted by Lodge. The American policy of "selfish isolation," House wrote, had resulted in Europe's remaining disorganized and mistrustful, while the United States itself had sunk to a "low level of materialism and official ineptitude." He contrasted the positions of the two parties on the tariff, monopolies and human rights versus property rights and regretted that the United States had no part in the League's efforts in disarmament, finance, economics, mandates and registration of treaties, all of direct concern to the United States. He pointed out that in 1916 Senator Lodge had himself stated "better than anyone" the Democratic attitude toward cooperative action for peace which he now rejected and condemned.

As a compromise of Republican and Democratic attitudes, House proposed that the United States become an associate member of the League and suggested that the Democratic Convention favor a joint resolution to that effect. This was the "half loaf" which I mentioned to Herriot and which he thought might be better than nothing. But it was rejected out of hand by the Republican leadership as a device for entering the League "by the back door" and by many pro-League Democrats who considered it a cowardly retreat.

V

Echoes of those battles of long ago come faintly over the years. The division inside the American public and among party leaders as to whether or not the United States had a positive role to play all around the globe finally ended not by argument but by bombs from two hundred Japanese aircraft over Pearl Harbor. Today we debate the policies designed to protect our global interests, but hardly the fact that they exist.

16

Ireland's Tragedy and Sir Horace Plunkett's

Through my father-in-law, who had many literary and political friends in Ireland, I came to know Sir Horace Plunkett, the benefactor of the Irish farmer who did more than anyone else to develop the rural economy of Ireland and bring it into the modern world. His associate in this work of a lifetime was George Russell, the poet AE, editor of the *Irish Homestead* and later of the *Irish Statesman,* founded by Plunkett as an organ of the Irish Dominion Party. Plunkett organized the party in 1919 in the hope that moderate political elements might coalesce to maintain a balance between rival fanatics bent on bringing the political and religious conflict in Ireland to open civil war.

The two seemed incongruous partners: Plunkett, son of the sixteenth Baron Dunsany, an Oxford graduate, slight in build, with a diffident manner, which, however, concealed iron determination, tremendously industrious in spite of being dogged by bad health and serious operations, practical, not interested in the looks of things so much as in their utility; AE, an ample rather shaggy figure who slouched back easily in a comfortable chair, puffing at his pipe and bantering about literary friends or reciting poetry in a mellow rumbling voice with an Armagh burr, painter as well as poet, mystic, concerned with the nature of things more than phenomena, yet Plunkett's best organizer of agricultural co-operatives, a brilliant editor (he stretched the purposes of the *Irish Homestead* to make room for James Joyce's first published fiction) and ready to intervene in political disputes with polemical fire.

I came to know them only when Plunkett was in his middle sixties and AE in his middle fifties, and never saw them together, but their evident differences were less than their union in love of Ireland, concern for its future as a nation, indignation at the misery of its rural population and dedication to mending it. W. G. S. Adams, Professor of Political Economy at Oxford, wrote that Plunkett was the "greatest" man he ever encountered.[1] There are many measures of greatness. Professor Adams' judgment was based on Plunkett's courage in fighting and overcoming political difficulties in spite of personal suffering; on his consistency, concentration of purpose, unselfishness and generosity; and, of course, on his practical achievements in lifting the level of Irish life and influencing thought and action on problems of the farmer all over the world.

In his twenties Plunkett had gone as a rancher to Wyoming in an effort to head off tuberculosis. Ten years on the plains had left him with many connections in America and a liking for Americans which later brought him back for visits to look after his business interests and exchange ideas about agricultural problems and especially the devolopment of cooperatives. On these visits he learnt useful things, but as the work of his Irish Agricultural Organization spread and began to alleviate the most backward features of the Irish countryside he began giving more than he received. President Roosevelt and Gifford Pinchot, Commissioner of Forestry, enthusiastically acknowledged his contributions to the Conservation Commission and the influential Country Life Commission. Later he met Colonel House in London and through him had an influence on the way President Wilson and Secretary of Agriculture Houston dealt with farm problems. During the First World War he became an interlocutor between House and his close friend Arthur Balfour. His introductions of House to Balfour and subsequently to Lloyd George created links between London and Washington which proved invaluable in view of the widening gap of misunderstanding over the British need to safeguard the flow of food across the submarine-infested North Atlantic and the American concern for the principle of the freedom of the seas. His correspondence and frequent meetings with House enabled him to expound to each side the legal and political aspects of the dispute as seen by the other; and in London he emphasized the importance of developing a sound psychology in dealing with American public opinion, something he found grievously lacking.

On his visits to America after the war Sir Horace often stayed with my wife and me at our little house on East Thirty-sixth Street. He was by conviction and temperament a moderate, by birth and inclination a

1. Margaret Digby, *Horace Plunkett, an Anglo-American Irishman*. Introduction by W. G. S. Adams. Oxford: Basil Blackwell, 1949.

Unionist, but following the Easter Rising of 1916 and its train of savage executions, reprisals and counterreprisals, and the failure of the Irish Convention of 1918, over which he presided, he saw that Ireland must have, would have, self-government. His solution was Dominion Home Rule, which would keep Ireland undivided, and on his visit to New York late in 1919, when I first met him, this was his counterproposal to the demand being made by Eamon de Valera, president of Sinn Fein, for an independent Irish Republic, something Ulster would never accept and which thus meant the division of the country. De Valera was conducting a stormy campaign in America for the Republican cause, soliciting funds and openly praying that Germany would defeat Britain in the war. I heard the two of them speak from the same platform in New York, and two more opposite characters in appearance and argument could hardly be imagined. De Valera was tall, menacing, rather saturnine, alarmingly sincere, with eyes that peered through heavy glasses and a dark face flushed with feeling. Plunkett's figure was slightly stooped; the expression on what George Moore described in *Vale* as his "well-designed oval face," bearded and divided sharply by a long straight nose, was one of such concentration on his argument that there was no room for any display of personal animus; his manner was composed, and only the sparkle of his eyes showed that he was as deeply committed to his opinions as de Valera's passion showed him to be to his.

Plunkett's conversion to Home Rule was gradual, and he delayed making public his support for it, knowing that it would damage his nonpolitical cooperative movement; for extremists on both sides looked on his effort to develop the economic structure, in order that Ireland would have a stronger basis for governing itself, as a diversion from their immediate political objectives. Confirmation that such fears were well-founded came later on when he became a supporter of the Irish Free State and hostile Republican bands sacked cooperative stores and burnt cooperative creameries.

Usually Sir Horace's American visits were broken by a sojourn at the Battle Creek Sanitarium, indeed that became one of his reasons for coming to America. The isolation and the vegetarian diet helped him recuperate from his illnesses, which he resented less for the suffering they caused than as time lost from useful occupations. The hardest part of the ordeal was the effort to do without the morphia which had first been prescribed by doctors during a severe bout with pneumonia and again after a dangerous operation for the removal of a malignant growth. His fight to break with the drug produced terrible insomnia. After dinner he would struggle to stay awake but would almost inevitably fail. Without warning his head would sag, his arms would fall alongside his chair and for half an hour he would quietly sleep. His revival was as abrupt. Suddenly you would find him joining animatedly in the conversation. Yet that brief nap would have been his last sleep for the night.

The summer of 1921 brought hopes of peace in Ireland. Lloyd George reversed his whole policy by inviting de Valera, President of the Dail, to negotiate an agreement with Downing Street, and a truce was proclaimed in July. Plunkett was particularly pleased because the prospective settlement was to be on the basis of Dominion Home Rule. On August 6 he wrote me that to understand the "amazing gyrations" by which this result was brought about "you must always bear in mind the *Realpolitik* of Lloyd George and eliminate principle and substitute expediency as the determining factor." He described how the use of secret service funds for propagandistic purposes and the control of a large part of the British press through wealthy political supporters had distorted every incident and accident of the political conflict and of the actual war into which it had developed. He continued:

> But it was essential to the substitution of force for negotiation that force should succeed—and force completely failed. The final collapse came with a blunder by the military in their policy of reprisals. It seems impossible to believe that the stupidest militarist could burn cottages as a means of terrorising a people in a district where they had no means of protecting castles from the people, but so it was. It was no change of heart which made Lloyd George, Birkenhead and Winston Churchill suddenly reverse their Irish policy and call a truce. They fled from the wrath of the Irish people just in time to avert a wrath of world opinion which would have overwhelmed them.

On this basis, Plunkett estimated, "there will be no renewal of hostilities." He wrote:

> The precise nature of Lloyd George's offer I do not know; but it is safe to assume that it is in substance the policy of the Irish Dominion League, with every kind of camouflage and, of course, no use of the word Dominion.

In all this, Plunkett said, he had been a silent spectator; and, with the only show of personal chagrin that I ever noted in him, he indicated the reason: "Such is the psychology of the politicians—who have, since they plunged the world into war been allowed to assume the role of statesmen—that the adoption of a policy is best promoted by the elimination of its advocates."

Ernest Boyd warned me not to be too optimistic, since Ulster would not make concessions and "Sinn Fein is not so green as it is painted."

His pessimism was correct and Plunkett's hopes were in the end dashed. The agreement of December 6, 1921, gave the Irish Free State the same status in the Empire as Canada or Australia, and under the leadership of Arthur Griffith the Dail ratified it in January, though by a narrow margin; Griffith became President and Michael Collins head of the provisional government. But de Valera repudiated the whole proceeding and by spring the Republican Army was in violent conflict with the forces of the Free State. Catastrophe followed catastrophe. The Republican headquarters in the Four Courts of Dublin was besieged and destroyed. Arthur Griffith died. One day in August, Lady Lavery brought Michael Collins to supper at Kilteragh, Plunkett's house at Foxrock near Dublin, where Bernard Shaw and his wife were staying; three days later Collins was shot dead in ambush.

Erskine Childers, a brilliant man who had worked closely with Plunkett in the Irish Convention, had joined the Republicans and was captured and shot in spite of Plunkett's plea for clemency. The special tragedy of civil wars marked Childers' request to his wife on the morning of his execution that she give his "affectionate farewells" to friends, "all on the other side, but dear." The first name on his list was Plunkett's.

Plunkett wrote me about that time from Kilteragh that he wondered how he could face Americans to whom he had given optimistic forecasts of Irish self-government. "Last night," he noted, "there was a small-scale battle close to this house." Kilteragh was central to all his activities. All his friends came there—Irishmen of different political convictions and both religions; young Sinn Feiners and Belfast businessmen; English statesmen like Grey, Milner and Bryce; Bernard Shaw, a close friend; H. G. Wells, George Moore and Yeats; always AE, of course; and often friends from America like James Byrne, Lawrence Lowell of Harvard, John Quinn, patron of Irish arts, and Gifford Pinchot. The house suited him in every respect, even to a small bedroom mounted on a turntable on the roof, manipulable by hand so that he could turn the open end away from the sun or moon or wind.

The "small-scale battle" was only one of many indications that Plunkett himself was in danger. It was enough that Collins had appointed him one of the thirty Senators of the Irish Free State, which the Irish Republican Army was resorting to every means to destroy. When he arrived in New York in December, 1922, I was away, for my wife had been ill; but he was to visit us on his return from Battle Creek. Before that, on January 30, the Associated Press called me to relay reports from Dublin that an armed band had appeared at Kilteragh that morning and after ex-

pelling the servants had blown up the front portion of the house. I telegraphed the terrible news to Plunkett at the University of Wisconsin,
where he was lecturing, and later that day forwarded an unsigned cable
from Dublin reading "Smouldering by mine" and the next day another
which said simply "Extinct." His reaction to our commiserations on this
disaster was typical. "The worry I am to you all," he wrote, "is distress-
ing. But soon I shall be with you, and then off to the ashes." And in a
postscript, "I want to be as quiet as I can. The news from Ireland is a bit
depressing."

The personal disaster did not keep him from discussing the Irish situation without rancor with House and the Lamonts at our house a few days
later, and with Coolidge, who was staying with us also. He still had hopes
that the final upshot would avoid partition. When I saw him off on the
steamer he was in fairly good spirits—"Game," he said to someone who
inquired how he was feeling. But the sight of the ruins of Kilteragh
brought home to him how devastatingly he had been uprooted—the record of his past gone, his future work jeopardized. The blow was the more
shattering because although he had realized he was surrounded by danger he had felt that even the most fanatical on both sides recognized that
all his political actions had been selfless. Nor was this the work of an
undisciplined band; the Republicans had returned the second day and
methodically set fire to the ruins. He was particularly sad that his secretary, Gerald Heard, who had used a few moments of grace before being
ordered out of the house to save some of the files, had chosen the financial
accounts of the estate and not the lifetime of correspondence with Balfour, Grey, AE, Bernard Shaw and others. He told me that for thirty
years he had been accustomed to exchange an almost weekly letter with
Lord Bryce. "All gone."

After another bad operation, Plunkett's doctors said he must live in
England, so he resigned from the Irish Senate, sold the land where Kilteragh had stood and settled in a little house in Surrey where, he wrote,
"I can work quietly for Ireland and other agricultural communities for
the remainder of my days." He arrived to stay with us again for a short
time at the end of the year, as usual on the way to Battle Creek. "Each
year Battle Creek lets me live one day more." On New Year's Day, 1924,
he was godfather to my daughter and sent her a porringer, "From one of
her earliest admirers." We spent most of that morning preparing caudle
from an old family recipe, very good.

At a dinner which I had for him at the Knickerbocker Club, he started
wearily, almost desperately, though he had said he particularly wanted to

meet the editors and certain friends that I had gathered together; but gradually he warmed up and talked well about what would have to be done to restore the rural economy of Ireland after the civil war. He thought the general effect on Ireland of Labour's imminent arrival in power in England would be good. He said afterward, "It was the only occasion of the sort where I wasn't asked a single foolish question." He ate no dinner, having fortified himself beforehand with a mess of Benger's food, which allowed him to stay awake longer than if he had filled up on a good meal; and he had another bowl of it when we got home.

On his way back from Battle Creek he spent a few days with us, revived sufficiently to want to be taken to see *Saint Joan,* Shaw's new play produced by the Theatre Guild. He said he couldn't face Shaw in London without being able to report on it. He said something about the way Shaw worked which was new to me, namely that he wrote in shorthand and transcribed later, which would account for the flash and run of his dialogue and for the length of some of the speeches in his plays. Miss Lenihan, though appealing as Joan, did not seem well cast in this production. Plunkett found her famous half-hour speech unconscionably long, and said he would tell G. B. S. so. Before sailing on the *Cedric,* amid reporters and photographers whom he fended off blandly, he undertook to write soon a long-promised article for *Foreign Affairs* (it appeared eventually in January, 1927) and said he would help us land one by AE (we finally succeeded in January, 1929) .[2] He also left injunctions that we should entertain his octogenarian friend Robert Bridges, the Poet Laureate, who was to arrive in America with Mrs. Bridges a few weeks later. When the time came, I made great efforts to give Bridges the best possible treatment, took him to lunch at the *Times* and gave him and his wife a dinner. On one occasion when I secured a police escort to rush him from one function to another, he gave the impression of not knowing whether to enjoy the spectacle of the traffic dividing before us as we sped, horns tooting, up Fifth Avenue, or fearing that he might be killed in such unimportant company as myself.

Any brief description of Horace Plunkett is bound to be a failure in communication, partly because his political influence was so often exerted through others, but mainly because to convey the sheer size of his material achievement would require pages of statistics of cooperative stores opened, cooperative creameries built, electricity brought to villages, steps taken to

2. I slipped in signing the article "A.E." He preferred AE with no periods and no quotation marks. In Alan Denson's volume, *Letters from AE,* there is a letter to Constance Sitwell in which he says, "I am unfamiliar with the name I was born with."

improve seeds and strains of cattle, all the details of the day-to-day work undertaken under his inspiration and supervision. Since he shied away from public recognition of his achievements, they often remained unrecorded. His desire to escape notice annoyed reporters. Once on arriving in New York en route to Battle Creek he slipped off the pier with the connivance of the customs officials, warned beforehand. A disgruntled newspaperman in revenge reported him dead. The worldwide eulogies which he read after he got to Battle Creek should have speeded an ordinary person's convalescence, but irritated him no end.

One honor he could not escape. It happened that he was a member of a committee to arrange for a visit by King Edward to the west coast of Ireland. After seeing that proper preparations had been made, he took a train home. On the way, he was handed a telegram informing him that the King wished to receive him. He obediently turned back, borrowed a frock coat (but failed to find black shoes to replace his brown ones) and presented himself on the deck of the royal yacht. King Edward without preliminary pointed to a cushion, told him to kneel (in which posture he felt that the protruding brown shoes were most conspicuous) and proceeded to knight him with a sword borrowed from a nearby naval officer. Plunkett told me he had discouraged an earlier offer of such an honor, not wishing to impair his usefulness as an Irishman not too closely linked with England to serve as a neutral negotiator. It crossed my mind that perhaps he also felt that the eight-hundred-year-old Dunsany family tree did not need to have a new little honorific twig grafted onto it.

It would be wrong to leave a picture of Sir Horace as one-track-minded. A touch of Wyoming always hung about him. He knew horses and enjoyed the annual Dublin Horse Show for that reason more than because it was the high point of Ireland's social activity. He was a masterly chess player (Capablanca used to visit him for matches) ; he laid out a small golf course at Foxrock; he took up bicycling and continued to ride in traffic even after twice falling off and breaking a thigh; he drove a car, recklessly according to universal testimony; and at seventy-five he took to the air, learnt to pilot a plane and continued to enjoy flying until his death two years later.

17

The End of the Old "Evening Post"

The situation of the *Evening Post* had become first parlous, then desperate. Receipts had been going up but expenditures had been going up faster. By 1923, Lamont found that the drain on his resources was unbearable and resolved to sell. By herculean efforts Gay put together a syndicate of thirty-four public-spirited New Yorkers to buy the paper and keep it alive; the alternative had been to let it be sold to Frank Munsey, a well-known executioner of newspapers, who would merge it into the *Sun*. (Gay himself went into debt to purchase a block of stock in the new corporation; it took him thirty years to pay the debt off.) The syndicate proved to be a palliative, not a solution. In Allan Nevins' phrase, the *Evening Post* tottered in forlorn dignity to its end. Cyrus H. K. Curtis of Philadelphia was the new purchaser. He took possession on January 1, 1924, and dismissed most of the staff, keeping one writer, Royal Davis, to supply fillers on local topics for the editorial page. Otherwise that page, which had been a monitor and guide for New Yorkers and a reflection of what was best in New York opinion from the days of Bryant and Godkin, became mainly an evening reprint of what Curtis' *Public Ledger* had told Philadelphia in the morning. The *New York Times,* which had earlier acquired Ogden and Noyes from the *Evening Post,* now secured Strunsky and Puckette. Mary H. Stevens, Puckette's secretary, escaping from the rigors of a daily paper's city room, came to *Foreign Affairs* and, to my unceasing gratitude, stayed.

The end of the old *Evening Post* had come on the last day of 1923. I say "old" in retrospect, in distinction from its present tabloid successor;

then it was the "new" *Evening Post,* as rejuvenated under Gay's direction. In the interval, Curtis' paper (destined in turn to be short-lived) would have the old name and carry the masthead saying it had been founded by Alexander Hamilton, but it would not be the independent and progressive organ planned by Lamont and Gay. The attempt to make it that had succeeded, but the attempt to maintain it had failed.

I went down to the office on Vesey Street on December 28 to say good-bye to the place and wish old friends there well. The sedate library with its shelves of well-used books, some from the time when William Cullen Bryant was editor, was not yet disturbed, but everywhere else there was the rustle of change and, it seemed to me, dissolution. Gay was getting together the last of his things in the corner office. The agonizing struggle to keep the paper going had been a long one, and though no emotion crept into his talk, his very black eyes under the overhanging black eyebrows lacked their usual piercing sharpness. Fight, for the moment, had gone out of him. As he talked philosophically with me, he would not have provoked the admiring remark of a colleague who watched him rout some of the "big fish" of wartime Washington: "He looks like a black bass and behaves like one."

Defeated in New York, Gay returned to his first love as professor of economic history at Harvard. Inevitably for one of his temperament, he continued from Cambridge his many wide-ranging activities, among them as a director and secretary of the Council on Foreign Relations and a member of the Editorial Advisory Board of *Foreign Affairs.* Thus he remained in my life (as he had been from the time he took me on at the *Evening Post*) a decisive force—I was about to write "factor," but my typewriter balked at applying so mechanical a word to someone abounding in Gay's enthusiasm, generosity and courage.

In the frantic period while Gay was scrounging around in every direction to find capital to keep the *Evening Post* alive, he asked me to see two or three people who might participate in the new syndicate. One was Mrs. Bayard Cutting, a public-spirited old lady with innumerable friends and admirers. I think she consulted Mrs. Whitelaw Reid, widow of our former Ambassador in London and after his death the owner of the *Tribune.* Advice from within the newspaper world was probably not very encouraging about the prospects for the *Evening Post.* A year before there had been ten daily newspapers in New York; in that year several had succumbed to higher costs and severe competition, and even in the narrowed field some of the survivors found themselves in trouble (later, when there were only three or four metropolitan papers, their difficulties seemed no less). At any rate, Mrs. Cutting declined. One morning in March, 1924, I read in the *Tribune* that it had just purchased the *Herald* from Frank Munsey. It happened that at dinner at Mrs. Cutting's that evening I sat next to Mrs. Reid, who filled in some details in the proceeding.

"Frank Munsey came to me," she said, "and announced: 'One of us must sell.' "

"Very well," Mrs. Reid had replied, "I'll buy the *Herald.*"

At which Munsey collapsed with surprise, as he'd expected to get the *Tribune* cheap.

"I couldn't do anything else," Mrs. Reid explained matter-of-factly. "Julian Mason had just sold his house in Chicago and moved to New York to manage the *Tribune.*"

Munsey stipulated that the Reids must pay employees of the *Herald* two weeks' salary. "So," said Mrs. Reid, "my son Ogden went down to the *Herald* office this afternoon and paid them all off with *Tribune* checks."

I noted down the next day, "This is the fourth set of good newspaper employees turned out onto the sidewalk in the last twelve months," and added the obvious observation, "Newspaper life is hazardous."

II

When the 1924 summer issue had been put to bed, with Lodge and House, Stresemann and Herriot standing in pairs, proof we had meant it when we promised that *Foreign Affairs* would offer "a broad hospitality to divergent ideas," Coolidge declared that I should not sit too long at an office desk but must take a short "refresher course" in Europe. He did not have in mind just the desk of his managing editor, but also the work being done at that same desk to get the Council on Foreign Relations going and show its members that they had other serious purposes besides sponsoring a magazine. The Clemenceau meeting had been a curtain raiser, and not, I was determined, a foretaste of the sort of Council program that was to follow: we would never again be inveigled into any such grandiose public operation.

I promise not to detail the activities of the Council as they grew year by year, but will say a few words about that first winter of 1922–23, the prototype in miniature of what we gradually developed on a widening scale. There were four full membership meetings, and to this program I added three small study groups. These groups, which afterward became a principal part of the Council's work, aimed to bring together two sometimes separate segments of American life—leaders in business, banking and the professions and writers, professors and former government officials. In those early days, the groups met monthly in the late afternoon around a table in my office. Then as their popularity increased they were transferred to less crowded surroundings at the Harvard Club and extended to include dinner and further discussion afterward. Later on, when a study led to substantial results, the secretary of the group was encouraged to use the group papers and discussions as the basis for a book, not representing the Council's views—since its charter precludes it from taking positions—but those of the author only.

Another of the Council's important functions was also coming into being more or less as a matter of course. Publishers were sending in their new books for review in *Foreign Affairs,* and I arranged that after the editors of our bibliographic section[1] had prepared their brief critical summaries, the books should come back to form the nucleus of a Council library. Soon they overflowed the shelves in my office and eventually became one of the arguments for getting the Council adequate quarters of its own.

Of the Secretaries of State who have addressed the Council over the years, the first was Secretary Hughes on January 23, 1924. General Bliss came up from Washington for the occasion and stayed with me. We picked up John W. Davis, who was to preside at the dinner, and then called for Mr. Hughes and escorted him to the Ritz. He was less austere than I had imagined him from his pictures, with a hearty chuckle and a comfortably curved waistcoat. (Mr. Byrne remarked that "The further Hughes gets from his Baptist upbringings and his crusading days at Albany the mellower he is, and the mellower he is the shorter he trims his beard.")

Afterward he went up to the Byrne apartment with Davis, Coolidge, Gay, Cravath, Morrow, Bliss and myself. At the meeting he had dealt with the hotly debated question of intervention in Latin America, and he now reverted to it in even more uncompromising terms. Of Mexico, he said: "We struggled to get the Mexican Government to recognize U.S. property rights, and now a personal revolution led by Huerta against the government of Obregón and his candidate for the Presidency, Calles, threatens to undo our work; and the papers say we have no interest and no right to intervene in support of Obregón. We have the right and the duty. This revolution is not a popular rising but a personal political campaign for the Presidency. As for our sending arms, it is not as though we were

1. At first, Harry Elmer Barnes, succeeded in turn by William L. Langer, Robert Gale Woolbert, Henry L. Roberts, and John G. Stoessinger.

supplying arms to one government to wage war on another; we help the forces of order; we help the forces of a legitimate government, at that government's request, against the forces of political revolution; we help order not disorder, peace not war."

As though I didn't have enough on my hands with *Foreign Affairs* and the Council, I had continued doing a column in the *Evening Post* called "Europe Week by Week." Coolidge had urged me to keep it up because it forced me to follow European events in detail. When the assignment stopped the last week in 1923, the *Times* suggested continuing the column for them, but I put the idea off until such time as, I fatuously imagined, the magazine would be so well organized that I would have free time regularly for my own writing. That time, of course, never came. However, when I sailed for my "refresher course" in the spring of 1924, the *Times* asked me to send them occasional articles, particularly what today would be called "profiles" of statesmen.

Waiting for me in my cabin on the *Paris* was a letter from Coolidge which bowled me over and (reversing the metaphor) very much set me up. If he wrote at all, it was bound to be in his usual friendly and considerate way. But this went further:

This epistle does not deal with business, but even if it comes in the commonplace category of steamer letters, it is a little less casually meant than some of them. Besides the ordinary desire for your health, happiness, prosperity and enlightenment which one lavishes on such occasions, I want to add a personal word in connection with the first real interruption, however short, of our work together. . . . *Foreign Affairs* will soon be two years old and we have had too many flattering testimonials not to feel assured that it has made good. How much of that is due to the intelligence, as well as energy and devotion, that you have put into it, I appreciate but shall not attempt to express; I quite fail to see what we could have done without them. At any rate, you have more than earned your vacation. . . . I don't much care where you go, believing that you will make the most of your time anywhere and that whatever interests you most has a good deal to be said for it for that reason if no other.

The reply I dashed off—but too late to catch the pilot—attempted to convey my feeling about what had been fun and high adventure as well as work.

There were several notables aboard, along with the usual mixed crowd. A six-day voyage had the advantage over today's six-hour flight in giving you time to sort out the passengers and observe their idiosyncrasies. Fifty transatlantic crossings have taught me not to go by a person's looks. I remember how once in my youth I crossed from Quebec and found my steamer chair beside that of a tiny old lady, a mouselike figure all in black

from black bonnet to sensible shoes. As it turned out, she made the crossing delightful with her shrewd but loving accounts of thirty adventurous
years in India as the wife of an Anglican bishop. Particularly with Eng-
lishmen, appearances are deceiving; in the course of time you find that
some diffident little man with a scraggly mustache has been risking his
life collecting a certain green butterfly in New Guinea, or for no particular reason at all lives for most of the year with his rubber bathtub, quinine
and hot-water bottle in Assam or Albania.

Colonel House had telephoned that morning to tell me Paderewski
would be on board and to be sure to speak to him. His political days
were over, but his disagreements with the reactionary military leaders
who had come to power in Poland had not wiped out the memory of
him among Poles everywhere—how he had organized Polish national
forces in exile during the war, played concert after concert tirelessly to
raise tremendous sums of money for Polish relief, and won recognition of
Poland's claims at the Paris Peace Conference by his magnetic influence
on Wilson, House and other Allied leaders. He was a national hero
whether he chose to live in Warsaw, California or Switzerland. Coolidge
had seen the play of his diplomatic virtuosity at Paris and had thought
of him as a possible writer for us.

I had been fascinated when I met him at lunch with House the year
before and looked forward to seeing him again. For several days, though,
I left him alone. He was politely aloof from his fellow passengers, sitting
in a corner in the smoking room playing cards, drinking chartreuse and
thinking very little, I imagined, about politics. Mention of House's name
made him spring to his feet. Pressing my hand and holding it close to
his heart he told me in a rush of gratitude and sentiment what he
thought of House and what he was prepared to think of House's friend.
His only reservation was that I was not a cardplayer, something which,
even if I had been, it would not have been wise for me to confess to him
and his experienced traveling companions.

Paderewski, who made innumerable trips back and forth across the
Atlantic, invariably by the French Line, was always importuned, of
course, to perform at the ship's concert. For much of the time after the
war, however, he had abandoned the concert stage and took that as a
reason to refuse; perhaps he felt that during the war he had done his
charitable share, which was certainly the case. But either on this or one
of his later voyages, I forget which, he counted without a wily American
master of ceremonies. This gentleman, a public-relations counsel who
knew the weaknesses of the great as well as the little, instructed the con-

cert volunteers to play either a Paderewski composition or one of his almost trademarked specialties. When he saw the program in the ship's paper, Paderewski found he could not stay away; and when he heard his pieces being massacred he did what the master of ceremonies had foreseen—hurried to the piano to do them properly. It was a rough evening, the ship was rolling badly, and at each sickening lunge the stool either slid away from the piano or brought the player so close to it that his elbows almost touched the keyboard. In his exhilaration Paderewski hardly noticed. The applause was immense, and even though many passengers had succumbed to the rough weather and retired to their staterooms, the collection for families of Breton fishermen lost off the Banks was double the usual take.

III

The year 1924 was momentous in Europe. In the first place, it saw the end of the French effort to extract reparations payments from Germany by force, thus opening up the possibility of a Franco-German reconciliation. The Dawes Committee reported in April that the evacuation of the Ruhr was a necessary factor in restoring German credit and productivity to a degree where Germany could remit considerable, though reduced, sums to France on a continuing basis. While Poincaré was hesitating, his ministry fell, and at the moment of my arrival in Paris (as I have described earlier) Herriot became his successor. The next six years were the so-called period of "fulfillment," marked by Locarno, Germany's admission to the League and the Kellogg-Briand Pact. Then, in the Great Depression, Hitler was able to inflame smoldering German resentments to a point where he could take power; the pause in Franco-German hostility begun in 1924 ended; and it would not be renewed until after another German defeat in another World War.

At Geneva, a turning point for the better in the prestige and influence of the League of Nations seemed at hand. Morale was still at a rather low ebb following the Assembly's rejection of a proposal to reinforce the Covenant by a draft treaty of mutual assistance. But Sir Herbert Ames, a member of the Secretariat, gave me the cheering news that Beneš and others were already at work on a new and more comprehensive project of collective security. The product of this planning, the Geneva Protocol, was introduced in the General Assembly that autumn and enthusiastically received.

In Rome, 1924 was a significant year for sinister reasons not immediately recognized and by many not recognized at all until too late.

It was the year in which Mussolini secured full and "legal" control of the Italian state, as Hitler later established the Nazi dictatorship in Germany on a "legal" basis.

In the period following the March on Rome on October 28, 1922, Mussolini had been granted temporary dictatorial powers by the King and Parliament to restore order. He used them to pass an electoral law, which in April, 1924, enabled him to win 60 percent of the seats in Parliament. Even without benefit of the new law he might well have won a majority anyway. A campaign of terror by the Fascist Squadristi outdid and overwhelmed the violence of the trade unionists, Socialists and Communists. Industrialists, landowners and in general the well-to-do either were cowed or were pleased that strikes, factory seizures and other social disorders were dealt with brutally. Mussolini dismissed recalcitrant officials, ousted legally-minded judges, suppressed opposition papers and expelled independent-minded professors from the universities. Then in June came the murder of Matteotti, a Socialist deputy, directed by high Fascist officials whose corruption he had documented. The Fascists had underestimated the reaction of horror, and there ensued a brief period of government disorientation and weakness. The non-Fascist deputies attempted to capitalize on it by withdrawing from Parliament, becoming known as the "Aventine Opposition" after the Roman plebs who had withdrawn to the Aventine Hill in the year 492 in order to exert pressure for the righting of their grievances. However, Mussolini recovered his nerve and by acts of terror succeeded in maintaining and then increasing his control.

I reached Rome from Geneva after the April elections and before the Matteotti murder. The royal coat-of-arms had not yet been replaced on public buildings by the Fascist bundle of rods and axe, and the carabinieri sauntered along in pairs as usual, as though they still embodied "law." There was, however, an unfamiliar bustle in and around the ministries and black-shirted guards at the doors looked at strangers with hostility. The clearest indication of underlying tension was the evasiveness that overtook conversations as soon as they verged on politics. When you asked the porter at the Hotel de Russie the address of some political figure, whether of the old regime or the new, he didn't know it, in fact had hardly heard of the gentleman; and the same reluctance to admit any current knowledge of controversial figures would appear even in polite conversations at tea in a ducal palazzo. Nobody was certain of anything, and not being certain kept still.

Probably there had been the same uncertainty in the last days of Papal

Rome. My father was there then as Consul to the Papal States. On the morning when he heard that Victor Emmanuel's troops would attack, he walked to the Porta Pia and watched them breach the walls, killing in the process seven Papal Zouaves, the total sacrifice exacted for the capture of the city and its transformation from the temporal capital of the Popes into the capital of united Italy. When the uncertainty of that day ended, the populace went wild with joy, hung out flags and feted the soldiers bivouacked in the Piazza del Popolo and other squares. Fascist propagandists never painted any such picture of Rome's reception of the Fascist marchers (Mussolini himself arrived from Milan the next day in a sleeping car) or claimed that anybody danced in the streets. The constitutional Italy of which Rome had become the capital fifty years before was finished, and so to all intents and purposes was the House of Savoy.

As yet nobody knew it, however. Even Mussolini could not have foreseen how swiftly and completely he would be able to gut the whole edifice of libertarian government. As for myself, I was only beginning to draw the correct conclusions from the prevailing uncertainty; until I got to Rome I had seen the future more in terms of Italian politics than as violent social revolution with worldwide significance.

The two Fascist officials with whom I talked—the Minister of Finance, De Stefani, and his right-hand man, Guido Jung—played down Mussolini's revolutionary character, much as in March, 1933, friends of mine in the Foreign Office in Berlin played down Hitler's after his capture of dictatorial powers. They did not suggest that it was all a flash in the pan, the illusion with which so many German officials and foreign observers would comfort themselves. However, they looked forward, after the restoration of "order," to the resumption of the constitutional government which Mussolini had pledged after the March on Rome, "purified," naturally, to accord with the precepts of Fascism.

I did not see Mussolini himself—that experience came several years later, by which time he was installed magnificently and apparently securely in the Palazzo Venezia. At the moment he was in Naples and would not be back until two days after I must leave for Fiume. I was only moderately disappointed, as I looked on him as an *opéra bouffe* character; it was a bad mistake, but with the useful result that when Hitler appeared I was not similarly misled. Afterward I really regretted that I had missed seeing him, for conceivably I might have persuaded him to write the article which we had in mind and which at one point he promised. His bombast and the arrogance of his demands might have conveyed a useful warning to Americans (among others, a university president and a future secretary of state) of what the world was going to be up against.

Lamont had recommended De Stefani as the brainiest man in the Mussolini government, and Jung offered him as a substitute writer. Jung had been with Ambassador Caetani in Washington, knew America and realized that a policy statement by a moderate like De Stefani would have useful effects there. It never materialized, which perhaps was just as well, for whereas a blast from Mussolini would have sounded a salutary warning, a careful article by De Stefani vetted by Jung would have been reassuring, and that was the opposite of what the world needed.

IV

The Italian who stood out was Count Carlo Sforza. Fascists dismissed him with one word, "Finito!" Our Ambassador, Henry P. Fletcher, who was favorably disposed toward the regime, an occupational risk of ambassadors, agreed. He was not as unqualified an admirer of Mussolini, however, as was his predecessor, Richard Washburn Child, who adored him for being among other things "a great humanitarian." Fletcher stopped short of telling me it would be unwise to see Sforza, merely saying I would find him uninteresting. That seemed to me unlikely. As Minister of Foreign Affairs, he had made the Treaty of Rapallo with the Jugoslavs in 1920, then had gone to Paris as Ambassador, resigned two days after the March on Rome in protest against the government's weakness in face of the Fascist coup and rejected Mussolini's request to reconsider and stay along. When I called at his house on the via de Rossi, on the outskirts of Rome, he said he would talk to me freely if I undertook not to quote him. He wanted to be able to stay in Italy to help form an alternative government in case the Fascists weakened, which he considered possible, even likely. When I showed surprise, he said I evidently had been hearing about the popularity of Mussolini's achievement in bringing Italy a new order, a new capacity for work.

"You are being told to count the beggars in the street and see how much fewer there are. You are being told that garbage is removed promptly instead of being left to rot in the cellars. But what is the use of having garbage removed if our souls die? Mussolini's 'order' is the 'order' the Prussian military gave Germany before the war. I didn't like it in 1914 and neither did the Italian people. I don't like it now, and neither do they."

How could the reaction come, I asked?

"Not from the old political class. Even Giolitti thinks we must 'live along' with Fascism. The fact is our political character is debased. Say I had a hundred friends in political life. Seventy-five of them if I meet them individually will wring my hand, whisper all they think of the regime. But will they join in a movement to put their convictions at work? Each one can find 300,000 reasons not to go into open opposition—Mussolini's 300,000 armed ruffians."

When I said this made the situation look pretty hopeless, he said no, other factors could come into play.

"First, the King. A year ago Mussolini thought of becoming King himself. Sycophants encouraged him to do so. But it was too bizarre even for him. He put the idea aside in favor of becoming a dictator, with the King in the background. As a symbol? Less than that, as a useful shadow, thin and timorous, throwing into relief the muscular decisiveness of the real leader. Now that is not a role that gives the King much pleasure. Three weeks ago he went to Sardinia on a state visit. He went in a torpedo boat. Last week Mussolini went on a political visit to Sicily. He went in the biggest battleship in the Italian navy, attended by fourteen torpedo boats.

"Second, the Pope. He knows that force provokes force. He might not be sorry to see the King reduced. But not in a civil war in which his own place might disappear also.

"Third, the Army. Certain high officers are Fascisti. But do you think a regular army likes to play second fiddle to a militia? Do you suppose it doesn't feel a professional jealousy when it sees these bands of boys and adventurers strutting around?"

Jealousy is a powerful force, I remarked, but would it lead men to risk their lives and property to get revenge?

Sforza did not consider the resentment superficial, but deep-rooted. And it was supported by other forces with positive reasons for action. One was freemasonry, "which is not dead," another was socialism. Further, no cabal was impregnable unless it had the support of the triangle of Italy's industrial strength—Turin, Milan, Genoa. All three gave majorities to the opposition in the last election. The press was another measure of power in Milan—"the moral capital of Italy." Of the two great papers there, the *Corriere della Sera,* openly critical of Mussolini, sold 500,000 copies, the *Popolo d'Italia,* with Mussolini's name on the masthead and edited by his brother, about 20,000.

After this, it was a little anticlimactic for Sforza to end by stressing that these forces of opposition were only potential. The Italian political character, he repeated, had become debased. It would take a moral shock to turn the latent opposition into definite planning and action.

Afterward, he offered to drop me at my hotel on his way to the Senate. I noticed that he paused at the gate and looked back before turning into the street. To my questioning look he said, "Oh, I always wait a bit to make sure my spy, who follows me on his bicycle, has had time to rub his eyes and get started. Poor fellow, if he lost track of me, he would lose his job."

When the moral shock of the Matteotti murder brought the Aventine Opposition into existence, Sforza became one of its leaders. He was now subjected to less casual surveillance, but was protected to a degree by his name, former high office and the fact that he was a Senator; perhaps the collar of the Annunziata helped, since that made him a "cousin" of the King, for whom the Fascists still were showing formal consideration. But the reconciliation between his conscience and his very limited field of action became more and more difficult. In January, 1925, he sent me an article which must be termed courageous in its description of the evolution of Fascism from diverse forces of the class struggle, some of them generous in purpose, others reactionary, callous and brutal, into the current dictatorship. Italian newspapers which published excerpts from this article were confiscated and Countess Sforza was attacked in the street. In September of that year he wrote me that one of his brothers had been arrested for having a mass celebrated on the anniversary of Matteotti's murder. He also wrote that his friend, Gaetano Salvemini, Professor of History at the University of Florence, had been arrested for refusing to give the Fascist salute at the opening of his classes, and he sent me an article on Italian wartime diplomacy which Salvemini had written during his imprisonment. Salvemini was later released and went to London, not to return to Italy until after the Second War; had he remained in Florence, he would likely have been murdered in his bed like some of his colleagues.

At the end of 1926, Sforza himself left Italy more or less permanently, going first to live mainly in Brussels (Countess Sforza was the daughter of a Belgian diplomat), then largely in America and the south of France. He visited China and Russia in 1927, came to America that summer to lecture at the Williamstown Institute of Politics, and later returned for longer periods. All told, he contributed to *Foreign Affairs* seven times. In addition, he persuaded his friend Benedetto Croce to write a brilliant article for our tenth-anniversary issue in the fall of 1932—also the tenth anniversary of the March on Rome. His title, "Of Liberty," might have carried a subtitle, "And Of Courage," for Croce had chosen to run the risk of remaining in Italy.

Sforza was always sarcastic about the complacent attitude of many leading Americans toward Fascism. Writing me from Brussels in 1932 he mentioned how Mussolini, in an interview with a London paper, had summed up his conception of American civilization: "The Lindbergh baby and Prohibition." Sforza was delighted, interpreting Mussolini's derisive comment as meaning that he had given up hope of any more loans from, in Sforza's phrase, "your silly bankers."

He was a man of contradictions. His weaknesses sometimes were more evident than his strengths because they were superficial, which means on the surface, while his constancy and courage were ingrained, which means inherent and deep. He made a fine figure, which in itself might provoke jealousy—tall, erect, with an oval face, a high forehead and a close-cut beard which curved up at the sides to meet a curving-down mustache. Jealousy was certainly not one of his own vices. He tended to be super-cilious, especially toward colleagues if they were his superiors and if he thought them inadequate. He had a politely distant manner with strang-ers until he placed them as interesting enough to bother with, when he unlimbered; otherwise, he dismissed them from his mind. This decision he reached rapidly. His black eyes searched you sharply when what you were saying held his attention, turned nonchalantly out the window when it did not. He talked well, but with silences that (when you knew him) were portentous: the remark which followed, perhaps an apothegm or a summary characterization of someone, could be devastating. He liked generalizations and particularizations equally.

Many people mistrusted Sforza, but they undervalued him at their peril. He took pleasure in unmasking deceivers and chastising mounte-banks. Two words he often used were "despise" and "serenity." The first he used as a noun: "I have a despise for him." I never got him to sub-stitute "contempt"; somehow, "despise" seemed more personal and satisfactory. "Serenity" he valued because, although he possessed it ex-ternally, it was achieved with effort; internally he would be seething. He could recognize honesty as well as hypocrisy, and praise a noble spirit like Salvemini's while criticizing his beliefs that history ever was accurate; and he would characterize disdainfully the errors of judgment which a great man like Churchill could make about Mussolini under the spell of a warm evening on a yacht on the Mediterranean.

Luigi Barzini (son of the noted journalist of the same name) mentions as a characteristic of Italians that they can be one thing and the opposite at the same time, and Sforza was fiercely Italian. Even in love. He loved his family; yet his romantic affairs were wide-ranging, going back to Peking, where as a young man he was chargé d'affaires before the First War. Polish girls he thought particularly attractive. And American girls? "Oh," he complained, "so beautiful, but even in the moment of surrender they look at you with those honest eyes." In little things, vanity overcame his sense of proportion; but when matters of moment were involved, it lost out to truth. Perhaps his most important characteristic was that in making critical choices of policy he subordinated his instinctive cynicism to his resolute idealism.

It did not occur to me that my meeting with Sforza in Rome would be the beginning of a long relationship, lasting till his death in 1952. His self-exile was a period of vicissitudes to which he paid very little attention. His property, never large in any case, had of course been expropriated, and he supported his family almost entirely by writing and occasional lectures. The fact of his straitened circumstances did not distress him; he never mentioned it. In their tiny apartment in New York, a supper of spaghetti cooked by Countess Sforza, with a bottle of Chianti, was always lively. They came sometimes with their children, Fiammetta and Sforzino, to stay with us on Long Island, and later when they secured a small villa near Toulon, on the Côte des Maures, we visited them, feasted on bouillabaisse concocted largely from the fish speared underwater by little Sforzino, and swam in the rocky cove beneath a hill covered with pine and pungent eucalyptus.

Sforza's adversity brought out the positive side of the vanity which people considered a flaw in his character; it kept him from supposing for a moment that he was in any degree dependent on anyone or that because his enemies were powerful and successful he had chosen wrongly in defying them. His courage was augmented by a self-esteem which made it impossible that he should not be right. When in the end he returned to Italy to become again Minister of Foreign Affairs, it seemed to him the most natural thing in the world.

18

Where the East Begins

When D'Annunzio defied the Peace Conference and seized Fiume in 1919 he placarded the streets "Italia o Morte!"—Italy or Death! Now in 1924 Fiume was both Italian and dead. As I looked out across the Quarnero it was bare of steamers to the horizon. Serpentine streaks marked where a breeze was passing; the wake of a ferry to Abbazia spread and disappeared; there was a touch of ochre or burnt sienna where a fishing boat idled. Otherwise the sea was lifeless.

So was the port, which for five years had occupied a place in world headlines out of all proportion to its intrinsic importance. Italy had been determined to annex it because otherwise Trieste faced a losing fight for the trade of the hinterland. The Jugoslavs needed it because it was their only adequate trade outlet on the Adriatic. For the world in general the importance of the struggle was that repeatedly it threatened to start a new war.

After his *coup de théâtre* in 1919, D'Annunzio reigned as "Commandant" of Fiume for about a year, playing what his supreme egoism told him was a heroic epic: and the world took it as such till suddenly the curtain went down. Learning that the Treaty of Rapallo recognized Fiume as an independent state, D'Annunzio declared war on Italy. The Italian Government responded by sending a battleship which put a couple of shells into his palazzo; whereupon he fled. Fiume functioned as a Free City until a Fascist coup overthrew the local government in March, 1922. With Mussolini as his antagonist, Premier Pashich thought better of his determination never to negotiate with Italy again. A division of interests in Fiume was agreed on as part of a general accommodation in which both Italy and Jugoslavia undertook to remain neutral in case the other were attacked.

The Fiume arrangement looked strange on the map, stranger still on the spot. A little stream, the Riječina, twenty feet wide, separates Fiume from the suburb of Sušak. Near its mouth the Rečina divides, forming a small delta where the lumber brought down to Sušak from Croatia was stored before being shipped out through the adjoining Baroš Basin. Which side of the delta should form the frontier? The dispute was now settled. Jugoslavia recognized Italy's annexation of the Free City which President Wilson had fought to establish, and in return retained Sušak and secured Baroš. King Victor Emmanuel visited Fiume in March, 1924, and celebrated its official annexation to Italy.

Now, two months later, grass was growing on the wharves built at enormous cost by Hungarian financiers to make Fiume a rival to Austria's Trieste. The quais were empty and children were using the mammoth derricks as jungle gyms. Some sloops were tied up at the public wharf along with two or three coastal steamers. The merchant ships which used to load freight for all parts of the world had been absent since 1914. D'Annunzio's legionnaires had blown up the old stone bridge across the Rečina and soldiers were guarding either end of the temporary wooden structure. The armed rushes and random rifle shots of past years had ceased, but neither side seemed comfortable. It took time and argument for me to get across to Sušak to visit the Jugoslav mayor.

In Rome, Count Sforza had arranged quietly for me to see General Giardino, just returned from serving as Military Governor of Fiume. He remarked, in humorous understatement, that the frontier was "not exactly the sort a soldier would choose." He warned me against taking too much stock in the complaints I would hear from both sides. "After all, they are small people," he said. "They honestly believe that personal interests of a very minor character constitute important international questions." He was right, of course, in stressing that Fiume was no longer a direct danger to world peace. The relics of the dispute were local commercial rivalries between Fiume and Sušak and Fiume and Trieste.

After talking with our Consul, North Winship, with leading Fiumiani (mostly "autonomists" at heart) and with the Mayor of Sušak, I had little doubt that Fiume would lose both contests. As a Free City, Fiume could have lived; its modern facilities would have attracted a large share of the Jugoslav trade. As an Italian port, it would be to a large extent boycotted by the Jugoslavs, who would prefer to build up their own

Sušak. In competition with Trieste, Fiume was bound to lose; the Italian Government would give the powerful shipping interests of that old established port all possible favors, and Venice, a city with great political influence, would be second in line for subventions. If anything was left, it would go to Fiume.

The leftovers were not enough. Fiume languished through the years, Sušak flourished. Then after the Second World War they became one again as the Jugoslav port of Rijeka.

II

When I saw the Grouichs in Rome they brought news of how outraged the Croats were by Pashich's compromise over Fiume. Had Wilson fought for the city's independence only to have Pashich concede that independence no longer existed even as a political fiction? They considered that Sušak even plus Baroš was wholly inadequate for their trade and that the arrangement was one more proof that the Serbs who controlled the central government cared nothing about their interests. The Croats also were aroused by the government's action toward the deputies elected to the Skupshtina by the Croatian Peasant party. In order to show his contempt for the whole Belgrade establishment, the party leader, Stjepan Radić, still refused to let his deputies take their seats. The government had replied by invalidating their mandates. Mme. Grouich said that Serb-Croat relations had never been worse.

To gauge how far Jugoslav unity was really cracking I stopped off at Zagreb on the way to Belgrade to see Dr. Ante Trumbić, the Croat wartime leader who had been most responsible for creating that unity. He had reacted strongly against the centralized structure of the Vidovdan constitution, but in spite of this had lost standing in Croatia. His efforts to get fair representation for Croatia's interests had been eclipsed by Radić's demagogic and often wildly implausible promises to the Croatian peasants. Now he was being buffeted from one side as a faint-hearted Croat, from the other as no longer a true Jugoslav. He, if anyone, ought to be able to give me a fair judgment of whether the two peoples were heading toward national disaster.

Trumbić admitted to being greatly disillusioned, but it was not, he insisted, because Radić's movement was leaving him by the wayside, but because national unity was being eroded by Pashich's use of his control of government finances to remake Serbia at the expense of other regions. The basic trouble with him as a national leader, said Trumbić, was that he was hopelessly provincial, in both his ideas of state organization and his concept of Jugoslavia's place in the new Europe. He was right to avoid conflict with Italy, but he had gone too far in compromise because in his heart he wanted, for selfish Serbian reasons, to orient Jugoslavia toward Saloniki and the Aegean instead of toward the Adriatic. Serbia's trade would most easily go southward, Croatia's to the west. He did not grasp the essential fact that with its six hundred kilometers of Adriatic coast Jugoslavia could belong to the great Mediterranean world and have a European future, whereas if it contented itself with a role in the Aegean it would have merely a Balkan future. The problem was not Serbian or Croatian but Jugoslav.

The sensational news had come recently that Radić, who had fled abroad to avoid arrest after abusing the King and advocating a Croatian republic, had arrived in Moscow to find Soviet support. The situation was farcical. During the war, while Trumbić was working to break up the Hapsburg Empire and form a Jugoslav nation, Radić had written sycophantic odes in honor of the Austrian Emperor. Now, monarchist turned republican, Radić was winning Croatian support by advocating Croatian self-determination even to the point of breaking up the nation which Trumbić had helped create.

"Radić is a complicated character," said Trumbić, "but he is not so erratic as he appears. He does favor a republic—for Jugoslavia if possible, but if not, then for Croatia. But he doesn't consider monarchy or republicanism important in itself. His aim is autonomy for Croatia and he works for it consistently under either system." As to whether Radić's visit to Moscow meant he was a Communist, Trumbić said no. Probably he had gone there simply to make Belgrade pay him more attention. Nor was he a violent revolutionary; he merely wanted to achieve revolutionary aims by political pressure. He was against using Croatian taxes for Serbian purposes and against a large national army.

"King Alexander and Pashich think we need a big army," Trumbić said, "to discourage Italy, Hungary and Bulgaria from attacking us. Radić wants to make friends with them by reducing the army."

To the question who would succeed Pashich, Trumbić answered: "Nobody in his own party. His place is unique because of his age and years of leadership. When he dies, his Radical party will go to pieces. The time of one-man government and one-man politics is over. It lasts in Belgrade simply because Pashich has outlived his time. Croatia is willing to wait. We shall not take to an Irish policy. When Pashich is gone we shall be able to make a new constitution. Centralized government is of the old Europe, federalism of the new. We are of the new."

III

Politicians in Belgrade worried less than Trumbić did about the future, and although this was wrong it was natural because Nikola Pashich's durability seemed endless. His cabinets might, and did, fall, but everyone knew that after an interval he would reappear as the head of a new government.

When I had been in Belgrade two years before, Pashich had been recovering from an automobile accident. Since then he had been severely wounded by a pistol shot while traveling in his automobile. Now the car windows were whitewashed and he was whirled over the rutted and gullied Belgrade streets in an opaque glass box. Despite these ordeals and the fact that in two months he would be eighty—the oldest prime minister in Europe—he had not relaxed control over state and party affairs.

The halls outside his office were crowded with petitioners, many of them peasants in baggy homespun breeches and braided jackets. He was sitting quietly with hands folded on his desk as though he had nothing to do; the bright red Pirot rug on the wall behind him set off his solemn face and made his long square-cut beard seem even whiter than usual.

Bishop Nicholai told me once that Pashich's lifelong characteristic was to be really contented only when he was alone, able to think things over free from the advice and importunings of even his closest associates. Nicholai had happened to have an appointment to see him the evening of the Sarajevo murder and on arrival found him in bed. Pashich said he had heard the news of the Archduke's death while he was dressing; he had taken off his clothes, lain down again and spent the rest of the day there alone, thinking. "It is very bad," he told Nicholai. "It is very bad. It will mean war." That first apprehension wore off, for when the Austrian ultimatum arrived he was away from Belgrade, electioneering in the south.

As Pashich began talking the effect of his stumbling words was contradicted as usual by the close regard of his sharp blue eyes. His halting speech did not give an impression of confused thought but neither did it seem considered strategy, like Balfour's technique of being overtaken by sudden deafness when asked an awkward question. The breaks in Pashich's conversation probably came from weakness of memory. He was said to forget even the names of members of his cabinet—but then how many cabinet members had come and gone in so many years!

When the subject of Radić's visit to Moscow came up his eyes crinkled into a smile. Radić really was too foolish, he said, touching his forehead; it was conceivable that he might even be honest, for he was too foolish to tell fact from fancy. He dismissed Radić's promises to end peasant taxes and abolish conscription as silly. A state could not exist without income, a state could not exist in the Balkans without an army. An independent Croatia would not be big enough to be prosperous or strong enough to be safe. Such talk was of no consequence. Jugoslavia would be there long after Radić was gone—"even," he said, though his evident amusement seemed to deny it, "after I am."

To rub in this point, he added that he wanted to live to see what had almost never existed in the Balkans—peace. With peace, Jugoslavia's population could grow by 50 percent in twenty years and the per capita income could increase three times. When I repeated this the next day to Foreign Minister Ninchich he did not even smile. The old man had dominated political life for so long that jokes about his immortality no longer had any point, either for enemies or for colleagues.

By early summer the Serbo-Croat wrangle reached such proportions that King Alexander decided he must resort to drastic measures to bring the Croats into the government. In June, taking advantage of Pashich's temporary loss of a parliamentary majority, he authorized Davidovich, Pashich's chief rival, to form a cabinet in which the Croatian Peasant party was expected to participate. And, in fact, Radić's deputy, Dr. Maček, came to Belgrade to negotiate with Davidovich for a coalition.

The King's action in turning to the leader of the second-largest party instead of allowing Pashich to adjourn parliament and make new elections was not strictly constitutional and has been much criticized by historians. He did it, he told me a year later, as a matter of conscience.

"I felt that the door had been slammed in the face of the Radić deputies," he said. "I disliked some of their program, but I felt it was not right—supposing, as Davidovich assured me, he could work with Radić —that this opposition bloc should not have the opportunity of governing."[1]

Typically, Radić rejected the opportunity, resumed his attacks on the army, called again for the separation of Croatia and verged on treason by announcing that Chicherin, the Soviet Commissar for Foreign Affairs, had promised him support in fighting Belgrade. This ended the King's hope of forming a Davidovich-Radić majority coalition. Thereupon he dismissed Davidovich and turned back to Pashich. Pashich ordered

1. This interview with King Alexander, March 21, 1925, important as giving his personal account of the much-debated 1924 crisis, is printed in full in Appendix II.

Radić's arrest, and the police found him hiding behind a washstand in a Zagreb apartment. It was announced that incriminating documents had been seized also, including the text of a treaty promising territorial concessions to Hungary in return for recognition of Croatian independence. (Radić explained it as merely a theoretical exercise.) Pashich doubtless hoped that Radić's arrest would disable the Croatian Peasant party. Yet even with its leader in jail it came through the elections in February, 1925, with undiminished strength.

Now both Pashich and Radić gave way. The Croatian Peasant party on March 27, 1925, renounced all ties with Moscow and accepted the Vidovdan constitution and the monarchy; and when Pashich invited it to join in a coalition it accepted and took four cabinet posts. To conclude the somersault, Radić himself shortly thereafter became Minister of Education. Moscow called him a "pitiful traitor."

It can be (and has been) argued that King Alexander committed a grave error in authorizing Davidovich to negotiate with Radić instead of ordering the elections advocated by Pashich, who was constitutionally authorized to advise the King as spokesman for the largest single party, even though he lacked enough votes in parliament to form his own cabinet. Five years later, in the great constitutional crisis of 1929, Croatian and other critics bitterly attacked the King's decision to establish a dictatorship. They saw it as an effort to protect the dynasty's Serbian base against demands of other peoples in his kingdom for a larger share in government; and they cited his action in 1924 as his first step toward seizing all power. The contrary was true. Alexander acted at that time to bring Croatian dissidents into the government against the opposition of the Serbian centralists.

I V

To return to 1924. Although politicians in Belgrade and Zagreb were absorbed in political rivalries and maneuvers, what I saw from a window of the Orient Express jogging along down the Morava Valley was reassuring. I was bound for Skoplje, the ancient Macedonian capital, where I hoped to find a car to take me to Ochrida for a visit to Bishop Nicholai. As the peasants turned to the train from following their teams of oxen their faces showed curiosity, but it was only momentary. They cared little about the great world; their concern was for their maize and wheat, their beets and (further south) their poppies, their pigs rooting in the ditches and their beehives near their orchards. Very good harvests were in prospect and it was predicted that the plums would yield a most abundant production of slivovitz. The smell of the earth when I jumped out of the leisurely train for strolls at tiny stations combined with all the busy signs of springtime country life to produce a sense of stability and continuity. Before the train came in sight of the minarets of Skoplje's dozen mosques and its old Turkish citadel I had added a postscript to a letter home saying that Jugoslavia, as Pashich had assured me, would be there tomorrow and the day after, one country still.

The visit to Ochrida was foreclosed by the refusal of the general commanding the division at Skoplje to lend me a military car for the trip. He was polite, gave me dinner, but stuck to his decision. The country to be traversed was rather wild and he feared that some incident with a band of *komitadji* infiltrators from Bulgaria would be built up in the Sofia press as a Serbian attack on defenseless Macedonian villagers. No other means of transport existed, so I could only send a telegram to the Bishop, without much hope of its ever reaching him, retrace my route north to Nish and wait for another branch of the Orient Express (one wagon-lit and one decrepit coach) to take me on to Sofia. Before starting the next morning I wandered around the old Turkish streets looking for a fabled tower built by the Turks with the skulls of a thousand Serbian rebels; but after being assured that it was just around the next corner, and then the next, and finally that it had been destroyed years ago, I gave up the rather grizzly search.

The possible presence of *komitadji* bands was not invented by the general, as I had thought at first, in order to discourage my trip to Ochrida. They had been a very real fact of life (and death) in Macedonia ever since such bands had been formed at the end of the nineteenth century to fight the Turks and, eventually, all non-Bulgarian inhabitants of Macedonia. No résumé can do justice to the conglomeration of nationalities that originated the culinary term *macédoine* or trace the reversals of fortune that, once the Turks had been expelled, switched segments of Macedonia back and forth between Bulgarian, Serbian and Greek rule. Each nationality formed its own guerrillas, that is to say terrorists. Of these, the Bulgarian *komitadjis* were the most notorious, and their principal organization, known from its Bulgarian initials as IMRO, was still powerful in Sofia as well as in the wild Macedonian countryside. They continued their operations until Bulgaria's defeat in the Second World War ended her pretensions in the area for the time being and settled it more or less securely in Jugoslav and Greek hands. One thing remains certain: at any promising opportunity the Bulgars will resume the struggle.

Two unusually spectacular acts of *komitadji* terrorism bracketed my visit to Sofia. One had been the assassination the previous spring of the Peasant party leader, Alexander Stamboliski, who had courageously opposed the war and had become Premier following Bulgaria's defeat and the abdication of King Ferdinand. Stamboliski had suppressed the Communists, antagonized the middle classes by land reform and offended the fearsome head of the IMRO, Todor Alexandrov, by negotiating with Jugoslavia to end the guerrilla warfare in Macedonia. He was assassinated in a coup staged jointly by IMRO and nationalist army officers. The second spectacular terroristic act was the assassination of Alexandrov himself, a few months after my visit, by a group of his own followers who disapproved of his effort to obtain arms and money from Moscow. Because the victims were so prominent the two murders stood out even in the atmosphere of plot and counterplot which made murder a part of everyday life in Sofia.

I had been lectured in Belgrade about the Bulgarian Government's hypocrisy in professing not to be able to control the *komitadji* raids into Macedonia; and the general in Skoplje had pointed out on a map the routes by which they came in from their bases in the Bulgarian mountains. Pashich looked on Alexandrov as a tool of the Bulgarian Government or perhaps even its master; and one of his counts against Radić was that he was in league with Alexandrov in soliciting Soviet aid. Foreign Minister Kalfov, who had been a member of the group that plotted to overthrow Stamboliski, though not involved in his murder, explained how helpless the government was to deal with all this. The Communist danger kept the country on the verge of civil war and Allied limitations on the size of the army made it inadequate either to establish internal order or guard the frontiers. Destitute refugees from Greek Thrace and what he called "Serbized" Macedonia had joined the *komitadjis* or else had become Communist revolutionaries, armed and supported by Moscow. A Communist rising the previous autumn had come close to success and now Moscow was spending money lavishly on preparations for another.

Like most of his colleagues in the reactionary Tsankov ministry, Kalfov was still short of forty. He tried hard to make a good impression. Everything wrong in Bulgaria was the fault of somebody else (except King Ferdinand's mistake in having chosen the losing side in two wars, which Kalfov left unmentioned). The country's misery and stagnation were explained by the influx of refugees and the heavy reparations being paid to Jugoslavia and Greece. The raids into Macedonia were not the result of government negligence but of Moscow's support of IMRO, Radić's collusion with Alexandrov ("which Jugoslavia seems unable to control") and the treaty requirement that the army must consist wholly of volunteers. He denied even thinking of treaty revision except as regarded the limitations on the army. The same story was repeated by everyone I talked with in Sofia—cabinet members, professors, journalists. Some of it was true, and in any case they could not be expected to say anything else to a foreigner, especially one arriving from Belgrade.[2]

During his reign, King Ferdinand had done his best to make Sofia over in German provincial taste, with the result that it was a rather uninteresting little city, a place a visitor was not likely to leave with much regret. This was especially so in a time when the inhabitants were overwhelmed by past misfortunes, cowed by the daily terror in the streets and apprehensive for their future in a world in which every neighbor was an enemy, made so largely by their own government's stupidity and cupidity.

V

Italy, Spain, Hungary—was Greece about to be added to the list of dictatorships? It seemed quite possible this spring of 1924. But it did not happen; and when a dictator did indeed take over Greece in January, 1926, his tenure was brief.

On arriving in Athens two years before, it may be recalled, I had asked the hotel concierge the address of a certain M. Papanastasiou, to whom I had been given a letter. I was told it was the city jail. Now Papanastasiou was the republican Prime Minister.

Greece had spent the interval playing musical chairs. The way in which everyone jumped or was shoved around made it look quite frivolous, but in fact the stakes were the highest: the throne. King Constantine had abdicated and had died abroad. His ministers, who had put Papanastasiou in jail, had been shot by a firing squad. Constantine's son and successor, King George, had held his place for only about a year; then Venizelos, the dynasty's chief enemy, had won a resounding electoral victory, George had found it expedient to leave the country and Venizelos had become Prime Minister. But in less than a month Venizelos too was out and Papanastasiou had succeeded him. Papanastasiou's government

2. Bulgaria increased her army only in 1938, when the members of the Balkan Entente—Jugoslavia, Greece, Rumania and Turkey—agreed as a gesture of friendship to permit it in return for a Bulgarian pledge of nonaggression. This was something of a formality, for by then Bulgaria was receiving arms surreptitiously from Germany. Hitler's seizure of Austria was already casting a shadow across all southeast Europe. Soon Nazi threats and promises put an end to attempts to solve disputes in the Balkans on a neighborly basis even if Bulgaria had wished it (which she probably did not, having less than the others to lose by war).

had begun with an overwhelming majority in parliament, but just as I reached Athens it was badly shaken by the resignation of the Minister of War, General Kondylis. The general looked very much like a dictator, and people were saying that he planned to knock Papanastasiou from his seat. Again the country's form of government seemed hanging in the balance.

Venizelos had lost his chair in this musical round partly because of poor judgment, partly because the general circumstances were unfavorable to him. The Treaty of Lausanne had deprived Greece of much that he had won for her at the Paris Peace Conference. He decided that in order to restore national harmony he must conciliate the moderate royalists, but this policy was unpopular with his own party and failed. Finally, although he favored a republic in principle, he refused to "impose" it (his word) without a plebiscite. His resignation followed. Papanastasiou, a former adherent, seized the chance to become Prime Minister and proclaim the Republic. Though this *fait accompli* was ratified in a plebiscite, the Republic evidently was rather shaky, and it was commonly believed that General Kondylis had provoked the crisis in order to replace it by a dictatorship.

Kondylis received me in his unpretentious villa in one of the new and still half-built outskirts of Athens. The whitewashed walls of his little study were hung with faded photographs of soldier groups in old campaigns in Macedonia and more recently Anatolia. Above his desk, strewn with cigarette stubs, was a small picture of Napoleon in an unvarnished wooden frame; another picture of Napoleon was propped up among piles of papers on a stand at one side. On a pine table in the center of the room stood a pickle jar, with label intact, filled with faded daisies. A thin film of dust which came in from the road through the skimpy lace curtains lay on everything. It was very hot and flies buzzed in an angry circle where there should have been a draft from a dormant fan in the ceiling.

The General motioned me to sit down at the table, took a seat opposite, and waited for me to explain why I had come to see him. He looked what he was, a peasant from Thessaly, now about forty-five, whose army life had been spent almost entirely in the field. His military education had been at a school for noncommissioned officers. His stained, furrowed face, set mouth, angry eyes, bushy hair thrust back in a mat, mustache turned up, proclaimed self-confidence and an ability to take and repel criticism but not to forgive it. William Miller, the historian who lived for many years in Greece (and wrote several times for *Foreign Affairs*), told me the next day that when Kondylis as Minister of War went into parliament he carried with him his riding crop and laid it on his desk, looking around unsmilingly as he did so.

As he spoke nothing but Greek, was not accustomed to interviews and distrusted interpreters, even his own aides, it was some moments before the conversation got going. I began by asking why although a long-time Venizelist he had joined an anti-Venizelos government. He said he had often disagreed with Venizelos on the "King question." He wanted, like Venizelos, to settle it, but by a plebiscite held only to ratify a *fait accompli,* whereas Venizelos insisted on a plebiscite as the first step, and this involved the danger of civil war. Then why, I asked, had he resigned from the Papanastasiou government which had held the plebiscite in the manner he wanted? It was for entirely different reasons, he replied—because the government kept shilly-shallying over what to do with the refugees from Anatolia and about how to handle Communist strikers (who ought to be jailed) and soldiers who were demanding to be demobilized (who were mutineers and ought to be shot). At hardly more than a hint from me that people were saying he wanted to become a dictator the General jumped from his chair and glared angrily at the terrified interpreter, whose only guilt was to have transmitted the question, a very mild one at that.

"The government delays and delays," he said, "and parliament talks and talks. I have no desire to work without parliament, but it must do more than talk. We must decide how to keep the refugees from starving next winter. The government is poor, but that is no excuse. If it decides what must be done, there are Greeks rich enough to help—or if they don't, they must be made to. We need foreign help, but the first thing is for the government to show that it knows its business and make a start at performing it. The Greek Government and the Greek people must be united in action. If necessary they must be united by force."

It sounded very authoritarian. However, Kondylis did not make a military coup either then or when a second occasion offered. A year later another general, Pangalos, voided the republican constitution, forced venerable Admiral Koundouriotis to resign as President and set himself up as dictator. His dictatorship lasted only seven months, and the man who destroyed it was General Kondylis. The expectation was that Kondylis would be tempted to take the same course. Instead he ordered parliamentary elections, refused to stand for office himself and after a new government had been installed and Admiral Koundouriotis reinstated as President he departed quietly for Paris. Obviously this was an exceptional Greek, as disciplined himself as he was ready to discipline others.

In the ins and outs of later years Kondylis was sometimes in, playing a decisive role in important events, sometimes out. Once during the Pangalos dictatorship he was sent into exile along with Papanastasiou and other former ministers. The place of exile was the island of Santorin, in the southern Cyclades.

It happened that at about this time Paul D. Cravath, the New York lawyer, was a guest on a yacht chartered for a cruise through the Greek islands by a rich lady, much publicized as one of America's "ten best-dressed women." Santorin, an interesting volcanic island, was on the itinerary. When the tourists landed they were surprised to find several gentlemen waiting on the quai, one in a morning coat and top hat, who greeted them courteously. The exiles, seeing the yacht approaching, and having nothing else to occupy them, had come down to the harbor to do the honors of the island. Among them was General Kondylis, though certainly he was not the one in a top hat.

Cravath later recounted how, continuing the voyage, the yacht arrived at night in the harbor of Piraeus. When he came on deck in the morning he asked his hostess when she planned to go up to Athens, five or six miles away. She said in some surprise that she hadn't thought of it.

"But I must see the Parthenon," said Cravath.

"Well, you can see it from here," said the lady, pointing to a white object just visible across the sloping plain, at that distance about an inch high.

In spite of the flurry over the Kondylis resignation and speculation over what would come next, the tension had lessened since my visit in 1922, when Athens had been split into two camps, with monarchists and republicans refusing to mingle. Cafés frequented by one set were avoided by the other; old friends cut each other in the street; nobody read opposition newspapers. Such hostility was bound to end in violence, and did. But the recent coup against King George had been different. He was requested to leave and complied with dignity. There was no terrible sequel like the executions which had followed his father Constantine's abdication the year before.

Intelligent royalists nevertheless feared the royal house was done for. The million refugees who had poured in from Asia Minor after the military debacle had blamed King Constantine for the loss of their homes, and they had voted against him to a man. The badly organized royalist coup the previous autumn led by General Metaxas, an officer trained in Germany and a strong supporter of Constantine's wife, Queen Sophie, had been a failure. The result for the monarchy had been further loss of face; and for Metaxas it meant exile.[3] Now a restoration of King George could be brought about only by a terrible convulsion, and this Greece could not stand. The only course for moderate monarchists seemed to be to work toward a coalition with moderate republicans and then once again let the public decide on the Greek form of government. It was dubious whether a decision of that sort would be possible, still more so whether it would be permanent. Nor from that day to this have the Greek people ever reached a consensus on the "King question."

V I

It used to be said in Vienna that the East began at the Landstrasse. If you left Vienna by that ancient route and came to Budapest you were warned there that if you proceeded further you would find nothing but filth, laziness and decay. "That," Hungarians said, "is the East."

Italians said that the East began when you came to the Quarnero, which Dante called the frontier of Italian civilization. One of Dante's heirs, the waiter in the Trieste café, flicking away the flies from the spotted tablecloth, would say: "You are going to Zagreb? A filthy place. My mother was a Croat but she had the good fortune to marry an Italian and escape to Europe."

The Croats, in turn, had the satisfaction of feeling more Western than their Serbian kinsmen: they said earnestly that when you reached Serbia you would see for the first time what it means to have been under Turkish rule for all those centuries.

Naturally, the Serbs told of the inferiority of their neighbors to the east, the Bulgars with their Tartar blood. And the Bulgars pointed out that the East began where Europe ends, at the Bosporus.

The East began at the Bosporus more clearly in 1924 than it does today. The Sultanate had been abolished in 1922 and the Sultan, whose predecessors held among other titles that of "Terror of the World," had slunk away almost unnoticed from his palace in Constantinople. The next year the Turkish Republic was proclaimed with Mustafa Kemal as President, and Constantinople, seated splendidly at the crossroads of two continents, was replaced as the capital by a little windswept town in the mountains of Asia Minor named Angora. To mark the decisive break with the past and with Turkey's Moslem neighbors, Mustafa Kemal abolished the Caliphate and ordered a sweeping overturn of political, reli-

3. Metaxas did better for the monarchy in 1936, when he helped bring back King George for the second time, became Premier and ran the country without benefit of parliament until the Italian attack in 1940, when he took Greece into the war on the side of the Allies.

gious and social law and custom. But at the time of my visit the bitterly resented transformation in habit and looks of the Turkish people had not yet taken place. The red fez still was universally worn, veiled women still were seen in the street, the music blaring from the black recesses of coffeehouses still sounded like cats caterwauling, beggars still tugged at your sleeves and couldn't be pried loose. As you stood on the famous bridge across the Golden Horn every type and color of face and dress passed by in the hustling crowd. Below, agile caïques darted about with loads of vegetables and fish, low-slung tartans with loose triangular sails on stumpy masts came sliding in from the Aegean or the Black Sea, while more steady slanted-masted lighters clustered several deep at the docks, or, further out, clung alongside the steamers in port from all over the world.

Mustafa Kemal would soon wipe out most of what was authentically Turkish in this kaleidoscopic scene. Holed up in Ankara, as Angora was to be called, he issued orders as his whim decided. Many of his original colleagues were antagonized by his disdain for popular feelings, his dictatorial manners and violent personal behavior. Among them was Rauf Bey, a signer of the National Pact and later Prime Minister. When the Greeks had been defeated in Asia Minor, Rauf felt that patriotism no longer required acquiescence in the trend of events; he resigned from the cabinet to show his disapproval of the concessions made at the first session of the Lausanne Conference by his rival, Foreign Minister Ismet Pasha (later Prime Minister and after Kemal's death President under the name Inönü). Rauf had the support of numerous deputies, but after Kemal retaliated brutally against those who first spoke up against him the rest subsided. Under the strange Turkish procedure of that time, ministers were elected by the National Assembly and could resign their posts or be dismissed without losing their seats. This was Rauf's position; he was still a deputy but had no other office and was little in Ankara.

Our chief diplomatic representative in Constantinople at the time was Rear Admiral Mark L. Bristol, with the title of High Commissioner. He had served there through all the troubles since 1919 and knew everybody and almost everything they were doing. Two of his staff, Howland Shaw and Pierrepont Moffat, were friends of mine and the military attaché, Colonel Sherman Miles, soon became one. I had read many of his reports to Professor Coolidge in Vienna from Carinthia and Dalmatia while I was in the Legation at Belgrade. I wanted to see one of Kemal's critics before going up to Ankara, where I hoped to see Kemal himself. So Admiral Bristol arranged for me to call on Rauf.

Rauf, about forty-five, just back from a visit to Western Europe, had kept the directness and smart appearance of his early days as a naval officer. He began by explaining in fluent English that the Turkish Government was organized like an army.

"Mustafa Kemal is the Commander in Chief," he said. "Ismet Pasha, Minister of Foreign Affairs, is Chief of Staff. The ministers are General Staff officers. The members of the National Assembly, having no powers as individuals and being for the most part automatons picked by the ruling clique, might be called privates. If they are privates, you may wonder what ordinary citizens are? The answer is simple: the citizenry, for government purposes, does not exist. Turkey is a republic; there are elections; but the people are inexperienced in voting and suspect anyway that how they vote will not affect the declared outcome. Well, we will compromise and call the members of the National Assembly corporals."

Despite this situation, which made it impossible to organize an opposition on a broad base, Rauf indicated that Kemal's troubles might force a change. Many deputies in Kemal's own People's party were restless; the government was divided by jealousies and snarled in red tape; costs of living were rising; commerce in Constantinople was fading away because of inefficiencies and delays in port management; military expenditures took two-thirds of the whole budget and until interest on old Ottoman loans could be met no new foreign loan was possible. Kemal was vigorous in political action against critics but bored by economic problems and when pressed to make decisions flew into senseless rages.

As the Republic would be a year old in October, might not that be an occasion to organize an opposition party? Rauf hedged on answering such a blunt question directly, but I felt he definitely had some such plan in view (and wrote an article to that effect for the New York magazine *Our World*). Admiral Bristol was not so sure but agreed it was possible.

Four months later, Rauf and several liberal colleagues formed the Republican Progressive party. On various pretexts, Kemal suppressed it. In many parts of the country there was rioting against the enforcement, just beginning, of Kemal's new laws, particularly the mandatory discarding of fezzes and the abolition of polygamy. A serious rising of the Kurds was also in progress. Taking these disorders as an excuse, Kemal executed most of the leaders of the new party although there was no evidence of their being implicated in any plot. By chance, Rauf Bey was in Europe and escaped, but was given *in absentia* a sentence of ten years' imprisonment. In exile (as Arnold Toynbee has recorded in his volume *Acquaintances*) he showed good judgment and admirable generosity, criticizing

Kemal's acts frankly but objectively without letting a note of personal bitterness creep in. Eventually he was able to return to Istanbul (as Constantinople was renamed) and in accordance with the new requirements dropped his title and became Rauf Orbay. For years he sent me boxes of raisins, figs, almonds and Turkish delight at Christmas, a substitute, perhaps, for the article he always begged off writing on the excuse that he would not speak ill of the regime abroad even though it differed so sadly from what he had hoped when he joined Mustafa Kemal in starting the revolution.

My plan to go up to Ankara was frustrated and I missed seeing one of the most formidable and successful revolutionaries of the twentieth century, his achievements in making a country remembered and his violences forgotten. One night I woke up in my room at the Pera Palace Hotel feeling violently ill. The bell brought no response and the Turkish telephone did not function before six. When at last it did I called up Sherman Miles, who came around at once, carried me downstairs on his back and took me to the old German Hospital, now being run by an American staff. The doctor in charge, Dr. Post, from East Williston, Long Island, had been a medical missionary for some years in Asia Minor. He took one look, said "amoebic," and started shooting me full of emetine. He told me afterward I had been lucky to come into the hands of someone experienced in tropical diseases, for by the time a well-organized Western hospital had gone through its routine of examinations and tests I would probably have been done for. Three weeks in the care of dozens of agile little Greek nurses followed, and gradually I began to take an interest in the view from the window—in the foreground a barren stretch of rocks and rubbish, traversed by three or four diagonal paths used at all hours by passers-by more miserable than picturesque; beyond, over reddish tiled roofs, the waters of the Bosporus, with many sails and occasional steamers; and in the distance Scutari, on the shore of Asia, where Florence Nightingale had had her hospital. Then Sherman Miles and his wonderfully kind wife, Yulee, took me to convalesce at their place at Therapia, on the upper Bosporus, where I got back my legs walking in the shady garden.

The special north breezes which cooled Therapia in summer still attracted foreign residents of Constantinople as it had the Byzantine emperors. From the garden of the Miles's villa overlooking the Bosporus I watched fisherman busy with their nets early in the morning and again at evening, when phosphorus trails marked their movements on the dark water. The sight was tantalizing, for by law all fish caught had to be shipped to Constantinople to be taxed and stamped before they could be sold. Even if they reached the Constantinople market in edible condition they certainly could not stand a second journey back. So Therapia went fishless.

The long, hot days were placid. Then in the evening half a dozen or more of the large contingent of White Russians from Wrangel's army who had found a temporary refuge in Therapia would drop in for a glass of tea. One usually had a balalaika, but though the songs were nostalgic no one ever allowed himself to bewail the lost past or express mistrust about the uncertain future. Some of them had reached Constantinople from Odessa in vessels commandeered by a friend of mine, Hamilton Bryan, an American naval officer on Admiral Bristol's staff. The operation saved many lives, but it had been done in an emergency without even the Admiral's authorization. Disciplinary action was threatened and my friend at one time thought he might be bankrupted by a fine levied on behalf of the shipowners. He was later exonerated.

Time was passing and I became restless to get home. My family were worried and although the office was temporarily in the charge of an able assistant, F. Rhea Dulles, editorial plans beyond the forthcoming issue were in abeyance. Also, the American political pot was boiling. Day after day an interminable stalemate was continuing in the Democratic Convention in Madison Square Garden as to who was to run against Calvin Coolidge. The news that the candidate was to be John W. Davis made me more than ever anxious to be on the scene.

The evening before I left about a dozen of the Russians appeared to say goodbye, bringing a large double-handled silver cup, saved somehow in the migration, and two bottles of champagne. As the cup passed around each took a sip and addressed a toast to me. The sips were small, so that by the time my turn came the cup was still half full, and I was instructed, on pain of committing an unforgivable insult, not to take my lips from the cup until every drop was gone. As I drank—and drank—and drank—the Russians sang a sort of gurgling and chirping refrain, climaxed with a great twanging of the balalaika and joyful shouts. When I remonstrated at the extravagance I was told: "But maybe we'll never have money for champagne again!"

19

Uproar over Count Károlyi

John W. Davis never had a chance of being elected President. He aroused neither great enthusiasm nor deep hostility. Either would have been a help. He urged America to join the League of Nations, but his stipulation that it must be on conditions which would not antagonize the old isolationist band in Congress was more opportunistic than inspiring. Calvin Coolidge, comfortably and cautiously negative, was made for just this sort of a campaign. He was against joining the League, against recognizing Soviet Russia, and most of what he was for was also negative—the enforcement of prohibition and discriminatory restrictions on immigration. Only a fiery campaigner would have disconcerted such a cold fish. That Davis was not. He was handsome, courtly, eminent in the law, the most accomplished afterdinner speaker of the day; but irony which would have been devastating in a courtroom was lost in a mass meeting. Cartoonists labeled him the most difficult person to caricature that had come along in years.

I kept out of any public activities during the campaign, but at Davis' suggestion gave him occasional memoranda, one on the dispute which had almost broken up the recent Conference of American States at Santiago, where Secretary of State Hughes rejected Latin American suggestions that the Monroe Doctrine be developed into a mutual policy of hemispheric cooperation, another stressing the rule of refusing full cooperation with the Latin American republics on hemispheric matters while counting on them not to take advantage of our absence from Geneva to follow independent policies there. The Coolidge and Hoover ad-

275

ministrations did ameliorate relations with Latin America somewhat, but it remained for Roosevelt in 1933 to urge a treaty which was the beginning of the "continentalization" of the Monroe Doctrine.

More interesting than dropping memoranda into the speech-writing hopper was an effort to unsettle the Republicans who had voted for Harding as the best way to "take the United States into the League" and who now, not yet undeceived, were preparing to repeat the performance by voting for Coolidge. I enlisted Gay and others in preparing a warning to pro-Leaguers not to be lured into the old trap and secured thirty-five signers, among them ex-President Eliot of Harvard, several college presidents, former Secretary of War Baker and others of eminence. The newspapers published the appeal widely but without visible effect. Nothing short of the Great Depression would dent American complacency.

Coolidge warned me humorously that if I became identified with Democratic politics he would take to the stump for the Republicans regardless of his personal opinions in order to maintain the review's neutrality. I replied that he need not worry; such desperate measures would not be necessary. Actually I was not sure at the time how he would vote. He barely knew Calvin Coolidge, a very distant cousin, but he conceded with a grin after Calvin became President that the relationship had become less remote.

Since most people were content with the status quo (some would have preferred the status quo ante), "Keep Cool with Coolidge" was a winning slogan. To the very end, nevertheless, Davis was buoyed up by the optimism that carries candidates through even the most desperate campaigns. The night before election, he told me at his house in Locust Valley that by last reports the odds were definitely in his favor. The next evening we watched Calvin Coolidge's plurality roll up past 700,000.

In the sequel, Democratic leaders counted on four years of cold-blooded Coolidge conservatism to reclaim the country from what they called its slump into materialism. Actually, of course, it took twice as long as that to produce FDR and the New Deal.

II

When the excitements of the Presidential campaign were over we settled down to the routine pursuit of authors. Actually, "routine" is misleading; the tactics are always different and never dull. The name of our infant periodical was not widely known, so that many prospective contributors had to be told about its character in detail. Only gradually did we begin receiving spontaneous offers to write, most often from historians and specialists of one sort or another who in those days could find few magazines (other than professional journals) which were interested in more than travel articles or discussions of superficial aspects of international affairs. Sometimes potential contributors who turned up in New York or Boston could be snared for future articles. Among them that winter were R. W. Seton-Watson, the historian; Sir Frederick Maurice, the military critic; Yusuke Tsurumi, a competent Japanese journalist; Dr. Hans Dorten, fleetingly President of a "Rhineland Republic"; and Philip Kerr, who as Lord Lothian became British Ambassador in Washington twenty years later. Coolidge knew Kerr well and occasionally asked him for advice about authors. But he was an elusive character, and sometimes went to Boston without letting Coolidge or other close friends know. This happened when he was absorbed to the exclusion of everything else in the affairs of the Christian Science Church, to which his friend Lady Astor had converted him from Roman Catholicism.

Dr. Dorten had become notorious as President of the "Rhineland Republic" in 1919, and when I heard he was in New York I was curious enough about his meteoric rise and fall in world politics to ask him to dinner. Coolidge, who came down for the evening, wrote me the next day that one could see that Dorten was a dreamer who had been used as a tool by people more clever and unscrupulous than he. Among those was General Mangin, who was looking for a device to separate the Rhineland from Germany, whereas it was Dorten's hope that the creation of an autonomous neutral buffer zone between France and Germany, but within the Reich, would help stabilize European peace. Before Dorten left New York I encouraged him to finish the rough draft of an article which he showed me, the first detailed description of his adventures. It included a highly interesting account of Konrad Adenauer's now largely forgotten attitude in the affair, which can only be described as vacillating. When we published the article it attracted the furious attention of the German Government and press.

On General Bliss's return from a disarmament conference in Geneva, he came with Coolidge for a weekend at our place near Oyster Bay. He was apprehensive that the proposed Geneva Protocol would provide grounds for a revival of isolationist propaganda to the effect that the League of Nations was a superstate. My inclination was rather to think that the Protocol would give the League a chance to become a really effective world force and that the American public would be more impressed by this than disturbed by the picture of the League as a danger to national independence. I remember Bliss stressing a fact which then was only beginning to be recognized, namely, that the increased power of the offensive and the new long-range instruments of war had rendered fortified frontiers anachronistic—a lesson still not learned by the French as late as 1939. It was two years before he finally wrote the article on disarmament which we discussed at this time. I was gradually learning to play for the long future as well as the issue just ahead.

Meanwhile the Council was expanding both in size—three hundred members—and activity. It was plain that we must have larger quarters, and with Gay's approval I suggested at a Board of Directors meeting on November 24, 1924, that a building be secured, perhaps as a gift from an individual or foundation, perhaps by subscription. Coolidge wrote me a day later that he heard from Gay that I had "put through my ideas," which he called "most interesting, not to say exciting." The congratulations were premature. One obstacle was that the directors were not agreed about the Council's function. Paul Warburg generously offered to give the first $25,000 to a building fund, on condition the house should serve as a sort of international club where members could put up foreign visitors. I hated to look a gift horse in the mouth, but was strongly opposed to this concept for fear the Council would become mainly social, with housekeeping and other problems that would divert us from scholarly pursuits. Fortunately, most of the board agreed, but in order not to rebuff Warburg's handsome offer the whole project was dropped for the time being. When it was revived on acceptable terms Warburg came forward with a contribution of the same amount he had originally offered.

III

An article in one of our early numbers set off an acrimonious public controversy involving the Hungarian Legation in Washington and the State Department on one side and a wide range of American liberals on the other. The author was Professor Oscar Jaszi, who had been a Social Democratic minister in the last-gasp non-Communist cabinet under Count Károlyi before Béla Kun took over the Hungarian Government in 1919. Jaszi criticized the Allied dismemberment of Hungary but suggested that what she needed to restore her strength was to adopt democratic methods—reform her agriculture, eliminate the unearned increment of her feudal classes, democratize her public life, suppress revanchist military organizations and develop sincere cultural and economic relations with her neighbors. This, he asserted, was the opposite of the policy being pursued by the Horthy regime, which secretly was aiming to restore the Hapsburgs, maintaining the great feudal estates and seeking allies for a new war. Count Széchenyi, the Hungarian Minister in Washington, urged us to print a reply and was supported by a friend in the State Department, William R. Castle, Jr., who accepted his assertion that Jaszi was in the pay of the Communists. The accusation, which Széchenyi spread widely, so enraged Jaszi that he was with difficulty persuaded of the futility of trying to break the Minister's diplomatic immunity and sue him for libel. Our first choice as spokesman for the Horthy government was Count Teleki, former Premier and famous geographer, but he ruled himself out after his appointment as chairman of a commission to draw the Iraq frontier. Teleki was a most honorable statesman. When later on he again became Premier, he felt forced to sign a pact with Hitler, but offset it with a mutual assistance pact with Jugoslavia. Then when Hitler insisted that Hungary invade Jugoslavia he committed suicide. In the end, the reply to Jaszi was written by the Hungarian Premier, Count Stephen Bethlen.

This flurry over Jaszi was only a preliminary to the public uproar created by the arrival in New York of Countess Károlyi, followed by that of her husband, the President of the former Hungarian Republic. The Hungarian Legation put out reports that they were dangerous Bolsheviks, and Castle supported the charge. Countess Károlyi, a lady of great determination as well as good looks, of which she was well aware, had come to America on a lecture tour to explain events at the time of the Communist takeover in Budapest and also to earn money, for although she and her husband belonged to enormously rich landed families they were now in exile and penniless. The Hungarian nobility (including Count Széchenyi, who happened to be the Countess' cousin) hated Károlyi for having favored social reform, advocating a separate peace and passing a law in 1919 for the division of the great estates (which Károlyi inaugurated himself by distributing his own land to his tenants). He was a traitor to his class.

The rumors set going in Washington caused excitement in the press; partisans and enemies defended and attacked the Károlyis; ladies joined committees to sponsor the Countess' lectures and quit them in confusion. In the midst of this, she was taken seriously ill and Count Károlyi applied in Paris for a visa to join her. The State Department demurred but under pressure agreed on condition he make no statements or speeches while on American soil. A day or so after Károlyi landed, he and Seton-Watson lunched with me and both expressed dismay at the display of what they considered the State Department's lack of knowledge about Hungary, both historical and current. Coolidge, who meanwhile had heard from his friend Castle that Károlyi was a Bolshevist, replied that he could not credit it. Seton-Watson agreed that under an unattractive exterior Károlyi was an honest and sincere man. He and Coolidge were competent judges, Seton-Watson having for years been a leading expert on Central European affairs, while Coolidge had watched the development of the Károlyi–Béla Kun crisis from nearby as head of the American Commission in Vienna.

Károlyi's physical appearance did certainly tend to put one off. He was tall and lanky, limped as a result of a broken hip and leant heavily on a cane. His face was cadaverous, his weak eyes behind heavy glasses seemed hostile, and the drawn-down corners of his mouth and deep creases on either side of his nose gave him a cynical expression. Worst, he had a harelip, which impeded his speech. It was testimony to his courage that thus handicapped he had entered public life. I came to share Seton-Watson's opinion of his sincerity (I was less certain about the Countess). The Károlyis had been put out of Italy, Castle said, for Bolshevik propaganda. "This," Coolidge commented, "if true, does not necessarily prove that the alleged reason was the real one or, even if it was, that the charge was correct and I have told Castle I am still unconvinced." The expulsion had indeed occurred, but it was carried out on the eve of Mussolini's takeover and, as Count Sforza later told me, because the Hungarian Government supplied the Fascists with forged documents about the Károlyis and pestered Rome to act against them.

A crisis now put these matters out of our minds. One evening during a little dinner at my house Károlyi received a telephone call that the illness of his wife, who was in a hospital, had taken a serious turn; gall bladder trouble had suddenly developed and she must be operated on immediately. I went with him to the hospital and found a young doctor in attendance who seemed to us hardly experienced enough to perform the major operation he was planning for early the next morning. The head surgeon at the hospital had a very high reputation. Having failed to reach him by telephone, Károlyi and I took a taxi to his house in the West Forties, where a sleepy maid reluctantly agreed to let us wait in the hall till the doctor and his wife returned from the theater.

Rather naturally, the doctor was not at all pleased to see us, and even less so when I introduced Count Károlyi, said that he was the former President of the Hungarian Republic, now in exile and penniless, and that his wife was in a dangerous condition at the hospital where he was chief surgeon. He said he had no responsibility and would not interfere in another doctor's case. Our pleas proved fruitless and the doctor pointedly opened the front door. I said I was not content to let the matter rest and that if he did not come with us to see that Countess Károlyi was in competent hands I would make sure that, if she died, the press knew of the circumstances.

This was blackmail but it worked. The doctor put on his coat again, went to the hospital with us, confirmed the diagnosis and the next day himself very generously performed the operation, which proved to involve far more than had been indicated. The Countess recovered after some weeks and left with her husband for France by way of Canada. There Károlyi was at last able to disclose how he had been forced to remain silent in the United States under attack.

The next autumn Countess Károlyi tried to return to the United States to finish her interrupted lecture tour, but this time was barred by the State Department. The Civil Liberties Union protested, Senator Wheeler introduced a resolution in Congress demanding disclosure of the reasons for the exclusion and the part played in it by the Hungarian Legation, Dean Gildersleeve of Barnard and other academic notables decried the suppression of free speech. Secretary Kellogg, driven into an intellectual corner, was obdurate. The *World* (at my instigation) had editorially compared the reluctant admission of Count Károlyi to the country with the immense public welcome extended in 1849 to the Hungarian revolutionary hero, Kossuth, when an official reception committee went down the Bay in gaily dressed boats to meet him and conduct him to City Hall. The editorial spoke sarcastically about a speech by Secretary Kellogg before the Council on Foreign Relations in which he said he was excluding the Countess in order to preserve the "priceless heritage of liberty" which "came from the struggles of our ancestors through centuries." "There stood the Secretary of State," said the *World,* "alone and unafraid in the Ritz-Carlton Hotel, pausing in his struggle just a moment to assure his anxious friends that he would not falter in his determination to protect the Republic against the Countess." It concluded that no more inspiring figure than Mr. Kellogg had appeared since Barbara Frietchie. The bar stood, however, and Countess Károlyi, who had gotten as far as Canada, returned to Paris.

The next time I saw the Károlyis was in Paris in March, 1925. The Countess was opening an antique shop on the Avenue Malakoff, and Károlyi came to my hotel to invite me to visit her there the next afternoon. I recall that he admired the cigarette case given me by King Alexander of Jugoslavia, made of two colors of gold in the Russian design, and remarked that it was heavy enough to fetch a good price at a pawn shop. "Ever since I became a refugee," he said, "I have lost all my artistic sense. My only reaction to a beautiful object is, how much would it bring?" He told me he had sold a painting by Zorn, which for a time he had left with us in New York for safekeeping, for about $7,000—"a godsend—we and the children have been living on it for a year." There had been news in the papers of the opening of the Countess' shop, and I found her being photographed. Later we went to the Károlyi apartment on the top floor of an old house off the Boulevard Montparnasse. Károlyi had preceded us and arranged teacups and some little speckled cakes on a table beside a large tin kettle on a gas burner.

Former Premier Nitti of Italy and his son had been invited to meet me. The conversation between the two exiles was interlarded with "Mais oui, M. le Président" and "Mais non, M. le Président" and "D'accord, M. le Président." The scene would have been pathetic if the two ex-Presidents had not so evidently been enjoying it. Nitti was pudgy and double-chinned, with beady eyes that twinkled sometimes and sometimes examined you suspiciously. His thesis, repeated in varying forms, was that Europe was suffering more from the peace terms than from the devastation of the war. The errors of the old order in Europe had been preferable, he maintained, to those perpetrated at Versailles because they had favored the "superior" peoples, the Germans and Magyars, while the new order favored "inferior" races, the Czechs, Serbs and Poles. Germany he considered the most cultured nation in the world and favored giving her a leading role in "reorganizing" Russia. He put the chief responsibility for the war on Russia, the chief responsibility for the peace on France. Károlyi had to demur at some of this, but I saw it would be useless to argue and more interesting to listen.

For two years Nitti had been saying that Fascism had reached the end of its rope and that he was on the eve of being summoned to return to office. He still said confidently that he would be back in Rome in a few weeks. I left the two ex-Presidents exchanging compliments.

20

Glittering Queen Marie

The first time I saw Queen Marie of Rumania was in Bucharest in the spring of 1925 when she came in for tea with our Minister, Peter Augustus Jay. She said at once that it was a pity the King would not be able to receive me as he was laid up with phlebitis.

"But it isn't really important," she went on. "He knows it's best that I play first fiddle. Anyway, I will tell you much more than he ever would" —this last perfectly true, of course.

The Rumanians liked to call Bucharest "Petit Paris." They were proud of their cosmopolitan society, the facility with which everyone who "belonged" spoke French and the chic of the court, dominated by a dazzling Queen. Split between her ambition to play an international political role and her love of pleasure, especially that derived from male admiration, and indulging both passions recklessly, Queen Marie seemed an unlikely and inappropriate granddaughter for Queen Victoria. Though she talked a blue streak about anything that came into her head, she was fascinated above all by her own dramatic personality and would stand apart, look at it as an interested connoisseur and discuss it with whoever was at hand. She was not a bore. Her husband, King Ferdinand, of the German house of Hohenzollern-Sigmaringen, may not have been of that opinion; certainly Queen Marie's references to him did not reveal an attitude which he could have relished.

The Jays were leaving Bucharest, and as a sign of friendship the royal family had come en masse that afternoon to say goodbye. Crown Prince Carol was there, evidently reluctantly, a washed-out-looking youth with pouting lips, self-conscious, bored and sullen. He had gotten a better matrimonial bargain than had his beautiful Greek wife, Crown Princess Helen, who was smartly dressed and seemed to keep up with the news of cosmopolitan society, since she at once informed me that most of Palm Beach, including the houses of some of her friends, had burnt down a couple of days before. Carol did not appreciate her, however, for he went from one mistress to another, ending with the notorious Magda Lupescu.

The Greek and Rumanian royal families were twice intermarried. Crown Princess Helen was a sister of ex-King George of Greece, who in turn was married to a Rumanian Princess, Elizabeth, and was now living with her in exile in Bucharest. Later he regained his throne, only to lose it again. My first impression of George, not changed later when I came to know him rather well, was that he was jolly, talkative, not brilliant but far from being a fool, in fact more fitted to be a ruler than many who had better luck in that role. His wife was pretty but plump (to put it politely), even plumper than her sister Marie, who was married to King Alexander of Jugoslavia. Her conversation was largely about her efforts to reduce—how she played battledore every morning, drank boiled milk and ate only certain kinds of meat. She was pleasant but seemed unable to rise above the burden of her bulk.

It would not have been easy in any case to retain much animation in in the overpowering presence of her mother, who came in late, in a cloud of white silk. A bandeau across her forehead held a long veil, which fell over her shoulders and lost itself in the many folds of her long, flowing dress. Three or four strings of pearls reached down to her waist. Everything was white or iridescent except a black Wall of Troy border on the dress. You saw at once that she was a "character" and knew it. She had been riding with Mr. Jay that afternoon and said in a loud voice that though she loved him he was the worst horseman she had ever seen. It was easy to understand that she had been a nuisance as well as something of a power when she appeared at the Paris Peace Conference.

Cotroceni Palace, where I went for lunch a day or so later, was a big stone-and-stucco edifice set on a hill among lovely woods thick with daffodils and surrounded by terraces with awful rockeries and wooden pergolas. I was ushered into a room where a dozen officers and court ladies of uncertain age were silently waiting. First Queen Marie appeared, then the former King and Queen of Greece. King Ferdinand was upstairs, with a fever, I was told, doing a crossword puzzle. At lunch I sat at the Queen's left, at her right was the ex-King of Greece, at the far end was his wife and in between on either side was a row of officers and ladies-in-waiting who said nothing but sat munching, turning their heads automatically when Queen Marie switched the conversation to her daughter at the other end of the table (who, ignoring her regime, was eating the lobster Newburg). Clustered around Queen Marie's place were gold, jeweled and enameled accouterments of Byzantine design—a cup and goblet, sugar and salt shakers, various gold boxes and two double-handled flasks the purpose of which was not clear since she said she never took wine. Once Queen Elizabeth suggested, perhaps by design, that her mother tell me about the articles she had been asked to write for an American syndicate. The topics were corny to a degree—"The King Business," "Love and Duty" and such. She took the assignment most seriously and hinted that one of the articles might go well in *Foreign Affairs.*

Royalty she considered useful and wonderful. "Like clowns," she said, "they amuse the people, even with their funerals, and keep them contented." Americans don't understand the mystique of royalty at all and, since they don't understand, shouldn't criticize. She had picked the Prince of Wales for Ileana, her youngest daughter, and since "that one is intelligent, pretty and not too plump," she hoped the match might come off. (I once played sardines with Ileana in Belgrade and think the Prince of Wales might have done worse—in fact did.)

After lunch there was a pause while Queen Marie went upstairs to see the King and I was taken to wait in a sort of boudoir study, a curious room with pillars carved in Byzantine designs, corner divans, high window seats piled with pillows, an open hearth with a swinging brass kettle, ikons and carved ivories on the walls and tables, with photographs, strings of amber beads and other knickknacks and bowls of flowers.

The Queen did not waste many minutes with her husband, for when she came back she had found time to change into a loose red teagown. She talked steadily until five o'clock, almost entirely on the engrossing topic of herself. Self-confidence, she said, had been her salvation. From the moment of her arrival in Bucharest at the age of seventeen she had been in hostile surroundings. She had had to deal with a husband whom she described as unenterprising and rather crude and who did nothing to protect her from his tyrannical uncle, the reigning sovereign, and from Carmen Sylva, the Queen, an *intrigante,* bored, jealous and insincere. She had arrived an "ignorant ninny," not knowing how a child came into the world, but in nine months had presented Rumania with a crown prince.

"There was steel in me which would neither bend nor break," she said dramatically, "otherwise I should have lost my mind or become a weakling like my husband."

By now King Ferdinand had come to realize, she said, that she was and always had been his best friend, and that it had been "the throne's salvation" that she had (repeating the metaphor) taken the fiddle out of his hands—"a habit I could never break once I had tried it."

She was determined to justify royalty to the world and her own royal role in particular. The articles she was writing for America she considered part of the educational process. The bits she read me were quite amusing but most so in places where she didn't intend them to be; I felt sure they would be laughed at in America, as they indeed were. She told me proudly she would get $2,000 for the set of ten and was disappointed when I said that was far too little. She hoped that Americans would respect royalty more when they realized how hard she worked at her job and also that members of other reigning families in Europe would profit from the things she said about royalty in general and take to heart her example of devotion and self-abnegation.

Once, she said, the King of Spain reproved her for riding alone. "I replied that I was as much respected alone as I would be surrounded by a bodyguard, and probably safer than he was with one. I had arrived in Bucharest, I told him, without his Velásquezes and his Escorials and with none of the thousand advantages that royalty enjoys in Spain and other less primitive countries. But I created compensations for myself. I refused to let myself be bound hand and foot and become a dummy like his Queen, my cousin. My substitutes for luxurious idleness were riding and writing and forever working, working, working for my people and my country."

In the war, she had opposed the powerful forces that wanted to take Rumania into the German camp and had staked everything on the Allies. She told how when the Peace of Bucharest was signed, with three-quarters of the country in German hands, she was terrified that her husband might "revert to type." Whichever way the war turned out this would have been fatal—if the Germans won he would have been their puppet, if the Allies won Rumania would be dismembered. She was determined to prevent it and set the stage for a tremendous scene with the King. Sending for her children, she advanced to the middle of the room and announced "in a loud, clear voice" (and here she stood up and assumed a commanding look):

"Ferdinand, we have had to come to terms with the enemy but that does not mean we are to accept them as friends. I warn you: at the slightest sign that you want to make friends with your Germans you will lose both your wife and your Queen."

The Crown Prince had jumped up, protesting that she was doing his father an injustice and he would not allow it. None of them, he said, would ever go over to the Germans. She replied that she liked his spirit and the way he had spoken; she simply wanted to make sure that everyone in the family realized that her determination was fixed. After this, she said, "I knew the King was safe."

Pointing to shelves filled with volumes of her diary, locked with clasps, she said her story was there for future generations to read. She had willed them to the Rumanian Academy with orders to publish them one by one as each became twenty years old, the proceeds to go to an orphanage she had founded. (Where are they now?) The current volume, open on her desk, was illustrated with pictures of herself and her family. She handed me one photograph that was loose, showing her holding a horse on a beach by the Black Sea. She had begun the diary only during the war, but as the entries were in a large, bold hand a few lines filled a page; this was already volume 49—coinciding, she remarked, with her age. A line which I noticed was typical: "My heart expands."

She complained that some people (including, specifically, Clare Sheridan, the well-known sculptor, journalist and adventurous world-traveler, whom she detested) described her as an actress. Her life had not been make-believe, she protested. She still looked forward to serving Rumania, as for instance by making a good-will visit to America. (When she did, the tour was an undignified fiasco, disfigured by commercial exploitation both of her and by her.) Was it by play-acting, she asked, that she "put Rumania on the map," held it on the Allied side, married two daughters to Kings, managed a dullard husband "to the Queen's taste," as she put it archly, and became renowned the world over as the most unusual and interesting of royalties?

"The Queen's taste" was often cheap. Much of what she said was, however, true, for example about her attitude in the war. That she was not an actress was not true. She was made for the stage, adored it, and in any role in life would have been a prima donna.

II

Most of the Rumanian politicians prominent in the twenties were men without unusual talent or character. Of those whom I met on this and later visits to Bucharest or during League of Nations meetings at Geneva the only ones who seemed to me to have European stature were Iuliu

Maniu and Nicolae Titulescu. Maniu, a stubborn patriot, respected as being incorruptible even by colleagues who were far from having that reputation, had formed the National Popular party in his native Transylvania after the collapse of the Hapsburg Empire, and at the time of my visit was reported to be negotiating a merger with the Peasant's party of the old Rumanian kingdom. Titulescu, who became Foreign Minister in 1927 after serving as Minister in London, made a European reputation by his astute performance at League meetings. He had a wizened, faintly Mongolian face, dry mousy hair brushed back from a high, slanting forehead, an effeminate voice, a manner at first playful, then abruptly sharpening as he prepared to skewer a lumbering antagonist on his gleaming rapier. You forgot his person in the brilliant display of his mind. Others had influential roles in the maneuvers of Rumanian politics, but I found these two, with Dr. Lupu, the peasant leader, the most interesting.

Queen Marie did not mention Maniu to me, though he was emerging as a powerful rival to Prime Minister Brătianu, the leader of the Liberal party, which contained most of her friends. She did not talk domestic politics with visitors and I was told that the reason for this untypical self-discipline was her ambition to be named Regent if King Ferdinand became incapacitated, for which purpose she must be known as politically neutral. The ambition was whetted by the antagonism which existed between her and her son Crown Prince Carol. She may have had an inkling, too, that Carol was so discontented with the "King business" that he might quit it altogether. And indeed Carol did leave Rumania with Magda Lupescu in December of that year, 1925, renouncing his rights to the throne in favor of his young son Prince Michael. Her ambitions were not fulfilled, however. She was not included in the Regency formed when her husband became completely incapacitated, and when he died she had no part in the choice of Maniu, by then head of the National Peasant party, to hold the first comparatively free elections in Rumanian history (won by him with 75 percent of the votes) .[1]

The Foreign Minister in 1925 was Ion Duca, clever, suave, too facile to be convincing. He asked me to lunch and gave me a rather complacent survey of Rumanian foreign relations under the guidance of his Liberal party. By his account, the peasants ever since the land reform of 1921

1. Maniu, an obstinate democrat, opposed the dictatorship established by King Carol after he had helped him return from exile; that of pro-German General Averescu (executed after the war by the Communists) ; and that of the Communists, who sentenced him to prison, where he died in 1953.

had been so busy enjoying their new acquisitions that they had become immune to radical agitation, as indicated by the failure of their demagogic leader, Dr. Lupu, to make them join a Peasant International and by their rejection of the Communist party's efforts to take them into the Cominform. Lupu was a native of Bessarabia, the great border province separated from Russia by the Dniester River and long claimed and fought over by both countries. At Paris in 1920 it had been recognized as belonging to Rumania on the basis of a vote by a Bessarabian provincial council. Duca claimed it was because Lupu himself had found the Rumanian peasantry there so strongly nationalist that he had renounced his earlier Communistic tendencies.

At breakfast with Dr. Lupu the next morning I looked for confirmation of this characterization. Breakfast consisted of stewed tea, the color of strong coffee and tasting like lye, which he said with pride he had learnt to make in England. He had also visited America and a few American and English books lay about in his apartment—Sinclair Lewis, Willa Cather, Graham Wallas, Seton-Watson. He was a former country doctor, the son of a priest, but had found that he could not be content with merely prescribing medicines for the peasants when the root of their troubles was social, agricultural and hygienic backwardness; he had gone into politics "as a matter of conscience." He told how the Liberals had "prostituted" the agrarian reform which they themselves had been obliged to introduce, and, contradicting Duca, claimed that the discontent of the peasants who still lived and worked as they had done five centuries ago was taking on overtones of desperation. Their need above all was for practical instruction in modern agricultural methods, for sanitation, for rural credit and to be organized into efficient cooperative units.

"The Liberals consider strong cooperatives Communistic," Lupu continued. "They oppress the peasants in Bessarabia for the simple reason that they are peasants, on the theory that all peasants are radical and that their tendencies are especially dangerous in territory adjoining Russia. In this way they make them radical. And they become more radical because for seven years there has been no trade across the Dniester with Russia. They are cutting down their fruit trees and vines and eating their sheep because there is no market for their produce in Rumania." He favored a different attitude toward Russia. France and England would like to make Rumania into a Chinese Wall against Bolshevism, but would they help her if that led to war? "We must look to the day when Russia becomes a great rural democracy and start arranging things."

He said the King had asked him recently how long he thought his dynasty would rule Rumania. "I said, 'Your Majesty, maybe five hundred years, maybe five years. It depends on whether you mix into politics and take sides with the Liberals against the people.' "

At the start, Lupu's heavy face, biggish nose and too-knowing look had made him seem somewhat untrustworthy, but as the morning wore on I liked him better and concluded that he was no less and perhaps more sincere than the usual run of Rumanian politicians.

By comparison, however, and even more so when measured against Duca, Iuliu Maniu seemed a statesman of real caliber. His appearance was solid and sober: high, broad forehead; high, stiff collar; courteous but not ingratiating manner. He did not look like an agrarian leader, although he was already sharing Lupu's popularity with the peasants and would soon eclipse him. He had sat in the old Budapest parliament as a deputy from the province of Transylvania; served as an artillery lieutenant on the Italian front; then when things began going to pieces there had slipped away to Transylvania, where he helped prepare the October, 1918, declaration that, following Wilson's principle of self-determination, Transylvania was free from Hapsburg rule. Two months later the provincial assembly formed a government with Maniu as its head and voted union with Rumania.

The freedom of the Danubian peoples, Maniu felt, was menaced from two directions in addition to the permanent threat from Russia. One was the Magyar threat, with or without a Hapsburg restoration. The other was the threat that Austria might unite with the German Reich. Actually, Austrian union with Germany as a whole would be less dangerous for the new Danubian order than the partial form of the plan which he asserted was being promoted by Vatican strategists—namely, to separate Bavaria from the Reich and unite it with Austria. Such a reactionary Catholic state would attract Slovenia, and in addition would have a powerful appeal for Catholic Hungary and for Croatia, where the Catholic majority was discontented with rule from Belgrade.

"This sounds like metaphysical politics," Maniu said, "but these are times when weird things happen and we must forestall developments that would destroy what we won in the war and produce new revolutions and new wars for liberation."

Surprisingly, Maniu considered that the confederation which he favored should eventually include Hungary, the still unreconciled enemy of all the Succession States. If they were to stop Russia's drive to the south they must be united by more than the legal ties of a limited organization like the Little Entente. It was with this development in view that he was favorable to Hungarians like Károlyi and Jaszi and not to extreme nationalists like Horthy and Apponyi. After the war, the first step had been disassociation. The second should be the reassociation of natural and logical national units to protect their common interests. This was ticklish ground and Maniu would not be drawn into a more explicit statement.

Anyone who traveled through the Rumanian countryside, as I did on this and other springs, would agree with the emphasis put by both Lupu and Maniu on the industry of the Rumanian peasants and the absolute necessity of bringing them into the twentieth century. From dawn to dusk they followed their oxen yoked to primitive wooden plows just as their forefathers had done, and their women still bent their backs double over the furrows, planting grain by grain the seed that in less primitive agricultures was distributed by machine. Which is merely to say that they were sturdy and patient like all Balkan peasants. I remember a remark by Voivode Mishich, who thought nothing of the Rumanian Army, that if the peasants in the ranks were given good officers it would be the equal of any army in the Balkans. The officers, however, had the reputation of being as indolent as the generality of upper-class Rumanians. In a now often-repeated story I was told that a notice in the Officers' Club set the easy tone of Bucharest society: "Members are requested not to bring ladies into the club unless they are the wives of other members." (For "ladies," read "mistresses.")

In that day Rumanians still could indulge their passion for entertaining. But if you by chance found yourself free at teatime there was Capsa's, with the best cakes anywhere (except perhaps Gerstner's in Vienna), and for a drink there was the great green salon at the Athénée Palace, where a series of mirrors multiplied the profusion of beautiful and talented young ladies prepared to converse with visitors in any of several languages. One had the illusion that identically the same young ladies reappeared in all the great Central European hotels—the Dunapalota in Budapest, the Grand and the Imperial in Vienna, the Europejski in Warsaw and the Adlon in Berlin. One evening as I went down the long corridor to my room at the Athénée Palace a girl burst out of a door and fled past me, gasping and moaning, pursued by a man in pajamas. The scene, piquant enough because the girl was naked, but nevertheless not in itself un-understandable, suddenly became mysterious when I saw another pajamaed gentleman holding a door open for her at the far end of the corridor. The pursuer turned back from the slammed door and walked past me without a glance. Vicki Baum might have told us who in that scene was who.

Pretensions to the contrary, Bucharest was not really the boasted "Petit Paris." Yet it was different from strictly uncosmopolitan capitals like Sofia and Belgrade, and even though it lacked Budapest's rundown grandeur and the baroque magnificence of Prague it was still a fine city for that part of Europe in those days.

21

Hungary and Austria: Could They Live?

Hungary and Austria were in process of being extricated from financial chaos. The loss of their tributary domains had destroyed their economy, political systems and social fabric and left them bankrupt. Now the League of Nations was administering life-saving transfusions in the form of international loans; and to make sure that the loans were not squandered it had sent teams of experts to Budapest and Vienna, each headed by a Commissioner-General to supervise budgets and expenditures.

In Budapest the man shepherding Hungary along sound financial paths was Jeremiah Smith, Jr., a ruddy-faced Boston lawyer, mild in manner, obdurate in purpose. As the League's Commissioner-General he was going about his duties with tact and firmness but without unnecessary displays of authority and consequently without provoking resentment. The way for the salvage action had been prepared by the Hungarian Prime Minister, Count Bethlen, who had won the necessary degree of confidence abroad by twice repulsing attempts by the former Emperor Karl to regain the Hungarian throne and by passing a new franchise law and winning an election victory over both the socialist left and the small but powerful remnant of legitimist forces. An essential factor in his success had been his persuasion of the Succession States which had reparations claims against Hungary that by reducing them they would not be helping Hungary equip herself for a new war. The Protocols of Agreement had been signed in Geneva March 14, 1924.

Now, a year later, Jeremiah Smith could assure me that Hungary's budget was in order and that she was not drawing on the League loans for current expenses. He also contradicted rumors that League funds were being used to build up Hungary's armed forces or that her military expenditures were inordinate.

Time, quoting from an article which I sent back from Budapest to the *New York Times,* commented that I was viewing Eastern and Central Europe with "an optimistic eye." This was, on the whole, true; but if the implication was that I was overoptimistic about the immediate future, I do not, looking back, concede the point. There were dark spots, but light did seem to be spreading gradually over the European landscape, chiefly as a result of the improving outlook for a Franco-German reconciliation. Locarno still lay ahead, but what afterward was called the Locarno spirit was definitely in the air. In Eastern Europe, Hungary and Austria seemed on the way to financial rehabilitation and once that was safely accomplished their rancor against their ex-enemies ought to diminish. Nobody foresaw the Credit-Anstalt crash and the ruinous Great Depression, which was to intensify old rivalries. There followed the assassination of King Alexander, an irreparable blow to stability in the area but even more significant as a portent because of Italy's collusion with Magyar and Croat Fascists in the murder plot. The advent of Hitler finally doomed any hope for peace in Europe as he and Mussolini proceeded to coordinate their plans of conquest.

Ten years later I would be publishing a book called *Europe Between Wars?* The question mark was added not because of any real doubts in my own mind but because I was told that otherwise I would be put down as a warmonger and that this would weaken my warnings. But for the moment the portents were not at all bad.

As a matter of fact, the editors of *Time* would have been justified in doubting my qualifications as a prophet. *Time* was then just two years old, *Foreign Affairs* a year and half older. Before the first regular issue of *Time* appeared there had been a "dry run" of several trial issues. Harry Luce sent these to various friends and acquaintances, myself included, asking opinions of the new venture. I told Harry that I thought Americans were accustomed to getting their news fresh each day and would not care for news—*Time* called itself a "news magazine"—a week old. *Time*'s circulation reached 100,000 within about a year and kept going up. So much for my foresight.

Harry Luce nevertheless always took a benevolent attitude toward *Foreign Affairs.* Years later, when its circulation had reached about twenty thousand, he told me it was a shame that it did not have at least five times the number of readers and offered to loan us temporarily one of his best promotion men to "jack the list up." I welcomed his help, though with just enough suspicion to ask how he himself thought the new campaign might be begun.

To start with, Harry said, he was not sure about our plain gray cover. Secondly, although he thought we were right not to scatter illustrations through the book we might consider carrying a supplement in the back with pictures of events and personalities. He recommended getting more reading matter onto a page by reducing the size of the type and setting it in two columns. He went on to say that we should explore the pros and cons of becoming a monthly and, if so, might station correspondents in the principal capitals to send us on-the-spot reports.

"That's a wonderful magazine you're outlining," I said when he got through. "Why don't you start it?" He admitted that maybe he was going too far, that there was room for many different sorts of magazines, that *Foreign Affairs* was good as it was, and so on. *Time* continued to show special interest in our progress and took occasion to praise us on our anniversaries. The worst adjective I can remember its ever applying to me personally was "thick-thatched."

II

Hungary's Prime Minister, Count Stephen Bethlen, an insignificant-looking little man with a drooping mustache, was anything but insignificant. He was a skillful politician and a man of principle, a combination not achieved by any other Hungarian of his time, except by his predecessor and fellow aristocrat, Count Paul Teleki. Eventually Bethlen was overtaken by the Fascist, anti-Semitic, militaristic and pro-German tide which engulfed and finally destroyed Hungary. In 1944 he hid successfully from the German invaders, but the Russian invaders, the next to arrive, transported him to Moscow, where he died in prison. At the time of which I am writing he had been Prime Minister for a longer period than any other holder of the office in Europe.

He considered that Hungary's treatment at the Peace Conference had been most unjust, but he told me that the wrongs done there would be righted, when the time came, "on a footing fair to all." The phrase indicated his dilemma. If he used it openly it would be taken as implying a mere revision of frontiers and not the recapture of all the lost lands. This would be unacceptable to most Hungarians, even those who were sensible enough to realize that wholesale treaty revision was impossible in the near future but were not prepared to abandon the dream forever; and it would infuriate the Awakening Magyars and other reactionary groups that had sprung up during the "white terror" of 1920 and who demanded immediate rearmament in preparation for a war of reconquest. To ask for trifling frontier rectifications would have been political suicide and would very likely have invited assassination.

In his bafflement Bethlen was playing for time, counting on the development of a new attitude toward treaty revision after Briand and Herriot had reached an understanding with Stresemann on reparations and Germany had been admitted to the League of Nations—"until then it is a league of victors." He hoped that when the atmosphere became more relaxed France might end her effort to encircle Germany with French "client states" and would urge them to work out compromises with their neighbors. I could not see the Little Entente states dismembering themselves sufficiently to satisfy even the most moderate Hungarians and suggested that membership in some Danubian Federation might offer an alternative solution. Talk about that was premature, he said; "other things come first."

In one respect Hungary was fully justified in complaining about the conduct of the Succession States. The rights of Hungarian minorities left outside the new frontiers had been guaranteed by treaty but complaints about violations were ignored. Hungary had oppressed her Slav and Rumanian minorities in the old days, but although this explained it did not excuse the violation by the new states of their promises regarding the Hungarian populations now under their rule. In one of my *New York Times* articles I urged that the Powers which had imposed the treaties recognize their responsibilities and either directly or through the League investigate complaints and exert pressure to secure compliance.

The Hungarian demand that all prewar Hungary must come back, sometime, somehow, to Budapest could not be achieved by direct pressure, since the physical means were lacking. Neither could the claim be pressed as a right, for it was flawed, as was made plain by the case of Transylvania, most lamented of the lost provinces. Transylvania had been awarded to Rumania at Paris because although certain districts were beyond doubt inhabited by a majority of Magyars and Saxons they were separated from Hungary proper by much larger districts inhabited by Rumanians. Count Apponyi told me loftily that it should be returned to Hungary anyway because the Rumanians were an inferior people. Mathematics, he said, did not matter. But it was not an argument that could secure support at Geneva.

There were other means of winning sympathy for Hungary's plight, of course, and a propaganda machine to publicize them had been established. Those of its activities which were directed at Western Europe were entrusted to a titled Englishman who occupied a handsome suite at the Hotel Dunapalota in Budapest. His assignment was to counteract the bad reputation being given Hungary by the warmongering of Magyar reactionaries; this was interfering with the resumption of old banking and commercial relations abroad and damaging the tourist industry. Sections of the foreign press were being subsidized to blame the threat of war on the Little Entente states which occupied Magyar lands rather than on Hungary, which was planning to get them back. The German press did not need much attention, for Germany was hostile to the Little Entente in any case. But France, where the government looked favorably on the Little Entente as an obstacle to a renewed German *Drang nach Osten,* was an obvious target for corrective indoctrination. Several French newspapers therefore received the propaganda bureau's monthly largesse and duly recited their lessons about the dangerous stubbornness of the Little Entente in resisting "peaceful change."

One French periodical which did not join the chorus was *L'Europe Nouvelle,* a political weekly edited by André Géraud, who in addition wrote a column of brilliant and mordant comment appearing five days a week in the *Echo de Paris* under his pen name "Pertinax." Géraud had begun his career before the war as a correspondent in London, where he was a protégé of the great French Ambassador Jules Cambon. He knew everybody worth knowing in Europe and was feared as well as admired because he was an uncommon phenomenon in the French newspaper world: he was incorruptible. He often referred in his column to Hungarian revisionist elements as a danger to peace second only to the German revanchists.

When I checked in at the Dunapalota I found a note from the titled Englishman inviting me to lunch the following day. He had some ostensible business agency in Budapest which gave him an excuse to make the acquaintance of foreign visitors, and he used it especially to get into touch with those who had press connections. I had a delicious lunch in his apartment overlooking the Danube and was able to leave afterward without having made any commitments in return, since I already had contacts with the government people to whom he offered to introduce me.

A year or so later when I came to know "Pertinax" I casually mentioned the Englishman's name to him. He said he ran into him occasionally in Geneva although he tried to avoid him as their encounters always ended in an argument over the Little Entente. Recently he had received a letter announcing that the Englishman was arriving before long in Paris, that he regretted not having seen "Pertinax" for some time and that he would like an appointment, since he wished to discuss a proposal which he hoped would prove attractive. He had heard, he wrote, that the Gérauds had a particular liking for the little isles lying off Hyères. Summer was approaching, and the Englishman wondered whether M. and Mme. Géraud would not like the loan of one of the islands for the season, or indeed indefinitely. It happened, the letter went on, that a Hungarian friend of his owned a charming and comfortable little villa on one of the islands, and since he had no use for it himself he would be happy to put it at their disposal. Would "Pertinax" let him know whether the proposal appealed to him? If so, when he came to Paris they could arrange the transaction.

"Pertinax" showed me his reply which ran something like this: "I am delighted to know of your intention to visit Paris. Is there anything I can do to make it agreeable? I know, for instance, of a charming and comfortable young lady whom I would be happy to arrange to put at your disposal. Let me know if I can help to arrange the transaction."

III

The war had left Austria in even more desperate straits than Hungary. By the time the League of Nations sent its rescue team to Vienna, late in 1922, the country was in collapse, helpless and hopeless, doubtful about even the wish to survive. Bereft of its empire, it lay like an exhausted tadpole in a dried-up marsh: Vienna an enormous hungry head, the rest a straggling tail of liabilities.

A principal difference in the League's tasks in the two countries, as described by Sir Arthur Salter.[1] was that the League did not begin work in Hungary until a year and a half later than in Austria and could point to its Austrian achievement as evidence that financial reconstruction was a practicable undertaking; this enabled it to raise the necessary credits for a similar Hungarian operation with less difficulty. On the other hand, the proposal to rehabilitate Hungary was handicapped by the fear of several countries that once she was reestablished in strength she would prove a dangerous neighbor. No such question had arisen in

1. In companion articles in *Foreign Affairs*, "The Reconstruction of Austria," June 15, 1924, and "The Reconstruction of Hungary," October, 1926. See also Salter's *Recovery* (New York: Reynal, 1932).

the case of Austria. Her weakness aroused genuine sympathy, unflawed by misgivings about her future behavior.

In Vienna a debate was going on as to how close the League's task was to completion, with Austrian officials on the one side and the League's Commissioner-General in Vienna on the other.

Chancellor Seipel and Foreign Minister Alfred Grünberger, who had negotiated the League loan at Geneva, recognized that it would not solve Austria's problem forever but did provide the necessary time for Austrians to lay plans how to survive on their own. Seipel, smooth and agreeable in the Jesuit tradition, was confident that by now Austria had been saved. "The first objective was simply to live. We have lived. The second was to see how Austria could accommodate herself to the peace treaties, not simply in order to continue living but to do so on a basis beneficial to both ourselves and our neighbors. We are now trying to find that basis."

A drastic solution which would lead in the opposite direction was being advocated in Germany and by the Pan-German party in Austria: union—*Anschluss*—with Germany. This had been banned in the Treaty of St. Germain and renounced voluntarily by Austria in the loan agreement with the League. In any case, said the Chancellor, such a desperate step was wholly unnecessary. Once Austria had been put back on her feet she could lead a satisfactory life of her own as merchant and banker for both East and West. Grünberger confirmed that progress in this direction was already being made, and he gave encouraging details of the commercial treaties negotiated with over a dozen countries, including one member of the Little Entente, Czechoslovakia. The great disappointment was Hungary, which feared the competition of Austrian industry and intensely disliked Vienna's powerful socialist trade unions.

But meanwhile the propaganda for *Anschluss* was spreading uncertainty and discord. France on principle opposed any change in the peace settlements as setting a dangerous precedent. The Succession States feared what would happen once a German "corridor" was opened into the Danube Valley. In particular, Czechoslovakia foresaw that if the German tide was permitted to flow around its southern frontier the German population in the Sudetenland would become increasingly troublesome. Italy was equally opposed; she was preparing to demand rectifications of the Tyrolese settlement and preferred to deal with a weak Vienna rather than a reviving Berlin. Further, she saw that a common frontier with a Greater Germany would open up the possibility that Trieste might become an objective of a renewed German push to the east.

The movement for *Anschluss* would lose its appeal in Austria, Grünberger felt sure, if neighboring countries would consent to do business with her on fair terms. A second requirement was to find credits in London and Paris to rehabilitate Austrian industry, in which case Vienna's excellent banking institutions and commercial experience plus its old tradition as a cultural center would provide the foundation for an independent national life—not the glittering life of the old imperial days, certainly, but one that was tolerably comfortable.

The League financial controller, Dr. Zimmerman, a stern Dutchman, was not made for a role of political conciliation. The time would come, he knew, for turning back financial control to Austria, but he was not convinced it was near; certainly it must not be before the federal government had asserted control over what he regarded as the outrageously reckless financial policies of the Social Democrats who ran Vienna's municipal government. "Until the socialist fortress of Vienna is subdued," he said, "Austria's finances will not be secure."

Although the "fortress" had not in fact been subdued, Dr. Zimmerman had to report at the end of that same year, 1925, that the Austrian budget was balanced; and the international control was ended the following spring. "Red Vienna" went on to develop ambitious working-class housing, education and health schemes on a scale that made it a model of socialist planning for all Europe. Contrary to Dr. Zimmerman's idea, these reforms in fact aimed to combat Communism. Despite the very great expenditures involved, Austrian finances remained in good order until shattered by the world economic crisis, when the League was again called in to help. Eventually the question whether Austria should unite with Germany was settled by Hitler in one gulp.

Interludes in my efforts to understand the Austrian financial situation were pleasant talks with my friend Dr. Joseph Redlich as we walked in the big garden of his house on Armbrustergasse in suburban Grinzing. There really was more stopping than walking, since he became so engrossed in what he was saying that he would constantly turn and seize me by the top button of my jacket and hold on tightly until his eloquent expression of a certain idea was complete and I had admitted that I agreed or at least understood. Sometimes we sat in the little classical pavilion at the end of one of the paths, but when the discussion grew animated he would jump up and tug me after him on another start-and-stop circuit. Before taking the tramway back to town I would recover my breath under the arbor of one of Grinzing's famous open-air taverns with a glass or two of *Heurigen.*

I had "inherited" Dr. Redlich from Coolidge, who respected him as a historian and had come to know him well in Vienna during the armistice period. It was partly due to Coolidge's urging that he was invited soon after the war to come to Harvard as a visiting professor. He had stayed at my house in New York and we corresponded frequently. His letters were as animated and disjointed as his discourse, and the same impatience that made his talk a tumbling torrent made his writing a series of half-formed wiggles, the deciphering of which provided my assistant, Miss Stevens, with the equivalent of a Double-Crostic.

Redlich admitted that the Austro-Hungarian Empire, where he had been the last Minister of Finance, had been fated to dissolve, but he criticized the fact that the forces which broke it up had not been required to take creative channels for future intercourse. The fact of dissolution of a great empire was not per se progress. A great organism admittedly had no more right to exist than a small one or than a group of small ones. Nevertheless, integration was a fundamentally productive force, represented one of the great processes of human progress, and should have been promoted by the peace treaties in at least equal measure with the principle of self-determination. Redlich was entitled to such views without being called reactionary and nationalistic. He had realized long before the war how closely the fate of the Hapsburg Empire was entwined with the problem of providing a satisfactory existence for its component nationalities, and had advocated recognizing their right to form separate political entities.

At the moment, Redlich was not at all sure Austria could live satisfactorily alone and feared that if her experience was disappointing she would be sucked inexorably into union with Germany. He doubted whether the League's "drops of temporary financial relief" would solve the problem. Masaryk and Beneš, with whom he maintained friendly contact, assured him that they recognized the necessity of helping Austria and Hungary create the basis for a tolerable future. His prescription of what this required went much further than Grünberger's. The Little Entente must be given a constructive rather than a negative purpose; it must at once begin planning for the time when Austria and Hungary would not simply be kept down by force but would have political and economic roles as partners in the organization.

In light of my visits to Belgrade, Bucharest and Budapest I saw little prospect that effective sentiment for this sort of partnership would develop soon on either side. Only Maniu in Bucharest had even hinted at a possibility of working in partnership with Hungary. Was not Redlich being misled by memory of the days when it seemed possible to solve the nationalities problem by creating autonomous ethnic states within the Hapsburg economic and political framework? The best to be hoped for was that the Successor States of the old Empire, constituted much as they were at present, might live and let live; in time, barring some new catastrophe, they might learn to work together on terms of mutual advantage. Redlich replied excitedly that there was not going to be time enough for that. Grabbing me by both lapels he argued out again the dangers of the course I seemed ready to accept as inevitable.

To Redlich every problem was intellectual and every solution speculative; to Dr. Frank, a former Vice-Chancellor, head of the Pan-German party, every problem was material and every solution pragmatic. He was a clean-shaven, businesslike man of about forty-five, not blustering like the German advocates of *Anschluss,* but sure of himself, didactic. He cited the reasons why when the League support ended there must be either a collapse or a steady retrogression which would convince the Austrian people that they simply could not live without their former sources of food and raw materials and their old markets. They would see that as things were going they had no chance of regaining their old standards of culture, education, scientific development and everyday comfort. Where could they turn except to Germany?

But it wasn't enough to give the reasons for *Anschluss,* I said, he must also answer the arguments against it. Was there nothing in the French fear, for instance, that it would encourage German reactionaries to prepare for a war of revenge? Frank answered that the union could occur only after a complete Franco-German reconciliation and that it would actually strengthen democratic forces in Germany and weaken the Prussian and Hohenzollern tradition by bringing in Catholic and "easygoing" Austria to reinforce what he had the temerity to call, in identical terminology, Catholic and "easy-going" Bavaria. I demurred. Hitler's National Socialists were not yet recognized as the principal menace to German democracy; they were only one of several nationalist, terrorist and anti-Semitic revolutionary movements in various parts of the country conspiring to destroy the Weimar Government. But Hitler's *Putsch* in November, 1923, had given Munich notoriety as a center of reactionary activity. It was not deserved, said Frank. Bavarians were law-abiding people. Anyway, the union of all Germans of all shades of opinion was a historical necessity. Even Czechoslovakia and Poland would soon see it was inevitable. Czechoslovakia would have to become a democratic state in which the rights of the German population were recognized, and Poland, which could not expect to keep Danzig and Upper Silesia indefinitely, would realize that she could not afford to have both Germany and Russia as enemies and would cede those territories to Germany as the price of friendship. Thus there would be peace.

It seemed to me an unlikely program for peace. Within ten years Hitler was to make us familiar with it, and more of the same.

22

Organizing Eastern Europe:
Masaryk and Beneš

President Thomas G. Masaryk and his Foreign Minister, Dr. Eduard Beneš, were a balanced team without equal in any other European government. Masaryk, philosopher and Platonist, quizzical, dry, mild in speech but audacious in crises, had a strong sense of direction based on a knowledge of history and experience in influencing it. Beneš, springy mentally and physically, reacting intuitively as well as logically to each new problem, was Masaryk's foil, complement and executor. Masaryk's power was immanent, like a natural phenomenon; Beneš was a dynamo, ready for action from minute to minute.

The construction of a new political basis in Eastern Europe after the war had been in the hands of the victors. Masaryk and Beneš more than any of the other national leaders had taken a view of the task that was not parochial. They believed that prosperity and security for Czechoslovakia depended on the prosperity and security of the continent as a whole. At Geneva, Beneš worked indefatigably to give the League of Nations the right and strength to deal with all threats of war. The Geneva Protocol, largely his handiwork, was designed to supplement the Covenant by establishing the principle that not only aggressive war but war in general was illegal and that every dispute carrying a threat of armed hostilities must be submitted for peaceful settlement. For the latter purpose the Protocol detailed a procedure for arbitration, defining the aggressor and applying sanctions when arbitration was refused or failed. The Protocol was accepted at Geneva in September, 1924. But the following March, Prime Minister Baldwin rejected what his predecessor

Prime Minister MacDonald had endorsed. The grounds on which Britain refused ratification was that the provisions were too sweeping. A powerful factor was Canada's insistence that Britain not engage Commonwealth members in commitments which might lead them into conflict with the isolationist United States. The opportunity to make the League an effective instrument for peace was lost, and did not recur.

At the time of my arrival in Prague two months had passed since the hopes placed in the Protocol had been shattered. The question before Europe was what to do next. Chancellor Luther of Germany had proposed that a pact be signed by the Great Powers guaranteeing the eastern frontiers of France and Belgium and demilitarizing the left bank of the Rhine, and further that arbitration conventions be entered into between Germany and the Great Powers and also between Germany and her neighbors to the east, Poland and Czechoslovakia.[1] For Czechoslovakia, as for Poland, the question was whether this would be an adequate substitute for the safeguards proposed in the Protocol.

Two long conversations with Dr. Beneš made clear that since the proposed Pact of Guarantee corresponded to the real situation, that is, reflected the extent to which each nation was prepared to go—and not to go—in maintaining peace, he accepted it. He preferred clarity to doubt and would make the best of the present state of fact. It held two advantages for Czechoslovakia. The political organization of Central and Eastern Europe was not nearly as complete as that of Western Europe. As in physics so in politics, expansion goes in the direction where resistance is weaker. Germany's pressure to expand and dominate in the East was therefore inevitable, even natural. Although Czechoslovakia would not be invited to sign the Pact of Guarantee, she would be included in its provisions. It was satisfactory that in this way Western Europe would be involved in the problems of Eastern Europe.

"Let me say something in strict confidence," Beneš added. "Even if the Geneva Protocol had been adopted and then disregarded it would have been of tremendous importance for us as a scrap of paper. The same thing is true of the Pact of Guarantee. If the warmakers are deterred, that is the supreme good. If they are not, if we are attacked, then all the world except the aggressor must be on our side."

He did not consider that the proposed pact would lessen Eastern Europe's need to organize itself. The Successor States had originated the Little Entente as a measure of defense, to keep the peace while they created stable economic and social structures. The danger that they

1. This was the genesis of the Locarno Treaty signed the following October.

would be destroyed either by their minority populations or by the Communists, working internally but also aided and directed from Moscow, had ended. Another threat had been a possible Hapsburg restoration. It was a threat not because the Hapsburgs themselves were particularly evil but because they were Hapsburgs; everyone would have believed that the dynasty was being brought back as a step toward recreating the old order, and even if this were not true, which it was, distrust and tension would increase to a dangerous point. Beneš said he did not care whether Hungary was a monarchy or a republic; that was an internal question. But whether it should be a Hapsburg monarchy or not was an international question. Now that too had been settled.

Another threat to security was the propaganda for Austrian union with Germany. If it was allowed, Hungary, Jugoslavia and Italy would have Germany as a neighbor, Czechoslovakia would be put in a parlous position and Rumania would be threatened at only one remove. Germany would resume her prewar policy of expansion. It was argued that the principle of self-determination gave Austria the right to join Germany. Austrians were like the weather, very changeable. It was far from certain whether they wanted to join Germany at this time or, if they did, would find they liked it; but even if the majority actually wished it, they must make the sacrifice of remaining independent, as the peace treaties had decreed, for the sake of peace in Europe. Their neighbors must take account of that sacrifice, if it was one, and help in a friendly way to make their independent existence successful. The balance in Europe would be jeopardized by either the creation of the reactionary Austro-Bavarian state in the center of the continent, which the Vatican was quietly urging, or by permitting the formation of a Greater Germany, ready to launch out once more on Kaiser Wilhelm's old course, the *Drang nach Osten*.

Several ways had been suggested for organizing Eastern Europe. One was to expand the Little Entente into a Danubian Federation. Beneš feared this would change its character and orientation. If Poland became a member, that would involve discussions about Danzig, Silesia and Lithuania; if Greece was added, the question of Saloniki and the future of Thrace would have to be considered. What was required was not to enlarge the scope of the Little Entente's defensive and negative function but to replace it or supplement it with an arrangement that was positive and constructive. The first steps in that direction should be economic, not however with a view to forming a *Zollverein,* but to promote economic collaboration on equal conditions for all—the conditions that should have prevailed in the old Empire but did not. In the future—the long future, perhaps—a political organization might be formed, a "League of Small Nations." Every member should have equal rights and responsibilities: no discrimination, no attempted domination, nothing, in fact, of the sort that Vienna and Budapest were afraid might develop in a Danubian Federation.

"Until that fear is dissipated," said Beneš, "I prefer remaining in my own castle and leaving my neighbors in theirs. We shall consult with them, do business with them, work on common projects with them, but not try to create a formal organization."

When Beneš became engrossed in his talk he would curl a foot up on the rung of his chair or throw a leg across the arm. First one and then the other now testified to his complete absorption in the problems of the little peoples in the zone between the Baltic and the Adriatic. Flanked as they were by great nations, they had always furnished those nations with the pretexts for their wars. That was why, Beneš said, they had needed so desperately the compulsory arbitration of the Geneva Protocol. Although the protection offered by the Pact of Guarantee now being proposed would be less specific, there was one hopeful element in the situation. The world was growing smaller as a result of new arms techniques, aviation, radio and other forms of communication. Prague was steadily becoming nearer to Paris and London, even to New York and Washington. "Maybe if one day a new crisis comes in Eastern Europe," he concluded, "the fact of our closeness will be realized in time to avoid catastrophe."

While I was in Dr. Beneš' office in Hradčany castle word was brought that President Masaryk was ready to see me in his room nearby. It was more a library than an office. Shelves ran up on three walls to the high ceiling and piles of books were everywhere waiting to be catalogued and arranged. As always, Masaryk's modesty and indeed shyness made it difficult to recall that he had won so many victories not merely in the realm of intellectual dispute but in desperate political battles in the world arena. The quietness with which he spoke heightened the impression he gave of nobility, even grandeur.

Masaryk was not sure that for all the ranting of the Pan-Germans the German Government really wanted to absorb Austria; it might fulfill its purposes better by following Bismarck's policy of using Austria without assuming responsibility for her. Also, Catholic Bavaria's desire for annexation was counteracted in some measure by the strong anti-Catholic sentiment in northern and eastern Germany. Other pressures must be taken into account, however. He reviewed the reasons I had heard cited elsewhere to suppose that the Vatican was working to form a new Roman Catholic state in Central Europe. But he thought that although the talk of Austrian union with Germany was stimulated by Rome, the Vatican's real objective was Austrian union with Bavaria, as a step toward union with Hungary and, if Jugoslav unity could be disrupted, with Croatia. The project was a logical sequel to the effort made during the war by Jacques Bainville and other French Catholic intellectuals to save Catholic Austria-Hungary.

He was worried by Fascism's tightening grip on Italy but did not believe it would last forever. Force begets force, and just as Communism would fail because—and so long as—it was founded on force and terror, so Fascism would fail in the long run. The danger of Communism was not its social revolutionary impact; the reforms it promised could be bested and eclipsed. The danger was its nationalistic egoism and cupidity. In Czechoslovakia, Communism had failed finally the past winter; the Communist-inspired strikes had fizzled out; the Communist party was split seven ways and for practical purposes was extinct. Its attempt to exploit grievances of the German minority had come to nothing. For the first time, the German deputies in the Czechoslovak parliament had voted for the statement of foreign policy made by Beneš on his return from Geneva, and as a result of their cooperative attitude German members would be brought into the cabinet shortly.

In some manner we got onto personalities. Masaryk, who had known Károlyi for years, was interested to hear about his experiences in America; he had always considered him sincere but a little "touched," not off his head, simply unable to see things whole or in proportion. "But not a Communist," he added. Radić he had also known in the past. "Inconsequential as a person, politically a plague." He was amused when I mentioned how Count Apponyi had complained to me three years earlier about not being able to go safely to his former estates, situated since the war in Czechoslovakia, saying, "They call that a country, and a civilized one, where they tell you openly that you had better not come for risk of being attacked"; and how, three minutes later, speaking of Károlyi, Apponyi had said venomously, "He had better not come to Budapest, because if he did he would be shot before he got out of the railway station."

Masaryk's chief worry was that German intransigence would harden under the increasing pressure of military and other reactionaries. For that reason, Chancellor Luther's proposed pact might well be the last conciliatory move that could be expected from Berlin. There had been a hopeful thaw in Franco-German relations, but if negotiations over the pact failed a full-scale crisis would follow. The discussion at Geneva over disarmament would end nowhere and the move to bring Germany into the League would be defeated.

On the eve of my leaving Prague for Berlin came the surprising news that Hindenburg had been nominated for the Presidency of Germany. Beneš was convinced that the old war hero, who had been pushed forward with the ex-Kaiser's blessing, would become a rallying point for all the reactionary forces against the democratic center. Nevertheless, the showdown would be useful whichever side won.

"If Hindenburg and the reactionaries are beaten," he said, "Europe can develop policies based on a new and hopeful situation. If he wins, all Europe—and even America—will be forced to realize the strength of the secret force against which we have been struggling and reckon with the open revival of German militarism and the growing demand for revenge."

II

In Berlin, this April of 1925, I found nobody thinking or talking about anything but the Presidential election, and in that connection not about the effect of one choice or another on the great international questions—European security, Luther's proposed pact, *Anschluss* and so on—but almost solely about the personalities of the two leading candidates. The first poll had not given the necessary majority to any candidate and a second was to be held on April 26. I was staying at the Hotel Adlon, facing on the Pariser Platz, at the head of Unter den Linden. Tremendous demonstrations were staged there during the last days of the campaign and at night the light of flares flickered on the ceiling of my room. The Centrists, Democrats and Social Democrats had joined to nominate the Centrist party leader, former Chancellor Wilhelm Marx. The Nationalists and the People's party had dropped their former nominees and in a surprise move had united to bring forward Field Marshal Paul von Hindenburg, aged seventy-seven. The Communists, though they could not hope to win, had put up their own candidate, Ernst Thälmann.

A most interesting feature of this 1925 campaign, in light of what came later, was that the Nazis did not figure as an issue, even as a side issue. Hitler was out of prison after serving about nine months for high treason, but he was barred from speaking in public and, as far as I can remember, nobody, either German or American, so much as mentioned his name to me. The economic situation was improving, the Dawes Plan on reparations was working, the Ruhr was being evacuated and people in general were in an optimistic frame of mind, receptive to revolutionary propaganda from neither the Communists nor the Nazis. Moreover, the issue in the campaign was not between the Republic, so long on the defensive, and a monarchical restoration. On the contrary, the rightists were endeavoring to convince the electorate that Hindenburg was not a monarchist and that his election would not compromise the Republic. The issue was Hindenburg himself, Hindenburg as a father figure. The betting was that Marx would win, but it failed to take account of the affection felt for the old war hero, particularly among women and ex-soldiers. Hindenburg was victorious by nearly a million votes. Ironically, the Communists made his victory possible, for even half the votes they gave Thälmann could have swung the result the opposite way.

Moderate Germans with whom I talked felt that it was a shame for Hindenburg to be drawn into politics and exploited, as his inexperience and age made certain he would be. One of Hindenburg's admirers told me he had boasted to him of not having read a book, except on military matters, for forty years. He was certain, he said, that the Field Marshal had accepted the nomination solely out of a sense of duty. Duty was such a powerful element in his character that if he found his administration becoming a failure he would feel it his duty to die, and would die. In the short run, supporters who denied that he would sabotage the Republic were proved correct. Once he had taken the oath to the republican constitution, he supported it loyally—so long, that is, as he retained his full mental faculties. That, fatefully, was not long enough. By January 30, 1933, when he faced the critical decision whether or not to name Hitler as Chancellor of the Reich, he had lapsed into senility.

The date 1925 thus became one for the German people to look back on with deep emotion. No one can say confidently that the Nazis would have been foiled if power had been entrusted firmly at that point into the hands of an alert and active President like Marx, working on terms of confidence and understanding with men like Luther, Stresemann and later Brüning. Opposite actions do not necessarily produce opposite results. Nevertheless, the election of Marx with the support of the three great moderate and centrist parties would have set the course of German history on different lines, events would have proceeded at a different pace and the result might perhaps have been different. The "perhaps" is enough to give the date tragic significance.

Parker Gilbert, the American who had been named Agent General for Reparations Payments, was away in Paris, but friends in the Embassy brought me up to date on how the Dawes Plan was working insofar as my limited understanding of such matters permitted. The plan, now in operation for eight months, was being called a success so far. Its prospects for the future were more dubious. Armed with such information as I could muster, I went out to Zehlendorf to see Dr. R. R. Kuczynski, recommended by Gay as the most competent German economist and statistician and given equally high marks in our Embassy and in the Reparations office. The accumulation of books in Kuczynski's library was overwhelming. Books filled each shelf up to the ceiling; on top of these other books were stuffed crosswise; and books were piled on tables, on chairs, on window ledges and on the floor. One pile was topped with a new book by Gay's colleague, Wesley Clair Mitchell. Kuczynski was as impressive a scholar as his bibliographic resources indicated and quite impartial in his views of the Dawes Plan. His preliminary opinion was that it was working successfully in two main respects—political and technical. In the economic field it was working satisfactorily for Germany and Britain but less so for France, who was receiving less than she was entitled to. For that reason the statement that it was acceptable politically might not be true by the end of the year.[2]

Before I left New York, Coolidge had agreed that I should press ex-Chancellor Marx to write for us, but that possibility vanished when he became a candidate for the Presidency and I turned instead to Hans Luther, who had succeeded Marx as Chancellor and was not involved directly in the campaign. As the Luther cabinet included Nationalists, foreign opinion considered that it marked a turn to the right in German politics; friends in the Embassy like Warren Delano Robbins disagreed and pointed to the fact that Luther supported the policy of reconciliation with France and had retained Stresemann as Foreign Minister to carry it forward. When I talked with Luther, he not unnaturally steered clear of election issues; instead he spent most of his time criticizing Dr. Dorten's article on the separatist Rhineland movement and blaming *Foreign Affairs* for having printed it. His article turned out to be rather thin; per-

2. Kuczynski promised to give *Foreign Affairs* an accounting at that time of the plan's successes and shortcomings. When his article appeared in the January, 1926, issue, Gilbert felt that it was too pessimistic in that it exaggerated what the Dawes Plan had been expected to do and damned it for not doing what it was never intended to do. He gave his reasons in an address before the Council on Foreign Relations in January, 1926, and the text was published as a supplement to the April issue of *Foreign Affairs*.

haps he watered down his views to suit the Nationalists in his cabinet, some of whom were hostile to his proposed pact. His article did not mention Dorten or his Rhineland Republic, against which he had inveighed to me. I was amused when later on Coolidge heard from his friend Count Lerchenfeld, the Bavarian statesman, that Luther was posing as being indignant that he had not known about the Dorten article; if he had, he assured Lerchenfeld, he would have made a point of refuting it.

I was worried that such a big name as Luther's should be attached to a rather unsubstantial article, particularly as the more severely I edited it for clarity the less weighty it became. On this Coolidge tried to set my mind at rest. He wrote: "Heavy, involved German cannot be rendered into pleasant, idiomatic English without getting too far away from the original to be genuine. When we have a thing like Luther's article which is practically an official statement from the chancellor of one of the great states of the world, I believe we should render it as accurately as we can whether we understand it or not and even whether he understands it or not. At any rate a thing should not be left out because we are not clear of its intention. The fact that some people may think we have made a mistranslation is relatively unimportant. A good many others are likely to feel that the more obscure a composition is the more thoroughly German it is."

A sophisticated comment on that delicate line which an editor is called on to draw between proper and improper editing comes from Ling Po: "Editing another man's copy is like giving a back-rub to another man's wife: if you are ethical, you do only what the situation requires, refraining from those services which the other man is perfectly capable of performing himself."

III

It was disappointing to have to leave Berlin before the election, but I would be late anyway in getting back to work in New York and must in any case stop a few days in Paris. For one thing, I had an engagement with M. Poincaré to discuss again his promised article. For another, I must follow up the effort I had begun there earlier in the spring to arrange for some Soviet official to write us an authoritative description of Soviet foreign policy. For that purpose I had gone to call on the Soviet Ambassador to France, Leonid Krassin, in the imposing old Russian Embassy on the rue de Grenelle. To my surprise, I had hardly begun my argument about how useful such an article would be when Krassin announced that he would like to write it himself. I had found him an impressive person, direct in manner, not at all stiff, self-confident but not aggressive, and showing a wide interest in matters outside his field of professional concern. The Soviet Embassy, I wrote Mr. Coolidge, was "better run, with politer employees, than any other place I have been in Paris." However, on my second visit I found that Krassin was away from Paris; shortly thereafter he was transferred to London, died there and his ashes were deposited in the Kremlin.

When I called on Krassin's successor, Christian Rakovsky, he agreed to take over the assignment. Rakovsky, a Bulgarian, dark and good-looking, was one of the original Balkan revolutionaries. The Embassy was even more elegant than before and my reception still more friendly. On the front steps I passed Mme. Rakovsky going out; she wore a fur stole and a string of pearls, and the car into which she stepped was large and sumptuous. In that era Moscow frowned on bourgeois elegance. Even more dangerous, Rakovsky belonged to the Trotsky opposition, which criticized Stalin for his support of Chiang Kai-shek and for his uncompromising attitude toward the British trade unions. He was recalled the next year (but not before sending me his article) and exiled to Siberia; ten years later, at the great treason trial staged by Stalin, he was sentenced to twenty years in Butyrka prison. Elegant Mme. Rakovsky was likewise jailed in Butyrka, as usually happened to wives of those convicted of political crimes.

On the steamer coming over to Europe I had struck up an acquaintance with an attractive young Frenchman, who now asked me to lunch at his family's *hôtel* on the rue Masseran. He had been making a tour in a small car of the United States—all forty-eight of them—and had been so taken with America and Americans that he wanted to marry an American girl. Could I find him one? Money, he assured me, was not an objective, as he was one of the richest young men in France. I laughed off the suggestion, but we remained friends and I promised to let him know the next time I was in Paris.

The house was very handsome, with a spacious courtyard and a large park. His family had made a fortune in, I think, the China trade and had been rewarded with a title in the splendid days of the Second Empire. The walls of the dining room were Chinese lacquer panels in pale pinks, yellows and greens, the most beautiful I have ever seen. My friend's mother pointed out my place midway down the table, took Count Boni de Castelane (as always wearing tight white kid gloves) at her right and some other French notable at her left. As we were sitting down my friend went around to his mother and there ensued a whispered conversation that became more and more intense, ending with his saying audibly, "Non, maman! Non, non, non! Il est l'étranger." After a tense pause, he came around to me, accompanied me, horribly embarrassed, to the place of honor at his mother's right and conducted Count Boni de Castelane to my more humble place. The Count behaved decorously and made no protest. The meal began in silence and, so far as I was concerned, continued in silence, for the lady of the house did not address a word to me. But afterwards, at my friend's whispered insistence, his father came up to me, bowed politely, asked me to forgive any misunderstanding that might have occurred and invited me to do him the honor of drinking a cognac with him on the sofa.

That was not the end of the story. When I was crossing to Europe a year later I noticed a very pretty girl dancing each evening with a man who was evidently her father. At the captain's dinner I found myself next to her. She told me she was on her way to Paris to be married. I guessed her fiancé's name before she mentioned it. I betrayed no secrets. I thought my friend had done exceedingly well for himself without my services as marriage broker.

Setting out for home, I wondered what conclusions might be drawn from my round of visits. The following seemed reasonable: Jugoslavia would not break up as a result of disputes between Serbs and Croats; she was now too strong for Italy to dare attack her directly; the Fiume settlement removed the immediate cause of contention and an agreement on remaining issues was in the making. The Little Entente was working. The Hapsburgs would never return. Hungary should be and would be contained within roughly her present frontiers. *Anschluss* should not and would not take place. Sectional and social divisions in Rumania were serious, but the popular leaders from both Transylvania and Bessarabia were loyal to dynasty and state, national unity would probably be maintained. Communism was not a menace in the area except possibly in Bulgaria, where it was a tossup whether repression by the Tsankov government stimulated or crushed Communist activity. Prospects for a regional political organization were nil; but the rehabilitation of Austrian and Hungarian finances would relax tensions and should open the way for discussions about an economic grouping. Rejection of the Geneva Protocol had set back hopes for making the League more effective; but Germany's proposal of a pact with France guaranteeing her western frontiers should inaugurate a new era in Franco-German relations and might by extension bring limited security to Poland and Czechoslovakia.

All these conclusions contained an implicit "for the time being." I knew too little about the localized Nazi movement in Munich to realize the full necessity of that saving clause. As of the moment, there seemed grounds for moderate optimism.

With his longer historical perspective, Coolidge was less optimistic. Before he had heard of Chancellor Luther's decision to write for us he had begun drafting an article of his own to be called "Dissatisfied Germany," in which he foreshadowed continuation of the Franco-German duel. France could require no more of Germany, he wrote, than that she accept the Versailles Treaty in the same way that France had accepted the Peace of Frankfurt in 1871; this involved the recognition that many Germans would dream of revenge now just as many Frenchmen had dreamed of revenge then.

I was forced to admit that Poincaré's ideas supported this pessimistic conclusion. In my talk with him in Paris only a few days earlier he had compared France's behavior after her defeat at Sedan with Germany's behavior since her defeat in 1918. He recognized that in 1871 the French press had made violent statements about Germany's punitive peace, especially the annexation of Alsace-Lorraine and the occupation of French territory until the indemnity of five billion francs had been paid; yet no French cabinet minister had ever indulged in such invective and threats as had come from German officials in the last years. And why? Poincaré thought it was because if French officials had behaved in such a manner German armies would have marched back into France and exacted fulfillment of French obligations without further wrangling. This intimation that the occupation of the Ruhr had been a right method and that only force would teach Germany to behave in the future supported Coolidge's foreboding. Regardless of Chancellor Luther's conciliatory moves and the somewhat promising turn of events which I had discerned in Eastern Europe, German dreams of revenge were to keep European peace in jeopardy.

23

Lindbergh, French Loans
and Other Matters

The Woodrow Wilson Foundation was a nonpartisan body, but when I was asked to become a trustee in the spring of 1925 I was of two minds whether I should accept. There were liberal Republicans on the board, such as William Allen White and Senator George W. Norris, but they were outnumbered by Democrats, including Franklin D. Roosevelt and Norman H. Davis. I decided that if anyone accused *Foreign Affairs* of being biased because I joined an organization to honor Wilson's name and works we could reply that we were busy at the moment negotiating for an article by Mussolini, Wilson's antithesis in every conceivable respect.

Our long-standing plan to get Mussolini to write for us had just been revived. Following my talk with Carlo Jung the previous year we had been notified that Mussolini's manuscript had actually been mailed, but that turned out to be a myth. Now on the boat coming back from Europe I had met the Italian journalist, Luigi Barzini, well known for such exploits as reporting the capture of Mukden and accompanying Prince Borghese on his famous trip by automobile from Peking to Paris. He showed me an angry Italian attack on Count Sforza's article in *Foreign Affairs*. Shouldn't we in fairness let someone set forth the other side? This gave me a chance to relate our experience with Mussolini. Barzini said he knew him intimately and felt sure he would never sit down and write out something by himself. But, if we composed several provocative questions, Barzini's correspondent in Rome would carry them to Mussolini, take down his comments in shorthand, put them into shape and submit them for his approval. Mussolini would become so interested that he would make additions and corrections and the result would be a powerful contribution for us. This came rather close to ghostwriting but we decided to make the experiment.

The result was neither a success nor a complete failure. In June while Coolidge was in Washington he dropped in to see his friend William R. Castle in the State Department. To his surprise, Castle handed him a manuscript which the Italian Ambassador had just delivered to him. It was an article by one of Mussolini's cronies, Roberto Cantalupo, Undersecretary for the Colonies. The Ambassador said Mussolini had read and approved the article and authorized *Foreign Affairs* to print it with a note saying it represented his views. The views were principally worth publishing as an exposé of what the Duce thought the American public might swallow. Fascism, the article explained, was a continuation of the Risorgimento in that it was creating a national consciousness, defeating antinational socialism and quelling treasonable internationalists. The glorious victory over Austria-Hungary had provided an opportunity to broaden the national foundations—spiritually, economically, politically and morally. Fascism had seized that opportunity from the fumbling hands of Italy's democratic leaders. Captained by Mussolini, the masses of workers had passed over from Socialism to Fascism. The Fascist era of regeneration was under way. And so on.

My interest in the Woodrow Wilson Foundation had begun quite by chance. Mrs. Charles L. Tiffany, one of the energetic women who had conceived the idea of creating a memorial to President Wilson, mentioned one evening that the trustees were wondering who should design the medal which was to be part of the Foundation's annual award for services in the cause of peace. My Jugoslav friend Ivan Meštrović, one of the great sculptors of our time, happened to be in New York supervising the Brooklyn Museum's first American exhibition of his works. At Mrs. Tiffany's suggestion I took him the next day to meet her and one or two other trustees. He volunteered to design the medal (as he wrote afterward) "as a labor of love and a tribute from the new nations of Europe which look upon Wilson as their greatest benefactor." The design of the medal, which was in reality a bronze medallion in low relief some ten inches across, showed a figure of Wilson as a lawgiver. While not a portrait, it conveyed what Meštrović believed had been three of Wilson's characteristics—wisdom, justice and love of humanity. The words *Sapientia, Justitia* and *Caritas* appeared on the rim; below was the inscription *Lex Mundi,* the law of the world. The effect was the opposite of sentimental; indeed, it was so severe that Mrs. Wilson never really liked it. Everyone else, I think, including the art critics, praised it as magnificent. The medal and an award of $25,000 were given for the first time to Viscount Cecil at a Foundation dinner on December 24, 1924, the anniversary of Wilson's birthday.

Meštrović, the son of a Croatian peasant and stone mason in Dalmatia, was a natural genius, as retiring and modest as some of his best works were vigorous and heroic. I visited him several times in his studio in Zagreb and later in Split, where he built himself a house, now a museum, on a height overlooking the Adriatic. He had spent much of the war in London, where he worked with Seton-Watson and Wickham Steed for the Jugoslav ideal and against both the Hapsburg dynasty and Pashich's first tendency to plan for a Greater Serbia. In 1916, Sargent (like Rodin, one of his admirers) organized an exhibition in London which gave Western Europe the first comprehensive idea of his work.

Out of friendship, Meštrović modeled a head of me, working in Malvina Hoffman's studio on East Thirty-fifth Street. He worked rapidly, almost feverishly, and completed the head in three long mornings. The first morning brought the lump of clay into the right size and proportions; on the second, the lump suddenly began to take on recognizable features; on the third, it was finished. I thought it made me look rather haughty, with head cocked a little to one side and chin up. But its destruction later on when my house on Long Island burnt to the ground left me feeling its loss more than that of anything else: only a weird lump of bronze remained in the rubble. (Strangely, too, there were masses of books from which the flames had bitten the edges but left the printed cores intact. How, I wonder, had Hitler's Storm Troopers burnt books so effectively that no contaminating heart of wisdom and charity would survive?) To show Meštrović my gratitude I asked which of his pupils he thought the most talented. He replied unhesitatingly Frane Kršinić and sent me photographs of his works. I bought two marbles, one a lovely head of a pensive girl, the other a seated peasant girl with a lute, mouth open, who now sings winter and summer among the wild azaleas on my place in Wainscott on the edge of Georgica Pond.

Meštrović felt that Tito betrayed the ideals of the Jugoslavia he had imagined and worked for, and soon after the war he left the country. In 1947 he came to the United States, joined the faculty first at Syracuse University, then at Notre Dame, and eventually became an American citizen. He did return once to Jugoslavia for a short visit, which was hailed there as a gesture of reconciliation. Actually he had not changed his political views but was nostalgic for his country and wanted to see some of his works there again—the monument to the unknown soldier on Avala, the famous mausoleum near Dubrovnik, and in Belgrade the figure of victory that looks out from Kalemegdan across "the great Pannonian plain"—"superb words," wrote Rebecca West, "the flattest I know."

While I am talking about the Woodrow Wilson Foundation I might jump ahead to 1926, when it gave its award and medal to Elihu Root as a founder of the Permanent Court of International Justice. At eighty-one, Root was rather terrifying for his ability to glare when indignant, the more so because you were never quite sure at whom the glare was directed, since one eye strayed off at a different angle from the other. Other nations had joined to form the League (he said in his address at the Foundation dinner) on the understanding, "based upon the judgment of our representative, our negotiator, our agent," that it would be acceptable to the American people. We had a right to refuse to join. Nevertheless, our repudiation of Wilson's action had left Europe to deal alone with the unsolved problems from the war and Versailles. "What," he asked, rapping sharply on the table with his knuckles and glaring at the large assemblage before him, "would any gentleman have said to another who had been brought to such an untoward condition by his representative and agent?" He would have expressed his most sincere regret, Root answered, and would have done everything possible to prevent his absence from injuring his friends. Instead, the Americans who had opposed joining the League had gone on to denounce the League itself and even to express pleasure at the thought it might fail. "Insensate prejudice" had prevailed. From "this hateful and contentious spirit," he ended in a low voice, "may the good Lord deliver us."

A sequel brought me mingled horror and delight. By this time I had become a trustee of the Foundation and was the only member of the board not to favor giving the award to Root, not from any lack of respect and admiration but simply because it seemed to me that it would be more stimulating if our awards instead of crowning recognized eminence sought out younger and less known persons who deserved recognition. My feeling may be imagined, then, when Root contributed the Foundation's check to *Foreign Affairs* as a nucleus of a permanent endowment fund.

After honoring Root, the Foundation's next award, in 1927, went to Colonel Charles A. Lindbergh. It created more excitement than any of the awards to statesmen, however eminent. Lindbergh was the hero of the day, especially with the teenagers, and when I escorted him into the Hotel Astor for the presentation dinner the police had as hard a time keeping the girls from mobbing him as they did to hold back a later generation from tearing the clothes off the Beatles. "I touched him!" I heard a girl shriek. "Anyway, I touched his coat!"

Following his transatlantic flight, Lindbergh had wanted to put his fame to some useful purpose. One day he came to my office to consult as to what it might be. Would a good-will flight to Soviet Russia be helpful? I was not sure that it might not be exploited there as an American effort to curry favor and suggested that it might be wise to arrange to be invited to make a visit. If the invitation didn't materialize, I suggested a flight to Mexico and other neighboring Latin American countries. This flight, arranged by Ambassador Morrow, was a tremendous success. It was shortly after this that the Foundation voted the award.

Lindbergh received an ovation. A telegram from Morrow said that he had come to Mexico "with healing in his wings." John W. Davis, in his welcoming address, said, "His name has been written in the skies." Nothing turned the young man's head. He replied extemporaneously, speaking slowly and with poise, saying exactly what he meant and no more. Our Union, he said, had been cemented by the railroad and the gas engine. He hoped that aviation would soon overcome the sea, jungle and mountains that separated us from the peoples of Latin America, as well as end the barriers that kept them apart. The aviation routes from North to South America were entirely feasible and should be opened soon. Let everyone help speed the day.

The next morning the *New York Times* called him "the young ambassador of good will" and "the greatest ambassador of modern times."

After the dinner, from which we escaped through the same pack of screaming admirers, we went for a drink at the Park Avenue apartment of Lindbergh's friend and lawyer, Henry Breckinridge. I say "for a drink," but that excludes Charles, who never drinks. I was conversing with someone when I vaguely heard Charles saying that he had always wanted to shy a phonograph record out a high window. With that, he jumped onto a chair, pulled up a window and made as if to sail his new bronze medallion out into Park Avenue. Without stopping to consider whether he was in fun or genuinely carried away by exuberance and relief that the sort of public ordeal he detested was over, I tackled him around the knees and we both fell to the floor, he laughing much more than I was able to do. He was known for his love of practical jokes, and this one may have been no more than a threat. But the bare possibility of a ten-pound bronze disk crashing down onto the traffic below didn't let me wait to find out.

In between its awards to Cecil and Root the Foundation had stubbed its toe badly. At a meeting of the executive committee at Roosevelt's house on East Sixty-fifth Street, in May, we discussed various ideas for a 1925 award and decided, as I remember, to wait and see what came of the British-French-German effort to strengthen European security. When the Locarno Pact was signed December 1, Norman H. Davis, the Foundation's president, suggested a joint award to the three responsible statesmen, Sir Austen Chamberlain, Aristide Briand and Gustav Stresemann. It was an ambitious plan, too ambitious as it turned out. There would be no problem with Chamberlain and Briand, but some reluctance was foreseen on Stresemann's part, for Wilson's name was still obnoxious in Germany for his role at Paris. To sound Stresemann out, Davis invoked the services of Paul Warburg's brother, Max Warburg, and Henry White, who had many ties with Germany. Stresemann's reply to Warburg was that he would never take an honor from any American foundation, most particularly one bearing the name of Woodrow Wilson, who (as reported by Warburg) had "betrayed Germany" by not remaining faithful to the Fourteen Points. With this news we considered the matter closed; but that, as we should have realized, was far too optimistic. Toward the end of December questions began to be asked why there was to be no award on the anniversary of Wilson's birthday, and rumors followed that an offer had been made to Stresemann and rejected. Meanwhile, we had also heard from Sir Austen Chamberlain that if no German participated he felt he ought not to do so either, "as it would weaken the Locarno spirit of solidarity." We met at Roosevelt's house on January 5 to discuss the situation. Since there was nothing we could do we decided to do nothing.

The next morning the bomb burst with publication in the *New York Times* of a Berlin dispatch confirming that Stresemann had been offered and had rejected the award. He denied that it was because President Wilson had "betrayed" Germany; he simply was too busy to come to New York. I helped Davis draft a statement on the subject. There really was little to say except that what had seemed a good idea had turned out to be a bad one.

German nationalists were delighted. A Berlin dispatch reported that Stresemann's action "is loudly commended and is held up as an example to all good Germans in perpetuating the hatred of Wilson as the deceiver of the German people." Only the *Berliner Tageblatt* expressed appreciation of the good will underlying the offer. A communiqué from the Foreign Office announced that Foreign Minister Stresemann "assumed no political position whatever in the matter." On hearing of Stresemann's statement to Max Warburg, James Speyer, a New York banker of German origin, commented, "Show a German a hole and he will leap into it." We had provided a tempting hole, and should have known better.

II

Caillaux, Minister of Finance in the Painlevé government, came to America in October, 1925, to negotiate a settlement of the French war debt—an essential step in his program for repairing French finances. He returned home defeated by President Coolidge's austere and self-righteous attitude in monetary matters. Instead of the hoped-for permanent settlement, all he was able to achieve was a five-year arrangement for annual payments with no final sum fixed. He had known that only a brilliant success at Washington would carry him through the forthcoming debates in the French parliament. He was also aware (as I was told by "Pertinax," who accompanied the mission) that Briand, who was his rival to succeed Painlevé as Premier, would attempt to bring down the cabinet in such a way that Caillaux would be held to blame and thus be put out of the running.

He was not in a jovial mood, then, at the lunch which I gave him in New York on his way from Washington to catch the *France* that evening. By coincidence, my wife and I were also sailing on the *France* as her sister was to be married the next week in Paris. At lunch, and afterward on shipboard, Caillaux made plain that it would be next to impossible to get the French parliament to agree to a series of cash payments which were not part of an agreed schedule of interest and amortization and would in the end bring nothing but the right to reopen negotiations five years later at the point left off. Answering questions at lunch, he said that his final proposal, rejected by the Treasury Department, represented the best terms that any French government was ever likely to offer. Later, on the steamer, he told me that if he were given time he would try to transform the five-year schedule into one for a longer period; but he realized that President Coolidge would probably veto such an amendment, that without it the French Chambre would reject the American terms and that he would resign.

Nevertheless, on shipboard Caillaux seemed to have reconciled himself to the inevitable and in public appeared in good spirits, playing bridge and joking with members of his mission. One of his anecdotes was that President Coolidge had received him with a laconic "Glad to see you," but then in an unusual burst of loquacity had added, "How is old Mr. Clemenceau?" Caillaux said he explained that he was not on good terms with Mr. Clemenceau, to which the President said, "Excuse me." Caillaux did not include in his story that the reason he was not on good terms with Clemenceau was that Clemenceau had wanted to have him hanged; and probably nobody told the President that either.

One of the only really unpleasant episodes in all my years with *Foreign Affairs* had its origins, indirectly, on the *France*. Obviously Caillaux was in no position to write just then on the French financial situation, and he recommended as a substitute Senator Henry Bérenger, a member of his mission, head of the Senate Finance Committee and rumored as likely to be the next French Ambassador in Washington. Caillaux said he himself would go over the manuscript. "Pertinax" told me that while he did not much like Bérenger, who was excessively ambitious, he would write a satisfactory article under Caillaux's supervision. Bérenger agreed to provide the manuscript before I left Paris for home, and did.

The trouble began when I gave the article for translation (as had been done with several previous French articles) to my friend, J. A. M. de Sanchez, a brilliant young financial expert on the staff of J. P. Morgan and Co. When he read the article he saw that Bérenger's statements would be of great concern to the Morgan firm and without saying anything to me showed it to one of the Morgan partners. The result was that Lamont telephoned me the following morning to say that Bérenger's article painted the French financial situation in such dark colors that its publication would damage French credit in the United States, and he asked me not to publish it. I explained that the article, by one of the highest officials of the French Government, had been written at my invitation; that it had the approval of the outgoing Minister of Finance (Caillaux had meanwhile, as forecast, resigned) ; that it had been accepted, and that we could not fail to publish it except at the author's own request. Lamont, usually very suave, for once let his Irish temper get the better of him and as much as ordered me to do as he said. He added that he could not understand my being so insensitive to the French national interest. By then I was really indignant and said I wasn't in a position to choose between his and Bérenger's opinion of that. He replied that he would "do everything in his power" to see that the article was never printed.

I was on a tough spot between on the one hand the author, who if we gave way to Lamont might reasonably think he had been made the victim of financial pressure on us, and on the other hand Lamont and his partners, personal friends, members of the Council. Actually, the article was not of vital importance to us; we could easily fill the space. But I felt in honor bound not to exclude it except at the direction of the author, and when I telephoned Coolidge he emphatically took the same view, as did Gay, who happened to be in New York, and my father-in-law, James Byrne, a leading member of the New York bar, not easily intimidated. I then cabled Bérenger informing him that his article had been shown without our knowledge to a member of the Morgan firm and warning him (using Lamont's words) that Morgan's was going to do everything in its power to stop its publication. At Coolidge's suggestion I later informed John W. Davis, whose law firm was counsel to the house of Morgan and who in addition was a member of our Editorial Advisory Board. On his side, Lamont cabled his partner in Paris, Mr. Harjes, to see Premier Painlevé and have him prevent the article's publication.

When Lamont heard from Paris that Bérenger had been warned of the pressure that was about to be put on him he telephoned me to say that my original action in refusing to cancel the article on my own responsibility "paled into insignificance" beside "this extraordinary discourtesy." I could only repeat that whether or not the article was to be printed was entirely up to Bérenger and said Coolidge and I had agreed that we could not leave him in ignorance of the fact that pressure was to be put on him to withdraw it. The conversation ended abruptly.

The cabled reply which I received from Bérenger stated simply that publication of the article "might be inopportune" and "authorized" me to stop publication "if you are yourself in accord." He evidently wished to transfer responsibility for the decision to me. I therefore replied that we could not undertake to decide what would be the effect of his article's publication, but we construed his message to mean that he did not wish it published. This left it to him to state a contrary desire if he so wished. The matter was finally settled when a cable came from Harjes, stating flatly that Bérenger now did in fact "agree fully" that the article should not be published.

Looking back at Bérenger's unpublished manuscript, I find it largely a statistical account of the increasingly heavy tax burden borne by the French people and a refutation of the idea that French military expenditures were unjustifiably high in view of French defense needs. In a section which undoubtedly was the one which so provoked Lamont he admitted frankly that "imprudent optimism" had often marked statements of past French ministers of finance about the state of the French economy and mentioned an unnamed American economist's reference to exaggerated official accounts of the French economic recovery at the time the Morgan loan was being issued in December, 1924. He excused such overoptimistic statements by the fact that France had to show her credit worthiness in order to be able to borrow in the American market at the same time she was stressing her dire need of reparations from Germany and asking American support in collecting them.

Senator Bérenger's withdrawal of his article ended a painful episode. Lamont had won his point: the article was not printed. But he had won it by pressure put on the author via the President of France and not as a result of any action by *Foreign Affairs,* which indeed had given him warning of what was impending. The principle had been established that, although *Foreign Affairs* owes its existence to the Council on Foreign Relations, its editors, so long as the Council retains them as editors, are not subject to dictation by Council members. After this incident, we realized the importance of this principle more than ever.

A postscript to the affair. Briand, as he had hoped, succeeded Painlevé as Premier and sent Bérenger, as he had hoped, as French Ambassador in Washington. Lamont asked Coolidge in January to suggest that the Council give a dinner for the new Ambassador. I said it would be a long cold day before that happened.

III

The fact that my father-in-law's name has come into these pages only incidentally is misleading, for his advice was always of great value, and I was especially grateful for it in an uncomfortable situation like that just described. What I say here will be briefer than such a brilliant and complicated character deserves; only a novelist could tell his story, and that he would have hated, for although he had inherited an extravagant Irish spirit he was shy as well as combative and recoiled from publicity as much as did his friend Horace Plunkett. He was a lawyer who believed in the law and would not and did not bend it. Yet great banks and corporations sought his services; and to become a law clerk in his firm, forbidding in its demands on a young man's time, energy and patience, was the ambition of many of the most brilliant law-school graduates of the day, among them Elihu Root, Jr., Winthrop W. Aldrich, William M. Chadbourne, Harrison Tweed and others successful in later life. He himself was president of the New York Bar Association and was the first non-Bostonian and the first Roman Catholic to become a member of the Harvard Corporation.

Stories and fables about him flourished. One will be enough to set the style. He was invited as *amicus curiae* in a case being heard by the Chancellor of the State of New Jersey. He took Winthrop Aldrich with him to Newark and entrusted a package to his care. The Chancellor asked Mr.

Byrne to sit beside him on the bench and at noon invited him to lunch and Winthrop with him. On the way back to the courthouse, Mr. Byrne asked Winthrop for the package. He explained that he had left it with the clerk of the court, who had locked it up in the office safe. Mr. Byrne was much annoyed; it seemed that there was a shoemaker in Newark better at resoling shoes than any in New York, and he had brought Winthrop along expressly to carry the package containing two pairs of shoes to be left for repair. Winthrop was crushed. His pride in being selected for a mission with Mr. Byrne evaporated now that the nature of the mission was revealed; and even in performing that mission he had failed. He did not seem, however, to lose confidence in Mr. Byrne's judgment. Later, when he was asked to become president of the Chase National Bank, he consulted Mr. Byrne about the wisdom of leaving the law for banking. Mr. Byrne told him that since almost all his legal work was for the bank he might as well be the one to ask for legal advice instead of the one who worked to provide it.

Although Mr. Byrne's temper was usually under control it was always in a state of alert. My own relations with him were, after a false start, most amicable. When his daughter and I became unofficially engaged in 1917 I was told that I should ask his approval, and a time was set for me to call on him late one afternoon. I was shown into a small reception room off the front hall. When Mr. Byrne came in he was polite but nervous and at the beginning seemed too shy to come to the point. When he finally did, his first remark was startling: "Er—er—Hamilton, you should understand that this is a Catholic family and that you can never be divorced." Luckily I was too stunned to make a quick reply. Collecting myself, I said chokingly that I had come to talk about marriage, not divorce, went out (without slamming the door), took my hat from the hall table and left. Mr. Byrne never mentioned the incident and for the rest of his life our relations were excellent, even when years later he found that a divorce could indeed occur in a Catholic family.

IV

Remembering the profitable years he had spent abroad as a young man, Gay suggested early in 1926 that I ought to go to Europe for a few months, partly to get a start at learning German, partly to finish research for a book on the Balkans which was progressing only slowly in New York. Coolidge concurred, and the plan was made possible by the fact that Malcolm W. Davis, whom we had persuaded to take over as executive director of the Council, was both eager to help Coolidge with editorial work and splendidly equipped to do so. It was agreed that in the spring I should set off with my family for Vienna, stopping on the way in Paris; plans beyond that would be made as we went along.

Things at the office seemed well in hand. The next issue was on the press. A number of articles were already scheduled for the summer issue, and I had plans for recruiting other writers abroad. Our circulation had been slowly creeping up. Sometimes our promotion circulars had brought replies that jounced us back into realization that our purposes were suspect among wide sections of the American public. Letters castigated us not simply for printing articles which the writers disagreed with but also for our basic assumption, which they considered "subversive," that the United States was not a fortress apart which was entitled and able, if bothered by the antics or threats of the outside world, to teach everyone by force to behave as it directed. These protests against the very reason for our existence left us cold. And what could one say to communications like one that came from T. E. Lawrence, of Arab fame, in reply to an invitation to subscribe sent him by Whitney Shepardson? He was not a likely quarry, he wrote, because he hadn't a red cent, was not concerned with politics and got rude when people mentioned the subject. "The ideal world," he said, "hasn't any humans in it." Coolidge was never fully reconciled to the need to solicit subscriptions, though gratified when they came in; he wrote me that one of our circulars describing the merits of our magazine reminded him of a work he had been fond of in his very early youth, *The Children's Book of Great and Good Men.*

All in all, when I sailed with my wife and small daughter on the *Leviathan* in late March it was without too many twinges of conscience and with great expectations for the things to be done and learnt in Europe. I was delighted, too, that Coolidge had undertaken ("with mute resignation") to write a short introduction to my book *The New Balkans,* which Harper's had contracted to publish and which I planned to finish in Vienna, where special sources of information would be available.

The French financial situation was even shakier than usual and everyone I saw when I passed through Paris was harassed by fears of a complete collapse. What was lacking, they agreed, was confidence—in the franc, in the political leadership, in France herself. The cabinet formed by Briand in succession to Painlevé had fallen a few weeks earlier; now he was again in office, but precariously. Tardieu said the Chambre des Députés was "intolerable," a situation he proposed to rectify by forming a new party of younger men led, of course, by himself (he was then fifty and had no seat in the Chambre, but was elected again that year) . A visit to the Chambre confirmed his description. The Communists had just won a by-election in the Paris "red belt" and were celebrating the appearance of their two new members by singing the "Internationale," banging their desk covers and raising such a hubbub that Herriot, who was presiding, burst the studs of his boiled shirt front in anger and suspended the session by clapping on his top hat.

Poincaré, less agitated and boastful than Tardieu, simply said he thought it was about time to hold elections. I had been anxious to see him because a French journalist named Ernest Judet, author of a book savagely criticizing Poincaré's conduct of French prewar diplomacy, had been threatening to sue *Foreign Affairs.* He based his case on harsh statements in Poincaré's article which without naming him made his identity unmistakable. Judet, claiming that the facts cited by Poincaré were false and perfidious, threatened to sue not the author but us because the article was published in America. This reason faded away when the first volumes of Poincaré's memoirs, *Au Service de la France,* were published in Paris, for Poincaré trampled all over Judet much more ruthlessly there than he had done in his article for us. Poincaré told me to pay no attention to Judet's threats: "He always talks of suing somebody. It's his only possible response when he is caught lying." And indeed we heard no more of the matter.

I squeezed as much as possible into a very short visit. Károlyi, bringing Szende, who had been his Minister of Finance in the Hungarian Republic, came to lunch at Foyot's, one of the best restaurants in Paris but since closed, a melancholy precedent followed by two others of great fame, Voisin and Larue. I had a brief talk with Herriot, who had suggested that he would like to write for us again but now was hesitating; he thought he would become Premier again in succession to Briand and in fact did —for three days in July, before Poincaré took charge and held things firmly in hand for the next three years.

What was to be a long friendship was established at a lunch with André Géraud ("Pertinax") and his wife Jaza in their apartment on the top floor of an old building on the rue de l'Université overlooking the Présidence du Conseil. It was the first of many visits that over the years made this the most familiar and congenial spot for me in all Paris. As you rang for the invisible concierge, pushed open the big varnished wooden door and started up the five flights of red-carpeted stairs—smelling in our earlier visits of the gas mantles that then provided the illumination, supplanted later by electric lights that presupposed you would ascend more rapidly than sometimes was the case, leaving you to fumble up the last flight in semidarkness—always you were encouraged on your way by the knowledge that though you arrived out of breath at the Géraud door delicious food and the best of company awaited you within. The first day we found Jean Parmentier there, one of our recent contributors; he was an Inspecteur des Finances, a guarantee of intellectual quality. Géraud and he agreed that we were fortunate to have been divested of the article by Bérenger, whose ambition made them rather mistrust him.

On one or two evenings we went with friends to Chez Fycher, not yet famous and crowded, to hear Lucienne Boyer. But the best entertainment in Paris was Edmond Rostand's little one-act play, *La dernière nuit de Don Juan*. Remembering his utterly boring *Chantecler,* one found difficulty in believing that this was by the same author. The scene is the loggia of Don Juan's Venetian palace. The Devil arrives disguised as the proprietor of an itinerant marionette show. At his summons, the girls whom Don Juan has seduced alight one by one from gondolas, and one by one Don Juan fails to recognize them. "Tu n'a rien vu," the Devil says to him scornfully. "Tu n'a rien su. Tu n'a rien eu." And he drags Don Juan, struggling and protesting, behind the little guignol, to appear above on the muslin-lined stage decked out in cheap crimson and gold.

V

Our first week in Vienna was spent in a futile hunt for something that turned out not to exist, an apartment or small villa for rent. The city was so crowded that proprietors were afraid to let it be known that they had space to spare lest the government commandeer it. After a discouraging search we decided to move to the Hotel Kobenzl on the slopes of the Wiener Wald not far beyond Redlich's house. The suggestion actually did not come from Redlich but from Count Coudenhove-Kalergi and his wife, Ida Roland, Vienna's most celebrated actress, who took us out to Kobenzl one afternoon for tea. The weather was still chilly and the hotel was not really open, but the countryside was beautiful with fruit trees in blossom, and the forest on the hills back of the hotel was a haze of feathery green. With Coudenhove-Kalergi's help we persuaded the management to open an apartment with a terrace overlooking the valley and the next day moved out there. Though it became less attractive when the Viennese began flocking there to make merry on warm spring evenings it served well for a time as a place to work. There were miles of walks through the beech forest and we usually ate our meals on the terrace, served by a waiter who had spent some time in America and announced each afternoon with unflagging pride that the "smashed cream" on my daughter's hot chocolate was heavier than any in New York. The rule of the road then was to drive on the right in Vienna but on the left in the Austrian countryside. This meant a switch at the city line. One quickly adjusts to driving on one side or the other in a new country, but a change several times a day was confusing.

House had introduced us to the Coudenhoves in New York, and I shared his doubts that the Pan-Europa movement, of which the Count was the founder and devoted proponent, was practicable. Since in addition I did not favor substituting regional alliances for the general provisions of the League Covenant, I had not become one of Pan-Europa's sponsors. Despite this, the Coudenhoves could not have been more friendly when we reached Vienna, and later on we paid them a short visit in their lovely Alpine chalet. Ida Roland had just had a terrific row with the Burgtheater, where she had been scheduled to play *L'Aiglon.* She fell and hurt her arm while rehearsing, and the theatre took the postponement as an excuse to cancel the production, which had been arousing violent protests in conservative circles because of Rostand's thrusts at Metternich and the Viennese Court. Now she was talking of resigning from the Burgtheater and suing for damages, but the quarrel did not go so far. With a lithe, boyish figure she had an advantage as the young Duc de Reichstadt in skin-tight breeches over Sarah Bernhardt, who had created the role when she was fifty-six. My father had taken me as a boy to see Bernhardt in an act of *L'Aiglon* during one of her "final" American tours. He was saddened that the old magic of her voice as he remembered it from Paris was gone; I was disappointed too, but pleased to be able to say I "had seen" the divine Sarah. As I never saw Ida Roland on the stage I cannot compare them, but while I do not suppose she rivaled Bernhardt in the exacting role of *L'Aiglon* she achieved an enormous success in it. Offstage she was temperamental but also amusing and kind-hearted. She treated Coudenhove-Kalergi like a small child, did not much understand his political views but supported them passionately.

We had many visits back and forth with the Redlichs and also saw something of Dr. Benedikt, editor of the *Neue Freie Presse,* who lived not far away on a steeply ascending road named Himmelstrasse. Both Redlich and Benedikt were in a pessimistic frame of mind. The Dawes Plan regulating German reparations would, they thought, fail. This would mean ruin for Germany; America would be liked there less than ever for seeming to do much and being found not to have done enough; and Dawes, pipe and all, would be burnt in effigy in the Potsdamerplatz. The prediction was wrong, for the Dawes Plan worked so well that many of the controls over German finance could be relaxed in the new Young Plan. The future of Austria was painted all in black; Redlich's opposition to *Anschluss* was still as strong as it had been the year before but he was more dubious whether it could be defeated. Both were critical of Stresemann's treaty of friendship with the Soviets, fearing it would free Germany to blackmail France and thus head Europe toward a new conflict despite the promises made at Locarno.

Dr. Gottfried Kunwald was ex-Chancellor Seipel's crony and, some said, evil genius. He was at any rate a man who made a great play of being omniscient and mysterious. When I called on him in his rooms in a baroque palace on the Stephans-Platz he was dressed in a flowing black silk gown with floppy white cuffs which he swept grandly across the desk as he talked. He confirmed that union with Germany was being more and more looked to as the only way out of Austria's blind alley but claimed that at heart Seipel was as thoroughly opposed to it as he was himself, only Seipel could not admit it since it was the only card left in Austria's hand. Most Austrians wanted union for economic reasons, but it had political attractions also. The Socialists, seeing that though they had Vienna in their hands they could never get control of Austria, had begun playing for *Anschluss* in the hope of gaining power in combination with the German trade unions. The conservatives in Vienna, Lower Austria and Styria had been quietly opposed, but now, as the industrial situation worsened, they had come around to believing that they might find new outlets for their products in a Greater Germany.

"This is a mistake," said Kunwald. "Northern Germans despise southerners and are in fact the stronger—stronger materially, stronger technically, stronger on the world scene, stronger, if you like, brutally. We would be gobbled up not just territorially and industrially but culturally and morally too—in everything, that is, that gives us distinction."

The Czechs, always jealous of Vienna, had failed, he said, to help Austria and now Foreign Minister Beneš was maneuvering with Poland and Italy to put her in a strait-jacket. "They will end not by getting an advantage over Vienna but by being taken over by Berlin." He looked on Mussolini, who had refused to make a treaty with Austria unless Italy were the only state so privileged, as the greatest troublemaker of all. "He wants to help us by eating us," he said. "Everyone around us is hungry, but the Italians can't excuse their appetite as the Germans can by pointing out that they are of the same race."

The Hapsburgs he dismissed as a political factor, more in commiseration than bitterness. "The war was not their fault. They simply didn't have adequate talents for avoiding it or, when it came, carrying the Empire through to safety." Hungary might want them back, Austria never.

When I saw ex-Chancellor Seipel a couple of days later I was not sure but that in some respects Kunwald was, contrary to rumor, a good rather than a bad influence. Seipel made a distinctly less favorable impression than he had the year before. True, he then had seemed a little too smooth, a little too wary. Now he was in addition more frankly reactionary, as came out sharply when I referred to Mussolini as a danger to peace. Yes, he said, a danger perhaps, but only one of the dangers, the chief one being Bolshevism. Then, unlike Kunwald, he began praising Mussolini for his strong personality and energetic reforms. If Fascism could be divorced from extreme nationalism it would prove a marvelous force for the good of the world; which struck me like saying that French dressing is good if one leaves out the vinegar. And in reply to a question whether Mussolini's reported efforts to line up Poland and Hungary as allies in Central Europe, thereby putting a squeeze on Austria, had not been the subject of discussion during Count Skrzyński's recent visit to Vienna, he denied that the Polish Prime Minister had come on any sort of political mission at all.

Now I had seen Count Skrzyński during his visit and had asked him whether Mussolini's apparent effort to get a firm grip on Austria had come up in his talks with the Austrian Government. Of course, he replied, but he thought Mussolini's eyes were now turning toward Ethiopia and Asia Minor, especially since England had agreed that western Ethiopia was to be an Italian sphere of influence. The answer clearly implied that Poland had refused to play Mussolini's game in Central Europe, and I deduced that this was the reason Seipel now felt at liberty to admire Mussolini at home without much fear that his policies abroad would threaten Austria.

Marcel Fodor, the *Manchester Guardian*'s correspondent, interpreted Skrzyński's visit to Vienna as signaling a victory for Foreign Minister Beneš of Czechoslovakia, who had been urging Poland to adopt a benevolent attitude toward Austria. Beneš' argument had been that to force Austria to make a choice between Italy and Germany would be bad for both Poland and Czechoslovakia, whichever the result; and he ridiculed the promise of assistance against Germany which Mussolini offered Poland as a quid pro quo as being worthless in view of Italy's military weakness. Beneš' attitude in the affair obviously had been dictated by self-interest rather than by kindly feelings for Austria, but it disproved Kunwald's theory that Czechoslovak aims were incongruous with Austria's and that Beneš was constantly looking for ways to do Austria in.

24

Summer in Slovenia

Vienna became hot, my book was finished except for a chapter on the Little Entente, and after an exploratory visit we set off by train for Bled, a village on a lovely lake in Slovenia, just over the Karawanken Mountains from the Austrian town of Klagenfurt. The journey was as unadventurous as any journey can be with a child of two and half years. We had canvassed several other sites but decided that Bled had the greatest attractions. For one thing, it was one of the most beautiful places we had ever seen. The fields around our little chalet, pink with cyclamen, sloped down to a lake of the deepest blue, suggesting coolness and endless depth. In the center was an islet with a tiny church, an attraction throughout the pious countryside because its Madonna could promise husbands to girls, children to wives, indeed almost anything a suppliant could desire. Almost, because when we rowed my daughter out there and she pulled the bell rope, the signal that a wish was being made, she was indignant that a cup of coffee for me didn't come sliding down. Across the lake a picture-postcard castle crowned a high rock and beyond rose a series of hills and ridges culminating in the snow-capped Triglav, the highest peak in the Julian Alps.

An hour's drive into the mountains toward the Triglav lay another lake, Bohinjsko Jezero, even bluer, deeper and colder than Bled, fed by the little Savica, parent of the River Sava, which gushed roaring from a steeply enclosed ravine a mile or so beyond. Between the source and the lake the Savica teemed with trout, reserved for the King, but since he did not care for the sport he later gave us permission to fish this and his other streams as much as we liked, to the delight of the old warden, who usually waited all summer without having a chance to entice out the fish of noble size lurking in the pools where huge mossy boulders momentarily hemmed in the rush of water. We often would motor out to Bohinj in the late afternoon, catch a dozen fish before sunset, and an hour later be eating *truite au bleu* that were no relative at all of the pulpy restaurant fish from tepid lakes and streams.

But I must get along to the reasons that made Bled, such unexpected pleasures aside, a place where I could spend part of the summer to advantage. For one thing, when King Alexander moved there out of the heat of Belgrade, followed gladly by the diplomatic corps, it became the summer capital of Jugoslavia. This year, moreover, it was to be the focus of political activities in which I was particularly interested, for the Foreign Ministers of the three Little Entente states were to meet there for a conference.

Secondly, as German was the second language in Slovenia, I soon was able to find a teacher, Captain Karl Mysz, a former officer of the Austro-Hungarian Navy. Captain Mysz had courtly manners, which he did not relax even after we became very good friends. To make up for being short in stature he held himself very erect and whenever we met bowed from the waist. He felt it his primary responsibility, however much I might explain and protest, to prepare me to conduct myself properly in polite society. This meant instructing me in the use of such phrases as "Ich habe die Ehre, Herr Doktor," and "Würden Sie mich bitte dem Herrn Geheimrat vorstellen?" So after I had done a stint of writing in the morning we would sit on the terrace overlooking the lake and exchange the rounded phrases of a vanished day, never to be useful in mine. As I do not have much aptitude for languages I can't judge how much greater my advance in German would have been under a teacher less polite, more willing to pound into me the essentials of a modern vocabulary. But when I found how much his modest fee meant to him I could not have turned him off in any case.

Coolidge assured me that he was not cynical enough to suppose that we picked Bled because of my liking for Jugoslavia, meaning that of course he did so suppose. Later in the summer he suddenly decided that he was going to make a flying visit to Europe, leaving the office in Malcolm Davis' competent hands. I induced him to pay us a visit; and when he had caught his trout, met the Foreign Ministers, had a talk with the King and motored to Zagreb with us to see Meštrović he professed himself in agreement with our choice and even thought I had not done too badly in the hands of Captain Mysz.

Soon after the Grouichs arrived to visit us, motoring all the way from Madrid, a gendarme came with an invitation to dine at the palace. The talk was not political, and when dinner was over an American movie was shown, something about Bogg's hogs, which fortunately seemed not to imply any insults to the great-grandson of Kara George, dealer in swine and cattle. At first Queen Marie was shy but gradually relaxed to the point where she told us that when her mother Queen Marie of Rumania had come recently for a visit little Prince Peter greeted her with "Granny, you *are* getting old." This was too much for her, since the goodbye of her other grandson, Prince Michael of Rumania, had been, "When you get back I'm going to plant you in the garden so you can come up *new.*" She had taken to bed with a cold and stayed there till she left.

The three Little Entente Foreign Ministers, Ninchich of Jugoslavia, Beneš of Czechoslovakia and Mitilineau of Rumania, arrived in Bled late in June for the conference. It was interesting in talking with them to note that they were modifying their ideas just as Seipel, Redlich and others in Vienna were doing.

Ninchich had been pursuing his attempt to put relations with Italy on a solidly friendly basis, but was not sure with what success; agreements had been reached on consular and commercial matters, but his plan for a Balkan Locarno had been rejected. The optimism which Jugoslavs had felt following the Fiume settlement had definitely waned. I mentioned to Beneš the deepening pessimism and trend toward reaction evident in Vienna, the increasing sentiment for *Anschluss* in industrial circles and Seipel's new caution in discussing it. Was this the result of Austria's waning hope that the Little Entente would do anything to ease her economic difficulties? Beneš retorted (in contrast to what he had said the year before) that it would be quite possible to work out a system of special commercial arrangements among all the Danubian countries, including Austria and Hungary, if it were not for the opposition of the major European powers. For example, the moment Czechoslovakia broached the idea of exchanging tariff concessions with Hungary or Austria, there would come a "me too" demand from Italy, Britain and France. "I'm ready to help Austria or Hungary," he said impatiently, "but not Sicily or Lancashire." He characterized Italy's greed as especially monumental; when there were responsibilities to be undertaken she was absent; when there were benefits to be secured she insisted on sharing in them as a Successor State.

Going back to a favorite topic, the old system of European alliances, Beneš said it was evil because it rested on the theory that all parties assumed mutual responsibilities—you take all my difficulties as yours and I take all your difficulties as mine. This was an immoral system, for you had to assume responsibilities which you might not at all approve of; worse, it didn't work, and he cited Italy's disregard of her obligations toward her partners in the Triple Alliance. The Little Entente on the contrary excluded promises of joint action against dangers which were not common to all three members. The fact that it was limited in scope meant that it would continue to exist as long as a vestige of its declared purposes was in danger.

II

Living in an old country house outside Bled was Dr. Ivan Shvegel, an admirer of Americans and especially President Wilson, after whom he had named his place "Villa Wilsonia." He was by nature an opposition-ist, sometimes for bad but more often for right reasons. His house was full of mementos of his uncle, Baron von Schwegel, a Slovene by birth but educated as an Austrian, who had been a high official in the Foreign Ministry in Vienna. Shvegel had un-Germanized the name as much as possible and renounced the title, or at any rate did not use it, because of his dislike of all things Austrian. Before the war he had been Austro-Hungarian Consul-General in Chicago but had been bounced for his Slav sympathies. He was a violent, arrogant, picturesque character, gen-erous and hospitable, rather pathetic in his heirless solitude, pondering resentfully the wrongs perpetuated by ruling classes—in former days by Austrians and Hungarians, now by Serbians—against the Slovenes and Croats, and by all exploiters of peasants and other helpless folk. (He did not foresee, fortunately, that after the next war the Communists would seize Villa Wilsonia and drive him to spend his last years in the stable.) He had hated the feudalistic structure of society under the Hapsburgs and now hated the ineptness and inefficiency of the new Jugoslav society. All around him he saw corruption, real and imagined, and considered every tax and cramping regulation retaliation for his having denounced it. He was interesting not only for his political information, expressed with impartial frankness, but also for his vast knowledge of the history, ethnography and art of the Jugoslav peoples.

Shvegel's liking for Americans had begun in Chicago but became cen-tered on Wilson at Paris, where he had been an adviser to the Jugoslav delegation on Trieste, Fiume, Klagenfurt and other problems inter-twined with his family traditions and his own passionate concerns. One of the most prolonged disputes had been over this very corner of north-western Slovenia where Shvegel lived, the so-called "Assling triangle," formed by the Karawanken Mountains on the north and the Julian Alps on the south. This is the region where German, Slav and Italian meet, but the triangle itself is inhabited overwhelmingly by Slovenes. Austria wanted it, and Italy wanted Austria to have it if she could not get it herself; for either way the segment of the Klagenfurt-Trieste railway which crossed the territory would be kept out of Jugoslav hands. For strategic reasons, however, the Peace Conference was disinclined to bring Austria over the Karawanken divide into the Sava River valley, and this plus the strong ethnic argument resulted in the decision to leave the triangle as part of Slovenia. In contrast, the dispute over the Klagenfurt area just to the north had been left to settlement by a plebiscite. Shvegel said he had been amazed by the resulting victory there for Austria. He had recognized that the factors as reported by Sherman Miles (noted in an earlier chapter) were strong, but what he had not foreseen was the republicanism of the peasants, who after living under the Hapsburgs preferred a future in an Austrian Republic to the idea of joining a new monarchy.

The politics of Jugoslavia disgusted Shvegel. He could not stand Pashich, thought Davidovich weak and hated Father Korošec's reactionary Slovene clericals. His only alternative was to join Radić's Croat Peasant party, and this he was about to do. He said that Radić, by now reconciled to Pashich, a member of the cabinet and an enthusiastic monarchist, had been staying at Villa Wilsonia recently in order to attend an audience with King Alexander. When he returned the following week would we come to dinner with him? Of course, I said eagerly.

On the agreed evening I arrived at Villa Wilsonia a bit in advance to meet Radić for what Shvegel said would be a quiet talk. Quiet and Radić were incompatible. He imprisoned my hand in a moist grip, and as sentence after sentence flowed on, well lubricated by saliva, he gave it a squeeze to emphasize each point. In looks he was exactly what the cartoons had depicted—short, round-bellied, with a rather foxy pointed nose and a projecting little beard. His nearsighted eyes blurred an expression that would otherwise have been watchful. His sight was so bad that when I offered him a cigarette in order to get back my hand he first tried to stick it into the wrong end of his holder and then when he had gotten it into the right end put the cigarette instead of the holder into his mouth. He was the pattern of the demagogue, first saying what he thought you would like to hear and then believing it because he had said it, ending by being swept along on the tide of words to the point where he was simply exhilarated by the noise he was making. Bits of what he said about the virtues of villagers and the deviltry that went on in cities were intelligible, but at the end you felt you had been read to from a badly-bound book in which odd pages made sense but the story as a whole did not.

During dinner Radić gulped down his wine and my impression that he had no idea who we were became a certainty. When he asked to be allowed to toast the foreign guests Shvegel agreed reluctantly, foreseeing that we were in for an oration. Forty-five minutes later Radić arrived at the toast: "To Wilson and all the English." There was present an old gentleman named Vlado Georgevich, who had been Prime Minister of Serbia under the Obrenovich dynasty, disliked all Croats and was very Austrophile. He listened to Radić with disgust and kept murmuring to my wife that it was not the right society in which to invite foreign ladies of distinction. When Shvegel in turn raised his glass to him Georgevich merely responded, without rising, "I remain seated in the presence of our Croatian Demosthenes," a compliment with which Radić was enchanted.

III

Not long afterward word came that King Alexander would receive me in audience at the palace, a not very imposing yellow stucco villa on the edge of the lake. While I was waiting on the terrace little Crown Prince Peter came along, dragging a toy train, followed by Miss Bell, his governess. He came straight up and asked me to go inside and play something for him on the piano. I responded with a one-finger performance of "Nelly Bly" while he watched the hammers hit the strings. When I was summoned upstairs to the King's study he gave me a kiss for my daughter.

The King said he had heard of my meeting with Radić and asked how he had impressed me. With his enthusiasm and underlying sincerity, I said; but his anxiety to please made you wonder where sincerity ended and demagoguery took over. This was the reason, the King said, that he never could rely on him; one day, because he thought it popular, he would abuse the monarchy, the next, to please him, he would protest his personal devotion. Nevertheless, said the King, the political situation had changed in the year since we had last talked, and for the better. Then there had been a conflict between the Croats and the Serbs; now there was a dispute between Croatian and Serbian politicians. Having once compromised, Radić could never return to quite his former intransigence; Pashich, though he did not believe that Radić's *volte-face* was sincere, had had to accept it as such and had been forced to yield part of his power—which, in the King's opinion, he had held far too narrowly and stubbornly to suit the modern day. Since both Pashich and Radić had lost some of their influence national unity was no longer in danger.

What was worrying him most, the King continued, was Italy's maneuvering in the Balkans, especially the trouble she was stirring up in Bulgaria and Albania. Everything indicated that she had no idea of establishing peaceful relations with Jugoslavia but intended to prolong what was in effect only an armistice. Under Italian influence Bulgaria had refused Jugoslavia's suggestion of a pact of nonaggression and friendship and lately irrefutable evidence had come that Italy was financing stepped-up *komitadji* raids into Serbian Macedonia. The Jugoslav General Staff now had to face the question where it could resist Italy on one front and Bulgaria on another. Either could be faced confidently, but to deal with both simultaneously would be difficult. He asked me directly whether I thought Italy planned to make war. I could only say that one never knew with dictators: often when they had troubles at home they created diversions abroad. In Mussolini's case, his craving for grandeur might lead him to jump into Asia Minor, Albania, Ethiopia or anywhere else that an excuse or opportunity offered. He repeated the question in a meditative tone and answered it himself: the likelihood that Italy wanted war was difficult to believe, yet too much pointed that way for it to be ignored.

Italy, he went on, had put Albania in her pocket. Jugoslavia had treated Albanian Prime Minister Ahmed Zogu in a friendly way but could not afford to give him the funds he demanded for founding an Albanian National Bank, developing railways and so on. Mussolini was only too delighted to do so in return for a stranglehold on the Albanian economy, finance and, as a result, foreign policy. Jugoslavia would like nothing better than to see Albania develop into a prosperous sovereign state, but if it was to be an Italian wedge driven into the eastern coast of the Adriatic the strategic problem for Jugoslavia would become difficult indeed.

The King emphasized that, although the Little Entente had the capacity to keep peace in the Danube Valley, it had only indirect value in strengthening Jugoslavia to meet an Italian challenge. And even in the Danube Valley it was strong only because of the power and determination of Jugoslavia and Czechoslovakia. It was a sad fact that the Rumanian Army was inefficient and that the governing clique in Bucharest was concerned only with their personal fortunes. His father-in-law, King Ferdinand, took no interest in his nation's problems and in any case had no power to influence how they were handled; he himself never talked with Ferdinand about Rumanian politics and it would be quite useless to make the attempt as he was so uninformed and indifferent.

As proof that he had to assume Italian hostility King Alexander referred to Ninchich's effort the preceding winter to secure Italian and French support for stabilizing the Balkan status quo. As Mussolini seemed to indicate preliminary approval, Ninchich went to Paris to discuss the project with Briand; it suited France perfectly, Briand said, and he promised to proceed whenever Jugoslavia was ready. But then the Italian Ambassador in Paris, Baron Avezzana, informed Ninchich on instructions from Rome that if France participated Italy would not; further, that if the two went ahead alone Italy would "remake the whole fabric of her European treaties." The threat forced Jugoslavia to let the plan lapse. Immediately afterward, Bulgaria became actively hostile.

Briand's complacent attitude toward Italy's behavior had shown King Alexander how little he understood Italian policies and how little he cared about Balkan problems. He seemed to be as much taken in by Mussolini's talk in contrast to his actions as Sir Austen Chamberlain was. If Briand had been clever he would have seen that Mussolini was not simply hostile to Jugoslavia as an obstacle to his expansionist plans but jealous of France herself. It was good that he had been replaced by Poincaré, a man of character, who had followed Balkan developments for years with particular care and who understood the deep currents of European politics in a historical sense. Briand promised much and performed little, whereas Poincaré promised little but performed exactly what he promised. The King expected to go to Paris himself in the autumn or winter but hoped I might meanwhile have a chance to see Poincaré and give him a preliminary report of his views.

As my résumé indicates, King Alexander could provide more information in an hour or two than a dozen ministers could in a week. It was clear from the precision of his thought (and his conclusions) why Poincaré had praised him to me as "le premier chef d'état de l'Europe." It was clear, too, why the leaders of Fascist Italy and Hungary came to see him as the chief obstacle to their scheme for securing control of the Balkans, determined to remove him, and eventually hired and trained a band of Croats to assassinate him at Marseilles in 1934.

IV

I seized one of the last days before Coolidge's arrival to drive down to Selče, on the Adriatic coast, to inspect the home for Jugoslav orphans founded by Mme. Grouich and supported by a committee which I had formed in New York and to which General Bliss had been persuaded to lend his name as chairman. I crossed the Italian frontier at Postumia, near the famous Adelsberg grottoes, a series of immense chambers, one of them over 150 feet high, hung with stalactites and threaded by a silent river that might be the Styx. Earlier in the summer we had gone there on an expedition organized by General Bodrero, the Italian Minister, who provided sumptuous fare both before and after the three-mile walk through the nether regions. Fiume, which I reached by mid-afternoon, seemed to have picked up very little since my visit there two years before; in spite of the splendid facilities, the docks were idle. I crossed by a new bridge to Sušak, where the controversial Baroš Basin had been enlarged and new freight yards built to handle the booming Croatian lumber trade.

At Selče there was time before dinner for a swim and afterward for a row with some of the older children in the *Gregor,* named after my daughter. Phosphorescent streaks trailed behind our oars, competing with the lights of fishermen off the dimly outlined island of Krk. In the morning I examined the ledgers, went over the premises and was greeted by the children, about fifty in number, the girls in neat blue dresses, the boys in shorts. They sang "My Country 'Tis of Thee" with much enthusiasm and about as much feeling as can be put into a purely phonetical rendering. Each group stayed at the home for four weeks, and since its opening over a thousand children, mostly orphans or half-orphans of soldiers killed in the war, had been given a seaside holiday, nourishing food and a set of clothes. Mme. Grouich's aim was not merely to give needy children a physical and moral pickup but by having them chosen impartially by social-service groups in all regions of the country to bring young representatives of the main Jugoslav races and religions into intimate contact. The home was run by Mme. Dedijer, widow of a well-known geographer who during the war had been on Dr. Grouich's staff in the Serbian Legation in Switzerland preparing maps and statistics to substantiate Jugoslav claims at the Paris Peace Conference. Mme. Grouich had brought her to Selče to act as matron and manager of the home, along with her two young sons, Steve and Vlado, both of whom afterward joined Tito's partisan fighters and later became distinguished, one in science, the other as a historian and biographer of Tito.

The Grouichs insisted that I return to Bled by way of the Plitvička Lakes, and they agreed to accompany me. First we drove south along the aromatic coast as far as Senj, a former pirate nest whence swift galleys used to prey on Ragusan argosies and Venetian galleons. There we turned up and up and up over the Velebit Mountains by a formidable zigzag road of loose, sharp rocks, then down into the valley of the Lika, an isolated region wholly Serb in population although forming part of Croatia. At sunset we came to the first of the chain of Plitvička Lakes, hemmed in by mountains, connected by a series of cascades, each lake its own distinctive hue of greenish blue. The next day's journey was even more of a test for my Fiat, for the roads alternately were deep in mud up to the axles or led steeply up bare mountainsides where hardly a track could be seen in the windswept dust. The Grouichs left me in the afternoon at a station on the railway to Fiume and I was back in Bled by midnight. There I found Coolidge, who had just arrived after a visit to Ambassador Houghton in Scotland and stops in Berlin, Copenhagen, Warsaw and Vienna.

Meštrović was working in Zagreb that summer on the great equestrian Indians to be placed in Grant Park in Chicago, and he suggested that we motor down to see the preliminary studies. Alongside his seventeenth-century house, sparsely but beautifully furnished, he had built a large studio, none too large, however, to accommodate the two heroic-sized Indians and their muscular steeds. He had chosen the subject because he vaguely associated the Indians of the plains with his favorite legendary Serbian heroes, in particular Marko Kraljevich and his fabled horse Sharats. In the center of the studio a sort of skeleton Trojan horse was being built up of lathe and wire. One of the Indians was already in plaster. The head had an almost Assyrian cast of countenance, fierce and disdainful; the lines of the upraised arms and of the horse's head and foreleg, all parallel, conveyed perfectly synchronized control; the thighs and legs, every muscle tense, grasped the horse's flanks as the rider drew back to thrust his spear at the enemy.

Prince Paul, King Alexander's first cousin and perhaps only intimate friend, had a small chalet at Bohinj, set on a knoll deep in pine woods through which a vista had been cut toward the lake and the Triglav, here closer and even more imposing than as seen from Bled.

The cousins differed in almost every respect. Whereas Alexander was a man of energy, decisiveness and absolute courage, essentially Serb, Paul was contemplative, cultivated and sensitive, European and cosmopolitan.

A man of Prince Paul's tastes and characteristics found very little to occupy himself with in Jugoslavia. Though the King saw much of him he did not ask him to take part in political life, and I never saw any indication that Paul attempted to advise the King on political matters. One reason the King did not turn to him was undoubtedly that Paul found politics quite uncongenial, but another must have been that political leaders would have been jealous of the influence of anyone so obviously in the King's confidence. The King's omission to bring Paul into the mainstream of national life was a grievous error. The effort might not have been profitable at the time and might have entailed some difficulties, but the fact that he remained without political experience was a handicap on him and a tragedy for the country when, following King Alexander's assassination, he became Regent for young King Peter. He found himself unprepared for the ordeal of dealing with Hitler; and, faced finally with the dreadful choice whether Jugoslavia should or should not fight, even if it meant another ordeal like that of 1914, he accepted the advice of weak ministers and then, overruled in a coup by determined generals and other leaders, left the country.

In less harrowing circumstances Prince Paul's natural qualities showed themselves to advantage. He had excellent taste, and chose the best works of representative Jugoslav artists for the art museum which he founded and largely supported in Belgrade. At one time I tried to persuade King Alexander to create a commission for the preservation of national art treasures and to put Prince Paul in charge of it. The main purpose would have been to safeguard the ancient monasteries and churches scattered throughout old Serbia and Macedonia and in particular to preserve and restore their superb frescoes, dating from as early as the twelfth century, many of which were in a dilapidated state and always in danger of mutilation. The riches and civilized amenities which had produced them before the Serbs lost their independence at Kosovo had not returned with the mere physical disappearance of the Turks, and the poverty-stricken local priests had neither the wit nor the funds to restore their sacred buildings. What had moldered for five centuries was moldering still and, worse, might at any moment be damaged out of sheer ignorance, as I saw in the monastery of Grachanitsa, on Kosovo Plain, where a priest had cut windows through twelfth-century frescoes. But the King said that the Orthodox Church would bitterly resent any interference with its prerogatives; he would remonstrate with the Patriarch, but he was not in a position to take any formal action which would add a feud with the bishops to his other difficulties.

Prince Paul's favorite cities were Munich and especially Florence, where he had a close friendship with Bernard Berenson. When we took Coolidge over to Bohinj to lunch with him and his beautiful wife, Princess Olga, a daughter of Prince Nicholas of Greece and a Russian Grand Duchess, he talked discriminatingly about the pictures at Fenway Court, in Boston, belonging to Coolidge's aunt, Mrs. "Jack" Gardner, although he had seen only photographs of them. Most of them had been bought on Berenson's recommendation. It likewise was on Berenson's advice that Paul had acquired El Greco's "Laocoön," which hung over the mantelpiece in the sitting room of his house at Topchider, outside Belgrade. I was told later that the price had been $45,000.

This magnificent and now celebrated picture reached its present place of honor in the National Gallery of Art in Washington only because of the timidity of the Art Institute of Chicago. In the summer of 1934, Prince Paul wrote me that an art dealer in Paris had told him that "a Mr. McCormick," a patron of the Chicago Art Museum, had expressed an interest in buying the "Laocoön"; and the dealer had offered on the spot to buy it from Prince Paul for twenty thousand pounds, obviously with the intention of reselling it at a large profit. Prince Paul had declined the offer and was now writing me to see if I could find out whether there was indeed a prospective buyer in Chicago and if so to tell him to write to him direct; he saw no reason why either the museum or he should pay a dealer's large commission. In reply to my inquiry, the director of the museum wrote me that he well remembered seeing the picture when it was in the hands of a New York dealer, Paul Rosenberg, and also when it was on exhibition at the National Gallery in London. "It certainly is a grand affair," he said.

The fact that nothing came of this correspondence was not due, as I understand it, to disagreement as to price. Prince Paul told me afterward that the Chicago Institute decided to hold to its rule of buying pictures only through dealers in order to protect itself with a guarantee of authenticity—a rather ludicrous precaution in this case in view of the fame of the "Laocoön" and its known history. When Prince Paul did eventually sell it to the National Gallery of Art the price was much more than twenty thousand pounds. The director, my friend John Walker, told me that the asking price—$450,000—was paid without haggling and was, at that, "one of the great art bargains of all time."

V

While we were engrossed at Bled mainly with Balkan problems—inflammable enough to start world wars but not Europe's chief preoccupation at the moment—desperate efforts were being made at Geneva and in the European chancelleries to find the basis for something more than an uneasy truce between Germany and France, the two hereditary enemies in the heart of the continent. For my part, I had been spending some time gathering bits of evidence on the war-guilt question, currently being exploited to support German and Hungarian demands for treaty revision, but not a central concern at the moment either.

The first bridge across the gulf separating Germany and France had been the agreements reached at Locarno in October, 1925, but they were to come into force only when Germany entered the League of Nations. The first effort to bring this about had failed. Germany had been urged to apply for admission, but when a special meeting of the League Assembly was held in March, 1926, to act on the application it rejected her requirement for a seat on the Council along with other Great Power members. This disaster was caused by demands from Spain and Brazil, and less urgently from Poland, that if Germany secured a permanent Council seat they must also. The Assembly refused and adjourned without fulfilling its purpose. Germany was so angered that she turned back to the policy of cooperation with Russia adopted at Rapallo in 1922; a German-Soviet neutrality pact immediately followed.

The summer of 1926 thus became a period of international crisis. France and Italy, in competition for control of the western Mediterranean, were moving troops to the Franco-Italian border. Italy made no bones about coveting the Riviera, and Fascist militiamen massed on the frontier were shouting to each other:

> "For whom Nice the Beautiful?" *"Per Noi!"*
> "For whom the shrapnel?" "The French!"

Tension was increased by Mussolini's maneuvers to gain a predominant position in the Balkans. Europe seemed about to be split into two irreconcilable camps.

In September, when the League was preparing a last attempt to ward off this threat, I motored Coolidge from Bled to Geneva to watch what would happen. We went by the magnificent route via Tarvis to Cortina d'Ampezzo and thence over the Vorarlberg into Switzerland. We saw heavy concentrations of artillery on the Italian side of the Jugoslav-Italian border, but no troops of any sort on the Jugoslav side; nor, when we crossed the Austrian frontier, was a single Austrian uniform to be seen. The customs officers on the western border of Liechtenstein were insulted that we had failed to notice that we were entering the country and sent us back to make a proper entry before they would let us exit.

Geneva was speculating excitedly whether this time Germany's conditions for acquiring League membership would be accepted; if it was not done now she would certainly assume that she was to remain an outcast from Western society and would play a vengeful role in collusion with Communist Russia. Elaborate plans for satisfying Spain short of electing her a permanent Council member failed, as did the effort to persuade Brazil to remain on the Council as a nonpermanent member. Both threatened to resign from the League altogether if their demands were rejected. But this time the Assembly refused to be blackmailed; and after their actual resignations were announced (they later reconsidered), Germany's former enemies rose one by one and voted "Yes."

The entry of the German Foreign Minister, Gustav Stresemann, into the Salle de Réformation, where the Assembly was meeting, did not provide the drama that might have been expected after such anguished suspense and given the historic importance of the event. He and his delegation filed in quietly and unsmilingly, to only a scattering of polite applause. Ninchich, who had just been elected president of the Assembly, gave them an official welcome in a few cordial but guarded sentences. As Stresemann walked heavily to the rostrum the double chin on the back of his neck bulged redly. Hugh Gibson, our Minister to Switzerland, no lover of Germans, whispered, "A typical square head." But Stresemann gave his speech with dignity, though in a hard, almost harsh voice, skirting successfully subjects of recrimination, such as war guilt, war crimes and reparations. He was warmly though not enthusiastically applauded.

Briand followed. The two were contrasts in every respect—in looks, in manner of speech and probably in subtle objective: Stresemann the pragmatist, the nonrhetorician, making few and wooden gestures, inaugurating a carefully thought-out program, very Teutonic; Briand the *illusionist,* the rhapsodist, his elbows and shoulders fluid with emotion as he invoked the reconciliation of the two nations in general and generous terms, very Gallic. Briand's task was harder than Stresemann's. Stresemann had to refrain from saying the wrong thing; Briand had to say the right thing. He did it, while avoiding the flaw of sentimentality that often ran through his oratory. Nobody grudged him the undertone of triumph that at last what he had been working for seemed to be coming true.

Geneva was crowded with celebrities, and the struggle to get into the meetings was ferocious. More Americans clamored for tickets (among them no less than fifty professors) than citizens of all the nations actually belonging to the League put together. Coolidge, who was staying with

Hugh Gibson, gained admission through him, and Arthur Bullard was able to get me a regular press ticket. Bullard was one of the several Americans who had eventually joined the League Secretariat despite the abstention of the U.S. Government, and like two of his colleagues, Arthur Sweetser and Huntington Gilchrist, performed valuable services.

One participant who seemed out of place in such a conglomeration of opposites as was meeting in Geneva was Radić, sent there as an associate delegate in a canny move by the Jugoslav Government to involve him in its foreign policy. Coolidge and I had an hour's talk with him, or rather he gave us an hour's speech, which quite stunned Coolidge, who had never encountered such a gale of words accompanied by so much spray. He expressed himself as a wholehearted admirer of King Alexander but he left his real intentions as regards Jugoslav politics unclear, partly by design, no doubt, but more, I thought, because they varied so rapidly that he did not remember at what point he was momentarily at rest. He said he welcomed Stalin's increasing grip on power in Russia. Coolidge and I were not sure whether this was because or in spite of Stalin's new policy of "socialism in one country," but thought probably the former because it betokened less Communist activity in the Balkans at a time when Radić himself was trying to shed the Communist label.

Among many others, I saw a great deal of André Géraud, and began to understand why his articles signed "Pertinax" had such influence in Europe and why he had many enemies. He was free of the vices of most French journalists and commentators: he was not ambiguous, he was not conformist, he did not mute criticism, he did not write for literary effect. Happily he had his likings as well as his antipathies, and he included me among them. One afternoon he took me out to Maurice de Rothschild's tremendous château near Geneva, with vast formal gardens, greenhouses, birdhouses and artificial cascades, where conversation with the dullest people imaginable was compensated for by the finest peaches and nectarines I ever tasted. By further way of variety, Professor Manley Hudson of the Harvard Law School, staunchest advocate of America's accepting the compulsory jurisdiction of the World Court, took a group of friends out to dinner one evening at a delightful little restaurant just across the French border, but his efforts to lead the somewhat staid company in barefoot dancing on the dewy lawn afterward did not meet with much success. Salvador de Madariaga, brilliant but irritatingly metaphysical in his political ideas, enjoyed the scene in cynical detachment.

My stop in Paris on the way home was mainly to see Poincaré, who had formed his ministry of "National Union" at the end of July and (as described earlier) was already moving successfully to reestablish faith in the franc. He spent more time at the Ministry of Finance in the Louvre than at the Présidence du Conseil, and it was there that he received me. I wondered how he would take Germany's entrance into the League, which meant that she must again be considered a subject and not an object of policy in Europe. He seemed thoroughly reconciled; indeed, he spoke as though he had in part inspired it. But the tone in which the new relationship with Germany was to be conducted, and how the Locarno agreements were to be applied, were not, he emphasized, to be settled by Briand alone. "M. Briand does not have a free hand at the Quai d'Orsai. The Council of Ministers decides." The intimation that he and Briand might not be able to collaborate for long was disquieting. Different as chalk and cheese, both seemed indispensable to France at the time.

One of the reasons Poincaré had given even partial support to Briand's efforts for a rapprochement with Germany was his mistrust of Italy. This became clear when he began questioning me about the Balkans. At my mention of King Alexander's fear that Briand did not realize the anti-French implications of Mussolini's refusal to join in a tripartite guarantee of the Danubian status quo Poincaré started visibly and said with great emphasis that at any rate *he* understood it. He then referred acidly to the unbridled language which Mussolini had been using about France in the past day or so, following an attempt on his life by an Italian émigré who had been living—"like a million other Italians"—in France. At this moment a secretary brought in a telegram over which Poincaré smiled, saying that it was a most mild and conciliatory reply to the congratulations which he had telegraphed Mussolini over his escape. I spoke then of the Jugoslav fear that Italy was getting a predominant position in Bulgaria, but commented that fortunately Count Bethlen's attitude toward Jugoslavia at the moment seemed friendly enough not to foreshadow Hungary's participation in the combination. Poincaré entirely disagreed. He said that even though Ninchich might be satisfied with Bethlen's professions of friendship he definitely was not. He would not state that Bethlen had been implicated personally in the great scandal of the day, the attempt to finance Hungary's revisionist propaganda by a wholesale counterfeiting of French francs, but he insisted that Bethlen had not handled the affair in good faith. "Hungary," he summed up, "remains one of the most disturbing factors in Europe."

The Bérenger story came up when I turned to the object of my visit, to secure his help in getting us the best possible writer on French finances. He remarked dryly that unlike Caillaux he would never have recommended Bérenger in the first place, and that we had not lost much when Morgan's persuaded him to recall his article. After going over a number of names, his recommendation was François-Marsal, former Premier and twice Minister of Finance, as someone not deeply committed either for or against the settlements reached by Caillaux in Washington. Eventually we procured a satisfactory if not brilliant article from him, stressing the difficulty that, whereas France's creditors would not consent to be paid in goods, Germany's reparations payments to France were precisely in merchandise.

My first day after crossing over to London was spent mostly at the Institute of International Affairs, inspecting with un-Christian envy its fine new quarters in Chatham House. I was particularly impressed with the development of the library, supported by a reference section and the beginnings of what would be a newspaper clipping file; and determined to get the latter going in New York if ever the Council could secure its own premises. The next day I had Professor Salvemini to lunch and was delighted to find that, partly with my help, he had arranged his passport difficulties and would be able to come to the United States to lecture the coming winter. His name headed the list of those declared by Mussolini to have forfeited Italian citizenship because of opposition to the dictatorship, and the State Department had hesitated to annoy the Italian Government by admitting him. But, remembering how strongly it had been criticized for its handling of the Károlyi affair, it was now wary of dealing arbitrarily with exiles of existing regimes merely because our government recognized those regimes; and when Senator Borah was induced to protest, it capitulated and put a visa on Salvemini's old passport. Salvemini said the principal aim of his lectures would be to combat the erroneous opinion that Fascism had saved Italy from Communism; that danger had already passed before the March on Rome.

There were several notables on the *Leviathan,* among them ex-Secretary Hughes and Will Rogers. Nobody noticed Hughes but Will Rogers was lionized, especially after he good-naturedly did his rope-twisting, gum-chewing stunt at the ship's concert. I found Hughes as fixedly anti-French as ever, even though he conceded that Briand had done well at Geneva and that Poincaré "had learnt a bit in the past year." He disclaimed any sympathy for Fascism but could not refrain from saying how much he thought Mussolini had done for Italy in forcibly restoring internal peace. He seemed surprised when I spoke of the offsetting dangers of Mussolini's adventurous foreign policy. My smug comment: "A very nice, honest man with banal views." Much of my time on shipboard was spent reading the third volume of Poincaré's memoirs, which he had given me; it was not as interesting as the earlier volumes, since by now he had become President of France and must tell the story of dress functions, visits to schools and orphanages, banquets for the King of Spain and such, but the thread of French policy running through it made it worthwhile. I also began Trevelyan's new history of England, lent me by Coolidge; I'd read nothing of his since the three *Garibaldis,* and was enchanted all over again with his combination of erudition and easy, flowing style.

Mounds of work were waiting at my office, but fortunately there was a few days' breathing spell before Coolidge returned. I was not able to meet him at the pier. But Malcolm Davis told me he came down the gangplank looking rather self-conscious, carrying a large Serbian doll which Ninchich had begged him to bring from his wife as a present for my daughter.

25

Light on the Assassination in Sarajevo

The discussion over who had been responsible for the war raged with increasing bitterness from 1925 on. Historians, partial and impartial, were turning up new evidence, and propagandists were using and misusing it to shift the blame from the shoulders of their particular clients. Accepted theories were being challenged and supported, not for the historical record so much as because the controversy provided arguments of immediate importance for slashing reparations payments and altering the territorial arrangements decreed at Paris.

The vast complex of moves and countermoves which culminated in the war cannot be broken down into neat national components. The Sarajevo assassination was only the proximate and not the deeper cause of the conflict; but it was the Balkan match that set the world conflagration going—rather, gave the excuse for it, according to Fritz Fischer's documented account.[1] After the war I talked with most of the Serbian officials who had played important roles in the decisive days of 1914. The information I gleaned is not of tremendous importance, but since my informants are now without exception dead and no further elucidation from them is possible I think I should add their testimony to the accumulated mass of historical evidence. Count Max Montgelas wrote in *The Case for the Central Powers* that the Great War (as we used to call it) ended with nobody knowing why it had been fought. If so, even slender threads that can be drawn from such a raveled skein are worth weaving into the final historical pattern.

1. Fritz Fischer, *Griff nach der Weltmacht.* Düsseldorf: Droste Verlag, 1961, revised edition (English translation, New York: Norton, 1967).

The "revisionist" historians of forty and more years ago made great play with a fifteen-page article written in 1924 by Ljuba Jovanovich, Serbian Minister of Education at the time of the Sarajevo assassination, in which he stated that late in May or early in June of 1914—that is to say, a few weeks before the crime—Premier Pashich had told him and several cabinet colleagues that he was aware of a plot to kill the Austrian Archduke. This disclosure, made in an obscure publication in Belgrade, *Krv Sloventsva* (*The Blood of Slavdom*), had at first passed largely unnoticed; but already when I saw King Alexander in March, 1925, we had spoken of it and I found that he knew of the angry letter written by the historian R. W. Seton-Watson a few weeks earlier to the London *Times* demanding that Pashich and Ljuba Jovanovich give a public explanation. The King said at that time that he could not understand how Ljuba Jovanovich could have written such a thing. He himself, he said, had been at every Council of Ministers in that period and "neither there nor elsewhere" had he heard "a single thing indicating that a plot was being prepared."

Ljuba Jovanovich's sensational story ran as follows. In April or May, 1914, he wrote, Pashich mentioned to some members of his cabinet that he had gotten word of a plan of some "people" to go to Sarajevo to kill the Archduke. It was agreed among them that the Minister of the Interior should issue instructions to the Serbian frontier authorities "to deny a crossing to the youths who had already set out from Belgrade for that purpose." However, the frontier authorities themselves belonged to the plot and did not carry out the instructions but reported back "that the order had reached them too late, for the young men had already got across." In Jovanovich's words, "the plot was hatched by a group of secretly organized persons and in patriotic Bosno-Herzegovinian student circles in Belgrade." He later confirmed that the first group were members of the organization Union or Death, often called the Black Hand, led by Colonel Dimitrievich, with the pseudonym "Apis," sworn enemy of Prime Minister Pashich and the Radical party; and that the "student circles" centered around two young Bosnians named Gavrilo Princip and Nedeljko Chabrinovich. Jovanovich continued: "Thus the endeavor of our Government to prevent the execution of the plot failed, as also did the endeavor made on his own initiative by our Minister in Vienna, Jotsa Jovanovich, in an interview with the Minister Bilinski, to dissuade the Archduke from the fatal journey he contemplated."[2]

2. "Jotsa" was the nickname for the Serbian Minister, Jovan Jovanovich. Count Leon von Bilinski, Austro-Hungarian Joint Finance Minister, was a nobleman of Polish descent in charge of Bosnian affairs.

Whatever Ljuba Jovanovich's motives were in publishing these recollections ten years after the event, they came as a windfall for writers seeking to exonerate Austria-Hungary and Germany from any share in the war guilt. The Hungarians acquired a valuable argument for demanding the return of their lost territory; and the Germans seized the opportunity to divert attention from the pressure which the Kaiser had put on Vienna to "make a clean sweep of the Serbs" and his offer of a "blank check" to Vienna to draw on Germany for full support.[3] The Germans also were glad to procure testimony offsetting recent damaging revelations, for instance that of Count Hoyos, permanent head of the Austro-Hungarian Foreign Ministry, who had been sent to Berlin to make sure of German intentions, but far from finding the Foreign Office wavering had discovered that its only worry was lest Vienna might weaken in the resolution to face Belgrade with an ultimatum. Hoyos had given assurances that the ultimatum contained demands which "were such as to make it really impossible for Serbia to accept them," and he reported back to Vienna that Germany promised unconditionally to stand by Austria even if the measures against Serbia which she advised should bring about "the big war."[4]

It was not surprising that King Alexander brought the subject up again when I saw him in Bled a year later, on August 5, 1926. What was surprising was that he apparently had come only slowly to realize that war guilt was not merely a theme for historical research but had current political importance. The German Minister, he said, had raised the matter in a conversation only the day before, and he had been amazed by the self-righteousness and apparent sincerity with which he had insisted on Germany's complete innocence, laying the blame instead on England. This was a new tune, I remarked; formerly it had been "Poincaré la Guerre." The King suggested that perhaps the Minister had suited his remarks to his own well-known partiality for France. In any case, he went on, the Germans had evidently decided that the war-guilt question might be turned to their political advantage and were giving it much study. This gave me a chance to emphasize how much Serbia's reputation was involved. The revisionist historians could not blame her for

3. Reminiscent of his attitude in the 1910 crisis when he placed himself behind Emperor Franz Josef in "shining armor."

4. *Cf.* Fritz Fischer, *op. cit.*, chap. 2; also Luigi Albertini, *The Origins of the World War of 1914*. London: Oxford, 1953, v. II, chap. 7, etc. In a privately printed pamphlet published in Chicago in 1923, *Interviewing the Authors of the War*, Professor Bernadotte Schmitt reports on a conversation with Count Hoyos, who told him that "he had explained to the German Government that Austria-Hungary desired war with Serbia and that Germany, in agreeing to support her ally, did not do so in ignorance of what was planned."

having resisted Austria's harsh demands, but they were exploiting the admission by Ljuba Jovanovich of the Serbian Government's fore-knowledge of the plot to make Serbia the main culprit for the war. Until his statement was explained, the Serbian case before history would be badly prejudiced.

I then mentioned the talks I had been having with Serbian statesmen who could throw light on the subject, including Ljuba Jovanovich himself, and I added that I was urging Foreign Minister Ninchich to try to find and publish relevant Serbian documents; to which the King nodded approval. From Pashich himself, all I could get had been a simple and oft-repeated: "Jovanovich a menti"—"Jovanovich lied." The King's comment was that Pashich simply did not understand, and never would, that anti-Serbian propaganda abroad had the slightest relevance to his concerns. He belonged to Old Serbia and a generation that looked on such matters as unimportant; what was important was acts. The previous winter, charges of corruption had been made against a member of Pashich's family. The King had suggested to him that he ought to isolate himself from those charges, vigorously and categorically. Pashich replied that he did not believe in denials and explanations; the attacks left him unmoved and uninterested.

I did not know then how much the question of the Serbian Government's behavior at the time of Sarajevo had become enmeshed in Serbian domestic politics. Pashich and Ljuba Jovanovich, both politicians of the old Balkan school, had been rivals for control of the Radical party, and each had been endeavoring to picture his relationship to the plot in a way to bring him credit with the Serbian public, who revered Princip and his fellow conspirators as patriots and martyrs. In other words, each was reluctant to disown knowledge of the plot entirely or admit that he had joined in steps to thwart it.

Another factor affecting their attitude was the role they had played at the sensational trial at Saloniki in 1917 where "Apis" had been found guilty of plotting treason and the assassination of Alexander, then Prince Regent. Prime Minister Pashich and Ljuba Jovanovich (in that period Minister of the Interior) had insisted on the death sentence's being carried out, and Alexander had agreed, though reluctantly and under great pressure. Enemies called this a political decision, claiming that Pashich and Jovanovich simply saw an opportunity to rid themselves of a mutual enemy who, they suspected, was planning a coup d'état.

A further reason might well have been that, as "Apis" had been involved in the Sarajevo plot against the Archduke three years earlier, his execution would satisfy the Austrian demand that persons responsible for that crime be punished—a demand being made in the secret negotiations then in progress between the French Government and Prince Sixtus, brother-in-law of the Hapsburg Emperor Charles, for a separate peace with Austria-Hungary without Germany's knowledge. Disclosure of the full facts about the Saloniki trial (to this day largely obscure) would have been politically damaging for Pashich and Ljuba Jovanovich, since Croatian and other critics were claiming that the projected separate peace would have reinstated Serbia's independence but left the Slavs of Austria-Hungary under Hapsburg sovereignty.

For a hostile opinion I went to Zagreb to see Dr. Hinko Hinković, one of Pashich's long-time rivals. He had played a great role in the Jugoslav movement during the war but opposed Serbian predominance in the new state, and when a Karageorgevich monarchy was established instead of the republic which he favored he retired in disgust from politics. He considered Alexander and Pashich linked in political misdeeds, and cited Alexander's agreement not to amnesty the death sentence of "Apis" on the charge of plotting *his* death, when "as everyone knew" the real plot was to overthrow Pashich. Hinković was still convinced that Pashich and other Serb leaders had intended to sacrifice the Jugoslav ideal in the negotiations with Prince Sixtus, abandon Croatia and come to a separate peace with Vienna. He admitted he had no proof of this, but upheld the thesis in blistering language; and when I noted Alexander's well-known antagonism for Pashich, he ignored this and included him in his charge. His theory was adopted by the *Kriegsschuldfrage,* the German periodical dealing with war guilt, and by many revisionist historians. It could never be either substantiated or disproved.

II

The historical threads most worth pursuing here are of two main sorts: those that lead to a fuller understanding of why the war came, indeed was bound to come, and those that add details to the story of just how it did in fact come. A thread of the first sort came into my hands at Bled when I obtained some material which threw extraordinarily interesting light on the ideas and motives of Gavrilo Princip, the twenty-year-old Bosnian youth whose pistol shot killed the Hapsburg heir. It consisted of notes of conversations with Princip, made while he was in prison, by Dr. Martin Pappenheim, an Austrian psychiatrist, professor at the University of Vienna. During the war Dr. Pappenheim was studying cases of shell shock and various abnormal types in Austrian military hospitals and prisons, and in 1916 he happened to come to the fortress of Theresienstadt where Princip was incarcerated. By then Princip, after two years in solitary confinement in a darkened cell, was dying of tuberculosis. Though only a wraith, hardly able to stand up, he had been loaded down, until two days before Dr. Pappenheim first saw him, with twenty-two pounds of iron shackles. Dr. Pappenheim was able to convince him that he was not a spy and could be spoken to freely.

Dr. Pappenheim's notes on four conversations with Princip, together with two passages which he persuaded him to write (he had not had a pen in his hand for two years), supplied new insight into the psychology and political background of the Sarajevo conspirators. Therefore, when the Jugoslav Minister in Vienna, Dr. Milojevich (who happened to be spending a few days with us in Bled), was able to verify the authenticity of the material as it appeared in a Serbo-Croat pamphlet in Zagreb, I had a translation made and later published it in *Current History*, with a short explanatory essay.[5] In the forty years since then nothing seems to have come to light to change the principal conclusions to be drawn from the material. Recently Vladimir Dedijer has quoted from it at length in his authoritative investigation of all the circumstances surrounding the assassination.[6]

Princip described to Dr. Pappenheim his grindingly poor childhood in a remote corner of Bosnia, his ideal love for a schoolmate ("never kissed"), his avid reading ("Books for me signify life"), the exalted talk among his comrades about freeing the land from Hapsburg rule and their plans to assassinate some high official as a means to that end ("a revolution, especially in the military state of Austria, is of no use"). "The older generation wanted to secure liberty from Austria in a legal way," he said; "we did not believe in such a liberty." He had read "many anarchistic, socialistic, nationalistic pamphlets, belles lettres and everything." But his generation did not occupy themselves with social ques-

5. *Current History*, New York, August, 1927. In a second article in *Current History* (October, 1927) I printed (for the first time) facsimiles of part of the Serbian reply to the Austrian ultimatum and of the telegram declaring war on Serbia, obtained by me from the Serbian Foreign Office. Sidney B. Fay made use of these two articles in *The Origins of the World War*, and Bernadotte E. Schmitt in *The Coming of the War, 1914*.

I also obtained from King Alexander a copy of an interesting letter found in the Vienna archives written by Count Tisza, Prime Minister of Hungary in 1914, to Count Bilinski, demanding that a Ministerial Council be called to discuss the Archduke's assassination. He wrote that in view of the remissness of the Austro-Hungarian administration in coping with sedition in Bosnia, they "can scarcely have the right to lay the blame on Serbia." This letter was printed in *Foreign Affairs* in April, 1928.

6. *The Road to Sarajevo*. New York: Simon and Schuster, 1966.

tions, "thinking that each of us had another duty—a national duty." He told how he took the idea of assassination with him when he went to Belgrade to enter high school and how when he and a fellow student named Chabrinovich were alerted from Sarajevo to the Archduke's prospective visit he decided the moment to act had come. He described how he secured revolvers from Major Tankosich, a Serbian army officer of Bosnian descent, a former *komitadji* leader in the wars of liberation against the Turks and a member of the Black Hand under "Apis." Major Tankosich, he said, knew [of the plot] at the last moment, when they [the conspirators] were already mentally ready." Carrying their weapons, Princip, Chabrinovich and another student named Gra-bezh succeeded in evading the Serbian police and with the assistance of frontier officers connected with the Black Hand crossed into Bosnia and reached Sarajevo some three weeks before the Archduke was due to arrive to attend army maneuvers.

The climax of the Archduke's visit was to be a reception in Sarajevo on, of all days, Kosovo Day, the anniversary of the Turkish victory, June 28, 1389, which ended the independence of the medieval Serbian state. For over five hundred years that anniversary had been observed as a day of national mourning, not only to commemorate lost freedom but also as a way to glorify tyrannicide: for a Serb nobleman had entered the victorious Sultan's tent and plunged a dagger into his heart. Thus it was an unpropitious date indeed that was chosen for the Hapsburg heir to demonstrate Austria's military control over his future subjects. Princip shot the Archduke and his wife (the latter, he claimed, by mischance) as the car carrying them backed slowly after making a wrong turn. At the trial, five of the accused were condemned to be hanged; Princip, Chabrinovich and Grabezh, being under the legal age for execution, were sentenced to twenty years' solitary confinement in darkened cells.

Princip, when Dr. Pappenheim saw him, had open tubercular wounds festering on his chest and his whole body was slowly putrefying. His brain, he told Dr. Pappenheim, was busy at night with "beautiful dreams" about life and love, by day with vague philosophizing and patriotic thoughts about his country (then being invaded and ravaged) and the ideal of South Slav unity free from Austria. "He had no thought of becoming a hero," Dr. Pappenheim reported him as saying, "he merely wanted to die for his idea." "Was a man of ideals, wanted to revenge the people. The motives—revenge and love." Suicide impossible. "Wait to the end." "Thinks about the human soul. What is the essential in human life, instinct, or will or spirit—what moves man?"

Dedijer quotes another doctor in the prison hospital to the effect that Princip's disease had destroyed his left elbow joint so far that the lower part of the arm had to be attached to the upper part by a silver wire. Dr. Pappenheim's last entry: "When permission has come, arm is to be amputated. His usual resigned disposition." He died April 18, 1918.

Both the psychiatrist and the historian can learn much about the psychology of revolution from Dr. Pappenheim's notes (of which I have room to quote only fragments). For the historian they bring light into the murky atmosphere in which the act of violence which led to the war, or another act like it, is seen to have been inevitable. No one who does not comprehend the degree to which exalted nationalism possessed the conspirators can understand the long series of political murders and attempted murders which culminated in the killing of the Archduke (there had been five previous *attentats* in less than four years) ; or why Austrian rulers decided that they must seize on this assassination as the occasion to end once and for all (as they thought) the threat to the Empire posed by South Slav nationalism and its dedicated terrorists—idealistic, remorseless, willing to run all risks and accept any punishment. As Field-Marshal Conrad von Hötzendorf put it: "If we miss this occasion, the Monarchy will be exposed to new aspirations. . . . Austria-Hungary must wage war for political reasons." To provoke this war, Vienna—encouraged from Berlin—determined to face Serbia with an unacceptable ultimatum, calculating that it would be a short and easy war ending in Serbia's collapse and subjugation. Instead, in the fragile structure of European peace at the time, it was a war of four years' duration, fatal to the Empire and changing the course of world history.

III

The ultimatum to Serbia was presented in Belgrade by the Austro-Hungarian Minister, Baron von Giesl, on July 23, 1914. It revealed clearly the purposes it was intended to achieve. Dr. Grouich, Secretary-General at the Serbian Foreign Office at the time, recounted the circumstances to me in detail. It happened that Prime Minister Pashich was absent from the capital, so that it was the Acting Foreign Minister, Mr. Pachu, who with Dr. Grouich received Baron von Giesl when he arrived carrying the document that boded so much tragedy. Grouich's account[7] leaves no doubt that Giesl was executing a carefully thought-out plan devised by Count von Berchtold, the Austro-Hungarian Foreign

7. For further details see my "Three Days in Belgrade," *Foreign Affairs*, January, 1927.

Minister, to bring the crisis resulting from the Sarajevo crime to a head at the precise moment intended and with the precise results foreseen. It corroborates, from the Belgrade end, Poincaré's assertion that at the very last moment presentation of the ultimatum was postponed until he and Viviani were certain to have left Kronstadt and be safely isolated at sea. It also shows Berchtold's full confidence that he would be able to reject Serbia's reply and proceed at once to invade and chastise her.

The timetable of Giesl's actions as given by Grouich varies from that in some other accounts. Thus he stated categorically to me that no notification of the imminence of an important communication from Vienna was received by the Serbian Government until the morning of July 23, when on his arrival at 9:30 at the Foreign Office he found a Secretary of the Austro-Hungarian Legation awaiting him. The Secretary expressed surprise at hearing of Pashich's absence, though the press had announced the fact,[8] and said that in that case his Minister would call at four o'clock on the Acting Foreign Minister. At five minutes before four o'clock the same Secretary appeared, very tense and pale, said the Minister was not yet ready and would come instead at six o'clock. These were the two hours needed to take account of a delay in Poincaré's departure from Kronstadt.

Giesl's words as he handed in the ultimatum at six o'clock were that "unless a satisfactory reply is given on all points by six o'clock on Saturday, the day after tomorrow, I shall leave Belgrade with all the personnel of my Legation." It was immediately clear that, even if Vienna's demands were met on every point compatible with the maintenance of Serbian independence and sovereignty, war was imminent. When Grouich had finished hurriedly turning over the pages of the ultimatum, reading bits aloud to the ministers present and translating as he went, Ljuba Jovanovich exclaimed, "Ne ostaje nishta drugo nego da se gine"—"There's nothing to do but die fighting." The expression "se gine" means literally "perish," but in the old Serbian ballads it was used in the sense of meeting violent death after combat. Both combat and death seemed certain. Belgrade lay at the mercy of the Austrian artillery across the Danube and could not be defended. At about four o'clock the government, seeing what was ahead, took the precaution of ordering mobilization and directed that a train be prepared to take the foreign diplomats and members of the government and their families south. All troops were withdrawn except for a hundred or so left to

8. Berchtold himself knew of it, as appeared later when his dispatch of July 21 giving instructions to Giesl was published in the collection of official Austrian documents.

maintain order, and a group of engineers to blow up the Danube bridge after Baron von Giesl's train had crossed.

The Serbian reply met seven of the ten Austrian demands unconditionally. Of the others, two were accepted with reservations, and one, the demand that Serbia at once open a judicial inquiry and that Austrian officials be permitted to take part therein, was accepted as regards the first half but declined as regards the second as being contrary to the constitution and the laws of criminal procedure. The reply emphasized Serbia's desire for a "pacific understanding" and her willingness to submit the question between the two countries either to the Hague Court or to the Powers. Every word was discussed and rediscussed by the cabinet, and changes ad infinitum were made up to the last moment. By the time the text, covered with elisions and corrections, was handed to Dr. Grouich for translation, the offices had been evacuated and he was alone with two assistants and a typist. As he was dictating the translation direct to the typist (there was no time to prepare a preliminary draft) the typewriter broke and one of his colleagues copied out the remainder in a shaky hand. Grouich put the document in an envelope and took it over to Prime Minister Pashich, who started off to deliver it at the Austro-Hungarian Legation—just ten minutes before the expiry of the time limit set by Vienna.

Baron von Giesl did not ask Pashich to sit down and dismissed him brusquely. He can barely have glanced at the note, a document of nine closely written pages, for hardly was the Serbian Prime Minister out of the room before he had signed the letter that was waiting on his desk. This stated that the Serbian reply was, as Berchtold had made sure it would be, unsatisfactory. Giesl and his staff had their luggage ready, within twenty minutes were at the railway station and less than an hour after receiving the Serbian reply were across the Danube in Austro-Hungarian territory.

Here I must make room for a postscript that would seem improbably apt if a dramatist used it as the final scene of a historical drama.

After the war, the Ministry of the Interior of the new Jugoslav kingdom installed itself temporarily in the old Austro-Hungarian Legation, which somehow had escaped destruction in repeated Austrian bombardments. One day in 1921 an elderly gentleman appeared there, a former Austrian subject, living in territory recently annexed to Jugoslavia. He wished to secure the pension granted to former enemy army officers in that situation. It was Baron von Giesl, seeking amid the ghosts of his vanished

Empire a favor from the authorities whom he had brushed aside seven years before as he strapped up his briefcase and rattled off to the station.

IV

More significant than the two historical threads pursued here briefly, would, of course, be any information I might glean as to whether the Serbian Government had had foreknowledge of the plot against the Archduke and had failed to sound a warning in Vienna. The British historian R. W. Seton-Watson, who had always been a partisan of the Jugoslavs (though strongly critical of Pashich for what he considered his narrow Serbism), was perturbed by the anti-Jugoslav crusade begun on the basis of Ljuba Jovanovich's article. After calling publicly on him and Pashich to repudiate or explain it, he visited Belgrade to press them personally to do so. We had discussed the subject several times during a recent visit of his to New York, and I was trying on my own account to get the Belgrade government to clear the record. Supported by my friend Pavle Karovich, formerly Consul-General in New York and then head of the Press Bureau in the Foreign Office, I suggested in 1925 to Foreign Minister Ninchich (as I mentioned to King Alexander) that he publish a White Book of relevant documents (Seton-Watson made the same recommendation, though he called the proposed book Blue), or, alternatively, appoint a commission of Jugoslav scholars to investigate and report. To explore the issues myself I had conversations with (besides King Alexander) Pashich, Ljuba Jovanovich, Jovan Jovanovich, Ninchich and, of course, Grouich; and I invited the two Jovanovichs to write articles for *Foreign Affairs*. Jovan Jovanovich accepted, but then put off writing until an electoral campaign in which he became involved was over.

When I saw Jovan Jovanovich again, on March 18, 1925, he went over Ljuba Jovanovich's story with me. He confirmed that he had warned the Austro-Hungarian Government of the grave risk the Archduke would run in attending the army maneuvers in Bosnia. However, he said he had not received specific instructions from Belgrade to do this but had acted on his own initiative, knowing the highly explosive situation in Bosnia at the time. The risk, he had emphasized, would be particularly great as the Archduke was "a declared enemy of Serbia," the more so as the maneuvers were to be deployed along the Serbian-Bosnian border and thus were plainly directed against Serbia.

People had largely forgotten, he continued, what universal hatred of

Hapsburg rule existed in Bosnia in those days and what wild desperation possessed the revolutionaries who had sworn to end it. He was so sure that terrorists would be "in every town and at every crossroads" where the Archduke would pass that he had decided to go to Bilinski, the Minister responsible for Bosnian affairs, to remind him of the danger involved. He said that if Belgrade had instructed him to make a *démarche,* he would have gone to the Foreign Office rather than Bilinski. But he knew Bilinski well and considered him a reasonable person, not hostile to the Jugoslavs; indeed, Bilinski had tried at one point to bring Bosnians and Croat and Serb elements in Bosnia into a single party with moderate reformist aims—of course without success. He said he told Bilinski: "The maneuvers are to be with blank cartridges, but what if one cartridge is not blank? What may not occur?" It was his impression that Bilinski agreed with him. But even if he did he held a merely civilian position and probably could do nothing to change the decision of the Archduke and the military hierarchy who had arranged the visit. At any rate, Bilinski called Jovanovich back a few days later to tell him the Archduke was determined to go. "After all," he said, "it's our affair. It's an internal matter."

Jovan Jovanovich concluded his story with a sentence I had heard and was to hear in one form or another from every Serbian official who talked about Sarajevo: "I always knew that if matters followed their course it was inevitable that an assassination would occur sometime, somewhere." And he followed it with the same conclusion as everyone else: "I knew that if anything like that happened, we Serbs would be the chief sufferers."[9]

The next day Grouich invited me to his house to meet Ljuba Jovanovich, now President of the Skupshtina, and I went eagerly.

Ljuba Jovanovich began with a general disclaimer of the importance of what he had written. He had not been making a studied and documented examination of events but merely giving "casual souvenirs," "impressions, recollections and hearsays" which were therefore "open to

9. The Austrian Government had dispatched a high official, Dr. Friedrich von Wiesner, Legal Counselor at the Foreign Office, to Sarajevo directly after the assassination to see if he could not procure evidence of the Serbian Government's implication in the plot. When I saw von Wiesner in Vienna in April, 1925, he was tired of the whole controversy and indignant that he had been made a central figure in it. For three days, he said, he had examined the dossiers of the military and civilian authorities in Sarajevo, including the files on Princip, but had been unable to find anything implicating the Serbian Government directly and had so reported by telegram to Vienna. A copy of his telegram (suppressed at the time, naturally) had been found in Sarajevo and transmitted to the American delegation in Paris. I could get nothing further out of him than that he considered the importance of the telegram much exaggerated.

correction." Now he was about to begin a careful study and write a more "deliberate" account. He would be handicapped, he said, by the fact that the Serbian archives were dispersed. Part of the Foreign Ministry archives had been left in Belgrade and seized by the enemy; other parts had been lost in the retreat, though some had been recovered from a hiding place in a monastery near Kraljevo. Nor did the archives of foreign governments contain important communications from those days, for the moment the ultimatum was handed in—or even before—Austria-Hungary had broken all communication between foreign legations in Belgrade and their home governments: the only exception was the British Legation, which had its own means of communication. Moreover, the French Minister, de Caux, was off his head and mistrusted his able assistant; the Russian Legation was entirely isolated. In any case, the Serbian response to the ultimatum was prepared entirely without communication with the Powers.

The plot itself (Ljuba Jovanovich continued) was hatched in Bosnia and any Serbian participation was of secondary importance; certain Serbian officers (meaning Tankosich and other members of the Black Hand) gave "personal encouragement" to the two or three conspirators who were in Belgrade, but this was not decisive. The fact was that no action or lack of action by any individual would have been decisive. Excitement and desperation had grown to such a height in Bosnia, and so many youths were pledged to acts of violence, that the attempt on the Archduke's life would have been made in any case, probably in Sarajevo on the Kosovo anniversary, but inevitably somewhere and at some time soon. (In fact, a first attack had been made on the Archduke the morning of the assassination, when a bomb exploded just behind his car; and several other conspirators were scattered along his route, armed with bombs and pistols.) It was now known, Ljuba Jovanovich went on, that foreign-based anarchistic elements hostile to both the Serbian Government and the Hapsburg monarchy were busy stimulating unrest and violence in Bosnia. A principal intellectual leader of the terrorists was an agitator named Gachinovich, a student of sociology at Lausanne, where he was in contact with the Bolshevik exiles living there (including, it was found later, Trotsky). The Vienna Government had agents everywhere and must certainly have been informed about this international movement.

On the main topic, whether the Serbian Government had knowledge of the plot, Ljuba Jovanovich was either confused or deliberately confusing; my impression was that he was both. He asserted that no word had ever been said in a cabinet meeting about any rumors of a plot. I interjected that his article had not stated that the discussion had been in formal cabinet meetings, only among cabinet members. Rumors were always circulating, he replied, of plots against this person or that—even against various Serbian ministers. Such rumors often cropped up in conversations with colleagues, but never anything that could be taken hold of. Pashich did, he thought, say something of the sort to him but he no longer remembered precisely what it was. On that point, I had no success in trying to push him further.

On the question whether a warning was sent to Vienna, he stood by what he had written in his article. Pashich had given Minister Jovanovich general instructions always to cooperate with Bilinski in any difficulty; this doubtless was the basis on which Jovanovich approached him personally. However, Bilinski was not on good terms with the Archduke, who despised him as a civilian bureaucrat: and the military commanders would have considered him a meddler if he had emphasized that it would be provocative to stage maneuvers at such a moment. As to whether a formal warning ought to have been given the Austro-Hungarian Government, Jovanovich refused to be drawn out. He said he intended to deal with the whole matter carefully in his "more deliberate" writing and, perhaps as a way out of our discussion, accepted my suggestion that he do so in an article for *Foreign Affairs*.[10]

The chief interest in my next interview, a not very enlightening talk with Foreign Minister Ninchich, was his statement—"I swear it"—that although he was a Deputy and in the center of political life, he had never heard of any plot to attack the Archduke at Sarajevo. All through 1914, and earlier still, there had been frequent rumors of plots by Bosnian or other terrorists to kill some Austro-Hungarian dignitary. Ninchich likened them to the rumors later on, following the war, of conspiracies by Bolsheviks, dissident Croats, and Italian, Hungarian or Bulgarian agents to assassinate Prince Regent Alexander, Pashich or other ministers, himself included.

"At first we took the reports of plots to kill us very seriously," he said, "and made all sorts of precautions. But little by little we became habituated to them and shrugged them off. That is how it was with the frequent rumors of plots against the Archduke, the Ban of Croatia and

10. Despite many promptings, Ljuba Jovanovich never sent us this article; and such occasional pieces as he wrote for Belgrade newspapers shed no new light on controversial matters connected with Sarajevo. Jovan Jovanovich's article, promised in 1924 and again in 1925, was sent to us in 1927, but it was too slight to be worth publishing. Bernadotte Schmitt, whom I consulted, agreed.

others. After a time they became so routine that they attracted little notice."

Another 1914 rumor had been about a coming insurrection in Bosnia. Ninchich thought that probably this was what "Apis" had aimed at rather than an assassination. In any case, the feud between Pashich and "Apis" would have kept Pashich from being aware of anything the Black Hand or its agents were up to. Ninchich thought that even "Apis" would have foreseen the fatal results that might follow the slaying of the Hapsburg Heir Apparent. But the various groups of young Bosnian conspirators ("Mlada Bosna") were in such a state of exaltation that nobody knew what might happen and nobody could have prevented something from happening.

When I saw Pashich that same afternoon he spoke as always in halting and abominable French, with the usual "comme-ça" after almost every phrase. There was no trouble getting him started, but it was a false start as far as I was concerned, for when I mentioned Sarajevo he went back to 1908, and earlier, to detail the remote and mostly well-known antecedents of the war. But when he came at last to Ljuba Jovanovich's account of the Serbian Government's action (or inaction) on the eve of the Archduke's assassination, he spoke quite categorically. Here are his remarks as I noted them down immediately afterward, unchanged except for the omission of a few repetitions and the transposition of some sentences into better sequence:

"I knew too much history from the inside not to know that Austria-Hungary always wanted war. But I always followed a peaceful policy so as not to give her provocation, for example in 1908, again in the Balkan Wars over the matter of Scutari and in our various demands concerning railways and commerce. But I knew she wished war, some way, some time.

"From far back I had been an opponent of Austria-Hungary, but I did not wish to fight her, only to keep our independence. For that reason I was opposed to Alexander Obrenovich. At first he and Emperor Franz Josef had a personal alliance, but then it was broken because he said derogatory things about the Austro-Hungarian Army, and the Emperor became very hostile to him. There is still alive a man who was one of the three who helped prepare the murder of Alexander and Draga. He has told me that he went with his colleagues to the Austro-Hungarian Legation here in Belgrade to tell the Minister of the plans, and then went with him to Vienna, where he received assurances that Austria-Hungary would not mix into the affair or take advantage of it. I mention this because when I was asked to join in these plots against Alexander I refused absolutely, although I was opposed to him. I have always pursued a fair and peaceful policy toward Austria-Hungary.

"After the murder in Sarajevo we closed the Bosnian border and gave strict instructions to let no one come from Bosnia into Serbia. We had always put suspicious characters in prison and had often communicated facts regarding them to the Austro-Hungarian Legation and Consulate. Princip had been locked up when he came to Belgrade but had been released at the Consul's request. I did not know him and I did not know who had crossed the border. What Ljuba Jovanovich says is wrong, and my colleagues will back me up in all this.

"I never said to Ljuba Jovanovich or anyone else that I had knowledge of this attack. Jovanovich lied. If I had known, I would have put anyone involved in jail. I ordered our Minister in Vienna to say we would do anything to help discover the culprits, and I told the same thing to the Austro-Hungarian Minister here. In reply to Austro-Hungarian complaints I said I was ready to use all Austro-Hungarian aid and information in the effort to apprehend and try the criminals. My whole policy was to avoid a quarrel with Austria-Hungary, for I knew that in every case Serbia would be the sufferer. But she was seeking an occasion to attack us, and found it.

"What Ljuba Jovanovich said must be considered in the light of the continuing situation at the time. The assassin was an overwrought young man. Young Bosnians and Croatians were coming into Serbia as a result of persecution and to get education, not in twos and threes but by dozens and hundreds. The Austro-Hungarian police knew all about this and were not in any need of warning. There had been several attempts on the Ban of Croatia and others. On a visit to Vienna I had heard that in Bosnian schools and in schools in Ljubljana boys of fifteen, girls even, formed societies to fight for Serbia. They drew up articles of union and agreed not to buy Austro-Hungarian candies and to boycott anti-Serb professors. They also got and circulated Serbian books. The Minister of Public Instruction in Vienna knew all this; he showed me samples. This shows how profound the feeling was. Nothing but a really systematic plan for meeting these nationalist desires could have prevented an outbreak of some sort. The Archduke was killed not by a bomb but by a revolver; and there were revolvers everywhere.

"My formal and repeated instructions were to do everything possible to calm nationalist feelings in the Austro-Hungarian provinces, to calm the Austro-Hungarian Government and to meet their wishes. We knew that war would probably obliterate us. We were weak, unprepared and poor. The only thing that can be said against us is that the frontier was not as well guarded as it ought to have been; but it was Austria-Hungary's frontier to guard, too. It was not a frontier of a kilometer or so; it was long, through difficult and mountainous country. There were spies and intriguers from Austria, Hungary, Russia and Germany all along it. Our Etat-Major certainly had agents there also—and maybe not, as was usual, of the most reputable character. It is possible that they were mixed up in this sort of intrigue. Who knows?

"The only legitimate imputation against us is that of negligence. But if we had kept on continuously warning Austria-Hungary we would have given ourselves into their hands; we would have proved their contention that our very existence was a menace to them."

This was the note on which Pashich ended. He avoided saying categorically that he had had no intimation from any source regarding a particular plot at Sarajevo. But his reason for not sending a specific warning to Vienna on that occasion even if he had heard rumors of it was characteristic of his way of reasoning and in itself not implausible.

It was the last time I saw Pashich, who died December 10, 1926.

V

Like everything connected with the Sarajevo plot, these bits of personal testimony are to be interpreted against a background much wider and more complex than the circumstances of the murder itself. Bosnia was in a frenzy of revolt, and the boiling-up of emotions revealed in Princip's talks with Dr. Pappenheim would certainly, at some point, have given the Austro-Hungarian military a pretext to start the war which they considered desirable, indeed essential. Baron Conrad von Hötzendorf, Chief of the General Staff, had long been preaching preventive war. When Princip provided the plausible excuse, the chance was not to be missed. His German colleague, General von Moltke, saw eye to eye with him. The Kaiser said, "Now or never!" The German Chancellor Bethmann-Hollweg (wrongly counting on Britain's neutrality), encouraged Austro-Hungarian Foreign Minister Berchtold to go the limit, even at the risk of Russian intervention. With Germany behind them, the Austro-Hungarian Government and military were confident of destroying Serbia and pressing on victorious to the Aegean.

26

Albania in Mussolini's Net

The controversies left from the war—war guilt, reparations, war debts, territorial settlements and the rest—were reflected in many of our articles and brought us brickbats as well as bouquets. Other subjects could do so also, as we found when we printed a piece by the President of Mexico, Plutarco Elías Calles. In this article he threatened to deal drastically with the still unsolved problems of the Mexican Revolution—land, oil, foreign investments and the concentration of wealth; pointed out that less than a third of the total wealth of the country was in the hands of the Mexicans themselves and that 60 percent of that one-third belonged to priests or institutions of the Roman Catholic Church; and warned that he intended exacting strict compliance with constitutional provisions against what he called the clergy's material and political domination of Mexican life. This notification of the phase being opened in the bloody struggle between Church and State in Mexico—which was to continue for more than a decade—incensed some of our readers and even led a few to cancel their subscriptions.

It seemed the right moment to find an authoritative statement of the social policies of the Catholic Church in backward countries, Mexico to be included but in a broad setting. Father Wynne, editor of the *Catholic Encyclopedia,* arranged for me to be received by Cardinal Hayes, an open-minded and cosmopolitan prelate, who at once saw the advantages of the project and agreed to forward a letter of invitation to Cardinal Gasparri, Papal Secretary of State. In reply, Gasparri sent us merely a copy of Pope Pius XI's recent encyclical, "Iniquis Afflictisque," and quotations from a papal allocution. The invitation to write a substantial article, although not definitely declined, was not taken up. Shortly after this interchange a would-be contributor recommended himself as a competent authority on theological aspects of international relations on the grounds that he was in touch with heavenly spirits. Coolidge remarked: "We thought we were getting pretty high when we were writing to Gasparri, but now we have an offer from higher still—a Direct Revelation."

Years later, in the course of a long audience with Pope Pius XII, I seized the chance to raise the proposition anew, arguing that it might be valuable for the Church to make known its changing attitude toward social problems in countries where the hierarchy had often been termed reactionary. The Pope took up the idea animatedly and asked me to send him details of just what I had in mind. Much to his surprise, I was able to whisk a two-page outline out of my pocket. He read it carefully then and there. The article, he said, should and would be written. My impression was that he would enjoy writing it himself—a "ghostwritten" contribution in reverse, to be signed with a lesser name. I asked how I should communicate with him further about the plan—perhaps, I suggested, through Cardinal Spellman in New York? "No, no, no," he said sharply. "Directly." Unfortunately, owing to his subsequent illness the project came to nothing.

The revolutionary slogan "Mexico for the Mexicans" brought the Mexican Government into sharp conflict with the United States over the petroleum laws, the ownership of railways and the laws governing the acquisition of land by foreigners. In 1927, at a tense moment, President Coolidge hurriedly sent his Amherst classmate Dwight W. Morrow, a partner in the Morgan firm, to Mexico as Ambassador. Morrow successfully negotiated various alterations in the discriminatory petroleum laws and also was helpful in tamping down temporarily the religious conflict. By coincidence, Morrow had earlier written an article for us which made a spirited appeal for good faith on the part both of bankers recommending investments abroad and of borrowing governments. I was told that it had played a part in deciding President Coolidge that Morrow was the right man for such a delicate mission.

I came to know Morrow fairly well and was tremendously taken with him. To look at, he was the reverse of impressive—small, very nearsighted, with mussed hair and rumpled clothes. If he had not been rather perky in manner you might have put him down as an absent-minded professor; absent-minded he was, but in spite of it a lawyer of unusual ability and a financial genius. His habit of concentrating on whatever was uppermost in his mind to the exclusion of all that was going on around him produced feats of abstraction that were proverbial.

One day I went to see Morrow at his office at 23 Wall Street. With a show of democracy, the Morgan partners sat at large desks ranged in rows on the ground floor (though each had his private office upstairs). As I waited in a small glass-enclosed room near the entrance I could see him coming across from his desk with decisive little steps, his chin thrust eagerly forward, and I watched helplessly as he banged headlong into the glass door. His pince-nez fell off but luckily didn't break, and as I helped him retrieve it he said apologetically, "I must have run into the door." Putting the glasses on again, he examined the door speculatively, took out his handkerchief and wiped off a small smudge where his nose had struck. Now convinced, but wanting to make sure I was also, he repeated, "I ran into the door."

Another time as I left Morrow's office I stopped to ask his private secretary, Arthur Springer, to remind Morrow of some promise he had made. Springer said I need make no apologies for referring to Morrow's absent-mindedness. Just the day before Morrow had called him in. "Take a letter," he ordered. Walking over to the window, he contemplated in silence the scene below for five or six minutes. Suddenly he completed his inner colloquy without having uttered a word and turned around. "That's enough," he said, "Yours truly."

I was with Morrow when Franz Schneider telephoned him the news of President Coolidge's laconic announcement: "I do not choose to run." Morrow obviously was flabbergasted. I began speculating whether Coolidge made the statement because he really didn't want to be President again or because it was a way of evading the prejudice against third terms by insisting on being drafted. This suggestion made Morrow very wrathful.

"I have known Coolidge since he was nineteen," he said, "and I have never known him to do an insincere thing."

My explanation that one didn't mean ordinary "insincerity" when talking about strategy in politics mollified him only partially. He added that he had thought all along that Coolidge wouldn't run again and that, unlike Teddy Roosevelt, he would leave a completely open field for competitors for the succession.

Many of the problems of that era are with us still, in essence little changed.

In January, 1927, the title of one of our articles was "Dictatorship in

Spain"; it was the dictatorship of Primo de Rivera, and after a grisly interlude of civil war came the present dictatorship of Generalissimo Franco. Patrick Duncan, a Minister in the government of South Africa, and afterward Governor-General set forth the alternatives in the racial dilemma there—"repression," "assimilation" or "segregation"? He called for a middle-road course between the second and third alternatives, thus reminding us that the subsequent choice of apartheid and the repression we now see was not inevitable. Duncan's son, of the same name, wrote for us thirty-seven years later in a situation which had deteriorated to the point where as a humane white South African he saw no acceptable course but constitutional government by the black majority. He has since died in exile, but the problem which both he and his father wished to cope with rationally remains in worse form than ever. A 1925 article by F. García Calderón, a Peruvian statesman, discussing dictatorship and democracy in Latin America, might be published today with only slight alterations; the phenomenon he describes, though not as discouraging as summed up in Bolívar's dictum "South America is ungovernable," survives as a perennial topic. Allen W. Dulles, after a disappointing experience as an American delegate at the 1927 Disarmament Conference in Geneva, wrote that so long as the United States was not prepared to offer the European states added security as an inducement to limit their forces, there was little expectation of being able to agree on arms limitation. Today, although the United States is bolstering European security with an army of a quarter-million men on the continent, the problem remains. Over and over, we find that though the dramatis personae and the stage setting vary, the scenario is, alas, much the same.

II

In the spring of 1927 the five-year underwriting fund for *Foreign Affairs* was due to run out and the problem of how we would continue to operate thereafter, though not my personal responsibility, was very worrying. As the fund had been somewhat oversubscribed, and as in addition some persons had made special contributions, the total received over the five years amounted to $146,085. Of this I had managed to save $41,153, by dint of economies and as a result of unpredicted increases in circulation. Frank Caruthers, our business manager, figured that with the additional income obtained by investing this nest egg and the Root Fund we would reduce our annual deficit to something under $14,000. This was the basis for my recommendation to the board of directors that they invite contributors to the underwriting fund to renew their pledges in half the original amounts for a further five-year term, to provide $12,000 annually. The sum did not seem stupendous even then; nevertheless for a time two or three directors demurred. They suggested increasing our subscription rate, which seemed a risky experiment for a new publication with a circulation of only about ten thousand, and in any case inadequate to meet the need; they also favored increasing Council dues and reducing the research and meetings program.

In the end, it was agreed to raise the new underwriting fund and not to diminish Council activities. The directors chaffed me a bit for having salted away the surplus from past years instead of returning it year by year to the original guarantors, but accepted the argument that a publishing venture ought to have *some* money in the bank against a rainy day, that the annual rebates would have been insignificant in any case and that I had given a full accounting to all concerned without awakening any protests. The new fund safeguarded publication for another five years, and at its end we continued the same procedure, persuading most of the contributors to continue their subscriptions at a quarter of the original amounts for a further five-year period. And in each period, with the consent of the contributors, an addition was made to a small but increasingly substantial capital fund. Anyone familiar with today's publishing costs will smile at the minuscule sum involved; and Cass Canfield, who bore the brunt of raising the first underwriting fund, will wonder, viewing the millions which foundations now disburse annually, why his task had been so hard.

At this point Walter H. Mallory became executive director of the Council in succession to Malcolm W. Davis, who resigned to accept the editorship of the Yale University Press. Mallory, who settled into his place in the fall of 1927, had had wide experience in various parts of the world—in the Balkans during the war and then for five years in the Far East as executive director of the China International Famine Commission. For thirty-two years he was to direct and expand the work of the Council without sacrificing excellence to size.

Two friends were star performers that summer at the Williamstown Institute. Bishop Nicholai's dramatic appearance and intense sincerity attracted even more attention there than Sforza's aristocratic bearing and intellectual brilliance. Sforza wrote me to introduce Rosetti, the Italian naval officer who single-handed had sunk the great Austrian battleship the *Viribus Unitis* in the harbor of Pola in the closing days of the World War. Rosetti sneaked into the harbor at night in a tiny rubber boat, swam under the hull and affixed there a destructive machine of his own invention. The exploit created a sensation and brought him a grant of money and the gold medal "Ad Valore," the highest Italian military decoration. But he had come to hate war, refused to sell or reveal his invention, gave his reward to charity and when the Fascists came to power escaped into exile. Now he was in New York and penniless. Could I help? He was ready, he told me, to do anything. I got him into touch, I forget how, with the engineers who were constructing the George Washington Bridge, and he went to work as a diver on the bridge foundations.

My first book, *The New Balkans*,[1] had been published in New York and London early in the year and had been serialized in newspapers in Athens, Belgrade, Vienna and elsewhere. The London *Times* was slightly condescending, implying that no mere American could thread without mishap the Balkan maze where even experienced English scholars could lose their way. Italian critics were harsher. Luigi Barzini wrote that my views were "the obstinate exhalations of an indigestible demagogy," which sounded painful for author as well as reader.

With my book off my mind and our October issue safely at press, I set off in September, 1927, for a few weeks in Europe, a trip that had been delayed by uncertainty about the magazine's financing and the change in executive directors. Coolidge had been suffering from sciatica and had not been down to New York lately; but he was writing his regular daily letters and Mallory was ready to go up to Boston to see him whenever desirable.

Paris I found in raucous occupation by the American Legion and as soon as possible went along to Rome. There I was received less uncordially than I had expected, apparently because we had established our impartiality by inviting a contribution by Professor Giovanni Gentile, the philosopher of Fascism and Mussolini's first Minister of Education. A conversation with Count Volpi, the Minister of Finance, was formal and unexciting, but it produced an offer to write an article on the economic crisis in which Italy quite plainly was about to be engulfed. His manuscript, when it arrived, showed it had given him some difficulty. Italy's economic problems were in fact hard to describe in other than pessimistic terms, as became plain in a talk with Professor Ruini, who had been Minister of Colonies and Minister of Industry in the last pre-Fascist cabinet. He spoke with grim humor about the box in which he and his anti-Fascist colleagues found themselves.

1. New York: Harper & Brothers, 1926.

"We are dead men," he said, "or at best living in the catacombs. We can only exist, think, study history and prepare to meet fresh dangers. And hope? Yes, in Italy everything is possible."

According to Ruini, the economic crisis was not crushing enough to break the government, but the contrast between the promises that had been made for this "Napoleonic year" and the dismal reality was most unsettling. If unemployment continued to grow, Mussolini had only two alternatives: to launch some foreign adventure to divert the public and win new lands, or to make a sharp turn to the left.

"Mussolini is a man of ideas and inspiration. Principles mean nothing to him. His object is to retain power. If he feels unable to wage a foreign war your American conservatives who have applauded his materialism and listened complacently to his bellicose tirades may find themselves uncomfortably arm-in-arm with a protagonist of the aroused proletariat."

An "audience" (as it was regally called) had been arranged for me with Mussolini, but on the morning of the appointed day he got word that an expected child was on the verge of being born to his wife in Milan and he departed to be present for the event. I did not meet him until May, 1933.

III

From the dry and dusty town of Bari I made a sleepless night crossing of the Adriatic to Durazzo. The harbor was crammed with Italian ships and the docks cluttered with Italian camions and matériel. A rickety car took me up from the malarial coast to Tirana, the capital of Albania, a town then of only twenty-five thousand inhabitants. The first morning as I walked through the market place and stopped to buy an orange I felt something bump against my head. It was a pair of wizened bare feet, bound together, belonging to some unfortunate who had been strung up and left as a warning to troublemakers. It was a suitable introduction to a visit where the pathetic and menacing mingled with the comic.

Since the war, Italy had moved into every Balkan situation holding the prospect of trouble and the possibility that it could be exploited. In Albania she was now hardly bothering to conceal her hand. Albanians were mostly primitive and untamed mountaineers, divided into feuding tribes, exploited by the landowners; the President, Ahmed Zogu, recently returned from exile in Belgrade, felt and was insecure; there was nobody to stand out against Italy's evident design to make the country a trans-Adriatic bridgehead. Moreover, Italy had quasi-legal standing there. In

1921, the Conference of Ambassadors in Paris, in order to be rid of one of its problems, had irresponsibly agreed that in case of trouble the maintenance of Albania's integrity should be entrusted to Italy. Exploiting this opening, Mussolini in November, 1926, had persuaded Ahmed Zogu to negotiate the Treaty of Tirana, which extended Italy's prerogatives to maintenance of the whole status quo—"political, juridical and territorial." Glittering economic and financial rewards were promised in return; these, as intended, tied Albania to Italy irretrievably. The Jugoslavs were outraged. They had succored Ahmed Zogu in exile and had aided his return to his country. The only outlet for their resentment was to blame Foreign Minister Ninchich for his naïveté and put a rival, Voja Marinkovich, in his place.

Now when I arrived in Tirana in the autumn of 1927 Italy's exploitation of her new position was in full swing. An Albanian National Bank had been established as a *succursale* of a group of Italian banks, and a newly founded Society for the Economic Development of Albania had given the Albanian Government a loan to finance public works, in return for which all revenues from monopolies and customs were pledged as security. Since there was not the remotest possibility that the interest could be paid from those or any other Albanian sources, Ahmed Zogu's only recourse was to beg off payments and ask Italy for further help. The Italian Government obliged, by advancing to the Society for the Economic Development of Albania the sum due it from the Albanian Government. Thus the expenditure was shifted to the shoulders of the Italian taxpayer (who knew nothing of what was being done), and Ahmed Zogu was tied still more tightly to Mussolini. Italy held a mortgage on Albania which Albania could never hope to pay off and on which she would never be able to pay a lira of interest.

To show that she intended to put this advantage to practical use Italy sent her Chief of Army Engineers to lay out a network of roads, which led mainly toward the Jugoslav and Greek frontiers from tiny harbors which did not exist in a commercial sense but might serve as convenient points for the debarkation of troops. From friends in the British and French legations who were more disturbed than their home offices by these developments, I secured a list of fifty-six Italian officers wearing Albanian insignia and serving as commanders of the general army depots at Durazzo and Tirana, of three army groups and of the artillery and engineering corps— even as commander of the President's personal guard. (A correspondent of the London *Times* ingenuously labeled them "instructors.") In addition, 40 mountain guns had arrived from Italy, plus 20,000 rifles and 120 Fiat machine guns. All uniforms were also Italian. In other words, the Albanian Army was practically a branch of the Italian Army.

Thus briefed I applied for an interview with President Ahmed Zogu. A formal written reply set a time and stipulated that I should arrive *en redingote,* i.e., clad in a frock coat. I replied that I would do so if I could procure one in Tirana. No objection was made when I presented myself at the palace in a flannel suit such as I usually wore in traveling.

I found Zogu in uniform, tall, younger looking than I had expected, flabby in face and cosmopolitan in manner. He indicated several times that he was scared of assassination, a usual occurrence in Albania. As there was nobody to step into his shoes if that happened, and Italy could seize on the resulting chaos as an excuse to occupy the country entirely, I could see that he was in real danger not merely from hostile tribesmen but from his protectors also. He told me that of the Italian loan (nominally for 50,000,000 gold francs but increased by bankers' fees, Italian taxes, advertising, etc. to 70,500,000 gold francs) he had received so far "about 6,000,000 gold francs," making it a not very advantageous transaction, the more so as he admitted that no gold had come into the country, all advances being in the form of paper notes issued by his own national bank.

Zogu expected that the next year the Italian Government would again supply the funds to rescue the Society for the Economic Development of Albania. But he claimed to be confident that by the year following the investment would begin to provide larger state revenues. He could not explain how this could be, as most of the expenditures were not of a sort ever to be productive, and some, for instance the railway being built from Durazzo to the capital, would always be a liability. His answer to a question how the complete reequipment of the army was being financed was complicated, but boiled down to the fact that it was being charged to the account of the Italian Government with the Albanian National Bank.

When I pointed out that Italy seemed to have acquired a mortgage on the country which she could foreclose at any convenient moment Zogu turned in desperation to the subject of sport. With no transition, he told me how fond he was of sport, that he hoped to persuade Americans to visit Albania to hunt and fish and that he intended having huts erected in the mountains to accommodate them. A liar who knows you know he is lying is a pathetic figure.

My impression was that he might like to wriggle out of the Italian net, but by now it was pinned down at every corner.

The year after my visit, Ahmed Zogu proclaimed himself King as Zog I and ruled as a dictator supported by Italian subsidies. Yet when Mussolini decided in the spring of 1939 to match Hitler's expansion into Czechoslovakia by making Albania virtually a part of Italy, demanding a customs union and the right to install an Italian garrison, Zog surprisingly refused. Mussolini invaded the country on Good Friday with 100,000 troops. King Zog fled and King Victor Emmanuel proclaimed the country an Italian province. The scene thus was set for Italy to use it as a launching point to invade Greece when she entered the World War. That military operation proved to be disastrous, however, to the point that Hitler had to send troops to the rescue. In the civil war which followed the Armistice the Communists established their rule by savage executions and expropriations, and have since maintained it, first as a satellite of the Soviets, later with the support of Peking. Zog, after years of exile in London, in Cairo and on Long Island, finally settled in the favorite haven of ex-royalties, Cannes; and died in Paris in 1961.

It was with some misgivings that I set off by road from Tirana for Scutari, on the great lake of the same name bordering Jugoslavia in the north. The countryside was far from tranquil and bands of mountaineers were liable to waylay and pillage travelers. In one incident members of a League of Nations mission had been attacked and killed, not, apparently, because of any particular objection to the League but because the individuals were foreigners, and Albanians had learnt from long experience dating back to Turkish times that most foreigners were better, from their point of view, dead. But I was told that the road to the north via Alessio was usually safe, and in any case it was the only way for me to get to Jugoslavia unless I took the same foul boat back to Bari and made a roundabout journey to Belgrade via Trieste. My English-speaking driver pointed out things of interest along the way and cheerfully changed tires when, as happened several times, they blew out on the jagged loose stones over which we bumped along. On a sharp curve between two rocky heights he drew up and remarked as an item of interest that it was just here that the League mission had been ambushed. I urged him to push ahead.

After a regrettable night at an inn in Alessio we skirted Lake Scutari, reflecting distant storm clouds on its brilliantly green surface, and crossed into Montenegro. I took another car along the spectacular coast of the Boka Kotorska to Dubrovnik (stopping once by the roadside, I remember, for warm purple figs bursting open in seams of crystallized sweetness) ; and from there went by the narrow-gauge railway which my wife and I had become acquainted with in 1919 to Brod and thence reached Belgrade.

IV

The year before, it may be remembered, the Jugoslav Government had hoped to persuade Italy and France to stabilize the situation in the Balkans by guaranteeing the status quo. Mussolini had refused to participate if France did and Briand had been unwilling to go into a pact with Jugoslavia alone. This year, I found, things were different. French policy had hardened, probably on Poincaré's insistence, influenced by the signature of the Treaty of Tirana and Mussolini's acquisition of a position in Albania which could be useful at any moment propitious for a Balkan adventure. At lunch, King Alexander told me that the French Ambassador in Rome had called on Foreign Minister Grandi only the week previous to inform him of France's decision to sign a bilateral treaty of guarantee with Jugoslavia. Grandi had merely replied that he would report the fact to Mussolini. The Italian Government was very angry. The treaty would nevertheless be signed the next week in Paris. The King referred to it as an "alliance," which brought France into a relationship with Jugoslavia like that binding the three Little Entente states to each other. This strengthened Jugoslavia not only materially but morally as well, for it showed French confidence that she was a factor for peace in the Balkans. The great war scare that Mussolini had raised in March, when he accused Jugoslavia of concentrating troops on the Albanian border and called on London, Paris and Berlin to stop the intended invasion, was seen now to have been a pure fabrication to cover his own projects in that neighborhood.

This interpretation jibed with what I had been told in Tirana by General Percy, the British head of the Albanian gendarmerie: there had been absolutely no evidence to support Mussolini's report of a threatened Jugoslav attack.

"No special trouble impended at that time on the Jugoslav frontier," Percy said, "so far as I know. And if anyone was to know it would be me, for I was responsible for internal security. Mussolini must have had some other motive."

As events proved, Mussolini did. In Balkan political geography all roads led from Rome.

The *komitadji* action in Macedonia was more than usually vicious this year, the King said. His Legation in Rome reported that three or four *komitadji* leaders had been there in the spring to obtain their annual subventions from the Palazzo Chigi and to receive instructions; and following the return of these men to Bulgaria the incursions into Macedonia had been stepped up. From time to time, too, disgruntled *komitadjis* who had "sold out" to the Jugoslavs reported that Italian money supported the whole operation, the object being, of course, to prevent a Jugoslav-Bulgarian reconciliation. Was not the only solution, I asked, for the Jugoslav Government to ignore so far as possible the terroristic acts in Macedonia, pass over the heads of the *komitadjis* and thwart Italy by coming to an accord directly with the Bulgarian Government? This was his precise object, the King replied, despite the protests raised by some of his military people. The trouble was that the Bulgarian Government did not dare offend the Macedonian émigrés who played such a great role in Bulgarian politics and who would unhesitatingly kill anyone favoring compromise.

Before I left New York, Ninchich had written me that progress was at last being made toward forming a committee of scholars to collate all the documents that could be found relating to the Sarajevo murder. Some hidden in Kraljevo during the Serbian retreat and found by the Austrians had been retrieved from Vienna by a mission sent there for the purpose; some taken personally by Pashich to Corfu had been turned over by his widow to King Alexander; others had been found in the Austrian archives in Sarajevo. I asked the King whether he in fact had documents bearing on the Sarajevo affair in his possession, and asked that if so I might have copies. He said he had received some of Pashich's papers but that they related to events long before the war. However, he said, there was an interesting letter from Count Tisza that had come from Sarajevo (mentioned in the preceding chapter) ; he would have it looked up and give me a copy, also copies of any of Pashich's papers that were relevant if they had not gone already to the Foreign Ministry.

He seemed more serious than I remembered his being even the year before, but perhaps it was because then he had been on a holiday in Bled. I noticed his first gray hairs. He showed me how much he had been Americanized; he now smoked Camels instead of the French Marylands he had adopted during the war.

V

In Sofia, the main topic was still in 1927, as it had been in 1924, Macedonia. With one exception, the dozen public figures I talked with professed to favor reaching an agreement with Jugoslavia, though some seemed more sincere than others. The exception was Stanichev, a member of parliament and head of the Macedonian National Committee (not to be confused with the even more fanatical IMRO), with headquarters in the blandly named Macedonian Scientific Institute. He asserted that the Macedonian Bulgars had started the Bulgarian national renaissance and were the only authentic Bulgars. Assassination and terror were the only practicable reply to the brutality of the Jugoslav administration in Macedonia. If ever an entente was established between Sofia and Belgrade it would have no effect on Macedonian tactics.

Neither of the two cabinet ministers whom I met was very hopeful that such an entente was in the offing. Molov, Minister of Finance, a funny little ball of a man, with a paunch and a pudgy face, admitted tacitly that the current bad relationship was to the advantage only of Italy. Burov, the Minister of Foreign Affairs, gave the reasons why the bad relationship was a fact. He struck me as a decisive and active sort of man despite a heavy-set body and a ponderous head sunk deep into a thick neck; and he replied sharply, when he had asked me what they were thinking in Belgrade, to my remark that there was a tendency there to accept Bulgaria's good faith but that stress was put on the difficulty of concerting any common policy with a government which was so much at the mercy of the Macedonian émigrés. This annoyed him, and he said very vigorously that he wished the government in Belgrade, which felt itself so strong and righteous, would speak and act plainly and directly. The only conciliatory moves possible in Sofia would be in reply to Jugoslav reforms in the Macedonian administration. His government disowned Bulgarian-sponsored acts of terrorism in Macedonia but it simply could not afford to open up a new civil war by taking on the whole half-million Macedonians in Bulgaria; with the support of sober opinion it could try to deal with those who took illegal action, but to do this successfully presumed a moderate attitude in Belgrade "and an extended hand." To stress individual incidents was to give too much importance and power to people who could always create them.

While I was with Burov word came that Prime Minister Liapchev was ready to see me. I remembered him as a gruff person from whom I had not gotten much three years earlier when he had not yet come to power. He was rather fat, heavy about the jowls, with an impassive expression and heavy-lidded eyes. He asked in bad French what I had seen in Albania and was amused by my frank description of Italian operations there. "It can never be made a country," he remarked. He denied any knowledge that Italy was acting directly to stir up trouble in Macedonia, though he admitted that it was easy enough to imagine it. I remembered the Belgrade story about the Italian stipends paid to *komitadji* agents but said nothing to contradict him. He gave the impression of wanting to talk further about the subject but restrained himself, merely adding that "it would be unfortunate if any foreign power got accustomed to thinking of itself as preeminently fitted to supervise the destinies of the Balkan states"—not a weak statement in the circumstances. He went on to say that he thought the Jugoslav regime in Macedonia was better than it had been a couple of years earlier, but that there remained much that a strong government could do there in the way of reform.

Only a couple of others need be mentioned. One was Minkov, Secretary-General in the Foreign Ministry, like many other Bulgarians in public life a graduate of Robert College in Istanbul. He talked loudly in a positive manner, tossed about matchboxes and pounded the table to relieve his feelings and emphasize his views. He spoke in favor of an accord with Jugoslavia, but asked why Bulgaria should give up outside support in order to get it. It wasn't a question of Italy's support but Britain's too; Sir Austen Chamberlain was such a champion of Italy that his interest in a reconciliation between Sofia and Belgrade was halfhearted.

In Belgrade I had heard gossip implicating King Boris in the 1923 murder of the Bulgarian peasant leader and popular hero Prime Minister Alexander Stamboliski, who had opposed Bulgaria's alliance with Germany in the war, deposed King Ferdinand, worked for union with Jugoslavia and won the hatred of the conservatives, the army and the Macedonians. King Alexander told me that a former associate of Stamboliski's had asserted that Boris was privy to the plot, but that he could not believe it. I thought he might be quoting Kosta Todorov, former Minister to Belgrade and now living there. But I came to know Todorov quite well, both in Belgrade and later in New York, and I never heard any such accusation from him; and in his book, *Balkan Firebrand,* he divided the guilt for the assassination between the Macedonians and the paid agents of Italy.

I thought it would be interesting to get the views on this of two men who had been close to Stamboliski—his nephew, Muraviev, and Tomov, who had been his Minister of War. Their stories were the same in essentials.

King Boris, they said, had telephoned Stamboliski shortly before the coup which led to his death to say that he was coming to visit him in his native village, Slavovitsa, and had asked him to wait for him there. The implication drawn from this was that Boris knew of the plot and wanted to be sure Stamboliski would be captured. Muraviev and Tomov said this was not at all the case. On June 5 King Boris did telephone from

Vranje to Stamboliski that he was going to stop to see him on his way to Plovdiv, but a mile or so after starting his car broke down, and this and a change in the weather decided him to put off the trip. Two days later he started again, taking with him two or three fine melons from his garden as a present. He stayed for lunch with Stamboliski, and in the afternoon went on to Kritchin, near Plovdiv. It was the following night, at about three o'clock on the morning of June 8, that the army coup occurred. Nobody knew exactly where the King was, and he did not get word until about 11 A.M. at Vranje. Meanwhile, Stamboliski had heard of the coup and had fled with some retainers, making for the Jugoslav frontier; but he was captured on the 13th and murdered on the 14th. All the indications were that Boris was not implicated. The organizers of the coup had been much worried what his attitude toward them would be, but decided to brazen it out. When the members of the revolutionary cabinet, led by the new Prime Minister, Tsankov, came to inform the King, he received them in silence. Tsankov thereupon said threateningly that if he did not accept the new regime the cabinet would retire to discuss the question of who should occupy the throne. My informants asserted that the King detested Tsankov, and in return Tsankov cut down his influence on affairs drastically.

Muraviev, an attractive young man, educated in France, had taken me to a café where we could talk quietly. He said that Boris had always shown a sincere fondness for Stamboliski "and Stamboliski liked him as a son." (Our Minister in Sofia, Charles Wilson, said the same thing; Boris always spoke to him about Stamboliski with sorrow and affection.) Muraviev maintained that his uncle had been killed not only because the reactionaries hated his reformist policies but because he made union with Jugoslavia the cornerstone of his policy, and this the Macedonians would not tolerate.

A few days later, passing through Belgrade a second time, I told King Alexander that some of Stamboliski's family and friends exonerated Boris from responsibility for his death. He expressed considerable relief; he had much sympathy for Boris, he said. "He always struck me as a well-meaning young man, but rather bewildered and out of his depth. He had suffered horribly from having King Ferdinand as a father, and the scars from his childhood still remain." When Ferdinand came into the room, he said, Boris' face changed completely and "he shut up like a mussel."

I wondered whether Boris' lost childhood accounted for his obsession with pastimes like driving locomotives; he loved being photographed leaning from the cab, peering ahead, goggles over his eyes.

PART THREE

On the Eve

Those who cannot remember the past are
condemned to repeat it.

—George Santayana

27

King Alexander, Poincaré,
Sir Austen Chamberlain

King Alexander was at Topola, about twenty-five miles from Belgrade on the road leading south into the Shumadija, the "Wooded Country," the most Serbian part of Serbia. He had a small villa there—a cottage, really, though built of stone, not wood. He sent a car to bring me down from Belgrade. The road led past the foot of Avala, a road I knew very well, though I remembered it best in the spring when it was rutted and muddy. Now the maize had been harvested and the grapes had been picked in the vineyards, but the air was calm and still smelt of summer.

Topola is identified with Kara George, the rude but brilliant strategist who led the first successful revolts against the Turks early in the last century. It was not his birthplace, but he had settled there as a dealer in cattle and pigs after coming back from exile in Austria following a youthful brawl in which he had killed a Turk; and it was from Topola that he started the risings against the janissaries that several times cleared the Turks temporarily out of the country. Later, a rival leader, Milosh Obrenovich, had him murdered and sent his head to Constantinople as a compliment to the Sultan, thus starting a fatal family and dynastic feud. Kara George's remains were buried in the village church at Topola but were moved by King Alexander to a fine modern church not far away, built originally by King Peter as a family mausoleum. It was largely destroyed in the Austrian invasion, but King Alexander rebuilt its cupolas and adorned it with magnificent mosaics based on the Byzantine frescoes at Dechani, Grachanitsa and other famous monasteries in Old Serbia. He placed the tombs of Kara George and King Peter in the church itself, under plain blocks of marble, and those of other members of the family in a dark crypt; eventually his body was buried in the crypt also, next to that of his Montenegrin mother.

Sentries of the royal guard stood on the side road leading to the house but otherwise there was no sign of special security, even though two armed Bulgars had been caught in the neighborhood the week before. The Maréchal of the court was also at lunch; Queen Marie appeared only afterward. The King talked sensibly about Macedonia and Albania and reported that the signing of the treaty with France had been postponed when the Jugoslav Minister in Paris was told that the question of the prewar Serbian bonds should be regulated in advance and an agreement about payment signed simultaneously. The King took the position that an important treaty, a fundamental cornerstone of Jugoslav foreign policy, ought not to be linked with a question of money and thereby diminished in importance in the minds of the public. The treaty with France was finally signed November 11. Perhaps the delay had really been due to a desire not to prejudice current negotiations with Italy. When hope of a general agreement with Italy was shattered by her signature of the Treaty of Tirana, there was no longer reason to wait.

Ninchich wrote me afterward that he believed Italy's policy toward Jugoslavia was inspired largely by her rivalry with France. Mussolini had offered to "let Jugoslavia do anything she wanted in the Balkans" if she would renounce her friendship with France. The Jugoslavs had not even considered the offer, said Ninchich, knowing it would have given them only temporary immunity.

The extent of Jugoslav worries over the Treaty of Tirana was revealed in a letter from Prince Paul. "We consider it a repetition of the annexation of Bosnia-Herzegovina in 1908," he wrote. "It's the first step of imperialistic Italy in the Balkans and we can't help wondering if it was worth getting rid of Austria to see her replaced by Italy."

II

In Paris, André Tardieu, now Minister for Colonies, said he knew I had been in the Balkans because Poincaré had read in the Council of Ministers a letter received from me after my visit to Albania. Tardieu doubted that Mussolini was actually preparing a war (so did I), but merely readying Italy to take advantage of any opening, political or military, which might offer (I agreed). "His attitude is that of a speculator waiting his chance to cash in." He scouted Ninchich's idea that Mussolini's main purpose in the Balkans was to hem in Jugoslavia so as to weaken and exasperate France. "What have we to fear from Italy?" he asked. "The real and permanent danger is Germany." There doubtless were many sincere Germans, but who could be sure of the future rulers of that ambitious people?

At dinner the night before, André Géraud had told me of Tardieu's aspirations to become Premier, but said that if he ever arrived at that peak it would not last for long. "He is a vigorous administrator but has no judgment and no grasp of ideas." Géraud tended to agree with Ninchich's assessment of Mussolini's strategy, and Professor Louis Eisenmann, who was there, accepted it even more emphatically. Elizabeth Bibesco, a sparkling conversationalist, dominated the dinner; for me, however, she had a very moderate charm. Talk tended to be episodic, as her relentless succession of bons mots jerked it from one scandal to another.

Lunch the next day at the Bibesco flat on the Quai Bourbon was more peaceful, as Princess Bibesco had gone to London. When I exclaimed on the quiet loveliness of the view down the Seine, Bibesco said the Ile St. Louis had the reputation of being the quietest spot in Paris; Anatole France had mentioned it favorably as the only part of the city where the New York *Herald* was not for sale. Bibesco gave me a pass to his play *Laquelle?*, the plot of which revolved around a man's efforts to discover which of three ladies at a country house he had slept with the night before. He said there was no satisfaction like that of writing a play: "You are father and mother and midwife too." I had no chance to see *Laquelle?* but Jimmy James of the *New York Times,* told me I was fortunate to miss it. In that husky voice of his he muttered, "Social double-entendres are always boring. Conversation in a brothel is more direct and more satisfactory." James's great concern at the time was which should take precedence—German reparations or payments on the American and other private loans supplied on a lavish scale to German industry, states and municipalities. The matter turned out to be largely academic.

As usual, Poincaré was at the Ministry of Finance. He had just read Coolidge's article on Anglo-French relations and his verdict was that "it could not be more complete, reasonable and fair—the work of a genuine historian." He was especially glad that Coolidge recognized that England had not been bound to come to the aid of France in 1914; the nature of the engagement had been made absolutely plain in an exchange of letters two years earlier, but people still mistook the facts. He said he was inserting a footnote in the next volume of his memoirs[1] contrasting Coolidge's account with that of Harry Elmer Barnes, a revisionist historian, who, he was "stupefied" to see, wrote that it had been practically certain that Britain would enter the war on the side of France and Russia.

Poincaré said that my letter about Albania had supplemented as well as confirmed what he already knew. I discovered that he tended to believe that Mussolini had saved Italy from Bolshevism, and he resisted any arguments to the contrary. Mussolini's vanity, he thought, handicapped his considerable intelligence. "Prestige is not a policy." When I asked about the possibility that Mussolini might land troops in Albania, he said that would be too serious a menace to the peace of Europe to be tolerated. Like Tardieu, he felt that Mussolini would not dare do anything so provocative, but he admitted that his action the preceding spring in accusing Jugoslavia of plotting aggression, for which he could present no shadow of evidence, did indicate a serious long-term design. And there was always the danger that he might do something rash in a crisis such as would arise if King Alexander was ever assassinated. "That would be a fearful blow. The King is one of the stabilizing factors in Europe. He is one of Europe's few statesmen."

King Boris had been in Paris recently and had come to see Poincaré at his house. Poincaré thought better of him than of his father. "King Ferdinand," he said, "was always suspect. You could never believe a word he said." Boris struck him as sincere in his wish for good relations with Jugoslavia and with France. "I told him," Poincaré said, "that in spite of the fact that Bulgaria had betrayed France I was prepared to be friendly with her, but that the extent to which friendship was possible would depend on the degree of friendship shown by Bulgaria toward France's nearby friends."

He professed to feel secure on financial issues for the present, and when I asked if it would not be risky to face elections early in the next year before the franc had been finally stabilized, he said: "On the contrary. It would be a risk to stabilize before a long period of political tranquillity is in sight. The Radical Socialists would not dare assume the responsibility of defeating the budget now, but they might think they could overturn my financial policy when it had set things firmly on the right course." He recalled that I had once said King Alexander was blamed for being too Serb in Croatia and too Jugoslav in Serbia. "I am like that here—too radical for the conservatives, too conservative for the radicals. And it

1. See *L'Union Sacré*. Paris: Plon, 1927, p. 436.

is a fact that I am a bit more conservative than the complexion of the Chamber as a whole."

That was true, but his underlying principles carried both sides, other than the extremists, with him. He was sufficiently acceptable to the Right because of his rectitude and financial soundness. He was sufficiently acceptable to the Left because of his record as an "old republican," who had opposed jingoist "Boulangism," who had been a Dreyfusard, who had voted for the separation of Church and State. The elections of April, 1928, gave him more than 330 out of 610 seats. He then proceeded to turn the *de facto* stabilization of the currency into stabilization *de jure* by vote of the Chamber and Senate. He remained Premier until the end of July, 1929; and he resigned then only because he faced a severe operation.

III

From London I wrote Coolidge of my meetings with Sir Austen Chamberlain, Sir William Tyrrell, Viscount Cecil, Lord Chelmsford and Ramsay MacDonald. "But I've kept my head," I hurried to reassure him. "Geoffrey Dawson, of the *Times,* asked me to do them an article on disarmament, and I refused, showing I'm more discreet and conscious of my limitations than I used to be." Anyway, Cecil was promising an article on the League and disarmament for our spring issue and I was saving such ideas and arguments as I might have to "steam him up."

Cecil I discovered to be one of the strangest figures imaginable. If he had not been so agreeable and so transparently honest he would have been decidedly unattractive, always scratching some part of himself and kicking his ungainly legs around. In his lankiness he was not unlike his brother, Lord Salisbury, the famous three-times Prime Minister. Unconsciously he revealed to me how the English are able to stand such frigid houses. As he sprawled with his long legs stretched out across a chair the flaps of his vest turned up, disclosing that it was lined with red flannel; moreover, an opening in his shirt revealed that under it he was wearing a red flannel undershirt.

We talked mainly about the League of Nations, of which he was England's most indefatigable advocate. He thought the Jugoslavs had made a tremendous mistake in not forcing the Albanian issue at Geneva when Italy made her quite plainly false charges; he could not understand why Briand had dissuaded them. He looked glum when I told him that everywhere in the Balkans British policy was accepted as a matter of course to be supporting Italy. He spoke feelingly of the League's diminishing chance of changing old habits of thought and diplomacy. Yet the League carried the one hope of averting a new and greater war. It had been the conception of an American President more than anyone else, but the United States had then decided to disown responsibility and left others to try to make it work. It could not be done.

I could not answer Cecil's inquiries as to what had become of traditional American idealism. Even more strange, he thought, was the disappearance of the liking Americans had always had for adventure and experiment. They used to be tireless, he said, in searching out new ways to get things done. It had been what made the country great. What had made them so cautious? All I could do was persuade him to ask these questions in *Foreign Affairs*. I went away respecting his integrity but somewhat depressed by what Arthur Salter called his "monastic presence."

In one of the boardinghouses on one of London's innumerable Crescents I found Salvemini, hemmed in by mountains of documents, books and newspapers which divided his room into cubbyholes. One narrow corridor between the teetering piles led from the door to the chair and table; a branch passageway gave access to the bed, on which he sat while I occupied the chair; and another passageway led to the lavatory. He was industriously and gaily at work, not regretting for a moment his exile but only the disaster into which he was certain Italy would be led by Mussolini—"the *malade imaginaire*." In their hearts the Italian people were ashamed of Mussolini, he said, and some of themselves for tolerating him. But this was of no account. Mussolini could not be displaced unless he made some great mistake, such as attempting to overthrow the King; or by a revolt of high army officers, which would really be a coup d'état on behalf of the Prince of Piedmont; or in a war which Italy began losing; or by assassination.

When Salvemini had some particularly good point to make his voice went up to a falsetto, and his sharp eyes looked at you humorously through his steel-rimmed spectacles to make sure that the sally had been understood and fully appreciated. He was in touch with colleagues at the University of Florence who had decided to "outlive" Fascism at home, but pitied their constricted life more than he envied its comparative comfort. I reminded him of a wonderful passage in an article he had written for us a couple of years before, in which he summed up the many advantages which Italy had obtained from the war, the last on the list being that the new generation of Italian statesmen had acquired the right to choose whether to be dogs or men—dogs, if they decided to fight new wars, men, if they chose to work for the peace of the world. Without waiting for my question, he said, "Alas, they are choosing to be dogs."

I felt qualms about my lack of appreciation for Princess Bibesco when she invited me to lunch at the Asquith house on Bedford Square to meet Geoffrey Dawson, editor of the *Times,* smug and catty (he later would play a role in the Cliveden set in support of Munich), and Gerald Barry, editor of *The Saturday Review.* Her talk reflected her father's uncertainty about the political good sense of Sir Austen Chamberlain, now Foreign Secretary. Dawson, disagreeing, offered to drop me at the Foreign Office.

Admittedly I went into the Foreign Secretary's old-fashioned Victorian office, smelling of coal gas from the open grate, somewhat predisposed against its occupant. Nor did his rather faded hair, eyes that gave the impression of not focusing exactly, monocle that seemed designed to conceal the fact and bouquet of discolored teeth argue for a change of heart. My mention that I had met him briefly at Geneva a year before was a mistake at the start, for it gave him a chance to open up at length on his favorite topic, Locarno. His little speech ended up, "It is seldom given to anyone to do anything thoroughly, which is why I am prouder of Locarno than any other achievement in my life." Seeing that he must somehow be shaken out of his platitudes, I seized on a passing reference to the Balkans to remark that one of the obstacles to a Jugoslav-Bulgarian rapprochement was Italy, and then repeated the statement of a Foreign Ministry official in Sofia that he saw no reason why Bulgaria, just in order to satisfy Belgrade, should give up the support not only of Rome but of London also. Sir Austen retorted sharply that he knew it was the fashion to say he was in Mussolini's pocket simply because he was one of the few statesmen in Europe who could talk to him. It was safer to have him as a friend, under surveillance, than a savage beyond the pale.

"Mussolini does not want or plan war," he said. "But Italy would be threatened if Jugoslavia secured Albania and bottled up the Adriatic." My suggestion that you couldn't bottle up the Adriatic unless you occupied *both* sides of the Straits of Otranto was, he said, a quibble; and he defended at some length Italy's requirements for self-defense. When I asked whether Italy hadn't in effect secured a mortgage on Albania, he agreed; but not that it was part of a nefarious plot; Mussolini aimed merely to exercise a restraining influence on Albanian behavior. Not Jugoslavia but Italy was the truly aggrieved party. The former Jugoslav Minister in Rome had written anti-Italian articles under a nom de plume and had been kept in the diplomatic service even after the fact became known. "No country with any discipline or sense of propriety would tolerate such a scandalous performance. It is contemptible, and shows the weakness of the Jugoslav Government." In any case, he went on, that government was a "pretty wretched" affair, with its constant cabinet crises, the attacks of politicians against former friends and their reconciliations with former enemies, all for reasons of expediency. "If it had a proper estimate of its power" (he meant, of course, its weakness) "and sincerely tried to come to terms with Italy, things could quickly be arranged." Then he shifted his ground. "The Jugoslavs have an inferiority complex. They still think of themselves as persecuted little Serbia. If they are to continue to exist as an important state they must take the responsibilities of one." Then he added, as an afterthought, "I must say that in the crisis last March when Italy made those silly charges they acted very well, very sensibly."

When I inquired why Austria, Hungary, Greece and Bulgaria had received the benefit of financial and administrative help from the League of Nations, whereas Albania, the most inexperienced, weakest and neediest of all, had been "turned over to the Credito Italiano," he stiffened and said resentfully that it did not befit an American to criticize the League for not assuming responsibilities; to which I was glad to agree, as it was my first opportunity to agree with anything he had said so far.

To amend this unfavorable picture, I must note that in later years I came to see the good points of honesty and high character that offset to some degree the fact (at least so I believed it to be) that his approach to Europe's problems was conventional and unimaginative. He was right in taking credit for being one of the authors of Locarno and thus bringing Germany into the League, and his fundamental partiality for France outlasted the period when he felt it so important to conciliate Mussolini. His petulance at our first meeting was not in fact usual, and when I found that he was often ready to exchange views in a most amiable manner I realized that my questions then had been unnecessarily irritating. They did bring out, however, the extent to which his conception of British interests was synonymous with Italian interests in that period, a fact which had its disagreeable effect on subsequent history.

My interview with Chamberlain had been arranged by Sir William Tyrrell, the powerful Permanent Undersecretary at the Foreign Office, and he had invited me to see him afterward. He evidently shared his chief's general attitude, but with qualifications. "Mussolini does not want war," he said; "he wants economic penetration. But he is clumsy and I feel sure he will find Albania a costly mistake." He would do better, he thought, to expand in Asia Minor. But if Mussolini sought only economic advantages, why had he made out a case for intervening in Albania last spring? "That I don't know," Tyrrell replied, "unless it is that unlike most statesmen he thinks nothing of writing high-sounding notes." Then he added reflectively, "We couldn't quite make that out." Of all the warborn states, Jugoslavia in his view stood the least chance of surviving. Like Chamberlain, he considered its government "altogether wretched." His conclusion: "The Jugoslavs ought to flatter Mussolini; he is very susceptible to good treatment."

Mrs. Ronnie Greville was a leading London hostess in those days, a tremendous snob, an adorer of royalty and the possessor of famous jewels. I had met her in New York; now she had heard via Austen Chamberlain that I was in London and asked me to lunch. I arrived to find a dozen or more persons standing around in the drawing room but no Mrs. Greville. We walked about looking at the pictures, giving each other furtive side glances. As a foreigner I didn't dare make any advances, and since the others either didn't know each other or didn't like each other the next forty-five minutes passed in silence. Then the doors were flung open and Mrs. Greville appeared saying that she had been caught on the telephone by the dear Queen of Spain, who had asked her to take her to the theatre that evening; they had to discuss what to see and she simply hadn't been able to break away. She may very well have been talking with the Queen of Spain but you suspected (and you felt everyone else suspected) that the entrance had been delayed to make the maximum impression. She then proceeded to describe me as this young man who had been so perfectly charming as to offer to introduce her—as though she didn't already know *everybody*—to political people in New York. Wasn't it charming of me, really too charming? I felt I had earned my right to escape the moment lunch was over. Later I read in Chips Channon's diaries that there was "no one on earth so skilfully malicious" as she, which, coming from a dear friend of hers who was himself a specialist in the art, is impressive. Harold Nicolson, who was not a friend, described her simply as "a fat slug filled with venom."

I went up to Cambridge for a night with Harold Temperley, the historian, at King's College, one of the loveliest of the noble buildings looking across the Backs to the River Cam. The beauties of Oxford and Cambridge have been endlessly compared; perhaps it is not invidious to say that the Backs give Cambridge a calm beauty not duplicated anywhere else. A group of Temperley's colleagues had been trying to get him appointed Regius Professor of History, but as he was a Liberal and the government was Conservative they were not sanguine of success. The reason seemed a poor one, but the situation was no more strange than that a Nonconformist Prime Minister should have the right to choose the bishops of the Church of England.

Not surprisingly we talked late into the night about the future of Central Europe, particularly about Hungary's bid to revise the Treaty of Trianon frontiers. Temperley considered some revisions possible and advisable, but thought almost insurmountable difficulties had been raised by the violence of the Magyar irredentist propaganda and the ignorance of many of those abroad who had been won over by it, especially Lord Rothermere and his *Daily Mail,* to say nothing of Lloyd George, who having had access to all the argumentation at the time of the Peace Conference ought to know better. One barrier would be removed, he thought, if the Hungarian Government would specify certain moderate demands that would be accepted as a final settlement; but this seemed most unlikely. Meanwhile, the Minorities Treaties might operate to calm the Magyar agitation somewhat. He agreed to spell out the problem in an article.

At Chatham House I told Arnold Toynbee that the Council was planning to publish an annual yearbook, but that it could not rival his wide-ranging work, since it would be mainly a review and appraisal of American foreign policy in the preceding year. At the behest of Lionel Curtis I agreed to speak to a Chatham House group of Balkan experts—a fair enough return, I had to admit, for all the visitors to New York I'd cajoled into doing the same sort of thing at the Council. The questions were good. The main argument was over whether Mussolini was keeping pots boiling in Albania, Bulgaria and indeed all over the map in order to maintain his domestic prestige or as preparation for making trouble at the first chance. Some maintained the former (as I remember, Toynbee among them), some agreed with me that the latter was the most likely (Seton-Watson was one of these). Noel-Buxton asserted with shattering self-assurance that both views were ridiculous; Mussolini was Bulgaria's and Albania's only truely unselfish friend.

I V

It was on the whole a satisfying bag that I brought back from Europe —articles or promises of articles from Cecil, Géraud, Temperley, Thyssen, Volpi and others, plus a manuscript of my own, "Italy, Jugoslavia and Lilliputia," the product of my experience in Albania.

But all my élan evaporated when I learnt that Coolidge's health had been deteriorating steadily and that the doctors seemed uncertain as to the origin of the sciatica that was plaguing him and of how to deal with it. X-rays were reported to show nothing serious. His brother Harold J. Coolidge writes in his biography that as early as June of 1927 "something in his face convinced me that he would not live long."[2] The Coolidge family was an unusually reticent one, even in a city by habit as reticent as Boston and in an era far more reticent than ours. At any rate, no hint of the suspicion entertained by his brother was conveyed to Coolidge's friends, and I myself was misled that summer by the clarity and vigor of his daily letters and the usual wide-ranging scope of his interests.

Writing me in June that he did not feel up to coming to New York for a meeting of our Editorial Advisory Board, he admonished me sternly: "It is not that I am really ill. I am not." He added that he had bought a new baby typewriter "so as to not waste my leisure" and was "also going on with my literary education, and having finished 'Evelina' have begun on 'Roderick Random.' " I agreed that Fanny Burney and Smollett were soothing fare. However, an occasional mention that he was feeling tired and that his mind was not functioning well was entirely uncharacteristic of him, and since he had never to my knowledge had anything worse than a cold or pinkeye I was brash enough to tell him (thirty-four advising sixty-one) that he should not rest content with treatment by a family doctor but ought to put himself in the hands of the best Boston specialists. He had, in fact, always seemed robust. One peculiarity disconcerting to me was his diet: he disliked vegetables and fruit and ate only meat and fish. Gay, I found, was giving him the same advice. But it was not until August that a new doctor took charge, ordered X-rays of his teeth and found that several badly needed extracting. It seemed that the focus of infection had been found; his condition improved and he was able at last to move into his "Stone House" at Squam.

Before I left for Europe, he had embarked on an article for our autumn issue, and we had many letters to and fro about it, criticisms and encouragements on my side, discontents on his. It turned out in the end to be one of his very best pieces (the one praised so highly by Poincaré). On my return he was active in criticizing the draft of my own manuscript which I brought back with me. He went into detail in two long letters. The Franco-German Treaty had been signed while I was at sea, followed almost at once by a new Treaty of Tirana between Italy and Albania. He considered the last more significant than I had suggested in calling it a "gesture of bad humor" and than the French would like to think it. He said it was "an effective score by which Italy makes a thumb at France

2. Harold Jefferson Coolidge and Robert Howard Lord, *Archibald Cary Coolidge, Life and Letters*. Boston: Houghton, Mifflin, 1932, p. 340.

and indicates (whether correctly or not does not matter) that she is not going to let her policy in the Balkans be interfered with by anything the French do." He liked the final text of the article and "ordered" that it be moved from the middle of the issue up to second place.

When the winter number had been safely put to bed I went up to spend a night with him in Boston. He was worried that I wouldn't be as comfortable as usual in a small upstairs room, since the main bedroom floor was monopolized by male nurses. Of course, I was perfectly comfortable (though I never understood why, like many Bostonians, he lived in what seemed to me luxurious discomfort). Though thinner, his face had not entirely lost its rather youthful look. His attitude to his illness, though not at all resigned, was stoical—the sciatica was acutely painful but something to be borne for the time being. Nevertheless I now realized fully how critical his illness really was, and though we had leisurely talks over editorial plans I left profoundly discouraged. Even though medical science forty years ago was not what it is today, I could not understand that no firm diagnosis could be made—and never was made, so far as I was aware.

In a letter the middle of December he complained about feeling disinclined to sustained thought; but, he admitted, "I can still make comments, especially of a snippy nature." For two pages he then proceeded to deal with a series of subjects running from the Hungarian frontiers to my suggestion of an article by André Siegfried, contradicting at every point that his mind was not in good order. He then allowed himself the pleasure of commenting without inhibitions on possible authors for a pair of articles, one Republican, the other Democratic, which we planned to publish the following summer. They were to deal with the foreign problems of the next administration and would appear on the eve of the party conventions. He dealt with my suggestions summarily:

"I think there is very little likelihood that Root would do it. Wickersham hardly counts as a Republican. Lawrence Lowell I might get if I bided my time and caught him in an unguarded moment but not otherwise, and I am doubtful about even this. . . . I really know little about Jimmy Wadsworth. If he wrote at all he would give us his policy and not that of the Republicans. Nick Roosevelt isn't important enough. Baker I have little line on. Lippmann is brilliant, though hardly a party leader. House is a back number and wouldn't say anything. Polk would be second rate. Strunsky is not eminent in politics. Glass is, and might give us something iridescent but I don't know what angle he would go off on. Franklin Roosevelt was not born a great man and I don't think he is on his way to becoming one. And other cheering remarks of the same sort, since you prefer me to commit myself before you do."

Not right in every appraisal (to my way of thinking), and certainly not prescient as regards the last, this nevertheless was cautionary advice to be pondered.

His "Merry Christmas" letter was signed "Yours as usual." On December 30 I wrote Gay in perturbation that contrary to all habit I had not had a letter from him for a week and asking advice as to how I should proceed. How much should I put up to him, to keep him from worrying, how much should I spare him? "There are some decisions I'll probably have to make without him—though I don't know just how I could justify myself to him afterwards." No need for that arose. He died January 14, 1928.

My relationship with him was unshadowed. Throughout these pages has run a thread of discourse between us that explains, I hope, how this was so, without need, here at the end, of elaboration about the affection I had for him and the feelings of friendship he so often showed for me. I knew, what was the essential, that he always had confidence in me if not always in my judgment. I learnt from him, not enough surely, but more than from any teacher. Some of the lessons were simple—not to be sententious, to avoid mediocrity, to realize that the most important thoughts if not rightly presented will not be read and might as well not have been written. In dealing with ideas, the reminders of history were always with him. Yet he did not think in remote or abstract terms, but directly, free from self-analysis and doubt. He believed that we live in a world of men where ideas are powerful in inverse proportion as they are abstract. His mind (as was emphasized in a memorial by members of the history department at Harvard after his death) was essentially political, and in considering political problems he had the advantage of a sense of realism not always possessed by academics. He knew, and not by report only, how things are done in the world, which to my mind is perhaps the greatest asset a political observer can have, and one of the rarest. He brought home to me gently but inexorably, by identifying my own errors and those of others, the immense difficulty of arriving at historical facts and the requirement to use humility and caution and to avoid sentimentality, not easy in my case, in judging and recording them.

The directors of the Council on Foreign Relations appointed me editor on January 27, 1928. I was then thirty-four. I imagine many of the members of the board were not far short of twice that age.

28

FDR in 1928

Nineteen twenty-eight was an election year. As Calvin Coolidge did not choose to run, the field was open on the Republican as well as the Democratic side. Carrying out my plan to publish a pair of political articles just before the nominating conventions, I asked Franklin D. Roosevelt (despite Coolidge's lack of favor for him) to give a Democratic view of the foreign-policy issues in the coming elections, and Ogden L. Mills, former Congressman from New York and at this time Undersecretary of the Treasury, to speak for the Republicans. Neither knew the name of his prospective antagonist at the time he accepted; but Roosevelt expressed delight as soon as he heard his was to be "stuffy old Ogden."

Mills started with an advantage. He had behind him the resources of the State Department, marshaled by his friend Assistant Secretary of State Castle. Roosevelt could call on no such reserve of ready information and advice. The Democratic national organization had been badly split ever since the calamitous defeat of the Cox-Roosevelt ticket in 1920, followed by the struggle in 1924 between the adherents of Alfred E. Smith, Roman Catholic and "wet," and the non-Catholic and "dry" forces led by McAdoo. Furthermore, Roosevelt himself had been out of commission politically for some time after being stricken with polio. Thus he did not look to the party professionals for help with his article but relied for supplementary ideas and data on what I could garner for him.

Cox and Roosevelt had waged a stout campaign in 1920 in support of the League of Nations, and following their defeat many Democrats favored dropping the League as an issue. Four years later, John W. Davis supported the League, but avoided making it a crucial point in his campaign. Smith, the likeliest choice to head the party in 1928, was not a strong League man. What would be Roosevelt's line toward the League in the third postwar election? The letters, memoranda, books and clippings which I sent him at Warm Springs, Georgia, where he was taking one of his periodic treatments, did not support a policy of expediency.

A new turn had been given to the controversy over the League by the movement to "outlaw war," an attractive slogan espoused by Senator Borah and others. It had entered the realm of practical politics when Foreign Minister Briand proposed in April, 1927, that France and the United States conclude a bilateral treaty renouncing war as an instrument of national policy. After much hesitation, Secretary of State Frank B. Kellogg replied in December, suggesting that the proposed treaty be open to signature by all countries. The idea that nations should simply pledge themselves not to go to war was vague enough not to awaken fears even among isolationists, and it had the advantage for Republicans of indicating that they did not stand heartlessly aloof from efforts to promote world peace. I was dubious about the idea that war could be abolished by fiat and without supporting enforcement measures and worried that people would suppose, quite erroneously, that something effective was being done to compensate for our refusal to join the League. Also, the League would be handicapped in any effort to impose sanctions on an aggressor, since that could be construed as an act of war. Professor James T. Shotwell and others were less pessimistic. They thought that once the pact had been adopted the American people would ask that a way be found to implement it. I was skeptical about such an evolution.

A long talk with Elihu Root reinforced these apprehensions. Republican though he was, he made no bones about calling the negotiations between Washington and Paris "vague fantasies of inexperienced persons." He thought that Secretary Kellogg had taken up Briand's proposal because of popular pressure to "do something" and because even inside the administration there was a feeling that American policy since the war had been far from brilliant. If Kellogg really had felt forced to act in response to public demand, that was encouraging; but what was proposed would weaken the efforts of Americans who were trying to accomplish something specific, for instance getting the country into the World Court. To satisfy high aspiration with something unreal was self-defeating and dangerous. "We are powerful, arrogant and bad-mannered," he said, as usual tapping the arm of his chair sharply to emphasize each individual word. "Our attitude is that we do not need friends. We feel that we can stand outside all international organizations and that our prosperity is such that it cannot be touched by external events. We are profoundly mistaken."

Along with a synopsis of Root's remarks I sent Roosevelt a copy of Secretary Kellogg's recent speech before the Council on Foreign Relations, noting that he had not so much as mentioned the World Court. Did this mean that the Republicans had abandoned the Court? If so, it left him an issue on which, as Root indicated, he could acquire considerable nonpartisan support. I also sent him a letter from Professor Manley O. Hudson detailing why Kellogg was in error in imagining that the so-called Bryan treaties of 1914, which he seemed to have just discovered, constituted a permanent machinery for maintaining peace. Hudson also criticized the idea that a simple declaratory statement like the proposed Kellogg-Briand Pact would usher in an era of world peace. History was strewn with the relics of disregarded treaties declaring "permanent peace." I arranged for Norman Davis to write Roosevelt directly in the same vein. A memorandum by Herbert Elliston raised questions about the Far East; and another outlined Latin American problems, especially those resulting from American intervention in Nicaragua, which had come under attack at the recent Pan American Conference in Havana.

Roosevelt, who had been Assistant Secretary of the Navy during the war, was a "Navy man"—as someone said later, really more so than Churchill, who liked masquerading as a "Former Naval Person." I therefore raised questions about maritime law, the "freedom of the seas" and limitations of naval armaments. Senator Borah had proposed calling a conference to "codify" maritime law, but this seemed premature so long as British and American policies were in direct conflict. Would our devotion to the ideal of freedom of the seas lead us to obstruct the League in trying to deal with aggression? For example, if Britain was willing to agree not to use her fleet except as an instrument of League policy would we nullify a League blockade by insisting on trading with the offending state?

When Roosevelt sent in the first draft of his article he called attention to the fact that he hadn't once used the word "Democratic" and said he had tried honestly to be as fair as possible. He asked for the fullest sort of criticism. After I had written him at length he telegraphed his thanks and asked me to meet him at his house immediately upon his return to New York a few days later.

I arrived on his doorstep as he was laboriously getting out of his car.

Archibald Cary Coolidge

Raymond Poincaré

Joseph Caillaux,
at Mamers

Sir Horace Plunkett

Count Carlo Sforza

President Thomas G. Masaryk

Greek Republican leaders in jail, Athens, April, 1922. Left to right: Professor Th. Petmezas; T. Stathopoulos, Manager, "Patris"; P. Carapanos, ex-Deputy; G. Villaras, Deputy; A. Papanastasiou, former Prime Minister; Theodoropoulos, ex-Deputy; Constantine Melas, Deputy.

King Constantine of Greece, in Palace Garden, Athens

King Alexander visiting the American Home for Jugoslav children

Queen Marie
of Rumania,
by the
Black Sea

Count Michael Károlyi
(Photo: G. D. Hackett)

Secretary General Avenol of the League of Nations and André Géraud ("Pertinax"), Geneva, January, 1932

Foreign Ministers of the Little Entente. Left to right.: Eduard Beneš of Czechoslovakia; B. Jevtich of Jugoslavia; N. Titulescu of Rumania. (Culver Pictures)

The Triglav,
from Bohinj, Slovenia

The White Fortress, Belgrade

Opening of the Council House, 45 East 65th Street, New York, November 28, 1930. Left to right: John W. Davis, Elihu Root, Newton D. Baker, and H.F.A.

Editorial office of *Foreign Affairs*, 45 East 65th Street, New York, 1930. (Wide World Photos)

As always, every move was a test of courage, met as a matter of course with dignity; he simply would not allow bodily disability to defeat his will. He arrived from Georgia exuding enthusiasm and high spirits and entered into the discussion of his manuscript with good-natured combativeness. Some of my suggestions he accepted; others he steered away from as too contentious, for example, the recommendation that we modify our policy of freedom of the seas. He did, however, add a paragraph urging that an effort be made to obtain agreement among the nations on the rights of neutral commerce in time of war, blockades and contraband, methods of submarine attack and similar subjects. All of this, he said, was bound up with the attitude of the United States toward Europe and the League. On the League he went further than I expected. Admitting that it was beside the point to agitate the question of League membership, he said he nevertheless could not believe that the American people would ever consciously handicap the League in its efforts to maintain peace. Further, without entering European politics, we should cooperate with the League and take an active, hearty and official part in all its proceedings which affected the general good. (The word "official" was, in the circumstances, courageous.) In another new paragraph he asked that "even without full membership we Americans be generous and sporting enough to give the League a far larger share of sympathetic approval and definite official help than we have hitherto accorded."

Ogden Mills's article was on the whole a more polished production. His principal theme was that it had been Republican policy since the war to maintain independence in foreign affairs but without being isolationist or indifferent to the interests of other nations. He skillfully omitted parts of the record which showed the contrary, for example, how the Harding administration rebuffed the League to the extent of hardly acknowledging letters from it. Norman Davis called the article "the same old materialistic piffle"; it was more than that. But Roosevelt (at least to my prejudiced eye) was not only more idealistic but also more frank and vigorous. The Democratic National Committee evidently liked it, as it ordered reprints for distribution to all the delegates at the national convention in Houston. At that convention Roosevelt put Al Smith's name in nomination and he was chosen on the first ballot. Roosevelt himself was later nominated to succeed Smith as Governor of New York. As everyone knows, Smith lost to Herbert Hoover; Roosevelt won, and was on the way to the White House.

When Secretary Kellogg sailed for Paris on August 17 to sign the pact that bore his name and Briand's, my wife and I were also on the *Ile de*

France. The text had been revised in the course of long international negotiation and no longer required that the signatories refrain from war in any and every situation. They were free to act in self-defense, or against a state which had broken the treaty, or in fulfillment of obligations as a member of the League or as a signatory of the Locarno agreements. These and other provisions made the pact more precise but did not make it more effective as an instrument for maintaining peace.

On shipboard we had many agreeable chats with Kellogg and his wife, who was accompanying him on a trip which he naturally looked on as a triumph. Nevertheless, he was worried about the fate of the pact in the Senate. I told him sincerely that I could not imagine its being turned down, but not that the reason for this confidence was that I thought it more innocuous than effective. I found it useless to mention any of the pact's possible weaknesses; a mere hint of less than total agreement that it would once and for all put an end to war, with him the ministering angel sent to accomplish the miracle, produced stuttering indignation. He was in every respect a nice and sincere person, but beyond his depth in dealing with great affairs. I felt that he knew it and that probably the knowledge unnerved him, with the result that in the State Department he was irreverently called "Nervous Nelly." This made me regard him with sympathy.

The ceremony at the Quai d'Orsay was conducted with much pomp in the great Salle de l'Horloge, the same room where the Allied representatives—Wilson among them—had signed the Covenant of the League of Nations with such great expectations in 1919. Mrs. Murray, the Embassy receptionist, who had been coping with the applicants for the meager number of tickets allotted the United States, said she had never imagined that President Coolidge had such a multitude of intimate friends or that Secretary Kellogg had so many near neighbors in his home town of St. Paul, Minnesota. One applicant asserted he had been a witness at the President's wedding, though he could not remember where it had taken place. I was lucky enough to get tickets for both my wife and myself. She, however, became ill and could not go. At lunch beforehand at Bibesco's flat on the Ile St. Louis, his cousin, Princess Marthe Bibesco, complained bitterly that the French had not given her a ticket. I was able to supply the lack, and took her with me to the Quai d'Orsay.

The delegates of the fifteen nations which were the original signers of the pact (sixty-three ratified it ultimately) were led to their places at a horseshoe table by ushers resplendent in blue coats with gold frogs, red velvet breeches, white stockings and pumps with gold buckles. Briand, the host, made the only address. He spoke with a feeling that was plainly sincere. He referred especially to Kellogg's optimism and tenacity, which "had got the best of the skeptics," and to his pleasure in welcoming Stresemann, the first German Foreign Secretary to be received on French soil in over half a century; and he greeted all who were gathered in the great hall "to mark a new date in the history of mankind," not in order to liquidate a particular war but to open a period of concord for all the nations of the world. On the way out, Secretary Kellogg stood at the doorway in something the manner of the father of the bride. To my warm congratulations he replied beamingly, "We have made Peace at last." The tone of triumph implied the capital "P."

Later that afternoon I had a talk with Poincaré. He had not attended the ceremony, since it was strictly Briand's show, but he refrained from making any adverse comment on the pact. Looking ahead to June, 1929, the tenth anniversary of the signature of the Treaty of Versailles, I wanted to persuade him to give us an article taking stock of what had been accomplished in the decade then ending and prescribing what must be done to restore Europe to a state of more certain peace. He agreed, and a year later, although by then he was in bad health (and soon afterward resigned), he sent us his manuscript as promised.

One task in Paris was to secure the visa for the visit I was hoping to make to Soviet Russia. It had not been easy to arrange. First I had had to apply for permission directly to Chicherin, the Commissar for Foreign Relations, enclosing an application made out with the help of Alex Gumberg, the principal figure in the American-Russian Chamber of Commerce in New York, and supported by Boris Skivirsky, the unofficial representative of Soviet interests in Washington. Six weeks had elapsed when, just on the eve of my sailing, Skivirsky informed me that I would obtain the visa from the Soviet Embassy in Paris. I was received courteously by the chargé, Mr. Besedovsky, and to my relief found that all was in order.

On the way to Moscow I visited first Berlin, then Warsaw.

II

The Dawes Plan seemed to be working so well that there was talk in Berlin of relaxing the controls over German finance and fixing a total sum for final payment. Parker Gilbert, the almost inhumanly efficient Agent-General for Reparation Payments, was determined to bring about a final settlement if possible. I was surprised to find, when we had dinner at his apartment on the Pariser Platz, that he feared the British would not agree and that they might be able to "seduce the French" (his phrase) into delaying tactics also. The British were beginning to realize that Germany was on the way to becoming a principal economic rival and that the danger would be magnified if the French and German coal concerns worked together. I said I could hardly imagine Poincaré's falling for such an obvious maneuver, but Gilbert's apprehensions remained. He said that in all his negotiations he had not encountered a single shifty or evasive act on the part of France, but that he had to be continuously on his guard in dealing with the British. They saw in Germany their new enemy, in a figurative sense of course, and were trying to rally the rest of Europe against her. I wondered whether Gilbert might not be overreacting to current difficulties, and when I mentioned his fears in a letter to Gay he replied that he thought Gilbert was "seeing spooks."

In delightful contrast to the discussion of reparations was leisurely conversation with Harold Nicolson, whom I now met for the first time. He was forty-two and Counsellor at the British Embassy. It proved to be his last diplomatic post, since he resigned the next year from the Foreign Service to pursue a career in letters and politics to please his wife, Vita Sackville-West, who refused to envisage a life spent in embassies abroad. He was quite boyish looking, with slightly rippled hair over a high forehead, a rather ruddy face and a neat small mustache. His manner was most amiable but sedate, and at first encounter I wrongly put him down as rather complacent. I had read *Some People* and was determined to make him write for *Foreign Affairs,* if possible about Lord Curzon, whose encounters with his tipsy valet Arketall had furnished the basis for one of that volume's unforgettable skits. I think that when he did so a few months later it was his first appearance in an American periodical. We lunched with him several times, once at Horcher's, where the food was excellent (later the Nazis made it their own), once at Peltzer's, a block or two from the British Embassy on the Wilhelmstrasse. Nicolson, who had been Curzon's assistant at the Lausanne Conference, attempted to unravel for us—with respect, admiration for Curzon's unrivaled diplomatic skill and even tinges of affection—the contradictions in the character of that formidable statesman and tortured and thwarted human being. To Nicolson, Curzon's defense of Britain's imperial role did not mean that he was an anachronism strayed out of the eighteenth century, but just possibly one of the few statesmen of the twentieth who had the audacity not only to see but to say what was going wrong with the world.

Curzon had developed curvature of the spine at nineteen and thenceforth lived a life of torment encased in a cage of steel. Nicolson told us how at the Lausanne hotel Curzon's bathroom adjoined his and how through the door he could hear Curzon groan as he removed his brace bit by bit to take a bath and then put it on again afterward, each operation involving five minutes of agony. To his other feelings for him, then, Nicolson added pity for the misery that led him to strike out in blind unreason at anyone differing from him in quality or opinion. One of my favorite passages in *Foreign Affairs* was Nicolson's summing up of Curzon's dissatisfactions:

He was Viceroy at 39; he was Foreign Secretary at a time of vast historical importance: he possessed riches and titles and many great houses and the glitter of the Garter at his knee. He rode on elephants whose trappings were of gold and emeralds; he sat on alabaster thrones while potentates bowed jewelled heads before him, he walked on the wide lawns of English houses, he purchased castles and palaces, he won the love of two of the most lovely women of our age. Yet all these were but a temporary solace in great bitterness. He did not get a first at Oxford; he did not get the better of Lord Kitchener, or of Mr. Lloyd George; and it was Mr. Baldwin, not George Curzon, who was appointed Prime Minister at the death of Mr. Bonar Law. These three disappointments remained for him the essential facts of his existence. His victories were for him but evidence of the injustice of his defeats.

Another friendship begun in Berlin at this time was with Dr. Gustav Stolper, an Austrian by birth, recently elected a member of the Reichstag and editor of *Der Deutsche Volkswirt*. He was a brilliant conversationalist and writer and proved a standby of information and criticism when he eventually emigrated to New York at the beginning of the Nazi regime. The contributions which I arranged to get from him, from Nicolson and from the Centrist leader Wilhelm Marx (who had been succeeded as Chancellor by Hermann Müller as a result of an increased Socialist membership in the Reichstag) made my Berlin visit productive as well as lively and interesting.

My stop in Warsaw, though brief, gave me a chance to see Count Skrzyński again; he had been Prime Minister since his visit to New York, but had been forced out of office by Socialist intransigence on the left and the imminent threat of a Pilsudski coup d'état on the right. Many Poles were gloomy. Soviet hostility persisted in every field. What Poland needed desperately was a market for her manufactured goods; but the Russians wanted to develop their own industries at any cost, refused to take even the consumer goods they lacked entirely and would accept only a few indispensable items such as electric machinery.

I was disappointed not to have time for a weekend at Count Joseph Potocki's famous estate close to the Russian border, where life was reputed to continue in unchanged feudal style, with a manservant sleeping at night across the doorway to one's room. I did go with him, however, to the Warsaw horse show, a characteristic exhibition of Polish insouciance despite the persistent hostility on every border and the internal tension, always on the point of snapping into violence. The gay life that went on at the luxurious Hotel Europejski gave one the same sense of unreality.

Professor Szymon Askenazy, a renowned Polish scholar, believed, erroneously as it proved, that Russia was undergoing an evolutionary process, and that the ups of moderation would gradually outnumber the downs of repression. "The course of the world about the sun alters, in time. The relation of the poles to the universe changes, in time. Human affairs also change, in time. The psychological factors which operate in the lives of individuals and peoples are more important than the material factors. If Russia is in fact in a phase of psychological change, we must be careful not to strengthen the virus, now losing its potency, which was the cause of her original breakdown." He was disappointingly vague as to the specifics of his recommendation, except that extremes of either coddling or of isolation should be avoided. The patient must be left to regain his equilibrium by degrees and by his own efforts. I went forward to Moscow encouraged by this diagnosis, hoping that the mellowing process discerned by the professor would not be so slow as the millennial changes in the world's course around the sun.

29

Moscow, a Study in Gray

The Eastern Express rolled all day across a vast plain of fen and moor and through endless forest of white birch just turned a golden yellow. After we crossed the River Bug the landscape was as much water as land. Late in the evening we reached the frontier at Negoreloye and the broad-gauge Russian railway. I was surprised by the comfort of my ample coupé and the friendliness of the attendant, who brought me hot water in the morning and all day long endless glasses of tea. At the October Station there was more confusion than ill will among the perplexed and apparently illiterate officials, police and other, who dealt in relays with my passport and luggage; after long delays as they scratched their heads, consulted with each other and examined me curiously, I found a rickety fiacre to take me to the Metropol Hotel, near one of the two entrances leading into Red Square from the Tverskaya, now named Gorkova. In 1928 the portal at the right still housed the Shrine of the Iberian Virgin, where peasants especially but other passers-by as well used to kneel and say a prayer to the ikon, as their ancestors had done before they carried it into battle. When the imperial family came to Moscow from St. Petersburg they had also been accustomed to pause there on their way to the Kremlin. A year after I was in Moscow the authorities concluded that the ikon was venerated to a dangerous degree and overnight the Shrine was completely demolished.

First impressions of a place are lasting, particularly if, as for me in Moscow, one stays only a week, and the more so if the new scene is extravagantly unlike anything ever set eye on before. Later, as Paul Schef-

fer, the *Berliner Tageblatt* correspondent, said, a visitor gets lost in the
paradoxes and contradictions of Soviet life and involved in sympathies
and dislikes that distort his judgment. I was not immune to those even
in a week, but the original impressions remained the strongest.

The first was of space. There were crowds in the wide avenues and
immense squares, but as I looked down from my hotel window, they
were mere trickles of black ants in all that space, not hurrying like ants
to a destination they wanted to reach but just going there doggedly because there was nowhere else to go. This was not quite true, for there
were popular cafés and even some night life for the diminishing tribe
of "NEP-men," the New Economic Policy profiteers, but the impression
of loneliness was strong. This was the basis of a second impression: not
of lassitude or physical weakness, but of activity without spontaneity.
People went singly more often than in couples or groups. Nobody called
out a greeting to a friend in the morning or waved a farewell at night.
Perhaps my preconceived idea of what life in a police state was like dictated this immediate impression of constraint, but the daily street scene
confirmed it. The uniformity of that scene depressed me, although I
realized it might not have that effect on those who had never seen another. The feeling that you were isolated and hemmed in was intensified
by warnings from the foreign correspondents that any Russian willing
to exchange words with a stranger was probably a police agent. Scheffer
said he had lost all of the hundreds of friends he had had five years before; in their place were half a dozen Russians he didn't want to see but
who were assigned to come and see him all the time.

The weather was rather cold and rainy, the usual routine, I was told,
for September; in a few more weeks the rain would turn to snow and
the snow would stay until April. Almost everyone in sight was in black
or some dingy variant of blackness. The exceptions were soldiers and
visitors from the provinces—Tartars, Chinese, Mongols and so on, in
their different dress, different caps, usually carrying bundles of their
belongings. Most of the men wore black shirts and knee breeches, some
leather jackets, almost all high boots. The only color was in the ker-
chiefs on women's heads. The buses bouncing over the cobblestones
looked like animated seesaws, with human beings in clumps clinging at
both ends; these external passengers, male and female, stuck out two
deep, those who could not find a footing clamped onto those who did.
Beggars were sometimes as many as six or eight to a block (they were
eliminated later by being shipped off to Siberia); even the most poorly
dressed women would give them small coins. At night one saw homeless

wanderers without enough spirit even to beg. There were stands with newspapers and cigarettes on corners and I saw some women selling apples out of barrels. All over the city, at any time of day, queues of thirty or forty waited outside the community stores, money in hand, to buy such elementary things as milk, eggs, ham; commodities which could be exported were unattainable.

In a city where as yet there had been almost no new building the Metropol Hotel was, from the outside, quite impressive. The foyer was much like those in many Central European hotels except that the personnel in charge, very numerous, were obviously more occupied in keeping track of the guests than in looking after their needs. The surveillance extended to each floor, where the kerchiefed old dame posted to take charge of your key also could note your exits and returns. The dining room became crowded at about four o'clock when NEP-men and members of the new ruling class appeared for dinner. They were better dressed than people in the street, but seemed not quite sure enough of themselves to enjoy an evening out with any display of gaiety. There was no white bread—had been none, I was told, for two months. For a Westerner, the only luxury was the bowl of caviar standing in the center of each table. On Saturdays, beginning at midnight, there was dancing, a joyless spectacle.

I may have been badly misled in what I deduced from the faces and gait of the Moscow crowd. Walter Duranty, with a long experience with the Russians (though less discriminating judgment than Paul Scheffer's), came to a different conclusion; he thought that patriotic pride and faith in a socialist future compensated to a considerable degree for the crowding, deprivations and bleakness of daily life. And of course my impressions, though vivid, were limited to a given moment, and not averaged out, like his, over years. As I have said, there were cafés in Moscow, and a certain number of people managed to visit them from time to time; there also were the ballet and the opera, but most of the tickets went to members of the party, the government and the trade unions, who paid only 15 percent of the official price. But to the eye of a transient such scattered reliefs from the grayness of life seemed to have left no imprint on the subdued multitude passing silently in the street.

The Kremlin was near the Metropol. At that time, indeed until after Stalin's death, it was inaccessible to visitors. Above its dark red walls, interspersed with towers, rose the shining domes and cupolas of churches and the great mass of palaces, certainly one of the most extraordinary agglomerations of buildings in the world. Whether viewed from the Red

Square or from across the river, where its brilliant colors shimmered on the water even on a gray day, it was stupendous, menacing and beautiful. As everyone knows, Lenin's tomb is in the Red Square, at the base of the Kremlin wall. It was then still a wooden structure, not replaced until 1931 by the massive red porphyry mausoleum that serves also as a podium from which the Communist leaders review their troops on May Day and other great occasions. Three days a week, from five to six, a queue of perhaps five hundred persons stretched across the square, waiting to enter the tomb and view Lenin's body lying on an unpretentious bier. A blanket was drawn up nearly to his chin, and one hand was laid across it. The face was yellowish, wax-smooth and expressionless except for a trace of the sneer at the corners of the mouth that photographs showed in life. To preserve the body, the veins had been pumped full of paraffin—some alleged Standard Oil paraffin. This unimposing lay figure was, incredibly, the relic of a man who, against logic and circumstance, had, in the words of his rival, Victor Chernov, overturned worlds by the force of his ironic, sarcastic and cynical intellect.

While I had been waiting my turn to enter the tomb, edging slowly toward the guarded door, I saw a little boy tugging at his mother's dress and pointing at me. She bought some sunflower seeds to keep him quiet but without effect. After resisting for some time, she left her place in the queue and came hesitantly up to me. "Douglas Fairbanks?" she inquired, in an accent I'll not try to reproduce. Only when I shook my head regretfully was the little boy satisfied.

A festival to celebrate the centenary of Tolstoy's birth was in progress, and one day when the foreign delegates were taken around the Kremlin I managed to get myself attached to the party. Few of the buildings now shown to the public were open, nor had the present museum been put in order; but the grandeur of the strangely deserted squares and the mystery of what might be passing behind those closely guarded doors produced a feeling something like awe. Our little company moved in silence across the cobblestones to the rhythmic click of the Western heels of its female members.

The Tolstoy celebration caused some embarrassment. The Bolsheviks wished to capitalize on Tolstoy's fame, and pictures of him barefoot were everywhere. But how account for his religious teachings, his opposition to the state and to bureaucracy, his title of Count and his Princess mother? Lunacharsky, Commissar of Education, delivered a two-hour oration praising him as a Russian artist, venerated the world over, but stating that he could not be recognized as a thinker or philosopher.

Lunacharsky was the liveliest and most matter-of-fact of the officials I met. He had a cosmopolitan air and seemed to enjoy talking with a foreigner about literary and artistic things. He admitted with a smile that students were not accepted in educational institutions according to their showing in entrance examinations but primarily in light of their social antecedents and current affiliations. Candidates from bourgeois backgrounds who passed exams with an A might be and in fact were refused admission, while those who had three times failed would eventually be admitted because they came from proletarian homes, Communist or otherwise; this, he said, was only a belated and necessary equalization of opportunity.

When I asked him to be more specific, he put the number of qualified applicants being barred that autumn from institutions of higher learning because of bourgeois antecedents at thirty thousand. The year before, the students admitted had been divided as follows: peasants, 35 percent; workers, 35 percent; "others" (bourgeois elements, that is, children of teachers, shopkeepers, doctors, lawyers, clerks, officials, etc.), 30 percent. This already represented, according to Lunacharsky, far too heavy a concession to bourgeois elements, for in the country as a whole the population was divided roughly into 80 percent peasants, 12 percent workers, 8 percent "others." He nodded when I noted the favoritism being shown the industrial over the peasant proletariat and accepted as a matter of course the obvious reason that the workers were Communists while the peasants were not. He agreed that candidates from worker and peasant homes could not be as well prepared for higher education as the "others" but denied that in the end they would not be such efficient engineers, doctors and so forth as those who had been better prepared in the first place. As he talked, I thought what a shock it would be for American radicals like Scott Nearing, who were demanding more free speech and intellectual integrity in our colleges, to have a look at education as it was conceived at that time in the Russia they held up as an example of progress.

Two persons in particular helped me get my bearings in Moscow. One was Paul Scheffer, who had been in Russia for five or six years and was by common consent of the foreign newspapermen the best informed of them all. The other was Bruce Hopper, a Harvard man, a special protégé of Coolidge's, who held the first of the Charles R. Crane fellowships abroad. Bruce, a native of spacious Montana, had a ruddy, open countenance, erect and brisk bearing, beguiling open manner and a trace of a Scottish burr. He had attracted Coolidge's interest not merely by his scholarship but by its scope; for the same concern for everything to do with the human condition that made him a historian made him also a humanist (a combination often suspect in American academic circles). For a guide, Bruce lent me his assistant, Walter Chumak, who had helped Sinclair Lewis in the same capacity when he followed Dorothy Thompson from Berlin to Moscow the year before. So far as I could tell, Chumak never twisted the answers to my questions or reported on me to the GPU beyond the minimum duty he owed them in order to keep alive.

The foreigners in Moscow were speculating about the changes still to come in economic policy as a result of the defeat of Trotsky's efforts to force the socializing process. The best source of information on this—indeed on everything—was Scheffer, who spoke the language and traveled widely and often. The other correspondents, like Ed Angley of AP and Ed Deuss of International News, knowing that I was not picking their brains in order to write second-hand pieces of my own, were generous with their ideas also. Offsetting them was Eugene Lyons of UP, who at that time was viewing Communist accomplishments through pinkish glasses; his colleagues debated whether this was the cause of, or the result of, his being so chummy with the Soviet press officials. Like Louis Fischer, who received much confidential information from Soviet authorities, he felt it needful to explain the Revolution to all comers. (Some years later both became critics of Kremlin policies.)

Scheffer's realism yielded to no such weakness. The New Economic Policy, instituted in 1921 to overcome the boycott of the peasants, who had reacted to the requisitioning of their produce by refusing to grow more than enough for themselves to eat, had failed. Trotsky, who had demanded that the fact be recognized and that socialization be pressed relentlessly, had been repudiated and with his partisans banished to the provinces. But Scheffer saw that this was far from the end. In fact, it was the "twilight zone," when the NEP was in process of liquidation and the socialist offensive was just beginning. Stalin was being constrained not only to adopt but even to exaggerate the very policies advocated by Trotsky. Incentives for both the peasants and the workers were being abolished. The forced collection of grain would lead to a peasant boycott. The consequences of breaking it by force could be shattering. I mentioned that Dr. Milyukov, Minister of Foreign Affairs in the Lvov provisional government before the Bolsheviks seized power, had prophesied in a talk at the Council on Foreign Relations in May that the deliberately reduced sowing of spring wheat by the peasants, particularly the kulaks, who were the chief producers, the increasing assaults on government officials and the burning of cooperative property meant that there would be a famine greater than that in 1921; and that this, with the sabotage in the coal mines and the reduced production in the factories presaged a breakdown in government control which would end socialism in Russia. Scheffer disagreed; Stalin would be as tough as necessary.

Scheffer foresaw that the crisis would compel Stalin and the other Soviet leaders to turn more of their attention inward. But this did not mean that they could cut Russia off from the West. The industrial program depended on capital to buy new machinery. For this they looked mainly to America. The terms set by America would be momentous for the whole world. Scheffer wondered whether we would insist on guarantees against Communist propaganda both for ourselves and the other Western countries, or would only demand guarantees of a commercial and financial nature and immunity from propaganda in the United States? Marx said that in the revolutionary struggle the proletariat's chief aid would be the greed of the capitalists. Would the United States be long-sighted enough to see that the crumbling-away of Europe would be a greater material blow than to be deprived of special advantages in Russia?

The forecast that the Soviet leaders would lessen their concern with foreign affairs was denied, naturally enough, by Maxim Litvinov, who because of Chicherin's illness was Acting Commissar for Foreign Affairs, as well as by Rothstein, head of the press department and chief brains of the propaganda machine, whom I saw later. The principal subject on Litvinov's mind was the coming American elections. What would be their effect on American foreign policy? Before I could attempt an answer he gave his opinion that whatever the result it would be all the same for the Soviet Union.

"We expect just as little from Hoover as we do from Smith," he said. "They are alike in their hostility."

I tried to explain various party and personal differences that might color their attitudes on diplomatic recognition, trade and a debt settlement. But neither he nor Rothstein, when the subject came up with him later, could believe that either candidate might reconsider the relationship with Russia and try to make a fresh start.

I questioned Litvinov as to whether if it became possible to enter into formal commercial relations with the United States, and if some compromises were made on the Russian as well as our side, the Soviet Government might not lose its influence over foreign Communist parties.

"Not at all," he replied. "They would realize abroad, just as our Communists would, that the chief need for the fulfillment of Communist aims is for the Soviet Union to be strong and prosperous."

He made no bones about the fact that after the so-called "intermediary period" of compromise the Soviets would be able to go ahead with the work of revolution. He tried to reassure me, however, that in describing Russia's essential and unvarying revolutionary aims he did not refer to the spread of revolution abroad but to completing the revolution at home. As though to support this claim, he referred several times to the Comintern as a "guest" that the Soviet Government would be glad to see move abroad, perhaps to Berlin or Brussels.

Litvinov rejected the idea that the reverse suffered by the Communists in China was anything more than temporary. In the long view, he maintained, it was really all to the good. The purge of the Russians and the Communists by the Nationalists and the establishment by Chiang Kai-shek of a capital at Nanking would in due course be "rectified." Meanwhile, it was of less importance that Russia shared in the general Chinese xenophobia than that China was becoming an independent power which later on could be made a political ally and "social equal." This was so much like Rothstein's prediction that the two interviews seemed rehearsed. Professor E. A. Adamov, the historian and head of the Foreign Office archives, also agreed with the analysis, on the basis that it was easier to pursue a clear and successful policy toward states that have a strong and stable government than toward those where there are chaos and weakness. Thus it was to the Soviet advantage that more stable governments were being formed in Persia, Afghanistan and Turkey, and after a time might evolve in China, even though at first their orientation might be against Russia. He ducked my question whether the Communist collapse in China signified the end of world revolution.

Professor Adamov, with whom I had several talks, had known and respected Coolidge and for that reason spoke with what seemed unusual frankness. The question of the Straits interested him particularly, as he had edited a volume of documents containing the correspondence of the Imperial Russian Ministry of Foreign Affairs and the Allies in which the latter promised to recognize Russia's right to Constantinople and the Straits, "the key to her house." He said that the Lausanne arrangement to demilitarize the Straits and assure free passage of warships of all nations had been made against Russia's will and interests. Russia (he pointedly used the name) would persist in her long-standing demand

for either control of the Straits or at the least joint control with Turkey—
"if it took a hundred years." In another connection, he told me it was
true that during the American Civil War sealed instructions had been
given to the Russian naval forces to assist the North in case Britain or
France took hostile action. He said he had the original of these instruc-
tions in his archives and asked me to look into the possibility that some
American scholarly review might like to publish an article on the subject.
Subsequently he did in fact send me a manuscript which I gave to
Professor Bernadotte Schmitt for publication in *The Journal of Modern
History*.

The greatest theatrical success in Moscow was *Dni Turbinykh*, a
sympathetic story by the playwright Bulgakov of the ordeals of a Rumanian family in Kiev during the Civil War. It was so wonderfully
acted at the Moscow Art Theatre that in spite of the language barrier I
managed to follow the action. It was suppressed soon thereafter because
it pictured White Russians not as brutes but as misled and rather sympathetic human beings; rehabilitated about 1931, it again fell out of favor
but recently has once more been revived. The most popular ballet was
"Krasnyi Mak"—"The Red Poppy"—with rather reminiscent music by
Glière, a second-rate ensemble but a brilliant première danseuse named
Adamova. The audience seemed to me rather indifferent both to the
dancing and to the crude propaganda that was lugged in. In contrast,
there was the wildest applause for the première danseuse in Tchaikowski's
"Sleeping Beauty," at the Bolshoi. She was an old favorite—and I mean
old—named Yekaterina Geltser, who had been Nijinsky's partner in
Tsarist times. The audience was so faithful to the tradition of her greatness that even in the most painful moments their cheers drowned out
the creakings in her knees that I imagined would otherwise have been
heard.

Other pleasures in Moscow (for the foreign visitor only) were the
magnificent collections of Impressionists and Post-Impressionists in the
huge and hideous mansions of two prewar millionaires, Sava Morozov,
who had been head of a textile combine, and Victor Shchukin, an equally
wealthy sugar baron. These collections abounded in Cézannes (twenty
or more), Van Goghs (including the grim "La Ronde des prisonniers"),
Gauguins (about thirty), Picassos, Rousseaus, Renoirs, Monets (I
marked in my catalogue especially "Déjeuner sur l'herbe") and every
other artist of similar fame one had ever heard of. Among the many
Matisses (sixty in all) was the famous "Ronde des danseurs," painted

for the grand staircase in the Shchukin palace. One had to get a permit to enter, but foreigners could obtain it without too much difficulty. These paintings, soon to be classed as decadent and stored away for years in the stacks at the Hermitage in Leningrad, are now on exhibition there and in the Pushkin Gallery in Moscow. The authorities need not have delayed so long for fear of contaminating the taste of the Russian public. In 1967 as I lingered in the rooms where they are now displayed, it was curious to see the Russian sightseers pour through without giving them a glance.

It was a fortunate moment to be in Moscow for anyone who wanted to make purchases, for the government in its search for foreign exchange was selling minor objets d'art from various museums and palaces, especially anything closely connected with the Tsars. Helped by Chumak, I found a number of beautiful things in shops on Arbat Street and near the Square of the Revolution, run by the Moscow Workmen's Soviet. Among accumulations of frayed bits of fur, strips of rubber from worn tires, Standard Oil cans and other rubbish would be piles of china from the imperial factories or bearing the famous mark of Gardner. My most extravagant purchase (actually, I found later, the prices were ridiculously modest) was a set of plates, platters and fruit stands with borders of pale blue and gold and a crown and initial A in the center, standing for Alexander I, in whose reign the design had originated. Successive Tsars had continued to use it as the pattern for the everyday service in the Winter Palace, as shown by the initials on the back; my plates were from the reign of Nicholas I. I would have bought more if I had thought they would ever arrive safely in New York; actually, Amtorg delivered them and my other purchases intact. Once, in my house in New York, Count Sforza asked about the significance of the monogram. I said the A stood for Armstrong but the crown did not. "Don't be snobbish," he said.

Also from the Winter Palace was an exquisite tiny miniature of the wife of Paul I, Maria Fëdorovna, the beautiful daughter of the Duke of Württemberg. His mother, Catherine the Great, was depicted on an ivory medallion with her husband, Peter III; he was feeble in mind and in body, and one can detect the visage of his evil genius peering forth from the folds of his neckpiece. Another miniature which I purchased was of later date; it was of Maria Alexandrovna, wife of Alexander II, and was described as coming from the palace of her son, the Grand Duke Paul, at Paley, where it had hung in his bedroom. There were many others, but they were inferior, besides quantities of framed photographs of tsars and tsarinas, grand dukes and grand duchesses. My miniatures were the pick of the lot. The one of Maria Fëdorovna was by far the most beautiful; but it was smaller than the less attractive one of Maria Alexandrovna, so it cost 20 rubles ($10), while that, being larger, cost 25 rubles.

At Zags, the bureau for registering marriages, divorces, births and deaths, I found that, in the words of one of the ladies in charge, "The only grounds necessary for divorce are marriage." A couple wanting to be married did not need to produce witnesses, sign any oath, go through any ceremony or pay any fee; and when one of them decided that he or she was tired of marriage, the other partner need not consent, or even know what was impending, but might simply receive by mail a notice of the change of status. I was told by the lady of Zags that in the province of Moscow about 29,000 marriages had taken place in 1927 and about 26,000 divorces. I felt afterward that the figures seemed so low that perhaps they applied only to one of several Zags offices in the city; but in any case the relative figures for marriages and divorces were interesting. The law was changed in 1935, but at that time a divorce could be obtained by mail; a postcard notification to Zags from either husband or wife was enough. That transaction was the only one that cost anything—a postage stamp. It was not necessary in every case that a man consent to the marriage; it was enough technically for the girl to prove that she had slept with him one night, but in practice she must show that they had lived together. If there was a child, the bureau decided whether some support must be given by the father. If a woman was sick or old, she was given some support from the government social service. I was told by Ed Deuss of a case where it was established that three men had slept with a girl within a short period; all three were required to contribute to the support of the child.

Of all the commissars, the one I was most anxious to meet was Nikolai Bukharin, the leading Communist intellectual, "the darling of the party." I thought that if any of them might be willing to write for *Foreign Affairs* it would be he, and that if he did it would be a ten-strike. All my efforts to meet him, seconded persistently (and rather courageously) by Chumak and by his brother, an official in the Narkomindel, came to nothing. Lenin in his dying statement had called Bukharin "the greatest and most valuable theoretician." He had since fallen out with Stalin, but I realized how far things had gone only when Chumak intimated one day that the reason for Bukharin's delay in answering me was that he would have to get the permission of Stalin as well as of every one of his colleagues, in writing, before he would be able, or would dare, to talk with a foreigner. Despairing of meeting him, I sent him in the end a written invitation. (His declination reached me later in New York, signed, incidentally, "Bookharin.")

Stalin had agreed with Lenin's enthusiastic estimate of Bukharin's theories only as long as they agreed with his. The split had become really dangerous for Bukharin about the time I was in Moscow. It presaged a fall from very great heights. He was editor of *Pravda* and a member of the executive committee of the Comintern. In 1924, he had been one of the eight men who had carried Lenin's coffin to its place in the mausoleum in Red Square; Stalin had been another of those eight. In that same year, he had become a member of the Politbureau. But he opposed Stalin's reversal of the Leninist policy of maintaining good relations with the peasants as the necessary basis for industrialization. He continued Lenin's opposition to forceful collectivization of farms. The showdown came in 1929; Stalin won. In November of that year he was expelled from the Politbureau and sent into exile in Siberia. He made a sort of peace with Stalin thereafter, but although he became editor of *Izvestia* and remained something of an oracle for the rank and file of the party, it was the end of him as a political power.

By a strange turn of events, this was not the end of my effort to get him to write for *Foreign Affairs*. In Paris, in April, 1936, my friend "Pertinax" told me of a rumor that Bukharin was there, staying in a hotel on the Left Bank. The rumor said that he was on his way to Spain to help plan the Communist resistance to the efforts of the reactionaries to overthrow the Spanish Republic. Without much difficulty I discovered that he was at the Hotel Lutétia. I went to the desk, asked the number of Bukharin's room, went up, knocked on the door, was admitted without any questions and a moment later was seated beside him on his bed. His face was vivid and expressive, with stubbly beard and rather wide mustache; his head was bald. We talked (on his side) in German, broken French and broken English and (on my side) in English, French and a few words of German. The result was his promise to write the article printed in *Foreign Affairs* the following autumn entitled "Imperialism and Communism."

I thought it better not to pry into why he was in Paris. Now it is known that he was not en route to Spain but had come to France to deal with Boris Nicolaevsky, who had been archivist in Europe for the Institute of Marx, Engels and Lenin in Moscow and had accumulated a vast store of his own of valuable books and documents.[1] The Institute was most anxious to purchase them, but failed (they went eventually to the Hoover Library in California).

Of fascinating interest was the Communist dogma which Bukharin set forth as we sat there on his bed. If it had been true it would have meant a revolution in the relations of states. Looking at me with the amiability of a tired professor, but with complete assurance, Bukharin explained at length that national rivalry between Communist states was an impossibility—"by definition an impossibility." What creates wars, he said, is the competition of monopoly capitalisms for raw materials and markets. "Capitalist society is made up of selfish and competing national units and therefore is by definition a world at war. Communist society will be made up of unselfish and harmonious units and therefore will be by definition a world at peace. Just as capitalism cannot live without war, so war cannot live with Communism."

Badly outclassed in dialectics, I managed nevertheless to express doubts. Could one explain national rivalries so neatly and dispose of them so rationally? Would groups of men with different inheritances, aptitudes and standards, possessing different natural resources and different productive machines, agree on what constitutes the common good and on how it should be divided?

Bukharin shook his head, but slightly, as if to imply that such queries were too feeble to deserve notice.

What tribunal of mere men (I persisted) was to decide the common good? And when they had figured it out down to the last decimal point of the master plan and up to the final plateau of the master graph, mightn't rebellious human nature upset all their calculations? People are quixotic. Even enlightened self-interest assumes unexpected forms at different times and places. History shows that often a nation chooses to lay down its life to save it.

Bukharin's answer was bland but final. The ultimate tribunal would be "the consensus of Marxist truth." What is truth? It does not need to be interpreted, only expounded. The unity and harmony of Communist society were not a theory but "eine spontane Realität"—"a spontaneous fact."

About ten years were to pass before these dogmatic statements could be put to the test. Until then there was no Communist state except the Soviet Union, no Communist international society and no way of as-

1. *Cf. Power and the Soviet Elite,* containing "The Letter of an Old Bolshevik," by Boris I. Nicolaevsky, edited by Janet D. Zagoria. New York: Praeger, 1965.

certaining whether Communist nations abandon competitive struggles because they are Communist, are content with the station in life to which they are assigned, cheerfully fulfill the tasks appropriate to that station and live together in harmony and peace.

After the Second World War, however, a Communist international society came into existence. Now there were other Communist states, and Moscow was called on to establish relations with them—states that were not bourgeois, capitalistic and therefore by nature antagonistic, but Marxist, brotherly and therefore deserving equality of treatment.

Almost at once the whole structure that Bukharin had reared in his mind collapsed. Within three years, one of the principal states belonging to the new Communist family was being branded as reactionary, bourgeois and nationalistic and its fellow members were being instructed to shun it politically, economically and culturally. According to the formal resolution of the Cominform, published at the end of June, 1948, Marshal Tito of Jugoslavia had been guilty of breaking "the unified Communist front against imperialism" and his party had "taken the road to nationalism." Tito's reply was that not he but the Bolsheviks themselves had succumbed to nationalist temptations. He said that they had attempted to dominate the Jugoslav Communist party and had aimed to exploit Jugoslavia as a Russian colony in the old capitalistic and imperialistic tradition.

As I wrote later in a preface to my book *Tito and Goliath,* Bukharin did not live to explain this rude contradiction of his maxim that rivalry and competition between Communist states is an impossibility. Nor, of course, was he there to see the rupture between the two greatest Communist states, the Soviet Union and Red China; or to hear Brezhnev's announcement in November, 1968, that developments within any Communist country which were unacceptable to the Soviets must be suppressed, a preliminary to the invasion of Czechoslovakia by the Soviet Army and the armies of four other Communist states.

Early in 1938, two years after I had been sitting with him in the Hotel Lutétia, Lenin's favorite theoretician was tried by Stalin for his particular deviation from the consensus of Marxist truth, and shot.

30

Dictatorship in Jugoslavia

For Jugoslavia, the year 1929 opened with a political bombshell. On January 6 King Alexander issued a proclamation dissolving the Skupshtina and rescinding the constitution. Parliamentary institutions remained his ideal, the King announced, but as practiced they had led to the brink of spiritual collapse and national disunion. Changes of government or new elections had failed to bring about stability. He would maintain the national union by his own efforts and on his own responsibility. The Jugoslav people thus woke up on the Sunday before the Orthodox Christmas with a strange present in their stocking, political silence.

This sensational act, the most important in the unified state of Serbs, Croats and Slovenes since its establishment in 1918, had already been in the back of the King's mind when I saw him in September, 1928. There was at that time a continuing crisis dating back to the preceding June when the leader of the Croat Peasant party, Stjepan Radić, had been shot in the Skupshtina by a member of the Radical party, a less disciplined organization since Pashich's death in 1926. The Croat deputies had thereupon left Belgrade, announced that they would never return to the parliament as then constituted and demanded that the constitution, a symbol to them of Serb hegemony, be got rid of. The King told me he considered it absolutely necessary to revise the constitution but he hoped that a split might occur among the Croat leaders and that the more moderate ones might be brought back into a working arrangement at Belgrade to formulate the needed reforms. However, he did not intend to fritter away his personal prestige in trying to bring this about by securing inconclusive concessions from the Radical party leaders. He would reserve his personal power to use at a moment when he could act effectively. I mentioned the risks of a resort to dictatorship; Primo de Rivera in Spain and Mussolini in Italy had so entrenched themselves that in each case the King was impotent to act against him; and if either fell the royal house was so involved that it must suffer also.

The King replied: "If ever the situation here demanded drastic action to save the state I would take the responsibility myself."

Although personal rule was contrary to his principles and involved great risks, the degeneration of political behavior rapidly reached a point where he saw no alternative. He had managed to devise a patched-up coalition to carry things along without Croat participation. But at this precarious juncture, the leader of the Democratic party, Davidovich, frivolously provoked a new crisis in the hope of himself forming a governing coalition with the Croats. This was the twenty-fourth cabinet crisis in the ten-year life of the state.

Pursuant to parliamentary procedure the King sent for the various party leaders, including Dr. Vlatko Maček, Radić's successor as head of the Croat Peasant party, the members of which had been breathing defiance from Zagreb, declaring, with a good deal of reason, that the crisis was not parliamentary but constitutional. Maček demanded that elections be held for a constitutional convention, which should divide the country into seven provinces, or states, each to have autonomy in all matters except foreign relations, which would be in the hands of a central body of delegates from the seven local legislatures. Each province would control its own education, religious matters, army, railways, finance and posts and telegraphs. For example, the military contingents raised for the army in each province would not be liable for service outside the borders of that province except with the local legislature's consent.

King Alexander considered that this would destroy the unity of the nation, throttle its economic development and render the army incapable of defending it against hostile neighbors. He thereupon took control of the government, appointed a nonparty cabinet representing different sections of the country, closed the offices of the political parties and ended newspaper discussion with a censorship law.

It was three months after the royal coup that I returned to Jugoslavia, stopping first in Zagreb to see what the Croats intended doing. Character-istically, the three principal leaders were of different minds. "Three Slavs always have four opinions."

Maček, a country-lawyer type, was, in contrast to his predecessor, Radić, rather quiet and modest, but he stuck firmly by the program he had put to the King. His colleague Pribichevich, black-haired, square-jawed, angular, arrogant, representing a party consisting largely of the Serb population of Croatia, had considerably modified his adherence to that program. He now agreed that the provincial delegations in the national capital should control not just foreign relations but everything except schools, local taxation and domestic commerce. A third view was held by the elder statesman Trumbić. He favored "Dualism," with Serbia and Croatia the two main units around which the other provinces would cluster in an undefined relationship. Influential with me was the opinion of Meštrović, with whom I had lunch. He was helping organize deputations of loyal Croat peasants to visit Belgrade, for he felt that if the King had not stepped in with his full authority the country would have gone to pieces.

In Belgrade three days later I had a talk of over two hours with King Alexander. He stated that for him there was only one matter of capital importance: to preserve the unity of the state. Everything else—the constitution, the Skupshtina, even the monarchy—must be considered secondary. For years the parliament had done nothing but talk, cabinet crisis had succeeded cabinet crisis, the economic situation had been deteriorating, the currency had not been definitely stabilized, which meant that foreign loans had been impossible. Extravagant abuse was being bandied about indiscriminately in the press. The electoral laws were faulty. The chiefs of parties were autocratic. Equality, the foundation of national unity, was lacking.

He recalled our conversation in September when in discussing various ways out of the situation I had spoken of the risks involved in dictatorship. "So you see," he said, "that what I did in January was not unpremeditated." I replied that I had thought of his words when I read the news of his coup and that I had been encouraged to suppose he had acted in order to avoid the establishment of a military or party dictatorship.

The King then went over in detail his interviews with party leaders before he decided to assume personal control. In discussing Maček's visits on January 4 and 5 he got out the notebook in which he had entered exactly what passed. He said he had frankly told Maček (whom he admitted to liking personally) the reasons why his proposals seemed absolutely impossible. In the second audience Maček held to his demands as a minimum, but admitted that what he termed the "historic frontiers" of the seven provinces might be modified.

When Maček had left, the King sent for Korošec, the Slovene priest who was Prime Minister of the current nonparty cabinet, gave him a communiqué prepared by Maček to publish and also showed him a brief declaration, to be given out at the palace an hour later, announcing that the King, having consulted the heads of the various parties, saw no way out of the parliamentary difficulties. When Korošec asked what that meant, he told him he had determined to dissolve the Skupshtina, annul the constitution and form a working cabinet. Korošec said he had only two remarks to make: nobody who had not been a minister could know how inevitable this step was; if the King was thinking of having a Slovene in the new cabinet, would he take him? The King asked Korošec if he had understood him clearly; he was at the moment the Prime Minister of a constitutional cabinet and this was to be a nonconstitutional cabinet. Wouldn't he like to consult his friends before committing himself? Korošec replied that he had no need to consult anyone and would accept any post the King offered him.

The King now dispatched messengers for the men he wanted in his new government. Meanwhile he went over his proclamation and sent it to the printing office for publication the next morning in the *Official Gazette*. He then sent for General Zhivkovich, head of the royal guard since 1917, outlined his plan, told him he was to be Prime Minister and asked him to wait with the others he had convoked. When all eighteen of the new ministers were there he invited them to undertake their respective posts and received their acceptances.

In the three months that had elapsed since then, the King noted, there had been no violence and nobody had been put in jail. Administrative work was being speeded up. Numbers of officials were being dismissed and power centralized in the ministers. Only the Prime Minister's consent was necessary to put ministerial proposals into action instead of as formerly the consent of the whole Council of Ministers. A "Supreme Legislative Council" of fifteen (six of them leading Croats) had been set up to advise the Prime Minister on proposed laws.

The King emphasized again that he remained a partisan of democratic government. When I remarked that I supposed he would return to a legal system "un de ces jours," he said, "Pas un de ces jours, mais un jour." What he had to do was produce results; if he did, the people would be content to wait. To my question whether he had ever heard of a dictatorship which relinquished power of its own accord, the King replied that this was because dictatorships usually were military or political, headed by persons who if their rule ended would become nobodies. He was in a different position. Nothing would suit him better than to be free of the burdens of direct rule.

Turning to international matters, the King said that as I was going to Athens he wanted to speak about Greek affairs. The question of a free zone for Jugoslav commerce in Saloniki was about to be settled satisfactorily. It was not of enormous importance in itself, nor was it important militarily, as the Greeks would not make any promises in that field. What was valuable was to have good feelings between the two countries and an understanding that if one was attacked the other would remain neutral. Greece agreed to this, but wanted the implication to be *must* remain neutral while Jugoslavia wanted it to be *will at least* remain neutral, leaving freedom of choice in a showdown.

Venizelos, the King said, had come through Belgrade after his visit to Paris and Rome the previous autumn, and seemed a changed man, much less decisive than before. Ever since Italy's bombardment and occupation of Corfu in defiance of the League of Nations in 1923 he had been skeptical of the willingness or ability of the Great Powers to cope with aggression. "He is terribly scared of Mussolini," the King said. But he admitted that he too had been impressed with the cowardice of the Powers in handling the Corfu affair.

King Alexander said he had asked Venizelos whether he might inquire what part Albania had played in his conversations in Rome. Venizelos answered that he had agreed not to mention Albania, since it was an Adriatic question and Greece was a Mediterranean and Balkan state. The King said he had replied: "But Albania is on your frontier and it is a Balkan state also. In deference to your high statesmanship let me doubt the exactness of your reply. No statesman could come to an agreement with Italy without touching that question."

Venizelos had continued to insist that it was true, and the King said that he was inclined on the whole to think perhaps it was, so uncertain of himself had Venizelos become. To me it seemed clear that Venizelos simply had been on the defensive in discussing a treaty which he had made with Jugoslavia's hostile neighbor.

The day before this talk I had been to lunch at the palace. The Queen, who was going to have a baby in a few months, was there, also Prince Paul and Princess Olga and Serge Obolensky. Talk was lively because

Serge had just arrived on a visit with plenty of gossip. There was a pair of large antlers on the wall at one end of the dining room. The King said he had shot the stag the only time he had been away from the capital since the coup—"the largest stag I ever shot," he said, "but that was natural as it was the first time I had shot as a dictator." Afterward Paul took Serge and me to see the old Turkish house which he had bought and was fitting up as a museum, with a number of modern pictures and some fine Meštrović statues, presented by him to the state at one time or another and never so far exhibited properly. There was talk of Paul's going to live in Zagreb as the King's representative. It might have been a good move to please the Croats, but Paul didn't relish the idea and nothing came of it.

My impression at the time was that the royal dictatorship would go on for at least two or three years; and by the time I went to Belgrade again in June, 1930, nothing had happened to alter this idea. The King meanwhile had moved into his new palace at Dedinje, on a hill on the outskirts of the city overlooking Topchider. It was built of white stone carved with motifs taken from Serbian peasant art and furnished in good taste. As I had lunch with him alone the conversation was free; and as usual I was startled by the frankness with which he talked. He began his "annual report" by speaking of the domestic situation, then of the new activities of the awakening Magyars and the Macedonian organization, fanned by a recent flamboyant speech of Mussolini's in favor of the revision of treaties. He was intent on widening the basis of government, but his first effort had been to promote unity. A law had been passed officially changing the national title to Jugoslavia, dropping the sectional names of the three component peoples, and the country had been divided for administrative purposes into nine *banovine* which had no historical associations. The present regime was, he emphasized, transitional, and he made plain that the next steps were very much on his mind. It might be possible to form the Legislative Council into a Senate, but he did not take to my suggestion that the Council of Ministers might at the same time be expanded into an Assembly. On the whole he thought it would probably be best to start fresh with a new legislative setup, but in no case was he going to be hurried into jeopardizing the progress that he felt had been made.

"This is the great chance," the King said, "and it must be used to the full, for it will not return."

My conviction remained that the son of King Peter, who had translated Mill *On Liberty* into Serbian, would eventually bring democracy back, though that it would be in the unfettered Western form was obviously dubious.

II

Political discussion in Athens in that spring of 1929 was being conducted for the time being in an unusually low key. The holes on the front of Venizelos' former house on University Street punched in by machine-gun bullets during the 1920 elections were still there; but the hostility between republicans and royalists, which had reached a savage climax with the shooting of King Constantine's ministers held responsible for the Asia Minor debacle, although not gone was in abeyance. The dictatorship of General Pangalos had been overturned in August, 1926, by General Kondylis, who, true to his democratic professions, had restored constitutional life and then retired from the scene. Meanwhile Venizelos had been living in his native Crete pursuing his studies of Thucydides. He had returned to Athens in the spring of 1928 and won the elections that summer by a big majority. Neither he nor the royalist leader, Tsaldaris, had changed his juridical position on "the King question" but neither was pressing it. George II was living quietly in Bucharest and making no overt efforts to regain his throne.

Venizelos, who asked me to lunch at the Petit Palais Hotel where he was living, looked younger than when I had seen him in New York seven years earlier. Those had been mournful days. The Greater Hellas which he had built up was being swept away. He was intensely miserable and seemed an old man. Now, though he told me he had been broken by the disasters in Asia Minor and by his country's hardships, nothing in his appearance showed it nor did his animated conversation reflect King Alexander's assertion that he had lost his self-confidence and drive. I had left a card at his hotel the previous day and within a couple of hours a note had come from him asking me to call. Like Poincaré's notes it was in his own hand and the promptness of the reply was like Poincaré also.

He evidently was thriving on being back in power and on the work it brought. His black skull cap had been discarded and there was light in his eyes and vigor in his voice. He spoke very warmly of King Alexander and said he had done "the only possible thing" in taking over power for a time. I asked whether the treaty of friendship to be signed with Jugoslavia within a few days was to be like the one which he had negotiated with Italy the previous autumn. Much like it, he said, but the Serbs did not want to use precisely the same phraseology. When I hinted that they probably wanted to show that Greece had a closer tie with Jugoslavia than with Italy he smiled and acquiescingly waved his hand. His ideal for the future, he said, was a Balkan Entente, but it was too early for it yet; there must be treaties of friendship and agreement on specific matters, mostly economic, and only then a broad treaty of mutual guarantee.

There was no longer any Greek "irredenta" question, Venizelos went on. Outstanding questions of property claims against Turkey resulting from the expulsion of Greeks from Asia Minor were being negotiated and this would be followed by a treaty. There still were from 80,000 to 100,000 Greeks in Constantinople, a few in Albania and, of course, Greek colonies in Egypt and elsewhere. But Greece at present was more homogeneous and more Greeks were under one rule than at any previous time.

When I raised the sore question of the Italian occupation of the Dodecanese islands, he said: "We signed a treaty recognizing Italy's presence there. It is a question today between the Dodecanesians and the Italians. As far as we are concerned, it is not under discussion. How can you discuss such a question with the Great Power which is nearest us and is, after all, the principal Power in the Mediterranean?" To a question as to whom he thought Italy's fortifications in the islands were directed against he answered: "Not Greece." The opinion of most Greeks, I had found, was that they were against Turkey, since Italy saw her most promising field of expansion in Asia Minor.

Venizelos spoke better English than I had remembered and had a most friendly air. From lunch, which we had alone, he went to take a nap, saying that as his habit was to work late at night he must catch up with an hour's sleep in the middle of the day. Charles B. Eddy, the American who headed the Greek Refugee Settlement Commission in succession to two other Americans, Mr. Morgenthau and Mr. Howland, told me that Venizelos was the only man in Greece who got things done in what he called "an American way," meaning that he attended to requests promptly and saw that his orders were carried out.

Eddy gave a figure of slightly over 1,400,000 for the refugees who had come into Greece from Asia Minor and Bulgaria; in exchange, about 350,000 Turks and Bulgars had left. In other words, the problem had been to find room for a million additional people in Greece proper. This immense influx had overwhelmed Greek resources and taxed foreign aid to the limit. By now, about half the number had been settled by the commission in new homes of their own, as many of them as possible on farms where they could be productive. Many more had been given the farms or homes of exchanged Turks and Bulgars. Others who had brought traditional skills with them, such as rug making, had been helped to set up their businesses anew. Members of the professional class, such as doctors and lawyers, could start life afresh without special help. The rest had been fending for themselves as best they could; I saw their hovels in the Piraeus and Saloniki, patched out of bits of board and loose stones mortared roughly together and roofed with the hammered-out oil cans which were to provide typical coverings for displaced persons on all continents after the Second War. Finding permanent homes for this remnant constituted the final phase of the commission's work.

Inevitably there had been friction between the established population and the new arrivals, especially in the professions and in Macedonia, where the refugee concentration was greatest. Eddy believed that time and intermarriage were lessening the differences and that these would soon be obliterated. This was also the opinion of A. Kyrou, the editor of *Estia,* who agreed that the "new" and the "old" were losing their sense of rivalry. "The danger that they might split into two Greeces is past." It was in the same belief that Venizelos had remarked to me, "The difficulties and sufferings of this generation are the price for a new and stronger Greece."

Not everyone was so optimistic. The "melting-pot" problem was not so much material—though that was stupendous—as psychological. The differences in background of the old and new populations might not create a geographical split between a radical and republican north, closely settled by refugees, and the older kingdom proper. The royalist leader, former Premier Tsaldaris, assured me he had no intention of letting "the King question" become entangled again in electoral politics. Yet the antagonism within the body politic remained and time would show, again and again, how disastrous it could be for Greek unity.

III

When I went for breakfast in the dining car on my way to Sofia I was beckoned to sit down by Baron Maurice de Rothschild, at whose château near Geneva I had visited with "Pertinax." He had been shooting in Africa, and his only concern in Athens had been to make sure that his guns were passed safely through the Greek customs. It was with this in view, and not for any political interest (although he was himself a member of the French Senate), that he had insisted on seeing Venizelos and securing his personal intervention. When he asked where I was bound for, and I said Nish, where I could change for Sofia, he was puzzled. "But

I thought that was in Turkey." He was noisily consuming a very large breakfast, calling out contradictory directions to the flustered waiter, dropping eggshells on the floor and shooting in all directions the pits from the oranges which he messily slashed open. When he paid his bill I lingered and out of shame added something to the tip which he left on the table and which was far from fitting his opulent family name.

Sofia had been put in good spirits, for once, by the news of King Boris' engagement to the Italian Princess Giovanna; Bulgaria needed somebody as a friend, and though Italy's friendship would have a price, that was not the chief factor in people's minds. Princess Giovanna's picture was everywhere and a new *pâtisserie* bearing her name was opening on the main square the next week.

The royal engagement was not the only cause of the better atmosphere. A détente in Bulgaria's relations with other Balkan states was in progress. The first fears awakened by the return to power of Venizelos, the "Maker of Greater Greece," had faded, and economic problems between the two countries were under negotiation. In Rumania, Prime Minister Maniu had shown a conciliatory attitude on questions connected with the disputed province of the Dobrudja. King Alexander, though concerned principally with internal problems, had opened the Jugoslav frontier and there was to be an early meeting to negotiate a commercial treaty.

Stamboliski's nephew, Muraviev, whom I had met here two years earlier, did not feel that the government was responding as it should to these openings for neighborly reconciliation. Instead, pacts of friendship were in process of negotiation with Turkey and Hungary. Were they harbingers of a new system of alliances under Italian leadership? If so, they were a threat of war and disaster. Boris was not a Fascist, but had become more military-minded since an attack on him in his auto by brigands; he did not understand the situation and feared Communism so much that he distrusted even the Agrarians, who, said Muraviev, were not Communist in the least. Five members of Stamboliski's Agrarian cabinet of five years ago had been killed—in bed, in prison, in the street or under convoy—and twenty-eight deputies. How many private individuals had been done away with could not be even estimated. There were four Communists in parliament, members of the Workers' party, supplied with money from Moscow (usually in dollars); everyone knew it, but the government allowed it since it gave them an excuse to point to the Communist menace. He had many similar tales of intrigue and terror.

These were contradicted by Burov, the Foreign Minister, who among other things said categorically that Italy had made no suggestions that indicated she had war in mind or wanted anything for Bulgaria except that she be truly independent. What else (I of course thought) could Italians be expected to say or Burov to repeat? From a number of sources I heard of the general disillusionment with the Macedonians since the rival factions of IMRO (Internal Macedonian Revolutionary Organization) had been killing each other freely. Various measures which the government had taken to deal with them had been popular; people were tired, I was told, of Macedonian "dictatorship."

This was admitted to me by Drangov, a lieutenant of Mihailov, whose faction had assassinated Protoguerov, who in turn had helped assassinate Todor Alexandrov, who in turn had been implicated in the murder of Stamboliski. Murder was a Macedonian specialty, but the objectives of murder were changing. Protoguerov had been a Macedonian leader for thirty years; and it was a sign of the times that Mihailov, who killed him, was only thirty years old. Protoguerov, said Drangov, had always thought as a Bulgarian, that is of creating a "Greater Bulgaria," whereas Mihailov planned for autonomy for Macedonia, which might then conciliate both Bulgaria and Jugoslavia and serve as a bridge between them. Another Macedonian named Kulichev, a deputy, condemned Mihailov roundly. "Who can one trust now?" he asked rhetorically. "One understands assassination, but not of one's colleagues."

IV

Where I crossed the Danube by ferry from Ruschuk to the Rumanian town of Giurgiu the river is broad and sluggish, very different from my recollection of it surging through the Iron Gates further upstream. In Bucharest, everyone told you how Prime Minister Maniu's first act when he came to power had been to abolish the state of martial law which the Liberal party had imposed in many regions, including Bucharest itself. His partisans announced with satisfaction that everywhere in the country there was a relaxation of tension, the minorities were feeling more contented, nowhere had there been disorders. Martial law had been retained only in a ten-kilometer strip along the Dniester River, facing Soviet Russia.

The Secretary-General in the Foreign Office was now Gregoire Gafencu, already recognized as one of Rumania's ablest diplomats and later Foreign Minister. He and his colleagues admitted that although expropriation of the large estates had been a social necessity it had reduced production, at any rate temporarily, and had cut down exports. The government's first aim was to aid agriculture as the basis of the national economy, a tremendous job after its long and systematic neglect. Bracketed with this in importance was the urgent problem of reorganizing and extending the school system. Here the language problem was a difficulty. In Transylvania and other regions which had been part of Hungary, government schools had been conducted only in Hungarian. That had to be changed. Now in over six hundred schools the instruction was still in Hungarian, but the Rumanian language was being taught also. This was in accordance with the minorities treaties, which gave states the right to teach the national language in all schools. Treatment of the minorities was improving; petty annoyances had been halted. Gafencu recited Maniu's formula: No liberty without order, nor order without liberty; both based on law.

Baron Vest, the Hungarian Minister, did not accept this picture. Justice for the minorities, as announced by Maniu, had not yet been realized. The letter of the law, Vest said, remained quite different from the execution of the law. No money was being given by the government for Hungarian schools in mixed or purely Hungarian districts, although Rumanian schools were being built. He nevertheless recognized what heavy burdens the Maniu Government had taken over from the Liberals. Maniu now was promising everything for "next year." The Liberals he characterized as tricky, the National Peasant party as dilettante. Somewhat contradicting this, he admitted that there was an entirely new sense of urgency in the government. Officials were really working, he said, especially Maniu himself.

Staying at the Palais de la Chaussée with Princess Helen, ex-King Carol's ex-wife, were Prince Paul and Princess Olga, on an Easter visit from Belgrade. I was invited to tea, and found there various other members of the family, including ex-King George of Greece and his wife. Conversation was freer than when Queen Marie had been the dominant figure; since King Ferdinand's death a year earlier she had retired to Sinaia and seldom came to Bucharest. The Greeks were amused that I had lunched with Venizelos, "the arch devil," and moreover in "their" house. For the Petit Palais Hotel had belonged to Prince Paul's father-in-law, Prince Nicholas, who luckily had been persuaded by Paul to make a timely transfer of the house to his name, so that even in exile the family was receiving via Paul four thousand pounds a year in rent. Speaking of Venizelos, Prince Paul said Lord Curzon had told him that at Lausanne in 1922 he had begged Venizelos to telegraph and save Premier

Gounaris and the other royalist ministers who had been condemned to death. According to this account, Venizelos agreed and drafted a telegram in Curzon's presence; but a few minutes later he secretly sent a second telegram with instructions to disregard the first one as having been sent for "diplomatic reasons."

Little King Michael was not there, but Prince Paul said that he was the image of his father, only fatter; not, I thought, a very promising start. He in fact turned out to have a good deal of spunk in trying circumstances. On the proposed marriage of King Boris of Bulgaria and Princess Giovanna there was general agreement that the Queen of Italy had as much to do with arranging it as Mussolini himself; as a member of the defunct Montenegrin royal house she was delighted at the prospect that one of its representatives would again figure on the Balkan scene.

I recalled that the Queen of Italy's father, old King Nicholas of Montenegro, had appeared at the Paris Peace Conference hoping to maintain his throne in face of the movement to merge Montenegro into the new Jugoslav state, and had sought by every means to win friends for his cause. The story went that one day coming out of Cartier's into a rainstorm he had been given a lift to his hotel by an American officer. That afternoon the officer received a messenger bringing him a Montenegrin decoration. He composed a suitable letter of thanks and dispatched it by his orderly to the King. Back came the orderly, much pleased, wearing the same glittering decoration.

The ex-King of Greece, whom I had a talk with the next day, was in good spirits in his bluff, rather boyish way. He said that he discouraged any thought of revolution in Greece. "What good would it be to return to an armed camp?" On the same premise, he had encouraged former royalist officers to resume their posts in the army and navy. "The snowball of foreign politics has," he remarked, "picked up some funny things." England had been encouraging Italy against France, which in turn caused Greece to look to Italy. But when Venizelos made the treaty with Italy, England was annoyed, as she did not want Italy to replace her as Greece's protecting power. This, in turn, King George said, had led England to begin being unusually polite to him and solicitous as to his wishes. Although he disclaimed any interest in returning to Greece at present he showed that he had hope for the future by the remark that the difficulties which Venizelos was running into might indicate the advantages of having a monarchy as a stabilizing force. I mentioned that, though the republicans and the monarchists fluctuated violently in power, the Greek people seemed to be divided into more or less equal halves. He observed sententiously: "Perhaps. But a half that has virility is sometimes greater than the whole."

V

On the train from Bucharest to Paris I was reminded, for a grotesque reason, of Maurice de Rothschild. I found myself sitting in the dining car with M. Cartier, head of the great firm of jewelers bearing that name. He had boarded the train in Budapest, where, he remarked, he had been visiting his wife. She was the former Countess Andrassy, member of a very distinguished family of great Hungarian landowners, and I remembered a story I had been told in Paris as to why she lived in Budapest rather than Paris. Soon after her marriage to Cartier they were dining with friends who happened to be going later to a ball being given by Maurice de Rothschild. They suggested taking the Cartiers with them. In the Rothschild mansion, where the Baron stood receiving his guests, they were introduced to him by their friends. The Baron looked at them stonily, said, "Je ne permet pas que mes fournisseurs viennent chez moi." (I don't receive my tradespeople in my house.) Saying this, he turned his back. After that Mme. Cartier said she preferred to live in Budapest rather than in a city where such a boor was a figure in society. Her husband had been making one of his weekly visits to her there.

In Paris at this moment negotiations were in progress, under the chairmanship of Owen D. Young, and with Thomas W. Lamont one of his team, to try once again to reach a final settlement of the German reparations question. A crisis had come just before Easter, when the negotiations between the creditor nations and the German delegation under Dr. Schacht reached a deadlock. As the debate developed, the creditor nations came to believe that Dr. Schacht was introducing political issues by emphasizing that Germany's capacity to pay would be very low unless there was an alteration in the existing regime in the Polish Corridor, which cut off Germany proper from her resources in East Prussia and Silesia; unless she gained access to the raw materials in her former colonies; and unless European tariffs were lowered. Schacht's personal ambitions were supposed to be making him less conciliatory than his German colleagues. According to Poincaré, whom I saw on April 5, the real difficulty was that Schacht refused to talk figures.

A few days later, Dr. Carl Melchior, one of the German delegates, asked me to come to see him. He thought (or at any rate said, perhaps with the idea I would repeat it to the Americans) that it would be best to adjourn the conference to the autumn. By then Germany's inability to transfer payments under the Dawes Plan would be obvious; there might be a Labour Government in England (why this would be advantageous to Germany's case was not clear); and President Hoover would have become "more educated," presumably on the linkage between demands for reparations and abilities to pay war debts. I suggested that adjournment would be a shock to American as well as European opinion and that American short-term money would undoubtedly be withdrawn from Germany, producing a new German inflation. He had on his side the argument that the total sum being demanded individually by the creditor nations was larger than current payments under the Dawes Plan. When I asked whether the reason the negotiations were bogged down was not because the Germans did not produce figures, he said they always stood ready to do so (which caused acid comments when I repeated it later in the day to friends in the American delegation).

"Pertinax" had quite severely criticized Owen Young in that morning's *Echo de Paris* for having put the Allies on the defensive by persuading them to state their reparations figures first. When I saw "Pertinax" that afternoon I pointed out that the first danger had been that the discussions would break up at the start; Young had deliberately strung them out, since it would be hard for the Germans to go home after six weeks with nothing done, whereas at the beginning it would have been easy. The sooner both sides talked figures the better. He said the French delegation was getting very restless and that he had written his article after talking with Vice-President Moret of the Bank of France. When I told this to Lamont at dinner he was startled and went off to tell Young. I made a note at the time that personally I didn't see how if the Allies made an offer considerably smaller than the Dawes figures Germany could refuse.

In the complicated settlement reached a few weeks later that was what happened. It terminated the virtual receivership of Germany, which was rewarded for agreeing to a definitive schedule of payments by the evacuation of the Rhineland. This seemed to dispose of the reparations problem; indeed, Lamont in telling the full story in *Foreign Affairs* in April, 1930, took as his title "The Final Reparations Settlement." He did not foresee that in 1931 the crash of the Credit-Anstalt in Vienna would add such impetus to the waves of the Great Depression then engulfing Central Europe that another revision of the reparations schedule, canceling a large section of the payments, would have to be accorded Germany. And of course the really "final" ending was written by Hitler, who repudiated any and all reparation payments.

One evening at dinner I sat next to the American wife of Sir Ronald Lindsay, former British Ambassador in Washington. She was amusing about her adopted countrymen: "I said to a silent Englishman before dinner the other evening, 'Don't you ever talk to women?' He replied stiffly, 'At dinner.' At dinner he was opposite me. I saw he was gazing at the ceiling, paying no attention to his poor partner's efforts to converse. So I leaned across and said, 'I thought you talked at dinner.' Fixing me with a cold eye, he said, 'Not across the table.' "

Among others I called on Jacques Seydoux, most brilliant of France's financial experts, a pathetic skeleton with shining eyes, propped up in a chair and living from week to week by force of will and the ingenuity of doctors. (He died within a month.) His comment on the reparations negotiations was that all the sums being talked of would seem very small in twenty years, given the increase in the world's wealth. Speaking of Poincaré as an extraordinary intellectual machine, he said that at the time of the Genoa Conference, where he was a member of the French delegation, he used every evening to send back eight or ten telegrams to Peretti, his contact in Paris, detailing the complicated maneuvering with the Germans and the Russians. Peretti would have them decoded overnight and take them around to read to Poincaré in the morning. Poincaré would sit at his desk hardly seeming to listen. As Peretti finished reading each telegram Poincaré would have composed his reply.

Poincaré himself, though he spoke incisively as always, said he was tired after the debates in the Chamber of Deputies and the state funerals of Foch, General Sarrail and American Ambassador Herrick. Herrick had died as he would have liked, Poincaré said, "in harness and in France." Mussolini as usual was on his mind. A visit just paid to him in Rome by Sir Austen Chamberlain he considered foolish. Chamberlain was wrong if he thought he could control or advise Mussolini.

"Besides," he said, "Mussolini has less direct power than is supposed. No man can head every division of government and know anything about any one of them. Whether he realizes it or not, he is at the mercy of the young and ambitious men around him." He might not plan war, not daring to risk it, but continuing tension and wild talk must be expected.

Poincaré assured me that as soon as the Chamber of Deputies adjourned he would start on his promised article to mark the tenth anniversary of the Treaty of Versailles. I had been thinking of inviting an article from Maurice Paléologue, who had been Ambassador in St. Petersburg until the outbreak of the Bolshevik Revolution, and I asked Poincaré's advice about the idea. He had reservations about Paléologue's qualifications.

"He has too much imagination," Poincaré said. "As a historian he has the traits of a talented novelist. I said as much when he was proposed for the Academy, and Barthou did too. However, he has a style *très vif*, and I like him and *tu-toi* him."

As I was leaving I mentioned that his victories in parliament meant that now, if he wanted, he could stay in office indefinitely. He gave a little laugh and a shrug and said dryly, "Merci!" Three years were quite enough; he needed some quiet. He was more than right. Although the "machine" was still functioning with precision, there were surface signs of wear. And in fact illness forced him to resign in July, just three years after taking over the government in the midst of what seemed an almost irremediable financial crisis and executing one of the most phenomenal financial reforms in history. It was his last public office.

31

Colonel House on Wilson

On "Black Thursday," October 29, 1929, the Wall Street crash spiraled the world down, down, down into the Great Depression, frustrating the hopes for European stability built on what seemed a final settlement of the reparations problem and Germany's signature of the Kellogg-Briand Pact. The stage was set for Hitler and the renewal of conflict.

Luckily for the Council on Foreign Relations, which had embarked that year on a campaign to raise funds to purchase a house of its own, it had reached its goal before the Wall Street collapse. The necessary total of $310,000 had been secured from seventy contributors to buy a five-story building at 45 East Sixty-fifth Street, remodel it and provide a modest amount for maintenance. This would be a change indeed from our crowded little offices in a commercial building. The goal was achieved after an intensive effort by the directors, spurred on relentlessly by Walter Mallory. Actually, since the Council was now a going concern, the job proved easier than it had been to raise the much smaller sum to launch *Foreign Affairs* seven years earlier.

The first public intimation that the Council's plan was about to come true was given at a dinner for Prime Minister J. Ramsay MacDonald at the Ritz-Carlton Hotel on October 11, when John W. Davis, president of the Council, announced that the next time the Prime Minister came to New York the Council expected to entertain him in its own habitat. And in fact we were able to move in on November 28, 1930. Davis presided at the ceremonies and Elihu Root spoke movingly of the necessity for the sort of careful but unspectacular work which the Council was doing. Gay, as secretary, read the names of the donors to the house fund and the congratulatory messages received from Secretary of State Stimson, Viscount Grey, president of the Royal Institute of International Affairs, and Raymond Poincaré, former President and Premier of France. He also referred to the valuable collection of books and Peace Conference documents given to the library by David Hunter Miller, the portrait of Coolidge presented by his family and the fact that William Adams Delano, the distinguished architect, had contributed his services in remodeling the building.

The Council House was next door to the double house shared by FDR and his mother. Roosevelt was then Governor of New York and spent a good deal of time there. Our staff used to watch him from the windows as he got out of his car, clicking the brace on one leg into place, then the other. Pulling himself erect by his powerful arms, he would then make his way slowly up the inclined boardwalk which covered one side of the steps. He never failed to pause, grin and wave a greeting to the girls in our windows. His house was comfortable but undistinctive. Like all the Roosevelts of both branches, he had little aesthetic taste. The Roosevelt ideal was bound up with activity outdoors, something to fight and overcome, like a storm at sea or the passes into Tibet, and Roosevelts liked the rough clothing that went with it. On a mantelpiece in FDR's New York house stood a ship's model in a glass bottle, his idea of a work of art.

I had known Roosevelt only slightly until we served together on the board of the Woodrow Wilson Foundation and then when he wrote his article for *Foreign Affairs*. Before being crippled by polio in the summer of 1921 he had practiced law in New York, been a liberal-minded State Senator in Albany and done good service as Assistant Secretary of the Navy during the war. But he was not regarded generally as a heavyweight, and although he worked and spoke indefatigably when he was a candidate for the Vice-Presidency in the 1920 campaign, he did not give evidence of possessing the courage and strength to inspire the country to overcome one of the most dangerous crises in its history and go on to become a world leader in a great war.

One of the orthopedic surgeons associated with Dr. Robert W. Lovett, of Boston, who helped take care of Roosevelt during his illness, was Dr. Robert Ober, who treated me also for some trouble I had with my back. Dr. Ober told me that all cases without exception in which some crippling accident or illness befalls an individual, whatever his or her age, can be divided into three categories: the patient resigns himself to the life of an invalid, takes to his bed or wheelchair without complaint, indeed rather likes being sympathized with and looked after; or he resents his handicap bitterly, is everlastingly complaining about the injustice of his lot, makes everything as hard as possible for his family, his friends and himself; or he rises above his affliction, sets himself with determination to mitigate it, and ends up more of a person than he had been before he faced the challenge. There was no doubt which was Roosevelt's category.

II

MacDonald's visit to Washington in the fall of 1929 aimed to patch up with President Hoover the Anglo-American naval rivalry which had grown to dangerous proportions since the Washington Naval Conference in 1922. Improbable as it now seems, it was much more than an academic question. As John W. Davis put it at the dinner in MacDonald's honor, the problem was not conditioned by the current relations of friendship between the two countries but by the behavior of a future enemy of one or the other. Exclude as we would even the contemplation of war with Britain, there still remained the possible strain which would come when one country or the other was at grips with a third party. These contingencies I had found being hotly debated in London when I had been there earlier that year.

Sir Ronald Lindsay, recently British Ambassador in Washington, told me of the "titanic battle" going on in the government between a group that might be labeled "the Admirals"—though not all of them were that —and more moderate elements, the former wanting to strengthen the Empire by every means for competition with the United States, the latter wanting by every means to arrange matters in harmony with the United States. He surprised me by saying that Winston Churchill was in the second category. Harold Laski, the Socialist writer, usually up to the minute on everything, was of the same view. He believed the Conservatives would win the election on May 30 and thought Churchill might become First Lord of the Admiralty in a new Conservative government and that he would then put through a settlement with the United States.

I was struck, lunching one day with Philip Kerr at the Travellers', to see Stanley Baldwin sitting in the library, smoking his pipe and reading a magazine as placidly as though in an hour the great budget debate was not to begin in the House—the debate which would decide the outcome of the election and the fate of his government. Labour won that election (Laski to the contrary), MacDonald succeeded Baldwin as Prime Minister and set himself to overcome "the Admirals." Then, in Washington, Hoover and MacDonald reached agreement on holding the Naval Conference which finally opened in London in January, 1930. The resulting three-power treaty between the United States, Britain and Japan was a compromise, but it recognized the American requirement for parity with Britain.

Underlying Anglo-American differences regarding types and sizes of naval vessels was doubt as to the circumstances in which they might be used. This uncertainty was emphasized by John W. Davis, who having been Ambassador in London was always especially concerned with any problem disturbing our relations with Britain. He pointed out the risks of determining national policies in this or indeed any matter by supposed advantages that might be gained by jockeying for position rather than by general principles. In talking with me about an article which he was writing for us on Anglo-American relations he noted how wrong nations could be in supporting policies for reasons of expediency. For example, at the Second Hague Conference in 1907, Britain, a trading nation which saw itself as a neutral in any prospective war, proposed that in order to diminish the risks to neutral shipping in wartime the principle of contraband be abandoned and that the right of search on the high seas be limited to ascertaining the neutral character of merchant ships. We voted against that proposal. Both sides were wrong. When the World War came, such a rule would have served us well in the period of our neutrality, whereas Britain would have suffered from the limitation on its ability to block our shipments and those of other neutrals to Germany. Davis favored a modification of the freedom of the seas principle, the subject which Roosevelt had not been willing to deal with quite forthrightly in his 1928 article. Davis argued that we should agree not to use our navy to frustrate the blockade of a nation which had gone to war in violation of the League Covenant, while Britain on its side should agree not to interfere with ships of neutral nations in a war in which the League was not involved.

This concept for a revision of the Freedom of the Seas seemed to call for an equally lofty statement of the British view. I therefore set myself to cajoling it from Viscount Grey, who as Sir Edward Grey, the British Foreign Secretary, had carried the brunt of defending British foreign policy during the first years of the war when the United States was insisting adamantly on its right as a neutral to trade with Germany, a course which led to a series of dangerous incidents between American mechantmen and the British warships ordered to maintain a blockade of Germany. Grey was sure to be elusive. He had retired because of failing eyesight after holding the post of Foreign Secretary for eleven years, longer than any predecessor, and was now out of public life. I realized how difficult it would be to capture him, and in the end succeeded only because I was able to enlist the support of Colonel House, his close friend.

Grey defined the issue between Britain and the United States as arising "not because each has differed in principle from the other, but because they have not always held the same views at the same time." He wrote: "It is as if each had used a telescope. Each when neutral looked at belligerent rights through the end of the telescope that makes all objects seem very small. Each when belligerent has looked at these rights through the end of the telescope which makes objects seem very large." When the United States entered the war it had reversed the telescope, and all differences of view or practice disappeared. But now that the war was over the Americans had reverted to their earlier position, and he delicately chided them by pointing out that Britain had been brought close to war with the United States for doing less than the United States was itself ready to do once it had entered the war but which it still denied Britain the right to do in future. Diplomatic revelations since the war had made plain that a real breach between the two countries had been much closer than anyone had realized at the time. The risk of a similar danger and disaster remained and must be eliminated through frank discussions, having especially in view the obligations of members of the League of Nations and of signatories of the Kellogg-Briand Pact.[1]

Actually, in the period of American neutrality in World War II no argument was to arise in terms of the rights and duties of League members versus those of non-League members, as Davis and Grey feared might be the case. In the early thirties such a difference had been possible, but President Roosevelt did his best to avoid it by collaboration with a world system. At his instructions, Norman Davis, American delegate to the Disarmament Conference in Geneva, offered in May, 1933, what might be called passive collaboration with the provisions of the League of Nations and the Kellogg-Briand Pact, conditional on the signature of a disarmament treaty. He undertook that if other states determined that a state was an aggressor in violation of its international obligations and took measures against it, the United States, if it concurred in the judgment, would "refrain from any action tending to defeat such collective effort which the states may thus take to restore peace." The Disarmament Conference failed, and with it this effort to put the United States into har-

1. See "Anglo-American Relations and Sea Power," by John W. Davis, *Foreign Affairs*, April, 1929; and "Freedom of the Seas," by Viscount Grey of Fallodon, *Foreign Affairs*, April, 1930.

mony with the general effort to organize peace. Nor can it be said that the proposal would not have met with opposition in the Senate, where the old confusion between "isolation" and "safety" still prevailed, as became clear two years later when Congress in a blind effort to safeguard neutrality in the application of an arms embargo refused to give the President power to discriminate between aggressor and victim and thereby avoid opposing the application of League sanctions.

Having failed in an attempt to strengthen the general effort to maintain peace by altering traditional American neutral rights and insistence on freedom of the seas, President Roosevelt then accepted the alternative of keeping the United States out of war on the basis of strict impartiality toward foreign warring forces. Yet this he modified as doubts arose during the first years of the war as to whether the United States could defend itself successfully if Britain fell; and he then urged departures from the requirements of rigorous neutrality such as lifting the arms embargo in favor of nonaggressors, the destroyer-bases deal with Britain and the Lend-Lease Act.[2]

III

A casual remark in one of my letters to Colonel House about the Grey article, to the effect that Churchill's latest volume, *The Aftermath,* took some hard cracks at the United States, led House to make some highly interesting comments in a series of letters to me, the first of them dated June 29, 1929. House, who was then at Magnolia, Massachusetts, recuperating from an operation, wrote that Churchill was in many respects unfair to the United States and that some of his observations were absurd. He said it had taken nearly ten years to drive into the consciousness of Europeans that Wilson had not forced the Allies to refrain from pushing forward to Berlin and making peace there rather than in Paris. Incidentally, he took credit to himself for having established, through questioning Foch, that it had not been Wilson who was responsible for the early armistice.

A European criticism of Wilson to which House took strong exception (Churchill, he said, was "obsessed" with the idea) was that Wilson had assumed to act for the United States at Paris although he knew that since the Senate was under Republican control it was liable not to ratify the Versailles Treaty. Actually, wrote House, responsibility for the defeat of

2. For details of the debates over neutrality see *Can We Be Neutral?* and *Can America Stay Neutral?* by Allen W. Dulles and Hamilton Fish Armstrong, New York: Harper, 1936 and 1939.

the treaty belonged to Democrats rather than Republicans. He called the
reservations associated with Lodge's name "unimportant" and pointed
out that they were rejected by twenty-three Democratic Senators and that
if these had voted for the treaty with the reservations it would have been
adopted eighty-three to thirteen.

One of House's surprising statements was that Senator Kellogg (who
was now Secretary of State) had told him that Lodge was in fact opposed
to reservations, but had been overruled in his committee and had been
forced to report the text of the treaty to the Senate with the "erroneously
known" Lodge reservations attached. My idea was that if Lodge had
wished to avoid reservations it was because he felt certain that without
them the treaty would be rejected—his real objective.

On second thought, House was afraid that some of his comments might
have made it look as though he had been criticizing Wilson for the defeat
of the treaty. He therefore came back to the subject in a letter in which
he emphasized that the President's health had been such that he was unable to gauge the sentiment in the Senate and that he had acted on the
advice of persons around him who were "utterly lacking in ability to ap-
praise the situation."

Both Churchill and Lloyd George, House noted, had tried to belittle
Wilson's authorship of the Covenant, claiming that it had been a British
product. Lloyd George had even written in an article that when President
Wilson visited Buckingham Palace in December, 1918, he had admitted to
him that he had no plan for the Covenant. As a matter of fact, wrote
House, from his veranda there in Magnolia he was looking across the
water to the house on Coolidge Point "where Wilson and I went over the
re-drafting of a convenant which I had written some weeks before and
which he took to Paris with him."

This attitude toward Wilson harmonized with the tone of a message
which House had sent to a meeting of the Woodrow Wilson Foundation
on April 29 of that year marking the tenth anniversary of the adoption
of the Covenant. He said that his thoughts went back with poignant feeling to the hour "when Woodrow Wilson gave to a torn and shattered
world a substitute for force and injustice," and he joined with those who
had gathered "to lay their affectionate homage at his feet."

I recall the rather banal message because when House used the word
"affectionate" I think he meant it. In the ten years since he had seen the
President off at the railway station in Paris to begin the attempt to get
Senate ratification of the Treaty—the last time the two ever met—things
had probably arranged themselves in his mind. He was able to separate

the Wilson whose intimate confidant he had been for years from the Wilson whose estrangement from him had begun in Paris. With a bit of rationalization he could decide that this had been due to the jealousy and overprotectiveness of others around Wilson and conclude that they and not Wilson had been responsible.

After the President's breakdown, Mrs. Wilson was a principal figure among those in control at the White House. I remember House uttering her name only once. It was in December, 1930, when I asked if he was ever going to elaborate on what was written in the last pages of *The Intimate Papers*. He said he couldn't add anything because he didn't know any more. "I don't know what happened," he said. I mentioned an assertion in Allan Nevins' life of Henry White that the Wilson-House split had been over the Adriatic question, the assumption being that House had gone too far in compromising with the Italians (the point of the Bliss-Bowman dialogue described in an earlier chapter). House replied that it had been his job to find a compromise and that the President had always professed to be in accord with his methods and with his recommendations. As for the cause of the split he added: "Well, it certainly wasn't Dalmatia. I guess it was Bernie Baruch, Grayson and Mrs. Wilson."

House's friendship had been extraordinarily useful to Wilson and, until near the end, must have been highly satisfactory to House, who cared more about the realities of power than about its outward appearances. He was a strategist, a conciliator, while Wilson's roads to his goals were determined intellectually. House was not, except in a rather broad sense, an intellectual, certainly not a highbrow. He absorbed ideas and developed policies in talk rather than from reading. Some of his biographers say he read widely. This did not show in his talk, at least in the period after the war when I saw him often. He preferred to talk rather than write, and his letters were usually brief. His articles for *Foreign Affairs* grew by a process of accretion, paragraph by paragraph, as ideas struck him or were given to him. Unlike his letters, his talk could be at length and leisurely. He would lay his hand on yours, if you were beside him, and you knew he was going to open his mind, beginning either with "This is between you and me and the angels," or, more solemnly still, "This is graveyard."

House happened once to mention something to me which indicates how much he acted as Wilson's alter ego. Our wartime Ambassador in London, Walter Hines Page, believed fervently in the British cause and frequently wrote the President personal letters to explain and defend British policy in the period when British interference with American shipping was causing serious disputes. House said that Page's extensive and repetitious epistles, written in longhand on both sides of thin paper, irked the President, who sometimes handed them over to House unopened with the remark, "Here's another from Page." House would glance through them to see if there was something new or vital that Page had to convey to the President and couldn't tell the State Department— "But there wouldn't be."

But it was as a reporter that House must have been supremely useful to Wilson. He was gregarious, and this Wilson was not, although in my recollection of him in Princeton in my youth Wilson was informal and delightful. I don't mean that House suffered fools gladly; he could easily sum up someone as a windbag. But he was able to listen and was willing to hear opposing views in order to deal with them effectively. Thus House liked doing what Wilson seems to have avoided doing when possible, namely, talking things over with critics and opponents, not to instruct them, but to bring them around gradually if not to agreement at least to an understanding that another view than theirs could be held, and thus to tolerance of it. He prided himself on the variety of his contacts and the fact that they spread all across the country and were not limited to the Eastern seaboard. Long after he installed himself definitely in New York, his notepaper still was embossed, "Edward M. House, Austin, Texas." Since he saw people of all sorts, often ones who would never come within the President's ken, his reports, gained in talk, were an invaluable complement to the President's knowledge, gained largely from the written word.

House was unassuming and mild in manner, persuasive rather than assertive. (As Bowman wrote: "His mind is like a sleeve valve; no friction!") But he had a strong will and confidence not only in his judgment but in the strategy he mapped out to give it effect. Since his judgment was in fact superior and his strategy usually successful, he was not lacking in quiet vanity. Thus he was convinced that if he had continued to have the President's confidence up to the end of the Peace Conference and during the Senate fight over the League he could have persuaded him to make concessions both at Paris and in Washington that would have saved the treaty. But when he revealed this feeling he did it without criticism of Wilson. His regret was at the failure of a great idea which denied the country the rewards of victory.

IV

House had the highest esteem for General Bliss. He had never met him, he said, until just before he was sent abroad by President Wilson in

1917 to consult with Allied leaders about the American role in the war. Wilson wanted him to go alone, but he thought it better to take a staff including an economist, an international lawyer and a military man.

When he asked Secretary Baker what soldier he should take, Baker said: "There is only one: Bliss."

Baker thereupon sent for Bliss and introduced him. House liked him from the start. Later on, when it came to drawing up the armistice terms, he consulted him frequently.

"I never talked to Pershing," House said, "because I never agreed with him about anything. While the armistice negotiations were under way, Pershing sent us a memorandum giving his views. I passed it across the table to Lloyd George, who handed it back to me with the one word 'Bunk!' I handed it to Clemenceau, who handed it back to me with the one word 'Theatricals!' "

I asked House what it was that Pershing wanted, whether he wanted to "go to Berlin." The Colonel said, "Yes."

House said that he thought Bliss had always been fond of him, "at least up to the time of the Peace Conference," but he wondered whether Bliss hadn't held it a little against him that he had not been given more to do at Paris.

"It really was scandalous," House said (I thought perhaps with more regret than he had felt at the time), "the way Bliss, Lansing and White were left to one side in the big decisions."

Henry White, he went on, used to come up to see him every morning to find out what was going on so that when newspapermen questioned him he wouldn't seem too ignorant. House said he used to beg the President to stop in and see the other principal delegates instead of always coming to his office. As a matter of fact, he said, Wilson had gone a number of times to Bliss's office and received people there; he thought Bliss saw more of the President than the other two.

There wasn't smugness in House's account, but one could not help feeling that he took some satisfaction in recalling, long after the fact, his absolute predominance in the early days at Paris.

Later, remembering House's different rating of Pershing and Bliss, I asked Newton Baker about the relationship between them. He said it was excellent. "Bliss was the soul of correctness and showed enormous tact and discretion." Pershing recognized those qualities, he said, and usually cooperated with him. I took up the word "usually." Well, said Baker, some of the younger officers around Pershing were jealous of Bliss, didn't understand why he was in France and disliked his opinion's being rated so highly by the President and in the War Department. Beyond that

Baker wouldn't go, not wanting to compare two generals both of whom had been responsible to him. But his personal regard for Bliss always stood out whenever the name came up. His nickname for Bliss was "The Mountain." General Hugh L. Scott, Bliss's predecessor as Chief of Staff, called him "the mountain on my life's trail."

General Bliss had great faith in *Foreign Affairs* and considered no trouble too much if he could help it along. As late as 1929 he still would send me a five-page penciled memorandum giving pointed advice about something I was writing or would himself type out laboriously an explanation of some opinions of his own. But early in 1930 I realized he was not at all well, and when I heard in the summer from his family that he had just been taken to Walter Reed Hospital with what was feared to be cancer, I ventured to telegraph the fact to Newton D. Baker, his former chief and close friend, suggesting that the best surgeon be brought in for consultation, perhaps from Johns Hopkins; and I believe this was done. On November 9 he died and was buried in Arlington. I followed the flag-draped caisson. It was the fifth time in history that the army had paid one of its sons its highest honors.

Bliss shared the title of full General with Pershing and March—the first full generals in the United States Army since Grant, Sherman and Sheridan. But although he rose from West Point cadet to the highest rank in the military he was not a militarist. He spent his last years in close study and reasoning as to how war, man's habit from primitive times, might be eliminated from the experience of nations just as it had been largely supplanted by processes of law among individuals. He pondered the lessons not only of the great war in which he had reached the climax of his own service but of war in general, or war as a human failure. He believed that disarmament by degrees was feasible, but he knew, as he said, that "disarmament is a political question, pure and simple," and that "while it is left in the hands of military men alone" there would be no progress. He believed that at the very least there must be in existence an international organization for consultation in times of crisis. He echoed what Root told me once: "An agreement to consult need only be feared by a nation which is not determined to maintain peace. The main object of a consultative pact is not to arrange steps to be taken against a possible aggressor, but to make sure that one will be in touch with that possible aggressor before things have gone to irreparable lengths. I cannot see how anyone in his senses can be opposed to the principle of consultation."

In the years I knew Bliss he was still craggily built. His powers, physical as well as intellectual, were unusual. His face in his old age had become rather gnarled, with quizzical eyes behind precariously perched eyeglasses and a conspicuously full mustache. His voice made him appear gruff, and he could use profanity (never of a vulgar sort) as an exclamation point to a statement. He spoke slowly, but meant exactly what he said, as colleagues in the Supreme War Council learnt. He believed in giving ideas action. Not in rebuke but as a simple statement of fact he told the Executive Committee of the Supreme War Council: "It is the duty of an executive committee to carry something into execution." No trouble was too great if the end was important. As someone said, he was "one of those elders who wear juniors down."

I am sure he took death calmly. As he wrote me when a member of my family died, even a Christian has to take refuge in the ancient Stoic's realization of the inevitableness of fate. Even an Epicurean like Horace, he wrote, could say nothing more than

> Durum: sed levius fit patientia
> Quicquid corrigere est nefas.

V

Two things took me to Europe in 1930, the first a conference of Institutions for the Scientific Study of International Relations, held in Paris, with representatives from associations in eleven countries as well as five international institutions. The Council on Foreign Relations acted as the coordinator for the American organizations participating. The word "Scientific" might have been omitted from the conference's high-sounding title; the discussions varied in interest, but most were of more value in arranging for cooperative research than in matters of substance, for which the term "scientific" would have been as inaccurate as it must be in any case where it describes something strictly political, that is, depending on human behavior. Annual meetings of the conference continued, but as Fascism tightened the reins on Italian intellectual life, and particularly after Nazism did the same in Germany, discussion became more and more difficult and the attempt to maintain communication between organizations in authoritarian countries and those where thought and comment were free had to be abandoned.

One day Sforza came down to see me from Brussels, where he was by now living, and took me to lunch at a tiny restaurant near the Bourse where the dessert had the lovely name, I remember, of "Coeur flottant de ma Tante Rose." His *Makers of Modern Europe* had just been published, dealing with historic figures whom he had known, some casually, some officially, beginning with Franz Josef, "the last monarch," all of whose small whims were gratified but to whom fate never accorded anything but disappointment, failure and sorrow. Sforza mentioned that when he had been Ambassador to France he had learned that Curzon had arrived there and begun discussions—without Italy—about the settlement to be made with Turkey after the Greek defeat in Asia Minor. "Sometimes," he said, "a diplomat on the spot who knows how to act quickly and sharply can nip a bad development in the bud." His instant protest brought an invitation to join the conversations. Sforza replied "that it was the first time in my life I was asked to dinner after the first course," but that he would go in the afternoon provided the minutes of what had been done in the morning were annulled.

The other reason for my trip was that the Woodrow Wilson Foundation had given its award this year to the League of Nations to mark its tenth anniversary, and because of the illness of the Foundation's President, Newton D. Baker, I was deputed as Vice-President to make the presentation in Geneva. The Secretary-General, Sir Eric Drummond, received the award, saying that the Meštrović plaque would always be preserved in the League headquarters and that the check would be used to create bronze front doors to the new League palace as a symbol of Wilson's leadership in inviting the nations "to establish their relations one with another on equal and open convenants of peace."

Passing through Paris on my way back I lunched with the Gérauds to meet Jules Cambon, famous as one of France's most distinguished diplomats. One of my editorial aims at this time was to organize a group of articles setting out the permanent bases of foreign policy of the principal powers, and with André Géraud's help I was able to persuade Cambon to lead off with the article on France. After serving as Ambassador in Washington and Madrid, Cambon had been transferred in 1907 to Berlin, where he did his best to combat the policies of the war party. Sir Edward Grey credited him, more than anyone else, with having staved off war between France and Germany in the Agadir crisis of 1911. He and his brother, Paul Cambon, for twenty-two years Ambassador in London, formed two-thirds of the famous French diplomatic team which played such an influential role in European policy in the first decades of the century, the other third being Barrère, French Ambassador in Rome. What is the quest for security, Cambon asked, but the quest for peace? He concluded, like Talleyrand, that the balance of power was its surest foundation; and this, he said, was still the view of France.

A visitor to New York about this time was a sandy-haired Scotsman named C. F. Andrews, who for many years had been an associate of Mahatma Gandhi. Indeed, although his name was hardly known in the West, Andrews had been one of Gandhi's closest collaborators since 1914, when he sought him out in South Africa and joined his cause. It took over a year to persuade Andrews to write for *Foreign Affairs* but the effort was worthwhile. As president of the Trades Union Congress of India he often visited foreign areas where Indian immigrants had been brought as indentured labor, sometimes under conditions very little different from slavery. Now he was on his way to British Guiana and other Caribbean territories to learn what social changes India must require if she was to encourage further emigration there; Indian labor formed an important part of the population in these areas and further quotas were being requested to work on the sugar plantations. On her side, India was most anxious to stimulate emigration in view of the rapid growth of her population—approaching 330 million, already a horrifying figure, and since, of course, far surpassed.

Andrews found that Indians lived in the Caribbean under conditions of equality side by side with Afro-Americans. He felt that to maintain harmony the Indian population should be kept roughly equal with the Afro-American, but that, to encourage further Indian emigration to accomplish this, various dietary deficiencies would have to be rectified. One necessary improvement, he told me, was that the rice which formed a main part of the Indian food must not be polished, thereby retaining the nutrient which prevents beriberi. As a believer in direct action he simply went to Canada, where much of the rice shipped to the Caribbean was milled, and arranged it. An Australian whom I ran into years later in Fiji, the head of the sugar industry there, but popular because of his liberal treatment of local labor, had a poor opinion of Andrews, who had spent some time on the island; he thought him hypocritical. But that was not at all my impression. He seemed to me a man of quiet determination, a Christian who nevertheless was in complete rapport with Hinduism, devoted to Gandhi but always ready to criticize him when he saw fit. Even today when I talk with Indians the fact that I knew this by now semi-mythological figure gives me a special standing.

VI

For several years the American public had been worried whether or not the United States should recognize the Soviet Union. Violently conflicting views were held on grounds both of morality and practical interest. The other principal powers had hurried to recognize the Moscow regime much earlier, Britain and France in 1924 (although Britain broke relations for a time in 1927 because of flagrant Soviet support of a general strike). The two sides of the argument were given in articles in *Foreign Affairs* in October, 1930, and January, 1931. One was by Paul Scheffer, for years correspondent of the *Berliner Tageblatt* in Moscow, now its correspondent in Washington; he gave the reasons against recognition. The other was by Paul D. Cravath, a leading New York lawyer, who argued the advantages of being in a formal relationship with the Soviet Government.

Scheffer's main point was that the Soviets could not be held accountable for their undertakings; they operated to advantage through two mediums: one the government, which was punctilious in its formal relations with foreign governments, the other, the Communist party, which did the "dirty work" of foreign propaganda, subversion, sabotage and revolution. He minimized the chances of profitable trade with Russia, pointing out that although Germany sent more goods to Russia than any other country these exports amounted to only 3 percent of her total exports. Nor had diplomatic relations with the West resulted in letting into Soviet society the "fresh air" that had been prophesied. He said American recognition would be taken as a sign of capitalist weakness and confirmation of Stalin's claim that ruthless policies did little harm to the Soviets abroad.

Cravath drew a sharp distinction between *de facto* and *de jure* recognition of a country; he thought confusion between the two was at the base of much popular opposition to recognizing the Soviet regime. *De facto* recognition did not involve approbation of a government; it might be autocratic and vicious, but that was not the point so long as it was in effective control of its territory. As a condition of recognition, he said, the Soviet Government must recognize the sanctity of international agreements; return, or make adequate compensation for, American properties confiscated after the 1917 revolution; recognize the debts contracted with our government and nationals by the Kerensky Government; and cease subversive activities against our institutions. He thought the first would be easily agreed to. The second and third, he admitted, involved difficulties, given that the abolition of private property lay at the very foundation of the whole Soviet structure. As for subversion, he thought that despite its bad record in promising other governments to refrain from propaganda the Soviet Government would find it in its own interest to terminate subversive activities in the United States, which in any case had proved futile.

Offsetting American claims, Cravath pointed out, was the Soviet counterclaim for damages resulting from Allied intervention in Russia and help to the White armies following the revolution. Instead of insisting on a settlement of this issue before recognition, it would be best to do as the United States had done with Mexico—first enter into diplomatic relations, then through prolonged negotiations bring about a settlement. Trade with Russia would be profitable, and American diplomats and consuls there could assemble useful information for American merchants and bankers and in addition influence the development of Soviet economic and social institutions.

Shortly after the appearance of the Cravath article I had a talk with Root about the whole question of recognizing Soviet Russia. As usual it was at his apartment and as usual he faced me in a large armchair, tapping on its arms to give staccato punctuation to his statements. Recognition of a country, he said, is a reciprocal affair, "not unlike marriage," in which both parties undertake certain responsibilities. "It is not a simple question of sending diplomatic officials who would help trade. It is a serious affair; it confers rights and validates claims."

The question of how long a regime must maintain itself in power in order to secure recognition Root found most interesting. A man who occupies a piece of land for twenty years without anyone questioning it obtains squatter's rights and cannot be evicted. On the other hand, he said, a murderer or forger may escape the police for forty or fifty years, but whenever he is discovered he is punished. Looking at me severely as though I might be in that category, he went on: "Some people pretend today that the fact that the Soviet regime has maintained itself in power for ten or fifteen years should in itself make the United States recognize it. That seems to me too short a statute of limitations. The Soviet Government stole the property of American firms and individuals; and it stole the property of the nationals of many other countries, including hundreds of thousands of Russians. It murdered a large number of persons and maintains itself by force and oppression. Of course it did these things for 'political' reasons. The word 'political' used in this connection would be an interesting subject for investigation. If I were twenty or thirty—or ninety—years younger I would write a book about it. Of course many acts for 'political' purposes are legal, as for example in time of war."

In the upshot, the United States recognized the Soviet Government in November, 1933, and President Roosevelt sent William C. Bullitt as the first American Ambassador since the overthrow of the Tsars. The degree to which Moscow fulfilled Cravath's requirements and predictions, indulged in the activities feared by Scheffer and offended the moral and legal injunction of Root has inexact but suggestive parallels in the situation that might result today from American recognition of Communist China. Today we look back with some wonder at our long delay in recognizing the Soviet Union. The thought arises that sometime Americans may wonder at the long lapse of time before the United States gave recognition to the People's Republic of China, proclaimed in Peking on October 1, 1949.

I was often in communication in those days (and fortunately for many years to come) with Bruce C. Hopper, now back from Moscow and taking his Ph.D. at Harvard. He was discriminating in his suggestions of Russian writers and helpful in vetting the translations of articles by men like N. Liubimov, of the University of Moscow, and Victor Chernov, the exiled Social Revolutionary leader, Kerensky's Minister of Agriculture, who turned up in New York and of whom I saw a good deal. Hopper's own first article for *Foreign Affairs* was on the subject of industrialization, especially baffling because even more than most Soviet undertakings it involved the unknown quantity x, a *lex economica* of revolution. As he wrote me: "You know it is the custom of foreigners to treat events in Soviet Russia as the outcome of attempts to put impossible theories into practise. The more I read of Peter the Great, of Count Witte, of the Tsarist Government's policy of whooping up industrial development and railway building, in the balmy days before the flood, the less I am inclined to view the Communists as tyrants extraordinary in the economic sense." He hesitated to label a project impossible simply because it seemed fantastic, and unlike many observers he did not predict that the Soviet fixing of prices regardless of supply and demand would cause the failure of the Five Year Plan and of the effort to finance industrialization without much aid from foreign capital.

I saw Paul Scheffer often. Late in October, 1930, though Hitler was still below the horizon, he was disquieted by the upsurge of passions in Germany. "The rapidity with which events move and leaders rise and pass," he said, "is one of the characteristics of pre-revolutionary days. There are symptoms of the sort among all the defeated peoples today. Leaders are usually unconscious of such developments. When peoples begin to make policy, leaders can no longer make policy: it is revolution. One has the feeling today that one might have sitting on some upland pasture if suddenly the whole face of the mountain began to slide."

It was a feeling many of us had entering the thirties.

32

❦

Paderewski; von Kühlmann; the Hoover Plan

On New Year's Day, 1931, I went to a lunch at Colonel House's for Paderewski, his friend from Peace Conference days. He was still the charmer he had been when he conquered Paris and London in the nineties. The hair that had been a flaming tumble of red above a low white forehead when he was painted by Burne-Jones now flowed back from a noble forehead and was sanded with a mixture of white. His face was pale, stern when in repose, the eyes sharp in rather deep slits; as usual he wore a very low collar and a loose white tie. The small company tried to pretend a deep interest in Polish affairs, which were in a sad state, with parliamentary government in eclipse under Pilsudski's dictatorship and continuing disputes with Germany, but really preferred talking about the somber economic situation and such subjects as whether or not to cancel the inter-Allied debts. On the latter subject everyone present but one, former Ambassador James W. Gerard, voted in an informal poll in favor of reduction or cancellation; among those favorable were, besides House himself, John W. Davis, Frank L. Polk, President Butler of Columbia, and Walter Lippmann, editor of the *World*. Although I had seen Paderewski only a couple of times since we crossed together in 1924, he motioned me to join him after lunch and we talked for half an hour or more.

"The Polish Government," he said, "is an oligarchy which pretends that it established the country, and that because of this it is entitled to rule it. It is wrong in both contentions. It did not establish the country, and if it had it would not necessarily be entitled to rule it."

455

He rejected the German proposal that the Polish Corridor as a whole be restored to German sovereignty. The population of the region was heavily Polish; not a single deputy of German nationality had been elected from it to the German parliament before the war. The Germans proposed that, if the Corridor was returned to them, the railroad from Warsaw north to the sea, with a narrow strip of land, be left under Polish sovereignty. Paderewski's proposal in return was that Germany be given sovereignty over the railroad and a narrow strip of land crossing the Corridor east and west and linking Germany proper with East Prussia. This change would not in fact alter the actual situation very much, since German traffic had unimpeded transit at present. But he felt that an important psychological change in German mentality would result from this concession.

Paderewski was not in favor of wholesale concessions to Germany. "Germany declares," he said, "that if she is given back large sections of territory, at the expense of Poland and others, as well as some of her former colonies, she will be satisfied. Her friends say that it is necessary to satisfy her if there is not to be another war. But Germany had all the territories and colonies in question in 1914. She was not satisfied, and there was a war."

He took my hand in both of his when I said goodbye to him on the sidewalk, and pressed it with great sentiment, thanking me over and over for the very insignificant help I had given his cherished Polish charitable causes.

Two months later I had occasion to talk with House about the situation in India, where Gandhi and Nehru were demanding independence and conducting a civil disobedience campaign. In view of the grave disorders that followed, a round-table conference had been held in London, where various Indian leaders (but not those of the Congress) agreed on the principle of an all-India federation. Now, a few weeks later, the Viceroy, Lord Irwin (later Lord Halifax), had signed a compact with Gandhi agreeing that political prisoners in India be released in return for a suspension of civil disobedience. An American banking friend of mine in London had cabled me asking about American opinion on this conciliatory step.

House said he believed American opinion was overwhelmingly in favor of the Irwin policy. Churchill was violently opposed to it and to Prime Minister Baldwin's program of evolution toward dominion government for India. But House felt that Irwin's was the only policy that Britain could follow. "The Churchill policy," he said, "might mean outright revolution and war. Irwin's is one of the finest pieces of diplomacy I know anything about." He went on to say that like many others he wondered whether self-government could be made to work in a country composed of heterogeneous racial masses and bitterly competing religions. "The attempt to exercise self-government may be very bad for India. But I don't see that there is any alternative."

House's doubts as to the success of Indian self-government were shared at the time by many Americans. Another friend that I consulted, Allen W. Dulles, who had spent a year after graduation from Princeton teaching in Ahmedabad, felt that anyone who knew India must have grave doubts whether self-government could succeed there. Nevertheless, he agreed that the Irwin policy was right and that the strong-arm policy urged by Churchill would be disastrous. Nor did I turn up any contrary view. For a time, conciliation did work; Gandhi himself attended another round-table conference in London, but was arrested on his return to India and remained in jail through 1932. Ironically it was while Churchill was Prime Minister during World War II that Britain proposed giving India a fully independent dominion status; and although it was rejected by the Congress, which demanded an independent national government, and by the Moslem League, which demanded an independent Moslem state, it was a prelude, after deeds of indescribable horror, to the creation of India and Pakistan as separate states and then complete independence.

II

That spring there arrived in New York a German diplomat of distinction, the subject also of much controversy, Richard von Kühlmann, former Secretary of State. The attitudes he had taken at several decisive moments in German history had led to his being praised by some as foresighted, condemned by others as weak-hearted and wrong-headed.

As Counsellor in the German Embassy in London in the six years before the war Kühlmann made himself something of a figure in English social and political life; he strove to develop good relations with the British Government and worked out with it the details of a prospective Anglo-German treaty, thereby arousing the scorn and hatred of the Pan-Germans, who considered Britain the arch-enemy. When war put an end to all such plans he went as Minister at the Hague and afterward as Ambassador at Constantinople. Then in the summer of 1917 he was appointed Foreign Secretary. In the military and political conditions of that time he felt it necessary to lay plans for peace, and since he considered Britain the most important enemy he prepared terms that he thought might satisfy her, in particular by restoring the independence of Belgium (furiously opposed by Ludendorff and Hindenburg). He meanwhile negotiated the Brest-Litovsk peace with the Bolsheviks and the Treaty of Bucharest. Then in July, 1918, he set off an uproar by stating in the Reichstag that the war could no longer be won by purely military means and that Germany might have to be content with "a so-called peace of understanding"—a famous phrase which was so immediately and violently repudiated on all hands that his fall was inevitable. He gave his resignation to the Emperor at the front on July 9, on the eve of the great offensive that began six days later, thus removing, as Franz Fischer put it, "the last man with a voice in the formation of German policy who hesitated to impose the approved war aims by force."

The offensive, as we all know, failed, and the Allied counteroffensive sealed Germany's military defeat in the West; the collapse of the front in Macedonia followed; and on September 29 Hindenburg and Ludendorff notified the Emperor that a request for an armistice must be made to President Wilson. Kühlmann had been right, but had spoken a few weeks too soon.

Talking of Kühlmann's arrival in New York, Paul Scheffer told me that he had pretty well run the German Embassy in London in the years he was Counsellor there. Recently he had told Scheffer that in looking back he wondered whether the exceptionally good relations he established with British statesmen might not have been one of the factors that helped bring on the war. The plans he and his British colleagues worked out for cooperation between the two countries had given encouragement in Germany to think that Britain might not join in a war, and also had led German militarists to feel that the last chance had arrived for settling accounts with France before Russia recouped her forces.

There was character in Kühlmann's face, not interfered with by an easy smile and the almost boyish expression that he still had at fifty-eight. While not exactly handsome, he was good-looking, dressed carefully, liked ladies and was liked by them. There was no doubt that he was very intelligent. Though he showed in office that he was willing to stand up to opposition, he did not look hard. He was what Germans today would call "old style," but not what a foreigner might think of as a Prussian type. He liked good food and good wine (at dinner at his house on Tiergartenstrasse in Berlin I remember five sets of glasses for the Rhine and Mosel wines, each more seductive than the last).

He was so agreeable and so full of interesting ideas that two or three days after his arrival I invited him to meet some friends at dinner at my house. In the course of talk about events on the eve of the war he remarked on how little understanding there still was of the broad scope of the group of treaties which England and Germany had been negotiating in the three years before 1914. Although the company included several knowledgeable people, nobody seemed to know much about those proposed treaties which, Kühlmann informed us, covered most of the principal outstanding problems between the two countries, including arrangements in the Balkans and the Near East, a division of spheres in Africa, a settlement of the shipping question and other matters. The treaties had actually been put in final form and were to be submitted for ratification in the respective parliaments on August 4. He wondered how much those treaties, if they had come into effect, would have changed the course of events in Europe.

That would have happened, I hinted, only if the balance of forces inside Austria-Hungary and inside Germany had been different, only if ruling circles in Vienna had not willed war and ruling circles in Berlin had not pressed Austria on. I could not argue this out in my own house, but it seemed to me that with those given facts, and regardless of different inclinations on Sir Edward Grey's part on account of any Anglo-German arrangements that might have been reached, the violation of Belgian neutrality and the invasion of France would have rendered inevitable the same British decision as was made on August 3.

The prewar British negotiations with Germany had greatly worried the French, Kühlmann continued, but they were put off with the statement that nothing under discussion in Africa concerned any territories north of a line running roughly through Fernando Po, in the Gulf of Guinea; but although true territorially speaking, said Kühlmann, the agreement was of general scope and would have come as a blow to the French and also the Russians. In the negotiations, he said, the English official with whom he dealt most closely was Sir William Tyrrell, who was of the "opposite party" in the Foreign Office from Sir Eyre Crowe and Sir Arthur Nicolson (then Permanent Undersecretary), both of whom were fearful of the growing strength of Germany in Europe and were working for a better understanding with France. Kühlmann thought that Sir Edward Grey was by nature sympathetic with the Crowe-Nicolson group but that Tyrrell had gradually won him around—"maneuvered" was his word—to acceptance of his emphasis on good relations with Berlin.

His relationship with Tyrrell, said Kühlmann, had gone back to before the First Balkan War of 1912. Tyrrell had had very precise information regarding the outbreak of that war, and the two had agreed that England ought to try to restrain Russia while Germany ought to hold back Austria-Hungary, and that the two should intervene to bring about a compromise settlement. It had been a particular cause for anger in London in 1914 that the Sarajevo incident had not been handled in the same way, the German Government instead throwing more support behind Vienna than was proper under the Anglo-German "gentleman's agreement." Kühlmann thought that the Sarajevo crime should not have been allowed to provoke war, nor, he said, did "the man most responsible for German foreign policy at the time" (presumably the Chancellor, Bethmann-Hollweg) think that it would. When this high official talked with Kühlmann a few days after the murder of the Archduke he referred to it as a "routine affair" to be handled in a "formal manner." (This would of course have been before the Austrian ultimatum.) As evidence that both he and his Ambassador, Prince Lichnowsky, were of the same opinion, he had been on holiday in southern Germany in July, resting after the completion of the Anglo-German negotiations, and Lichnowsky had not felt it worth while for him to interrupt his vacation. It was only on the Friday before the declaration of war that Lichnowsky telegraphed him and he started back to London. He went through Holland, where the bridges were already being mined, and arrived in London Sunday morning. War was declared Tuesday and the German Embassy staff were evacuated on Thursday.

At this point Colonel House remarked that the Kaiser's cruise in July, 1914, on the yacht *Hohenzollern* could not have been arranged as a deliberate camouflage of German warlike intentions because when he, House, had been planning in December, 1913, to go to Europe in the spring ("Wilson and I were very much worried about the possibility of a European war"), the German Embassy in Washington had informed him of the Kaiser's schedule for most of the coming year, and the yachting trip already appeared on it. Kühlmann said that whoever plotted the war—if anyone did—the Kaiser was not one of them. The Kaiser, he said, was a vigorous man of a good deal of ability but not good judgment, and that he was not kept closely informed of matters of high policy. He was half English at heart, at least "in aspirations," and wanted to have the favor of King Edward, who, however, was "rather gruff" to him. He really would have liked nothing better than to be received as an English gentleman and asked to shoot grouse.

Kühlmann told an interesting anecdote about the Kaiser's reception by wireless of the text of the Austrian ultimatum, as recounted to him by Prince Albert von Schleswig-Holstein, who was on the *Hohenzollern*

at the time. Early one morning, the Kaiser sent for two or three inti-
mates, among them Prince Albert, and read them the wireless. He had
ordered the yacht, he said, to head back for Germany. He then told the
following story: "My grandfather and the Tsar of Russia, as evidence of
particular friendship, exchanged personal ADCs. There were rumors of
war at one moment between Russia and Turkey, so my grandfather
sent to the Tsar's German ADC and asked for a confidential report. The
Tsar told this German ADC there was nothing in it, adding, 'I do not
wish it, and it will not occur.' Not long afterward when the Tsar was on
a trip his train passed some troops headed south. The Tsar asked what
they were there for and was told that they were going to the 'theatre of
war.' He told his German ADC to telegraph at once to my grandfather,
informing him of the fact and saying, 'I know nothing about it.' Gentlemen (said the Kaiser in conclusion), 'if I don't hurry back to Berlin I
shall find myself in the same position.' "

Answering a question from John W. Davis as to who had been Germany's best military men, Kühlmann broadened it to include the
Austrians also, saying that he thought the best general on "our" side was
Conrad von Hötzendorf, the Austrian chief of staff, and next to him
General Hoffmann, who succeeded Ludendorff as chief of the general
staff on the eastern front, and who was Kühlmann's colleague in negotiating the Brest-Litovsk Treaty. "Hoffmann," he said, "was the best instinctive military man we had. Conrad was the best equipped technically,
being thoroughly grounded and trained in the Moltke school." He had
had three days of talk with Conrad in Marienbad in 1921, when they
decided to sit down and go over everything each of them knew about the
origins and conduct of the war. Conrad explained his desire for war by
saying, "We thought it better to die with honor than to rot." Kühlmann's
remark on this was, "That was all right for them, but not for us. We were
not in any danger of rotting." He added that when he informed Conrad
of the point to which Anglo-German negotiations had progressed in
June, 1914, Conrad said that if he had known this he would not have
favored war, on the assumption that a decisive turn was about to be
taken in European politics and that Austria would benefit therefrom. I
asked Kühlmann at this point whether he could deny that there was a
very large percentage of deliberation in Austria's choice of war. He replied: "Conrad never concealed his desire for a 'preventive war.' " But
Kühlmann's theory was that in general, to use Lloyd George's phrase, the
world "stumbled into war," and that "few people" in any country really
wanted it. (This was a loose statement; the vital point was who the

"few people" were who did want war and what their positions of power were.)

III

Several weeks of that summer my family and I spent abroad, mostly at Dubrovnik on the Dalmatian coast, where we took a house, the Villa Argentina, since then very much enlarged and turned into a hotel. It stood on the road that leads south along the coast, overlooking the town. A flight of 164 steps led down to the sea, where a boatman would row us off to spend the day in some inlet edged with flat warm rocks on which we sunned ourselves between plunges in the blue-green crystalline water. There was a terrace overhung with oleanders where we ate dinner, looking across olive trees and aloes at the golden walls of the town and the tiny harbor behind a breakwater, an unlikely place in modern eyes to have been the site of immense mercantile power and wealth, the city republic of Ragusa, which sent its "argosies" trading throughout the Mediterranean and the Levant and ran trade caravans over the Balkan mountains to the Black Sea. From the terrace in the evening we would watch the sun sink in the Adriatic and the darkness gradually dim the outlines of the island of Lacroma, where Richard Coeur de Lion was shipwrecked; or saunter down to the café in one of the arcades by the harbor for a glass of Dalmatian black wine or a maraschino.

Not many motorcars were on the roads in those days, so that without the flaw of dust and honkings we made many expeditions—up the inland road beyond Trebinje to where the massive carved boulders of the Bogomils, a schismatic twelfth-century sect, stand scattered on the hillsides; or down the coast to Cavtat, where the hospitable Bozo Banats family of shipowners would provide tea before we went up the nearby hill to the memorial chapel built among cypresses by Meštrović. I remember a calm evening when my daughter and I walked along the coastal road to where the mass of mountains on the left gives way to a wide and fertile valley. It lay spread out below us, the air clouded here and there by a motionless wisp of smoke from the evening fire of a farm. We sat and identified the sounds that came from the distance below— the bark of a dog, then of another, the lowing of a cow, the treble tinkle of a bell on a sheep, the deep tone of a bell on a distant and unseen church, the twitter of birds, a girl's call, a child's cry, the gurgle just at our feet of a stream that passed by a culvert under the road and down to the sea. We counted, I think, about twenty distinct sounds, outside of time, before a noisy cart came by and ended the game.

Coming by car from Paris to Dubrovnik we had stopped in Selče for a couple of nights at a guesthouse built by the Grouichs near the Children's Home. When I told Dr. Grouich I intended very soon to motor from Dubrovnik over the mountains to the Sanjak of Novi Pazar and the plain of Kosovo, he said that the last time he had been at Kosovo he had talked with the guardian of the tombs of Sultan Murad and of the Grand Vizier and his standard bearer, slain there at the time of the famous battle that extinguished the Serbian medieval kingdom. It was a hereditary office, passed from father to son, and the old man was the sixteenth in line. In showing Dr. Grouich the battlefield, he had pointed out where the Sultan Murad's tent had been in 1389 and then how the Serbs had moved in such and such a way, but really referring to the battle at Kumanovo, many miles distant, where the Serbs beat the Turks in 1912. He mixed up the battles; for him there was no interval between them, they were two incidents in one struggle. The body of the Sultan is not now at Kosovo, having been taken later for burial to Brusa, but his tomb was kept holy and in 1919 the Serbs arranged that the line of old guardians be preserved and the tomb kept from desecration. To this day the round red cap of the Dalmatians carries a band of black in memory of the defeat that ended Dushan's empire more than five and a half centuries ago.

In accordance with its traditions, Dubrovnik had many intellectuals and they spoke freely about King Alexander's dictatorship. An Oxford graduate, to whom my friend Roland Bryce had written, saw no good in the regime whatsoever, called it pure Serb hegemony; things had been better under the Austrians. The Mayor, who had been a member of the Jugoslav Committee in London during the war, had been put in office by the regime and was its strong partisan. He said that if one took a poll of all the prewar Dalmatian patriots—deputies in the Vienna parliament, members of the Jugoslav Committee, mayors and others who had been opposed to the Hapsburgs when that was dangerous—most would be counted favorable to the present regime, a few would be holding back "waiting to see," and two or three, Trumbić among them, were definitely hostile. He said the doubters had the same motives as Radić, who had told him once, "A politician must be like the pilot of an airplane, ready to veer at a moment's notice to right or left, to soar or duck."

The leading citizen of Dubrovnik was Pero Cingrija, who had been one of the eleven Dalmatian members of the parliament in Vienna and had worked as far back as 1905 with Trumbić and others for cooperation between Croats and Serbs. He said frankly that whether one liked dictatorships or not—and he did not—there was no doubt that the present one was necessary. It was less meddlesome, less expensive, less insistent and less unreasonable than the dictatorship of the parties which had strangled the country and spent its forces in an orgy of vapid talk and recrimination. Nobody in his senses could question the King's sincerity and good will or think he had wanted to take on responsibilities in which he "risked everything." For instance, the King had ordered only the national flag to be flown and had even made Serbian regiments with glorious records turn in their colors and receive new Jugoslav ones, a real test of his sincerity and also of his strength. Those who opposed him, if they did not do so naturally because they had lost office, were mainly impractical persons who wanted everything good to happen at once and in just their way.

Trumbić was a special case, he said. He had always wanted Croat independence or, if not that, Croat hegemony in a Jugoslav state. He recalled how when he went to Geneva in 1918 for a conference on war aims with Pashich and others it was the first time that he had been able to see Trumbić in four years. The first thing Trumbić said was, "Pero, we have no time to talk fully. Our first duty is to bring about the fall of Pashich."

"Now Pashich was not a real Jugoslav," said Cingrija, "and his training and age forbade his ever becoming one. But that was not a crime, simply a factor to be reckoned with. To talk of overthrowing the Premier of the Serbian people, who had been suffering a terrible ordeal and were just winning the struggle as part of the Jugoslav program was ridiculous, and I said so at once. And I say now, that if it was a crime for Pashich not to be a real Jugoslav, it is a crime for Trumbić not to be one, for we all professed to be Jugoslavs for years, when Pashich had never heard of us and was busy with the Turkish and Balkan wars and the politics of his little medieval state."

Cingrija had been on the train that brought members of the government from Corfu to Belgrade at the end of 1918. When the train passed through Sarajevo, he said, Pashich was called on to make a speech. He said, "I salute you, Serbs of three religions," and never understood that this remark, meant to be inclusive and generous, was really an insult to half the people of the country, who of course were not Serbs. The old man could not adjust his mentality to the new situation, but that did not mean he was an enemy; he had to be worked with and brought along. Now he was dead, and in spite of him and because of him the nation stood.

Soon I determined to act on my plan to see the Field of Kosovo with its ancient monasteries, and early one morning set off down the coast, then turned abruptly up over a twisting road between masses of rock under the brow of Mt. Durmitor, the great peak that rises to over eight thousand feet on the border between Montenegro and the inland plain. I had with me "Steve," once the major-domo of King Nicholas of Montenegro, who went with him first to Italy, then to France, and was with him when he died. He was both mechanic and guide, much-needed talents in the primitive country through which we were going. The whole day's drive provided evidence of the old Slav legend that when the Lord made the earth he found at the very end that he had nothing left in his sack but rocks and dumped them all out in one place, which was Montenegro. Steve admired King Alexander even though he had ousted his own King Nicholas. Alexander had gotten rid of "the talkers," he said. "Besides, his mother was a Montenegrin and so he belongs to us."

It was a long day to Niksich and another to Pech, with the usual misadventures of travel on roads not meant for cars in a car not meant for mountain roads of sharp loose rocks; but when I went out in the morning to the Dechani monastery it was worth it all. Against a distant background of Albanian snow peaks the church lies low to the ground in a gorge of rock and pine. It was built in the fourteenth century of blocks of reddish and cream-colored marble, and at the time of my visit it had not been touched by a modern hand. Frescoes of menacing or benign prophets and saints and of members of the royal Nemanjich family completely cover the interior, some of them damaged by time but luckily not yet inexpertly tampered with. I was sure they would someday have to be restored, and by now I am told they have been; but I was glad to see them as they had survived after six centuries of both veneration and neglect. The French-speaking priest had the marble tomb of the founder Stefan III opened for me, and showed me Stefan's mummified body with the pearl-and-diamond-studded bracelet on his withered arm, and his royal red slippers.

Also on the undulating plain of Kosovo, at one moment deep in dust, the next, after a sudden torrent of rain, slimy with mud, is Gračanitca, perhaps the most famous of all the medieval churches in the Balkans that survived the Turkish flood. It is larger and more majestic than Dechani, with a lovely dome and a cluster of four subsidiary domes with many roofs, but because these are of brick, even though rose-colored, and even though the rest of the church is of polished marble, the effect is perhaps less exquisite.[1] The shadows of the storm clouds sweeping down from the mountains which eventually overtook and mired us turned the rose to a sullen red. About ten years before our visit, a priest who did not see very well and found the church too dark had cut two arch-shaped windows through the frescoes in the transepts and fitted them with rough wooden frames. It was this naïve vandalism that made me urge King Alexander (unsuccessfully) to appoint a national monuments commission to prevent similar mutilation of works of art.

On the track between Grachanitsa and Mitrovitsa, where we spent the next night, we came to the two tombs mentioned by Dr. Grouich on the sites where Sultan Murad and his Grand Vizier had been buried. The Turkish guardian, ninety-five years old and eighty-two years in his present office, was delightful, full of wit and life. He had been thirteen, he said, when his father died, leaving him a sum of money and the "living"; and when he died his son, now studying in Constantinople to be a *hodjah,* would come to Kosovo to succeed him. He lived happily surrounded by the turbaned graves of his predecessors who, with their families, alone had the right to be buried on the hill around the tomb. Much of the population on the plain was Albanian, which here meant squalor. When the Albanians and the Mohammedan Serbs die they are buried by the roadside in shallow graves under a few rocks. Only the more important had gravestones, and few of these had the traditional stone turbans, more often a fieldstone stuck on end.

The drive the next day to Sarajevo was over 350 kilometers, something of a feat considering the mountain heights we scaled and the twisting and uneven roads, often no more than upland tracks. The route lay by Novi Pazar, a primitive and interesting place, lively with market-day crowds, then up over grazing lands and rough mountainous country to Prijepolje, and again up and across the old Bosnian-Turkish border. By now, Durmitor, the high mountain that had been our companion for some time near Nikshich, again was in sight, this time to the south. Then we descended by a series of wooded valleys to Sarajevo. There my wife met me, and we motored back to Dubrovnik by way of Mostar, where the women still wore the local costume of long, loose black gown and a high black headpiece with flaps on either side, "blinders" that left only a

1. For a fuller picture of the Kosovo monasteries, and indeed of all the people and landscape of Jugoslavia, see Rebecca West's magnificent *Black Lamb and Grey Falcon* (New York: Viking, 1941).

narrow slit through which to see. The impression was of a menacing bird of prey.

Before we left Jugoslavia I spent a day in Belgrade for a talk with King Alexander, who was in a good frame of mind because of steady improvements in the domestic situation. He felt that soon he could take a first step toward returning to a more democratic system. He had been all over the country, and he said that everywhere, including Croatia, he had found patriotism and loyalty. He now had in mind a two-chamber parliament, with an elected lower house and an upper house partly elective and partly appointed to represent different elements in national life. The first step would be to draw up a constitution, and work on this was well along. He would build into it what he called a "trench" around the state's essential functions, leaving to parliament all matters not touching national unity and security. Elections might even be held before the end of the year, and then the way would be clear for parliamentary powers to evolve.

As usual, Italy and Albania were the King's chief preoccupations. He said he would like to come to a real understanding with Italy before the disarmament conference scheduled for 1932. The Albanian Army was now for practical purposes part of the Italian Army and must be counted as such. Unless the Adriatic "front" could be neutralized Jugoslavia would have to remain on guard there. Foreign Minister Marinkovich had several times proposed the neutralization of Albania to Foreign Minister Grandi and as recently as May had suggested that the two countries join to guarantee Albanian independence. Grandi reminded him that Italy had *dans sa poche* the 1921 mandate of the Powers to act on their behalf in case Albanian independence was threatened; to which Marinkovich replied that what Jugoslavia wanted was precisely to guarantee that independence. So the danger on the Adriatic remained and Jugoslavia would have to step very cautiously in any move toward disarmament.

At this point the King took me in to lunch. General Zhivkovich was there, evidently rather puzzled why this American should make up a party of three. He hardly opened his mouth except to eat. The King said he had been pressing forward the publication of Serbian documents on events preceding the outbreak of the war. The work would be in two volumes, and was progressing well. It contained much correspondence with Russia and, of course, a section on Serbia's alleged part in the Sarajevo assassination.

In international finance Jugoslavia was facing what the King called a

staggering *Diktat,* President Hoover's proposal of a one-year moratorium
on all international debts. Since Serbia had been completely occupied by
the enemy after 1915, she had had no opportunity, like the other Allies,
to acquire foreign debts; thus, while the Hoover Plan released Jugoslavia
from paying the comparatively small sum of something over 9 million
marks on wartime debts, it deprived her of over 79 million marks in
reparations, a terrible blow to the Jugoslav treasury. "If we don't accept,"
the King said, "we incur everybody's ill will, if we do we ruin our finances." (In the end, of course, Jugoslavia had no choice but to accept.)

When I got to Paris I found in a number of talks that French banking
opinion considered the Hoover moratorium, though painful and unfair,
a better way of keeping Germany afloat than to offer her a massive international loan. The French felt that she had deliberately let herself drift
toward the current crisis by indulging in immense short-term loans for
unproductive purposes; these were now "frozen." The collapse of the
Credit-Anstalt in Vienna had brought the deepening Great Depression
to a climax in Central Europe, and Germany had now thrown herself on
the mercy of the financial world in the hope of being saved from the
further reparation installments agreed on only two years earlier in the
Young Plan. Parker Gilbert while Agent-General for Reparation Payments had frequently denounced the extravagant borrowing by the
Reich and especially by scores of German municipalities (in which New
York bankers had been prominent) ; and now some way had to be found
of saving them and with them the finances of France, Britain and other
creditors.

One trouble was that all the governments concerned were weak—
Chancellor Brüning was weak, so was Prime Minister Laval, so was
Prime Minister MacDonald. Even the position of President Hoover was
far from ironclad; he had found it necessary at last to deal with reparations and war loans together, but still faced stone-wall resistance in
Congress to any mingling of the two issues. The French fear was that
even the part of the reparation payments marked down in the Young
Plan as unpostponable might be postponed under the Hoover Plan. In
the end, that part was maintained, but only in form, for France made a
loan to the German Railways of an equivalent sum.

As I was writing an article on these problems I went to Basel to talk
with officials of the Bank for International Settlements. Leon Fraser, the
assistant director, a friend of mine, was critical of the manner in which
Hoover had introduced his plan. When Chancellor Brüning had said that
Germany was at the end of her resources he evidently was motivated

by political reasons; everyone knew that her situation was bad, but not that it could not be saved. But when the President of the United States announced it, all doubts were removed and the last remnant of German credit was destroyed. As André Géraud put it: "Hoover came along, said he was going to save Germany, clapped her on the back and knocked her flat."

French faith in international contracts was now gone. The reputation of Briand and the financial people who had worked to get the Young Plan accepted by the Chamber of Deputies had suffered badly. General Mangin and other military people who had all along favored taking a hard line with Germany were saying that France must insist that agreements made be carried out, that further compromises must be refused, that if there were a default an equivalent must be taken by force. Nevertheless I told Fraser that hotheads like Mangin were not being taken seriously in Paris. In the Ruhr crisis a Boulangist coup might have been feasible if Poincaré had not set himself firmly against any adventure. But not now. If a military man became influential in case of a deadlock with Germany it would be General Weygand, cool and precise. The French people were in a sober and thoughtful mood; if they turned to a general it would not be because he was a demagogue but as a temporary expedient above party.

Fraser said his French colleagues were much annoyed by Montagu Norman, the governor of the Bank of England, who made no bones about being a partisan of Germany's. They held him responsible for Britain's war-debt settlement with the United States and felt that if he had not wanted to glorify British prestige by being the first to settle, a common settlement could have been reached on better terms. Also, he had done nothing to discourage Germany from its reckless financial course, calculating that if she stopped paying reparations Britain would have a good argument for getting off paying her debts. And so on. Fraser did not corroborate these allegations but obviously had a good deal of sympathy with them.

I repeated a remark which Bernard Baruch had made a few days earlier to my father-in-law in London: "When we look back two years from now, the present stage of this depression will look like a mountain." Fraser gloomily agreed he might be right. Everybody was broke, only some did not know it yet and had not begun to save. Everybody would have to save before things got better.

33

Hemingway in Madrid

Madrid in August of 1931 was empty of tourists, discouraged by the political upheavals that had culminated in the flight of King Alfonso in the spring. He had departed secretly from the royal palace by a back door one evening in April, leaving the Queen and other members of his family to follow. An immense crowd which packed the square before the palace that night did not know he was gone and threatened to break in to try to kill him. To divert them, Luis Quintanilla, a painter whose studio had been used for secret meetings of the Republican leaders during Primo de Rivera's dictatorship, clambered to the roof and to wild applause pulled down the royal standard. Now the Republican provisional government under Alcalá Zamora, legitimatized by an immense majority in elections in June, was at work trying to draft a new constitution. On the surface, Madrid was serene and lazy in the summer heat, but there were tension and intrigue inside the Republican-Socialist coalition.

As government offices did not open until about eleven, I spent the first part of my mornings at the Prado. One afternoon I went for a look at the Cortes, which was discussing the new constitution—one of the last chances, I surmised, for a European bourgeoisie to show what it could do in such a matter. A priest was making a fiery defense of religion. He looked like an Irishman, and I found he came from Galicia—a Celt. One of the cabinet members whom I very much liked was Fernando de los Ríos, Minister of Justice, a professor of political science, afterward Ambassador to the United States, where I came to know him well. He was busy planning the agrarian reform, an especially thorny undertaking in the case of the great estates of southern Spain owned mainly by absentee landlords. I also talked with Luis Araquistain, an intellectual, Under-Secretary of Labor, who was not enthusiastic about certain members of the cabinet; he especially suspected that Foreign Minister Lerroux did not intend to carry through the revolution with enough energy and looked on him as more of a danger to the regime than the Syndicalists. In addition I saw Sánchez Román, a deputy and leading lawyer, affable and cagy, and Jaime Carner, Vice-President of the Generalitat of Catalonia and head of the Catalan delegation to the Cortes. Salvador de Madariaga, who was staying at my hotel, gave me an introduction to Ortega y Gasset, then editor of *Revista de Occidente,* and he arranged an appointment but to my lasting regret contracted a fever and had to cancel it.

A formidable strike was raging in Barcelona, with many casualties, generated by the struggle between the Syndicalists, to whom the left-wing leader Francisco Macía had promised everything under the sun to get their support for a Catalan Republic, and the more moderate trade unionists who joined in the demand for autonomy but wanted the form worked out in harmony with the central Republic in Madrid. Jaime Carner said that a statute providing for autonomy would certainly be adopted, according important local prerogatives but stopping short of independence (as indeed happened, though it was limited in 1934 and finally terminated by Franco in 1939).

On my first day in Madrid I had a call from my friend Jay Allen, correspondent of the *Chicago Tribune,* and he and Ernest Hemingway and I had lunch in the grill of the Savoy Hotel. I believe it was bombed out in 1936. Hemingway swore us to secrecy when he told us the title of his new book on bullfighting, *Death in the Afternoon.* "It's a serious book," he said, "and I want a sober title." It seemed to us a magical choice. He already had shown a genius for titles, *The Sun Also Rises* and *A Farewell to Arms.* He didn't want this one talked about ahead of time because "the bastards will steal anything, and if they can't steal it they run it down." "They" were unspecified.

The next evening we had drinks at the Cervecería Alvarez, on tables set in the open air in the Pasaje Alvarez. I arrived a good deal after the others, who besides Jay Allen and Hemingway included Luis Quintanilla, Sidney Franklin, the Jewish boy from Brooklyn who became a bullfighter, with his retainer, about four feet six inches high, and a large man named Wickersham, picked up by Jay in Lisbon when he went there to cover the Masonic-Republican rebellion, "a bloody little affair," as Jay said.

They were drinking beer and eating shrimps and a sort of barnacle that I had never seen before, with a long neck, or stem, and that I learned was called *percebes*—not appetizing to look at, but sweet to the taste. On the pavement around the table was a circle of pink shrimp shells, and at each place was a pile of the cardboard disks put under glasses to keep track of sales. They had been at it since six or seven, and as it was now about nine the piles were high. Before we went to dinner they were higher, and mine was higher than I usually accumulate.

Franklin's retainer, a toothless and grinning little wretch, very much in need of a shave, hovered behind his chair, solicitous about ordering new rounds of beer so that he could drink what was left in all the glasses. Franklin himself must have been six feet tall, and by contrast with his retainer seemed taller. In a good profile of him in *The New Yorker*, Lillian Ross described him as almost bald, with only wisps of sandy-colored hair; but that was in 1949, and eighteen years earlier he had plenty of hair and it was really red. He had a well-knit body, slender, but without the elegance that one thinks of in a young matador. He had gone to Mexico, I think as agent for a Chicago concern, selling calendars and greeting cards, and was there over a year before he saw his first bull-fight. He told me he fought his first bull six weeks later. When he decided to try his luck in Spain he first won curiosity and then admiration from fans in Seville and Madrid; but the leading Spanish matadors soon became jealous of him, then furious and then refused to fight anywhere that he appeared. They forced the managers of bull rings to join in a boycott, and this summer he had no contracts. Hemingway said the other matadors disliked Franklin because he was unselfconsciously reck-less and took risks whenever he fought, whereas most of them accepted serious risks only on the big days in the big rings; at other times they used tricks to give the illusion they were working dangerously close to the bull. He had put the "big names" on the spot, so was out of a job. He was less egocentric then than Lillian Ross described him later. He said being a good bullfighter was being born that way. What else was needed, I asked? To give up love, he said. Sex was bad for bullfighters and ballet dancers; it made them weak in the legs. I believe he never married. Of course he could not be blackballed for long and soon came back to great acclaim. The Spanish crowds called him "Fracking."

Jay Allen has told me that Hemingway and Quintanilla originally planned to cook a *paella* that evening down on the banks of the Man-zanares, for which purpose they had acquired a couple of live chickens from a street vendor and parked them, legs tied together, under my chair. I don't remember the arrangement, and at any rate if there was such a project it was abandoned. Wickersham proposed settling the account for drinks for all of us and brought out a hundred-dollar bill. That of course meant nothing to the waiter and the rest of us looked at the display rather sourly. At about eleven, average for Madrid, we went to dinner at Botin's, where Jake took Brett in the last pages of *The Sun Also Rises*. We went to the upstairs restaurant, which had, as I remember, a wainscot of white tiles. The huge square oven was in the center of the room, with a door that the host opened to haul out a whole lamb or a suckling pig and slice off your piece. Tradition said the fire hadn't gone out since Cervantes' day. We took a square table near the head of the stairs. Ernest took off his jacket, hung it on the back of a chair opposite the one where Wickersham had sat down, and said slowly to Wickersham: "I don't like you." Without waiting for what might come next Wickersham got up and jumped for the stairway. Ernest sat down quietly. It was the only time in those days that he acted in the combative character so often ascribed to him. We had thick bean soup, tunny fish, suckling pig, melon and a crisp white wine for a total for all four of us of sixteen pesetas—forty cents apiece. I had paid sixteen pesetas for my dinner at the Palace Hotel the evening before.

When we left to go to a flamenco dance hall, Ernest tried with his jacket to illustrate the difference between good and bad veronicas on the little taxis racing around the Puerto del Sol, but had difficulty as they all veered away. At the dance hall, the girls who flocked to Don Ernesto's table smelt overpoweringly of scent, applied generously over an unwashed foundation, and seemed to be pancaked with flour all over, judging by what was exposed in a friendly and matter-of-fact way, including what one girl called her two plump white *palomas*.

One day Quintanilla took me out to Toledo, and on the way we stopped at his studio to see the portrait he was painting of Hemingway. He had sat for only six hours, but that had been enough to finish the head, which I thought vigorous and very like.

As you approach Toledo it grows on the horizon, like Chartres. It was a morning of transparent clarity, but when we stopped across the river for an early lunch the city seemed to swim in the wavering heat up into the limitless blue of the sky. Under the grape arbor of an inn in the fields we had partridge, shot that morning. Crossing the Tagus by one of the bridges, we went to visit the Moorish city walls, with a marvelous view, the Casa del Greco and the adjoining museum, the old synagogues, the cathedral with El Greco's "Espolito," and the Church of Santo

Tomé with his magnificent "Burial of Count Orgaz." Several of the pictures in the El Greco museum Quintanilla assured me were fakes. He knew it not by internal evidence, since El Greco's style is not too hard to copy, but because they had been painted by acquaintances of his to the order of one of the royal ministers, who paid them a moderate price, then "discovered" the pictures with appropriate éclat and sold them to the state at El Greco prices. In any case, there was nothing in the El Greco museum, nor for that matter in the Prado in Madrid, to match the "Espolito" or the "Burial of Count Orgaz." The only other El Greco in the same class seemed to me the "St. Maurice and the Legion" at the Escorial.

We arrived at the cathedral to find the great silvered and gilded gates of several of the chapels closed and locked. A drowsy verger, reluctantly answering a summons, told Quintanilla they would not be opened again until the next morning, and when Quintanilla protested shrugged and said we must see what we could through the grilles. Quintanilla was not at all pleased with this, and seizing one of the gates with both hands rocked it back and forth till the whole cathedral reverberated. The echoes chased the pigeons in the clerestory around in confusion, and priests came running, shouting to Quintanilla to stop. "Who presumes to close national treasures to the public?" he demanded. "Open at once or I'll see that they are moved to museums where all Spaniards can see them." I didn't understand the words until Quintanilla told me afterward, but it was pleasant to see the way the priests tumbled to unlock the gates.

Ernest would not take me to a bullfight although there was to be one at Aranjuez, some thirty miles from Madrid. It was out of season and wouldn't be much good. "You must begin with a first-class fight," he said, "not necessarily famous matadors but expert enough not to botch things up and disgust you with the whole thing for good." Jay Allen told Ernest he was an Eagle Scout, but did not get a rise. He simply said the bulls were bad at that season; they were sending anything into the *plazas* that had two balls and a tail.

I was very much taken with Hemingway; he was in a relaxed mood after finishing his book and there were no histrionics. Since there was no animal or bird to shoot and no fish to catch he was not in competition with anyone, and thus had no reason to show the unattractive aspect of his character which Carlos Baker bears down on rather heavily in his admirable biography. One afternoon we went rummaging through back-street shops for things for his new house in Key West. Old Spanish tiles had become rare, but he found a number that he liked, and I bought two, with figures on a creamish ground, also a dozen old Spanish plates made of the lovely pure silver that has a soft light rather than a shine. Ernest offered to ship my tiles to America with his. Luckily I sent the tiles only and not the silver plates. When I asked him later how I could get my tiles I found that without his knowledge his wife had embedded them with the others in the wall of the Key West patio.

Jay Allen was a top-flight reporter in an era when there were many competitors for fame in the profession. It is a loss that he has never set down his experiences in a book as have his friends and peers Jimmy Sheean, John Gunther, Bill Shirer and John Whitaker. He was fearless of authority when it stood in the way of a story and he wrote it as he saw it. Without his dispatches the massacre at Badajoz would never have been known in its full horror. Already in 1931 he was very deeply involved in the Republican cause, and became increasingly so after Franco raised the army in revolt in 1936 and made Spain the bloody battleground of rival ideologies. The lines were already discernible in 1931 but had not yet been drawn so that every citizen had to choose, as in the end was bound to happen. It is the tragedy of civil wars that everyone must make a choice, even though it means that he finds himself fighting on the same side as extremists with whom he disagrees on everything except the one central issue. So it was in the Spanish Civil War, with the choice between democracy struggling to be born in a country where it had never existed, and privilege entrenched since the Middle Ages determined to abort the new order however cruel the price. Masses of Spaniards were horrified to find themselves in the same camp with Communists, supported by Stalin, or with Nazis and Fascists, supported by Hitler and Mussolini, but where could they have taken another stand except on the other side where some of their allies would have been equally repulsive?

As the early September heat was scorching, Jay left to join his wife in Torremolinos, Quintanilla disappeared on a political errand and Ernest decided to return to Paris. His wife, Pauline, had been with him in Madrid earlier but had left. He said he was really fed up with bullfighting; the last straw was the way Franklin was being treated. He talked of quitting Spain for good and going to East Africa. I said he might run into Louis Bromfield there, to which he replied that if there was danger of that he'd go to West Africa. I didn't see why he had such a skunner against Louis, a likable fellow and a successful writer, but not in a class that could arouse Ernest's jealousy.

He asked me if I would come and wake him in time to have a drink before catching his train. He was staying in an unpretentious hotel in the Calle de la Victoria; a rather bare room, the tiled floor scattered with clothes and newspapers. He was lying naked on the mattress. As nothing was packed I helped stuff things into a couple of valises as one might clothes into a laundry bag. Then we met Quintanilla at the toreros' bistro and had so much beer and talk that Ernest almost missed his train.

When Ernest said he was going to stop off at St.-Jean-de-Luz the reason for his grudge against Louis Bromfield appeared. On the way down he had run into Louis on the platform there. Louis, who must have been seeing somebody off, asked him to come out and stay a night with him and his wife, Mary. A few days later a friend in Paris had sent him a sarcastic note with a clipping from the society column in the Paris *Herald* recording his visit as a house guest of the Bromfields. He said, "I'm going to stop over long enough to beat Bromfield up." I told him that would be silly; Louis probably had had nothing to do with his appearance in the society news. I suppose he had no intention of doing it anyway. At the station I carried one valise, Ernest the other and a large straw-covered bottle of *rioja alta*. As we walked down the platform toward his wagon-lits he and his bottle were greeted with hopeful cheers by the occupants of each compartment we passed.

II

The Spanish Civil War tested liberal convictions everywhere. For me, and especially for those a few years younger, it became an embodiment of the struggle against Fascism and Nazism. Many volunteered in the Republican forces and many gave their lives. My revulsion from Nazism had begun long before the start of the war in Spain and grew as Hitler went from one barbarism to another. The Spanish War should have been a warning to civilized governments, but instead they adopted the strangling policy of nonintervention which, as Clement Attlee said, was "really devised to prevent the Spanish Government from exercising its rights under international law." I was against that evasiveness and against the arms embargo adopted by our Congress on January 8, 1937. Throughout the war I was closely in touch with Jay Allen, who made his apartment on Washington Square a center of activity on behalf of the Loyalist cause.

When Luis Quintanilla was sent by his government to the United States early in 1939 he brought me a set of Goya's famous series "Los Proverbios," just drawn from the original plates in besieged Madrid by order of the Spanish Republican Government. Herbert L. Matthews later described this special edition of Goya's etchings in the *New York Times* on Sunday, September 8, 1954, as follows:

The idea of this edition was primarily to raise foreign currency for the hard-pressed Loyalists, but also to prove that reverence for Spanish art was as great among the so-called "Reds" as among their critics abroad. So, the famous engraver Adolfo Rupérez was commissioned to make 150 sets of the four great Goya series. The first five of these, on Antique Japan paper, were destined for very special presentation. Fifteen sets, numbered 6 to 20, were to be on Imperial Japan paper and the remaining 130 on Arches paper.

The "Los Proverbios" series consisted of eighteen etchings, accompanied by a covering plate stating that it had been completed at the Calcografía Nacional on November 9, 1937, also a map of Madrid showing where bombs had dropped while the work was being done.

As Matthews gave the story of the undertaking, which he said had never appeared in print even in Spanish publications, the full number of the engravings was not completed, but those that had been were sent to London, where three sets of each series were placed in an exhibition of Spanish art at the Victoria and Albert Museum in the summer of 1938. As a result of protests by representatives of Franco, the exhibition was closed and the material was sent out of the country, probably to Paris. What happened to most of it thereafter remains a mystery. The Spanish Government wanted to sell the entire lot, according to Thomas Harris, the print collector, for what he called a "huge" sum. Matthews commented:

Dealers generally were doubtful of the ability of Rupérez either to draw good prints from the old worn plates or to complete the contract. On the latter score they were right, but not on the former. Rupérez himself modestly characterizes the results as "not bad," but where the plates permitted, as they often did, his performance was remarkable and in any case he did as good a job as any human being could do, considering the state of the engravings.

He added that "Rupérez says that it will never be possible again to make a complete drawing of the four sets. On the other hand, Luis Alegre, present director of the Calcografía Nacional, believes that another edition can be made 'with much care.'"

When Matthews visited Rupérez in Madrid he had retired from government service and had his own workshop near the Prado. He told Matthews he could throw little light on what happened to the etchings after London, but that he knew one of the five sets on Antique Japan paper went to the Spanish Republican President, Manuel Azaña, who died in

Switzerland during World War II, and that set number 2 went to Mrs. Eleanor Roosevelt, who, said Matthews, still had it. That a set was given Mrs. Roosevelt was told me by Quintanilla at the time he gave me mine. Who received the other copies on Antique Japan paper is not known. Mine is not one of them, since it bears the number 24. Quintanilla inscribed it to "Friend Armstrong" as a "gift of the Spanish people, which is given to you officially, in the name of my Government." He dated it January 25, 1939.

That was an ominous moment. The great insurgent drive in Catalonia had begun on December 23, and on January 26 Franco's forces, with Italians playing a major role, took Barcelona. On March 28, Madrid, having suffered appalling losses, ended its resistance. The bloody struggle was over. Soviet Russia had sent the Loyalists quantities of military equipment and many military advisers. Nazi Germany had sent Franco about ten thousand men, Fascist Italy up to seventy-five thousand, and both had supported him in the air and at sea. Five months later, on September 1, 1939, Hitler's armies, profiting from the experience gained in Spain with new matériel and its use, invaded Poland.

34

The Losing Fight for Disarmament

Fifty or more nations were to meet at Geneva in February of 1932 to discuss disarmament. It would be a dangerous occasion, since where national security is concerned popular feelings are hard to control. But the Allies had a definite obligation to do something about disarmament. They had replied to German protests against the Versailles requirement that Germany limit her military establishment by undertaking to make the general reduction of armaments one of the first duties of the new League of Nations. Over ten years had passed and Germany was saying that unless the Allies made good their pledge she would feel relieved of her obligations. This would of course jeopardize French security. Since France was unlikely to reduce her land forces or approve of an increase in Germany's, and since Germany would not continue her military inferiority to France, it seemed uncertain whether on this count alone the conference would succeed; and there were a dozen other reasons for pessimism.

What was to be the American position? On November 13, 1931, I telephoned Secretary of State Stimson offering him the first ten or a dozen pages in the winter issue of *Foreign Affairs* to set the public straight on the American interest in the conference and what he thought it might reasonably accomplish. He confessed it would be impossible for him to write anything frank "without dashing the hopes of the world." For the past year, he said, he had been trying to steer events so that the conference might do something useful.

"These efforts have failed," the Secretary said, "and if I were to speak my mind now it would have the same effect that Senator Borah had when he spoke out during the visit of Premier Laval. There would be consternation everywhere, and blame for the failure of the conference would be hung around our necks."

He was referring to Laval's visit to Washington in October, when the American and French governments issued a statement declaring that some agreement on intergovernmental indebtedness might be necessary during the period of depression; which brought Senator Borah's quick rejoinder that any arrangement could not include the war debts, thus torpedoing any influence the United States might have exerted in helping regulate the reparations question. I commented that if the conference was destined to have rough going a realistic statement from him might put everyone on their mettle and add to the incentive to overcome difficulties and make at least some progress.

After a long pause the Secretary said he must hold to his decision. His whole tone was very sober and very discouraged. I concluded that he was disillusioned about our government's ability to do anything effective in world affairs. He had just run into strong opposition from isolationists in Congress when he tried to help the League cope with the developing Manchurian crisis, which he saw clearly held a threat to world peace. He had gone so far as to appoint an American observer to sit with the League Council during its effort to keep Japan and China from open war, and to take part in the discussions when they related directly to the Kellogg-Briand Pact, but for this he had been scathingly attacked by Senate isolationists, with the result that when the Council reconvened in Paris early in November there was no official American observer. Instead, Stimson merely sent Ambassador Dawes from London to be available for consultations. He nevertheless did not abandon his effort to bring American influence to bear for world peace, and on January 7, 1932, announced his famous policy of not recognizing the fruits of aggression—a direct retort to Japan's action in Manchuria.[1]

Pessimism over the continuing depression, the Far East crisis and forecasts of the failure of the Disarmament Conference was not lessened by reports from Europe, especially Germany. Paul Scheffer, back from a visit home, said he had found great changes both there and in France. A policy of fulfillment had become impossible in Germany and a policy of moderation had become impossible in France. The German situation was going from bad to worse. Big industry was at a standstill, shipping was paralyzed, German coal couldn't compete with British coal while the pound

1. Eventually, in April, 1933, *Foreign Affairs* published Stimson's description of the nonrecognition policy and his other policies during his four years in office.

was low, unemployment was growing. The middle and lower classes were in despair; they were turning away from reason and more and more listening to Hitler.

It was a bad mistake, Scheffer said, to suppose that Hitler's power lay simply in phraseology and not in ideological appeal. He aimed to create a conscious national proletariat, and was on his way to doing it. Scheffer had heard him speak in Hamburg at a mass meeting of thousands of well-behaved but dispirited middle-class persons. One statement drew particular applause: "Some say we should work for a rapprochement with France, some with England, some even that we should draw closer to Russia. None of these propositions means anything so long as there is no 'We.' The first task is to create a German 'We.' "

Scheffer's feeling was that Hitler was preparing a reservoir of nonparty national power to take advantage of the impending German collapse. Chancellor Brüning had said to Scheffer that Hitler told him he would accept no part in any Brüning government; what he wanted was the power behind the throne. Scheffer asserted (what I could not get him to substantiate) that certain American bankers were contributing to Hitler so as to dispose him favorably toward repaying American credits when he came to power. I was struck that he said not "if" but "when."

At a recent Council meeting an American banker had said that it would be better for American creditors of Germany to settle for whatever they could get—even twenty-five cents on the dollar—because later they would get nothing. Scheffer agreed: "German capital is disappearing like a mouse." He diagnosed the world situation as a cumulative series of crises to which statesmen had become accustomed, thinking as each crisis passed that a climax would never come. The world's economic structure was tottering. "We ought to put gold in our safe-deposit boxes."

II

When I saw Colonel House just before New Year's he showed me a sheaf of letters from Europe, all pessimistic. One was from William Bullitt in Vienna, where he was collaborating with Freud on a book psychoanalyzing Wilson (Freud had never laid eyes on Wilson, and the book was properly criticized as analysis at second hand when it was published thirty-five years later). Bullitt, who had been in England, wrote that Baldwin was loyal to MacDonald in the National Coalition cabinet but that many Conservatives were far from that, among them Churchill, Rothermere and Beaverbrook. They would like to resume close collaboration with Japan, so that when the Conservatives came back to power they could cooperate with the nationalist Japanese in Asia—"the Japanese to do the shooting in China," as Bullitt phrased it, "the English to do the shooting in India." The aim would be to build up a strong power against Bolshevism and also a counterweight to American influence in world affairs. The Labour party was all at sea. Oswald Mosely had definitely gone Fascist and was organizing "cells" all over the country. When I raised the question of Bullitt's reliability, House agreed that it was dubious so far as facts were concerned, but he thought his general sense of the trend of events was good.

Norman Davis had told me of Hoover's invitation to go to Geneva as chairman of the American Delegation at the Disarmament Conference. When I mentioned it to House he said it indicated that the President expected the Conference to fail and wanted to give the Democrats a generous share of the responsibility.

House could seldom keep away for long from the current political scene, and now told me at some length how he had become an adviser to Franklin D. Roosevelt in his campaign to get the Democratic nomination for the Presidency. He did not know the Governor (as he then was) very well, he said, and had been somewhat surprised when Roosevelt asked him about a year ago to come to see him and told him he felt in need of political advisers and wanted him and Owen Young to act in that capacity. House replied that he was not greatly interested in the details of the coming campaign, any more than he had been in those of 1920, 1924 and 1928, but he was much more interested in its general conduct than he had been then, for whereas he had known that they were doomed to failure, he felt that, with reasonably good management, the coming Democratic campaign could be made successful. He said he had suggested to Roosevelt that he keep on good terms with Owen Young but not ask his political advice; this was not, he told Roosevelt, because he didn't want a colleague, but because, as he put it, Young's advice on political matters "couldn't be of any conceivable use to Roosevelt" and because his advice on general matters was available without any special understanding. House's conditions of acceptance had been that he should not be asked to pass on specific problems and that their relationship remain absolutely confidential. Roosevelt had found it impossible to maintain this last condition as regards his private political secretary, Louis Howe. After Howe divulged it to a *Herald Tribune* man it seemed best to be quite open about the matter, and Roosevelt had gone up to the North Shore the previous summer and spent the day with House.

House then gave an estimate of Roosevelt's capacities. "Between you and me and the angels," he said, he did not consider him a great man, nor would he say that he was the best man in sight for the Presidency. He would say that he was honest and able, that he was the most available candidate and the one that stood the best chance of being elected if nominated. He pointed out that Roosevelt had a definite following in about the same states where Wilson had been strong before his first nomination. Although Al Smith and the central party machine were opposed to him, he had the support of the progressive wing of the party. House said he felt that Newton Baker came nearer to being the Wilson type than any other man in the country. But he thought that by talking too much about the League of Nations Baker would raise an unnecessary and unfortunate issue.

"I'd very much like to see Baker President," he said, "but it would be much harder to elect him than to elect Roosevelt, and I don't at all agree with the people who say any Democrat can be elected this year."

Smith's recent decision to become a definite candidate was made because he was one of those who believed that any Democrat could be elected. House said: "The only Democrat in sight for the nomination that I think definitely could *not* be elected is Smith."

One of House's objectives in having a close relationship with Roosevelt was to influence his appointments. His candidate for Secretary of State would be Baker, he said, and after him he would put Frank Polk and Owen Young. He would prefer to see Young as Secretary of the Treasury.

When I mentioned John W. Davis, he said Davis wouldn't take the job. I pointed out that there was a difference between refusing "a job" and refusing to be Secretary of State in the first Democratic administration in twenty years. He replied: "Well, I'd rather have Davis than any of the others." I wasn't sure he was wholehearted about this, since it conflicted with what he had said about Baker previously. As if to confirm this suspicion, he then remarked: "I think we would get just as much of what you and I want with Roosevelt as President and Baker as Secretary of State as we would with Baker as President; and the first is much easier to get than the second."

House claimed that Smith was more to blame than Roosevelt for the split between them. "Smith looks on Roosevelt as a sort of Boy Scout," he said, "doesn't really think of him as an equal. Roosevelt wanted to have Smith's advice on state matters, regarding which Smith knows more than any living man, but this didn't suit Smith, who wanted to be Roosevelt's mentor in national politics as well." On the prohibition issue, for instance, Smith tried to bully Roosevelt and didn't even consult him before defining the "party" attitude.

Many people in politics believed, said House, that a social overturn was coming in the United States. (By "social" he really meant "political.") Then, interjecting his highest injunction to secrecy, "This is graveyard," he said that McAdoo had come to him a few days earlier and revealed that he was holding himself in readiness to be spokesman of a new group aiming to profit from the overturn of the two major parties. Young La Follette and other progressives of both parties were with McAdoo and were looking to him for leadership. House termed McAdoo a man of "great drive, courage and intellectual power." When I noted that "character" was lacking from this reference, he replied, "Well, I don't mean he lacks character; I just didn't put it in among his chief characteristics."

III

I left at the end of February for Europe, planning to spend some time in Geneva, where the Disarmament Conference would be in session. On the way I stopped in France, mainly to visit Poincaré, who since his stroke in January, 1931, had retired to his place in Lorraine. Passing through Paris, I had a talk with Caillaux. He had very much aged; he still had the shining poll, but there were wrinkles around the edges and the small fringe of hair was gray. His figure had become more stocky and his knees seemed to creak, but he still gesticulated violently, clasping his hands above his head as he invoked the gods against what he considered the *bêtises* of his political enemies.

In a broad way Caillaux attributed the economic crisis to the development of science and mechanization, without a corresponding drop in costs to compensate for the resulting unemployment. Reparations were finished, he said, and as soon as that fact was ratified debt payments would be finished too. "Oh, we shall promise to resume debt payments as soon as Germany resumes reparations payments," he said with a shrug, "but neither will ever happen."

He drew a parallel between what Stalin was attempting to do overnight in Russia and what Count Witte had tried earlier to accomplish in a decade. It was exactly thirty years, he said, since he had talked with Witte, then the Tsar's Finance Minister, about Russia's finances.

"I told Witte that, as Finance Minister of France, I was far from pleased with all the Russian loans being floated in Paris. I said I doubted they could be repaid. 'They will be ready for amortization in twenty years,'

Witte replied, 'for by then the factories and railways we are building with them will begin producing a return.' I said how about a revolution, or even a European war? Witte replied that the first was out of the question, the second most unlikely."

From this recollection Caillaux concluded that the sufferings being imposed by the Bolsheviks on the Russian masses to bring about industrialization were too great to be borne indefinitely, and that since sufficient experts and managers could not be developed rapidly enough, nor the workmen trained, the immense Bolshevik effort would fail. Already the failure was foreshadowed by the fact that factories had been built but could not function efficiently and railways operated badly over badly maintained roadbeds. Did he think there would be another revolution, I asked, or another war, the results which Witte had not thought conceivable thirty years earlier and which Stalin did not think conceivable now? Caillaux evaded answering.

I had not seen Poincaré since his stroke, but he had written that he would be glad to have me visit him. I left the train from Paris at Commercy and took a car up the valley of the Meuse to Sampigny. The willow shoots were red and spring plowing had begun, but the streams were still partly frozen and snow lay in the hollows. Poincaré's house, Le Clos, stood among evergreens on a rise above the river, with the village of Sampigny right at its feet. It was one of those French villas, not a very happy combination of red brick and stone, with a high mansard roof, that would seem more at ease in a Paris suburb.

Poincaré came in with Madame Poincaré, followed by a lap dog. His face had filled out, he dragged his feet slightly and instead of his usual briskness and precision he seemed to collect his thoughts with difficulty and express them almost painfully. The sad impression was accentuated by the comfortlessness of the house, with its formal rooms, ugly ornaments, stiff chairs and no rugs to make the floors seem less cold and less dangerously slippery for an invalid to move around on. But he greeted me in a very friendly way and I felt he liked the diversion of a visitor. Evidently his wife was there to make sure I didn't tire him, but she joined in the conversation whenever she got a chance, which was oftener than either he or I wanted, for if he hesitated for a word she found it and was off.

He spoke of his disillusionment over the League's lack of action when faced with Japan's occupation of Manchuria and landing in Shanghai, which suggested to him that it should develop a police force, perhaps beginning with an air arm. He praised Secretary Stimson's initiative and was interested to hear that in America there was a revival in some quarters of the earlier idea of a league to "enforce" peace. This, he noted, accorded with the French thesis that the basis of peace was security. He was worried, naturally, by the rise of Hitler—"evidently a maniac." The latest evidence of this was that in speaking of Poincaré he had said that if he had done any service to France it was because he was not a Frenchman, being from Lorraine.

"I'd like him to know," said Poincaré with sudden energy, "that if he has ever done any service to Germany it is because he is not a German, but an Austrian."

Poincaré tells in *L'Invasion,* one of the volumes of his memoirs, how he heard from the Préfet of the Meuse on September 25, 1914, that his house in Sampigny was being bombarded by the Germans. In all, forty-eight shells of large caliber landed on it. He had seen the house again for the first time, he told me, on September 13, 1918, when he invited Pershing to lunch with him in his railway car on a siding at Sampigny. After lunch they walked up the hill to the house, which was caved in and in utter ruin. Apparently some American soldiers had done additional damage, chipping off bits of mantelpieces and so on for souvenirs. When Pershing said he would see that they were punished Poincaré asked as a favor that nothing of the sort be done.

We went into a room in the front of the house, facing in the direction of St. Mihiel, to see where the shells had come from. Poincaré took pleasure in the fact that the Germans never set foot on his property, being retained on the other side of the Meuse. As the room was cold, Madame Poincaré threw a shawl—baby blue—over his shoulders. This made him indignant and he flung it off with a shudder. He chafed terribly at being inactive. "Nothing takes the place of work," he said. He was allowed an hour and a half's work in the morning, the same in the afternoon. When he heard that *Foreign Affairs* was to be ten years old in the autumn he offered to write for the anniversary issue, and though I of course accepted eagerly I felt the article was unlikely to materialize. He was busy now with the ninth volume of his memoirs, to be published in the autumn. The tenth appeared in 1933 and the eleventh was under way at the time of his death, October 15, 1934. The assassination of King Alexander at Marseilles six days before that was a blow to him, but more particularly the death in the same attack of his friend and colleague of many years, Foreign Minister Louis Barthou, who had had an appointment to lunch with Poincaré the very day Poincaré died. As I was leaving, he almost neglected to say goodbye, and when he realized it was much chagrined. It was a sad last glimpse of him.

Poincaré and Caillaux, politicians so different in method and men so antithetic in character, had parallel careers for over thirty years, continuously in conflict. The first serious break was in the Agadir crisis in 1911, which came close to bringing France into war with Germany; Poincaré severely criticized Caillaux, then Prime Minister for the first time, helped force his resignation and succeeded him. In 1928, during Poincaré's last term as Prime Minister, in which he triumphantly restored the French currency, Caillaux maneuvered the fall of his cabinet—though in a few days Poincaré remade it. Both had powerful intellects. Both committed errors. Caillaux's errors came chiefly from vanity and a general lack of character; Poincaré's every action, even his effort to exact what he considered just reparations from Germany by military force, was dictated by rectitude.

I V

In Geneva the Disarmament Conference was marking time; a special session of the League Assembly had been called at China's request to consider the Japanese seizure of Shanghai, and this was monopolizing all attention. Japan's moral and juridical position seemed untenable to almost everyone, doubtless including the Japanese delegation, headed by Tsuneo Matsudaira, but her material position was a strong one, and she was determined to exploit it. The world was in the grip of the economic crisis, elections were pending in several great nations,[2] and her antagonist and victim, China, was thoroughly disorganized; moreover, Geneva was on the other side of the world from the scene of action, and reports of what happened there arrived late and confused. France was unwilling to antagonize Japan; England felt unable to do so. Japan, therefore, was not at all disposed to let the League thwart her bid for power on the Asian mainland.

The representatives of the Great Powers did not instill confidence—Paul-Boncour of France, verbose, rhetorical, sentimental; Sir John Simon of Britain, pompous and vacillating; Dino Grandi, when present, a figurehead and mouthpiece for his master in Rome. (Like Premier Tardieu, Grandi had come to Geneva for the Disarmament Conference, but both

2. The German presidential election took place on March 13, 1932. President Hindenburg fell short of securing a majority over Hitler and the Communist Thälmann, but was reelected in a second round on April 10.

had hurried off so as not to become involved in the Far Eastern mess.)
In a long and very eloquent opening speech Paul-Boncour defended the
League for not having been able in five months to come to any terms with
Japan which would save the League's face or bring peace in East Asia.
It fell completely flat. There followed a couple of days of recriminations
between Matsudaira and the Chinese representative, Dr. Yen.

The little states did not know what to do. They trembled for the sanctity of the agreements which they counted on to protect them in some
emergency of their own, yet were loath to attack the sincerity of the
Great Powers. They aimed to press the Great Powers to execute the
Covenant, but not to press them so far that they came to think of the
League as a danger and handicap that must be gotten rid of. In other
words, they had to vindicate the prestige of the League, but not at the
risk of destroying the League.

Obviously nothing would be easier than to force Japan out of the
League, but what could the League do then to protect China from further injury? Matsudaira emphasized that China was not an organized
state and that Japan must therefore protect the interests of her nationals
there by her own means. But Japan had supported China for membership
in the League and had made treaties with her. Was China organized
enough to make agreements and grant concessions but not entitled to
appeal to the League if they were forcibly violated? From the League's
standpoint (it seemed to me), the touchstone for deciding its position
was whether or not the alleged aggressor, a member of the League, would
accept its commitment to enter into conciliation and arbitration; if not,
it was in fact the aggressor. In that case the only way for the League to
save its moral position was to state that its members would not recognize
whatever Japan might achieve by force, leaving for the future the task
of deciding how much, as a result of this decision, the duties of states
under the Covenant must be enlarged or abbreviated.

Geneva was swarming with journalists from every part of the world.
The two best Americans were Clarence Streit, of the *New York Times*,
able and hard-working, a convinced believer in the League, and Frank
Simonds, of a quite opposite temperament, caustic, cynical, always
prophesying that things would go wrong and delighted when they did.
The foreigner that interested me most, apart from André Géraud, with
whom I had at least one meal daily, was Karl Radek, an editor of *Izvestia,*
who besides being the leading Soviet publicist was a member of the Soviet
delegation. Like so many who came to the top in the Soviet hierarchy,
Radek's career ended in official disgrace and death. Stalin ordered him

tried for treason in the great purge of 1937, which wiped out Bukharin and hundreds of other leaders and hundreds of thousands of those less conspicuous. Radek was spared instant execution but his fate was not less harsh; he was imprisoned in an Arctic labor camp, where he was shortly murdered by another prisoner. I had several talks with him in Geneva, the first in his hotel room, where I found him half in bed, a cigar in his mouth, his boots on the mantelpiece, the table and floor littered with books and newspapers.

Radek was a brilliant talker, if given to hyperbole. He saw Japan establishing herself as the most powerful state in the Far East, an economic force of the first rank, with a Germanic energy and a total disregard of secondary considerations. Nevertheless, opposed as she was by three mighty forces—the eventual consolidation and industrialization of China, Russia's development of Siberia and the expansion of American economic power in China—she was doomed to a debacle, whether soon or late. He believed that even while Japan's representatives in Geneva were going through what she considered a League rigmarole she would not hesitate to undertake any power move that seemed to her advantageous. She might well press it too far, involving Western powers against their will, which in turn would put Soviet Russia in a dangerous position by forcing her to support whatever states opposed Japan. Or if France should support Japan that would also be dangerous, for the Soviets would be faced on their borders by two French satellites, Poland and Rumania. Such were his alarmist views, very much condensed. He said that Moscow had become more worried by recent events in the Far East, and although no new forces were being sent to Siberia those already there were being concentrated on the Manchurian border.

The member of the American delegation to the Disarmament Conference responsible for handling Far Eastern problems was Hugh Wilson. It seemed plain that Japan's exploitation of her conquests on the mainland would increase vastly her reserves of raw materials and her military potential, and since this would concern both us and the Soviet Union I suggested to Wilson that it might not be a bad idea for him to meet Radek. I said I could easily arrange to have this happen "by chance" on neutral ground. The idea came to Wilson as a terrific shock, and he dismissed it with a sharp "certainly not." Ted Marriner, another member of our delegation who was with him, blanched to the back of his bald head. But although our delegates were handicapped by not being able to deal directly with any matter before the League, even though it might affect the world balance of power, they were well posted on the twists and turns in the disarmament labyrinth. One of the most experienced of them, Hugh Gibson, acting chairman of the delegation in Norman Davis' absence, had the drawback that he could not refrain from making a joke of everything. Admittedly this was easy enough in the circumstances in which the Conference was operating. Hugh Wilson, perhaps the most active member of the delegation, hoped that whatever the League did it would not endanger its future existence or take drastic measures that might eventually involve us. He thought that the "Stimson doctrine," as it had come to be called, might prove a way of implementing the Kellogg-Briand Pact, even though by negative action.

One evening Walter Lippmann arrived from Rome, and after dinner, when I brought him up to date on events, we went to the rooms of the American delegation and had a long talk with Gibson, Wilson and Marriner about everything under the sun—the limitations on security under any conditions, the practicability of distinguishing between offensive and defensive weapons, humanizing war, naval problems as changed by Japan's aggression and so on. The next evening we again had dinner together and afterward we again visited Gibson. While we were there Radek arrived to see me. The disgust and amazement on the face of Gibson's secretary as he came in to tell me that Radek was downstairs made me laugh. This time we talked mostly about changes in American life, Soviet economic problems and the mechanization of both city and rural life. Radek had a strange theory that the development of electrical energy, advances in chemistry and scientific progress in general would prevent the return of world prosperity.

If Radek reflected the views of the Communist International, in which he had once been secretary of the Executive Committee, that organization had pretty well given up hope of making revolutionary progress in the United States. As he freely admitted, America had an insufficient historical radical background, the radical leaders there had no ideology and relations between factory managers and workers were not "feudal."

"We did not succeed in Germany," said Radek, "a country where Marxism had been nourished and propagated for years, even after a fearful war and defeat, and following a civil war in which we lost thirty thousand men. And in England, where the roots of economic distress go deep, we see as the socialist leader a mild and tired man like Arthur Henderson. What, then, can we think our prospects are in a country with twenty-four million automobiles? Labor troubles will come there, of course, and there will be unemployment insurance and various kinds of state socialism, but the structure will remain as it is for some time to come. The pioneering spirit is not dead, there will be energetic adaptations to new conditions and these will meet with comparative success due to the large home market and the wealth of the population."

On the question of the Polish Corridor, Radek made a remark which struck me particularly in view of Churchill's account in *The Unknown War* of the part played by that territory in the terrible fighting on the Eastern Front. Neither Germany nor Poland, said Radek, spoke of the essential strategic factor in the dispute over the Corridor, namely that without it Germany could not threaten Warsaw and that with it Poland could threaten Berlin, and would do so even more effectively if she could secure East Prussia. "The strategic line for Germany," he said, "is on the Vistula."

I didn't know whether many American officials had spoken with Soviet representatives since the war; certainly not any great number. However, when I suggested a talk with Radek to Norman Davis, after his return from a visit to Paris, he was not alarmed (unlike Hugh Wilson) and asked me to bring him to see him. In their talk Radek repeated much of what I have noted above, but on one point was more explicit. The Soviets would not agree, he said, to a division of Manchuria. Japan had several times proposed that she take the southern half. Nor would Soviet Russia agree that any "independent" state which Japan set up in Manchuria could be free to repudiate Russian interests and rights in the Chinese Eastern Railway; Russia would not fight for those rights but would reserve them for future adjustment. (As it turned out, Soviet Russia sold her interest in the Chinese Eastern Railway to the Japanese puppet state of Manchukuo in March, 1935.) To recognize an independent Manchuria would be to go against China, said Radek; this Moscow would not do. Japan could not capture Vladivostok from the sea, nor could she do it by land, provided China was Russia's ally. The Soviet Union must and would remain friendly with China.[3]

The two ablest among the representatives of the smaller states at Geneva were the Foreign Ministers of Czechoslovakia and Rumania, Beneš and Titulescu. Titulescu was often called a cynic and Beneš a believer, but the terms of comparison were not quite correct. Their methods were different. Beneš was a busy spider, spinning threads back and forth between the European chancelleries, trying to create something—anything —to safeguard the peace on which his country's existence as a nation de-

3. As a result of this meeting in Geneva, Karl Radek wrote two articles for *Foreign Affairs*, "The War in the Far East: A Soviet View," published in July, 1932, and in January, 1934, an analysis of the bases of Soviet foreign policy.

pended, producing idea after idea, always producing. Titulescu felt it important to blow strongly on any structure that might be erected in order to test its durability and not be disappointed in an hour of need. When I lunched with him one day he said frankly that he felt the League was failing; it was not because the Powers lacked the courage specifically to antagonize Japan but because they had never dared really accept the obligation to maintain peace in all such conditions. When I suggested that to have done so would have put a heavy responsibility on certain Powers, he replied that if I meant he was talking in abstractions or trying to shift responsibilities he stood ready to send a thousand Rumanian soldiers to Shanghai as part of a League expeditionary force to police a neutralized zone between the Japanese and the Chinese.

Titulescu said he was trying to make sure that the resolution to be adopted by the Assembly should refer to Japan's breach not only of the League Covenant but of the Kellogg-Briand Pact also, for Rumania had no protection under the Covenant, which Russia had not signed, but did under the pact, of which Russia was a signatory. I had not thought of the fact that the United States had a similar interest in this respect, and when I saw Beneš later in the day I mentioned it to him. Later at dinner with Hugh Wilson I pointed out that the omission broke the common front between the League and the United States regarding the Stimson doctrine; also, Soviet Russia's participation could perhaps be secured under the pact even if not under the Covenant, something that might be highly useful in the Far East. Wilson thereupon asked me to telephone Beneš, who in his usual energetic way promised to act at once to rectify the omission. When Norman Davis called Beneš later, Beneš told him that he had gone at once to see Drummond, the League Secretary-General, who had promised to try to put back the reference, and in fact when the Assembly met the next morning Sir John Simon got up and proposed that this be done. Beneš scurried around among the delegates getting support, and the suggestion was finally adopted.

The Disarmament Conference adjourned in July without concrete achievement, although having recognized various principles which, optimists hoped, could be embodied later in an international agreement. The debate disclosed the possibility of qualitative rather than quantitative disarmament, that is, the abolishment of certain weapons adapted to breaking down national systems of defense; and there was agreement, too, on the need to reduce and limit the size of standing armies. But no agreement could be reached on how to apply these principles. In September, Germany announced that she would not participate further until her right to equality with other nations in all respects was recognized. Satisfaction was given her on this, and the Conference reconvened on February 2, 1933, the first anniversary of the original meeting. But three days earlier, on January 30, Adolf Hitler had become German Chancellor. This hardened France's requirements for security against what she saw as an increasing threat. What number of guns, airplanes and tanks should each country have, and of what types? How, for example, to rate aircraft —by weight alone or by horsepower, wing area and weight combined? The possibilities of disagreement on technical matters were endless, and behind them lay insoluble political problems. On October 14, 1933, Hitler took Germany out of the League of Nations and out of the Disarmament Conference.

35

Economic Chaos in Eastern Europe

While the diplomats in Geneva were wrangling over the Far East crisis and marking time on disarmament they were discussing on the side a proposal put forward by Premier Tardieu of France to deal with the economic chaos in the Danubian states. Strangulation of trade, starvation prices for agricultural products and government bankruptcy threatened social collapse in Czechoslovakia, Austria, Hungary, Rumania and Jugoslavia. Could they be persuaded to join in necessary action to ward off a common catastrophe? Would the Great Powers step in and help in order to avoid being caught in the results of the catastrophe themselves?

Earlier salvage proposals for the area had come to nothing. But the events following the collapse of the Credit-Anstalt had shown that disaster and panic in Austria could spread like wildfire to the centers of the world's wealth and power. Now in 1932 Tardieu was making another try at inducing reform. Specifically, he asked the Danubian states to cut existing tariffs among themselves by 10 percent, do away with import and export prohibitions and abolish exchange limitations. He suggested that outside states waive most-favored-nation treatment and indicated that France would give her share of an international reconstruction loan. He hoped that the world was sobered enough by the remorseless deepening of the economic crisis for the plan to be accepted. Everywhere stock exchanges had closed, currencies tottered, capital migrated hither and yon seeking a safe refuge, emergency restrictions had been rushed through in many countries in efforts to keep capital at home, trade was slaughtered by embargoes, unemployment increased, commodity prices slumped lower and lower.

Germany and Italy indicated at once, however, that they would have nothing to do with such a scheme. They had large trade interests in Danubia and would not waive most-favored-nation treatment. In essence, too, Germany deeply opposed the plan because it would have ended any idea of *Anschluss* or of a revival of the *Drang nach Osten*. Italy feared the restoration of the power that had been Austria-Hungary in some new form, the end of the influence she had built up in Hungary and the wreck of her effort to become arbiter of Balkan affairs. Both dreaded the creation of a bloc under the domination of French diplomacy and finance.

"Pertinax" told me that Beneš had had a hand in developing the Tardieu plan, but when I talked with him he did not claim joint authorship. He emphasized that the project, which might take as much as a year or two to realize, was not for a federation or union, since that would put many new enterprises in the Danubian states out of business; nor was any Great Power to participate, especially neither Germany, who would look for benefits in Austria, nor Italy, who would support Hungary. The Little Entente would remain a political and military force, unaffected by the new arrangement. When he was twenty-four, he said, he had written a book called *Save Austria-Hungary*. Ten years later, in Paris, he had written one called *Destroy Austria-Hungary*. Now his enemies would allege that he was writing one to be called *Recreate Austria-Hungary*. But necessity was forcing the states of the area to collaborate instead of strangling each other.

In the capitals that I visited after Geneva I found mixed feelings about Tardieu's proposal—indifference (surprisingly) in Belgrade, hidden opposition in Budapest, open hostility in Berlin, a division of opinion in Paris and London. One of Tardieu's chief concerns, of course, was what the American attitude would be. When he asked Norman Davis he was told that the United States could approve of the idea of a Danubian customs union provided the common tariff wall applied to all the outside world. Davis rejected Germany's and Italy's claim to have a privileged position because they took Danubia's agricultural surplus; they did this not as a favor but because they needed it.

II

In Vienna, Redlich took me out for lunch at his house in Döbling. The garden was still winter-bound, but the cozy library and his hospitality

were warm as always. He had been ill the previous summer and had resigned as Finance Minister. The experience of the past year had made
him more than ever opposed to *Anschluss*. The Prussian spirit was far
from dead, he said. Germany was laying far-sighted plans, the motif of
which was to keep Europe in turmoil just short of a collapse by Germany
herself. She would never permit such a settling-down in the Danube states
as would follow adoption of the Tardieu plan. "History teaches very
little," he said, "even to those who live through it." During the afternoon
Count Lanzkuronski came in, a towering old gentleman of eighty-three
who had been the custodian of the Emperor's art and was himself a great
collector. He was a Pole, a figure out of the past, and exceedingly agreeable. He repeated an interesting remark that he said the Archduke Franz
Ferdinand had once made to him: "Two people ruined the Hapsburg
Empire—the liberal Emperor Josef and Metternich."

The next day Nick Roosevelt, our Minister to Hungary, drove me over
to stay with him in Budapest. He had been in Vienna for a couple of days
of holiday to hear some music. He said that the world depression was
carrying Hungary steadily down a descending spiral. What was bound in
any event to be hard times was worsened by the trade restrictions with all
the surrounding states. Unsold goods piled up, cash was scarce, taxes
were hard to collect. The Great Powers differed as to remedies; the concern of the French and British on one side was financial, the interest of
Germany and Italy on the other was to get the largest possible share of
trade. Perhaps Tardieu's scheme would help; at any rate it was worth a
try, but the opposing forces were powerful. I got little reflection of these
difficulties when I called on Count Paul Teleki, who, although one of the
Hungarian counts able occasionally to assimilate new ideas, had a closed
mind on the plan for a Danubian agreement. If it should come to pass,
he said, it would not survive, for in the better times which would follow
people would shift their interest back from their stomachs to their heads
and revived nationalism would destroy the economic cooperation. Apart
from this rather premature reason for condemning the Tardieu plan, he
thought that Central Europe should be used as an interpreter between
East and West and not fitted into one political or economic mold.

Dr. Desiré Kiss (what a name to carry around!), an agile and highly
intelligent little man who was foreign editor of the *Pester Lloyd,* took a
more favorable view. He repeated a remark that Clemenceau once made:
"Jaurès is a great orator; but his verbs are all in the future." As with
Jaurès, Tardieu's hopeful words were all in the future. Yet something
had to be tried. A chief obstacle, Kiss said, was the psychological factor,

almost incomprehensible to an outsider. Sovereignty could hardly be said to exist for the small states of the region, so helpless were they on the world currents carrying them this way or that, yet they held to it as an absolute fetish. Their frustration was aggravated unbearably by the "elbow-room problem," especially acute in Hungary with ninety-three inhabitants per square kilometer. Tardieu's aim was certainly right. How could there be neighborliness in such a stifling atmosphere?

After a talk in his office he took me in to see his chief editor, Dr. Veszi, thirty years in parliament before the war, a hardened old sinner who was always on the side of the government of the day, a strong nationalist. "We will continue to eat our wheat and potatoes," he said. "Let Beneš feed his starving Czechs on pottery and paper." Yet his dislike of doing anything that might help the Czechs did not prevent him from pretending that he favored the Tardieu plan. He said he was writing an editorial for the next day urging that Poland be asked to join the group. I noted that this would add to the farm surplus that must find a market, but he brushed this aside. On the way out, Kiss whispered to me that the proposal was inspired by the Hungarian Foreign Office, because it would arouse Germany and make the plan fail. Foreign Office officials, he said, despised considerations of economics and finance, which were for "professors."

In Belgrade, John Dyneley Prince, our Minister, said that the Jugoslav economic situation was so bad that the government was considering centralizing exports and instituting export and import licenses, yet there was little support for the cooperative salvage operation proposed by Tardieu. And when I had dinner with former Foreign Minister Ninchich he talked little about economics and mainly about domestic politics. He said the chiefs of the old parties were meeting privately and making plans to reconstitute a parliament that would be "the real thing." The obstacle was that the Croats still held aloof.

At lunch at Dedinje the next day, King Alexander seemed cheerful, much engrossed with a secret negotiation he was having with Mussolini through a young Italian intermediary, the son of a former keeper of the archives in Venice whom he had known twenty-five years before when he was studying under Count Voinovich. The objective was a treaty guaranteeing the independence and integrity of Albania. Mussolini had consented to such a treaty, but on condition Jugoslavia recognize that Italy had special interests there. This Alexander had refused, and he had further suggested that in order for the treaty not to seem too much like an alliance some third party be added, perhaps France, or, if Mussolini preferred, England. This, in turn, Mussolini had refused, and Alexander expected the young Italian back in three days with a counteroffer. The King said I was the fourth person to know of the project, the other three being the King himself, Mussolini and the young Italian.

The King also told me of visiting Paris the preceding December, when for the first time he had met Premier Laval. Laval informed him he was preparing to go to Rome to come to an agreement with Mussolini. He considered Laval's assumption that this could be achieved on satisfactory terms very naïve, and found that Berthelot, the Secretary-General at the Quai d'Orsay, agreed. Berthelot said he had been begging Laval not to go to Rome without a clear understanding of what would be talked about. A few days later the Italian Ambassador came to Berthelot "with good news for our two countries," namely, that Mussolini would indeed be glad to welcome Laval in Rome provided it was understood that they would talk about Tunisia, where the right of Italian settlers to maintain their Italian nationality was being pressed, much to the annoyance of France, and provided that France accepted Italian naval parity. This, to King Alexander's satisfaction, torpedoed the project.

There had been little change in the domestic situation, King Alexander felt, since my last visit. He was aware of the discussions among leaders of the old parties for a return to open political activity and said he was quite prepared to work with them at any time on only one condition, that the unity of the state be preserved. He would accept any arrangement that did not bring back the situation of three years ago. The difficulty was that the Croats expected war in Europe and thought that their chance to secure their most extravagant demands for autonomy would come then.

Our talk was broken by lunch, which I had with the King and Queen alone, very good but too quickly served. The King took little interest in food and swallowed what was put before him without much noticing it. In England, I thought, where the food is indifferent, you don't dare lay down your fork for an instant for fear your plate will be whisked away. Why should the same thing happen in Belgrade, where admiration for everything French ought to dictate that you have enough time to enjoy a good meal?

I discovered that the project which I had been pressing for the publication of the prewar Serbian documents was now in the hands of a Professor Vladimir Chorovich. In a talk with him I found that the Foreign Office had given him access to its files and that he was making a systematic study of the records, going back to 1903. He had also been working in the archives in Vienna and Sarajevo. He said he would have a book of his own ready in a few months and that it would be followed by publication of the documents.[1] I made a strong point that they should appear in French as well as in Serbian, and later that day at tea with Prince Paul I urged that he make sure this was done. It was a nursery tea, with little Alexander and Micky and two boys of one of the secretaries at the American Legation.

III

The run-off in the German Presidential election was to take place a couple of weeks after my arrival in Berlin, but there was little talk about it; everyone assumed Hindenburg would be reelected. Chancellor Brüning had taken advantage of the Easter "truce" to have a short holiday, which meant I would not see him. However, I had a number of talks with officials at the Foreign Ministry and the Reichskanzlei. While I was with Planck, the youngest of Brüning's assistants but said to be the closest to him, a message was brought in reporting Poincaré's death, afterward found untrue. Planck said: "He was the greatest enemy of Germany, but a clean and honest antagonist. I would rather make peace with him than with someone of the left." He spoke disparagingly of the Tardieu plan. So did Dieckhoff at the Foreign Ministry, who said it came "comme la moutarde après le dîner." Both of them indicated that Germany was in a good position to bargain. What the Danubian states needed was not merely money but markets. And who could provide markets except Germany and to some extent Italy? Another Foreign Ministry official remarked that France and Germany should cooperate in the area, France furnishing the money, Germany the experience. The contributions didn't seem to me equivalent.

At our Embassy there was not much concern about Hitler. True, in the first round of the election he had received about eleven million to Hindenburg's eighteen million votes; but there was confidence that "Brüning would deal with him," backed by the army.

Scheffer had told me that the best agricultural expert in Germany was Dr. Karl Brandt, and I therefore paid him a call in the Landswirtschaftliche Hochschule. It was the beginning of a long friendship, in the course of which Brandt wrote several times for *Foreign Affairs*. Following Hit-

1. Vladimir Dedijer has informed me that Chorovich, who in 1935 published a volume of Serbian diplomatic documents covering 1902 to May, 1903, published in 1936 a book of his own, *Odnosi izmedju Srbije i Austro-Ugarske u XX veku*, dealing among other matters with the Sarajevo crime, but that it was banned and never circulated. He said it in general confirmed the thesis given in Chapter 25.

ler's expulsion of Jews from public life Brandt emigrated to America and became a professor at the New School in New York. This was not because he was himself Jewish—tall and large-boned, he came from the Frisian coast—but because he refused to dismiss assistants who were. Brandt felt that the chief German opposition to the Tardieu proposal came from the big landowners, especially in East Prussia, who were for self-sufficiency and who had a great hold over Hindenburg, himself an East Prussian. German exports were decreasing, but a reaction would set in only when protection began to produce real distress, and then it would be too late in the German political calendar for cooperative plans. He said German intellectuals were becoming extremists; in advanced groups like the "Tat-Kreis," which included some of the best scientists, professors and lawyers, the only lively debate was over the merits of Fascism and Communism.

At the station in Brussels I was met by Count Sforza, who said Emile Vandervelde had asked us to lunch with him and some friends in a little restaurant for a "Good Friday meal." Chez Georges was warmed by a stove at one side and crammed with good, plain people intent on getting a fish lunch that was good but not plain. Apparently Good Friday lunches were a Brussels institution. We had mushrooms on toast, trout, lobster à l'Américaine and crêpes. When I remarked how delicious it all was, Vandervelde said, "L'amour, ça passe, mais la gourmandise, ça reste."

Vandervelde, for some time Minister for Foreign Affairs, President of the Second International and a famous orator, was now rather deaf but charming and a real character without any pretensions in that direction. He was sticking loyally to his socialism but one felt it lacked drive in a world full of Fascists and Communists. He tried to speak well of Briand, who had died a few weeks earlier, but admitted that he was too amiable and too lazy to be as effective as he should have been. He thought Tardieu the ablest man in French politics. "Since he is really intelligent, and since he isn't hampered by scruples, he is capable of anything, even good actions." The Germans, he said, were unrepentant, at any rate unchanged in their mentality; they kept ruffling the Belgians unnecessarily. A propos of what Vandervelde called German insensitivity, Sforza told of a meeting between Wilhelm II and Victor Emmanuel just before the war. The Kaiser informed the King that he had found a fine old engraving as a present for him, and had it brought in. It depicted a fourteenth-century Brandenburger dismounting, while a Savoy chevalier held the stirrup.

At dinner Sforza told of his first "big job" in diplomacy. He had been secretary of the Italian Embassy in Constantinople and for the moment chargé d'affaires. The Sultan sent for him, and as it was a time when matters in Africa were very tense he thought something important was afoot and that he could make his name in handling it well. When he was ushered in, the Sultan spoke to him through an interpreter. "Would he do the Sultan a favor?" This was promising. He had a vision of being called on to execute a mission of great delicacy. The Sultan's request was deflating: "The chief soprano at the court opera, an Italian, was threatening to break her contract. Would he use his influence to pacify her?"

Sforza saw few signs of change in Italy, except possibly a lessening of élan among the Fascist hierarchy, mainly because Mussolini had become more sober. "The less like Mussolini he is, the less he mesmerizes them." He claimed that the bulk of the population were anti-Fascist or non-Fascist, but passive, while intellectuals like Croce were waiting for some moment of confusion in Europe when they might make a positive move. He made no claim beyond that, and even that I felt he did not make with much confidence.

In Paris, Salvemini agreed that Mussolini was somewhat subdued, because, he said, the economic situation was desperate; but that did not mean that the political situation was desperate. Revolution was a technical impossibility. As usual, Salvemini was occupying a very small room, this time four flights up, surrounded by books and papers, furiously at work. He made a clear place among the papers spread out on the bed so that we could sit side by side. His book *Mussolini Diplomate* was just out; he said he had relied on my article on Albania of three years before to document that part of the story. What was most difficult about the Italian economic situation, he said, was that Italy must import from ten to twenty thousand tons of wheat each year to take care of the four months before a new harvest; for this she needed a couple of billion francs, and as they were to be paid abroad they had to be real francs. If France would loan Mussolini that sum, and find a means to save his face in doing it, she could have her way with him. Britain's influence in Rome, which was strong, tended the other way; she encouraged Italy, and Germany as well, to resist France.

"The British Foreign Office," said Salvemini, "wants peace in Europe but not the pacification of Europe. No crisis must lead to war or chaos, but when the moment for a real compromise appears the Foreign Office does not consider it in the British interest for thoroughgoing reconciliation to take place. The basis for the entente between MacDonald and Mussolini is that neither likes France, and both find material support for that dislike in German hostility to France."

After lunch with Louis and Mary Bromfield (no mention of Hemingway), I went to tea with Jan Ciechanowski, former Polish Minister in Washington, and there found Lord Tyrrell, the British Ambassador to France. He entirely repudiated the Salvemini theory of British policy, though he admitted that the idea that the Foreign Office played a double game was very common in Paris. He thought France could give satisfaction to Italy at any moment if it was done in a way (as Salvemini had also said) to save Mussolini's face; and he recalled a characterization made by Lord Salisbury in the nineties, "The Italians, a nation of sturdy beggars."

Tyrrell told of a talk he had had with Mussolini in Rome two or three years before, when Il Duce asked him what they thought of him in England. Tyrrell said: "They admire what you have done to make Italians orderly and washed and ready to pay taxes, but they think that in foreign policy you talk too much like the Kaiser."

To which Mussolini had replied: "Oh, it is all for home consumption. If I were a French leader I couldn't say those things, because when the French get excited they act. But Italian excitement is always very restrained."

In talking about Italy's relations with Germany, I repeated an idea of Kühlmann's that Italy was useful to Germany "to hold the line from the Balearic Islands to Sicily." Tyrrell said he was afraid the Germans still thought in those geopolitical terms. Germany was in the same situation as regards Italy, he said, as a woman who is being courted by a suitor who can't support her. The door is left open, but no answer is given. Italy had made overture after overture to Germany but so far had not convinced her that the alliance would be a good one.

"The danger," he said, "is that France will leave Italy unsatisfied for so long that the moment will come when Germany thinks Italy worth accepting as a partner, and then we shall have trouble in Europe."

Osusky, who had been Czechoslovak Minister in Paris for ten years (in fact I had met him there in 1922), did not describe Italy's policy very differently from Tyrrell. It was a negative policy—she would not sell her friendship in return for collaboration but she would buy collaboration by promising to cease hostility. The great obstacle to the Tardieu plan was Germany's demand for preferences. Would she be swayed more by political or by economic advantage? Her decision would determine much about the future of Europe. There was no economic reason for her to oppose the expansion of the Danubian market on an impartial basis, indeed there would be great commercial advantages in it for her. But she must decide whether she wanted those advantages or would attempt to fix her hold on the Danube Valley. In that case hostility with France was inevitable. Stresemann had been at fault in not exploiting the very considerable victories he had won over France but in minimizing them in order to get more. His actions had been good for Germany and for Europe, but he had failed as a psychologist and educator; he had not convinced the German people that cooperation with France was productive. Now the German masses were disillusioned, and the tendency of the government, though still not yet quite decided, was to exploit the general European disorder in preparation for getting "revenge." If that was to be the final decision it meant tragedy for everyone.

At the Bank of France I was told by Lacour-Gayet, as I had been by so many others, that any scheme to reconstruct the bankrupt states of Eastern Europe depended on finding them markets. Since Germany, their natural market, declined to play her part the outlook was black. As always in history, the creditors must now take their losses, a moral but disagreeable procedure, with the only advantage that it distributed money around and would keep any one nation from feeling too cocky. Some would come through the wringer better than others. Britain and France were close-knit nations, capable of taking punishment and surviving by their own efforts.

All was not dismal economics and finance. For the weekend I went to friends at Senlis, where everybody picked daffodils in the woods. One evening I dined with the Gérauds, another with Professor Louis Eisenmann and his family, another with Professor André Siegfried (the best society in Paris is among the professors, whom Embassy people seldom bother with), and one evening I went with friends Chez les Clochards to hear Lucienne Boyer, brimming with pathos and sentiment.

I V

I crossed the Channel with the French delegation bound for London to discuss the Danubian project. MacDonald, Simon and others were on the platform to meet Tardieu and Finance Minister Flandin. MacDonald's greeting seemed to me stiff and perfunctory, and I wondered whether maybe he was piqued at Simon's success at Geneva in reconciling British policy with Tardieu's. At any rate, the four-power consultations in the following two days did nothing to advance the project. The opposition of the German and Italian delegates was decisive. Simon, I was told, characterized it to their faces as shortsightedly selfish.

One morning I called on Lord Cecil at his house in Eaton Place. He confessed that at the start of the occupation of Manchuria he had been quite taken in by protestations of the Japanese that it was only to be partial and temporary and that they themselves considered it unpleasant and dangerous. The League (in which he believed ardently) should have taken a strong stand against the operation as soon as its real nature became plain; after that it was too late. He was imprecise as to what that strong stand should have been. He considered the Stimson doctrine of nonrecognition effective only temporarily, if at all, and saw dangers in it of the sort pointed out by President Lowell of Harvard in the April issue of *Foreign Affairs,* which he had just read. He said he agreed with Lowell in objecting to an interpretation of the Kellogg-Briand Pact which laid no obligation on the signatories to prevent war yet gave them the right to disregard its results.

Speaking of the situation in Ireland, where de Valera had just been elected President on a program of abolishing the oath to the King, Cecil said: "We don't care tuppence about Ireland now, except that if we gave way there, as we are tempted to do, it would have a bad effect in India." I remarked that the Danes would probably be glad to take the oath which de Valera refused if they could get the same preferential treatment as the Irish did for their dairy products. Cecil thought I was speaking seriously and said gravely that Denmark's strategic position was too precarious for England to be interested.

The rest of my day was spent with England's two leading economists, Sir Walter Layton, editor of *The Economist,* and Sir Arthur Salter. They were divided by Layton's pessimism and Salter's innate optimism. Layton thought the resistance and rigidities of the strongly developed cartels and trusts and the interference of governments in normal processes of readjustment had postponed the day until a great crash became inevitable. "No more reparations can be expected from Germany, or perhaps one fifth of what is due. Is it worth offering the United States one-fifth of the war debts? Wouldn't it be flung back at us like a tuppence tip to a taxi driver?" He thought it would be better to say frankly that Europe wouldn't pay at all, without trying to save faces that could not be saved. On the contrary, Salter, with whom I had tea, thought the Tardieu plan was feasible and a step in the right direction. His book *Recovery* was just out, and when I asked him a question he would reach out and read me a paragraph.

In the evening I went with Henry Clay, of the Bank of England, to an interesting dinner of the Political Economy Club, a long-established institution. A financial editor of the *Times* drew a gloomy picture of the budget outlook. One speaker suggested selling the Post Office to a concern that would put in a businessman as manager, "someone like the manager of the Midland Railway." F. W. Hirst remarked that the stockholders of that railway ought not to be deprived of the services of a manager who in three years had reduced the value of their shares from 100 to 16.

On every hand Londoners were being urged to "Buy British." In Knightsbridge a notice in a grocer's window read: "Only strictly English laid eggs." And as I left Chatham House to go to the Reform Club to lunch with Ramsay Muir I saw a sign at a restaurant off St. James's Square: "Oysters only from British beds."

Muir, who held the difficult position of chairman of the Liberal party, was furious with Jowett, the Attorney-General, who to his mind had betrayed the Liberal party to secure office, and of whom, he said, Churchill had remarked: "He has disgraced the Noble Order to which I belong, the Order of Rats." The Reform Club had fine old portraits of Bright, Cobden, Lord John Russell and such, also, most welcome, an open fire in the library; I hadn't been warm since getting to London.

As we walked back across the Green Park, Muir pointed to the back of Lord Haldane's house and said that on one occasion when he had been in the library there Haldane had remarked that he was sitting in the chair in which the Kaiser had once sat. Haldane, a former Secretary for War and Lord Chancellor, was a student of German philosophy and criticized by some for being pro-German. Another time, said Muir, when he had spent the night in the house, Haldane had told him his bed was the one in which Lord Grey (then Sir Edward Grey) had been sleeping when they came to wake him and tell him of the invasion of Belgium; and with Haldane sitting on the edge of the bed Grey had decided that mobilization should be ordered but that the rest of the cabinet should not be told yet "so as not to prejudice their decision about war or peace." An extraordinary tale.

One day I took the tube out to Wimbledon to lunch with Seton-Watson. We spent most of the morning in a good-natured set-to over King Alexander's character and the aims of his dictatorship. Seton-Watson began by asking if I was very angry with him over his articles criticizing the Serbs in general and the King in particular. I said not at all, I was only sorry that in addition to lambasting the Serbs, he hadn't used his great prestige with the Croats to tell them some disagreeable truths, particularly urging them to put forward a program of national union which people like himself wouldn't have to repudiate. He sighed and got out a letter just received from Maček, Radić's successor as head of the Croat Peasant party, suggesting a harebrained scheme that plebiscites be held in seven "historical districts" of the country to elect delegates to local parliaments, which in turn would choose delegates to meet and determine a new basis for the state. Seton-Watson agreed the idea was childish and also admitted that the efforts of opposition Serb leaders to outline a program was disappointing.

When I pressed him as to what he had meant when he wrote in one of his articles that he had "lost confidence" in the King, Seton-Watson replied that he thought the King liked personal power and was seeking to prolong it. I said we both recognized how disastrous the state of affairs had been when the King had taken control. What now should he do to end the dictatorship? I said I was prepared to disagree amicably whether the King had ability and good judgment, but had to disagree fundamentally on whether he had acted and was still acting in good faith. "Well," said Seton-Watson after much argument to and fro, "we are really in agreement as regards the question of state unity and as regards the role of the Croats, and I think we have come to agreement about the King's real aims." With that we went down to lunch, I rather pleased with having gotten so far with a stubborn Scotsman who knew twice as much about the Balkans as I ever would.

Stuyve Chanler took me to lunch another day at the Rothschild bank with Anthony Rothschild, who sat at the head of the table and helped his guests in patriarchal style. The food was the best I had ever had in England, with Mosel to match; I wondered what Rothschild thought when he came to New York and lunched at the office of one of his banker friends. He asked what I predicted was going to happen in Central Europe and looked glum when, following Lacour-Gayet's lead, I told him that as usual in history, the creditors would lose. After lunch he showed me the original accounts kept by his grandfather as banker for the British Government in the hundred days before Waterloo. In the evening I saw Noël Coward's *Cavalcade,* a snapshot history of England since the turn of the century, deftly steering between fun and feeling with the balance just rightly weighted toward the latter.

I had written Lord Grey, who lived in the north, asking whether if he happened to come to London I might not call on him. He replied that he would be in London on April 9 and would drop in that morning at my hotel. I found him just the sort of person you would expect from this lack of side, rarer in other countries, I think, than in England.

In the Manchurian affair Grey's sympathies were with Japan. He reminded me that his interest in the Far East went back to the Sino-Japanese War of 1895, at which time he had been Undersecretary for Foreign Affairs. The Powers had intervened to force Japan to give up a large part of her gains, some of which, notably Port Arthur, were then appropriated by Russia, "most immorally and in a way to awaken contempt in Japanese minds." He thought that Japan had lived in fear of suffocation and had often been badly treated, and he was not surprised that she had been stung into action by Chinese pinpricks. He did not condone the seizure of Shanghai but accepted the view that it was an act of military hotheadedness and not a deliberate play by the civil government.

There had been lively discussion of the question whether the Liberal party should have participated in the National Coalition government under Ramsay MacDonald. Lord Grey approved of it and thought the government would last out its full term (actually it continued for three and a half years, despite the withdrawal of the free-trade Liberal members of the cabinet following the Ottawa Imperial Economic Conference). He said that personally he opposed protection; however, that was not the primary issue, but retrenchment and national union. He did not consider that Britain had become protectionist but merely a low-duty country pending the world's recovery from its orgy of economic nationalism.

"Without trade, gold is nothing," said Grey. "Gold is only a medium of exchange. You can't eat it or keep warm with it. You in America will sometime discover that gold is not useful unless it is acquired by selling something and used to buy something."

The feebleness of his eyesight was evident. He found it a great trial, he said, to sit still while someone read the news aloud to him, and snippets of the articles and books he wanted to know about. He went off with his bag to attend a meeting at the British Museum and then take a train north.

At lunch at Rutland Gate, Sir Austen Chamberlain talked interestingly about Stresemann and Briand, his colleagues at Locarno. His highest praise he reserved for Stresemann, despite the fact that he thought the Germans could never be a great nation "because of their psychological defects" and because, quoting a phrase that he said was Lord Salisbury's, "They always ask too much." Stresemann, he said, had had no great faith in the Locarno idea when it was first put to him, but he felt in a secure enough position not to be afraid to experiment with it. Then it grew on him, and he made it his own "and cared more about it than anyone else did." Herriot at first had seen little of advantage for France in the plan. "You cannot picture more of a contrast," Chamberlain said, "than between the Herriot I went into a room with after dinner in our Embassy in Paris and the crestfallen man I came out with after telling him that my government would have nothing to do with a treaty of alliance but would be willing to join in a general treaty of guarantee along the lines acceptable to Stresemann."

Chamberlain gave a more pleasant impression personally than I remembered from an earlier meeting or from a lunch at Geneva where he had managed to speak about Locarno with hardly a mention of Briand or Stresemann. He talked nostalgically of the Berlin and Paris he had known forty years before, comparing the French stage of Bernhardt and Coquelin with that of the present, much to the latter's disadvantage. However, he got out and showed me with relish a photograph which the Guitrys had given him recently when he went across to Paris for Briand's funeral.

I observed him with interest, a figure from another era (he had made his maiden speech in the House of Commons in April, 1893, the month and the year in which I was born). His eye behind his monocle was glassy and his manner rather too elaborate; certainly he hadn't a light touch. Sir Arthur Salter's memoirs describe him rather mercilessly as "formal, rigid, precise, correct in thought, in manner, in costume." But essentially he was a friendly human being, more so, at any rate, than I had remembered.

36

Roosevelt Nominated at Chicago

There was little to give cheer in a visit I made to Washington soon after getting back to America. Everyone agreed that Europe was in a mess and that France was responsible. Secretary of the Treasury Ogden Mills, in a bellicose and rah-rah mood, thumped his desk as he related Europe's stupidities, failures and iniquities and emphasized that the United States had best leave Europe out of its calculations for the next generation or so.

"The French," he said, "are the most stupid and obstructionist people in the world. They were responsible for the failure of the Hoover moratorium last year. It was their last chance to get American cooperation. We will never again take the initiative to help save Europe. If anything was needed after that experience to give a measure of the puny men who are running Europe it was supplied the other day in London when they couldn't agree on measures to save the miserable little Danube states which had been established by the insane people at the Paris Peace Conference and allowed to set up insane tariff barriers."

I said mildly that perhaps the war might be blamed more than the Versailles Treaty for nationalism in Europe, and that it was hard for Americans to talk much about tariffs when we, although off by ourselves and menaced by nobody, had shown the way in establishing prohibitive rates. He glared at me and said American tariffs were "traditional" (hence presumably moral), that he thanked God for them and that Europe was done for and deserved to be. Another glare answered my query whether it might not be advisable for all Europe's obligations to be pooled in a common effort to get rid once for all of the postwar financial burden under which she was still staggering.

To my amazement, Mills apparently had not thought about the financial problems of unemployment relief which would have to be faced the following winter and which would certainly have to be a federal responsibility. I remarked that to have begun public planning on means for financing the operation might have been a way to head off the soldiers' bonus in Congress. The idea seemed to strike him as novel, just as it had Eugene Meyer, governor of the Federal Reserve Bank, when I had brought it up earlier at lunch. Meyer was optimistic that the crisis had about run its course. Enough "dead wood" had been brought down in the financial storm for it to be time to halt the deflationary process. He made no attempt to extenuate the faults and sins of big business, but I was not sure he realized that probably full payment for them was still to be made.

The next day I went over to the Capitol to meet Senator Borah of Idaho, the redoubtable chairman of the Senate Committee on Foreign Relations. I had never so much as laid eyes on him, and from the newspapers expected to find him opinionated, emphatic and abrupt. Cartoonists usually depicted him as a bad boy, overturning something or banging into somebody. On the contrary, he received me very quietly and talked frankly and pleasantly. He at once brought up a favorite subject of his, the war debts, which from the earliest days in 1921 he had adamantly opposed reducing. He told me he was now preparing to announce that the whole complex of debts and reparations ought to be canceled in the interest of world recovery and world confidence. This was most surprising, as only two weeks earlier, on April 19, he had made a major speech in the Senate opposing cancellation of the debts as being a "mere bagatelle" in the question of adjusting Europe's economy, something that was Europe's responsibility and hers alone. He had held the Allies responsible for not revising the Versailles Treaty, settling reparations, reducing armaments and freeing channels of commerce, and had minimized the usefulness of talk about aiding Europe by canceling war debts until those things were done.

Everyone knew, said Borah, that the United States was not going to get any more money on the debts, or at any rate very little, but nobody had the courage to say so. He gave the strong impression that what Congress would really like most would be for Europe to repudiate the debts completely, for this would relieve it of having to make any decisions and still provide a field day for demagogic oratory. One of the chief troubles of the world, he said, was that nobody would speak out, nobody would assume the risks of leadership; and nowhere were initiative and ingenuity more lacking than in Washington. President Hoover knew as well as anyone else that the war debts were dead, but was afflicted by the same disease: "Republics make cowards of us all."

It was easy to draw the Senator out on another of his favorite topics, the iniquity of the postwar frontiers in Europe. When I suggested that the new states were not the product of the peace treaties so much as of historical processes which had simply culminated in the war he listened with interest but with some impatience. He referred to the Versailles Treaty several times as "Clemenceau's treaty." The name Clemenceau obsessed him. But he admitted that a general revision of the treaties by another conference was impossible and that Germany had obtained a great deal out of the piecemeal revision procured by Stresemann.

Forgotten now are the prestige and power of this difficult, blindered and transparently honest Senatorial figure, "The Great Opposer." The title, first earned in the debate over the League of Nations, in which he played a role second only to that of Senator Lodge, held good through thirty years of service. He seemed to me to display a greater affection for general principles than for facts; but maybe this impression was fixed in my mind before I ever saw him.

I remained mystified by his statement that he favored cancellation of the whole complex of debts and reparations. And, in fact, when the chance came to take a step toward that end, he did not find it a policy which he was able to support, or perhaps he did not have enough imagination to gauge the opportunity correctly. In June and July of that year, Germany's creditors met at Lausanne and agreed to transform her reparations debt into 5 percent bonds to be deposited with the Bank for International Settlements, to be issued whenever they became marketable. A qualification to the agreement was that the United States in turn agree to a settlement of war debts. The proviso proved decisive, for Congress by resolution formally rejected any policy which "in any manner" canceled or reduced the indebtedness of a foreign power. This action, in which Borah concurred, meant a return to the Young Plan. In fact, Germany made no further payments and Hitler's government repudiated it entirely. Perhaps if Borah's stubbornness had allowed him to help work out a settlement he might have played a useful role at that juncture.

At lunch at the German Embassy I found that Ambassador von Prittwitz (whose moderation was before long to lose him his place in

the German diplomatic service) agreed that Central Europe was threatened by chaos, the climax likely to come in the autumn unless the Lausanne conference could reach—once again—a "final" solution on reparations, and this time make it stick. A section of German officialdom, he
admitted, favored a *Katastrophen Politik*. That policy—aiming at a
showdown regardless of consequences—was given new vigor by the decision of Congress not to make any accommodation on the war debts.

II

The country devoted the first part of the summer of 1932 to preparations for the party conventions. Republican plans attracted little notice;
Hoover's renomination was taken as a matter of course. But the Democrats were in a ferment, with strenuous competition for a nomination
which this year was believed to carry a better-than-good chance of victory. Through Colonel House I secured tickets to the Democratic Convention for my wife and myself and on June 25 we took the Twentieth
Century to Chicago. A few days earlier I had been at Arthur Sulzberger's
for a dinner for Walter Duranty. Duranty said he couldn't understand
the excitement; the country was broke, the world was broke, and whoever was elected President couldn't do much about it.

The Democrats gathering in Chicago showed none of that pessimism.
Al Smith and Franklin D. Roosevelt, the leading candidates, held out
promises of successful change on almost every topic. A third candidate
was Governor Ritchie of Maryland, and there were several others formally
in the running but actually aiming at the nomination for the Vice-
Presidency, including the House Speaker, John Nance Garner, of Texas,
and Governor Harry F. Byrd, of Virginia. I personally favored Newton
Baker, but unlike the others he had not announced his candidacy, did
not have a headquarters and was represented mainly by his former
secretary, Ralph Hayes, who had two rooms remote from "Candidates'
Row" and affirmed that he was not in direct touch with Baker. An immediate topic of interest was Roosevelt's proposal to abolish the century-
old two-thirds rule in order to profit from already having a majority of
the delegates rounded up. I ran into John W. Davis, who called this
proposal "the most damned fool thing a politician ever did"; and in
effect a tide of hostility rolled up and overwhelmed it.

After breakfast the first morning with Lippmann, we went to see the
sights of the Congress Hotel, where the dark corridors, the poster-
hung assembly room and the candidates' headquarters were jammed
with pushing and perspiring crowds. Everybody was buttonholing some-

body or being buttonholed. At Ritchie's headquarters one of those in charge was my friend Dick Cleveland, who had led a famous revolt against the club system at Princeton just after my time there; he professed the confidence in Ritchie's nomination which seizes all candidates and their troops. Roosevelt's rooms were boiling with activity but no more so than those where Al Smith, his coat off figuratively and actually, was rallying all those who opposed the plan to abolish the two-thirds rule. He was very confident and very aggressive. His chief lieutenant, Belle Moskowitz, who was holding the door, radiated confidence from her ample person.

We had a talk, too, with Ralph Hayes, who said he had no authorization to act from Baker but was working for him as hard as though he did. He said there were many demands that Baker come to Chicago, but this was unrealistic; he was not an avowed candidate and for him to inject himself into the convention would be to reverse his role; and as he was not a delegate it was even doubtful whether he could secure the unanimous consent necessary to get the floor. To clinch the argument, Baker had told Hayes that if he yielded to importunities and came to speak at the convention his first words would eliminate himself from the possibility of being a candidate. Yet he remained a strong dark horse.

We had lunch with William Allen White and his wife, refreshingly Kansan in independence and optimism. Afterward we joined up with Bernie Baruch's party, which included Clare Boothe (an editor of *Vanity Fair,* not yet Mrs. Luce) , but rather quickly decided to retreat to the Art Institute on the lake front for a look at the French impressionists. Revived by cold baths, we had dinner at the Blackstone with Mrs. Bordie Harriman and Mark Sullivan. Smith came in with his wife and a party. Mrs. Smith had been libeled outrageously by Smith's opponents. She was a good-looking woman in a nice foulard dress, plump but not fat, with trim ankles and an agreeable voice. She would have been a more acceptable President's wife than many others who have presided at the White House. After dinner, Smith came over and spoke to those at our table, calling my wife and me by name, which I thought pretty good even for an experienced politician twelve hours after meeting us for the first time. Then came another tour of the headquarters with Mrs. Harriman, who barged in everywhere with gusto.

By the time the stage was set for the nominating speeches it already looked like Roosevelt. Smith was determined, if he could not get the nomination himself, to stop Roosevelt at any cost; and this it was supposed he would do by releasing some of his delegates to Ritchie or Baker. The first ballot, which was conducted to the accompaniment of constant din and incessant calls for polls of state delegations, was not completed until 4:30 A.M. It gave Roosevelt about 100 short of the necessary 769 votes. The second and third ballots showed little change. By now it was 9:15 in the morning and everyone was stunned with fatigue. We stumbled away from the hall and fell into bed. Not so the candidates' managers. Hayes had taken a poll which showed enough Baker strength in almost every delegation to indicate that a break to Baker would occur on the fourth ballot and might be successful. This threat made it imperative for Roosevelt to acquire the Garner strength controlled by Hearst and McAdoo. That evening McAdoo climbed to the rostrum and, against clamorous interruptions from Smith supporters in the balconies, announced California's shift from Garner to Roosevelt. The Roosevelt-Garner ticket was the result. Ralph Hayes let me know later that he received a telegram from Baker which read: "I wish you could be as contented as I am." Since Roosevelt was my second choice I did not feel too badly.

John W. Davis was on the train with us coming back from Chicago. I asked him whether a large part of Smith's animosity toward Roosevelt lay in the story that Roosevelt had remarked to a group of friends: "I never knew what a bad governor Smith had been until I became governor myself." Davis said the story was accurate. It went a long way toward explaining the depth of bitterness which, as revealed at Chicago, had taken hold of Smith's soul.

While the air was filled with campaign speeches, the crescendo coming, of course, in the fall, I was busy preparing the tenth-anniversary number of *Foreign Affairs*. The leading article, "Of Liberty," was by Benedetto Croce. To those who questioned the future of the ideal of freedom, he answered "it has more than a future; it has eternity." In other articles, Beneš wrote of the successes and failures of the League; Wickersham of the political factors in American foreign policy, citing the similarities as well as the diversities in the two party platforms; Harold Laski on the prospects for Communism, which he said depended on the ability of capitalist society "to solve the contradictions between its power to produce and its inability to distribute income in a rational and morally adequate way"; Kühlmann on Franco-German reconciliation as the cornerstone of European peace, stressing the need for French patience in face of the rising tide of German nationalism, the result of former French faults; and Sir Frederick Whyte on postwar developments in the

Far East. There were half a dozen other articles, and the issue ended with a piece of my own, "Versailles: Retrospect."

By exception, the Council arranged a dinner in the middle of the summer for Secretary of State Stimson, who wanted to make public his efforts—and hopes—to develop the Kellogg-Briand Pact into a more effective treaty. John W. Davis presided, giving the dinner a nonpartisan tone. Arnold J. Toynbee, Director of Studies at Chatham House, happened to be in New York and we invited him to represent our sister organization. Stimson's speech was a reply to criticisms that the Pact was not a treaty but merely a group of unilateral statements declaring a pious purpose on the part of each signatory, of which purpose each was to be the sole judge and executor. This interpretation would reduce the Pact to a mere gesture. He denied it was correct, and implied that no further action to implement the Pact was necessary (although planks suggesting just that were contained in the platforms of both political parties). President Hoover and Prime Minister MacDonald, he pointed out, had declared in a joint statement that their countries accepted the Pact as imposing positive obligations to direct national policy in accordance with its pledge. Consultations under the Pact had become a fact when the League Assembly adopted a resolution on the Sino-Japanese controversy stating that it was incumbent on members not to recognize any situation brought about by means contrary to the Covenant or the Pact. (So my effort at Geneva to make sure that the resolution did not omit reference to the Pact had been useful.) Recognition that signatories must consult when faced with the threat of violation would, Stimson was convinced, become "one of the great and permanent policies of our nation."

The Secretary's sincerity and the force with which he spoke were impressive, but his belief in the importance of his nonrecognition policy, and his linkage of it with the Kellogg-Briand Pact, led him to a too optimistic conclusion.

I must skip ahead to wind up the story of the Manchurian affair. Less than a year later, on March 4, 1933, the League finally found that Japan's organization of the puppet state of Manchukuo was opposed by the population there and agreed that League members would not recognize it either *de facto* or *de jure*. Stimson's doctrine was incorporated in the League resolution. A week later his term as Secretary of State ended.

On March 27, Yosuke Matsuoka, who had been Japan's negotiator at Geneva and had led his delegation out of the League, was returning to Japan via New York, and the Council on Foreign Relations invited him to address its members. Stimson was perturbed that an invitation had been issued to the spokesman of a nation declared by the League to be a treaty breaker. Walter Mallory replied to his complaint by pointing out that the Council did not sanction Japanese policy by its invitation, merely gave Council members a chance to hear the other side of the argument. Matsuoka's speech was defensive and defiant. The problem of the Far East, he said, was not Manchuria; it was China. Communism was spreading there. China needed to be reorganized and this could be done "only by force." The Japanese "are by no means a perfect or an innocent people," but they had not had a fair deal either at Geneva or in the United States. Americans should keep their feeling for China in their hearts, if they must, but use their heads to understand Japanese action. He said nothing about the "incident" that had been the excuse for Japan's intervention.

Herbert Feis later described Matsuoka as the "excitable and voluble individual who, fervidly admiring Germany and hating the United States, was to become Foreign Minister in the cabinet of Prince Fumimaro Konoye in 1941 and was more responsible than any other civilian for bringing the United States into the war."[1] At that time probably Stimson felt more convinced than ever that he had been right in objecting to the Council's giving him a forum.

I I I

Even before the election I was confident enough of Roosevelt's coming victory to begin casting about for an authoritative Democrat to write an article on the probable foreign policy of the new administration. Colonel House finally agreed to undertake the task and asked me for a memo-randum of points to be covered.

The general aim of the Roosevelt administration, I suggested, must be to help liquidate the war once and for all. This was essential in order to create economic stability and renew confidence in the ability of govern-ments to govern. Roosevelt would be able to point to the fact that three Republican administrations had failed to do this and thereby had post-poned the restoration of the world economy.

In attempting to liquidate the war the new administration must begin by putting the war debts on a basis where they no longer were a world political question. In negotiations with the debtor countries the tariff

---

1. *1933: Characters in Crisis.* Boston: Little, Brown, 1966.

would be an important factor. In tariff reform the aim should be stability of rates as well as reduction. In disarmament, political solutions must precede technical solutions. A supplement to the Kellogg-Briand Pact providing for consultation in crises might relieve other Powers of fear that if they employed League sanctions against an aggressor the United States might thwart them. The Manchurian crisis had shown that collaboration with the League from outside was not effective. On a favorable occasion we might join the League as an associate member with limited but clear responsibilities based on implementation of the principles of the Kellogg-Briand Pact.

This went about as far as I thought House was likely to commit himself. He did not take up the suggestion of closer association with the League but accepted the idea of consultation under the Briand-Kellogg Pact. He prepared several drafts of his article, and when the election gave the Democrats a resounding victory of 472 to 59 electoral votes it was decided that I should go over the final draft with Roosevelt himself.

My wife and I therefore motored up to Hyde Park for lunch on Sunday, November 20. We arrived about noon, just as the family were getting back from church. Lord and Lady Astor were with them; also staying in the house were Amelia Earhart and her husband and Robert Brand, Lady Astor's brother-in-law.

The house, big, comfortable and rather ugly, belonged to the Governor's mother, Mrs. James Roosevelt. She was "Hudson River," as my family were, and although seventy-eight she bustled around making all the arrangements. One of her grandsons had just turned up for lunch without notice. "I always like having the children," she said, "but don't like having extra vegetables picked just on the chance they may come. They never bother to telephone." Then she added matter-of-factly, "But of course they have had no bringing up." At lunch she was at the head of the table, the Governor at the other end. I sat beside her and during lunch she spoke a great deal about my father and mother and about the many Delano connections they knew in common. Mrs. Eleanor Roosevelt, near the center of the table, disappeared unobtrusively before lunch was over —"off on one of those things she's always busy with, I suppose," old Mrs. Roosevelt remarked in a somewhat sarcastic tone when she noticed it.

Lady Astor sat next to Roosevelt and kept that end of the table in an uproar. Shaking her finger under his nose, she said: "Franklin, don't get the idea you want a second term. If you do you'll be a flop. If you can be a successful President for one term you will be better remembered in history than if you're a bad President for two terms." Roosevelt took it with a laugh but obviously was a little nettled.

After lunch Roosevelt had a talk with Brand, signed letters out of one of several waiting suitcases of papers, and then it was my turn. The coatroom had been turned into a sort of a study for him, very dark and crowded. Piles of papers were on the chairs, on the desk, on the floor. He asked me to wait a minute while he wrote a check for the son who had appeared for lunch. "He's in a jam, and though I can't afford it I really haven't a choice."

The check having been written and handed out the door to a waiting hand, Roosevelt started right in talking about the conference he was to have with Hoover the coming Tuesday about the war debts. It was perhaps the chief subject on which the world was speculating as to the President-elect's likely approach. He said it was a nasty situation which shouldn't have been allowed to develop in its present form; for one thing, it had been a mistake for the British and French governments to send Washington such full notes, not merely asking for deferment of the December 15 installments but going into the whole question of future payments.

Throwing up his hands, he said: "It's fearful. When I am President I want to try and make sure that no note is ever presented by one of the leading Powers to another without a draft having been talked over beforehand." He went on to say that even if he and Hoover were to recommend deferment of this payment, Congress would say, "Who are you to dictate to us? Get the hell out of here."

What was in Roosevelt's mind, evidently, was that the nations would have to make their December 15 payments and then come individually to agreement on how to go on from there. He dictated a sentence to me in this sense for insertion in the article: "It is to be hoped that without default or postponement of present installments the individual debtor governments will in the spring request conferences with the United States Government in order to deal with the whole problem in a systematic way." He admitted that for England to pay her installment would have a bad effect on sterling and would cause much resentment. "France can pay this time without difficulty," he threw in. My impression was that England might get special treatment.

After this preliminary, Roosevelt took up the House manuscript and prepared to read it aloud. But first he said that I must understand that he didn't have time to examine the article closely and that if anyone ever raised any question about it he would disclaim responsibility. I followed his reading with a carbon copy and made additions and deletions at his dictation. In the opening paragraph where a reference was made to the policies adopted by the Republican party out of implacable hatred for Woodrow Wilson, he suggested attributing those to the Republicans' "selfish and uncooperative attitude" rather than to their "isolationist principles." When he came to the tariff, I suggested he might draw an example from our relations with Canada, where resentment caused by our recent tariff policy had been the last straw needed to turn the British Empire into a protectionist unit, a momentous event which would have unfortunate results for us and for which "we have only ourselves to blame." "That's fine," he said.

Taking this as a cue, Roosevelt paused for a little talk about the tariff, saying that it and the farm problem were his chief preoccupations. He agreed that it was fortunate that Hoover had stressed the tariff issue, because this, taken with the statement in the Democratic platform, gave him a stronger position than any recent President to deal with tariff matters. When I asked whether the most-favored-nation clause wasn't "on the skids," he said he was sure it was. But when I asked whether that meant it might be waived in dealing with Canada, he said the trouble was that what Canada would send us was mainly agricultural products, and it was our farmers who at present needed to be protected.

"I have the feeling," he said, "that agricultural products are the real currency in the world and that we shan't get out of our present mess until that currency has been given some new value."

One sentence on the tariff stated that for the Tariff Commission to ascertain the relative costs of production at home and abroad was "an impossible task." He thought the phrase had better come out. "We may have to try something like that and it's just as well not to bring it up now."

Reading along, he came to a paragraph on the war debts, the greater part of which was verbatim from my memorandum to House. He seemed to think that the amounts of principle should not be brought into question, but that it might be possible to negotiate about rates of interest and length of period for repayment. There followed a statement that England was unable to return to the gold standard while the war-debt question remained open, also a reference to the Lausanne agreement on reparations and to the fact that Germany remained in standstill owing to the same cause. He asked that this reference be dropped, evidently because he did not want to have an analogy drawn between what was done at Lausanne and what might be done with the debts.

At the end of each paragraph he would pause and say, "Right." Toward the conclusion, there was a bit to the effect that Americans had acted sometimes in a rather arrogant way because of their prosperity. He didn't object to that statement, he said, but he would like it pointed out also that the situation in America had changed in the last few years and that we were having difficulties of our own. While it was all right to stress that Americans must realize that the nations "were all in one boat," the article should note that pictures of the fabulous and everlasting prosperity of the United States were misleading. Our budget had been nearly three billion dollars out of balance the year before and might be perhaps two billion out in the current year. "The duty to take account of another nation's resources and capacities doesn't fall on the United States alone."

When he finished reading he handed the manuscript back to me and said, "That's a good article and I think it's a good plan to print it." A couple of phrases he particularly liked, he said, one the reference to Harding's "having had a particular liking for the tariff as a political issue," the other to Hoover's argument, typical of the "new era" economics of 1928 and 1929, which implied that debts could be created without consideration of how they were to be paid. As a result, foreign trade and foreign loans had collapsed together. If this was "the American system," the article said, we were well through with it. Roosevelt liked that. "Those two are kind of mean cracks," he said, "but they're both deserved."

The press had been waiting for quite a while out in the cold and it was time to go. We hurried back to town as quickly as possible because we were having dinner with the Nicholas Murray Butlers to meet Dr. Curtius, Stresemann's successor as German Foreign Minister. He was hardly given a chance to open his mouth. After dinner, President Butler told us to draw up our chairs in a circle and ask Curtius some questions. As a witticism, Curtius said he supposed we would like to begin by asking him how he had voted in the American election. That was his first and last remark. Butler was reminded of a story, and he talked for the next forty minutes until it was time to join the ladies and soon after that to go home.

The next evening it happened that Russell Leffingwell and Parker Gilbert, both partners in the Morgan firm, were at the Council House for a dinner for Brand. Before dinner they took me aside, having seen in the paper that I had been at Hyde Park, and asked what I thought Roosevelt's attitude would be on the war debts when he met with President Hoover the next day. Without quoting Roosevelt, I said I supposed that he would leave the question where it belonged, in Hoover's hands, without making any attempt to influence Congress itself, and that this meant, if I understood Hoover's attitude correctly, that the December 15 installments should, could and would be paid. Leffingwell and Gilbert were horrified, Leffingwell especially. He said Roosevelt didn't seem to realize that the future of the incoming Democratic administration rested in Hoover's hands unless he took part of the responsibility into his. Leffingwell considered that the European nations would default on the December 15 payments, and that this would be the signal for economic warfare. England would make an effort to ward off the disastrous collapse of sterling by putting an embargo on such things as cotton.

"The world will go into another tailspin," Leffingwell said, "and if so the United States will go with it. The Roosevelt administration will never recover from the black eye it will receive before it ever gets started. I'd hoped the present crisis could be gotten over by a display of joint strength and leading by Hoover and Roosevelt, giving Roosevelt time in the next few months to learn the complexities of the situation." Gilbert joined in to say that it seemed essential from the Democratic point of view that a world crisis should not occur before Roosevelt took office in March.

They then asked if I had any lines to Roosevelt, and pointed out that the time left for bringing their view of the gravity of the situation to him was short, since he was going to Washington in the morning. At the moment Roosevelt was right next door—"just that wall away," said Leffingwell, tapping it. Wouldn't I communicate with him and suggest that Leffingwell drop by for a talk? I said I could not do that.

Instead, at their request, I called up Colonel House, who listened to the story carefully. He felt that Roosevelt was more open-minded on the debt question than I did and also that the dangers inherent in either a default or a payment were less serious than the two Morgan partners did. I made plain that I had not quoted Roosevelt to them and that I was repeating to him what they had said without associating myself with their point of view on a matter on which I had no competence. I added that although they belonged to the banking firm which was financial agent for England and France, he would agree that they were men of the highest honor; and I reminded him, incidentally, that both of them had voted for Roosevelt. House said he would think the matter over and decide whether to communicate with Roosevelt during the evening if Roosevelt didn't communicate with him.

In the morning when I talked with House again he said that on reflection he had decided that having had general conversations with Roosevelt on the war debts, and Roosevelt having not himself called him up during his day in New York, he had not felt justified in taking the initiative and telephoning him late in the evening.

This attempt by Leffingwell and Gilbert to make contact with the President-elect was a preliminary to a long series of abortive efforts, described by Herbert Feis in his book *1933: Characters in Crisis,* to arrange some collaboration between Roosevelt and President Hoover on how to deal not only with the war debts but also with disarmament and the Far East crisis. As Feis describes it, the discussion on the debts went round and round, "more like a tumbleweed than a vine." Perhaps Roosevelt preferred default to a large reduction which would have to be defended in Congress.

In the event, Britain, Italy and several smaller debtor countries paid their installments, France, Belgium and others deferred. In England, economic nationalism became pronounced, with managed paper currency and control of foreign exchange. In France, the Chamber's refusal to agree to payment led Herriot to resign as Prime Minister. Actually it was only the proximate cause. French fears following Hindenburg's substitution of reactionary von Papen for Brüning as Chancellor and the growing strength and menaces of the Nazis had ended French confidence in the Locarno spirit and in the policy of reconciliation that had been pursued by the Cartel des Gauches.

I was glad I had refused to involve myself directly with Roosevelt in the matter, especially when Roosevelt told me later that he had never thought that Wall Street "gave orders to the Treasury Department under the Republicans," only that the line was always open for advice back and forth. "That line I intend to cut," he said.

37

Wotan Chases Apollo

The year 1933 held great portents for the world, for it brought Hitler to power in Germany. The first event of the year for the Council on Foreign Relations, however, did not look toward a new war but backward to the last one. On January 18 a portrait of General Tasker H. Bliss was unveiled at the Council House, a duplicate by Dana Pond of the one he had painted at the Château of Versailles in March, 1918. Newton Baker, in a speech of presentation, praised Bliss not only for his soldierly qualities but also, in what in others might seem a contradiction in terms, as "the most scholarly person I ever knew."

Baker had arrived with John W. Davis, and a knot of reporters waiting outside Roosevelt's house next door scented an important political development. Neither Baker nor Davis had been received or consulted by Roosevelt since the Chicago convention; indeed, Davis told me that his telegram of congratulations, including an offer to take part in the campaign, was not even acknowledged. At any rate, when the reporters saw those two step out on the sidewalk they rushed up to tell them they were going into the wrong house and were much disappointed to find it was they who were in error.

When Baker and Davis came up to my office they were still talking about it. Davis said, "Newton, there but for the grace of God go you," to which Baker answered that the Lord had been kind to him in many ways, but in none more outstanding than in sparing him the Presidential nomination. He said that just after the convention his wife, who had furiously opposed the idea of his nomination and had even begged him to state categorically that he would refuse it if it were offered, had said that she wondered whether after all he had not been derelict in his duty. "My dear," he said he had replied, "if I had been nominated, in that room on the left there would now be eight reporters, and in that room on the right there would now be eight photographers, and in this room with us there would now be eight politicians, and if I wanted to speak to you privately we would have to go into a closet." After that, said Baker, she decided she had been right all along.

Before starting for Europe on a trip that would take me to Berlin and also to the capitals of two other dictators, Belgrade and Rome, I spent a couple of days in Washington. Under-Secretary William Phillips and others in the State Department were intensely concerned about events in Germany, especially the accumulating reports of outrages against the Jews. Phillips told me the Department was endeavoring to persuade Jewish organizations to refrain from actions which could be seized on by Hitler as an excuse for added excesses. What positive action was the Department taking, I asked? Urgent private representations were being made, he said, through the German Ambassador, von Prittwitz, and through our Embassy in Berlin to Foreign Minister von Neurath. Also, our Embassy was being asked for a full report of events and a summary of the answer would be made public.

When I saw Prittwitz that afternoon his criticism of what was happening in his country was surprisingly frank, even given the fact that he was about to be relieved of his post as Ambassador. The wave of anti-Jewish fury would, he knew, damage Germany irreparably. Germany's reputation would suffer, and along with it her trade, with the result that she could not pay interest on her foreign loans abroad, foreigners would be furious and Germans in desperation would give way more than ever to xenophobia. He did not mean to criticize the situation for materialistic reasons alone, I felt sure; he viewed it as raising grave moral issues, but saw also the practical losses it entailed for his country. He had some hope that the German Army might take control, or even the *Stahlhelm,* as a counterforce to the Nazi Storm Troopers. But that would mean civil war. In any event, he said, those military leaders who had political sense were out. Hindenburg at eighty-six had relapsed into the arch-Junker, steered by his son and his East Prussian cronies. Opposition among Catholics, business leaders and the trade unions had crumpled up.

What was the weakness, I asked, which had led to such disaster? Was it—I apologized for putting it baldly—because Germans were simply "like that," or was this rather a strategic retreat by opposition elements who hoped that the Nazis would hang themselves? (Years later, President Eisenhower gave me a similar hope as a reason for not dealing with Senator Joe McCarthy when I begged him to do so; fortunately in that case, after bitter experiences, McCarthy did hang himself.) Prittwitz thought that this might in fact be the opposition's tactic. As I left I realized that whichever way things went lay terrible risks. The reaction might swing too far to the left, I thought, or Hitler, finding no opposition which he could not otherwise overcome, might push on to new enormities. The first alternative need not have worried me.

Phillips had let me read a memorandum just left with him by the Italian Ambassador, Rosso, describing a four-power pact between Britain, France, Germany and Italy which Mussolini was proposing and which MacDonald had endorsed during a visit to Rome. Its professed aim was to halt the deterioration of the Locarno spirit, for which purpose the four Powers would discuss a common line to be taken on all controversial questions, disarmament especially, and to assure that, if the Disarmament Conference failed, equal rights in armaments would be given gradually to Germany, Austria, Hungary and Bulgaria. Such a treaty would not be innocuous, I suggested, if it meant that Germany and Italy were to collaborate in establishing their special spheres of influence, one in Eastern Europe, the other in the Balkans and the Mediterranean. Later when I saw Ambassador Rosso (whom I knew from Geneva) the first thing he did was read me the memorandum on the treaty, to which I listened with as much attention as though I had not already just read it. He placed store on the treaty as a brake on Germany's determination to obtain revision of the arms limitations, even by force. "It is not based," he said, "on the idea of coercion, nor does an Italian rapprochement with Germany indicate we wish to impose unfair revisions on the Little Entente states." Precisely that seemed to me to be its plain objective.

Crossing on the *Europa* early in April, my wife and I had dinner one evening in the Sun Deck restaurant with Kühlmann, Fritz Kreisler and Jules Sauerwein, Foreign Editor of *Paris Soir*. A rather tense conversation kept us till after one o'clock. Three contradictory observations were made about the origins of the 1914 war, one German, one French, one Austrian. Kühlmann: "The war came because Germany could not fail to support Austria and thereby risk seeing her withdraw from the Triple Alliance." Sauerwein: "The war came because Russia would not permit German power to become predominant in the Balkans." Kreisler: "The war came because we foolishly made it, because the Empire was disintegrating, because it seemed better to die with honor."

Sauerwein saw another war on the horizon, not declared formally, perhaps, but growing out of a confused conflict of peoples in distress and revolution. On the contrary, maintained Kühlmann, war was not possible. Germany was disarmed; Polish airplanes could be over Berlin in twenty-five minutes, French airplanes over the Ruhr in forty-five minutes. There was no gamble in a war like that, merely defeat. We talked amicably, except that Sauerwein laughed at Kühlmann's statement that Germany was not already partially armed. "I have been to Germany forty-four times since the war," he said. "Don't tell me fairy tales."

We agreed that Vienna was now one of the critical points, with either a Nazi *Putsch* or a Hapsburg coup in the cards. Kreisler said that the Socialists were almost ready to accept a constitutional monarchy as the lesser evil. He himself would like a monarchy, though he ruefully remarked that this was because of his nostalgia for a day when Vienna was a gay imperial capital; the Emperor's ministers, he granted, were blind and giddy, but what did an artist have to do with that? He was a sensitive and sympathetic soul; his face twitched as we spoke of the possibility of a new war, and the next morning he told me he had not been able to sleep because of it.

Paris was as lovely as it should be on Easter Day, the Tuileries gardens filled with crowds enjoying the spring sunshine. I went to Versailles to see Norman Davis, where we lunched at the Golf Club and in the evening had dinner at a little restaurant overlooking a lake with him, Allen Dulles, the Hugh Wilsons and Ethel Bullard. Both Ramsay MacDonald and Herriot were then at sea on their way to Washington to discuss the coming economic conference and disarmament. Roosevelt was anxious to dramatize his plans for economic reconstruction, for he knew that only as part of some spectacular program could he touch the war debts. Dulles had a suspicion that the visits of the two statesmen were partly the result of Raymond Moley's desire to transfer the field of negotiations to Washington, where he could be in charge, and away from Norman Davis in Europe. Davis was still determined to push ahead with disarmament and thought it might be possible to secure agreement to progressive cuts in certain offensive arms, such as tanks and bombers, with inspection by the League—what was called "controlled disarmament." He said the United States would agree to take part in the inspection. Fortifications, with emplacements for heavy guns, would not be included. There was difficulty about the neutralized Rhineland zone, but when Davis had been in Berlin a week earlier he had gotten the impression that Germany might be content to build fortifications back of the neutralized zone. There was talk that the Disarmament Conference, which was due to reassemble in a week, might adjourn pending a discussion of political questions; everyone at last agreed that there would be no progress with either disarmament or economic reforms until broad political decisions had been reached.

France seemed to me to have taken Mussolini's proposed pact with surprising calm even though it referred to possible treaty revision. Actually, she was less concerned about the risks of such talk than she had been before the Nazis lined up world opinion against them. The Polish Ambassador in Paris, Ciechanowski, told me of Premier Daladier's reassuring message to his government that France was no more willing to allow Poland's frontiers to be revised than her own. I could not make out whether Davis had taken any part in discussions of possible treaty revisions. I hinted to him that the American influence in the Disarmament Conference would be jeopardized if the impression spread that we might favor increasing German armaments instead of pressing for a general arms cut which would gradually bring Germany to a position of equality. I said I hoped Roosevelt wouldn't let the word "revision" pass his lips while MacDonald was in Washington.

I I

I arrived in Berlin on Hitler's birthday, and already in the early morning while going from the station to the Adlon Hotel I passed groups of shouting Brown Shirts on their way to various celebrations. At noon a crowd assembled in the Pariser Platz while a loudspeaker blared forth slogans in angry tones. But spirits were dampened by sleet and rain, and the swastika banners flapped dejectedly alongside the black-white-red of the old Empire; the flag of the Republic was not to be seen. It was a contrast with the sun and the relaxed gaiety of the strollers in Paris.

In a small book which I wrote at full speed following my experience in Berlin and which was published in July,[1] the first sentence made the stark statement, "A people has disappeared." The discovery took little time. Almost every German whose name the world knew as a leader in government, business, science or the arts in the Republic of the past fourteen years was gone. There were exceptions, but the waves were swiftly cutting the sand beneath them, and day by day, one by one, the last specimens of another age, another folk, were toppling over into the Nazi sea.

To the Nazis it meant nothing that a compatriot had shouldered more than his share of the load in the long uphill struggle to reestablish Ger-

---

1. *Hitler's Reich: The First Phase.* New York: Macmillan, 1933.

many's prestige and means of existence in the years after the military collapse. If he was not a Nazi he was wiped out, and more, to have even a memory of him became risky. When I asked about acquaintances from the days of the Republic I was given vague answers: "Oh yes, but is he still alive? Maybe he is abroad. Or is he in a nursing home?"

This was true not just of Jews or Communists, fled, imprisoned or being attacked in the streets, but of men like Otto Braun, leader of the Social Democratic party, perennial Premier of Prussia, the strong man of whom Germans used to say, "When Hindenburg dies we have him." Ill and broken, he had escaped to Switzerland the day *before* the election —significant of the confusion and timidity of the Left and Center. The generals who had been talked about as embryo dictators were no more heard of and not to be found—von Seeckt, whom I especially asked after as I had been impressed on a previous visit by his sharp words and steel-like demeanor; Groener, successor to Ludendorff as Quartermaster General of the Army, whom I had counted on seeing, as he had written in the current *Foreign Affairs* on the results of the Versailles disarmament provisions; and even the once-powerful and tricky von Schleicher. Dr. Brüning, last of the chancellors furnished by the powerful Center party, was still in Berlin but (I was told) had isolated himself in a Catholic clinic.[2] The trained city officials—Dr. Adenauer and other burgomasters who wielded power far outside their own great cities—had been abruptly dismissed. Stresemann was not merely dead, but dead as long as the last Pharaoh.

Hindenburg himself was a legend, a fable. His picture hung on the walls of coffeehouses, for he had played a role for the Nazis, but their need for him was finished since he had signed the Enabling Act that ended German parliamentary democracy and turned over the powers of the Reichstag to Hitler's cabinet. It also ended the President's constitutional right to issue emergency decrees; now Hitler had the power to change the constitution. Hindenburg still occupied his residence on the Wilhelmstrasse, his Presidential flag still flew over it, the guard changed with formal precision in the courtyard, witnessed at noon as usual by Hindenburg himself. The difference was that police shooed you to the other side of the street whether or not this brief ceremony was in progress.

2. Later, in May, 1934, John Wheeler-Bennett helped Brüning to get to Holland, thence to England and eventually to America. On the Dutch border a customs official who was a double agent tried to kill him with a poisoned cigar but the attack failed. In America he lived at first in a seminary near Huntington, Long Island, under the name Henry Anderson; I had several letters from him at that time signed with that alias.

This all was pretense; it did not matter whether Hindenburg was there or not. All that mattered went on in the Chancellery further down the street or, just beyond, in the Hotel Kaiserhof, the rendezvous of the Nazi leaders.

The *Stahlhelm,* organization of the front-line veterans, credited with having saved the country from anarchy and Communism in several post-war crises, but feared by the Nazis as a possible rival to their own *Sturm Abteilung,* was broken and subjugated. The *Reichswehr,* which as recently as the previous December would have supported a determined move to establish authority in the name of the flickering Republic, was standing glumly aside, knowing its day for action had slipped by. The last citadels of military defense against uncontradicted Nazi dictatorship had fallen.

Federal Germany was gone. The *Gleichschaltung* law had disposed of the prerogatives of the separate states, and Nazi leaders had been named *Statthalter.* The Socialist trade unions, active for fifty years in German life, were helpless, and ten days after I left Berlin I heard that their buildings had been occupied by Storm Troopers, their officers jailed as "Red' criminals" and their funds appropriated. Jesuits and Free Masons had been ranked almost with Jews as hated objects of the Nazis; some were imprisoned already, and more would be soon. Newspapers on the day of my arrival disclosed the resignation of the President of the Supreme Court of Prussia, and printed an announcement of the Commissioner for the Prussian Ministry of Justice that in future judges would be tested for their patriotism and martial ardor, and before being appointed would serve in a training camp and be schooled "body and mind" in "martial sports." Even the great Nationalist party, co-party with the Nazis in the election of only a few weeks before, supported by the monarchists, the landed proprietors, former army officers and many of the industrialists, which Chancellor von Papen had used in the thought of swallowing up the Nazis, had instead been swallowed up. Its leader, Dr. Hugenberg, was wringing his hands and complaining about his lack of even the slightest influence; I was told he would not see a foreigner.

The Spanish Ambassador, my friend Luis Araquistain, repeated to me a remark by Professor Moritz Bonn which summed it all up: "We made a Republic; but there were no republicans."

Hitler had made the whole race of Jews scapegoats for Germany's miseries even though they numbered less than one percent of the whole German population of some sixty-five million, and on them he had set a special curse. Norman Ebbutt, the objective correspondent of the London

Times, afterward dismissed from his post for sending dispatches objectionable alike to the Nazis and to the editor of his paper, Geoffrey Dawson, did not support the most sensational reports of widespread atrocities in this first period of the Nazi regime; he thought they might well have been more numerous in view of the horrifying propaganda that had preceded the Nazi victory, for example the expectation held out by Dr. Alfred Rosenberg, the party's philosopher, that the head of a Jew would be stuck on each telegraph pole from Munich to Berlin. With this attitude the American correspondents agreed, although they could not get a denial from government quarters of specific rumored atrocities. They told me they no longer needed to give interpretations of what was going on; they simply quoted statements by Nazi leaders and reported events, of which the meaning was self-evident. The number of political prisoners in Prussia at that time was officially given as ten thousand and estimates of those in internment camps and jails in other parts of the country brought the total up to about twenty thousand. No court process, of course, had been gone through to confine these people, and the figures could not be checked. Many persons were escaping abroad; a few weeks after my visit I saw an estimate of fifty thousand.

The Communist leaders had been arrested or gone underground. They had not fought the Nazis wholeheartedly in the elections, hoping that if the Weimar Government disappeared they could profit from the ensuing disorder. Our chargé d'affaires, George Gordon, whom I had known as a boy at our little summer place in Quebec, told me that now they were refraining from sponsoring strikes or sabotage, probably thinking that the Nazis would come into conflict with the army or the *Stahlhelm,* which in either case would mean civil war and be grist to their mill. The ablest of our officials, I thought, was Consul-General George Messersmith. He could hardly restrain himself when he talked about the Nazis, biting his cigar into two pieces and tossing them away in disgust as he catalogued his difficulties in trying to protect American citizens from molestation. Proper consideration of his representations was made almost impossible by the fact that government officials were powerless to cope with actions by Nazi party members. He spoke of the way the Nazis were propagating militarism and said frankly that he had little hope of peace for long.

In the evenings I usually went to Paul Scheffer's apartment and there met various officials of the Foreign Office, men like Dieckhoff, later Ambassador in Washington, and Ritter, an economics expert, especially on affairs in Eastern Europe. They were holding on to their offices and keeping quiet. They said they did this out of a sense of duty; the Nazis were a flash in the pan, and they would simply outwait them, doing what they could meanwhile to keep German foreign policy from error and ready to serve the new German regime which would eventually take over. They thought that even if Hitler remained he might just possibly be sobered by his responsibilities. They were not unintelligent men, but I knew in my bones that they were wrong. I was not certain that Scheffer shared my view, but I believed he did; and his eventual action in leaving the post in London to which his newspaper transferred him and coming as an émigré to America proved that if he did not already know that Hitler was more than a temporary phenomenon he came to understand it the hard way.

Dieckhoff gave the impression that the Foreign Office was pathetically isolated from Nazi centers of power; even its press bureau had been bodily removed and put at the disposal of Dr. Rosenberg, "unofficial" director of the party's foreign policy. Without saying so, he also indicated the childlike conception of the Nazis as to how foreign policy works. Their attitude to hostile foreign criticism had gone through three phases: first they believed it didn't exist, then they said it didn't matter if it did exist, now they were beginning to say that something ought to be done about it. Dieckhoff himself seemed to see through their illusions. For instance, they were pleased with Mussolini's assurances that he would like to help them because Italy also was a Fascist state and wanted treaty revision; but they hardly noticed when he added that world hostility to Germany made any moves to give expression to that sympathy impossible at present.

I asked Scheffer and his friends about some of the men in academic life whom I had known—Karl Brandt; R. R. Kuczynski, the statistician; Dr. Moritz Bonn, the economist, whom I had met at Paul Warburg's in New York; Dr. Ernst Jäckh, founder of the Hochschule für Politik, with which the Council on Foreign Relations had had dealings. They had disappeared, I was told, and in any case it was better for them that I should not try to look them up. The toll throughout the ranks of Germany's best talent in literature, the arts, medicine and science was already formidable, and growing. At least four Nobel prize winners had been dismissed. It was staggering to think of what the resulting intellectual vacuum would mean in a country bled white and defeated in a devastating war.

There were two ways in which I might make contact with the Nazis. One was through a letter given me by Dr. Hans Luther, former Chancellor and President of the Reichsbank, now Ambassador in Washington, to his successor at the Bank, Dr. Schacht. The other was through Ernst Hanfstaengl, nicknamed "Putzi," a graduate of Harvard, whose mother was a Sedgwick of Boston. He had given a helping hand to Hitler in the early days in Munich, where his father was a well-known publisher of art books and reproductions of pictures; he had lent him money, hid him after the failure of the 1923 putsch and solaced him on evenings of discouragement by playing for him on the piano.

In appearance, Putzi was an overgrown boy, broad-shouldered, bulky, with hair parted in the middle and a long nose between deep-set eyes. His political ideas were primitive, positive, exaggerated. He was easily flattered and very proud of his access to Hitler and his ability to soothe his overwrought nerves with emotional passages from Wagner.

Now Putzi had become liaison officer for the Nazi party with the foreign press. Even if it had not been his duty he would probably have helped me, for he liked Americans and spoke often of his American connections. In the end he became troublesome to Hitler and lost his confidence. He claims in his memoirs[3] that there was actually a plot to do away with him and that he escaped just in time to Switzerland, then to England. He was interned when war came, then was transferred to Canada and ended up helping American psychological warfare by interpreting news from Germany.

Schacht without doubt deserved his reputation as a financial wizard, for he guided the economy of Hitler's Germany away from the abyss of inflation and at the same time made it pay for German rearmament. My meeting with him was extraordinary. When I called at the Reichsbank I was taken to the great empty kitchen, where on a chair placed on top of a large table was perched Schacht. A sculptor who was making a bust of him thought it would be a good idea to view him, while he worked, from the same angle that the statue on its pedestal would later be viewed. Whether for that reason or not, he plainly was having a hard time with Schacht's screwed-up ugly face. Schacht, a great worker, did not want to lose time in posing, so even though it made him rather ludicrous he had invited me to fill the time for his sitting.

Looking down at me, while the sculptor pottered and scraped with the plaster, Schacht told me, in a harsh voice but with an ingratiating manner, about the strides the German economy was making under his direction. He spoke enthusiastically of the Nazi "reforms" as a necessary reaction against "wild" capitalism—speculation, the cycle of giddy profits and

3. Ernst Hanfstaengl, *Unheard Witness*. Philadelphia: Lippincott, 1957.

fearful drops, the power of money, banks and big business. It was a humorous thesis for a man who was said to have brought in heavy contributions from certain big industrialists who had not liked the social and welfare policies of the Weimar Republic and in any case thought it wise to pay "insurance premiums" to the Nazis. (He was accused at Nuremberg of having been Hitler's accomplice but was acquitted, and died only in 1970, aged ninety-three.)

Schacht offered sometime to write an article for *Foreign Affairs* (and eventually did so, in October, 1934, under the title "German Trade and German Debts"), and said he thought he could persuade the Führer to receive me. He was a man of great vanity, and it evidently pleased him to display his influence. Also, as he was going to visit America in May in the hope of securing a loan to finance German exports (he failed) he may have thought it advantageous to demonstrate that influence. My vertical interview was not much of a success intellectually, but it did procure me what I most wanted, a chance to meet Hitler.

38

Hitler in the Pulpit

When Putzi Hanfstaengl arrived at the Adlon to take me to see Hitler he was in uniform. Nothing matched. The tunic was olive drab, the shirt a rather sickly greenish brown, the breeches were yellowish brown, the puttees still another brown.

"Why, Putzi," I said, "I've never seen you in uniform before. How magnificent!"

Looking down at himself with satisfaction, he said: "Yes, it is rather good, isn't it? Don't tell anyone, but it's English stuff. That does make a difference."

Hitler's office at the Chancellery was filled with flowering plants, left from his birthday a week earlier. He greeted me with a slight bow from the waist. He was not in uniform and there was no Nazi salute. Instead, he shook hands and motioned me to a low round table on which reposed a pad with some headings in pencil. Evidently he was prepared with a speech. I sat opposite him, with Hanfstaengl on one side and Hans Thomsen on the other. Thomsen I had already met. He had been German Consul in Naples under the Fascists and had come easily to the belief that a similar movement in Germany was, as he put it, "obligatory." He and Putzi were to serve as interpreters, each, I suppose, to watch the other. Neither fulfilled the assignment very well, for when I asked an uncomfortable question both were reluctant to incur Hitler's displeasure by putting it to him in German. They undoubtedly knew, besides, that Hitler's format did not provide for interruptions.

In press photographs, Hitler usually posed, but evidently the gallery on this occasion was not large enough to make that worthwhile, or perhaps he thought simplicity was a better tack. At any rate, he looked me over calmly, without any of his usual grimaces. I was interested to find that he had rather nice, wide-open eyes, which dilated and became intense only when he was irritated. People disagreed as to their color; some said they were blue; Dorothy Thompson wrote later that they were gray; and Anthony Eden said in 1934 that they were pale and glaucous. My observation was that they were light brown with perhaps a greenish cast.

While he was talking he did not look at me but kept his eyes fixed on the upper distance, which made it seem as though he were in communication with God. He brought them down to me only when I tried to interject a remark or ask a question, and when that happened he looked surprised, as a clergyman might if interrupted in the middle of a sermon by someone in the congregation. He waited impatiently till the disturbance was over. His nose was large, with rather large nostrils. His general appearance was insignificant. Several small wrinkles around the eyes, particularly above, gave him an inquiring look which was misleading, for although I had come from the West where his policies had aroused such fierce antagonism he did not ask me a single question or by any remark or reference reveal that he was in the least concerned by what the world thought of him or of the position in which he had placed his country.[1]

Without preliminary, then, Hitler began addressing me. He spoke quietly. Two or three times, however, he seemed to lose control. A few words at the start of a sentence about some indignity inflicted on Germany would suddenly carry his voice up to the breaking point, his eyes flashed and a wisp of hair fell down over his left eye in the way the whole world knew. The rocket went up with a whiz, then there was a splutter, he smoothed his hair and went on again comparatively calmly.

He started with a formal statement that Germany was for peace, noting that he had emphasized this in his very first pronouncements after coming into office. How could it be otherwise, he said, in a country which had eight million men out of work? This did not carry conviction, for I had learnt that statesmen always said their country wanted peace, and to prove it cited equally well either prosperity or bad times and unem-

---

1. This was characteristic. In 1937, Hans Thomsen was brought back from Washington, where he was chargé d'affaires, to act as interpreter for Hitler in talks with Mussolini in Rome. James V. Compton writes in *The Swastika and the Eagle* (Boston: Houghton, Mifflin, 1967) that Thomsen told him later that neither Hitler nor Ribbentrop had asked him anything about the United States.

ployment. He went at length into the iniquities of Versailles but said
that the moment had not come to rectify them. "We must look ahead;
we must make a new Germany; we must consolidate our strength." All
this was conventional stuff. The Polish frontier, he went on, was *un-
möglich und unerträglich,* impossible and intolerable, and to accept it
permanently was unthinkable, *absolut undenkbar.* How would Americans
feel, he asked, if they were bound by a foreign *Diktat* that prevented
them from having adequate troops while their neighbor Mexico, which
bore the same cultural relationship to the United States as Poland did to
Germany, had enormous armaments, was increasing those armaments
and threatening the American frontier? "Poland holds a naked knife in
her teeth," he said, clenching his teeth in demonstration, "and looks at
us menacingly," glaring at me as though I were a regiment of Polish
soldiers.

The question was rhetorical, but it seemed a good moment to arrest
what had become a flood of words. I therefore answered that if the United
States found itself in such a position of inferiority regarding Mexico, it
would be grateful that it had a friendly country like Canada on the other
frontier; whereas Germany had France on the other frontier. As neither
interpreter liked the idea of translating that remark, I had to repeat it in
my bad German. Hitler nodded vehemently in agreement, evidently
thinking I had confirmed his argument. So I again asked Hanfstaengl to
translate it, whereupon Hitler froze for a second with jaw set, then continued without comment.

It would have been much better, said Hitler, if Germany had been
entirely bereft of soldiers by the Allies rather than allowed a miserable
100,000. That number was entirely useless to protect her frontiers, yet
furnished her neighbors with an excuse to call her chauvinistic. This
argument, he added, was one which he had not used before, and for a
moment I thought he wanted a foreigner's reaction to it, but that was
not the case, and he proceeded to ask, again of course rhetorically,
whether the United States would consider that the peace of the world
would be served if it scrapped its fleet? I interjected that it might be, if
Britain and Japan did also. To this he paid no attention. Europe, he
went on, was armed as it never had been before. This was the fault entirely of the Allies. For every soldier in the *Reichswehr* there were fifty
in the armies of France, Poland, Czechoslovakia and Belgium. Again and
again he repeated that if there was a clash it was the Allies who must bear
the responsibility. "To say the contrary," he said vehemently, his voice

rising and the lock of hair coming down menacingly over his eye, "is to say that a toothless rabbit would start a battle with a tiger."

Wasn't the present question, I asked, whether there would be sufficient time to agree on action to bring the German Army into a condition of more equality with neighboring armies before the situation deteriorated further? Both disarmament and treaty revision had seemed nearer six weeks ago than they were now. How soon could consideration begin of disarmament, not only as an end in itself but as one way of giving Germany equality? Hanfstaengl translated this, and Hitler made a reply, though he did not give an answer. Instead of commenting on what had become the most promising manner for Germany to achieve arms equality peacefully, he said that the bad *Stimmung* at the Disarmament Conference was not the result of any act of Germany's but of a deliberate plan by France to wreck it. Everything being done at Geneva, he continued, was a "maneuver" and amounted to nothing but a "swindle." The mentality of 1919 was back again.

I protested that wars were not always made deliberately by governments or individuals but often came simply because things had been allowed to drift on a dangerous course. Could not Germany join to halt the drift? He disregarded the appeal and returned to Poland. To allow Poland to continue arming while Germany remained disarmed was a plot against Christian civilization. The world had two courses open to it—to accept Bolshevism or to stabilize nation states. On one side was acceptance of the disproportion of arms and the illogic of the present frontiers; on the other side was a determination to undo those wrongs. One course led to Bolshevism, the other to building defenses against Bolshevism by the strengthening of the system of nation states.

"We are armed today," said Hitler, "with spears, bows and arrows and swords. Does that condition represent a danger to the peace of the world? Or does the danger of war come from the vast arms possessed by Poland?" The answer, he concluded, was obvious, and the sooner the world recognized it the better for the world—he did not say for Germany, but for the world. "We have waited months and years for justice. To get it, we must rearm. We cannot and will not wait longer. The *sine qua non* of any agreement which Germany will join must be, at the very minimum, equality in arms."

Further generalizations followed, during which I found a chance to put a question to him about the national boycott of Jewish businesses on April 1, which had caused tremendous repercussions abroad. Would it be repeated? The world, I said, was following the campaign against German Jews with intense concern. Actually, I had taken his omission of any reference to the Jewish question as perhaps indicating, though in a negative way, that he might after all take some slight interest in foreign opinion. For the boycott had allegedly been staged in retaliation for foreign criticism of the Nazi persecution of the Jews, and threats were being made to repeat it if foreign criticism continued. Did Hitler's avoidance of the subject indicate indirectly that after all he was sensitive on the subject? I hoped to smoke him out. He ignored my question, and after a peroration to the effect that the Versailles Treaty was not binding because it had been entered into under duress he rose and solemnly bowed.

Hitler accompanied me to the door—a great compliment Putzi told me afterward. To pay him back for giving me a lecture rather than accepting a give-and-take of ideas, I thanked him for addressing me alone when usually he addressed sixty millions. The sarcasm he took as a compliment, said he had enjoyed what he miscalled our "animated talk" and again bowed slightly. He waited just inside the open door as Putzi followed me into the elevator. The Führer had been in excellent good humor, Putzi said over and over as we drove back to the Adlon; never had he heard him talk to a foreigner with such consideration, so openly, so concretely. He repeated to me two or three times, with a sigh of relief and satisfaction, "Wasn't he *lovely* to you?"

Loveliness is relative, and what Putzi meant was that I had not been treated to Hitler's usual hectoring. Some dramatics there had been, but it was halfhearted; I realized that inspiration had been lacking. It was only some time later, when I was talking in New York with Dr. C. G. Jung, that I came across a possible clue. I mentioned to Jung a rumor, never confirmed, that Hitler's mother had been a medium. This quite excited Jung because, he said, it would account for Hitler's behavior when he faced one of his tumultuous mass meetings—a slow and tight-throated beginning, but then, as he drew inspiration from the hysterics of the crowd, responding to each wave of adulation with a fresh wave of frenetic oratory. The theory formed by Anthony Eden after meeting Hitler was different; he put him down as a self-hypnotist. But maybe it was more in Hitler's character to suppose that he was hypnotized from without, that he drew power from the swelling chants of "Sieg Heil!" and the shrieks of the adoring women and that he transmitted that power back to them in magnified form, each side feeding on the other's frenzy. Facing me, however, across a small round table, there had been no pool of emotion from which he could draw; without it his performance was pallid—"lovely," as Putzi put it.

II

Hitler had shied away from the suggestion that progressive disarmament by Germany's neighbors offered a way for her to acquire arms equality. This implied that he favored an opposite course of action. It materialized almost at once. Foreign Minister von Neurath announced that, regardless of the results of the Disarmament Conference, Germany would create a military and naval air force, arm with big guns and build up her manpower. And von Papen, trying to "keep up," made a belligerent speech at Münster aimed at strengthening the public determination to be satisfied with nothing less. "Mothers," he said, "must exhaust themselves to give life to children. Fathers must fight on the battlefield to secure the future of their sons." Plainly, Hitler was determined to have the means to acquire what he demanded, by blackmail or force, and to have it at once; and he had the support of a people in a feverish mood, ready to respond to his every call at whatever risk. The word pacifism had been struck from the German vocabulary.

What specifically, once he had the arms, did Hitler intend to achieve? He had itemized the list in many speeches, and even at this early stage it was a long one. He wanted the Polish Corridor and Silesia back from Poland, and Danzig back from its truancy as a Free State. He wanted *Anschluss* with Austria. He wanted Northern Schleswig back from Denmark, Memel back from Lithuania, Eupen and Malmédy back from Belgium and the former German colonies from their present possessors. It went without saying that he counted on getting back the Saar after the 1935 plebiscite. Alsace, for the moment, was being mentioned only indirectly, as when the Nazi Premier of Bavaria said at about the time of my visit that the Nazis would take an oath "never to rest or relax until the Rhine flows to the sea once more as Germany's river, not as Germany's frontier." In Hitler's words, "the revolution will only be complete when the entire German world is inwardly and outwardly formed anew." Since the Nazis never stopped proclaiming by radio and in the press and in textbooks for the children the right and duty to use force to attain Nazi demands, it could not be claimed that this program excluded a general European war.

It was not only the wreck of a civilization, then, that I had observed; it carried the threat of disaster for all the world. Yet as I left Berlin I speculated whether I might not be wrong, whether the current passions and violence might not be phenomena of a first era of revolutionary fervor only. Was there not the ghost of a chance that Hitler might modify the means he threatened to use to reach his promised goal? The German spirit had been purged at least in part of its pent-up store of hate and envy. Full legal and moral equality had been declared and the material evidence to support it would mount rapidly. Might Hitler decide, from his new vantage point of total power, total responsibility, that the cost of gaining his ends by war were too immeasurable and might be won instead by skillful diplomacy? There might be real reasons for caution. It was said that there were divisions in the party leadership, that Hitler sometimes had to hold back Goebbels and other especially reckless colleagues. There were rivalries between the secret police and the S.A., and, of course, between the S.A. and the *Reichswehr,* who still clung to the hope of controlling Germany's military future. Instead of laying plans to seize his requirements by force, might Hitler gradually revert to the methods of piecemeal revision exploited by his predecessors?

Nothing that I had heard or seen in Berlin really seemed to me to justify such a hope. And, even if the next to impossible did happen, was it conceivable that the world would accept it in good faith? Would France believe in "a new Hitler" and make concessions to him which she had not been ready to make to a Stresemann and a Brüning? Everything in Hitler's make-up seemed to echo Lenin's dictum: "He who undertakes the storming of a fortress cannot refuse to continue the war after he has taken the fortress." Hitler had taken the old German fortress, and citizens who had not shouted "Sieg Heil!" had been beaten to their knees. In the little book which I wrote in the next few weeks I questioned most pessimistically both the hope that Hitler, armed, would draw back from the ultimate test of wills and the thesis of many that his reign would prove to be only a flash in the pan. A people had, in sober and awful truth, disappeared. I could not see the possibility of their rebirth as a part of Western civilization under Hitler or the possibility of their resurgence against him.

39

Between Hitler and Mussolini

Danzig, a lovely old Hanseatic town at the mouth of the Vistula, with gabled houses on the waterfront and along its narrow streets, had been established as a free city in 1919 under the protection of the League of Nations. The intention was that it should serve as a Polish outlet to the sea, and Poland received privileges in trade as well as control over its foreign relations; but as the inhabitants were something like 97 percent German, they were given a democratic constitution which enabled them to run their local affairs. The inevitable conflict of interest and authority which developed, and which was aired in acrimonious hearings each year in Geneva, had been brought in 1933 to a new pitch of intensity by the Nazi takeover in Germany.

A campaign was in progress for elections to the city legislature, to be held May 28—destined, I was told by our consul and others, to give the city to Nazi control (as in fact it did). Nazi meetings had been banned, but "concerts" and other deceptive festivals were being held daily in the Sport Halle. Nazis in uniform were everywhere in the streets and drilled in the outskirts of the city. A Nazi newspaper, *Der Danziger Vorposten,* was filled with claims, threats and recriminations against the Poles. Nazi flags decked the streets in spite of Polish protests that the swastika banner was no longer that of a party but of a foreign state since it had been adopted as a flag of the German Reich along with the old Imperial black, white and red.

The campaign was being fought over the fact that the port of Danzig was dying. Since the Danzigers openly wanted to rejoin the Reich, and

Berlin propagandized them day in and day out to demand it, Poland had built a port of her own, Gdynia, some ten miles away, and was using it more and more both for exports and imports. At the moment, the tonnage passing through the two ports was approximately equal, but plainly Gdynia would be the eventual winner. I was reminded of the conflict over Fiume, and the threat to its prosperity posed by Italy's favor for Trieste.

Two years earlier Hitler had sent Albert Forster to Danzig to organize the Nazi element there, and he had done it most effectively. He had been a Nazi leader in Bavaria, indeed was among Hitler's first collaborators, one of the so-called "First Seven"—a number that the last election in Germany had brought from seven to seventeen million. Forster was not much over thirty, energetic, rather attractive in an impetuous way, though afflicted with the Nazi habit of speaking to you in a loud voice and with too much emphasis. He was enormously impressed by my having been received by the Führer and wanted me to tour the city in his car, which I declined. He was sure his party would win the election but denied that even if not there would be any violent coup. He said he realized that Danzig was only a part of a great international complex and that all his actions were under instructions from Berlin.

The German Government was represented in Danzig by a consul, Baron von Thermann, who although having more formal status than Forster had less local influence. When I asked him what compromise short of a solution by force he could suggest, he naturally hesitated to reply, but finally said that the maximum German concession would be that if the Corridor and Danzig were returned to Germany, Danzig might be made a free port (with Königsberg and Stettin free ports also), leaving Gdynia as a Polish enclave served by an internationalized railway. An intelligent German expert on the area, Fräulein Gaertner, admitted that the Polish Corridor, perhaps 80 percent German before the war, was now not more than 15 percent German, but agreed with the consul that nevertheless it must go back to Germany, and certainly Silesia with it, "since that would diminish Poland's reliance on Gdynia." Like Thermann, she favored internationalizing the railway to Danzig and Gdynia and the Vistula also. She did not deny it when I said it seemed evident to me that Germany was intent above all on getting Silesia, with its great wealth in coal and iron, but was harping on the Corridor because on the map it appeared such an anachronism.

I had several talks with the Polish diplomatic delegate, Mr. Papee, intelligent and informative, with two officials of the so-called Foreign Office of the Free City, named Blume and Herschfeld, and with our consul, Mr. Heiser. Herschfeld took me around the harbor in a police launch, and with Heiser I paid a visit to Gdynia. The number of workers employed in the Danzig shipyards had sunk to three hundred, compared to ten thousand before the war, but this was not the result of competition from Gdynia, where there was no shipbuilding to speak of, but of world economic conditions. Heiser agreed, however, that Danzig was gradually being choked, as Riga and Libau had been choked (Fiume also).

Danzigers stressed that the idea of the free city had been that Poland needed Danzig and Danzig needed Poland, but the benefits had turned out not to be mutual. Poland discriminated in favor of Gdynia and against Danzig in harbor charges, in terms of free warehousing and in innumerable other ways. To live, Danzig must go back to Germany, but it must not go back without the Corridor, for that would isolate and ruin it. The Danzigers were stubborn and contentious people, who had thought to prove to the world by their numerous complaints to the League (many of them well-grounded) that the situation was fantastic and could not last. They proved their point to the Poles only too well, and the result had been the creation of Gdynia. They thought of the Poles as barbarians with whom they must do business but from whom they could expect nothing but deceit; and the Poles thought that regardless of how they treated Danzigers they could aim at nothing except to rejoin Germany.

To Danzig's complaints that Poland was killing it in favor of Gdynia, Papee replied that it was German hostility, in Danzig and in Berlin, that had forced Poland to develop Gdynia. Traffic through Danzig, though being overtaken by that through Gdynia, was nevertheless double what it had been before the war, and if the political conflict abated Poland would continue to use them both. He had to admit that this was unlikely. The police and customs guards were Nazis and the local Nazi party was campaigning for revenge and reunion with Germany. East Prussia had always been separated from Germany proper, as he called it, by a band of territory that remained Slavic through the centuries. "In fact," he went so far as to say, "East Prussia is only a German colony." Poland had tried to make German transit across that band of territory as convenient as possible; but she could not and would not give it up. Her lifeline to the sea lay through Danzig and Gdynia.

"The Corridor question," said Papee, "was settled in its present form by war; it will be changed only by war." It was a true prediction, although the changes would be more than one.

II

In Warsaw no Pole would admit to the slightest doubt about the future of the Corridor; it was Polish and would stay Polish come what might, in peace if possible, by war if necessary. This was stated flatly by Colonel Joseph Beck, Minister of Foreign Affairs, right-hand man of the dictator General Pilsudski, and by his chief opponent, General Wladyslaw Sikorski, to whom I had an introduction from Paderewski. I heard the same thing at the Foreign Office in talks with Joseph Potocki and his colleagues, with former Minister of Finance Ignatius Matuszewski, with others at dinner with our chargé, Crosby, and at lunch with Princess Lubomirski—a broad sampling of government and opposition opinion.

Beck was later to become Prime Minister, and it was he who in a last effort to ward off Hitler's threats in 1939 persuaded Britain to sign the treaty of alliance which brought her into the war. His manner was tough and so were his principles. Like his chief, Pilsudski, he was patriotic without limits. In talking with me he would hear of no initiative that might conciliate Germany (although not many months later he did conclude a nonaggression pact with her—which turned out to be valueless—to balance Poland's agreement with the Soviets—which also proved useless). Specifically as to the Corridor, he brushed aside the possibility of any change, however small, as for instance Paderewski's idea of facilitating east-west transit by according Germany sovereignty over the railway; Germany needed nothing of the sort and it would only give Hitler the idea that pressure would bring further concessions. The Corridor was Poland's lifeline. Without access to the sea Poland would be dominated either by Germany or by Russia or once again divided between them. (When in fact Germany and Russia did divide Poland in 1939, Beck was interned in Rumania and died there.)

Since Hitler's demand for the Corridor was part of his declared intention to reestablish German hegemony in *Osteuropa,* Beck considered it wrong to concentrate attention on the Corridor as such; it was only one item in the central question: was Germany to be restored, even expanded? This was not a Polish question; it was a European question, a world question. Poland had been divided before, and she might be again. It could be done only by force, over the bodies of millions of Poles; then it would be undone again by force, no matter what the cost.

This was one of the few things on which General Sikorski agreed with Beck. He had been a hero of the defeat of the Soviet armies before Warsaw in the summer of 1920 and was not intimidated by armed threats.

He was confident that Poland could handle Germany by herself. This may well have been true at that time (our Embassy people thought so too) even though it was not to prove the case in 1939 after Germany had rearmed. Sikorski estimated that even when Germany had rearmed, a German-Polish war would last at least several months, within which time all Europe would be in flames and Poland would have powerful allies. Among these certainly would be France. He recalled the inspiration given Poland by General Weygand in 1920; next time, France would send more than generals, for she could not afford to let Poland be overwhelmed and must fight *à l'outrance* to prevent it.

Sikorski sketched a map to show the strategic necessity for Germany to regain the Corridor if she meditated aggression, since it cut away the heart of the great prewar system of German fortresses stretching from Breslau to Marienburg and Königsberg. Poland's answer to German propaganda was the single question: "Will you sign a nonaggression pact guaranteeing the Polish-German frontier?" The fact that she would not implied her determination to revise it by force.

The only glimmer of optimism came from Matuszewski, who wondered, as I had done myself, whether there might not be a faint possibility that Hitler, faced with realities, might adopt peaceful rather than warlike lines. I said I did not believe he had either the mental or moral capacity—perhaps even the physical power—to make a dramatic turnabout. Matuszewski's answer was that realities would not wait. Germany could not isolate herself politically without ruining her export trade, on which fifteen million Germans lived directly or indirectly. That fact could not be swept away by a speech in the Sportpalast. His point was emphasized by Potocki, who came down to the station to see me off. He said many Polish merchants, especially in the textile trade, were receiving orders from England stipulating that consignments not be shipped through Hamburg or Stettin, but via Gdynia, to avoid patronizing German railways and ports. These were either Jewish traders or their sympathizers, acting in retaliation for the Nazi mistreatment of Jews. It was one more sign of the compression of forces being built up inside Germany and (to my mind) of the probable explosive end.

III

Austria, always intrinsically weak, was now split politically in three ways. The Social Democrats had made Vienna a model workers' city; they had built imposing blocks of apartment houses for trade-union members and instituted admirable social services. But although in their citadel they seemed invulnerable, the government of the country was not theirs. The national government of Chancellor Engelbert Dollfuss was anti-Marxist, clerical and authoritarian. It too was weak, however, for its majority in the parliament was only one. Now, menacing both, Hitler's Nazis stood on the borders, blaring radio threats and cajolings into Austria night and day; and within the country their partisans were carrying on the same campaign of violence that had brought success in Germany—riots, bombings, assassinations, blackmail.

Dollfuss had had two choices. He could try to beat the Nazis in an all-out drive without the help of the Social Democrats. In this he could secure the support of Mussolini, who like him was hostile to the socialists, was against the *Anschluss,* which would bring a Greater Germany to the Brenner, and was favorable to a Hapsburg restoration since it would weaken Jugoslavia by setting up a Catholic attraction for the Croats. Or he could make an armistice with the Social Democrats, who were against both the *Anschluss* and a Hapsburg restoration and hoped to avoid either by proclaiming Austrian neutrality and coming to terms with the neighboring states of the Little Entente. Dollfuss had chosen the first course, to fight both the Nazis and the Social Democrats. His position had been strengthened since he had suspended the parliament a few weeks earlier, taking advantage of a series of procedural errors. Whether the suspension was temporary or permanent nobody yet knew, but for the time being, at any rate, Dollfuss had no legal rival.

I talked with the two leaders of the Social Democrats, Dr. Karl Seitz, the Burgomaster of Vienna, former President, and Dr. Otto Bauer, the powerful leader of the party's left wing, former Foreign Minister. Both were to suffer a few months later—Seitz by imprisonment, Bauer by exile—for their part in the tragic and bungled rising of the Viennese workers against Dollfuss' attacks on the privileges of the socialist trade unions and his decree dissolving all political parties except his own coalition. By mismanagement I failed to see Dollfuss, but heard much about him from John Gunther, correspondent of the Chicago *Daily News,* whom I now met for the first time. We became lifelong friends. One evening I went with him and his wife to see Fritz Kreisler's *Sissy,* a pleasant trifle, and afterward we talked till late about Dollfuss. The Chancellor was only four feet eleven, and John referred to him as "millimeter dictator," "Jack the giant killer" and "fly-weight champion." He admired his spunk and showmanship, and thought that in spite of his precarious political position between left and extreme right (if the term had meaning as applied to the Nazis), he was Austria's best chance of avoiding being swallowed by Hitler.

Seitz I met in his office at the *Rathaus*. He was sarcastic about the stupidity of German industrialists who had supported Hitler's rise to power. They had imagined that once the Nazis had destroyed the socialists and the trade unions they would be able in turn to destroy the Nazis.

"But the dead cat that was to have been swung against the socialists," he said, "turned out to be a live tiger, which devoured those who had it by the tail."

His colleague Bauer spoke bitterly of the colossal error Dollfuss had made in refusing to accept the cooperation of the Social Democrats against the Nazis. He considered him mad to suppose he could win alone, or even with the help of Mussolini, with whom there was talk of a treaty of mutual defense. Did Dollfuss imagine Mussolini would fight Germany to save Austria? Mussolini's only interest was self-interest.

I thought the Social Democratic solution—neutrality for Austria— might not be a bad idea for the long run (and in fact it was how Austria found salvation after World War II), but as an immediate way of deflecting Hitler it seemed irrelevant.

One important enemy of the Social Democrats, not yet an open ally of Chancellor Dollfuss but soon to be, was young Prince Starhemberg, a leader of the *Heimwehr,* army of the Fascist right. He was tall, handsome, pleased with his looks in a pale gray uniform, a playboy in politics, not very bright. His program was simple: be hard, self-reliant, authoritarian. Dollfuss realized that this was not enough, and shortly afterward visited Italy and reached an agreement for close relations with Mussolini, part of which was that he would form a corporative state and let the *Heimwehr* destroy the Social Democrats. Early in 1934 in a four-day civil war he put down an uprising by the Viennese workers and smashed their great blocks of modern housing with howitzers. Austrian defenses against the Nazis were weakened irretrievably. Six months later Dollfuss was shot by a Nazi gang that invaded the Chancellery and left him to bleed slowly to death on a sofa in his office.

It was a loss not to be able to talk with Redlich, who was in Cambridge, lecturing at the Harvard Law School. But I saw something of his friend Dr. Benedikt, of the *Neue Freie Presse*. He was as pessimistic as the politicians but more philosophic. He mused aloud over what he called the destruction of the German *Geist,* a word meaning either spirit or intellect, two qualities we consider quite different. We were witnessing, he said, the triumph of German philistinism. Democracy had become tedious; the young barbarians were taking charge. We talked of the novel by Ernst von Salomon, *Die Geächteten* (*The Outlaws*), which describes the mentality of young Germans like the S.A. who had come out of the war with nothing to do—no work, no play, no culture, no faith, no history—their ignorance, dilettantism, childishness, hardness, terrorism, heroism. "It is the Middle Ages in the twentieth century," said Benedikt. Or more primitive, I said, "Wotan secondhand."

IV

In Belgrade I first received an orientation course from Foreign Minister Jevtich on recent changes in Jugoslavia's relations with her neighbors. They were not very great. Bulgaria: A slight détente in relations between the two countries was noticeable, perhaps due to the fact that Italy, being hard up like everyone else, was not able to support her anti-Jugoslav propagandists in Bulgaria as generously as before. Also, the Macedonian question was largely quiescent, partly for the same reason, but also because so many Macedonian leaders had killed each other. Albania: Italy was displeased with King Zog's manifestations of independence since her subventions had tapered off. Zog was talking, too, of asking the League of Nations to help in reorganizing Albanian finances, something that Italy would fear and resent. Italy: Mussolini still pursued a policy of prestige, looking around for clients, but he seemed to have begun worrying about Hitler's excesses and the worldwide condemnation of them. Austria: This was a German land, and Italy was foolish not to realize that eventually it was bound to be absorbed by Germany. This would hold dangers for Jugoslavia. On the other hand, when Germany was on the Adriatic, or close to it, would not Italy see that Jugoslavia was a natural ally?

Not greatly to my surprise, King Alexander greeted me with the news that his secret negotiation with Mussolini over Albania had come to nothing. But first he spoke in detail of affairs at home. There still was a crippling lack of men who could be entrusted with power and still the same absence of any constructive program among the opposition parties, either Serb or Croat. He was disappointed that Maček, successor to Radić as leader of the Croat Peasant party, had not become a substantial power in Croatia; it would have been a risk if he had, but at least there then would have been someone with whom to negotiate a solution. It was not the nature of Croat peasants to be much moved by political issues, the way Serbian peasants were, and the leaders who spoke for them had little authority and no ability. In Serbia, the best men were staying out of politics "as from a plague," and those who came forward were mostly mediocre. Both lacks would have to be filled.

Meanwhile, he was trying gradually to create a better administrative system, and here real progress was being made. Reports to the contrary had been spread abroad, especially in England, by well-meaning friends of the country who considered themselves its godparents and could not bear that their advice was not taken. (He evidently had in mind Seton-Watson and Wickham Steed.) They spoke of the suppression of parliamentary life in Jugoslavia as though it were an incident by itself and not part of a wave of similar experiences going on in many countries. The recent murder of a professor in Zagreb, for instance, was deplorable, but that single crime was talked about as though there was not a murder every day in the streets of Sofia and as though there had not been wholesale murders during the past fourteen years in Germany, a great, cultivated state in the center of Europe. He had told me many times, he said, that he intended to return by degrees to a more democratic system. He still did. If that was the proclaimed aim of national leaders who had assumed dictatorial powers in other countries he had not heard of it.

After lunch the King returned to the negotiation with Mussolini. It had progressed, he said, to the point where Mussolini had actually drawn up a document which would guarantee Albania's territorial integrity and independence. But then toward the end of the summer there had been a shuffle in Mussolini's advisers; Grandi was sent to the Embassy in London and Aloisi came to the fore, along with other advisers who were "more adventurers than statesmen." They persuaded Mussolini that Jugoslavia was in dissolution and there was no need to come to terms with her. Mussolini sent word that though the matter was not closed he was for the time being "waiting by the window."

Alexander could not make up his mind whether Mussolini had started the negotiation sincerely or merely to find out the extent of Jugoslav demands. He inclined to think the former. He still believed Mussolini did not want war but veered around in search of a profitable opening here or another there. Without mentioning names, I recounted what Mussolini had said to Nick Roosevelt when he saw him in Rome in March, just before MacDonald's visit there. Mussolini told him he had a vast plan for revisions in Central Europe and the Balkans—a plebiscite for the Slovaks, a shuffling of the Hungarian-Rumanian border at many points, and so on. The King said he had heard of these projects, also of one for

Jugoslavia to "offer" Hungary some Magyar villages in Croatia. Meanwhile, the Italian press harped on Italian claims in Dalmatia and Mussolini was encouraging Dollfuss to "go Fascist." Evidently Italy was shopping around for friends and hinting at bonuses to get them. If the program was ever initiated it would lead to clashes that might well end in war. But this was only a risk of war, which Mussolini was willing to take; it did not mean he would seek or start war.

40

The Axis in the Making

Hitler and King Alexander were as different in character, temperament and objectives as two dictators could be. Now within a span of less than two weeks I was to see a third. My train from Trieste, confirming the cliché of American tourists that Mussolini had been a boon to Italy, arrived in Rome on time.

Ambassador Rosso in Washington had written on my behalf to the Italian Foreign Ministry, so that when I called at the Palazzo Chigi I was politely received by Fulvio Suvich, the Under-Secretary. He had taken over from Foreign Minister Grandi when Grandi went to London as Ambassador and Mussolini himself assumed direction of foreign affairs. Suvich was anxious to learn as much as possible about Hitler's personality, for as yet neither Mussolini nor any of his top advisers had seen him. What did I think of him? How had he received me? My replies took him aback. I said Hitler had addressed me, point by point, from a sheet of paper, like a public meeting. He didn't ask questions or answer questions. He lived for and by himself alone. He was impervious to world opinion and cared for it so little that he didn't even inquire about it. It must be exhilarating, I said, to feel able to operate in a vacuum, but for a statesman it might lead to unfortunate miscalculations. (Mussolini, when I saw him a few days later, on May 16, asked plenty of questions; perhaps Suvich had briefed him.)

At this early stage in their relationship, Mussolini's opinion of Hitler was still tentative. Hitler had taken him as a model, and this of course was flattering. The Italian press was under orders to acknowledge the compliment and had restricted its accounts of what had been happening in Germany in the last few months to eulogies of the German spiritual renaissance and had passed over unpleasant details. Its allusions to the treatment of the Jews (for whom Mussolini had no personal antipathy) had been indirect, consisting of vague regrets that unfavorable reactions abroad should have resulted from hostile propaganda and newspaper exaggeration. Just before my arrival in Rome the *Giornale d'Italia* had spoken of the partnership of Italy and Germany in lyrical terms: "Two peoples, and one idea, one faith! Two revolutions, and one revolution! Two races, but one attitude, the same Roman salute!"

Nevertheless, Mussolini's feelings about Hitler were ambivalent. It was uncomfortable to have his own Fascist dictatorship, which had managed to win a measure of tolerance even in some respectable circles abroad, identified with the Nazi imitator whose excesses were meeting with universal opprobrium. Also, Nazi rhetoric about Austria was unsettling, even though Mussolini in this period could hardly believe that Hitler meant it to be taken seriously. Added to these discontents were twinges of jealousy for the successful new arrival who was creating such a stir. As the lines in *Bombastes Furioso* put it:

> So I have heard on Afric's burning shore
> Another lion give a grievous roar;
> And the first lion thought the last a bore!

Mussolini would have real difficulty, I saw, in maintaining a partnership with Hitler on terms of equality. Italy was not Germany and Italians were not Germans. Hitler could equip Germany out of Germany's own resources in preparation for any struggle he might undertake. Italy did not provide Mussolini with that capacity and he would have to attain his goals by less direct methods. Further, Mussolini would have to struggle to counteract an Italian weakness for individualism, ridicule of authority, "disorder"; whereas Hitler would be aided by the German weakness for obedience, respect for power, "order." In one important respect, Mussolini had the advantage. Hitler was the neophyte. While he was learning and organizing, Mussolini would have time to make the Mediterranean Italy's *Mare Nostrum* and spread the new Roman imperium into Africa and the Levant.

The Counsellor of the American Embassy in Rome, Alexander Kirk, lived in a huge and gloomy villa on the via Nomentana, just outside the city. He was a bachelor, tall, thin, stately, whose mother presided at his social functions. His formal manner was said to conceal an unusually good mind, and I had hoped for some hints from him as to what Musso-lini might be most disposed to talk about. But there was no chance for serious conversation during an elaborate lunch. I remember in the pauses the scratching of knives on silver plates. More easy and productive were meals with Ambassador de Jouvenel of France and his colleague Charles-Roux, French Ambassador to the Vatican.

II

The room in the Palazzo Venezia where Mussolini received visitors was vast and high-ceilinged, with walls of marble interspersed with fres-coes and two tiers of windows permanently curtained so that the only light was artificial. Presumably the curtains were part of the security system, although I saw only liveried servants, no Black Shirts or other guards. The great fireplace, in which no friendly fire evidently had ever burned, was surmounted by a monumental stone *fasces,* the bundle of rods and axe. The floor, of marble of many colors, stretched before the visitor in a glassy expanse from the door where he entered to Mussolini's working table in the far corner. While the visitor made his slippery crossing, Mussolini remained seated behind his table, watching him.

Not according to plan was the fact that, when I entered, Mussolini was talking on the telephone, leaning on one elbow, so that I made my way across the room unperceived. As the conversation continued, I went quietly after a moment to a chair standing beside the table, sat down and waited. Although I knew hardly any Italian, I soon made out that the person at the other end of the wire was Cerruti, the Italian Ambassador in Berlin. I had dined there with him and his wife, a handsome and high-spirited Jewess from Budapest. Both were anti-Nazi; indeed she spoke to me quite freely of her antipathy for Hitler and all his works. After a couple of minutes, Mussolini banged down the receiver, turned abruptly and looked up to where he supposed I was standing, thrusting out his head and bugging his eyes. To his surprise, I wasn't there, and he had to turn and repeat the thrust of jaw and the bugging of eyes when he discovered that actually I was sitting alongside him.

Without any introductory remark, Mussolini hissed (a detective-story word, but in this case accurate), "What news?"

I replied that I had been across Europe from Paris to Berlin, Warsaw, Vienna and Belgrade, and everywhere had found the same extreme nerv-ousness caused by Hitler's arrival in power, his threats of treaty revision and revenge and his unconciliatory attitude on disarmament. Mussolini commented that this was natural enough; the Disarmament Conference was done for and the situation was indeed very serious. I said I agreed, that is, if Hitler was in fact determined to rearm, as he had told me he must and would do. Mussolini asked if that was exactly what Hitler had said. I replied yes; Hitler had told me he could not wait any longer while the maneuvering at Geneva dragged along without result, that Germany must have at the very least equality of arms.

What impression did I have of Hitler as a person, Mussolini asked? I described in more detail than I had done to Suvich his looks, manner of speaking and general attitude; I spoke of his indifference to outside opinion and even mentioned the paralyzing effect he seemed to have on his interpreters. He nodded several times to show he understood the nuances of what I was saying, looking at me attentively, not so much with suspicion that I might be suggesting parallels with his own behavior as with interest in my thumbnail sketch. When I was finished, he observed that Hitler had made several bad mistakes, notably in the persecution of the Jews.

"I have sent word to him personally," he said, "and told him it is a great error. I said he will have all the Jews in the world against him, and the Christians also."

I referred to the violent methods being used by Hitler not only in dealing with the Jews but to enforce all his principles—"if they can be called that." Mussolini paid no attention to the addition, but shifted his emphasis to the error that he thought Hitler made in pressing ahead so fast. "Remember," he said, "what I do now I do after ten years of experience."

He then turned to the question of European security. "Locarno is dead," he said. "The British Minister of War has actually mentioned the possible need of sanctions against German rearmament." I commented that if Germany did begin to rearm singlehanded, that would be taken by France as a threat she could not accept; and since Britain in the present state of public opinion against Germany might agree, a policy of sanctions by degrees might actually be adopted.

"Yes," said Mussolini, "France is frightened. She was not six months ago, but now she is. You saw that the French Socialists voted for the war budget for the first time since the end of the war."

It was to prevent the isolation of Germany, he said, and to dissuade her from abrupt action that he had proposed the Four Power Pact; and he outlined at length but not very convincingly what he considered its positive advantages. "It fits into the League framework," he said. "It is not outside the League. It is not against anyone." I interrupted that the

Little Entente states felt it was directed specifically against them, but Mussolini pressed on. "It merely recognizes the responsibility of the Great Powers in the same manner that their possession of permanent seats in the League Council recognizes it. It provides the only way to keep Germany's actions within limits.

"There is no question of revision at this point," he continued, disavowing what Nick Roosevelt had said he had told him recently. "But if ever we are to have real peace political solutions must precede economic ones. Someday my proposals for revision must be revived. The Polish Corridor, for instance, is not insoluble. Yes (when I shook my head), even the question of the Corridor can be solved. I gave my ideas on it to Prime Minister MacDonald the other day. But that is not a priority question now. The question is how to keep Germany from rearming in spite of the discussions at the Disarmament Conference."

I referred to a gradual and agreed reduction of arms by Germany's neighbors as a way for Germany to attain parity in the course of time; and I said that when I mentioned it to Hitler he had ignored it and that Neurath's open demand for rearmament "regardless" had followed.

Mussolini made a grimace and commented that nothing gradual suited Hitler. "Your Mr. Norman Davis has a role to play there," he said. "He made suggestions for a solution of our naval question with the French. Let him make concrete suggestions for a solution of the Franco-German military question. The nub of the conflict there is Germany's refusal to count members of semimilitary organizations among military effectives. Let Mr. Davis persuade the Conference to take up questions of matériel first. After Germany has been given satisfaction there she probably will be willing to back down on effectives. If there could be agreement on general principles, without going into too much detail, then any two powers could proceed to make agreements on specific questions without seeming to act exclusively, that is, against the others."

Wouldn't it be risky, I asked, to leave everyone to act by just general principles? As for Davis, he had already associated himself with a number of proposals brought forward by MacDonald. For instance, he had said we might be willing to agree that as part of a broad treaty we would consult about our rights as a neutral in case of aggression in Europe. But as the United States was not going to undertake political and military commitments there, it was hard for Davis to press solutions on those who would. I said I hated to think what would happen to American opinion if the Disarmament Conference failed and left the World Economic Conference to take place under such handicaps that it failed also.

Our government had gone quite far in consulting with the League in the Far Eastern crisis. Now if we found that nothing could be done with regard to either armaments or the depression I was afraid we might draw back again from Europe, and this time for good.

Mussolini shook his head. "Then the economic crisis will continue and the political crisis will get worse. Anything can happen." Then suddenly he added, as though to reassure himself as much as me, "But I do not believe in war."

As I had done to Hitler, I commented that it is not necessary that anyone plan war in order for war to come. "War can spring from unforeseen circumstances or the stupidities of individuals." And for emphasis I repeated, "especially from individual stupidities, when leaders do not take account of possible reactions to their actions." In view of Mussolini's longer experience in world affairs, I said, he was in a position to exercise a useful influence over Hitler. Mussolini smiled a sour smile, pulling down the corners of his mouth. He wondered, he remarked, half to himself, whether he really had any influence over Hitler, and again mentioned his unaccepted advice about the Jews.

Jugoslavia came into the conversation when I rather boldly asked why he didn't reach an agreement directly with King Alexander; having talked with Alexander, I said, I imagined it could be done relatively easily. Yes, Mussolini agreed, very easily. But when I said that everything necessary could be put in a dozen words—simply a mutual guarantee of Albanian neutrality and integrity—he dropped the subject. Instead he asked me how I assessed the internal situation in Jugoslavia —"Can the present regime last?" I replied that probably it was less unstable than reports abroad suggested. "The Croats are more obstructionists than revolutionaries," I said. "The King's difficulty is to find leaders to negotiate a settlement with." I asked what his reports of the situation were, and he said much like mine. He summed it up: "Our relations with Jugoslavia are indifferent."

When I mentioned the delicate situation in Austria, and the fact that some people there seemed to hope for Italian support against the *Anschluss*, he said that the preservation of Austrian independence was absolutely necessary if there was to be peace in the Danube Valley. But he pointedly said nothing about Italy's concern that Austria remain independent and continue to block Germany from appearing on the Brenner, within sight of Italy's South Tyrol with its quarter-million Austrian-Germans.

To get away from topics which obviously made him uncomfortable he went back to Hitler. Was he popular? What did the man in the street think of his policies? I answered that if he didn't like them he knew enough to keep still. Mussolini grinned. I said I wondered whether Hitler would demonstrate the adaptability to direct a mass movement when he became responsible for turning promises into results. He had taught the German people that violence was the road to success. They were in a state of exaltation. If he faltered, might they apply to him the same sort of violent revenge he had used against his enemies?

The possibility of this seemed to me small, but the interview was evidently coming to an end and this seemed a sobering idea to leave behind. His response was to lay his hands palms down on the table, look at me with big, serious eyes and sigh a sigh that might have been for the woes of the world but probably was regret that he was being copied by an inferior artist. He walked with me over to the door, repeating platitudes that I must come back to Rome often and expressing disbelief that my father had lived there sixty years before. He shook my hand more cordially than his feelings probably dictated and, as he opened the door, put a hand casually on my shoulder, a final application of charm.

He looked to me fit, though a little stout for his height, and with too heavy jowls. He was dressed in a dark jacket and gray flannels, a soft white shirt and a rather loose dark blue tie. His eyes were his principal feature, expanding and contracting remarkably rapidly, giving the probably erroneous impression that his emotions were deep and troubling. Doubtless he adopted whatever manner he considered appropriate to his visitor. With me, informality and responsiveness were what he thought would work best. I had heard nothing startling from him, nor had I expected to. What was most interesting was the strong reservations he expressed about Hitler, not reflected in his public statements or the Italian press. What, I wondered, would be Sforza's reactions to this, or those of Salvemini, now at Harvard, lecturing and working on his next book? He had written me, perfectly happy in his exile: "I am the richest man in the world. I have the Widener Library."

Even though I knew that Mussolini's display of charm was an act, it nevertheless left me feeling that this was a man, certainly not of humanity, for of this he had given too many disproofs, but with human reflexes. In contrast to Hitler's thin-lipped smirk and automaton manner, he could grin and carry on an ordinary conversation. I found him, though, too ingratiating. Nothing was sincere, whether his friendly arm on your shoulder, or the grim visage and jut of chin with which he reviewed his troops, throwing out their legs in the ridiculous *passo romano* copied from the German goose step, or his harangues from the balcony of the Palazzo Venezia, where his chest puffed out to incredible dimensions as the roar reverberated across the square: "Duce! Duce! Duce! Duce!" He wallowed in the adulation. Hitler, by contrast, took the hysterics of his followers as something they owed him, his due, accepted but barely appreciated. With him nothing was put on or superficial. A mystical sense of destiny, lacking in his self-consciously theatrical partner, gave him a conviction of eventual triumph that sustained him even when toward the end there in fact was nothing left but ashes.

III

Mussolini had avoided commenting on my remark that the states of the Little Entente considered the Four Power Pact, with its mention of possible treaty revision, as directed against them, or on the possibility of concerting plans with them to check a German move into Austria. That would have meant abandoning his long-standing project for an Italo-Austrian-Hungarian bloc. In particular it would have involved coming to terms with Jugoslavia. Although he had toyed with this idea in his recent negotiations with King Alexander, he had now evidently decided against it. The best he could say of relations with Jugoslavia was that they were "indifferent." His present plan seemed to be to deal with the German threat to Austria by underwriting Dollfuss. It was in accordance with this that, about a month after I had been in Rome, Mussolini received Dollfuss there and encouraged him to deal decisively with the Social Democrats at home; and at a second meeting with him in Riccione in August he gave him a promise of full support against Germany.

In talking with me in Vienna, Otto Bauer had ridiculed the idea that Hitler would ever take a threat of war by Mussolini seriously. So it proved. But it was only when Mussolini met Hitler for the first time in Venice in June, 1934, that he began to understand that his calculations might be wrong, for although Hitler agreed that the *Anschluss* was not at the moment an acute issue he spoke of the need to replace Dollfuss and bring Nazis into a new Austrian Government. Then on July 25, 1934, came the murder of Dollfuss by a gang of Nazis. This was confirmation with a vengeance, in the true meaning of the term, that Hitler had no fear of Italy and that *Anschluss* figured on his calendar at an early date.

A series of events, however, both inflated Mussolini's ego and caused him to accept by degrees the idea that he might do better in collusion with Hitler than in opposition.

The first was his success in conquering Ethiopia and the failure of the

League's attempt to prevent it by sanctions (in which attempt the United States refused to help). Another was Hitler's reoccupation of the Rhineland in March, 1936, when the French and the British failed to move. With the League ineffectual and British and French power at a low ebb, Mussolini realized that if he tried to prevent Germany's occupation of Austria he would have to do it alone. Meanwhile, he and Hitler found themselves partners in the Spanish Civil War; their help to Franco caused the nonintervention policy of the non-Fascist powers to fail.

On a visit to Germany in September, 1937, Mussolini was enormously impressed with Germany's military strength and intoxicated with dreams of what he might accomplish with such an ally. The *Documents of German Foreign Policy* have since revealed that the two dictators agreed there that in general "Italy will not be impeded by Germany in the Mediterranean whereas, on the other hand, the special German interests in Austria will not be impaired by Italy." The two realms were being defined. In any case, the hard fact was that with Italian troops in Ethiopia and Spain, Mussolini lacked the power to attempt a defense of Austria against a German coup even if he wished it. By now he was not sure he wished it, and by March, 1938, he accepted the inevitable and made no protest when German tanks entered the country. It was not a significant sacrifice, he persuaded himself, compared with the glory and material dividends to be obtained from partnership in the Axis.

Postscript: General Bliss's Prophecy

General Bliss told me once of an evening during the war when he was sitting late in the War Department with Secretary Baker. It was the night when the first American convoy of troops was reaching the submarine zone, and in their anxiety neither of them could go home to sleep.

"General," asked Baker, "how long do you suppose this war will last?"

After hesitating a time, Bliss replied that by the analogy of other great wars it might last thirty or forty years. There might be a pause, he said, an armed truce, while both sides licked their wounds and collected their forces. Maybe some of the contestants would disappear; perhaps some would even change sides. But then the war would go on again, until one side was obliterated as a fighting force or until civilization ended in a chaotic breakdown.

At what point, I wonder, would Bliss have decided that the truce which began in November, 1918, would not last much longer? He told me that he had hoped, since that anxious evening in June, 1917, that he had guessed wrong; he had counted on the League of Nations as a new factor to limit the power and modify the aims of both victors and vanquished. But I think that by 1933, if he had been still alive, a realistic appraisal would have warned him that the balance was swinging against peace.

After snatches of sun at Locarno, or when the Kellogg-Briand Pact was signed, or when the reparations negotiations moved toward good sense and adjustment, the European landscape had turned uniformly black under the pall of disillusionment and despair spread by the Great Depression. States lived from moment to moment, and in their convulsive struggle to protect their trade and currency provoked retaliatory measures from their neighbors and worsened their own plight. It was Spengler's "struggle on the keel of the overturned boat."

Political anguish kept pace with economic deterioration. As their misery increased, people asked whether there was no superman able to arrange that millions would not go workless and starve in a world of unexploited resources. Why did not governments that in wartime had assumed control of every department of life look after them now in times which many of them found just as hard?

Here was a chance for anyone who had a ready-made economic panacea and who promised to solve all political questions if only he were freed from the stupid harness of democracy. Italy gave a model, and all over Europe Fascist movements were gaining followers—Iron Guards in Rumania, Croix de Feu in France, Mosleyites in England. Hitler's advent in Germany was decisive. His repudiation of the "Geneva swindle," his swift creation of a great war machine, his glorification of death on the battlefield, his mystical evocation of happiness in the spirit land of Norse heroes, his claims to lands that could be won only by war or at the risk of war, his elimination of every element that might oppose taking that risk—all indicated his intentions. A new arms race began, or, reverting to General Bliss's theory, the truce ended and the old race was resumed. Laggards in the race were the victors of last time; the defeated pushed ahead.

The United States was not very influential in these years. Our objectives since 1919 had been negative; we had not developed policies either for maintaining peace or, much less, fighting an unimaginable war. Like the rest of the world, too, we were sunk in the Great Depression—banks closed, savings gone, mortgages foreclosed, farms without markets, unemployed in 1932 at the staggering total of twelve millions. Roosevelt's First Hundred Days changed the psychology of despair to hope. But it was not a time when Americans were disposed to think about the troubles of others or question the established isolationist credo.

In the first issue of *Foreign Affairs*, Elihu Root had written: "When foreign affairs were ruled by autocracies or oligarchies the danger of war was in sinister purpose. When foreign affairs are ruled by democracies the danger of war will be in mistaken beliefs." A mistaken belief of the American democracy for many years had been that American security was separable from the security of other nations. The slow evolution of informed and sober opinion combatting that belief was about to be overtaken by events that had passed beyond American control.

It would be an exaggeration to say that World War II began in 1933. The exaggeration nevertheless contains a kernel of truth. The power of a dictator includes the power to make war. And from the moment Hitler assumed absolute control in Germany on March 23, 1933, his actions warned that he might exercise that power. Six years later, his preparations complete—Austria annexed, Czechoslovakia annihilated, the Axis solid, Russia seduced into complicity—he sent the German armies into Poland. Those were six years of counterfeit peace, as the months between the invasion of Poland and the invasion of the Low Countries were "the phony war." There followed the fall of France, the battle of Britain, the turnabout attack on Russia and, suddenly, Pearl Harbor.

Appendices

I

Members of the American Institute of International Affairs,
merged in 1921 with the Council on Foreign Relations

General Tasker H. Bliss

Edward M. House

Herbert Hoover

Thomas W. Lamont

Martin Egan

George Barr Baker

Stanley K. Hornbeck

Clive Day

James T. Shotwell

Charles Seymour

Louis H. Gray

Robert H. Lord

Douglas Johnson

Archibald C. Coolidge

James Brown Scott

T. B. Kitteredge

Christian A. Herter

Manley O. Hudson

Charles H. Haskins

Whitney H. Shepardson

Ray Stannard Baker

George Rublee

Charles P. Howland

Jerome Greene

Raymond B. Fosdick

Alonzo E. Taylor

Edwin F. Gay

Hamilton Fish Armstrong

Vanderbilt Webb

Gerard C. Henderson

F. Trubee Davison

"This is the list of people to whom the first correspondence was sent with regard to the American Institute. Those names down to and including Ray Stannard Baker are of men who were at the Paris Peace Conference at the time when the formation of an American Institute was discussed and who took some part in those discussions when we met with Curtis and his British group to consider the formation of a joint Institute. The names from George Rublee to the end of the list were added in New York by a process of cooption, though in some cases I believe that they did not carry over their election to the Institute into membership in the Council."—Excerpt from letter from Whitney H. Shepardson, to H.F.A., September 26, 1932.

II

King Alexander's Statement to H.F.A., March 21, 1925

I had always wanted to have the Croatian deputies participate in Parliament and I had often urged Pashich to find means of getting them in. He had professed the same wish, and when the first 20 presented themselves last year their mandates were ratified; then, when another group of them came, and when his majority was becoming jeopardized, Pashich decided to adjourn parliament (as technically he had a right to do) and asked me to empower him to make new elections. This I was unwilling to do, as Ljuba Jovanovich,[1] when questioned, assured me he felt the existing Skupshtina could still work. I felt the door had been slammed in the face of the Radić deputies and, however much I disliked much of their program, I felt it was not right if, as Davidovich assured me, he could work with Radić, that this opposition bloc should not have the opportunity of governing. I therefore refused Pashich and, after asking Ljuba Jovanovich to form a cabinet (which he failed in doing), gave a mandate to Davidovich to form one. In this I really exceeded my powers; certainly I went as far as I could possibly go, and I did it as a matter of conscience.

Before determining upon this course I had explicit assurances from Davidovich that he had agreed upon the main lines of an entente with Radić, as also of course with the Slovenes, etc., that the program supported the national State and dynasty, and disowned Moscow, and that details could be worked out speedily, so that Radić's full support for the new government could be obtained and he might be represented in the cabinet, thus assuming his share of the responsibility for what was done.

We waited only a very short time before it began to be clear that

1. President of the Skupshtina, himself a Radical.

Davidovich was having real trouble with Radić; this did not appear in his conversations with me, but from the speeches which Radić began making in Croatia, in which he attacked the army, called for the separation of Croatia, etc., all of which was quite contrary to the form in which Davidovich had agreed the policy of the new government should be cast. I began inquiring of Davidovich when he expected to be able to report progress, and he held me off. Radić's speeches grew more provocative, until General Hadjich, Minister of War, declared to me he could not, as a matter of conscience, remain longer in a government which was predicated on cooperation with such a man. I said that if it was a matter of conscience I must accept his resignation. Davidovich then proposed that he appoint a new Minister of War and take four of the Radić deputies into the Cabinet. I said this seemed to me a strange time to suggest that, just when Radić had made it plain that the expected cooperation between them was impossible on the basis agreed upon between Davidovich and myself, as it would be a victory for Radić instead of the rebuke he should receive at Davidovich's hands.

Davidovich expressed himself also as outdone with Radić, but said the matter was not yet by any means hopeless, and on his assurance I agreed to go forward provided he could have an undertaking from Radić that, one, the integrity of the country was not to be impaired, two, that he sever, openly, all dealings with Moscow. Davidovich said this was quite easy; but as Radić was making speeches every Sunday, and as these were the occasions when he was most violent, he sent a representative especially to Zagreb the next Saturday, to point out the seriousness of the situation to Radić, and to tell him to be moderate. This was the occasion chosen by Radić to speak of the support which Chicherin had promised him in Moscow and to renew his demand for an autonomous republic. The Minister of the Interior, Nastas Petrovich, telephoned me to say that he had disagreeable news for me, and proceeded to give me the main substance of Radić's speech. I sent for Davidovich, told him the thing was hopeless, that this was Radić's reply to his efforts. I pointed out to him the position he had put me in, said that I thought he must feel his own position also, and asked him what must be done. He suggested new *pourparlers* with Radić. To this I said I could not consent, that I had given him the mandate to form a cabinet because he assured me it would be a majority cabinet (even though it was not actually as yet a majority cabinet, and in this I went out of our exact constitutional practice, but I thought the unusual situation warranted it), that it would be based on certain principles, that he had been unable to get the collaboration of

Radić on those principles, that I saw nothing for it but to have him admit failure. But I said that if he would do so publicly I would stand by him and allow him to order new elections—which (with a smile) is a great part of the battle in this country. To this he agreed.

In the morning, Marinkovich[2] came to me with a long statement, which he spoke of as the statement I had directed Davidovich to make. I replied that I had not directed or asked him to make a statement: I had told him that if he chose to make a statement explaining explicitly the effort he had made to form a united cabinet and the reasons for its failure, I would feel he had done his duty and tried his best to carry out his undertaking to me, and that I would feel justified in asking him to remain in office and make the elections. Marinkovich thereupon showed me the statement. It was vague and wobbly—it showed Davidovich still thought of his task as coming to a compromise with Radić and that if I let him make the elections it would not be he but Radić who would in reality do it. I therefore said it was unsatisfactory, and that I must return to my belief that the only course left for Davidovich was to resign. I said that as it was hard for him in his letter of resignation to state that he had failed in what he had undertaken he could do, let him say he thought it wiser to reform the cabinet on broader grounds, and that I would accept the resignation on those terms. This he did. I then gave the mandate to Timotievich, a moderate Democrat on good terms with the Radicals; but he could not get their cooperation, though many Radicals wished to give it.

I had now exhausted all my resources. I could only turn back to the representative of the largest single group in the Skupshtina, Pashich, and allow him to make the elections which at the request of Davidovich I had refused to let him do before. In the course of Timotievich's negotiations I had seen more than ever that the question was one of personal pride and ambition, and of the smallest sort of party politics. I am afraid that is in our blood, but more than anywhere else it is evident in the Croats—they have the *mentalité Russe,* much talk and little definite accomplishment. I am done with meddling in the affairs of Parliament. I did my best, and was able to accomplish nothing. From now on I am a King of the English type!

2. Minister of Foreign Affairs, a Democrat.

Index

Adamov, E. A., 414–15
Adams, W. G. S., 236
Adenauer, Konrad, 277, 528
Adriatic question, 39, 41, 48, 66, 106, 425, 445
AE, *see* Russell, George
Agadir crisis (1911), 450, 487
Albania, 34, 146, 339, 391, 394, 425; Italian guarantees for, 339, 374–77, 378, 386, 388, 467, 497–98, 548, 549; *see also* Tirana, Treaties of; Mussolini on, 392–93, 548–50, 556; neutralization of, 467
Albert, Prince von Schleswig-Holstein, 460–61
Albrecht-Carrié, René, 105*n*
Aldrich, Winthrop W., 325
Alegre, Luis, 477
Alexander I, King of Jugoslavia, 95, 146, 163, 338–40, 385–86; assassination of, 294, 388, 486; Bled residence, 334; dictatorship of, 421–27, 463–64, 467; on King Boris, 382; and Jugoslav unity, 262, 423–24; and Mussolini, on Albania, 497–98, 548–50, 556; and Sarajevo plot, 352, 353–54, 356*n*, 379; Seton-Watson on, 505–506; statement to HFA (March 21, 1925), Appendix II, 566; and Venizelos, 425, 427; *see also* Prince Regent *below*
Alexander, Prince of Greece, 158
Alexander, Prince Regent of Jugoslavia, 35, 41, 60, 165–66; HFA meeting with, 77–78; on land reform, 63; and Russian refugees, 169–70
Alexander II, Tsar of Russia, 416

Alexandrov, Todor, 265, 266, 431
Alexandrova, Maria, 416, 417
Alfonso, King of Spain, 470
Allen, Jay, 471–73, 474, 475, 476
Alliance for Progress, 121
Aloisi, Pompeo, 549
Alsace-Lorraine, 126, 315
American Field Service, 202
American Institute of International Affairs, 182–84; list of members, *see* Appendix I, 565; *see also* Royal Institute
Ames, Sir Herbert, 249
Anderson, Henry W., 92
Andrassy, Countess, 434
Andrews, C. F., 451
Angley, Edward, 412
Anschluss, 299–300, 301, 302, 309, 314, 331, 495, 496; Beneš on, 306, 335; and Czechoslovakia, 299, 331, 332; and Italy, 546, 556, 558; Masaryk on, 307–308; *see also* Austria; Germany
"Apis," 352, 354–55, 357, 365
Apponyi, Count, 172–73, 174, 291, 296, 308; *FA* article, 223
Araquistain, Luis, 471, 529
Armée Française d'Hongrie, 68, 73, 74, 92
Armenia, 157
Armstrong, D. Maitland, 251
Armstrong, Hamilton Fish: becomes managing editor, *FA*, 143–46, 159–62; becomes editor, 397; and *New York Times*, 247; *Hitler's Reich*, 527*n*; *The New Balkans*, 327, 373; *Tito and Goliath*, 420; *see also Foreign Affairs; New York*

71 72 73 10 9 8 7 6 5 4 3 2 1